Beowulf Cluster Computing with Linux

Scientific and Engineering Computation

William Gropp and Ewing Lusk, editors; Janusz Kowalik, founding editor

Data-Parallel Programming on MIMD Computers, Philip J. Hatcher and Michael J. Quinn, 1991

Unstructured Scientific Computation on Scalable Multiprocessors, edited by Piyush Mehrotra, Joel Saltz, and Robert Voigt, 1992

Parallel Computational Fluid Dynamics: Implementation and Results, edited by Horst D. Simon, 1992

Enterprise Integration Modeling: Proceedings of the First International Conference, edited by Charles J. Petrie, Jr., 1992

The High Performance Fortran Handbook, Charles H. Koelbel, David B. Loveman, Robert S. Schreiber, Guy L. Steele Jr. and Mary E. Zosel, 1994

PVM: Parallel Virtual Machine–A Users' Guide and Tutorial for Network Parallel Computing, Al Geist, Adam Beguelin, Jack Dongarra, Weicheng Jiang, Bob Manchek, and Vaidy Sunderam, 1994

Practical Parallel Programming, Gregory V. Wilson, 1995

Enabling Technologies for Petaflops Computing, Thomas Sterling, Paul Messina, and Paul H. Smith, 1995

An Introduction to High-Performance Scientific Computing, Lloyd D. Fosdick, Elizabeth R. Jessup, Carolyn J. C. Schauble, and Gitta Domik, 1995

Parallel Programming Using C++, edited by Gregory V. Wilson and Paul Lu, 1996

Using PLAPACK: Parallel Linear Algebra Package, Robert A. van de Geijn, 1997

Fortran 95 Handbook, Jeanne C. Adams, Walter S. Brainerd, Jeanne T. Martin, Brian T. Smith, Jerrold L. Wagener, 1997

MPI—The Complete Reference: Volume 1, The MPI Core, Marc Snir, Steve Otto, Steven Huss-Lederman, David Walker, and Jack Dongarra, 1998

MPI—The Complete Reference: Volume 2, The MPI-2 Extensions, William Gropp, Steven Huss-Lederman, Andrew Lumsdaine, Ewing Lusk, Bill Nitzberg, William Saphir, and Marc Snir, 1998

A Programmer's Guide to ZPL, Lawrence Snyder, 1999

How to Build a Beowulf, Thomas L. Sterling, John Salmon, Donald J. Becker, and Daniel F. Savarese, 1999

Using MPI: Portable Parallel Programming with the Message-Passing Interface, second edition, William Gropp, Ewing Lusk, and Anthony Skjellum, 1999

Using MPI-2: Advanced Features of the Message-Passing Interface, William Gropp, Ewing Lusk, and Rajeev Thakur, 1999

Beowulf Cluster Computing with Linux, Thomas Sterling, 2001

Beowulf Cluster Computing with Windows, Thomas Sterling, 2001

Scalable Input/Output: Achieving System Balance, Daniel A. Reed, 2003

Beowulf Cluster Computing with Linux

Second Edition

Edited by William Gropp, Ewing Lusk, and Thomas Sterling

The MIT Press
Cambridge, Massachusetts
London, England

© 2002, 2003 Massachusetts Institute of Technology

All rights reserved. No part of this book may be reproduced in any form by any electronic or mechanical means (including photocopying, recording, or information storage and retrieval) without permission in writing from the publisher.

This book was set in LaTeX by the authors and was printed and bound in the United States of America.

Library of Congress Cataloging-in-Publication Data

Beowulf Cluster Computing with Linux / edited by William Gropp, Ewing Lusk, and Thomas Sterling.—2nd ed.
p. cm.—(Scientific and engineering computation)
Includes bibliographical references and index.
ISBN 0-262-69292-9 (pbk. : alk. paper)
1. Parallel computers. 2. Beowulf clusters (Computer systems) 3. Linux. I. Gropp, William. II. Lusk, Ewing. III. Sterling, Thomas Lawrence. IV. Series.
QA76.58.B46 2003
004'.35–dc22 2003059364

Dedicated with respect and appreciation to the memory of
Seymour R. Cray
1925–1996

Contents

Series Foreword

Computing is one of the fastest changing areas of technology. Keeping up with these changes is hard, making the practical use of the most advanced algorithms, technology, and methods difficult. The Scientific and Engineering Computation series focuses on rapid advances in computing technologies, with the aim of facilitating transfer of these technologies to applications in science and engineering. It includes books on theories, methods, and original applications in such areas as parallel computing, large-scale simulations, and scientific software.

The series is intended to help scientists and engineers understand the current world of advanced computation and to anticipate future developments that will affect their computing environments and open up new capabilities and modes of computation.

This volume in the series describes the highly successful distributed/parallel system called Beowulf. A Beowulf is a cluster of PCs interconnected by network technology and employing the message-passing model for parallel computation. Key advantages of this approach are high performance for low price, system scalability, and rapid adjustment to new technological advances.

This book covers how to build, program, and operate a Beowulf system based on the Linux operating system. The second edition is a complete update of the book, with new material in every chapter and several new chapters on cluster setup, management, and programming.

Beowulf hardware, operating system software, programming approaches and libraries, and machine management software are all covered here. The book can be used as a textbook as well as a practical guide for designing, implementing, and operating a Beowulf for those in science and industry who need a powerful system but are reluctant to purchase an expensive massively parallel processor or vector computer.

William Gropp and Ewing Lusk, Editors
Janusz Kowalik, Founding Editor

Foreword

*Super*computers! What computer scientist would not want one? After all, when I was growing up (in the dark ages), everything good was "*Super*." Super*man*, Super*girl*, Super*dog*, Super*size* . . . everyone and everything wanted to be "Super." And so, with the work of a lot of very intelligent people, the Super*computer* was born. People like Seymour Cray, who expended much money, time and effort in creating machines that could solve problems very quickly.

Unfortunately these *Super*computers were also Super*costly*. Often built by hand, they would cost millions of dollars (and that was when a million dollars was a lot of money) to design and build, then a relatively few systems were produced. In addition, these systems tended to be handmade, or at least produced in relatively small qualities, which also drove the production costs up. Finally, each style of supercomputer (whether it be a Cray, a CDC Cyber, an ECL or others) would have a different instruction set, and run a different operating system, which caused the people writing software for them to learn this new operating system, and write their applications to it. Likewise a lot of the software tools for writing applications (compilers, debuggers, profilers, etc.) had to be created for each line, if not each model, of supercomputer. This made these software tools and operating systems costly to develop and maintain.

As general-purpose computers started getting more and more prevalent, the ability to manufacture machines of increasing speed and size at lower and lower prices made the lifetime of supercomputers shorter and shorter. After all, the purpose of purchasing and using a supercomputer was to be able to run your application in the shortest possible time. When this speed transitioned from the previously purchased supercomputer to the latest mass-produced "mainframe" or "super-mini," the justification for running a supercomputer became more difficult.

Because of these and other financial issues, a lot of the supercomputing companies started to go out of business. This was bad for a lot of reasons. First of all, we need supercomputers, or at least we need to have the ability to solve large problems quickly. Whether it is trying to prospect for natural resources, or trying to protect the environment; whether it is analyzing aerial photographs for weapons of mass destruction or trying to predict the weather precisely for a shuttle launch; whether it is generating real time computer graphics or analyzing a mammogram to determine if a woman has cancer or not, the time needed to analyze the problem can mean the difference between success or failure, life or death. Too long in analysis, and you miss the window for the answer to do you any good. For iterative processes, you may find that your competitor, who is using a faster computer, comes up with a better answer or a better product faster than you do.

A good example of this is the computer industry itself. In designing a CPU, a lot of simulation of the new chip is done by already existing computers. The faster the simulation can be done, or the faster a checkout of the finished design can be accomplished, the faster the next iteration of the design can be started. This is why, for years, many chips were designed by supercomputers, even if those supercomputers were from rival chip manufacturers.

As the fortune of supercomputer companies declined, the need for high-speed computing still continued to grow. Two people in NASA, Dr. Thomas Sterling and Dr. Donald Becker, realized that something had to be done. They hypothesized that using inexpensive, off the shelf computer systems (COTS) hooked together with high-speed networking (even with speeds as low as 10 Mbit/sec Ethernet) could duplicate the power of supercomputers, particularly applications that could be converted into highly parallelized threads of execution. They theorized that the price/performance of these COTS systems would more than make up for the overhead of having to send data between the different nodes to have that additional computing done, and sooner or later this concept became known as "Beowulf clusters," or just "Beowulfs."

At first these systems were built from individual PCs built from individual boxes, mounted on commodity racks (and sometimes just stacked on the floor), but as time went on various small companies started to sell pre-packaged, pre-built units in ever-smaller packages with more and more CPUs in them. Boxes kept getting smaller and smaller so you could put more boxes in each rack, and customers were able to order pre-built and pre-wired systems. And because these Beowulfs were made with high-volume manufactured chips, the cost was often one-fortieth that of a conventional supercomputer. Over time even the larger manufacturers such as HP and IBM began building rack-mounted Beowulf systems to order.

Of course there were a few other problems to think about, such as the time it took to send the data back and forth (usually called "latency"), sizing the system, or coordination of the flow of data and instructions to the many, many nodes that might be required. And these were just the beginning of the issues. As the number of COTS nodes increased, so did the amount of power needed, the amount of air conditioning, and even the amount of floor space and floor loading needed to support that many individual units.

These systems were made up of what we call "commodity architectures." While some of these "commodity architectures" were made up of relatively low volume Alpha chips, or SPARC chips, the majority of the Beowulfs were 32-bit Intel chips. And finally, the bulk of the systems used a newly developed operating system called "Linux." The combination of a commodity architecture with a free and high-volume operating system allowed supercomputing to have a volume binary interface for the first time. Applications that worked on a single CPU Intel system running Linux would also work on a Beowulf.

Linux was royalty free, and came with all the source code needed to create it, which allowed people to change the kernel to help make it work better on a Beowulf cluster. People wrote new libraries, and contributed to changing existing libraries to make them work better in the new environment. Compilers were made more efficient, and newer interconnects were developed that had higher throughput, lower latency, and lower overhead than the original ones. New algorithms allowed applications that could not utilize Beowulfs before to utilize the new technique. However, the open source nature of Linux and these compilers and libraries allowed a pseudo-standard for Beowulf systems to emerge. For the first time we could think about mass-produced supercomputers ... units that could duplicate the power of a supercomputer for less than *one-fortieth* of the price.

Still, a lot of people did not foresee how Beowulf systems would change the face of computing. It was only when certain projects happened that people began to realize the excitement generated by affordable supercomputers.

The first project came from Oak Ridge National Labs, where a "mistake in planning" left a project without budgeted money for computing. By going to their colleagues who had recently had upgrades to their desktop systems, the project managers were able to collect forty-eight cast-off units and make the Beowulf needed to do their calculations. They called it the "Soupercomputer" after the old story of "Stone Soup" and the man who fed a village by making a soup only out of water, fire and a white stone. After all, they had made their soupercomputer at "no cost" to the facility.

The second success was a CD-ROM made by Red Hat Software in conjunction with NASA, more as a marketing gimmick than anything else. Declaring the Beowulf software on the CD-ROM as "rocket science," the CD-ROM that was expected to sell as a sleeper flew off the shelves of Red Hat, and became one of their largest sellers. Whether the CD-ROM was ever installed or not made no difference, everyone wanted to have supercomputing software on their bookshelf, particularly for the low, low price of a Linux CD.

Another success started happening in high schools and small colleges. These schools never dreamed of owning a traditional supercomputer before, but with the concept of Beowulf systems, either with donated "Stone Soup" computers or new ones bought through a small grant, the schools were able to create that computing power. This was important to not only the computer science department, but to areas such as chemistry, biology, animation, music, physics, and other areas needing high performance computations for real-time visualizations and simulations.

As the use of Beowulf systems grew into other areas such as bio-informatics and genome research, new uses for supercomputers were derived that had never been considered before. A major financial company had to maintain a certain amount of monetary reserve as required by the SEC. Since this company was so large, the amount of money that it had in this reserve at any one time took over twelve hours to calculate. Since it took so long to come up with a correct answer (which by definition was no longer correct), they had to keep a significant buffer to meet a potential audit. By purchasing a Beowulf system, they were able to calculate the amount of reserve accurately in fifteen minutes, and therefore calculated it every fifteen minutes of the day. This allowed them to reduce their reserve, and with the reclaimed money re-invested, they were able to make fifteen million dollars in profits the first year. This (of course) paid for their Beowulf system many times over.

There are other points to programming these Beowulf systems. The techniques used in programming them (message passing, parallel threads of execution, memory locks, and latency speeds) are all considerations of programming what are known as "workstation farms," which these days are simply desktop PCs hooked together with Ethernet. One moment these machines could be used as a high school or college computing laboratory. But within a few moments and with the right operating system software you could have a "horizontal Beowulf" capable of solving anything that a dedicated, rack-mounted Beowulf could solve.

A hospital, for instance, could use the nurses and doctors stations standing idle between accesses to do the analysis of a mammogram, something that was modeled using a Beowulf, and which reduced the analysis time from twenty hours on a single SPARCstation 20 to ten minutes on a 160 unit Intel Beowulf. By utilizing the excess cycles of idle PCs throughout the hospital, the hospital was not required to buy a Beowulf system for this speedup in mammogram analysis. They simply utilized the idle CPU cycles that they already had.

We are entering into a new age of computing. Sixty-four bit computers made out of commodity chips will allow us to more easily solve problems of almost any size. Pulling together hundreds, if not thousands, of CPUs in various configurations (SMP, Beowulf, and NUMA) will allow us to tackle problems where we could not have afforded the solutions ten years ago. Use of the Grid will use a lot, if not all, of the same programming and systems administration techniques that are used in the classic Beowulf system.

Finally, I believe that all of the programming techniques used in Beowulf systems are relevant to even single-CPU desktop machines today. Multi-threaded, distributed programming should be the normal way of thinking about programming, not the exception. Therefore I think that every high school and college computer science student should at one time or another learn how to program a Beowulf system, and the sooner the better.

This book is an excellent place to start.

Carpe Diem.

Jon “maddog” Hall, President
Linux International
Amherst, NH, USA
July 4th, 2003

Preface to the second edition

The purpose of this book is to help you understand the Beowulf approach to parallel computing. We describe here how to select the hardware components of computers and networks, how to configure and install the necessary system software, how to write parallel programs to take advantage of your new machine, and how to manage it for use by others.

This book concentrates on the *concepts* of Beowulf computing, since computing changes too fast for any detailed "Beowulf manual" to stay up to date for long. Many concepts are common to multiple generations of systems, and provide the basic for understanding the changing details of assembling, configuring, using, and managing a cluster.

We don't take a purely abstract approach, however. We give detailed examples drawn from current systems, which will be immediately useful. This book can thus serve as a practical guide to the current state of Beowulf computing as well as a map to the central issues, an understanding of which will have long-lasting value.

Since the first edition appeared, Beowulf computing has expanded rapidly, at all ranges of cluster sizes. The continuing drop in prices of both computers and networks has meant that more and more users are acquiring small and medium-sized systems for departmental and even personal use. At the high end, clusters are now amply represented in the Top500 list of the most capable machines in the world. Clusters available from cluster hardware vendors such as Dell and Linux Networx are even in the top 25.

Another development contributing to the expansion of the Beowulf community has been the emergence of effective automated cluster setup software. We survey some current systems in Chapter 6.

The fact that both pre-packaged cluster hardware and cluster software are available greatly simplifies the effort required to get a cluster up and running. Of course it is also possible (and common) for clusters to be assembled "by hand." This book will help you build your Beowulf yourself if that is your choice, and to understand both its hardware and software structure well even if you let others attend to the hardware construction and systems software installation.

About the Second Edition

Many additions and updates to the first edition make this second edition timely and more complete.

1. A new introductory chapter explains what sorts of applications Beowulf clusters are good for and provides a "road map" for reading the book.

2. The chapter on PVFS has been entirely rewritten to cover parallel file systems for clusters, including the three systems that are hot in the Beowulf community: GPFS, Lustre, and PVFS.

3. A new chapter on managing clusters covers the issues faced by systems administrators.

4. A new chapter on tuning networks for clusters includes information on network security. As Linux has matured, the typical Linux distribution has been optimized for interacting with the Internet, which requires strict security policies. This new chapter discusses how to configure your cluster for performance while retaining a secure system.

5. A new chapter describes the Scyld environment, which provides an illusion of a single system image to the user and the administrator.

6. A new chapter describes library and application software for numerical applications. Using a Beowulf no longer requires writing programs; there are already many available applications. Even if it is necessary to write software, existing powerful parallel libraries make it relatively easy to write many kinds of parallel applications. A new section in Chapter 8 shows how libraries written in MPI may be used to write programs that have no explicit use of MPI. Two sample programs that solve a linear and a nonlinear system of equations in parallel illustrate this approach.

7. A new chapter on parallel programming covers both the basic terms and ideas and presents some simple programming methods based on the manager/worker approach and using powerful scripting languages such as perl and python.

8. The MPI chapters now emphasize the new version of MPICH2 that supports all of MPI-1 and MPI-2, including the use of `mpiexec` (recommended in the MPI-2 standard) over `mpirun`.

9. As the software for Beowulfs matures, changes are inevitable. Each chapter has been updated to cover the current state of the software. Cluster hardware changes even faster than the software, and hence the hardware chapters have been rewritten, covering new processors and networks.

The high-level structure of the book breaks the huge topic of cluster computing into three parts.

Part I, Enabling Technologies describes the components, both hardware and software, that go into a Beowulf.

Part II, Parallel Programming shows how to write application programs for clusters, either by using functions built into Linux or by using any of a number of both general and special-purpose libraries.

Part III. Managing Clusters covers administration of clusters large and small, and includes a case study of a specific large cluster.

Acknowledgments for the second edition

We thank first the authors of the chapters contributed to this book:

Peter H. Beckman, Argonne National Laboratory
Ralph Butler, Middle Tennessee State University
Narayan Desai, Argonne National Laboratory
Jack Dongarra, University of Tennessee
Victor Eijkhout, University of Tennessee
Remy Evard, Argonne National Laboratory
Al Geist, Oak Ridge National Laboratory
David B. Jackson, University of Utah
James Patton Jones, Altair Engineering
Jim Kohl, Oak Ridge National Laboratory
David Lifka, Cornell Theory Center
Walt Ligon, Clemson University
Miron Livny, University of Wisconsin
Karen Miller, University of Wisconsin
John-Paul Navarro, Argonne National Laboratory
Bill Nitzberg, Altair Engineering
Daniel Nurmi, University of California, Santa Barbara
Philip Papadopoulos, University of California, San Diego
Erik Paulson, University of Wisconsin
Rob Ross, Argonne National Laboratory
Dan Stanzione, Jr., Clemson University
Brian Toonen, Argonne National Laboratory
Todd Tannenbaum, University of Wisconsin
Derek Wright, University of Wisconsin

Many other people helped in various ways to put this book together. Thanks are due to Philip Carns, Anthony Chan, Andreas Dilger, Michele Evard, Tramm Hudson, Rob Latham, Andrew Lusk, Richard Lusk, Neill Miller, Bill Nickless, Craig Stacey, Rick Stevens, and Edward Thornton.

Don Becker, Tom Quinn, and the people of Scyld Computing Corporation provided particular help with Chapter 18 on the Scyld approach to Beowulf.

Special thanks go to Karen Toonen for her tremendous help in making the network tuning chapter more understandable. Gail Pieper, technical writer in the Mathematics and Computer Science Division at Argonne, once again improved every chapter's style and readability.

William Gropp
Ewing Lusk
Thomas Sterling

Preface to the first edition

Within the past three years, there has been a rapid increase in the deployment and application of computer clusters to expand the range of available system capabilities beyond those of conventional desktop and server platforms. By leveraging the development of hardware and software for these widely marketed and heavily used mainstream computer systems, clusters deliver order of magnitude or more scaling of computational performance and storage capacity without incurring significant additional R&D costs. Beowulf-class systems, which exploit mass-market PC hardware and software in conjunction with cost-effective commercial network technology, provide users with the dual advantages of unprecedented price/performance and configuration flexibility for parallel computing. Beowulf-class systems may be implemented by the end users themselves from available components. But with their growth in popularity, so has evolved industry support for commercial Beowulf systems. Today, depending on source and services, Beowulf systems can be installed at a cost of between one and three dollars per peak megaflops and of a scale from a few gigaflops to half a teraflops. Equally important is the rapid growth in diversity of application. Originally targeted to the scientific and technical community, Beowulf-class systems have expanded in scope to the broad commercial domain for transaction processing and Web services as well as to the entertainment industry for computer-generated special effects. Right now, the largest computer under development in the United States is a commodity cluster that upon completion will be at a scale of 30 teraflops peak performance. It is quite possible that, by the middle of this decade, commodity clusters in general and Beowulf-class systems in particular may dominate middle and high-end computing for a wide range of technical and business workloads. It also appears that for many students, their first exposure to parallel computing is through hands-on experience with Beowulf clusters.

The publication of *How to Build a Beowulf* by MIT Press marked an important milestone in commodity computing. For the first time, there was an entry-level comprehensive book showing how to implement and apply a PC cluster. The initial goal of that book, which was released almost two years ago, was to capture the style and content of the highly successful tutorial series that had been presented at a number of conferences by the authors and their colleagues. The timeliness of this book and the almost explosive interest in Beowulf clusters around the world made it the most successful book of the MIT Press Scientific and Engineering Computation series last year. While other books have since emerged on the topic of assembling clusters, it still remains the most comprehensive work teaching hardware, software, and programming methods. Nonetheless, in spite of its success, *How to Build a Beowulf* addressed the needs of only a part of the rapidly growing commodity cluster community. And because of the rapid evolution in hardware and software, aspects of its contents have grown stale in a very short period of time. *How to Build a Beowulf* is still a very useful introduction to commodity clusters and has been widely praised for its accessibility to first-time users. It has even found its way into a number of high schools across the country. But the community requires a much more extensive treatment of a topic that has changed dramatically since that book was introduced.

In addition to the obvious improvements in hardware, over the past two years there have been significant advances in software tools and middleware for managing cluster resources. The early Beowulf systems ordinarily were employed by one or a few closely associated workers and applied to a small easily controlled workload, sometimes even dedicated to a single application. This permitted adequate supervision through direct and manual intervention, often by the users themselves. But as the user base has grown and the nature of the responsibilities for the clusters has rapidly diversified, this simple "mom-and-pop" approach to system operations has proven inadequate in many commercial and industrial-grade contexts. As one reviewer somewhat unkindly put it, *How to Build a Beowulf* did not address the hard problems. This was, to be frank, at least in part true, but it reflected the state of the community at the time of publication. Fortunately, the state of the art has progressed to the point that a new snapshot of the principles and practices is not only justified but sorely needed.

The book you are holding is far more than a second addition of the original *How to Build a Beowulf;* it marks a major transition from the early modest experimental Beowulf clusters to the current medium- to large-scale, industrial-grade PC-based clusters in wide use today. Instead of describing a single depth-first minimalist path to getting a Beowulf system up and running, this new reference work reflects a range of choices that system users and administrators have in programming and managing what may be a larger user base for a large Beowulf clustered system. Indeed, to support the need for a potentially diverse readership, this new book comprises three major parts. The first part, much like the original *How to Build a Beowulf,* provides the introductory material, underlying hardware technology, and assembly and configuration instructions to implement and initially use a cluster. But even this part extends the utility of this basic-level description to include discussion and tutorial on how to use existing benchmark codes to test and evaluate new clusters. The second part focuses on programming methodology. Here we have given equal treatment to the two most widely used programming frameworks: MPI and PVM. This part stands alone (as do the other two) and provides detailed presentation of parallel programming principles and practices, including some of the most widely used libraries of parallel algorithms. The largest and third part of the new book describes software infrastructure and tools for managing cluster resources. This includes some of the most popular of the readily available software packages for distributed task scheduling, as well as tools for monitoring and administering system resources and user accounts.

To provide the necessary diversity and depth across a range of concepts, topics, and techniques, I have developed a collaboration among some of the world's experts in cluster computing. I am grateful to the many contributors who have added their expertise to the body of this work to bring you the very best presentation on so many subjects. In many cases, the contributors are the original developers of the software component being described. Many of the contributors have published earlier works on these or other technical subjects and have experience conveying sometimes difficult issues in readable form. All are active participants in the cluster community. As a result, this new book is a direct channel to some of the most influential drivers of this rapidly moving field.

One of the important changes that has taken place is in the area of node operating system. When Don Becker and I developed the first Beowulf-class systems in 1994, we adopted the then-inchoate Linux kernel because it was consistent with other Unix-like operating systems employed on a wide range of scientific compute platforms from workstations to supercomputers and because it provided a full open source code base that could be modified as necessary, while at the same time providing a vehicle for technology transfer to other potential users. Partly because of these efforts, Linux is the operating system of choice for many users of Beowulf-class systems and the single most widely used operating system for technical computing with clusters. However, during the intervening period, the single widest source of PC operating systems, Microsoft, has provided the basis for many commercial clusters used for data transaction processing and other business-oriented workloads. Microsoft Windows 2000 reflects years of development and has emerged as a mature and robust software environment with the single largest base of targeted independent software vendor products. Important path-finding work at NCSA and more recently at the Cornell Theory Center has demonstrated that scientific and technical application workloads can be performed on Windows-based systems. While heated debate continues as to the relative merit of the two environments, the market has already spoken: both Linux and Windows have their own large respective user base for Beowulf clusters.

As a result of attempting to represent the PC cluster community that clearly embodies two distinct camps related to the node operating system, my colleagues and I decided to simultaneously develop two versions of the same book. *Beowulf Cluster Computing with Linux* and *Beowulf Cluster Computing with Windows* are essentially the same book except that, as the names imply, the first assumes and discusses the use of Linux as the basis of a PC cluster while the second describes similar clusters using Microsoft Windows. In spite of this marked difference, the two versions are conceptually identical. The hardware technologies do not differ. The programming methodologies vary in certain specific details of the software packages used but are formally the same. Many but not all of the resource management tools run on both classes of system. This convergence is progressing even as the books are in writing. But even where this is not true, an alternative and complementary package exists and is discussed for the other system type. Approximately 80 percent of the actual text is identical between the two books. Between them, they should cover the vast majority of PC clusters in use today.

On behalf of my colleagues and myself, I welcome you to the world of low-cost Beowulf cluster computing. This book is intended to facilitate, motivate, and drive forward this rapidly emerging field. Our fervent hope is that you are able to benefit from our efforts and this work.

Acknowledgments

I thank first the authors of the chapters contributed to this book:

Peter H. Beckman, Turbolinux
Remy Evard, Argonne National Laboratory
Al Geist, Oak Ridge National Laboratory
William Gropp, Argonne National Laboratory
David B. Jackson, University of Utah
James Patton Jones, Altair Grid Technologies
Jim Kohl, Oak Ridge National Laboratory
Walt Ligon, Clemson University
Miron Livny, University of Wisconsin
Ewing Lusk, Argonne National Laboratory
Karen Miller, University of Wisconsin
Bill Nitzberg, Altair Grid Technologies
Rob Ross, Argonne National Laboratory
Daniel Savarese, University of Maryland
Todd Tannenbaum, University of Wisconsin
Derek Wright, University of Wisconsin

Many other people helped in various ways to put this book together. Thanks are due to Michael Brim, Philip Carns, Anthony Chan, Andreas Dilger, Michele Evard,

Tramm Hudson, Andrew Lusk, Richard Lusk, John Mugler, Thomas Naughton, John-Paul Navarro, Daniel Savarese, Rick Stevens, and Edward Thornton.

Jan Lindheim of Caltech provided substantial information related to networking hardware. Narayan Desai of Argonne provided invaluable help with both the node and network hardware chapters. Special thanks go to Rob Ross and Dan Nurmi of Argonne for their advice and help with the cluster setup chapter.

Paul Angelino of Caltech contributed the assembly instructions for the Beowulf nodes. Susan Powell of Caltech performed the initial editing of several chapters of the book.

The authors would like to respectfully acknowledge the important initiative and support provided by George Spix, Svetlana Verthein, and Todd Needham of Microsoft that were critical to the development of this book. Dr. Sterling would like to thank Gordon Bell and Jim Gray for their advice and guidance in its formulation.

Gail Pieper, technical writer in the Mathematics and Computer Science Division at Argonne, was an indispensable guide in matters of style and usage and vastly improved the readability of the prose.

Thomas Sterling

Beowulf Cluster Computing with Linux

1 So You Want to Use a Cluster

William Gropp

What is a "Beowulf Cluster" and what is it good for? Simply put, a Beowulf Cluster is a supercomputer that anyone can build and use. More specifically, a Beowulf Cluster is a parallel computer built from commodity components. This approach takes advantage of the astounding performance now available in commodity personal computers. By many measures, including computational speed, size of main memory, available disk space and bandwidth, a single PC of today is more powerful than the supercomputers of the past. By harnessing the power of tens to thousands of such low-cost but powerful processing elements, you can create a powerful supercomputer. In fact, the number 5 machine on the "Top500" list of the world's most powerful supercomputers is a Beowulf Cluster.

A Beowulf cluster is a form of parallel computer, which is nothing more than a computer that uses more than one processor. There are many different kinds of parallel computer, distinguished by the kinds of processors they use and the way in which those processors exchange data. A Beowulf cluster takes advantage of two commodity components: fast CPUs designed primarily for the personal computer market and networks designed to connect personal computers together (in what is called a local area network or LAN). Because these are commodity components, their cost is relatively low. As we will see later in this chapter, there are some performance consequences, and Beowulf clusters are not suitable for all problems. However, for the many problems for which they do work well, Beowulf clusters provide an effective and low-cost solution for delivering enormous computational power to applications and are now used virtually everywhere. This raises the following question: If Beowulf clusters are so great, why didn't they appear earlier?

Many early efforts used clusters of smaller machines, typically workstations, as building blocks in creating low-cost parallel computers. In addition, many software projects developed the basic software for programming parallel machines. Some of these made their software available for all users, and emphasized portability of the code, making these tools easily portable to new machines. But the project that truly launched clusters was the Beowulf project at the NASA Goddard Space Flight center. In 1994, Thomas Sterling, Donald Becker, and others took an early version of the Linux operating system, developed Ethernet driver software for Linux, and installed PVM (a software package for programming parallel computers) on 16 100MHz Intel 80486-based PCs. This cluster used dual 10-Mbit Ethernet to provide improved bandwidth in communications between processors, but was otherwise very simple—and very low cost.

Why did the Beowulf project succeed? Part of the answer is that it was the right solution at the right time. PCs were beginning to become competent computational platforms (a 100MHz 80486 has a faster clock than the original Cray 1, a machine considered one of the most important early supercomputers). The explosion in the size of the PC market was reducing the cost of the hardware through economies of scale. Equally important, however, was a commitment by the Beowulf project to deliver a working solution, not just a research testbed. The Beowulf project worked hard to "dot the i's and cross the t's," addressing many of the real issues standing in the way of widespread adoption of cluster technology for commodity components. This was a critical contribution; making a cluster solid and reliable often requires solving new and even harder problems; it isn't just hacking. The contribution of the community to this effort, through contributions of software and general help to others building clusters, made Beowulf clustering exciting.

Since the early Beowulf clusters, the use of commodity-off-the-shelf (COTS) components for building clusters has mushroomed. Clusters are found everywhere, from schools to dorm rooms to the largest machine rooms. Large clusters are an increasing percentage of the Top500 list. You can still build your own cluster by buying individual components, but you can also buy a preassembled and tested cluster from many vendors, including both large and well-established computer companies and companies formed just to sell clusters.

This book will give you an understanding of what Beowulfs are, where they can be used (and where they can't), and how they work. To illustrate the issues, specific operations, such as installation of a software package are described. However, this book is not a cookbook; software and even hardware change too fast for that to be practical. The best use of this book is to read it for understanding; to build a cluster, *then* go out and find the most up-to-date information on the web about the hardware and software.

Each of the areas discussed in this book could have its own book. In fact, many do, including books in the same MIT Press series. What this book does is give you the basic background so that you can understand Beowulf Clusters. For those areas that are central to your interest in Beowulf computing, we recommend that you read the relevant books. Some of these are described in Appendix B. For the others, this book provides a solid background for understanding how to specify, build, program, and manage a Beowulf cluster.

We begin by defining what a cluster is and why a cluster can be a good computing platform. Since not all applications are appropriate for clusters, Section 1.3 introduces techniques for estimating the performance of an application on a cluster, with an illustration drawn from technical computing. With this background, the next two sections provide two different ways to read this book. Section 1.4 provides a procedural approach, from choosing which components will constitute the cluster to determining how applications can be tuned on the cluster. Section 1.5 provides a topical approach, such as how to program it, run jobs on it, or specify a cluster's components.

1.1 What Is a Cluster?

Before we talk about cluster computing, we need to define our terms. For the purposes of this book, a *cluster* is a parallel computer that is constructed of commodity components and runs (as its system software) commodity software. A cluster is made up of *nodes*, each containing one or more processors, memory that is shared by all of the processors in (and only in) the node, and additional peripheral devices (such as disks), connected by a *network* that allows data to move between the nodes.

Nodes come in many flavors but are usually built from processors designed for the PC or desktop market. Chapter 2 describes processor choices in detail. If a node contains more than one processor, it is called an *SMP* (symmetric multiprocessor) node.

Networks also come in many flavors. These range from very simple (and relatively low-performance) networks based on Ethernet to high-performance networks designed for clusters. Chapter 4 describes network choices in detail.

Clusters can also be divided into two types: do-it-yourself and prepackaged. A do-it-yourself cluster is assembled by the user out of commodity parts that are purchased separately. A prepackaged cluster (sometimes called a turnkey system) is assembled by a cluster vendor, either before or after shipping it to the customer's location. Which you choose depends on your budget, need for outside help, and facility with computer hardware.

1.2 Why Use a Cluster?

Why use a cluster instead of a single computer? There are really two reasons: performance and fault tolerance. The original reason for the development of Beowulf clusters was to provide cost-effective computing power for scientific applications, that is, to address the needs of applications that required greater performance than was available from single (commodity) processors or affordable multiprocessors. An application may desire more computational power for many reasons, but the following three are the most common:

- Real-time constraints, that is, a requirement that the computation finish within a certain period of time. Weather forecasting is an example. Another is processing data produced by an experiment; the data must be processed (or stored) at least as fast as it is produced.

- Throughput. A scientific or engineering simulation may require many computations. A cluster can provide the resources to process many related simulations. On the other hand, some single simulations require so much computing power that a single processor would require days or even years to complete the calculation. An example of using a Linux Beowulf cluster for throughput is Google [13], which uses over 15,000 commodity PCs with fault-tolerant software to provide a high-performance Web search service.

- Memory. Some of the most challenging applications require huge amounts of data as part of the simulation. A cluster provides an effective way to provide even terabytes (10^{12} bytes) of program memory for an application.

Clusters provide the computational power through the use of *parallel programming*, a technique for coordinating the use of many processors for a single problem. Part II (Parallel Programming) discusses this approach in detail. What clusters are *not* good for is accelerating calculations that are neither memory intensive nor processing-power intensive or (in a way that will be made precise below) that require frequent communication between the processors in the cluster.

Another reason for using clusters is to provide fault tolerance, that is, to ensure that computational power is always available. Because clusters are assembled from many copies of the same or similar components, the failure of a single part only reduces the cluster's power. Thus, clusters are particularly good choices for environments that require guarantees of available processing power, such as Web servers and systems used for data collection.

We note that fault tolerance can be interpreted in several ways. For a Web server or data handling, the cluster can be considered up as long as enough processors and network capacity are available to meet the demand. A well-designed cluster can provide a virtual guarantee of availabilty, short of a disaster such as a fire that strikes the whole cluster. Such a cluster will have virtually 100% uptime. For scientific applications, the interpretation of uptime is often different. For clusters used for scientific applications, however, particularly ones used to provide adequate memory, uptime is measured relative to the minimum size of cluster (e.g., number of nodes) that allows the applications to run. In many cases, all or nearly all of the nodes in the cluster must be available to run these applications.

Of course, many uses of clusters are a blend of these two approaches. Part III describes tools for sharing a cluster among users and, in many cases, providing support for both performance-oriented and fault-tolerant computing.

1.3 Understanding Application Requirements

In order to know what applications are suitable for cluster computing and what tradeoffs are involved in designing a cluster, one needs to understand the requirements of applications.

1.3.1 Computational Requirements

The most obvious requirement (at least in scientific and technical applications) is the number of floating-point operations needed to perform the calculation. For simple calculations, estimating this number is relatively easy; even in more complex cases, a rough estimate is usually possible. Most communities have a large body of literature on the floating-point requirements of applications, and these results should be consulted first. Most textbooks on numerical analysis will give formulas for the number of floating-point operations required for many common operations. For example, the solution of a system of n linear equations; solved with the most common algorithms, takes $2n^3/3$ floating-point operations. Similar formulas hold for many common problems.

You might expect that by comparing the number of floating-point operations with the performance of the processor (in terms of peak operations per second), you can make a good estimate of the time to perform a computation. For example, on a 2 GHz processor, capable of 2×10^9 floating-point operations per second (2 GFLOPS), a computation that required 1 billion floating-point operations would take only half a second. However, this estimate ignores the large role that the performance of the memory system plays in the performance of the overall system. In many cases, the rate at which data can be delivered to the processor is a better measure of the achievable performance of an application (see [45, 60] for examples).

Thus, when considering the computational requirements, it is imperative to know what the expected achievable performance will be. In some cases this may be estimated by using standard benchmarks such as LINPACK [34] and STREAM [71], but it is often best to run a representative sample of the application (or application mix) on a candidate processor. After all, one of the advantages of cluster computing is that the individual components, such as the processor nodes, are relatively inexpensive.

1.3.2 Memory

The memory needs of an application strongly affect both the performance of the application and the cost of the cluster. As described in Section 2.1, the memory on a compute node is divided into several major types. *Main memory* holds the entire problem and should be chosen to be large enough to contain all of the data needed by an application (distributed, of course, across all the nodes in the cluster). *Cache* memory is smaller but faster memory that is used to improve the performance of applications. Some applications will benefit more from cache memory than others; in some cases, application performance can be very sensitive to the size of cache memory. *Virtual memory* is memory that appears to be available to the application but is actually mapped so that some of it can be stored on disk; this greatly enlarges the available memory for an application for low monetary cost (disk space is cheap). Because disks are electromechanical devices, access to memory that is stored on disk is very slow. Hence, some high-performance clusters do not use virtual memory.

1.3.3 I/O

Results of computations must be placed into nonvolatile storage, such as a disk file. Parallel computing makes it possible to perform computations very quickly, leading to commensurate demands on the I/O system. Other applications, such as Web servers or data analysis clusters, need to serve up data previously stored on a file system.

Section 5.3.4 describes the use of the network file system (NFS) to allow any node in a cluster to access any file. However, NFS provides neither high performance nor correct semantics for concurrent access to the same file (see Section 19.3.2 for details). Fortunately, a number of high-performance parallel file systems exist for Linux; the most mature is described in Chapter 19. Some of the issues in choosing I/O components are covered in Chapter 2.

1.3.4 Other Requirements

A cluster may need other resources. For example, a cluster used as a highly-available and scalable Web server requires good external networking. A cluster used for visualization on a tiled display requires graphics cards and connections to the projectors. A cluster that is used as the primary computing resource requires access to an archival storage system to support backups and user-directed data archiving.

1.3.5 Parallelism

Parallel applications can be categorized in two major classes. One class is called *embarassingly* (or sometimes *pleasingly*) parallel. These applications are easily divided into smaller tasks that can be executed independently. One common example of this kind of parallel application is a parameter study, where a single program is presented with different initial inputs. Another example is a Web server, where each request is an independent request for information stored on the web server. These applications are easily ported to a cluster; a cluster provides an easily administered and fault-tolerant platform for executing such codes.

The other major class of parallel applications comprise those that cannot be broken down into independent subtasks. Such applications must usually be written with explicit (programmer-specified) parallelism; in addition, their performance depends both on the performance of the individual compute nodes and on the network that allows those nodes to communicate. To understand whether an application can be run effectively on a cluster (or on any parallel machine), we must first quantify the node and communication performance of typical cluster components. The key terms are as follows:

latency: The minimum time to send a message from one process to another.

overhead: The time that the CPU must spend to perform the communication. (Often included as part of the latency.)

bandwidth: The rate at which data can be moved between processes

contention: The performance consequence of communication between different processes sharing some resource, such as network wires.

With these terms, we can discuss the performance of an application on a cluster. We begin with the simplest model, which includes only latency and bandwith terms. In this model, the time to send n bytes of data between two processes can be approximated by

$$T = s + rn, \tag{1.1}$$

where s is the latency and r is the inverse of the bandwidth. Typical numbers for Beowulf clusters range from 5 to 100 microseconds for s and from 0.01 to 0.1 microseconds/byte for r. Note that a 2 GHz processor can begin a new floating-point computation every 0.0005 microseconds.

One way to think about the time to communicate data is to make the latency and bandwidth terms nondimensional in terms of the floating-point rate. For example, if we take a 2 GHz processor and typical choices of network for a Beowulf cluster, the ratio of latency to floating-point rate ranges from 10,000 to 200,000! What this tells us is that parallel programs for clusters must involve a significant amount of work between communication operatoins. Fortunately, many applications have this property.

The simple model is adequate for many uses. A slightly more sophisticated model, called logP [31], separates the overhead from the latency.

Chapter 7 contains more discussion on complexity models. Additional examples appear throughout this book. For example, Section 8.2 discusses the performance of a master/worker example that uses the Message-Passing Interface (MPI) as the programming model.

1.3.6 Estimating Application Requirements

What does all of the above mean for choosing a cluster? Let's look at a simple partial differential equation (PDE) calculation, typical of many scientific simulations.

Consider a PDE in a three-dimensional cube, discretized with a regular mesh with N points along a side, for a total of N^3 points. (An example of a 2-D PDE approximation is presented in Section 8.3.) We will assume that the solution algorithm uses a simple time-marching scheme involving only six floating-point operations per mesh point. We also assume that each mesh point has only four values (either three coordinate values and an unknown or four unknowns). This problem seems simple until we put in the numbers. Let $N = 1024$, which provides adequate (though not exceptional) resolution for many problems. For our simple 3-D problem, this then gives us

$$\begin{aligned} \text{Data size} &= 2 \times 4 \times (1024)^3 = 8 \text{ GWords} = 64 \text{ GBytes} \\ \text{Work per step} &= 6 \times (1024)^3 = 6 \text{ GFlop} \end{aligned}$$

This assumes that two time steps must be in memory at the same time (previous and current) and that each floating-point value is 8 bytes.

From this simple computation, we can see the need for parallel computing:

1. The total memory size exceeds that available on most single nodes. In addition, since only 4 GBytes of memory are directly addressable by 32-bit processors, solving this problem on a single node requires either a 64-bit processor or specialized out-of-core techniques.

2. The amount of work seems reasonable for a single processor, many of which are approaching 6 GFlops (giga floating-point operations per second). However,

as we will see below, the actual rate of computation for this problem will be much smaller.

Processors are advertised with their clock rate, with the implication that the processor can perform useful work at this rate. For example, a 2 GHz processor suggests that it can perform 2 billion operations per second. What this ignores is whether the processor can access data fast enough to keep the processor busy. For example, consider the following code, where the processor is multiplying two vectors of floating-point numbers together and storing the result:

```
for (i=0; i<n; i++)
    c[i] = a[i] * b[i];
```

This requires two loads of a `double` and a store for each element. To perform 2 billion of these per second requires that the memory system move $3 \times 8 \times 10^9 =$ 24 GBytes/sec. However, no commodity nodes possess this kind of memory system performance. Typical memory system rates are in the range of 0.2 to 1 GBytes/second (see Section 2.3). As a result, for computations that must access data from main memory, the achieved (or observed) performance is often a small fraction of the peak performance. In this example, the most common nodes could achieve only 1–4% of the peak performance.

Depending on the application, the memory system performance may be a better indicator of the likely achievable performance. A good measure of the memory-bandwidth performance of a node is the STREAM [71] benchmark. This measures the achieved performance of the memory system, using a simple program, and thus is more likely to measures the performance available to the user than any number based on the basic hardware.

For our example PDE application, the achieved performance will be dominated by the memory bandwidth rather than the raw CPU performance. Thus, when selecting nodes, particularly for a low-cost cluster, the price per MByte/sec, rather than the price per MFlop/sec, can be a better guide.

We can parallelize this application by breaking the mesh into smaller pieces, with each node processing a single piece as shown in Figure 1.1. This process is called *domain decomposition*. However, the pieces are not independent; to compute the values for the next time step, values from the neighboring pieces are needed (see Section 8.3 for details). As a result, we must now consider the cost to communicate the data between nodes as well as the computational cost.

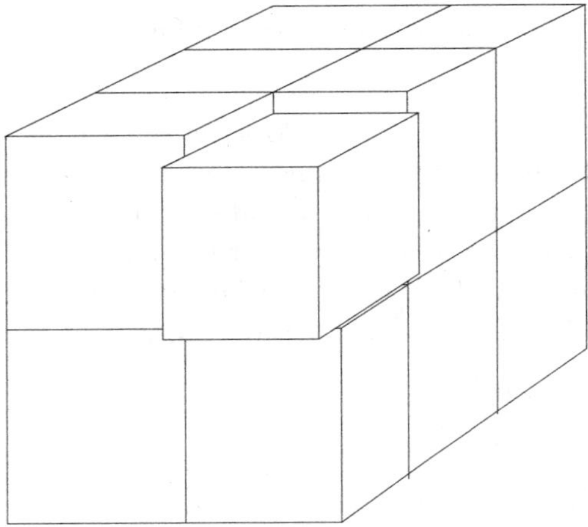

Figure 1.1: Sample decomposition of a 3-D mesh. The upper right corner box has been pulled out to show that the mesh has been subdivided along the x, y, and z axes.

For this simple problem, using the communication model above, we can estimate the time for a single step, using p nodes, as

$$T = \frac{1}{p}N^3 f + 6\left(s + r\frac{N^2}{p^{2/3}}\right). \qquad (1.2)$$

The first term is the floating-point work, which decreases proportionally with an increase in the number of processors p. The second term gives the cost of communicating each of the six faces to the neighboring processors, and includes both a term independent of the number of processors, and a term that scales as $p^{2/3}$, which comes from dividing the original domain into p cubes, each with $N/p^{1/3}$ along a side. Note that even for an infinite number of nodes, the time for a step is at least $6s$ (the minimum time or latency to communicate with each of the six neighbors). Thus it makes no sense to use an unlimited number of processors. The actual choice depends on the goal of the cluster:

- Minimize cost: In this case, you should choose nodes so that each subdomain fits on a node. In our example, if each node had 2 GBytes of memory, we would need at least 32 nodes (probably more, to leave room for the operating system and other parts of the application).
- Achieve a real-time constraint such as steps per second: In this case, T is specified and Equation 1.2 is solved for p, the number of nodes. Beware of

setting T very small; as a rule of thumb, the floating-point work (the $N^3 f/p$ term) should be large compared to the communication terms. In this case, as p becomes large, and since

$$T \approx \frac{1}{p} N^3 f + 6s,$$

in order to make the communication a smaller part of the overall time than that computation, we must have

$$\begin{aligned} \frac{1}{p} N^3 f &> 6s \\ p &< \frac{N^3 f}{6s}. \end{aligned}$$

For the typical values of s/f and for $N = 1024$, this bound is not very strong and limits p to a only few thousand nodes. For smaller N, however, this limit can be severe. For example, if $N = 128$ instead and if fast Ethernet is used for the network, this formula implies that $p < 10$.

Some notes on this example:

- We chose a three-dimensional calculation. Many two-dimensional calculations are best carried out on a single processor (consider this an exercise for the reader!).
- The total memory space exceeds that addressable by a 32-bit processor. But because we are using a cluster, we can still use 32-bit processors, as long as we use enough of them.
- The expected performance is likely to be a small fraction of the "peak" performance. We don't care; the *cost* of the cluster is low.
- If there are enough nodes, the problem may fit within the much faster cache memory (though this would require thousands of nodes for this example). In that case, the computing rate can be as much as an order of magnitude higher—even before factoring in the benefits of parallelism! This is an example of *superlinear speedup*: speedup that is greater than p on p processors. This is a result of the nonlinear behavior of performance on memory size and is not paradoxical.
- Latency here has played a key role in determining performance. In other computations, however, including ones for PDEs that use different decompositions, the bandwidth term may be the dominant communication term.

- Since each time step generates 64 GBytes of data, a high-performance I/O system is required to keep the I/O times from dominating everything else. Fortunately, Beowulf clusters can provide high I/O performance through the use of parallel file systems, such as PVFS, discussed in Chapter 19.

1.4 Building and Using a Cluster

In this section we review the issues in configuring, building, and using a cluster and provide references to the corresponding sections of this book. Section 1.5 provides an alternate view of this book, organized around particular tasks, such as programming or managing a cluster.

1.4.1 Choosing a Cluster

When choosing the components for a cluster, or selecting from a prebuilt cluster, you must focus on the applications that will be run on the cluster. The following list covers some of the issues to consider.

1. Understanding the needs of your application. Some of this has been covered above; you will find more on understanding the performance of applications in Part II.

2. Decide the number and type of nodes. Based on the application needs, select a node type (e.g., uni-processor or SMP), processor type, and memory system. Chapter 2 covers node hardware. As described above, raw CPU clock rate is not always a good guide to performance, so make sure that you have a good understanding of the applications. Other issues to consider when choosing the processor type include whether you will run prebuilt applications that require a particular type of processor, whether you need 64-bit or 32-bit addressing, or whether your codes are integer or floating-point intensive.

3. Decide on the network. Determine whether your applications require low latency and/or high bandwidth in the network. If not, for example, running a throughput cluster with embarassingly parallel applications, then simple fast Ethernet with low-cost switches may be adequate. Otherwise, you may need to invest in a high-performance cluster network. These network choices are covered in more detail in Chapter 4. Note that the cost of a fast Ethernet network is very low while a high performance network can double the cost of a cluster.

4. Determine the physical infrastructure needs. How much floor space, power, and cooling will you need. Is noise a factor?

5. Determine the operating system (OS) that you will use. Since you bought this book, you have probably selected Linux. Chapter 3 will help you select a particular distribution of Linux as well as understand how to tune Linux for your cluster. The choice of cluster setup software may also influence which distribution of Linux you can use; this is covered in Chapter 6. In choosing the operating system, consider the following:

    - Do your applications run on the chosen system? Many applications and programming models (Part II) run under many operating systems, including Windows, Linux, and other forms of Unix.
    - Do you have expertise with a particular operating system?
    - Are there license issues (cost of acquiring or leasing) software, including the operating system and compilers?

6. Cost tradeoffs. The cost of a node is not linearly related to the performance of that node. The fastest nodes are more expensive per flop (and usually per MByte/sec of memory bandwidth) than are lower-cost nodes. The question is then: Should a cluster use the fastest available nodes regardless of cost, or should it use mid-range or even low-range nodes? The answer depends, as always, on your needs:

    - If price is no object, go with the fastest nodes. This approach will reduce the *number* of nodes needed for any given amount of computing power, and thus the amount of parallel overhead.
    - If total computing power over time is the goal, then go with mid- or low-end nodes, but replace them frequently (say, every 18 months to two years) with newer nodes. This strategy exploits the rapid advances in node performance; buying two low-end nodes every two years will often give you a greater amount of computing power (integrated over time) than spending the same amount every four years on a high-end node.
    - If a targeted amount of computing power (e.g., for a specific application) is the goal, then analyze the tradeoffs between a greater number of slower (but possibly much cheaper) nodes and a smaller number of faster but individually less cost-efficient nodes.

1.4.2 Setting Up a Cluster

Once you have specified your cluster, you need to assemble the components and set up the initial software. Chapters 2 and 4 cover some of the issues in assembling the hardware for both the nodes and the network. Chapter 20 discusses cluster setup in the context of two generations of clusters used at Argonne National Laboratory.

In the past few years, great strides have been made in simplifying the process of initializing the software environment on a cluster. Chapter 6 covers the most popular packages and provides advice on setting up your new cluster.

At this point, you may wish to benchmark your cluster. Since such benchmarking will require running a parallel program, information on this topic is provided in Part II, Sections 9.10 and 9.10.3. Alternatively, you may prefer to run a prepackaged performance suite, such as the Beowulf Performance Suite (BPS), available at `www.plogic.com/bps`. BPS contains both single node and parallel performance tests, including the following:

bonnie++: I/O (disk) performance; `www.coker.com.au/bonnie++`

Stream: Memory system performance; `www.cs.virginia.edu/stream`

netperf: General network performance; `www.netperf.org/netperf/NetperfPage.html`

netpipe: A more detailed network performance benchmark; `www.scl.ameslab.gov/Projects/ClusterCookbook/nprun.html`

unixbench: General Unix benchmarks; `www.linuxdoc.org/HOWTO/Benchmarking-HOWTO.html`

LMbench: Low-level benchmarks; `www.bitmover.com/lmbench`

NAS parallel benchmarks: A suite of parallel benchmarks derived from some important applications; `www.nas.nasa.gov/Software/NPB`

1.4.3 Developing New Applications

Before deciding to develop new applications, check out what is already available for clusters. Chapter 12 provides a guide to software that is already available, either as full programs or as libraries that can be used to build new applications with little or no explicitly parallel programming. New applications are constantly being developed, so check the web and the Beowulf mailing lists before starting to develop your own application. If what you need is not yet available, then Part II provides an introduction to parallel programming, covering both the most popular tools for building embarrassingly parallel applications as well as the two most popular libraries for parallel programming, MPI (Chapters 8 and 9) and PVM (Chapters 10 and 11). These chapters also contain information on tuning and testing applications. Section 9.10 covers the most common cluster performance benchmarks, including High Performance LINPACK (Section 9.10.3).

1.4.4 Operating a Cluster

Once your cluster is up and running, you (or someone) will need to operate it. Chapter 13 covers the basics of system management for clusters, including account administration, security, monitoring, and file system backups. Chapter 19 discusses parallel I/O in general and the systems administration issues for the Parallel Virtual File System (PVFS) in particular.

One of the biggest decisions is whether the cluster will allow provide interactive use, batch use, or a mixture of both. Since batch use is a common way to use clusters, Chapter 14 provides an overview of the issues and many of the available batch systems. This chapter is followed by chapters on individual batch systems.

1.4.5 Getting Help

Many resources are available to which you can turn for help. One of the best is the Beowulf mailing list. To subscribe, visit `www.beowulf.org/mailman/listinfo/beowulf`. The Beowulf Web site, `www.beowulf.org`, also provides much valuable information.

A major strength of Linux is the community. The Beowulf mailing list (`beowulf@beowulf.org`) is a good place to go for answers to all kinds of questions.

1.5 Another Way to Read This Book

This book may also be used as an introduction to the various areas of Beowulf computing. Each part, and to some extent, each chapter may be read independently of the others. This section makes recommendations based on how you intend to use your cluster, providing a different persective on the book than that presented in the preceding section. Additional information on all of these topics may be found in the reading list in Appendix B and the URLs in Appendix C.

1.5.1 Using a Cluster Operated by Someone Else

If you are using a cluster that someone else is operating, you need only learn how to program and run applications.

Part II covers programming clusters. Even if you do not intend to develop your own parallel applications, we recommend reading Chapter 7, which provides an overview of the technologies. For a deeper understanding of the parallel programming technologies, read the chapters on MPI (Chapters 8 and 9) and PVM (Chapters 10 and 11). Even if you plan to write your own parallel software, you should read Chapter 12 on parallel software and libraries. You may find that what you need has already been written!

Once you have your application, you will need to run your program. Part III covers tools for managing and using a cluster. Many clusters will use some kind of workload management system to mediate use of the cluster among the user community. Chapter 14 provides an overview of the concepts and capabilities of these systems. You should also read the chapter that corresponds to the workload system that is used on your cluster: Condor (Chapter 15), Maui (Chapter 16), PBS (Chapter 17), or Scyld (Chapter 18). If your application requires a high-performance, parallel I/O system, read Chapter 19 on the Parallel Virtual File System. These chapters cover information of interest to both the system administrator and the cluster user, so skip over material that doesn't apply to you.

1.5.2 Choosing Cluster Components

First, re-read this chapter and pay close attention to the discussion of application requirements. These requirements will guide you in your choice of cluster components. Chapters 2 and 4 describe the choices of processor, network, and other hardware. Even if you plan to buy a preassembled cluster, these chapters will help you understand the various choices of components and aid you in understanding the specifications of a cluster. Chapter 2 also covers some of the issues of assembling your own cluster.

1.5.3 Operating a Cluster

Operating a cluster requires an understanding of the operating system. Chapter 3 provides a brief introduction along with a discussion of cluster-specific issues. Chapter 6 describes tools for setting up a cluster. An introduction to managing a cluster from the point of view of the system administrator is presented in Chapter 13. Chapter 14 provides an overview of the concepts and capabilities of these systems. The chapters on the individual systems provide information on both the use and management of workload management systems: Condor (Chapter 15), Maui (Chapter 16), PBS (Chapter 17), or Scyld (Chapter 18). Once the cluster is up and running, you may need to tune the network and operating system. Chapter 3 provides some information on tuning the OS; Chapter 5 discusses techniques for tuning the network and communication systems. Finally, Chapter 20 provides a case study of two generations of a major cluster system, illustrating particular choices and best practices.

I ENABLING TECHNOLOGIES

2 Node Hardware

Narayan Desai and Thomas Sterling

Few technologies in human civilization have experienced such a rate of growth as that of the digital computer and its culmination in the PC. Its low cost, ubiquity, and sometimes trivial application often obscure its complexity and precision as one of the most sophisticated products derived from science and engineering. In a single human lifetime over the fifty-year history of computer development, performance and memory capacity have grown by a factor of almost a million. Where once computers were reserved for the special environments of carefully structured machine rooms, now they are found in almost every office and home. A personal computer today outperforms the world's greatest supercomputers of two decades ago at less than one ten-thousandth the cost. It is the product of this extraordinary legacy that Beowulf harnesses to open new vistas in computation.

A Beowulf cluster is a network of nodes, with each node a low-cost personal computer. Its power and simplicity are derived from exploiting the capabilities of the mass-market systems that provide both the processing and the communication. This chapter explores the hardware elements related to computation and storage. The choice of node hardware, along with the choice of a system area network, will determine the basic performance properties of the Beowulf for its entire operational lifetime. Neither of these choices should be taken lightly; tremendous variation exists among instances of all components involved. This chapter discusses the components included in a cluster node, their function in a system, and their effects on node performance. Communication hardware is discussed in detail in Chapter 4.

The purpose of a Beowulf cluster is to perform parallel computations. This is accomplished by running applications across a number of nodes simultaneously. These applications may perform in parallel; that is, they may need to coordinate during execution. On the other hand, they may be performing an embarrassingly parallel task, or a large group of serial tasks. One key factor in application performance in all cases is local node performance.

2.1 Node Hardware Overview

A cluster node is responsible for all activities and capabilities associated with executing an application program and supporting a sophisticated software environment. The process of application involves a large number of components. An application is actually executed on the main CPU. The CPU loads data from its cache and main memory into registers. All applications use peripherals, such as persistent storage or network transmission, for noncomputational tasks. All peripherals load data into or process data from main memory, where it can be accessed by the system CPU. Applications can be characterized in terms of these three basic operations:

- Instruction execution: operating on data in registers, storing the results in term in registers. This operation is implemented entirely by the CPU.
- Register loading: loading data from main memory or processor cache into processor registers to facilitate instruction execution. This operation involves the CPU, front-side bus, and system memory.
- Peripheral usage: copying data across an I/O bus into or out of main memory to allow for a noncomputational task to occur. This operation involves the peripheral, the I/O bus, and the interface from the I/O bus into system memory, and system memory itself.

The system *CPU* is the main processor, on which most code is executed. A node may have more than one of these, operating in SMP (symmetric multiprocessing) mode. This processor will have some amount of cache. *Cache* is used for fast access to data in main memory. Cache is typically ten times faster than main memory, so it is advantageous to load data into cache before using it. *Main memory* is the location where running programs, including the operating system, store all data. It is not persistent; data that should survive beyond a reboot is copied to some persistent medium, such as a hard disk. An *I/O bus* connects main memory with all peripherals. The peripherals (disk controllers, network controllers, video cards, etc.) operate by manipulating data from main memory. For example, a disk write will occur by copying data across the I/O bus to the disk controller. The disk controller will then actually write the data to disk.

In detail, when an application is executed, it is loaded from disk or some other persistent storage into main memory. When execution actually begins, parts of the application are copied into processor cache. From here, the data is written into on-processor registers, where the processor can directly access it. When the processor is done with this data, it is copied back out to main memory. When the application is dependent on data from a peripheral (e.g., data read from hard disk, or data received on a network interface) loading data into registers becomes much more complex. For example, a kernel call will result in a disk controller's reading of data from hard disk into local storage on the controller. The controller will copy the data across the I/O bus to system main memory, from which it can be loaded into registers for the processor to operate on. Each of these steps is faster than the proceeding step; indeed, there are several orders of magnitude difference between the speeds of the first step and the last step. All applications can be characterized in terms of these basic three types of activities.

2.2 Microprocessor

A microprocessor (also referred to as the CPU or processor) is at the heart of any computer. It is the single component that implements instruction execution. Processors vary in a number of ways; we focus on the more important characteristics. The lowest-level binary encoding of the instructions and the actions they perform are dictated by the microprocessor instruction set architecture (ISA). The most common ISA used for cluster node CPU is IA32, or X86. This family of processors includes all generations of the Pentium processor and the Athlon family. A shared ISA doesn't imply an identical instruction set; newer processors have extra features that old processors do not. For example, SSE and SSE2 are numerical instruction sets that were added in Pentium III and Pentium 4 processors, respectively. The earliest clusters were composed of 486 processors, which implement this ISA.

A processor runs at a particular clock rate. That is, it can execute instructions at a particular frequency, measured in terms of megahertz or gigahertz. For example, a 2.4 GHz processor can execute a rate of 2.4 billion instructions per second. Note that a processor's clock rate is not a direct measure of performance. Frequently, processors with different clock rates can perform equivalently for some tasks; likewise, two processors with the same clock rate can perform quite differently for some tasks. Current clock rates range from 1 GHz to slightly over 3 GHz.

Any processor has a theoretical peak speed. Theoretical peak is the maximum rate of instruction execution a processor can achieve. This is determined by the clock rate, ISA, and components included in the processor itself. This rate is measured in floating-point operations per second, or flops. A current generation processor will have a theoretical peak of 3-5 gigaflops. As one might guess from the name, theoretical peak is just that, *theoretical*. A processor rarely, if ever, runs at that rate while executing a real user application.

Both the instructions and the data upon which they act are stored in and loaded from the node's random access memory (RAM). The speed of a processor is often measured in megahertz, indicating that its clock ticks so many million times per second. RAM runs at a much slower clock rate, usually measured in hundreds of megahertz. Thus, the processor often waits for memory, and the overall rate at which programs run is usually governed as much by the memory system as by the processor's clock speed.

The slow rate at which data can be copied from RAM is mitigated by a processor's cache. The cache is a small amount of fast memory usually co-located on the CPU. When data is copied from main memory, it is also stored in cache. If the same data is accessed again, it can be read from cache. This is highly advantageous: applications can be optimized to access memory in patterns that take the best possible advantage of cache speed. The quicker access to memory in cache leads to better processor utilization; the processor spends less time waiting for data from memory. Processor caches vary in size from kilobytes on some processors to upwards of four to eight megabytes on processors specified to provide good floating point performance. Obviously, the larger the cache is, the easier it is to reuse entries stored in it.

2.2.1 IA32

IA32 is the most common ISA used in clusters today, and for the foreseeable future. This is caused by the enormous economies of scale at work. Processors implementing this ISA are used in the majority of desktop PCs sold. IA32 is a 32-bit instruction set. It is treated as a binary compatibility specification. Multiple processors, implemented in vastly different ways, all implement the same instruction set to allow for application portability. The three most common processors used in clusters today are the Pentium III and 4 processors, manufactured by Intel, and AMD's Athlon processor. Recent additions to the IA32 ISA include SSE and its successor SSE2. (Streaming SIMD Extensions) SSE and SSE2 are instruction set extensions that define instructions that can be performed in parallel on multiple data elements; these are not necessarily implemented in all instances of IA32 processors. These features can yield substantially improved performance, so care should be taken when choosing the processor for a new system. Hyperthreading is another feature recently added to the IA32 ISA. It allows multiple threads of execution per physical CPU. This feature typically impacts application performance negatively and can be disabled, so it really isn't a decision point when choosing a CPU, as SSE and SSE2 are.

Pentium 4. The Pentium 4 implements the IA32 instruction set but uses an internal architecture that diverges substantially from the old P6 architecture. The internal architecture is geared for high clock speeds; it produces less computing power per clock cycle but is capable of extremely high frequencies. This architecture is also the only IA32 processor family that implements the SSE2 instruction set, providing a substantial performance benefit for some applications. This is also the only architecture that implements hyperthreading, but (as was mentioned previously) this feature is not terribly important for computational applications typically run on clusters.

Pentium III. The Pentium III is based on the older Pentium Pro architecture. It is a minor upgrade from the Pentium II; it includes SSE for three-dimensional instructions and has moved the L2 cache onto the chip, making it synchronized with the processor's clock. The Pentium III can be used within an SMP node with two processors; a more expensive variant, the Pentium III Xeon, can be used in four-processor SMP nodes.

Athlon. The AMD Athlon platform is similar to the Pentium III in its processor architecture but similar to the Compaq Alpha in its bus architecture. It has two large 64 KByte L1 caches and a 256 KByte L2 cache that run at the processor's clock speed. The performance is a little better than that of the Pentium III and Pentium 4 in general at similar clock rates, but either can be faster depending on the application. The Athlon supports dual-processor SMP nodes. Newer Athlon processors support SSE, but not SSE2.

2.2.2 Other Processor Types

HP Alpha 21264. The Compaq (now HP and originally DEC) Alpha processor is a true 64-bit architecture. For many years, the Alpha held the lead in many benchmarks, including the SPEC benchmarks, and was used in many of the fastest supercomputers, including the Cray T3D and T3E, as well as the Compaq SC family. Alpha are still popular with some users, but since the Alpha processor line is no longer being developed and the current Alpha processor will be the last, Alphas are rarely chosen for new systems. However, a few large clusters make use of Alphas, including the ASCI Q system at Los Alamos National Laboratory; ASCI Q is one of the fastest systems in the world, according to the Top500 list.

The Alpha uses a Reduced Instruction Set Computer (RISC) architecture, distinguishing it from Intel's Pentium processors. RISC designs, which have dominated the workstation market of the past decade, eschew complex instructions and addressing modes, resulting in simpler processors running at higher clock rates, but executing somewhat more instructions to complete the same task.

PowerPC G5. The IBM PowerPC is an processor architecture used in products from IBM and from Apple. The newest processor is the G5, a sophisticated 64-

bit processor capable of running at speeds of up to 2GHz. Other features include a 1GHz frontside bus and multiple functional units, allowing the G5 to perform multiple operations in each clock cycle. Apple sells Macs with the G5 processor, and a number of groups have built clusters using Macs, running Mac OS X (a Unix-like operating system).

IA64. The IA64 is Intel's first 64-bit architecture. This is an all-new design, with a new instruction set, new cache design, and new floating-point processor design. With clock rates approaching 1 GHz and multiway floating-point instruction issue, Itanium should be the first implementation to provide between 1 and 2 Gflops peak performance. The first systems with the Itanium processor were released in the middle of 2001 and have delivered impressive results. For example, the HP Server rx4610, using a single 800 MHz Itanium, delivered a SPECfp2000 of 701, comparable to recent Alpha-based systems. More recent results with a 1.5 GHz Itanium 2 in an HP rx2600 server gave a SPECfp2000 of 2119. The IA64 architecture does, however, require significant help from the compiler to exploit what Intel calls EPIC (explicitly parallel instruction computing).

Opteron. Another 64-bit architecture is AMD's Opteron. Unlike the Intel IA64 architecture, the Opteron supports both the IA32 instruction set as well as a new 64-bit extension, allowing users to continue to use their existing 32-bit applications while taking advantage of a 64-bit instruction set for applications that require easy access to more than 4 GB of memory. The Opteron includes an integrated DDR memory controller and a high-performance interconnect called "HyperTransport" that provides up to 6.4 GB/sec bandwidth per link; each Opteron may have three HyperTransport links. Early Opterons have delivered a SPECfp2000 of 1154. The AMD Opteron is used in the Cray "Red Storm," that will use over 10,000 processors and have a peak performance of over 40 Teraflops.

2.3 Memory

A system's random access memory (RAM, or memory) is a temporary storage location used to store instructions and data. Instructions are the actual operations a processor executes. The data comes from a variety of sources. It may be data supplied by some peripheral, such as a hard disk or network controller. It may be intermediary results generated during program execution. Instructions and data are both required for the processor to compute a meaningful result. Hence, the processor constantly is issuing commands to load or store data from memory across the memory bus. Memory buses operate at rates between 100 MHz and 800 MHz. This bus is also referred to as the front side bus, or FSB.

Because of the constant usage of system RAM and the large gap between processor clock rate and memory bus rate, the memory bus is one of the largest impediments to achieving theoretical peak. Memory bus performance is measured in terms of two characteristics. The first is peak memory bandwidth, the burst rate that data can be copied between the DRAM chips in main memory and the CPU. The FSB must be fast enough to support this high burst rate. In the case of some proprietary systems, memory accesses are pipelined to improve aggregate memory bandwidth. In this case, data is bursted from multiple groups of DRAM chips. However, this technique is not used in PC systems. The second characteristic is memory latency, the amount of time it takes to move data between RAM and the CPU. RAM bandwidth ranges from one to four gigabytes per second. RAM latency has fallen to under 6 nanoseconds.

Except for very carefully designed applications, a program's entire dataset must reside in RAM. The alternative is to use disk storage either explicitly (out-of-core calculations) or implicitly (virtual memory swapping), but this usually entails a severe performance penalty. Thus, the size of a node's memory is important in parameter in system design. It determines the size of problem that can practically be run on the node. Engineering and scientific applications often obey a rule of thumb that says that for every floating-point operation per second, one byte of RAM is necessary. This is a gross approximation at best, and actual requirements can vary by many orders of magnitude, but it provides some guidance; for example, a 1 GHz processor capable of sustaining 200 Mflops should be equipped with approximately 200 MBytes of RAM.

Two main types of RAM are used in current commodity systems. SDRAM has been in use for several years. RDRAM is a newer standard used only in Pentium 4-based systems. RDRAM tends to be faster and more expensive.

2.4 I/O Channels

I/O channels are buses that connect peripherals with main memory. These peripherals will range from disk and network controllers to video controllers, and USB and firewire. Machines will have several of these buses, each connected by a bridge (also referred to as the PCI chipset) into main memory. Because I/O is one of the most common tasks on computers, this subsystem is an integral part of any system.

2.4.1 PCI and PCI-X

The most common I/O channel in commodity hardware is the PCI bus. Every machine sold today has at least one; many have multiples of these buses. Many flavors of PCI exist; these buses have been included in commodity hardware since 1994. Earlier versions of the PCI bus were 32-bit, 33 MHz buses. The theoretical maximum rate of data transmission on these buses is 132 MB/s. Good implementations of the PCI chipset are able to provide nearly this rate; maximum observed bus rates greater than 125 MB/s are not uncommon.

Newer revisions of PCI buses are 64-bit buses, running at 66 MHz or higher. These buses have become quite common over the last three to four years. The theoretical maximum rate for these is upwards of 500 MB/s. Good implementations of this PCI chipset provide between 400 and 500 MB/s of read and write bandwidth. Good PCI-X implementations, running at 133 MHz, provide upwards on 900 MB/s of read and write bandwidth.

2.4.2 AGP

AGP is a port used for high-speed graphics adapters. It is connected closely with main memory, providing better peak bandwidth than that offered by PCI or PCI-X. AGP devices are able to directly use data out of main memory. AGP is not a bus, like PCI. It is only able to support one device, and systems only have one port. AGP 2.0 provided a peak bandwidth over 1 GB/s to main memory. The successor to this, AGP 3.0, provides upwards of 2.1 GB/s to main memory.

2.4.3 Legacy Buses

Older machines will also have other buses. The ISA bus is an 8 or 16-bit bus, commonly used in older machines. Vesa local bus is a 24-bit bus, common in some generations of 486 machines. EISA is an extension to ISA that was common in older servers. All of these buses should be avoided if possible: They are slow, and peripheral choice is non-existent.

2.5 Motherboard

The motherboard is a printed circuit board that contains most of the active electronic components of the PC node and their interconnection. The motherboard provides the logical and physical infrastructure for integrating the subsystems of a cluster node and determines the set of components that may be used. The motherboard defines the functionality of the node, the range of performance that can be exploited, the maximum capacities of its storage, and the number of subsystems that can be interconnected. With the exception of the microprocessor itself, the selection of the motherboard is the most important decision in determining the qualities of the PC node to be used as the building block of the system. It is certainly the most obvious piece of a node other than the case or packaging in which it is enclosed.

The motherboard integrates all of the electronics of the node in a robust and configurable package. Sockets and connectors on the motherboard include the following:

- Microprocessor(s)
- Memory
- Peripheral controllers on the PCI-X bus
- AGP port
- Floppy disk cables
- ATA or SCSI cables for hard disk and CD-ROM
- Power
- Front panel LEDs, speakers, switches, and so forth.
- External I/O for mouse, keyboard, joystick, serial line, sound, USB, and so forth.

Other chips on the motherboard provide

- the system bus that links the processor(s) to memory,
- the interface between the peripheral buses and the system bus, and
- programmable read-only memory (PROM) containing the BIOS software.

As the preceding lists show, motherboards are an amalgamation of all of the buses and many peripherals in a cluster node. The memory bus is contained within the motherboard. All I/O buses a system supports are also included here. As data movement is the most serious impediment to achieving peak processor performance, the motherboard is one of the single most important components in a system.

We note that the motherboard restricts as well as enables functionality. In selecting a motherboard as the basis for a cluster node, one should consider several requirements including

- processor family,
- processor clock speed,
- number of processors,
- memory capacity,
- memory type,
- disk interface,
- required I/O slots
- number and types of I/O buses

2.5.1 Chipsets

Chipsets are a combination of all of the logic on a motherboard. Typically included are the memory bus, PCI, PCI-X and AGP bridges. In many cases, integrated peripherals are also part of the chipset. This may include disk controllers and USB controllers. Because the chipset combines all of these components, performance properties of single components are often attributed to the chipset itself.

The chipset is split into two logical portions. The north bridge connects the front side bus, which connects the processor, the memory bus, and AGP. AGP is located on the north bridge so as to have special access to main memory. The south bridge contains I/O bus bridges and any integrated peripherals that may be included, like disk and USB controllers. This provides controllers for all of the simple devices mentioned later in the peripherals section.

2.5.2 BIOS

The BIOS is the software that initializes all system hardware into a state such that the operating system can boot. BIOSes are not universal; that is, the BIOS included with a motherboard is specifically tailored to that motherboard. The BIOS is the first software that runs after the system is powered up. The BIOS will start by running a power on self test (POST) that includes this ubiquitous memory test. POST also checks other major systems. The BIOS runs initialization code present

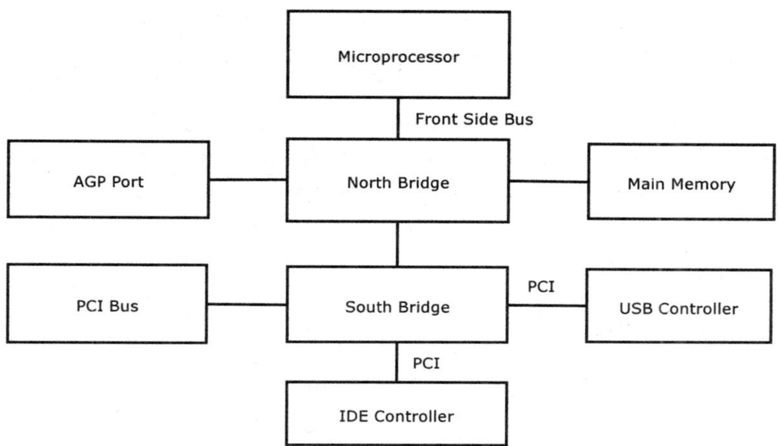

Figure 2.1: Block diagram of a motherboard chipset. The chipset consists of the entire diagram excluding the processor and memory.

on peripherals, including controller-specific code that initializes SCSI or IDE buses. Once these steps are completed, the BIOS locates a drive to boot from, and does so.

PXE (Pre-execution environment) is a system by which nodes can boot based on a network-provided configuration and boot image. The system is implemented as a combination of two common network services. First, a node will DHCP for an address. The DHCP server will return an offer and lease with extra PXE data. This extra data contains an IP address of a `tftp` server, a boot image filename (that is served from the server), and an extra configuration string that is passed to the boot image. Most new machines support this, and accordingly many cluster management software systems use this feature for installations. This feature is implemented by the BIOS in motherboards with integrated ethernet controllers, and in the on-card device initialization code on add-on ethernet controllers.

LinuxBIOS is a BIOS implementation based on the Linux kernel. It can perform all important tasks needed for an operating system to boot. These tasks are largely the same as proprietary BIOSes, but some of these steps have been streamlined in such a way that all operating systems do not function properly when booted from LinuxBIOS. At this point, Linux and Windows 2000 are supported. Work is under way to supply all BIOS features necessary to run other operating systems as well. This approach offers several benefits. Since source code is available for LinuxBIOS, the potential exists for users to fix BIOS bugs. LinuxBIOS is also performs far better than proprietary BIOSes in terms of boot time. This reduction has yielded boot times under five seconds. This speed is far better than times in the ten to ninety second range seen with proprietary BIOSes. This performance increase doesn't affect user applications, as most user applications don't require node reboots.

2.6 Persistent Storage

With the exception of BIOS code and configuration, all data stored in memory is lost when power cycles occur. In order to store data persistently, non-volatile storage medium is required. Specifically, data from a system's main memory is usually stored on some sort of disk when applications are not using it. It is then loaded when the application needs it again.

2.6.1 Local Hard Disks

Most clusters have a hard disk on each node for some storage. This is usually used in addition to a central data storage facility. Hard disks are magnetic storage media that interface with some sort of storage bus. A hard drive will contain several platters. Data is read off of these platters as they rotate. Logic in the drive optimizes read and write requests based on the geometry of the disk to provide better collective performance. This logic also contains memory cache, which is used to prevent the need for multiple reads of the same data.

Disks also have an interface to any of a number of disk buses. The three most common buses currently in use for commodity disks are IDE (or EIDE or ATA), SCSI, and Serial ATA. IDE disks are the most common. Controllers are integrated into nearly every motherboard sold today. These controllers support two devices per bus and typically include two buses, for a total of four devices. The fastest of these buses, UDMA133 (Ultra DMA 133), run at rates up to 133 MB/s. IDE devices are typically implemented with less logic on each drive, leading to higher host CPU utilization during I/O when compared with SCSI.

SCSI disks are typically used in servers. Everything but the bus interface logic is nearly identical in many disks, regardless of disk interface bus. Many vendors sell multiple versions of many of their drives, one for each bus type. That said, the major difference between IDE and SCSI disks is the obvious one: the data bus.

SCSI buses support many more devices and run at higher speeds. Current SCSI buses support up to fifteen devices and the controller, which functions as a SCSI device as well. Current-generation SCSI buses operate at rates up to 320 MB/s. This higher data rate is needed because of the larger quantities of devices sharing a single bus. The largest differentiating characteristic between IDE and SCSI disks is the cost at this point; SCSI disks are more expensive.

Serial ATA, or SATA, is the newest commodity disk standard. New, high-end motherboards are beginning to incorporate controllers. Nominally, Serial ATA is similar to IDE/ATA. Those older standards are now referred to collectively as Parallel ATA, or PATA. SATA is poised to take over the market segment of PATA; drives are not quite price competitive at this time, but their prices are close enough that in the next few months, they should drop to PATA levels. Serial ATA, as the name suggests, is a serial bus as opposed to the parallel buses used PATA and SCSI. Hence, the cables attached to drives are smaller and run faster: current SATA connections function at 150M̃B/s. Because SATA buses are only used by two devices, the aggregate data rate doesn't need to be as high as those on parallel buses to perform comparably. Because of the serial nature of SATA, bus speeds will increase rapidly, when compared with parallel buses like PATA and SCSI. SATA is natively hot-pluggable, and its cables are far smaller than the ribbon cables used by PATA and SCSI. The increased speed of SATA buses doesn't provide a real benefit at this point; most drives don't function at speeds high enough to congest a high-speed PATA controller.

The same basic disk technology is used in disks using any of the three previously mentioned buses. Hence, the basic measures of performance are the same as well. The platters in disks spin at a variety of rates. The faster the platters spin, the faster data can be read off of the disk, and data on the far end of the platters will become available sooner. Rotational speeds range from 5,400 RPM to 15,000 RPM. The faster the platters rotate, the lower latency and higher bandwidth are. The other main indicator of performance of a disk is the amount of cache included in the on-disk controller. As was mentioned previously, this cache is used to avoid disk reads when particular blocks on the disk are requested multiple times.

2.6.2 RAID

RAID, or Redundant Array of Inexpensive Disks, is a mechanism by which the performance and storage properties of individual disks can be aggregated. Aggregation may be done for a variety of reasons. Simplification of disk layout is the most common. Basically, the group of disks appear to be a single larger disk. This approach is commonly used when disks are in use that are not as large as the data that will be stored. Performance is another common reason. Multiple disks will perform better than single disks. The last reason RAID is used is to guard against hardware failure. When multiple disks are used in a RAID set, data can be stored in multiple places. This approach allows the system to continue functioning with no loss of data after disk faults. These solutions can be implemented in software, usually as an operating system driver, or in hardware, typically consisting of disk controllers, a processor that handles RAID functions, and a host connection. Hardware solutions tend to be more expensive but also tend to perform better without impacting host CPU utilization. Software solutions typically allow more flexibility, but the computational overhead of some RAID levels can consume large amounts of computational resources.

A variety of allocation schemes are used in RAID systems. With RAID0, or striping, data is striped across multiple disks. The result of this striping is a logical storage device that has the capacity of each of the disks times the number of disks present in the array. This array performs differently from a single larger disk. Reads are accelerated; each byte of data can be read from multiple locations, so interleaving reads between disks can double read performance. Write performance is similarly accelerated, as actually disk write performance is improved compared with that of a single disk.

With RAID1, or mirroring, complete copies of the data are stored in multiple locations. The capacity of one of these RAID sets will be half of its raw capacity. In this configuration, reads are accelerated in a similar manner to RAID0, but writes are slowed, as new data needs to be transmitted multiple times, to both parts of the mirror.

The third common RAID level is RAID5. It works similarly to RAID0, in that data is spread across multiple disks, with one addition. One disk is used to store parity information. This means for any block of data stored across the N-1 drives in an array, a parity checksum is computed and stored on the last disk. This allows the array to continue functioning in case of drive failure, as the parity checksum can be used in the place of a block off of any one of the data disks. Read performance on RAID5 volumes tend to be quite good, but write performance lags behind mirrors because of the overhead of checksum computation. This overhead can cause performance problems when using software RAID.

RAID is typically used on storage nodes in clusters. The reasons for this are the performance and capacity differences when compared to standalone disks. These disk I/O characteristics are not of prime import on compute nodes, so RAID is not typically configured there.

2.6.3 Nonlocal Storage

Nonlocal storage is used in similar ways to local storage. Data that needs to survive system power cycles is stored there. The physical medium on which data is stored is similar, if not identical, to the hard disk technology described in the preceding sections: the difference lies in the data transport layer. In the case of nonlocal storage, the storage device bus traffic is transmitted across a network to a central depot of storage. This network may or may not be dedicated to storage; standards exist for protocols of both types.

ISCSI is a protocol that encapsulates SCSI commands and data inside IP packets. These are typically transmitted over ethernet. It allows a single network to be used for disk I/O and regular network traffic, however, this can form a serious performance bottleneck. Fiberchannel is similar to ISCSI in character, but uses a dedicated network and data protocol.

Network filesystems are most common in clusters. Examples of this include NFS and PVFS. (PVFS is discussed in detail in Section 19) Network filesystems transmit persistent data across a network, but differ from the previous two storage types in the nature of the data being transmitted. Network filesystems transmit data with filesystem semantics across the network; the previous two protocols transmit block-based data.

2.7 Video

Video devices are the part of computers that users are most familiar with. A computer's video card renders the current state of the computer into a user interface displayed on a monitor. Because users don't interact with clusters in the same way, video cards on clusters are typically used for visualization. That is, a graphical representation is developed for the purposes of user interaction. Most video or graphics devices are currently connected with AGP (see Section 2.4.2). Previous generations of graphics adapters were connected with PCI (see Section 2.4.1), but the PCI bus did not adequately provide bandwidth for video-intensive applications.

The main usage scenario for graphics adapters in clusters is the driving of tiled displays. Tiled displays are large installations wherein the output of multiple video cards are used in parallel to provide higher resolution than would be possible with a single device. These displays are generally used for displaying regions of 3D visualizations, so a graphics adapter's performance in this area is important. Many gaming web sites post reviews of current video adapters. As this is an area where new hardware is released from week to week, these sites are the sources of the best, up to date information. In most clusters, where visualizations are not displayed on local hardware, the particular graphics adapter present in a system is not important; it is most likely used to debug hardware problems and update BIOS settings.

2.8 Peripherals

In this section, we discuss most of the miscellaneous ports that haven't been discussed in preceding sections. We give only a cursory description because these components aren't generally used in cluster configurations.

USB and Firewire are peripheral buses. Devices can be connected into these buses. The bus controller bridges the devices onto the primary I/O bus (in most cases, some flavor of PCI) so that the devices can be used. USB keyboards and mice are common; other than these two cases, it is unlikely that any USB or firewire devices will be used in these systems. Generally, devices of these types are consumer electronics, such as cameras, printers, and handheld devices.

The other major group of peripherals is quite old; all have been included in all PCs sold in the last 15 years. Included in this group are dedicated keyboard and mouse ports. These are typically used to debug problems, as setting up a keyboard and mouse for every node in a cluster isn't a particularly space-efficient decision to make. Also, all machines have serial (RS232) and parallel ports. These were historically used for peripherals, much like USB and firewire; however, in modern clusters, RS232 is used for a hard-wired system console, and parallel ports aren't used at all.

Since these devices have little to no bearing on cluster manageability or performance, they don't enter into any decisions in the node hardware specification process. If a choice is offered between nodes with 2 or 6 USB ports it doesn't matter which is chosen.

2.9 Packaging

"Packaging" refers to the container into which a computer is installed. Packaging ranges from cases that sit vertically beside a desk to high-density rack-mounted units. As space is frequently a key design constraint, choice of packaging is instrumental in determining a maximum cluster size. The decision can affect both the type of storage a cluster will use and the overall cluster storage density.

Desktop cases are the most common example of packaging. Also referred to as pizza box cases, they are typically twelve to sixteen inches wide, four to six inches tall and twelve to sixteen inches deep. The earliest clusters were build out of these.

Another common type of packaging are the tower cases that many consumer-level computers and built from. They typically stand one to three feet tall, six inches wide, and one to two feet deep. Because of the large size, cooling is usually not a serious problem with this type of machine. On the other hand, shape and design of desktops make rack mounting relatively difficult, and leads to a lower density than can be achieved with other designs. Laptops are occasionally used to construct low-profile clusters. These lead to small clusters, but are typically low-performance as well.

Rack-mounted cases are low-profile cases usually marketed to businesses for use in locations with large numbers of machines. These cases are designed to be mounted into a rack unit about six feet tall, and are almost universally nineteen inches wide. The machines are typically mounted on sliding rails, making service on an individual node a matter of sliding it out of the rack. These cases range in size from one to four rack units tall. One rack unit is 1.75 inches. Some manufacturers have even managed to fit complete machines with commodity parts into cases less than one rack unit in volume. Rack-mounted machines provide high machine density and good serviceability. However, because of the high density, care must be taken to provide adequate cooling.

The final option in node packaging is blade servers. These are machines that have been packed into cases as tightly as feasible. In many cases, common parts such as power supplies are shared between machines. This configuration provides extremely high machine density. The disadvantage is that blade server hardware is still somewhat specialized, and nodes, similarly, are not necessarily expandable.

Packaging is clearly an important decision point when choosing a cluster. Typically, this decision involves considering space constraints, along with cost and serviceability concerns. Generally, desktop machines are the least expensive, followed by rack mount machines, and then blade servers.

2.10 Node Choice and Cluster Construction

When building a cluster, a variety of issues must be considered. A choice of hardware suitable to the goal must be chosen. A vendor must be chosen. Environmental issues, such as availability of space, cooling, and power must be considered. Extra services, like hardware and software maintenance can be opted for. See Chapter 6 for a discussion of post-purchase cluster setup. A variety of paths to this goal can be taken, each with pros and cons.

2.10.1 Cluster Vendors

A common approach to building clusters is to find a vendor that provides integrated solutions. Many large system vendors now have products in the cluster space. They are experienced with the problems that customers will have in the initial stages of cluster setup, and know the questions that should be asked initially. These vendors are able to ship integrated solutions. In many cases, the cluster can be powered on when delivered, and be running applications in hours. Experienced cluster vendors optionally offer on-site hardware and software support. This approach is certainly the simplest, but can be more expensive than the following options; all of the extra services provided by the vendors cost money to provide. However, in many cases, the extra cost is well worth it.

2.10.2 White Boxes

Another common approach to building clusters is to find a vendor that builds custom computers, but has no cluster expertise. The vendor builds machines to the customer's specifications. This allows the customer to specify the exact parts the cluster should be assembled from. While on-site hardware maintenance may be available, software maintenance isn't. Experienced cluster builders may choose to take this route, as the difference between white box vendors and cluster vendors largely consists of help with cluster specific issues.

2.10.3 DIY

The final approach taken to building clusters is to do everything yourself. Every detail of system configuration is controllable; from the type of power supply to cables, and fans used for cooling. Hundreds of boxes will be delivered containing each of the parts required for each cluster node. Nodes must be assembled, and software can then be installed. This approach provides the most flexibility, but also has the highest potential for pitfalls.

2.10.4 Pitfalls

Many problems can manifest themselves during the construction and operation of a cluster. Some can be avoided by making proper decisions during the specification process. These problems can make clusters virtually unusable, so they should be taken seriously. Problems mentioned here could be treated as a laundry list of issues to be checked before a cluster is setup.

It should be verified that enough power and cooling exist to properly operate the cluster. Underpowered or overheating clusters rarely perform well, and in many cases exhibit strange problems that can consume days, weeks, or months of administrator time to properly debug.

The use of some sort of console solution should be employed. Many hardware errors are displayed during the BIOS boot sequence. Whether the BIOS supports a serial console or not, the hardware needed to see these errors should be available. The simplest solution for this problem is a crash cart. This consists of a single keyboard, monitor and mouse on a cart that can be connected to machines in case of problems. More elaborate solutions can be constructed using serial concentrators to provide usable consoles on each machine, or KVM switches.

Real profiling of target applications should be performed. Performance on artificial benchmarks is better information than no information at all, however, these results aren't important unless the primary application run on a cluster will be benchmarks.

Finally, remember that everything is harder when it needs to be done multiple times. While it is an easy process to assemble a single new machine, assembling 32, 64, 96, or 128 machines is a much harder process. Remember that time has value. Cutting corners for the sake of small amounts of money almost always causes problems.

3 Linux

Peter H. Beckman

Since the original AT&T and Berkeley Unix operating systems of the early 1970s, many variants of the operating system have been launched. Some have prospered, while others have fallen into obscurity. Have you ever heard of Concentrix or nX? Many customized Unix derivatives are no doubt still occupying obsolete Winchester drives and 8-inch floppies in the dusty storage rooms of businesses and laboratories, right there next to the paper tape readers and acoustic modem couplers. Even Microsoft tried its hand and sold a Unix back in 1980, when it released XENIX.

3.1 What Is Linux?

Simply put, Linux™ is a flavor (clone) of the original Unix™ operating systems. While Linux is relatively new on the operating system scene, arriving about two decades after Ken Thompson and Dennis Ritchie of AT&T presented the first Unix paper at a Purdue University symposium in 1973, it has rapidly become one of the most widely known and used Unix derivatives. Ever since Linus Torvalds, the creator of Linux, released it in October 1991, developers from all over the world have been improving, extending, and modifying the source code. Linus has remained the godfather of the Linux source code, ensuring that it does not get overwhelmed with useless features, code bloat, and bad programming. As a result, Linux has become one of the most popular operating systems in world.

3.1.1 Why Use Linux for a Beowulf?

Linux users tend to be some of the most fervent, inspired, and loyal computer users in the world—probably in the same league as Apple Macintosh users. Both groups of users are likely to rebut any criticism with a prolonged, sharp-tongued defense of the capabilities of their system. For scientific computational clusters, however, a cute penguin named Tux and lots of enthusiasm are insufficient; some pragmatism is required.

Linux is the most popular open source operating system in the world. Its success is the result of many factors, but its stability, maturity, and straightforward design have certainly been keys to its growth and market share. The stability and availability of Linux have also created a booming commercial marketplace for products, unmatched by any other open source operating system. Companies such as IBM, Fujitsu, NEC, HP, and Dell have all incorporated Linux into their business model, creating a marketplace around a distribution of kernel source code that is free. Other companies are simply using Linux because it makes practical business sense.

The enthusiastic backing of multibillion dollar companies is certainly a vote of confidence for Linux, but it is by no means sufficient for deciding to choose Linux. Probably the most important reason for using Linux to build a Beowulf is its flexibility. Because Linux is open source, it can easily be modified, rearranged, and tweaked for whatever the task. Some individuals may grow pale at the idea of modifying the operating system, but never fear: Linux is actually very friendly. Because of the distributed development environment that has helped it become so successful, it is also easily modified and tweaked. Later in this chapter, some simple instructions will show just how easy modifying Linux can be.

Does Linux really need to be modified before you can use it to build a Beowulf? Well, no. However, scientists are generally by their very nature extremely curious, and even though a wonderfully fast and easy-to-use Beowulf can be constructed with "stock" kernels, most cluster builders will soon give in to the nearly irresistible urge to roll up their sleeves and pop the hood to see what is really inside their Linux system. Be warned: many a plasma physicist or molecular biologist, fully intending to spend all of her time solving the mysteries of the universe and writing technical papers, has instead become completely drawn into the wonderful and creative release that comes from modifying the source code. You can often see these expatriates roaming the HPC and Beowulf mailing lists answering questions about the latest kernel and support for new chip sets or features.

Another reason to choose Linux is that you will not be alone. The available talent pool for knowledgeable system administrators that have Linux experience and actually enjoy working with Linux is large. System administrators are scrambling to find excuses for building a Beowulf with Linux. The same cannot often be said for other operating systems. Furthermore, remote administration has been a part of all Unix derivatives for decades. Many simple interfaces are available for updating the configuration of remote machines and organizing a room full of servers. The talent pool of Beowulf builders is enourmous. Linux clusters are popping up in every nook and cranny, from small departments on campus to the world's most prestigious laboratories. A quick look at the Top500 list (`www.top500.org`) shows that Linux is extremely popular. In fact, about one out of every 6 teraflop computers in the world are running Linux.

Google (`www.google.com`), one of the most popular and acclaimed search engines, is using thousands and thousands of servers running Linux to index and provide advanced searching capabilities for the web. While Google is not a scientific computing cluster, its size demonstrates the flexibility and adaptability of Linux. From an embedded palm-sized computer to running on clusters with thousands of nodes, Linux has demonstrated its utility and stability for nearly any task. There are even real-time versions of the Linux operating system. No legacy operating system can even come close to such flexibility and dominance among the largest clusters in the world.

Another reason to choose Linux is its support for many types of processors. Alpha, PowerPC, IA32, IA64, Opteron, and many others are all supported in Linux. You can choose to build your Beowulf from the fastest Apple Macintosh servers or IBM pSeries servers, or you can buy the biggest and hottest (literally) chip on the market, the Intel IA64. As an example of the flexibility and speed with which the Linux community ports to new hardware, take a quick look at the Intel IA64 or the AMD Opeteron. Both are already available in many places, and the operating system of choice is Linux. Several distributions have already been released, and for many users, removing Linux and installing a legacy 32-bit OS for their 64-bit system is certainly not in their plans.

Finally, many people choose Linux for what it does not have, or what can be removed. Linux is a sophisticated multitasking virtual memory kernel. However, it can be trimmed down to a very small set of functions representing the bare necessities. In fact, Linux can easily be compiled to use as little as 600 KBytes of compressed disk space on a floppy. Linux can be made small. It can fit on embedded devices. Although counterintuitive to some legacy PC operating system software companies, where adding a new feature and urging all the users to upgrade are the status quo, smaller and simpler is better when it comes to operating system kernels for a Beowulf. The first reason that smaller is better comes from decades of experience with source code development and stability. Whenever a line of code is added to a source tree, the probability increases that a hidden bug has been introduced. For a kernel that controls the memory system and precious data on disk, robustness is vital. Having fewer functions running in privileged mode makes for a more stable environment. A small kernel is a kernel that is more likely to be stable. Although it did not run Linux, the NASA Sojourner that traveled to Mars was also designed with the "smaller and simpler is better" mantra. The Sojourner sported a 2 MHz CPU and less than 1 MByte of combined RAM and nonvolatile data storage. While NASA certainly could have afforded a larger computer, as well as a large commercial operating system, simpler was better. Making a service call to Mars to press Ctrl-Alt-Del was not an option.

More down to earth, although nearly as cold, the NSF-funded Anubis project used Linux machines to monitor seismic conditions at unmanned monitoring stations on Antartica [3]. The stations upload their data via ARGOS satellite transmitters.

The average annual temperature for the stations is -28 degrees Celsius to -54 degrees Celsius. Linux was chosen for its stability, robustness, and the ease with which it could be modified for the task. Traveling hundreds of miles across an ice sheet to repair a blue screen of death was not seriously considered.

The second reason for a small kernel is that the most stable code path is the most used code path. Bugs (and programmers) tend to congregate in poorly lit out-of-the-way locations, away from the well-worn code paths. The smaller the kernel, the fewer the hidden and rarely tested code paths. Finally, smaller is better when it comes to kernel memory and CPU cycles on a Beowulf. For scientific computing, nearly every instruction not being performed by the scientific application, usually in the form of a floating-point operation, is overhead. Every unnecessary kernel data structure that is walked by the kernel pollutes the precious cache values intended for the scientific application. Because kernel operations such as task switching are run extremely often, even a small amount of additional kernel overhead can noticeably impact application performance. Linux's heritage of development on small machines forced developers to pay extremely close attention to performance issues. For Beowulfs, a small kernel is advantageous.

With its modular and easy-to-modify code base, support for a wide variety of the hottest CPUs on the planet, and incredibly enthusiastic talent pool, Linux is a winner for building Beowulfs.

3.1.2 A Kernel and a Distribution

The term "Linux" is most correctly applied to the name for the Unix-like kernel, the heart of an operating system that directly controls the hardware and provides true multitasking, virtual memory, shared libraries, demand loading, shared copy-on-write executables, TCP/IP networking, and file systems. The kernel is lean and mean. It contains neither an integrated Web browser nor a graphic windowing system. Linux, in keeping with its Unix heritage, follows the rule that smaller and simpler should be applied to every component in the system and that components should be easily replaceable and composable. However, the term "Linux" has also been applied in a very general way to mean the entire system, the Linux kernel combined with all of the other programs that make the system easy to use, such as the graphic interface, the compiler tools, the e-mail programs, and the utilities for copying and naming files. Strictly speaking, Linux is the kernel. Nevertheless, most users refer to a "Linux system" or "Linux CD-ROM" or "Linux machine" when they really mean the Linux kernel packaged up with all of the free software tools and components that work with the kernel—a *distribution*.

A Linux distribution packages up all the common programs and interfaces that most users think of when they imagine Linux, such as the desktop icons or the Apache Web server or, more important, for scientific users, compilers, performance monitoring tools, and the like. Many Linux distribution companies exist. They take the freely available Linux kernel and add an "installer" and all the other goodies just described. In fact, those companies (Red Hat, Mandrake, SuSE, and a host of smaller companies) have the freedom to customize, optimize, support, and extend their Linux distribution to satisfy the needs of their users. There are also companies that supply integrated hardware and software Beowulf solutions. They deliver their Beowulfs with Linux installed. They derive the Linux used on their systems from a standard distribution, such as Red Hat, then add their own utilities, reconfigure many of the basic software packages for scientific computing, and preinstall it on the cluster. Since these companies are adding value via integration, their customized Linux distribution is generally not available without purchasing their cluster.

There are also several volunteer efforts to bundle up all the software packages with the kernel and release a distribution. Understanding how the Linux kernel and Linux distributions are developed and maintained is key to understanding how to get support and how to get a Beowulf cluster up and running on the network as quickly as possible.

3.1.3 Open Source and Free Software

Of course, before getting very far in any discussion about the Linux kernel or Linux CD-ROM distributions, some time must be spent on the topic of open source and free software. Several well-written books on the topic have already been published. The book *Open Sources* [33] details the many intertwined and fascinating stories of how the code bases that began as research projects or simply hobby tinkering become the fundamental standards that are the lifeblood of the Internet. It is important, however, to understand some of the basic concepts of freely distributable software for building a Beowulf with Linux. Of course, the most important reason for understanding some of the fundamental licensing issues surrounding the Linux kernel is so that they can be adhered to. Even though the term "free" is cavalierly used within the community, there can often be strict rules and practices that must be followed. Another reason why it is important to understand these basic issues is so that you can understand how the code base came to exist in the form it is today and how you can contribute back to the community that provided the software for your use.

The open source software movement has gathered both publicity and credibility over the past couple of years. Richard Stallman began work in 1984 on creating a free, publicly available set of Unix-compatible tools. He uses the term "free software" to describe the freedom users have to modify it, not the price. Several years later, the GNU General Public License (GPL) was released. The GPL (sometimes called the "copyleft") became the license for all of the GNU products, such as `gcc` (a C compiler) and `emacs` (a text editor). The GPL strives to ensure that nobody can restrict access to the original source code of GPL licensed software or can limit other rights to using the software. Anyone may sell a copy of GPL software for as much as people are willing to pay (without any obligation to give money back to the original author), but nothing prevents the person who bought the software from doing the same. Moreover, all users must be given a copy of the source code so that those users are able to fix and enhance the software to suit their needs. However, probably the most important aspect of the GPL is that any modifications to GPLed source code must also be GPLed.

For most Beowulf users, the strict rules for how free software may be distributed will never come up. However, if code licensed under the GPL is modified, its binary-only distribution is forbidden under the license. For example, if a Beowulf user extends or patches one of Donald Becker's Ethernet drivers or uses it as the basis for writing a new driver, that driver cannot be redistributed in binary-only form. The Linux kernel also uses a clarified GPL license. Therefore, modifying the Linux kernel for private use is fine, but users may not modify the kernel and then make binary-only versions of the kernel for distribution. Instead, they must make the source code available if they intend to share their changes with the rest of the world.

More recently, Eric Raymond and others coined the term "open source" to refer to freely distributable software (`www.opensource.org`). There are, however, differences between the two monikers associated with freely distributable software. GPLed source code cannot be the basis for a privately developed set of enhancements that are then sold in binary-only shrink-wrapped form. Derived software must remain essentially free. On the other hand, licenses that follow the open source definition but are not the GPL are not so restricted. An open source–compliant license that is not using the GPL permits programmers and users greater flexibility in what they do with the code. They are free to use the source code however they wish. They may develop private, "closed" code repositories and then sell products that may be distributed in binary-only form.

Many licenses conform to the open source definition: Mozilla Public License (Netscape), MIT License (used for the X-Windows Consortium), and the amended

BSD License. A company can enhance an open source–licensed program that is not using the GPL and then sell a binary-only version. In fact, software developed by the X-Windows Consortium and the BSD project was commercialized and used as the basis for a wide range of products. For the Beowulf user, this means that code licensed with a BSD or X-Windows–style license give the users the freedom to use the software in whatever manner they see fit. Specifically, the MPICH version of MPI, available from Argonne National Laboratory and explained in greater detail in Chapter 8 of this book, is licensed using a non-GPL open source license. Beowulf users may make changes to the source code and distribute binary-only versions, or even create products based on the work done by the original authors. Many people believe the careful choice of license for the MPICH project helped make the MPI standard as successful as it is today.

Of course "giving back" to the community that has worked collectively to provide the sophisticated toolset that makes Beowulf computation possible is part of the scientific process and is highly encouraged by the authors of this book regardless of what kind of license a particular piece of software uses. The scientific process demands repeatability, and the freely distributable nature of most Beowulf software provides an ideal environment for extending and corroborating other scientists results. Whenever possible, changes to the source code should be sent back to the authors or maintainers, so the code can continue to grow and improve.

3.1.4 A Linux Distribution

A Linux distribution generally arrives on several CD-ROMs or a DVD, with the Linux kernel actually using a very small portion of that CD-ROM. Since a distribution can be fashioned around a Linux kernel in practically any manner, Linux distributions can vary quite widely in form and function. Since the Linux kernel is probably the most portable kernel on the planet, it is running on an amazing array of CPUs and devices, everything from handheld devices such as the HP iPAQ and the IBM Linux wrist watch to the IBM S390, a large corporate enterprise server getting a new lease on life with Linux. With such an incredible range of users and hardware devices that can run Linux comes a plethora of distributions built around those kernels and their target users. It can be quite daunting to choose among the dozens of popular (and hundreds of specialized) Linux distributions. Linux Web sites list dozens of distributions created with the Linux kernel. Of course, not all such distributions are suitable for use in a Beowulf. Many are designed for the embedded market, while others are built for a single-purpose appliance server, such as a firewall or a file/print server.

One of the first steps to using Linux to build your Beowulf Linux cluster is to pick a distribution and get comfortable with it. While it is beyond the scope of this book to help you become a rabid Linux user, there are plenty of books on the topic that can help guide you through the different installers and different graphic desktops optimized for each distribution. Table 3.1 shows some of the most popular Linux distribution companies or groups and where to find more information about them.

Company	URL
Red hat	`www.redhat.com`
Turbolinux	`www.turbolinux.com`
Mandrake	`www.mandrake.com`
Debian	`www.debian.org`
SuSE	`www.suse.com`
Slackware	`www.slackware.com`

Table 3.1: Some companies or groups that release Linux distributions.

Which distribution is best for building a Beowulf? Unfortunately, there is no easy answer. Usually, the choice comes down to three factors: support, language, and ease of use. While the core of all Linux distributions are, by nature of the GPL, available for free and may downloaded from the Internet, the question of support is very important, especially to the new user. Most commercial distributions include access to either phone or e-mail support. Some include the option of purchasing additional support. Some integrate software that is not freely distributable.

Local familiarity and popularity can be a factor in your choice. If everyone else in your office or on your campus or at your laboratory is using the same Linux distribution, getting their help when things go awry may be easiest if you share a common distribution. Another consideration is support for your native language and e-mail support in that language. The SuSE distribution is very popular in Germany, and naturally has very good support for the German language. Certainly, you can e-mail your questions in German to their support staff. Likewise, the Turbolinux distribution is very popular in Japan and China and supports double-byte characters and special input methods for typing in Japanese or Chinese. Your choice of distribution may also be influenced by what the hardware company can preload on your Beowulf nodes if you are not building them from scratch. Having your nodes arrive preloaded with a Linux distribution can save a lot of time.

There are also several rebundled distributions designed especially for cluster use. These systems start with a basic Linux distribution, usually from Red Hat, and then add a cluster installer and cluster-specific software packages. The cluster installer makes remote, network-based installation easier. Essentially, these cluster distribtions, such as NPACI ROCKS (`rocks.npaci.edu`) and OSCAR (`www.openclustergroup.org` are sets of "diffs" to a basic installation, replacing some of the packages and adding new ones. For the beginner, they can be an excellent place to start with a standard configuration.

Another key detail for building a Beowulf with Linux is the licensing of the distribution. Almost every commercial vendor, has, at times, included software that could not be freely distributed. In some cases, a portion of the purchase price is used to pay royalties for the software that is not freely distributable. Using such a distribution to install 16 nodes would violate the licensing unless you actually purchased 16 copies. Luckily, most distribution companies try to make it very clear whether their distribution can be freely distributed and, in many cases, offer a freely distributable version of the distribution on the Web site.

3.1.5 Version Numbers and Development Methods

The Linux kernel, Linux applications, and even the Linux distributions have different development models, different version numbers, and different schedules. While picking a Linux distribution for your Beowulf, a basic understanding of version numbers and distribution versions is required. A relatively small team of core developers develops the Linux kernel. Yes, many many people from around the world, representing more than fifty different countries, have contributed to the Linux kernel, but its stability and the organized introduction of new features are made possible by a well-coordinated band of core programmers. With Linus Torvalds sometimes called the "benevolent dictator," core developers such as Donald Becker, Alan Cox, Stephen Tweedie, and David Miller maintain and extend sections of the kernel with the help of hundreds of programmers who send in contributions to the kernel. This hierarchical model is clearly more efficient than everyone sending Linus their patches and new ideas for how the kernel can be extended (not that they don't try). Of course, not all patches and extensions are included in the main line, or "stock" kernel, no matter who sent them. Significant restraint and conservatism are used for most sections of the code. Some programmers must lobby Linus or other code developers for extended periods of time before their improvements are incorporated. In some cases, the suggestions are never accepted and are therefore made available only as a patch and not part of the "official" kernel tree.

Your Linux distribution will, of course, arrive with a Linux kernel, but upgrading the kernel is one of the most common ways to update a Beowulf node, and will be discussed later. It is important to understand that the version number of the kernel and the version number of the distribution are in no way related. At any point in time the Linux kernel has two most-up-to-date kernels: the "stable" release and the "development" release. Stable kernels use an even minor kernel number, such as 2.2 or 2.4. Similarly, development kernels use odd minor kernel numbers, such as 2.1, 2.3, or 2.5. As work on a development kernel becomes more stable, the rate of change begins to slow, and finally the core kernel developers stop adding new features. There exists no definitive set of tests that indicate when a development kernel is ready for general use, but at some point, Linus will "release" a new stable kernel. After that, patches and updates take the form of incremental versions, such as 2.4.9 or 2.4.11. With few exceptions, a kernel that is part of a popular CD-ROM distribution comes from the "stable" kernel releases. Of course, nothing prevents a would-be Beowulf builder from using the latest, most unstable versions of the development kernel. However, the main kernel developers take the stability of the Linux kernel very seriously, and it would be wise to be conservative in choosing a kernel.

Linux distributions, on the other hand, can create version numbers for their distribution however they please. Red Hat 9.0 simply means that it is newer than Red Hat 8.0. Since distribution companies are separate, they use completely different versioning schemes. Red Hat 9.0 is not necessarily any newer, or better, than SuSE 8.2. In fact, because it is clearly to their advertising advantage, don't be surprised to find out that the distribution on the shelf with the highest version number is in fact not the most recent release. Furthermore, distributions are free to use whatever basic version of the Linux kernel they believe will make their end-users most satisfied. Then, they often add in a couple more changes to the kernel that may not be in the mainline kernel. For example, a hardware company working with a distribution company may ask for some special drivers or special options be added to the kernel, so their hardware can work well with Linux. While certainly common practice, it can lead to some confusion in infrequent cases because upgrading the kernel for such a distribution may not always work unless the upgraded kernel came from the distribution's Web site and therefore contained the special additions, or the special additions are added to the basic main-line kernel that can be downloaded from `www.kernel.org`.

For the Beowulf user, this situation means that getting help with kernel issues may involve some investigation. Generally, the distribution companies support their product. However, that does not mean they wrote the code or are on a first-name basis with the person who did. The commercial support company can certainly provide front-line support, but what the industry often calls level-3 support requires some extra work. Generally, open source programmers such as Donald Becker make a portion of their time available to answer questions about the code they authored. However, the author of the code could also have moved on to other endeavors, leaving the source code behind. Kernel and Beowulf mailing lists help, but the burden can often be on you to find the problem or find the person who can help you. When trying to track down what you believe to be a kernel or driver issue, please follow these guidelines:

1. Read the documentation. Because Linux support has traditionally been ad hoc in nature, a large number of `HOWTO` documents have been written, ranging from ones that are probably very important to you like the '`Kernel-HOWTO`', the '`Beowulf-HOWTO`', and the '`Parallel-Processing-HOWTO`', to more specific ones like the '`Slovenian-HOWTO`',the '`Kodak-Digitalcam-HOWTO`', the '`Quake-HOWTO`', and the '`Coffee-mini-HOWTO`'. These documents are located in the directory '`/usr/doc/HOWTO`' on most distributions.

2. Second, search the Web. Modern search engines such as Google `www.google.com` are amazing. Many a perplexing, nasty bug or software incompatibility has been easily solved with fifteen or twenty minutes of Web surfing.

3. Get some help from local Linux users. Often, there is a very simple answer or widely known work-around for a problem. Talking to someone can also help you better understand the problem, so Google can once again be queried or intelligent e-mail sent.

4. Read the relevant mailing lists, and search for your topic of interest on the mailing list. Several archives of Linux-specific mailing lists exist, such as can be found at `marc.theaimsgroup.com`.

5. After the difficulty has been narrowed down to a very clear, reproducible example, mail the appropriate mailing list, and ask for help. To make your bug report useful to the readers (and get you a fix much faster), follow the guidelines given in the kernel sources as '`REPORTING-BUGS`', '`Documentation/BUG-HUNTING`', and '`Documentation/oops-tracing`'.

6. If you don't make any progress, try looking at the source code and mailing the author directly. Naturally, this should be used as a last resort. Authors of key portions can often get dozens or hundreds of e-mail messages a day about their code.

3.2 The Linux Kernel

As mentioned earlier, for the Beowulf user, a smaller, faster, and leaner kernel is a better kernel. This section describes the important features of the Linux kernel for Beowulf users and shows how a little knowledge about the Linux kernel can make the cluster run faster and more smoothly.

What exactly does the kernel do? Its first responsibility is to be an interface to the hardware and provide a basic environment for processes and memory management. When user code opens a file, requests 30 megabytes of memory for user data, or sends a TCP/IP message, the kernel does the resource management. If the Linux server is a firewall, special kernel code can be used to filter network traffic. In general, there are no additives to the Linux kernel to make it better for scientific clusters—usually, making the kernel smaller and tighter is the goal. However, sometimes a virtual memory management algorithm can be twiddled to improve cache locality, since the memory access patterns of scientific applications are often much different from the patterns common Web servers and desktop workstations, the applications for which Linux kernel parameters and algorithms are generally tuned. Likewise, occasionally someone creates a TCP/IP patch that makes message passing for Linux clusters work a little better. Before going that deep into Linux kernel tuning, however, the kernel must first simply be compiled.

3.2.1 Compiling a Kernel

Almost all Linux distributions ship with a kernel build environment that is ready for action. The transcript below shows how you can learn a bit about the kernel running on the system.

```
% ls -l /proc/version
-r--r--r--    1 root  root     0 Jun 19 13:49 /proc/version
% cat /proc/version
Linux version 2.5.67 (root@terra.mcs.anl.gov) (gcc version 2.96 20000731
(Red Hat Linux 7.3 2.96-110)) #4 SMP Fri Apr 18 09:36:21 CDT 2003

% cd /usr/src
% ls -ld linux
lrwxrwxrwx 1 root root 21 Apr 22 07:19 linux -> /usr/src/linux-2.5.67
```

The '/proc' file system is not really a file system in the traditional meaning. It is not used to store files on the disk or some other secondary storage; rather, it is a pseudo-file system that is used as an interface to kernel data structures—a window into the running kernel. Linus likes the file system metaphor for gaining access to the heart of the kernel. Therefore, the '/proc' file system does not really have disk filenames but the names of parts of the system that can be accessed. In the example above, we read from the handle '/proc/version' using the Unix cat command. Notice that the file size is meaningless, since it is not really a file with bytes on a disk but a way to ask the kernel "What version are you currently running?" We can see the version of the kernel and some information about how it was built.

The source code for the kernel is often kept in '/usr/src'. Usually, a symbolic link from '/usr/src/linux' points to the kernel currently being built. Generally, if you want to download a different kernel and recompile it, it is put in '/usr/src', and the symlink '/usr/src/linux' is changed to point to the new directory while you work on compiling the kernel. If there is no kernel source in '/usr/src/linux', you probably did not select "kernel source" when you installed the system for the first time, so in an effort to save space, the source code was not installed on the machine. The remedy is to get the software from the company's Web site or the original installation CD-ROM.

The kernel source code often looks something like the following:

```
% cd /usr/src/linux
% ls
COPYING        Makefile        crypto   init    mm        sound
CREDITS        README          drivers  ipc     net       usr
Documentation  REPORTING-BUGS  fs       kernel  scripts
MAINTAINERS    arch            include  lib     security
```

If your Linux distribution has provided the kernel source in its friendliest form, you can recompile the kernel, as it currently is configured, simply by typing

```
% make clean ; make bzImage
```

The server will then spend anywhere from a few minutes to twenty or more minutes depending on the speed of the server and the size of the kernel. When it is finished, you will have a kernel.

```
% ls -l /usr/src/linux-2.2.14/arch/i386/boot/bzImage
-rw-r--r-- 1 root root 906584 Jun 19 00:13
              /usr/src/linux-2.5.67/arch/i386/boot/bzImage
```

3.2.2 Loadable Kernel Modules

For most kernels shipped with Linux distributions, the kernel is built to be modular. Linux has a special interface for loadable kernel modules, which provides a convenient way to extend the functionality of the kernel in a dynamic way, without retaining the code in memory all the time, and without requiring the kernel be recompiled every time a new or updated module arrives. Modules are most often used for device drivers, file systems, and special kernel features. For example, Linux can read and write MSDOS file systems. However, that functionality is usually not required at all times. Most often, it is required when reading or writing from an MSDOS floppy disk. The Linux kernel can dynamically load the MSDOS file system kernel module when it detects a request to mount an MSDOS file system. The resident size of the kernel remains small until it needs to dynamically add more functionality. By moving as many features out of the kernel core and into dynamically loadable modules, the legendary stability of Linux compared with legacy operating systems is achieved.

Linux distributions, in an attempt to support as many different hardware configurations and uses as possible, ship with as many precompiled kernel modules as possible. It is not uncommon to receive five hundred or more precompiled kernel modules with the distribution. In the example above, the core kernel was recompiled. This does not automatically recompile the dynamically loadable modules.

3.2.3 The Beowulf Kernel Diet

It is beyond the scope of this book to delve into the inner workings of the Linux kernel. However, for the Beowulf builder, slimming down the kernel into an even leaner and smaller image can be beneficial and, with a little help, is not too difficult.

In the example above, the kernel was simply recompiled, not configured. In order to slim down the kernel, the configuration step is required. There are several interfaces to configuring the kernel. The 'README' file in the kernel source outlines the steps required to configure and compile a kernel. Most people like the graphic interface and use `make xconfig` to edit the kernel configuration for the next compilation.

Removing and Optimizing

The first rule is to start slow and read the documentation. Plenty of documentation is available on the Internet that discusses the Linux kernel and all of the modules. However, probably the best advice is to start slow and simply remove a couple unneeded features, recompile, install the kernel, and try it. Since each kernel version can have different configuration options and module names, it is not possible simply to provide the Beowulf user a list of kernel configuration options in this book. Some basic principles can be outlined, however.

Think compute server: Most compute servers don't need support for amateur radio networking. Nor do most compute servers need sound support, unless of course your Beowulf will be used to provide a new type of parallel sonification. The list for what is really needed for a compute server is actually quite small. IrDA (infrared), quality of service, ISDN, ARCnet, Appletalk, Token ring, WAN, AX.25, USB support, mouse support, joysticks, and telephony are probably all useless for a Beowulf.

Optimize for your CPU: By default, many distributions ship their kernels compiled for the first-generation Pentium CPUs, so they will work on the widest range of machines. For your high-performance Beowulf, however, compiling the kernel to use the most advanced CPU instruction set available for your CPU can be an important optimization.

Optimize for the number of processors: If the target server has only one CPU, don't compile a symmetric multiprocessing kernel, because this adds unneeded locking overhead to the kernel.

Remove firewall or denial-of-service protections: Since Linux is usually optimized for Web serving or the desktop, kernel features to prevent or reduce the severity of denial-of-services attacks are often compiled into the kernel. Unfortunately, an extremely intense parallel program that is messaging bound can flood the interface with traffic, often resembling a denial-of-service attack. Indeed, some people have said that many a physicist's MPI program is actually a denial-of-service attack on the Beowulf cluster. Removing the special checks and detection algorithms can make the Beowulf more vulnerable, but the hardware is generally purchased with the intent to provide the most compute cycles per dollar possible, and putting it behind a firewall is relatively easy compared with securing and hampering every node's computation to perform some additional security checks. Section 5.6.2 discusses the use of firewalls with Beowulf clusters in more detail.

Other Considerations

Many Beowulf users slim down their kernel and even remove loadable module support. Since most hardware for a Beowulf is known, and scientific applications are very unlikely to require dynamic modules be loaded and unloaded while they are running, many administrators simply compile the required kernel code into the core. Particularly careful selection of kernel features can trim the kernel from a

1.5-megabyte compressed file with 10 megabytes of possible loadable modules to a 600-kilobyte compressed kernel image with no loadable modules. Some of the kernel features that should be considered for Beowulfs include the following:

- *NFS:* While NFS does not scale to hundreds of node, it is very convenient for small clusters.
- *Serial console:* Rather than using KVM (Keyboard, Video, Mouse) switches or plugging a VGA (video graphics array) cable directly into a node, it is often very convenient to use a serial concentrator to aggregate 32 serial consoles into one device that the system administrator can control.
- *Kernel IP configuration:* This lets the kernel get its IP address from BOOTP or DHCP, often convenient for initial deployment of servers.
- *NFS root:* Diskless booting is an important configuration for some Beowulfs. NFS root permits the node to mount the basic distribution files such as '`/etc/passwd`' from an NFS server.
- *Special high-performance network drivers:* Often, an extreme performance Beowulf will use high-speed networking, such as Gigabit Ethernet or Myrinet. Naturally, those specialized drivers as well as the more common 100BT Ethernet driver can be compiled into the kernel.
- *A file system:* Later in this chapter a more thorough discussion of file systems for Linux will be presented. It is important the kernel is compiled to support the file system chosen for the compute nodes

Network Booting

Because of the flexibility of Linux, many options are available to the cluster builder. While certainly most clusters are built using a local hard drive for booting the operating system, it is certainly not required. Network booting permits the kernel to be loaded from a network-attached server. Generally, a specialized network adapters or system BIOS is required. Until recently, there were no good standards in place for networking booting commodity hardware. Now, however, most companies are offering network boot-capable machines in their high-end servers. The most common standard is the Intel PXE 2.0 net booting mechanism. On such machines, the firmware boot code will request a network address and kernel from a network attached server, and then receive the kernel using TFTP (Trivial File Transfer Protocol). Unfortunately, the protocol is not very scalable, and attempting to boot more than a dozen or so nodes simultaneously will yield very poor results. Large Beowulfs attempting to use network boot protocols must carefully consider the number of simultaneously booting nodes or provide multiple TFTP servers and separate Ethernet collision domains. For a Linux cluster, performing a network boot and then mounting the local hard drive for the remainder of the operating system does not seem advantageous; it probably would have been much simpler to store the kernel on hard drive. However, network booting can be important for some clusters if it is used in conjunction with diskless nodes.

3.2.4 Diskless Operation

Some applications and environments can work quite well without the cost or management overhead of a hard drive. For example, in secure or classified computing environments, secondary storage can require special, labor-intensive procedures. In some environments, operating system kernels and distributions may need to be switched frequently, or even between runs of an application program. Reinstalling the operating system on each compute node to switch over the system is generally difficult, as would maintaining multiple hard disk partitions with different operating systems or configurations. In such cases, building the Beowulf without the operating system on the local hard drive, if it even exists, can be a good solution. Diskless operation also has the added benefit of making it possible to maintain only one operating system image, rather than having to propagate changes across the system to all of the Beowulf nodes.

For diskless operations, naturally, Linux can accommodate where other systems may not be so flexible. A complete explanation of network booting and NFS-root mechanisms is beyond the scope of this book (but they are documented in the '`Diskless-HOWTO`' and '`Diskless-root-NFS-HOWTO`') and certainly is a specialty area for Beowulf machines. However, a quick explanation of the technology will help provide the necessary insight to guide your decision in this regard.

In addition to hardware that is capable of performing a network boot and a server to dole out kernels to requesting nodes, a method for accessing the rest of the operating system is required. The kernel is only part of a running machine. Files such as '`/etc/passwd`' and '`/etc/resolv.conf`' also need to be available to the diskless server. In Linux, *NFS root* provides this capability. A kernel built with NFS root capability can mount the root file system from a remote machine using NFS. Operating system files such as dynamic libraries, configuration files, and other important parts of the complete operating system can be accessed transparently from the remote machine via NFS. As with network booting, there are certain limitations to the scalability of NFS root for a large Beowulf. In Section 3.2.6, a more detailed discussion of NFS scalability is presented. In summary, diskless operation is certainly an important option for a Beowulf builder but remains technically challenging.

3.2.5 Downloading and Compiling a New Kernel

For most users, the kernel shipped with their Linux distribution will be adequate for their Beowulf. Sometimes, however, there are advantages to downloading a newer kernel. Occasionally a security weakness has been solved, or some portion of TCP/IP has been improved, or a better, faster, more stable device driver arrives with the new kernel. Downloading and compiling a new kernel may seem difficult but is really not much harder than compiling the kernel that came with the distribution.

The first step is to download a new kernel from `www.kernel.org`. The importance of reading the online documents, readme files, and instructions cannot be overstated. As mentioned earlier, sticking with a "stable" (even minor version) kernel is recommended over the "development" (odd minor version) kernel for most Beowulf users. It is also important to understand how far forward you can move your system simply by adding a new kernel. The kernel is not an isolated piece of software. It interfaces with a myriad of program and libraries. For example, the Linux mount command file system interfaces to the kernel; should significant changes to the kernel occur, a newer, compatible mount command may also need to be upgraded. Usually, however, the most significant link between the kernel and the rest of the operating system programs occurs with what most people call `libc`. This is a library of procedures that must be linked with nearly every single Linux program. It contains everything from the `printf` function to routines to generate random numbers. The library `libc` is tied very closely to the kernel version, and since almost every program on the system is tied closely to `libc`, the kernel and LibC must be in proper version synchronization. Of course, all of the details can be found at `www.kernel.org`, or as a link from that site.

The next step is to determine whether you can use a "stock" kernel. While every major distribution company uses as a starting point a stock kernel downloaded from `kernel.org`, companies often apply patches or fixes to the kernel they ship on the CD-ROM. These minor tweaks and fixes are done to support the market for which the distribution is targeted or to add some special functionality required for their user base or to distinguish their product. For example, one distribution company may have a special relationship with a RAID device manufacturer and include a special device driver with their kernel that is not found in the stock kernel. Or a distribution company may add support for a high-performance network adapter or even modify a tuning parameter deep in the kernel to achieve higher performance over the stock kernels. Since the distribution company often modifies the stock kernel, several options are available for upgrading the kernel:

- Download the kernel from the distribution company's Web site instead of `kernel.org`. In most cases, the distribution company will make available free, upgraded versions of the kernel with all of their distribution-specific modifications already added.
- Download the kernel from `kernel.org`, and simply ignore the distribution-dependent modifications to the kernel. Unless you have a special piece of hardware not otherwise supported by the stock kernel, it is usually safe to use the stock kernel. However, any performance tuning performed by the distribution company would not have been applied to the newly download kernel.
- Port the kernel modification to the newer kernel yourself. Generally, distribution companies try to make it very clear where changes have been made. Normally, for example, you could take a device driver from the kernel that shipped with your distribution and add it to the newer stock kernel if that particular device driver was required.

Of course, all of this may sound a little complicated to the first-time Beowulf user. However, none of these improvements or upgrades are required. They are by the very nature of Linux freely available to users to take or leave as they need or see fit. Unless you know that a new kernel will solve some existing problem or security issue, it is probably good advice to simply trim the kernel down, as described earlier, and use what was shipped with your distribution.

3.2.6 Linux File Systems

Linux supports an amazing number of file systems. Because of its modular kernel and the virtual file system interface used within the kernel, dynamically loaded modules can be loaded and unloaded on the fly to support whatever file system is being mounted. For Beowulf, however, simplicity is usually a good rule of thumb. Even through there are a large number of potential file systems to compile into the kernel, most Beowulf users will require only one or two.

The de facto standard file system on Linux is the second extended file system, commonly called EXT2. EXT2 has been performing well as the standard file system for years. It is fast and extremely stable. Every Beowulf should compile the EXT2 file system into the kernel. It does, unfortunately, have one drawback, which can open the door to including support for (and ultimately choosing) another file system. EXT2 is not a "journaling" file system.

Journaling File Systems

The idea behind a journaling file system is quite simple: Make sure that all of the disk writes are performed in such a way as to ensure the disk always remains in a consistent state or can easily be put in a consistent state. That is usually not the case with nonjournaling file systems like EXT2. Flipping off the power while Linux is writing to an EXT2 file system can often leave it in an inconsistent state. When the machine reboots, a file system check, or `fsck`, must be run to put the disk file system back into a consistent state. Performing such a check is not a trivial matter. It is often very time consuming. One rule of thumb is that it requires one hour for every 100 gigabytes of used disk space. If a server has a large RAID array, it is almost always a good idea to use a journaling file system, to avoid the painful delays that can occur when rebooting from a crash or power outage. However, for a Beowulf compute node, the choice of a file system is not so clear.

Journaling file systems are slightly slower than nonjournaling file systems for writing to the disk. Since the journaling file system must keep the disk in a consistent state even if the machine were to suddenly crash (although not likely with Linux), the file system must write a little bit of extra accounting information, the "journal," to the disk first. This information enables the exact state of the file system to be tracked and easily restored should the node fail. That little bit of extra writing to the disk is what makes journaling file systems so stable, but it also slows them down a little bit.

If a Beowulf user expects many of the programs to be disk-write bound, it may be worth considering simply using EXT2, the standard nonjournaling file system. Using EXT2 will eke out the last bit of disk performance for a compute node's local file writes. However, as described earlier, should a node fail during a disk write, there is a chance that the file system will be corrupt or require an fsck that could take several minutes or several hours depending on the size of the file system. Many parallel programs use the local disk simply as a scratch disk to stage output files that then must be copied off the local node and onto the centralized, shared file system. In those cases, the limiting factor is the network I/O to move the partial results from the compute nodes to the central, shared store. Improving disk-write performance by using a nonjournaling file system would have little advantage in such cases, while the improved reliability and ease of use of a journaling file system would be well worth the effort.

Which Journaling File System?

Once again, unlike other legacy PC operating systems, Linux is blessed with a wide range of journaling file systems from which to choose. The most common are EXT3, ReiserFS, IBM's JFS, and SGI's XFS. EXT3 is probably the most convenient file system for existing Linux to tinker with. EXT3 uses the well-known EXT2 file formatting but adds journaling capabilities; it does not improve upon EXT2, however. ReiserFS, which was designed and implemented using more sophisticated algorithms than EXT2, is being used in the SuSE distribution. It generally has better performance characteristics for some operations, especially systems that have many, many small files or large directories. IBM's Journaling File System (JFS) and SGI's XFS files systems had widespread use with AIX and IRIX before being ported to Linux. Both file systems not only do journaling but were designed for the highest performance achievable when writing out large blocks of data from virtual memory to disk. For the user not highly experienced with file systems and recompiling the kernel, the final choice of journaling file system should be based not on the performance characteristics but on the support provided by the Linux distribution, local Linux users, and the completeness of Linux documentation for the software.

Networked and Distributed File Systems

While most Linux clusters use a local file system for scratch data, it is often convenient to use network-based or distributed file systems to share data. A network-based file system allows the node to access a remote machine for file reads and writes. Most common and most popular is the network file system, NFS, which has been around for about two decades. An NFS client can mount a remote file system over an IP (Internet Protocol) network. The NFS server can accept file access requests from many remote clients and store the data locally. NFS is also standardized across platforms, making it convenient for a Linux client to mount and read and write files from a remote server, which could be anything from a Sun desktop to a Cray supercomputer.

Unfortunately, NFS does have two shortcomings for the Beowulf user: scalability and synchronization. Most Linux clusters find it convenient to have each compute node mount the user's home directory from a central server. In this way, a user in the typical edit, compile, and run development loop can recompile the parallel program and then spawn the program onto the Beowulf, often with the use of an *mpiexec* or *PBS* command, which are covered in Chapters 8 and 17, respectively. While using NFS does indeed make this operation convenient, the result can be a B3 (big Beowulf bottleneck). Imagine for a moment that the user's executable was 5 megabytes, and the user was launching the program onto a 256-node Linux cluster. Since essentially every single server node would NFS mount and read the single executable from the central file server, 1,280 megabytes would need to be sent across the network via NFS from the file server. At 50 percent efficiency with 100-baseT Ethernet links, it would take approximately 3.4 minutes simply to transfer the executable to the compute nodes for execution. To make matters worse, NFS servers generally have difficulty scaling to that level of performance for simultaneous connections. For most Linux servers, NFS performance begins to seriously degrade if the cluster is larger than 64 nodes. Thus, while NFS is extremely convenient for smaller clusters, it can become a serious bottleneck for larger machines. Synchronization is also an issue with NFS. Beowulf users should not expect to use NFS as a means of communicating between the computational nodes. In other words, compute nodes should not write or modify small data files on the NFS server with the expectation that the files can be quickly disseminated to other nodes. This is discussed more fully in Section 19.3.2.

The best technical solution would be a file system or storage system that could use a tree-based distribution mechanism and possibly use available high-performance network adapters such as Myrinet or Gigabit Ethernet to transfer files to and from the compute nodes. Unfortunately, while several such systems exist, they are research projects and do not have a pervasive user base. Other solutions such as shared global file systems, often using expensive fiber channel solutions, may increase disk bandwidth but are usually even less scalable. For generic file server access from the compute nodes to a shared server, NFS is currently the most common option.

Experimental parallel file systems are available, however, that address many of the shortcomings described earlier. Chapter 19 discusses PVFS, the Parallel Virtual File System. PVFS is different from NFS because it can distribute parts of the operating system to possibly hundreds of Beowulf nodes. When done properly, the bottleneck is no longer an Ethernet adapter or hard disk. Furthermore, PVFS provides parallel access, so many readers or writers can access file data concurrently. You are encouraged to explore PVFS as an option for distributed, parallel access to files.

3.3 Pruning Your Beowulf Node

Even if recompiling your kernel, downloading a new one, or choosing a journaling file system seems too adventuresome at this point, you can some very simple things to your Beowulf node that can increase performance and manageability. Remember that just as the kernel, with its nearly five hundred dynamically loadable modules, provides drivers and capabilities you probably will never need, so too your Linux distribution probably looks more like a kitchen sink than a lean and mean computing machine. While you may now be tired of the Linux Beowulf adage "a smaller operating system is a better operating system," it must be once again applied to the auxiliary programs often run with a conventional Linux distribution. If we look at the issue from another perspective, every single CPU instruction performed by the kernel or operating system daemon not directly contributed to the scientific calculation is a wasted CPU instruction.

The starting point for pruning your Beowulf node will be what the Linux distribution installer set up. Many distributions have options during installation for "workstation" or "server" or "development" configurations. As a general rule of thumb, "server" installations make a good starting point. Workstation configurations often have windowing systems running by default, and a myriad of background tasks to make Linux as user-friendly as possible to the desktop user. Fortunately, with Linux you can understand and modify any daemon or process as you convert your kitchen sink of useful utilities and programs into a designed-for-computation roadster. For a Beowulf, eliminating useless tasks delivers more megaflop per dollar to the end user.

The first step to pruning the operating system daemons and auxiliary programs is to find out what is running on the system. For most Linux systems there are at least two standard ways to start daemons and other processes, which may waste CPU resources as well as memory bandwidth (often the most precious commodity on a cluster).

inetd: This is the "Internet superserver". Many Linux distributions use a newer version of the program, which has essentially the same functionality called `xinetd`. Both programs basic function is to wait for connections on a set of ports and then spawn and hand off the network connection to the appropriate program when an incoming connection is made. The configuration for what ports `inetd` or `xinetd` listening to, as well as what will get spawned can been determined by looking at '`/etc/inetd.conf`' and '`/etc/services`' or '`/etc/xinetd.conf`' and '`/etc/xinetd.d`' respectively.

/etc/rc.d/init.d: This special directory represents the scripts that are run during the booting sequence and that often launch daemons that will run until the machine is shut down.

3.3.1 `inetd.conf`

The file '`inetd.conf`' is a simple configuration file. Each line in the file represents a single service, including the port associated with that service and the program to launch when a connection to the port is made. Below are some simple examples:

```
ftp     stream  tcp     nowait  root    /usr/sbin/tcpd  in.proftpd
finger  stream  tcp     nowait  root    /usr/sbin/tcpd  in.fingerd
talk    dgram   udp     wait    root    /usr/sbin/tcpd  in.talkd
```

The first column provides the name of the service. The file '`/etc/services`' maps the port name to the port number, for example,

```
% grep ^talk /etc/services
talk 517/udp # BSD talkd(8)
```

To slim down your Beowulf node, get rid of the extra services in '`inetd.conf`'; you probably will not require the `/usr/bin/talk` program on each of the compute nodes. Of course, what is required will depend on the computing environment. In many very secure environments, where ssh is run as a daemon and not launched from '`inetd.conf`' for every new connection, '`inetd.conf`' has *no* entries. In such extreme examples, the inetd process that normally reads '`inetd.conf`' and listens on ports, ready to launch services, can even be eliminated.

3.3.2 `/etc/rc.d/init.d`

The next step is to eliminate any daemons or processes that are normally started at boot. While occasionally Linux distributions differ in style, the organization of the files that launch daemons or run scripts during the first phases of booting up a system are very similar. For most distributions, the directory '`/etc/rc.d/init.d`' contains scripts that are run when entering or leaving a run level. Below is an example:

```
% cd /etc/rc.d/init.d
% ls
anacron    functions     kdcrotate nfslock     sendmail   wine
apachectl  gpm           keytable  nscd        single     xfs
```

```
apmd       halt           killall   ntpd        snmpd      xinetd
arpwatch   http_sanity    kudzu     portmap     snmptrapd  ypbind
atd        http_sanity~   lpd       radvd       sshd       yppasswdd
autofs     identd         netfs     random      syslog     ypserv
crond      ipchains       network   rawdevices  vncserver  ypxfrd
cups       iptables       nfs       rhnsd       winbind
```

However, the presence of the script does not indicate it will be run. Other directories and symlinks control which scripts will be run. Most systems now use the convenient **chkconfig** interface for managing all the scripts and symlinks that control when they get turned on or off. Not every script spawns a daemon. Some scripts just initialize hardware or modify some setting.

A convenient way to see all the scripts that will be run when entering run level 3 is the following:

```
% chkconfig --list | grep '3:on'
syslog 0:off 1:off 2:on 3:on 4:on 5:on 6:off
xinetd 0:off 1:off 2:off 3:on 4:on 5:on 6:off
lpd 0:off 1:off 2:off 3:on 4:on 5:on 6:off
mysql 0:off 1:off 2:on 3:on 4:on 5:on 6:off
httpd 0:off 1:off 2:off 3:on 4:on 5:on 6:off
sshd 0:off 1:off 2:off 3:on 4:on 5:on 6:off
atd 0:off 1:off 2:off 3:on 4:on 5:on 6:off
named 0:off 1:off 2:off 3:on 4:on 5:on 6:off
dhcpd 0:off 1:off 2:off 3:on 4:on 5:on 6:off
gpm 0:off 1:off 2:on 3:on 4:on 5:on 6:off
inet 0:off 1:off 2:off 3:on 4:on 5:on 6:off
network 0:off 1:off 2:on 3:on 4:on 5:on 6:off
nfsfs 0:off 1:off 2:off 3:on 4:on 5:on 6:off
random 0:off 1:off 2:on 3:on 4:on 5:on 6:off
keytable 0:off 1:off 2:on 3:on 4:on 5:on 6:off
nfs 0:off 1:off 2:off 3:on 4:on 5:on 6:off
nfslock 0:off 1:off 2:off 3:on 4:on 5:on 6:off
ntpd 0:off 1:off 2:off 3:on 4:on 5:on 6:off
portmap 0:off 1:off 2:off 3:on 4:on 5:on 6:off
sendmail 0:off 1:off 2:on 3:on 4:on 5:on 6:off
serial 0:off 1:off 2:on 3:on 4:on 5:on 6:off
squid 0:off 1:off 2:off 3:on 4:on 5:on 6:off
```

```
tltime 0:off 1:off 2:off 3:on 4:off 5:on 6:off
crond 0:off 1:off 2:on 3:on 4:on 5:on 6:off
```

Remember that not all of these spawn cycle-stealing daemons that are not required for Beowulf nodes. The "serial" script, for example, simply initializes the serial ports at boot time; its removal is not likely to reduce overall performance. However, in this example many things could be trimmed. For example, there is probably no need for `lpd`, `mysql`, `httpd`, `named`, `dhcpd`, `sendmail`, or `squid` on a compute node. It would be a good idea to become familiar with the scripts and use the `chkconfig` command to turn off unneeded scripts. With only a few exceptions, an X-Windows server should not be run on a compute node. Starting an X session takes ever-increasing amounts of memory and spawns a large set of processes. Except for special circumstances, run level 3 will be the highest run level for a compute node.

3.3.3 Other Processes and Daemons

In addition to '`inetd.conf`' and the scripts in '`/etc/rc.d/init.d`', there are other common ways for a Beowulf node to waste CPU or memory resources. The `cron` program is often used to execute programs at scheduled times. For example, `cron` is commonly used to schedule a nightly backup or an hourly cleanup of system files. Many distributions come with some `cron` scripts scheduled for execution. The program `slocate` is often run as a nightly `cron` to create an index permitting the file system to be searched quickly. Beowulf users may be unhappy to learn that their computation and file I/O are being hampered by a system utility that is probably not useful for a Beowulf. A careful examination of `cron` and other ways that tasks can be started will help trim a Beowulf compute node.

The `ps` command can be invaluable during your search-and-destroy mission.

```
% ps -eo pid,pcpu,sz,vsize,user,fname --sort=vsize
```

This example command demonstrates sorting the processes by virtual memory size.

The small excerpt below illustrates how large server processes can use memory. The example is taken from a Web server, not a well-tuned Beowulf node.

```
  PID %CPU   SZ   VSZ  USER COMMAND
26593  0.0  804  3216   web httpd
26595  0.0  804  3216   web httpd
 3574  0.0  804  3216   web httpd
```

```
  506  0.0  819  3276  root squid
  637  0.0  930  3720  root AgentMon
  552  0.0 1158  4632 dbenl postmast
13207  0.0 1213  4852  root named
13209  0.0 1213  4852  root named
13210  0.0 1213  4852  root named
13211  0.0 1213  4852  root named
13212  0.0 1213  4852  root named
  556  0.0 1275  5100 dbenl postmast
  657  0.0 1280  5120 dbenl postmast
  557  0.0 1347  5388 dbenl postmast
  475  0.0 2814 11256 mysql mysqld
  523  0.0 2814 11256 mysql mysqld
  524  0.0 2814 11256 mysql mysqld
  507  0.0 3375 13500 squid squid
```

In this example the proxy cache program `squid` is using a lot of memory (and probably some cache), even though the CPU usage is negligible. Similarly, the ps command can be used to locate CPU hogs. Becoming familiar with `ps` will help quickly find runaway processes or extra daemons competing for cycles with the scientific applications intended for your Beowulf.

3.4 Scalable Services

Modern operating systems take network connectivity for granted, and are almost always configured by default to rely on basic network services for everything from the correct time of day to DNS name resolution. This can cause performance bottlenecks for large clusters. Consider a 1024 node cluster launching a job yet configured to use the campus-wide DNS server for resolving names. Often, as TCP connections are made nodes are configured to do a reverse lookup. This could result in thousands of near-simultaneous requests to a server that could scale poorly. As mentioned earlier, NFS can also fall in to this category, usually scaling only to about 64 nodes. NIS can be another potential bottleneck. NIS, the Network Information System is often used to provide network-shared configuration data, such as password files. Every time a user logs into a node, the computer consults the remote NIS server. Naturally, spending a few moments to examine the remote services the operating system uses can be important. Many Beowulf builders simply eliminate, wherever possible, the use of remote services such as NIS for synchronizing accounts.

3.5 Other Considerations

You can explore several other basic areas in seeking to understand the performance and behavior of your Beowulf node running the Linux operating system. Many scientific applications need just four things from a node: CPU cycles, memory, networking (message passing), and disk I/O. Trimming down the kernel and removing unnecessary processes can free up resources from each of those four areas.

Because the capacity and behavior of the memory system are vital to many scientific applications, it is important that memory be well understood. One of the most common ways an application can get into trouble with the Linux operating system is by using too much memory. Demand-paged virtual memory, where memory pages are swapped to and from disk on demand, is one of the most important achievements in modern operating system design. It permits programmers to transparently write applications that allocate and use more virtual memory than physical memory available on the system. The performance cost for declaring enormous blocks of virtual memory and letting the clever operating system sort out which virtual memory pages in fact get mapped to physical pages, and when, is usually very small. Most Beowulf applications will cause memory pages to be swapped in and out at very predictable points in the application. Occasionally, however, the worst can happen. The memory access patterns of the scientific application can cause a pathological behavior for the operating system.

The crude program in Figure 3.1 demonstrates this behavior.

On a Linux server with 256 megabytes of memory, this program—which walks through 300 megabytes of memory, causing massive amounts of demand-paged swapping—can take about 5 minutes to complete and can generate 377,093 page faults. If, however, you change the size of the array to 150 megabytes, which fits nicely on a 256-megabyte machine, the program takes only a half a second to run and generates only 105 page faults.

While this behavior is normal for demand-paged virtual memory operating systems such as Linux, it can lead to sometimes mystifying performance anomalies. A couple of extra processes on a node using memory can push the scientific application into swapping. Since many parallel applications have regular synchronization points, causing the application to run as slow as the slowest node, a few extra daemons or processes on just one Beowulf node can cause an entire application to halt. To achieve predictable performance, you must prune the kernel and system processes of your Beowulf.

```
#include <stdlib.h>
#include <stdio.h>
#define MEGABYTES 300
main() {
  int *x, *p, t=1, i, numints = MEGABYTES*1024*1024/sizeof(int);
  x = (int *) malloc(numints*sizeof(int));
  if (!x) { printf("insufficient memory, aborting\n"); exit(1); }
  for (i=1; i<=5; i++) {
    printf("Loop %d\n",i);
    for (p=x; p<x+numints-1; p+=1024) {
      *p = *p + t;
    }
  }
}
```

Figure 3.1: A simple program to touch many pages of memory.

3.5.1 TCP Messaging

Another area of improvement for a Beowulf can be standard TCP messaging. As mentioned earlier, most Linux distributions come tuned for general-purpose networking. For high-performance compute clusters, short low-latency messages and very long messages are common, and their performance can greatly affect the overall speed of many parallel applications. Linux is not generally tuned for messages at the extremes. However, once again, Linux provides you the tools to tune it for nearly any purpose.

The older 2.2 kernels benefited from a set of patches to the TCP stack. A series of in-depth performance studies from NASA ICASE [68] detail the improvements that can be made to the 2.2 kernel for Beowulf-style messaging. In their results, significant and marked improvement could be achieved with some simple tweaks to the kernel. However, most people report that the 2.4 series kernels work well without modification to the TCP stack.

Other kernel modifications that improve performance of large messages over high-speed adapters such as Myrinet have also been made available on the Web. Since modifications and tweaks of that nature are very dependent on the kernel version and network drivers and adapters, they are not outlined here. You are encouraged to browse the Beowulf mailing lists and Web sites and use the power of the Linux source code to improve the performance of your Beowulf.

3.5.2 Hardware Performance Counters

Most modern CPUs have built-in performance counters. Each CPU design measures and counts metrics corresponding to its architecture. Several research groups have attempted to make portable interfaces for the hardware performance counters across the wide range of CPU architectures. One of the best known is PAPI: A Portable Interface to Hardware Performance Counters [75]. Another interface, Rabbit [53], is available for Intel or AMD CPUs. Both provide access to performance counter data from the CPU. Such low-level packages require interaction with the kernel; they are extensions to its basic functionality. In order to use any of the C library interfaces, either support must be compiled directly into the kernel, or a special hardware performance counter module must be built and loaded. Beowulf builders are encouraged to immediately extend their operating system with support for hardware performance counters. Users find this low-level CPU information, especially with respect to cache behavior, invaluable in their quest for better node-OS utilization. Three components will be required: the kernel extensions (either compiled in or built as a module), a compatible version of the Linux kernel, and the library interfaces that connect the user's code to the kernel interfaces for the performance counters.

3.6 Final Tuning with `/proc`

As mentioned earlier, the '`/proc`' file system is not really a file system at all, but a window on the running kernel. It contains handles that can be used to extract information from the kernel or, in some cases, change parameters deep inside the kernel. In this section, we discuss several of the most important parameters for Beowulfs. A multitude of Linux Web pages are dedicated to tuning the kernel and important daemons, with the goal of serving a few more Web pages per second. A good place to get started is `linuxperf.nl.linux.org`. Many Linux users take it as a personal challenge to tune the kernel sufficiently so their machine is faster than every other operating system in the world.

However, before diving in, some perspective is in order. Remember that in a properly configured Beowulf node, nearly all of the available CPU cycles and memory are devoted to the scientific application. As mentioned earlier, the Linux operating system will perform admirably with absolutely no changes. Trimming down the kernel and removing unneeded daemons and processes provides slightly more room for the host application. Tuning up the remaining very small kernel can further refine the results. Occasionally, a performance bottleneck can be dislodged with some simple kernel tuning. However, unless performance is awry, tinkering with parameters in '/proc' will more likely yield a little extra performance and a fascinating look at the interaction between Linux and the scientific application than incredible speed increases.

Now for a look at the Ethernet device:

```
% cat /proc/net/dev
Inter-| Receive | Transmit
face |bytes packets errs drop fifo frame compressed multicast|bytes
packets errs drop fifo colls carrier compressed
lo:363880104 559348 0 0 0 0 0 0 363880104 559348 0 0 0 0 0 0
eth0:1709724751 195793854 0 0 357 0 0 0 4105118568 202431445
0 0 0 0 481 0
brg0: 0 0 0 0 0 0 0 0 0 0 0 0 0 0 0 0
```

It is a bit hard to read, but the output is raw columnar data. A better formatting can be seen with '/sbin/ifconfig'. One set of important values is the total bytes and the total packets sent or received on an interface. Sometimes a little basic scientific observation and data gathering can go a long way. Are the numbers reasonable? Is application traffic using the correct interface? You may need to tune the default route to use a high-speed interface in favor of a 10-baseT Ethernet. Is something flooding your network? What is the size of the average packet? Another key set of values is for the collisions (colls), errs, drop, and frame. All of those values represent some degree of inefficiency in the Ethernet. Ideally, they will all be zero. A couple of dropped packets is usually nothing to fret about. But should those values grow at the rate of several per second, some serious problems are likely. The "collisions" count will naturally be nonzero if traffic goes through an Ethernet hub rather than an Ethernet switch. High collision rates for hubs are expected; that's why they are less expensive.

Tunable kernel parameters are in '/proc/sys'. Network parameters are generally in '/proc/sys/net'. Many parameters can be changed. Some administrators tweak a Beowulf kernel by modifying parameters such as `tcp_sack`, `tcp_timestamps`, `tcp_window_scaling`, `rmem_default`, `rmem_max`, `wmem_default`, or `wmem_max`. The exact changes and values depend on the kernel version and networking configuration, such as private network, protected from denial of service attacks or a public network where each node must guard against SYN flooding and the like. You are encouraged to peruse the documentation available at www.linuxhq.com and other places where kernel documentation or source is freely distributed, to learn all the details pertaining to their system. Section 5.5 discusses some of these networking parameters in more detail.

With regard to memory, the `meminfo` handle provides many useful data points:

```
% cat /proc/meminfo
MemTotal:       1032828 kB
MemFree:          24916 kB
Buffers:         114836 kB
Cached:          436588 kB
SwapCached:       58796 kB
Active:          720008 kB
Inactive:        210888 kB
HighTotal:       130496 kB
HighFree:          2016 kB
LowTotal:        902332 kB
LowFree:          22900 kB
SwapTotal:       530136 kB
SwapFree:        389816 kB
Dirty:               64 kB
Writeback:            0 kB
Mapped:          390116 kB
Slab:             57136 kB
Committed_AS:    761696 kB
PageTables:        7636 kB
ReverseMaps:     202527
```

In the example output, the system has 1 gigabyte of RAM, about 114 megabytes allocated for buffers and 25 megabytes of free memory. The handles in '`/proc/sys/vm`' can be used to tune the memory system, but their use depends on the kernel, since handles change frequently.

Like networking and virtual memory, there are many '`/proc`' handles for tuning or probing the file system. A node spawning many tasks can use many file handles. A standard ssh to a remote machine, where the connection is maintained, and not dropped, requires four file handles. The number of file handles permitted can be displayed with the command

```
% cat /proc/sys/fs/file-max
4096
```

The command for a quick look at the current system is

```
% cat /proc/sys/fs/file-nr
1157 728 4096
```

This shows the high-water mark (in this case, we have nothing to worry about), the current number of handles in use, and the max.

Once again, a simple echo command can increase the limit:

```
% echo 8192 > /proc/sys/fs/file-max
```

The utility '/sbin/hdparm' is especially handy at querying, testing, and even setting hard disk parameters:

```
% /sbin/hdparm -I /dev/hda

/dev/hda:

 Model=DW CDW01A0 A , FwRev=500.B550, SerialNo=DWW-AMC1211431 9
 Config={ HardSect NotMFM HdSw>15uSec SpinMotCtl Fixed DTR>5Mbs FmtGapReq }
 RawCHS=16383/16/63, TrkSize=57600, SectSize=600, ECCbytes=40
 BuffType=3(DualPortCache), BuffSize=2048kB, MaxMultSect=16, MultSect=8
 DblWordIO=no, maxPIO=2(fast), DMA=yes, maxDMA=0(slow)
 CurCHS=17475/15/63, CurSects=16513875, LBA=yes
 LBA CHS=512/511/63 Remapping, LBA=yes, LBAsects=19541088
 tDMA={min:120,rec:120}, DMA modes: mword0 mword1 mword2
 IORDY=on/off, tPIO={min:120,w/IORDY:120}, PIO modes: mode3 mode4
 UDMA modes: mode0 mode1 *mode2 }
```

Using a Beowulf builder and a simple disk test,

```
% /sbin/hdparm -t /dev/hda1

/dev/hda1:
Timing buffered disk reads: 64 MB in 20.05 seconds = 3.19 MB/sec
```

you can understand whether your disk is performing as it should, and as you expect.

Finally, some basic parameters of that kernel can be displayed or modified. '/proc/sys/kernel' contains structures. For some message-passing codes, the key may be '/proc/sys/kernel/shmmax'. It can be used to get or set the maximum size of shared-memory segments. For example,

```
% cat /proc/sys/kernel/shmmax
33554432
```

shows that the largest shared-memory segment available is 32 megabytes. Especially on an SMP, some messaging layers may use shared-memory segments to pass messages within a node, and for some systems and applications 32 megabytes may be too small.

All of these examples are merely quick forays into the world of '/proc'. Naturally, there are many, many more statistics and handles in '/proc' than can be viewed in this quick overview. You are encouraged to look on the Web for more complete documentation and to explore the Linux source—the definitive answer to the question "What will happen if I change this?" A caveat is warranted: You can make your Beowulf node perform worse as a result of tampering with kernel parameters. Good science demands data collection and repeatability. Both will go a long way toward ensuring that kernel performance increases, rather than decreases.

3.7 Conclusions

Linux is a flexible, robust node operating system for Beowulf computational clusters. Stability and adaptability set it apart from the legacy operating systems that dominate desktop environments. While not a "cancer" like some detractors have labeled Linux, it has spread quickly from its humble beginnings as a student's hobby project to a full-featured server operating system with advanced features and legendary stability. And while almost any Linux distribution will perform adequately as a Beowulf node operating system, a little tuning and trimming will skinny down the already lean Linux kernel, leaving more compute resources for scientific applications. If this chapter seems a little overwhelming, we note that there are companies that will completely configure and deliver Beowulf systems, including all the aforementioned tweaks and modifications to the kernel. There are also revolutionary systems such as the Beowulf software from Scyld Computing Corporation (www.sycld.com). The software from Scyld combines a custom Linux kernel and distribution with a complete environment for submitting jobs and administering the cluster. With its extremely simple single-system image approach to management, the Scyld software can make Beowulfs very easy indeed. Chapter 18 is devoted to a discussion of the Scyld approach.

One final reminder is in order. Many Beowulf builders became acquainted with Linux purely out of necessity. They started constructing their Beowulf saying, "Every OS is pretty much like every other, and Linux is free...free is good, right?". On the back of restaurant napkins, they sketched out their improved price/performance ratios. After the hardware arrived, the obligatory LINPACK report was sent to the Top500 list, and the real scientific application ran endlessly on the new Beowulf. Then it happened. Scientists using Linux purely as a tool stopped and peered inquisitively at the tool. They read the source code for the kernel. Suddenly, the simulation of the impending collision of the Andromeda galaxy with our own Milky Way seemed less interesting. Even though the two galaxies are closing at a rate of 300,000 miles per hour and we have only 5 billion years to wait, the simulation simply seemed less exciting than improving the virtual memory paging algorithm in the kernel source, sending Linus Torvalds the patch, and reading all the kernel mailing list traffic. Beware. Even the shortest of peeks down the rabbit's hole can sometimes lead to a wonderland much more interesting than your own.

4 System Area Networks

Narayan Desai and Thomas Sterling

Clusters are groups of machines, meant to be harnessed to perform a task or tasks in parallel. In order for a group to coordinate itself and efficiently perform a task, the individual nodes in the cluster must be able to communicate with one another. As these messages are used for synchronization in many cases, the pace of the continued progress of the computation is dependent on the performance of the communication network.

Networks are among the most important components of clusters. A network is a group of peers that share an interconnection fabric. These peers are able to use this fabric to communicate with one another. The peers are usually hosts with network interfaces, and the fabric consists of devices that help to deliver network traffic to the intended receiver.

System area networks vary with respect to bandwidth, latency, scalability, and cost. Network performance determines cluster performance for many applications. Therefore, the initial choice of a network will affect the usability of a cluster for its entire operational lifespan.

Another type of network, a storage area network, might also be connected to nodes in a cluster. These networks carry I/O traffic to remote storage resources. Unfortunately, these networks carry the same acronym as system area networks, leading to some confusion. Storage area networks are discussed in Chapter 19; we concern ourselves only with system area networks, although these networks share many characteristics.

4.1 Network Hardware

Networks are composed of a several types of components. First, there are the nodes (or peers) on the network. Each of these will have one or more network interface card on its I/O buses. The term "card" is figurative in some cases; network interfaces have been integrated into many motherboards in recent years. Every interface will be connected to the network fabric by a network link. The network fabric is composed of some number of network devices, interconnected into some topology. The functionality and performance of networks are composites of particular components used.

4.1.1 Host Interfaces

All peers in a network must have an interface into the network itself. These interfaces usually take the form of add-on network peripherals. These network interface cards (NICs) are usually I/O boards that plug into the system. On PC hardware, the most common bus type is PCI (or its newer replacement, PCI-X).

The function of these NICs is to allow nodes on the network to send and receive messages on the network. In order to support these operations, NICs have several parts. One component is hardware that interfaces with the physical layer of the network, the wires that carry data in a network. This hardware will work with either copper or fiber physical layers. It can convert messages from data used on the NIC and in the host stack to wire format messages for transmission, and provides the reverse functionality for message receipt.

Another portion of the NIC performs a similar task for the I/O bus. For the purpose of simplicity, we will assume the NIC in question is PCI based. In order for applications running under the host operating system to transmit a message, the message data needs to be copied to the NIC from the application so that the actual message can be prepared for transmission. This copy is done over the PCI bus from the system's main memory. So this second part of the NIC is responsible for collecting data from the PCI bus for network transmission and transmitting data received off the network over the PCI bus to the system main memory.

All network access on a peer will go through a NIC. This means the rate at which data can be transmitted is limited by the rate at which data can be copied into and out of the NIC via the I/O bus, and it is also limited by the rate at which the NIC can transmit and receive data from the network. In the days of 100 Mbps Ethernet, the link speed of links connecting nodes to the network were typically the limiting factor in hardware performance. At this point, high-end network vendors are able to nearly saturate even the fastest of I/O buses available.

4.1.2 Network Links

Network links are the channels connecting interfaces to devices and interconnecting devices. The link medium affects several other properties. Fiber and copper are typical link media. Link speeds vary widely; 10 and 100 Mb (Megabit, not to be confused with MB, or MegaByte) Ethernet is still in common use, running at 10 and 100 Mb/s, respectively. Current-generation high-end interconnect links function at rates in excess of 2–3 Gb/s. Emerging technologies, like 10Gb Ethernet and 4X Infiniband feature link speeds near 10 Gb/s.

Some network links are full duplex. If a link is full duplex, no action of two devices on the network segment can cause a collision on the link. If a link is half-duplex, or not full duplex, multiple hosts' simultaneous transmission can cause a collision. Collisions cause a few types of performance degradation. First, the average latency of messages varies with the overall usage of the network, since messages will frequently need to be retransmitted, or will have to wait before transmission can occur. Second, the aggregate bandwidth available to the entire network is lower because of the cost of collision detection and retransmission. Also, in a network featuring half-duplex links there will typically exist a single collision domain. This means that the amount of bandwidth available to all hosts is that of a single link. This is undesirable when compared with switched, full-duplex network that provide up to full bandwidth of all links.

We note that the ability to operate in either full or half duplex mode for any link in a network is governed by the devices at either end. Some devices are limited in terms of supported operational modes. Hubs are unable to function in full-duplex environments due their basic design. Some Ethernet interfaces are unable to run in full-duplex mode. All Ethernet devices, by specification are able to run in half-duplex mode.

4.1.3 Network Devices

A network device is hardware that interconnects some number of network links. The network device uses one of a number of algorithms to process and forward the traffic between hosts. The style of traffic forwarding affects the properties of the whole network greatly; different algorithms yield different behavior of the network under load. These devices also vary widely in terms of media, performance, and price.

The two main classifications of network devices are hubs and switches. Hubs implicitly contain a single broadcast domain. That is, any traffic received on any port is transmitted to all other ports on the switch. All links connected to these devices are half-duplex. These are typically among the least expensive network devices. They were most common in the days of 10 and 100 Mbps Ethernet. Gigabit hubs are unheard of. Hubs will only function with network link types that allow for contention. Ethernet does this, though many other networks currently in use do not. This sort of contention detection and correction come at some cost. When all of the links connected to a hub are suffering from contention simultaneously, the aggregate bandwidth available to clients drops to about 35%. As we mentioned previously, hubs cannot use full-duplex links, due to their basic design. For this reason, hubs are less desirable in the cluster environment.

Switches have become the standard network device in the last few years. This has occurred because of their plummeting cost and performance benefit. Ethernet switches maintain network state information that maps known Ethernet hardware addresses to the port they were last seen on. This means that when a packet is processed by the switch, the switch will have only have to flood (broadcast on all links) the first packet; the client's response will cause an entry to be created in the MAC address table of the switch and all subsequent packets will be directly forwarded to the proper port. This approach is extremely effective in small environments. A relatively small number of packets are flooded allowing all links to be used efficiently. The switch is able to cache near complete network state and the network can be near-optimally used. In more complex networks, the simplicity of this approach makes it difficult to get as good performance as one might want.

Many switches have limitations in terms of the quantity of traffic they can process. This limit is described in one of two ways. The term backplane bandwidth is used to describe the aggregate amount of bandwidth a switch can handle at once. For example, a switch that has a backplane bandwidth of 16 Gbps is able to process the load generated by 16 clients each with a 1Gbps NIC. The other way this capacity is described in specifications is in packets per second, or PPS. Also, a switch may be said to be non-blocking. This means that any configuration of clients that can be connected can be supported by the switch without packet loss because of internal bandwidth limitations. The backplane bandwidth in these cases is higher than the sum of the individual bandwidths of all links in the network.

In complex networks, many network switches will be interconnected. This is required because of the bandwidth and port counts of single switches. In large configurations, multiple switches must be used in conjunction to provide enough capacity. All clients on one switch will be limited to the link speed of the connecting link when communicating with clients on another switch. For this reason, switches are typically connected with multiple links. This allows for more packets to be exchanged by clients on different switches. This is referred to as trunking, or link aggregation.

The algorithm used to forward packets in Ethernet switches has been modified to allow for multiple link channels. These channels are treated like normal links. A variety of hashing algorithms are used to distribute the network traffic across the underlying links. Many of these algorithms use peer configuration information, like IP address or NIC hardware address. Many of these hashing algorithms do not work very well in cluster environments because of the uniformity in hardware and software. In most clusters, hosts are configured with sequential IP addresses. Also, most clusters also have homogeneous hardware. It is not uncommon for cluster nodes to have sequential, or at least very similar NIC hardware addresses. Both of these facts make many hashing algorithms suboptimal in clusters. Round-robin hashing algorithms distribute traffic well, but tend to cause packet reordering to occur. This causes problems in higher layers of the network software. Because of these problems, Ethernet switch complexes tend to be reserved for network-intensive tasks in smaller environments. In small environments, clients will have good connectivity to a large fraction of the system because of a shared switch. In larger configurations, inter-client connectivity is diminished because inter-switch connectivity is typically poor.

In order to address these sorts of problems in large switch complexes, some vendors, such as Myricom, use source routing. This means that each packet handled by the network will contain a complete route to its destination. If packets contain this information, the switch needs to simply use the stored route to forward the packet to the next hop in the stored route. This is a more scalable approach, because the switches process traffic identically whether there are 2 or 1024 nodes in the network. On the other hand, the clients need to do a lot more work. Each client needs to maintain a set of routes to all other clients in the network. This can be a complicated task; it involves complete knowledge of the whole network topology. However, it allows more flexibility for the clients of the system. This leads to better network performance overall, especially on large systems.

4.1.4 Topology

Many small cluster networks are extremely simple, consisting of a single network device and a number of clients. This configuration is advantageous in the following way. A single network device, by definition, needs to connect to other devices in the network. This means that all hosts are equally well connected to all other hosts in the system. There are no issues of traffic distribution as discussed previously. The MAC address-based forwarding scheme described previously for Ethernet switches works beautifully. Hardware performance in these configurations is typically governed by the performance of the single switch.

Once multiple switches become involved, things become more complicated. Hosts on the same switch enjoy lower latency to one another than hosts on different switches do. All of the switches need to be inter-connected. Depending on the network topology, packets may be handled by multiple switches during delivery. Depending on the particular case, packets may even by handled by all switches.

Multiple network links may be aggregated in order to improve connectivity between switches. Traffic needs to be distributed across these links. If these switches are multiply-interconnected, the path from any given host on the network may not be fixed any more.

The topology of the system will impact the overall performance of the network for clients. The primary metric of this is *bisection bandwidth.* Bisection bandwidth is the maximum amount of bandwidth that an arbitrary half of nodes on the network can use to communicate with the other half. In simpler networks, this is usually determined by finding the limiting factor in communication between two regions in the network. In a single switch case, this is usually the backplane bandwidth of the switch. In a multiple Ethernet switch case, this is usually the set of uplinks between switches.

Complex networks are usually built in order to provide full bisection bandwidth to cluster nodes. This means that any half of the network can communicate with its conjugate at line rate; i.e., the network itself doesn't limit communication between any set of nodes in the system. In small configurations, this task can be achieved with a single switch. Once the network outgrows a single switch, topology becomes more complicated. These configurations are composed of two types of switches. Some switches connect clients to switches. Others only connect switches to other switches. On any switch connected directly to clients, one port must be connected to another switch for each port connected to a client. This is required to allow data to flow between clients connected to different switches. Switches connected only to switches are used to distribute traffic between the switches connected to clients. As these configurations get larger, the second category of switches grows in size quickly. In larger configurations, half or more of the ports available on switches are used as inter-switch links, not as client ports.

4.2 Example Networks

The networks used in clusters vary greatly based on the users' particular needs. The following are example networks (from a hardware perspective). The first example is an inexpensive Ethernet network for use in a small cluster ($<$ 32 nodes). The second example is an Ethernet network with moderate bisection bandwidth.

4.2.1 Single Switch Ethernet Network

In Figure 4.1, we show a simple cluster network, consisting of a single switch and 8 cluster nodes. This is probably the most common network configuration for clusters. The performance is generally governed by a combination of network link speed, and aggregate backplane bandwidth of the switch.

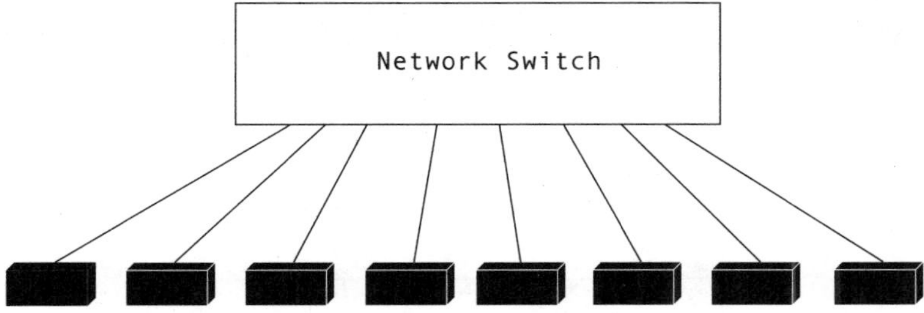

Figure 4.1: A simple cluster network.

4.2.2 Multiple Switch Ethernet Network

In Figure 4.2, we show a slightly more complicated cluster network, consisting of two switches and 16 cluster nodes evenly distributed across the switches. The performance of this configuration is dependent on more factors than the previous example. In this case, it is limited by a combination of link speeds, backplane bandwidth of both switches, and the effectiveness of the hashing algorithm used to aggregate the 4 uplinks between switches. This may seem like a similar performance limit to the previous example, but in these multi-stage switch networks, single switch limitation are aggregated non-linearly based on system usage.

4.3 Network Software

In order for applications to use the network, applications need to access the network via a set of software. This software stack will provide a range of functionality, and will exist in a number of forms. At the highest level, there are communication libraries, for example, MPI implementations. These are typically used by applications because they provide a transport and platform independent interface to communication. (These libraries won't be discussed in detail in this chapter; see Chapters 8–11 for details.) At a slightly lower level, protocol stacks are used. These protocol stacks provide transport properties like reliable message delivery, ordered message delivery, message framing, and flow control. The lowest level of network software is the driver layer. Network drivers interact directly with network interfaces to control transmission and receipt of packets on the network.

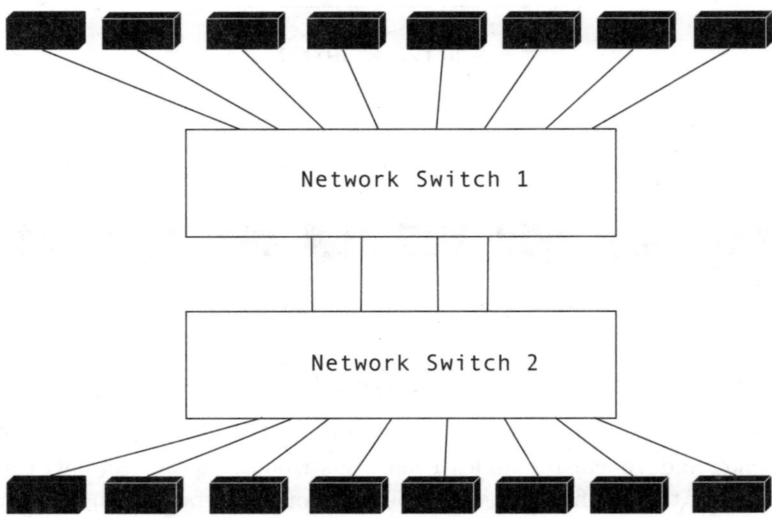

Figure 4.2: A complex cluster network.

4.3.1 Network Protocols

Network protocols are a series of procedures used to setup and conduct data transmissions between a group of machines. Such protocols abstract the physical transmission medium to provide some portability to applications. Protocols are used to provide various properties to network communications sessions. Note that not all protocols provide all of these properties, and the following list is by no means exhaustive.

- Media contention: work around collisions and other physical errors.
- Addressing: A station addressing scheme that is network layer independent.
- Fragmentation: A means to break down messages into smaller pieces (called datagrams) for transmission, and reassemble them at the receiver.
- Reliable delivery: A means for the client to determine if transmission completed properly or an error has occurred.
- Ordered delivery: Messages are delivered in order to the application from end to end.

- Flow control: Transmission can be slowed to improve performance or prevent the exhaustion of resources at the destination or along the route to the destination.

Most applications will actually use a combination of network protocols in the course of communications. This means that all protocols do not need to provide all of the above properties. For example, the IP protocol only provides an addressing scheme and message fragmentation: the IP protocol provides an addressing scheme that allows a message to be delivered to another end station and that it is fragmented and reassembled if necessary. Most IP applications also use either TCP or UDP. TCP is used when reliability and ordered delivery are desired. The following are descriptions of a number of common network protocols and the properties they implement.

Ethernet provides media collision detection and avoidance. The Ethernet protocol also provides an addressing scheme. Each client uses a 48-bit address, assigned by the vendor of its network interface.

IP is a protocol that provides the features of addressing and fragmentation. Addressing is implemented in the following way. Each client address has a 32 bit address, broken into a network address and a host address. Network addresses are used to route packages from one network segment to another. Fragmentation is implemented using a identification field in the header. IP also includes a header field that specifies the transport layer protocol as well. This will in most cases be either TCP or UDP, but other protocols can be used as well.

The IP protocol must be adapted to the underlying physical network type. IP addresses must be able to be mapped to physical network addresses. In the case where IP is used on top of Ethernet, the address resolution protocol (ARP) is used to determine the Ethernet address of the intended recipient. This process consists of a broadcasted query for the MAC address of an IP address. The owner of that IP address will respond with the MAC address. This value is cached. At this point, IP can be used on top of Ethernet transparently. See Section 5.2 for a more detailed discussion of IP, TCP and UDP.

TCP specifies a set of steps required to establish a communication session. Once this is established, it provides reliable, in-order delivery of messages.

UDP provides about the same functionality as IP. It is generally used so that an application can implement its own network protocol for reliable delivery of messages. UDP is also used in cases where reliable message delivery is not as important as low latency or jitter. UDP is frequently used for streaming audio and video.

GM is the driver, firmware, and user-space library used to access Myrinet interfaces. It provides all of the properties necessary to use the network for reliable communications. Addressing is implemented in GM using interface hardware addresses and a routing table that exists on each node. This routing table has a set of source routes for all nodes on the network. Fragmentation is not necessary, as GM messages are not limited in size. GM also implements reliable, in-order message delivery. Because of the switched nature of myrinet switch complexes, media contention is not an issue.

The kernel driver providing support for GM on Myrinet interfaces also provides Ethernet emulation. This means that protocols like Ethernet and IP (TCP and UDP) can be run over Myrinet hardware.

4.3.2 Network Protocol Stacks

Network protocol stacks are the software implementations of the network protocols mentioned in the previous subsection. These implementations are typically operating system specific. Many of these are implemented inside of the kernel, but this is not universally the case. These stacks provide a `syscall` interface for user-space programs. The most common example of this interface is the socket interface used by all IP-based protocols. An application will set up a socket, and then send and receive data using this socket. All of these function calls are implemented as system calls. The network stack uses network drivers to actually send and receive data. The purpose of the `syscall` layer is to provide portability between different implementations of facilities provided by the kernel. This layer is tightly coupled with network drivers, as it is the sole consumer of their functions.

4.3.3 Network Drivers

Network drivers are the software that allows network interface hardware to be used by the kernel, network protocol stacks, and ultimately user applications. Network drivers have a few responsibilities. First, the driver will initialize the network card, so that it can be enabled. This setup consists of internal setup like on-card register initialization, but also includes external setup like link auto-negotiation. After these steps are complete, the network hardware should be initialized. This does not mean the interface is completely configured, as some configuration processes like DHCP use the network interface itself to configure settings like IP addresses.

The driver also provides functions necessary to send and receive packets via the network. The send functions are typically called from a protocol stack. The set of transmission steps is as follows: an application makes a system call, providing data to be sent. This data is processed by the network protocol stack. The protocol stack calls functions provided by the driver to copy the data across the I/O bus and actually transmit the data.

When receiving data, the network interface will receive data from the network. It will then do some amount of processing of the data. This processing varies from card to card. Some cards implement parts of the protocol stack in hardware in order to improve performance. When the card is finished processing the packets received from the network, it causes an interrupt. This causes the kernel to call functions defined in the network interface driver. These functions are called interrupt handlers. An interrupt handler will copy the data from the network interface to system main memory, via the I/O bus. At this point, the network protocol stack finishes processing the packets, and copies the data out to the application.

The process of servicing interrupts is very invasive; it typically causes other operations to be preempted. Under high network receive load, this causes the primary computational task of the system to be frequently stopped. As context switches are not free, this constant switch comes at a high performance price. In order to address this issue, most high-end (gigabit and custom network) NIC manufacturers have implemented interrupt mitigation, or coalescing strategies. This means that the NIC will buffer some number of processed packets before issuing an interrupt. This means that instead of interrupting after every packet is processed, the NIC may only issue an interrupt after 10 or 100 packets. This allows the spend less time switching between the network and computational task, and more time executing the user's application. See Sections 5.5.4 and 5.5.5 for more information about driver performance settings and techniques.

4.3.4 Network Software In Action

In general, cluster use is characterized by the execution of parallel applications. These applications consist of many instances of the same application, running on multiple cluster nodes simultaneously. These instances of the application use the system area network to communicate. These messages are typically used for coordination between instances of the parallel application.

When communication occurs, a complex series of actions is performed. First, the application makes a library call to initiate message transfer. This call usually does a variety of things; it will frame the message and potentially split the message into multiple packets if the message size is too large. At this point, the packet is passed to the network driver stack. The data is transferred across the I/O bus to the NIC.

The network controller transmits the packets to the network controller on the intended recipient. The packet reaches receiving network controller, where it is processed by the hardware and processed by the network driver stack. These packets are reconstituted into the original message by the protocol stack, and this message is passed to the application when if calls a receive function in its messaging library.

4.4 Performance

As was mentioned earlier, clusters are built in most cases to harness the resources of many machines to solve a single problem. In order for any problem to be solved on many hosts in a faster time than the single machine execution time, these hosts need to coordinate.

During application execution, this coordination takes the form of messages transmitted from one node to another. The communication patterns of these messages vary widely; some programs will spend most of their execution time performing computation, with very occasional messages reporting results and receiving a new assignment. This sort of program will typically perform independently of network performance. Other programs are constantly communicating between the parallel processes; small variances in network performance can cause huge differences in application performance in these cases.

4.4.1 Hardware Performance

Network performance can be characterized in terms of three basic metrics: latency, bandwidth, and topology. Latency is the time for a message to travel from the sender to a receiver via the network. Bandwidth is the rate at which data can be transmitted. The topology of the network is the underlying "shape" of the network. These attributes are the key determinants of network-based application performance for all applications. However, the nature of the application determines which of these attributes, if any, are important with respect to performance. Section 1.3 introduced the analysis of application performance with respect to latency and bandwidth in abstract terms; in this section we'll discuss these from the standpoint of the network hardware.

Latency is the measure of time for a message to transit the network from a sender to a receiver. Latency is important to application performance for a number of reasons. Whenever synchronous communication occurs, the receiver is waiting for messages to arrive. Fundamentally, this is the speed at which nodes in the cluster can coordinate themselves during a parallel computation. Application latency can range from upwards of 100 microseconds down to approximately 4 microseconds.

Bandwidth is the most straightforward metric of networks. It is the rate of data transmission. This is also an extremely important metric, as it governs how fast data can be exchanged between nodes.

There are many types of descriptions of bandwidth in a system, so some clarification is necessary. A network is composed of nodes with network interfaces, a set of switches, and network links connecting these parts together into some topology. All components in this system have individual bandwidth limitations, so determining what the actual available network bandwidth can be tricky. Also, as all of these function as limiting factors, many factors must be considered together in order to form a complete picture of available network bandwidth.

The most common network bandwidth quoted is the bandwidth of an individual link in the system. For example, gigabit Ethernet networks are composed of links running at 1 gigabit per second. Current generation single link bandwidths currently range from 100 Mbps (12.5 MB/s) to nearly 4 Gbps (500 MB/s). In the next year, products featuring link speeds between 4–10 Gbps are expected. It is worth noting that some network interfaces include multiple links in order to increase the available aggregate bandwidth.

Bandwidth available within network switch complexes also effects the usable bandwidth for nodes on a network. In a network composed of a single switch, the switch backplane bandwidth is an important factor. Backplane bandwidth is how much traffic the switch can handle simultaneously. Some switches, typically cheaper ones, are also limited in the number of packets per second (PPS) they are able to handle. While all of the links will still run at full speed, these two limitations cause packets to get dropped within the switch itself.

Bisection bandwidth is the other important measure of network bandwidth. Bisection bandwidth is defined as the minimum of the aggregate bandwidth between any two halves of a system. When communication is occurring between a number of stations on the network at the same time, contention inside of the switching complex can reduce the bandwidth available to communications regardless of the speed of links in the network. In many cases, individual links may not be usable because of a lack of available bisection bandwidth.

4.4.2 Software Performance

Network software is essentially responsible for moving data from system main memory to the NIC for transmission, and vice versa. This involves translating data into a format suitable for transmission, and translating data back from this formate upon receipt. Performance in this process is limited by a few factors. The first of these is the use of data copies in libraries and protocol stacks. In many cases, data starts in the user application, where it is copied into the network stack and processed. After this has completed, the data is copied across the I/O bus and is transmitted. In the case of inbound messages, data is received on the NIC, copied across the I/O bus into the network stack, processed, and finally copied into the application's memory.

A more optimized scheme would be to copy data directly from application memory to the NIC for transmission. This would avoid one of the copies mentioned in the previous scenario for each direction. This has been implemented in two ways. The first is user-level networking. In this case, all networking code exists in the user application; kernel facilities are used only to access the NIC. The other way to implement this is to use NICs with hardware network protocol processing support. This allows the NIC to process packets into an application usable form without involving the kernel at all.

Another performance problem is caused by the network stack's usage of the system CPU for computationally intensive tasks. One example of this is computation of TCP checksums. The performance of early generation gigabit Ethernet NICs were severely limited by the ability of the system CPU to compute TCP checksums quickly enough. Moreover, this computation also hampers the node's ability to perform its primary computational tasks, like the execution of user applications. This problem can only be solved by the addition of NIC support for network protocol processing.

As we mentioned previously, performance problems are caused by the frequent generation of interrupts during the usage of high speed network interfaces. Any time an interrupt is received, the current running task is stopped, causing a context shift. If this occurs every time a packet is received on the network, the host CPU will spend all of its time context shifting, without accomplishing much in between. NIC hardware assistance can help with this issue in two ways. Interrupt coalescing helps with this issue quite a bit. However, even when using interrupt coalescing, interrupt load scales with the number of packets received, not with the number of messages received. If more network protocol processing can be done in hardware, the host CPU will get interrupted less often, with more benefit.

Many of these issues have been addressed in both software and hardware. High end NIC manufacturers have begun addressing these issues, interconnect vendors more so than Ethernet NIC vendors. Myricom already addresses most of these issues in their software releases, because their hardware already supports these features. More details on tuning network software are presented in Chapter 5.

4.5 Network Choice

Choosing the appropriate system area network for a cluster can be complicated process. Two factors weigh heavily in this sort of decision. The first is cost. Realistically, most clusters are built with a fixed budget. This means that a higher-priced, higher-performance network will probably come at the cost of needing to purchase a smaller cluster. In many cases, specialized network interconnects can cost upwards of $1000–2000 per node. At this point, this cost approximates the cost of a high performance compute node. This means that building a high-performance network can reduce the cluster size by a factor of two, when working with a fixed budget. As we saw in Section 1.3.6, a high-performance network can be a very reasonable use of resources because of the greatly improved performance it can provide.

Another important factor is the performance of the network, and accordingly, the cluster itself. Many applications need particular performance properties to function effectively. Serviceability is a third concern. When the scale of a cluster increases beyond 32 or 64 nodes, many low-cost solutions become quite unwieldy, and result in largely unusable clusters. Fundamentally, all of these factors are pieces of the same puzzle: how to get the best value out of a cluster for its intended uses.

If a cluster is being built for a small number of applications, thorough application benchmarking is in order. The spectrum of communication patterns exhibited by application ranges from occasional communication from one node to another, to consistant communication from all nodes to all other nodes. At one extreme are applications that behave like SetiAtHome, wherein compute nodes will infrequently query a master node for a work unit to process for hours or days. At the other extreme are many scientific applications, where nodes will be in constant communication with one or more other nodes and the speed of the computation is limited by the performance of the slowest performing node. As is obvious from the communication pattern description, basically any interconnect would perform admirably in the first case, while the fastest interconnect possible is desirable in the second case.

The range of network options available to clusters ranges from the integrated Ethernet that is included with nearly any computer sold today, to higher speed interconnects with substantially higher costs. Performance varies greatly between these options. Integrated gigabit Ethernet will typically provide 100 MB/s of bandwidth, with latencies measured in the tens to hundreds of microseconds. Cluster interconnects generally provide five to ten times the bandwidth, providing latencies in below ten microseconds. As with many of the technologies described here, the state of the art is a fast moving target. Precise high-end performance figures would be out of date within months; check online sources for up to data figures.

5 Configuring and Tuning Cluster Networks

Daniel Nurmi and Brian Toonen

Cluster network configuration is a commonly overlooked aspect of many cluster design issues. Although designers think about details regarding the required network hardware, they frequently overlook the network design until after the cluster is installed and users start running code on the system.

The cluster network, the topic of this chapter, is most simply defined as the methods employed to connect various cluster entities via networks. This high level definition leads us to consider equally high level issues of node connectivity, node visibility, and cluster networking services. We will quickly discover that these seemingly simple issues encompass more complex topics, such as how cluster users interact with the machine, how security requirements imposed on the system impact the network design, and how application performance varies based upon the cluster network design. The methods used to handle these issues are implemented in the *cluster network design*, which we define as an administrative network topology imposed on the cluster to organize security, performance, and usability policies.

This chapter aims to bring the concept of cluster network design and tuning to the forefront of cluster designers' minds during the design phase. Fundamentally, we hope to leave the reader with the sense that a cluster's network design heavily impacts its core operation.

The rest of this chapter is arranged in the following manner. First, we will introduce some important issues that face the cluster designer and show how these issues can be directly affected by the choice of network design. Next, we introduce some fundamental concepts that will be used throughout the rest of the chapter, such as the Internet protocols and simple Linux networking concepts. Then, we will construct a simple cluster from the leftmost side of the cluster network design continuum (fully connected, fully visible). We will cover some of the most fundamental configuration issues involved by taking some machines and setting up the network and network services so that the machines act as a cluster running parallel codes. We then use this theoretical system as a vehicle to introduce the concepts of performance and security optimization techniques. We conclude with a brief discussion of diagnosing and correcting network problems.

5.1 Cluster Network Designs

Just as many styles of node and network hardware exist, so do a wide variety of cluster network designs. To understand why such variety exists is to understand how the choice of network design directly affects the operation of the cluster as a whole. In general, the motivation for such variation comes from the striving to achieve a perfect balance of usability, performance, and security. As a result, the cluster designer has realized that network design impacts all of these in important ways.

5.1.1 Impact of Network Design

Although it would be impossible to fully enumerate how a cluster network design impacts the overall look, feel, and operation of a cluster, there are some key aspects that are directly and substantially affected.

One of the first issues affected by the cluster network is security. Questions include how secure the system is from outsider attacks, how we maintain security over time, and how the cluster fits within institutional security requirements. The cluster network design should directly address all of these issues since the primary security defenses are often implemented inside the institution's network itself.

The cluster's usability is defined by how users interact with the system and what types of applications will use the cluster. Application requirements impact every aspect of the cluster design, and the cluster network is no exception. If the cluster is designed to run a single application, the designers can make very focused decisions about how the user(s) can employ the machine. If the cluster is meant to be a general resource for students, researchers, etc., then intuitiveness and ease of use must be considered.

Finally, we cannot overlook the impact of the cluster network design on application performance. The cluster network may impose bottlenecks that could limit the performance of an application. The designer must be aware that some decisions, while bolstering the security and usability of the cluster, can seriously impact the performance of applications.

5.1.2 Example Designs

Over time, cluster network designs have evolved from simple networks of desktops and servers. Modern designs focus more on the specific realm of high performance computing and thus often mirror network designs that large site administrators have been employing for years. The cluster community has built upon this substantial groundwork to generate a wide variety of network topologies. As we examine some common network designs, we should remember that the examples are a small subset of the many possibilities. For each of the following design descriptions, we could imagine a dozen permutations, each having a different positive or negative impact on overall cluster issues.

The first, and probably the simplest, style of cluster is the fully connected system. In this case, all nodes in the system, as well as any front end servers or login machines, are simply connected to the Internet the same way as any non-cluster server or workstation. The major benefit of this design is obvious: very little work is required to initially bring the system online. While the simplicity of such a design is attractive, the users and administrators of these systems must constantly be aware of all the implications. Security, for instance, will be a major concern. Although each node is easily accessed by legitimate users and administrators from anywhere on the Internet, each system is equally accessible to malicious outside attackers.

A simple optimization would be to reduce the number of systems visible to the Internet. Such a system would have a publicly available front end login machine, with all other nodes hidden behind a firewall and only visible from that front end machine. A user would log into the front end and then have access to cluster nodes. Although such a design provides tighter system security, we still have a machine visible to the Internet. Internet visibility is inherently problematic, but certainly does not make the system impossible to tightly secure. One interesting disadvantage of this design is that users whose work requires compute resources to be Internet accessible are unable to use such a system.

Going one step further, measures could be taken to completely block all access to compute nodes, even from the user. The user would log into a cluster front end (login) machine and would perform local operations such as compilation or preliminary testing. When the user's program is ready to be run on the cluster, it is submitted as a job to the cluster scheduler. When sufficient compute nodes become available, the scheduler runs the job on the user's behalf. Notice, in this design, the cluster nodes are never directly accessed by the user. The nodes are therefore completely hidden to all entities except the scheduler and other cluster services. We further could extend this concept by disallowing users access to the front end machine. Instead, the cluster would only accept jobs from a meta scheduler.

One interesting design simulates a large multi-processor computer with a single system image on a Linux cluster. By running custom operating systems, nodes become nearly invisible to users or outside influences. On such a system, users would employ an OS level mechanism present on the login machine (which may or may not be externally visible) to run processes on the cluster compute nodes. The biggest advantage of this design is ease of use for the application user. The user interface to a single system image avoids the common problems of managing remote processes. Disadvantages may arise when a user needs direct access to the compute nodes, which is prohibited by the nature of the system.

Cluster designers have put tremendous efforts into creating network topologies

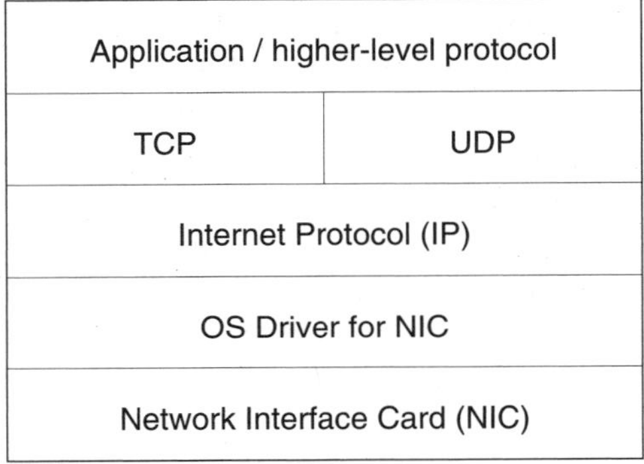

Figure 5.1: Layering of network protocols

suited to their individual needs. Many designers have made their experiences and technologies available for other cluster designers to use. For some real life examples of cluster designs, see Chapters 6, 18, and 20.

Armed with an awareness of various cluster network configurations, as well as some of the most importantly impacted issues, the cluster designer can embark on designing a network that optimally addresses individual needs. However, knowing the issues and possibilities at hand is only the first step. We must understand the simplest case of cluster network designs and some of the concepts surrounding their construction. In the sections that follow, we introduce customary communication protocols and give a short overview of Linux networking concepts and services, before delving into the construction of a simple cluster network.

5.2 Internet Protocol Stack

Simple Beowulf clusters are built with commodity networking hardware, typically Ethernet based, and communicate using standard networking protocols such as TCP/IP. Before examining UNIX networking concepts and services, as well as the configuration of a simple cluster, it is important that you understand the protocols involved in network communication. Understanding the protocols will be necessary when performing advanced configuration, troubleshooting problems or attempting to improve performance.

Networking protocols are built, at least conceptually, in layers. Figure 5.1 depicts the layers involved in TCP and UDP communication. In the paragraphs that follow, we will describe the layers from the bottom up, focusing on details important to our later discussions. While a full discussion of IP networking is beyond the scope of this chapter, the interested reader will find that [28, 110] discuss the topic in great detail. In addition, a more general discussion of network hardware, software, and protocols can be found in Chapter 4.

A combination of the network interface card and the associated driver is responsible for sending frames out to other devices on the local area network. The maximum amount of data that can be placed in a frame is otherwise known as the maximum transmission unit (MTU). The MTU for an Ethernet device depends on which specification the device implements, but most devices have a MTU of 1500 bytes. Some newer Ethernet devices can be configured to send and receive jumbo frames, resulting in a MTU as large as 9000 bytes. Jumbo frames and their implications will be discussed further in Section 5.5.4.

The Internet Protocol (IP) is the building block for TCP and UDP. IP is a communication protocol for transferring messages known as datagrams between machines, even machines on different networks. An IP datagram consists of a header plus data. The header contains, among other things, the addresses for the source and destination machines and the length of the datagram (in bytes). The destination address is used by special network devices known as routers to forward (or route) the datagram between networks until the datagram reaches its destination. Section 5.3.1 contains a more detailed discussion of IP addresses and routing.

The length field of the datagram header is only 16 bits wide. As a result, the combination of the datagram header and data can be at most 65,535 bytes in length. However, as you might have guessed, IP datagrams are transmitted on the underlying network using frames, a network whose MTU is generally much smaller 65,535 bytes. To solve this problem, IP datagrams larger than the MTU are fragmented into a series of IP packets and reassembled by the receiver. In addition, fragmentation may occur if a packet is routed through any network having a smaller MTU.

IP is what is known as an unreliable, unordered, and connectionless protocol. Unreliable suggests that datagrams sent using IP may not arrive at their destination. Although the protocol makes every effort to deliver the datagram, network misconfiguration, resource exhaustion, or outright failure may result in data loss. Unordered indicates that datagrams that do arrive at their destination may arrive in a different order from the one in which they were sent. And finally, connectionless implies that no state is maintained at the sender or the receiver between datagrams.

The User Datagram Protocol (UDP) is a thin layer on top of IP. Like IP, UDP is unreliable, unordered and connectionless. The primary contribution of UDP is the addition of ports. IP only identifies the source and destinations machines, not which application or service was involved in the communication. The port is an integer identifier that allows multiple flows of communication to exist between a pair of machines and ensures that the datagrams are delivered to the appropriate application or service.

The Transmission Control Protocol (TCP), also layered on top of IP, is substantially more complex that UDP. TCP provides a bidirectional connection over which a stream of bytes is reliably communicated. Like UDP, TCP uses ports. A connection is uniquely identified by a four-tuple (source address, source port, destination address, destination port). Using this four-tuple, the TCP layer can locate the structures maintaining the state of the connection.

With TCP, data in the stream is divided into segments for transmission. These segments, plus a TCP header, are encapsulated into an IP datagram. To avoid fragmentation, which can adversely affect performance, the maximum segment size (MSS) is advertised when the connection is formed so that the segment data plus the TCP and IP headers do not exceed the MTU of the underlying network. On a local-area network (LAN), the MSS can be computed by subtracting the size of the TCP header from the network device's MTU.

TCP connections that reach outside of the LAN are more difficult as the MTU of all the networks involved is unknown when the connection is formed. In this case, most TCP/IP implementations assume an initial MTU of 576 bytes, unless an alternative value is specified by the system administrator. A discovery process is then employed to determine a MTU that is acceptable for all networks involved in the connection. Since the primary focus of this chapter is the cluster network, a discussion of wide-area network MTU discovery is unwarranted. However, the interested reader will find introductions to the topic in [28, 110] and a detailed discussion in [74].

TCP uses a coupling of positive acknowledgments and a sliding window protocol. Positive acknowledgments and data buffering along with timeouts and retransmission provide the reliability. The sliding window protocol allows the sender to have multiple unacknowledged segments outstanding, substantially increase throughput. Additionally, the protocol provides the receiver with the ability to advertise the amount of buffer space available at its end of the connection. By knowing the amount of available space at the receiver, the sender can avoid transmitting more data than can be accommodated by the receiver. This is known as flow control.

More detailed discussions of these topics, and TCP as a whole, can be found in [28, 110, 87].

This concludes our high-level overview of the Internet Protocol stack. Building and operating a Beowulf cluster by no means necessitates mastering these protocols; however, a basic understanding is required. After all, it is these protocols that enable network communication. In the coming section, we will discuss a series of networking concepts and services which are built upon these very protocols.

5.3 Networking Concepts and Services

Before constructing a cluster, it is important to understand the concepts and services that are involved in UNIX networking. This section presents the basics in preparation for the step-by-step configuration of a simple cluster coming up in Section 5.4. Additional information on the topics presented here can be found in [56].

5.3.1 IP addresses

Each node in the cluster must be assigned a unique *IP address.* IP addresses consist of 32 bits or four octets[1] and are usually expressed by writing each octet in decimal and separating the octets with a decimal point. This is known as dotted decimal notation. As an example, `192.168.13.24` is a valid IP address.

A *netmask* is used to split the IP address into two parts: the network address and the host address. The netmask expresses how many of the high-end bits of an IP address are part of the network address. The low-end bits of the IP address then form the host address. Using the previous example address of `192.168.13.24`, asserting a netmask of `255.255.255.0` would mean that the network address is `192.168.13.0` and the host address on that network is 24. Two special host addresses are reserved and may not be used to identify an actual host. All bits turned off (or zero) is the address of the network, and all bits turned on (or 255 in our example) is the network broadcast address.

Hosts that share the same network address are generally part of the same physical network and can talk directly to each other. Hosts on different networks require a router to talk to each other. The router uses the network portion of the destination

[1] An octet is just 8 bits, which is the same as a byte in most modern systems. The term octet is used in networking to specify precisely 8 bits. Once was a day when machines with 6-bit characters and 36-bit or 60-bit words were common, and the term octet was coined to ensure that 8 bits were used.

IP address to determine onto which physical network link to forward the data packet. In complex networks, the data packet may be forwarded by several routers before it finally reaches the destination network and ultimately the destination host. To begin this forwarding process, the sending host must know the address of the router on its local network. The address of this router is know as the gateway address.

Not all IP addresses are routable to the Internet. Three address ranges have been reserved for private (internal) networks:

- 10.0.0.0 – 10.255.255.255
- 172.16.0.0 – 172.31.255.255
- 192.168.0.0 – 192.168.255.255

These address ranges may be used by clusters that either have no need to communicate with Internet resources or are hidden behind a firewall that does network address translation (NAT). Discussion of network address translation is beyond the scope of this chapter; however, the interested reader will find the topic covered in [127].

5.3.2 Hostnames

In addition to an IP address, each node in the cluster will require a unique name. Names generally come in two forms: short and long. The long name is used when referring to the host from outside of the local domain (or subdomain) in which it is present. The long name for the first node in our Beowulf cluster might be `bc1-001.phy.myu.edu`. Notice that the long name is hierarchical. It refers to the node `bc1-001` in the `phy` (short for the Physics department) subdomain which is part of the `myu.edu` domain. The short name, `bc1-001`, is often used when referring to the node from within the local subdomain, the Physics department.

With clusters, it is common practice to name the cluster nodes after their host addresses. For example, nodes in a 128 node cluster with IP addresses ranging from `192.168.13.1` through `192.168.13.128` and a netmask of `255.255.255.0` might be named `bc1-001` through `bc1-128`. Computer scientists who prefer to begin counting their nodes from zero should recall that host address zero is reserved for the network address (`192.168.13.0` in our example). To avoid having the host address and the node name differ by one, it is best to number nodes starting from one [108].

An additional side effect to starting the node number and host address of the first node at one is that the gateway address must follow that of the nodes. To allow room for expansion, the gateway address is generally given the maximum *available* host address. Remember, that the maximum host address is reserved for the network broadcast address, so the gateway address is generally assigned the address just prior to the network broadcast address. In our continuing example, the gateway address would be `192.168.13.254`.

5.3.3 Name resolution

Given a set of hostnames and IP addresses for the nodes in the cluster, a mechanism is needed to map from one to the other. For a small number of nodes, this can be accomplished with a hosts file ('`/etc/hosts`'). The hosts file will include a line for each node in the cluster. Each line contains the IP address of the node followed by the names the nodes is known by, usually the long name first followed by the short.

The hosts file traditionally contains one additional mapping from the names `localhost` and `localhost.phy.myu.edu` to `127.0.0.1`. The address `127.0.0.1` is tied to the loopback device driver that funnels all messages sent from it back to the same host. The combination of the loopback device and the mapping in the hosts file allows a host to communicate with itself as though it were any other host on the network simply by using the name `localhost`.

One caveat of using a hosts file is that it must be replicated and kept current on every node in the cluster. However, for most environments, the hosts file does not change that often. A master copy can be kept on one node of our cluster and then pushed to the other nodes when changes are made. This push operation would be tedious to do by hand, but it is not very difficult to write a script to copy the hosts file to the other nodes using a program like `scp`. A brief description of `scp` can be found in Section 5.3.5. Chapter 6 describes tools that can handle all of these setup steps for you; the material in this section describes some of the operations that those tools must perform and provides some background for understanding how those tools work.

As an alternative, the Network Information Service (NIS) exists to perform this type of replication automatically. NIS allows the system administrator to manage a single copy of important files like the hosts file on one node designated as the NIS server. The other nodes, acting as NIS clients, obtain the host information from the NIS server as necessary.

In addition to maintaining a single copy of the hosts file, NIS can also be used to propagate account ('`/etc/passwd`') and group ('`/etc/group`') information, as well as other important system files. A more detailed explanation on the capabilities of NIS can be found in [109]. An example configuration of a NIS server and clients will be shown in Section 5.4.

Another option for avoiding the replication of the hosts file is the Domain Name Service (DNS). DNS differs from NIS in two major ways. First, its sole purpose is to return information about a host or domain. Second, it performs resolution for hosts outside of the local domain. DNS is by design a scalable distributed database capable of handling name resolution for the entire Internet. Further information on DNS and Berkeley's implementation (BIND) can be found in [1].

DNS and NIS are designed to work together. It is not uncommon to use NIS for resolution of local hostnames and DNS for resolving names external to the local domain (or subdomain).

5.3.4 File sharing

In most networked computing environments, the ability to share files with other machines on the network is extremely useful. Such a capability allows system administrators to install a software package once an make it accessible to a set of machines. File sharing also allows users to create a file on one machine and access it from a variety of other machines on the local-area network. For Linux environments, this file sharing capability is traditionally provided by the Network File System (NFS).

File sharing is useful on Beowulf clusters for the same reasons. Application programs built by users typically reference libraries from other software packages. If these software packages use shared libraries, ones that are dynamically loaded at runtime, then those libraries must be accessible on all nodes where the application is being run. Thus the system administrator has two choices: installing the necessary packages on each of the nodes or using a network based file system like NFS to make the packages available to each of the nodes.

Likewise, the typical user of a Beowulf cluster will wish to run their application on several nodes, perhaps simultaneously. Most users find copying their application's executable and input data files to each node before executing the application undesirable. Instead, they would like to build their application on a single machine, construct any necessary input files on that same machine, and have the executable and input files automatically available on all nodes of the cluster. Again, a file sharing system like NFS can help. Using NFS, the users' home directories can be exported from one machine to each of the cluster nodes, allowing access to these home directories from anywhere in the cluster. A detailed explanation of NFS and its capabilities can be found in [109].

5.3.5 Remote access

The purpose of building a Beowulf cluster is to run user applications. In a networked computing environment, users typically do not have access to the console of all the compute resources. Even if they did, it is much more convenient to access those resources from the workstations present on their desktops. Clusters are simply an array of compute resources with which users wish to interact, execute programs, and share files.

A traditional UNIX system has programs like `telnet` and `rlogin` to establish an interactive terminal session with remote compute resource over the network. In addition, `rsh` executes commands on the remote resource without user interaction, and `rcp` transfers files between a local and remote resource when direct file sharing is not available. The last two commands are especially powerful because they allow complex remote operations to be scripted and executed without user interaction.

The problem with all of these commands is security. None of the data transferred between the local and remote hosts is encrypted, thus allowing the data to be easily read if captured by someone monitoring network traffic. While a user might not care if someone saw their interactions with a remote resource, `telnet` transmits the user's password over that same unencrypted channel. All users should care if their passwords are visible to potential outside attackers.

The `rsh` and `rcp` commands do not send passwords, making them somewhat more secure. Instead they use host based authentication. If the host is listed in the system's or user's authorized hosts file on the remote machine, then the command is allow to proceed. The `rlogin` command will also use host based authentication if possible; but, if the host is not authorized, `rlogin` will ask for the user's password.

Clearly, host based authentication is preferable to sending a password in clear text. However, host based authentication is not without its problems. First, all hosts on the local network must be strictly controlled. Physical security is important. If a malicious host is allowed to attach to the local network, it can be configured to appear as an authorized host, thus compromising security. Second, access to the authorized hosts files must be tightly controlled. If these files can be compromised, so too can the machines for which they control access. Hence, many system administrators disallow the use of user controlled authorization files (i.e., '`~/.rhosts`').

SSH, or the Secure Shell, was designed as a replacement for the previously mentioned remote access tools. However, SSH is more than a just remote execution shell. It is a suite of tools utilizing public-private key based authentication and modern day encryption to provide a secure means of remote access. As might be expected, it contains programs like `slogin`, `ssh`, and `scp` to replace their less secure counterparts. SSH also contains tools for creating and managing authentication keys, the foundation of its security. In addition, recent implementations like OpenSSH also provide a secure form of FTP.

SSH uses host authentication keys to verify that a host is the expected host and not a malicious decoy. During connection establishment, these keys are used to verify that the connection is with the expected remote host before vital information, such as the user's password, is sent. If host based authentication is employed, the connecting host can be verified before authorization is granted. It is still important to strictly control which hosts are authorized and to disallow user controlled authorization files; but, on a properly configured system, SSH's use of host authentication keys substantially reduces the security risk associated with host based authentication.

SSH can also use authentication keys as a replacement for user passwords. The advantages may not be immediately apparent; however, when combined with the SSH agent, user authentication keys can be very powerful. A more detailed discussion of authentication keys, both host and user, and the SSH agent will be presented in Section 5.4.6.

5.4 Simple Cluster Configuration Walkthrough

Now that we have discussed basic UNIX networking concepts and services, and briefly described the protocols involved in network communication, it is time to walk through the configuration of a simple cluster. Since we cannot cover the variety of Linux distributions in existence, we have chosen to use Red Hat Linux 9 for our example. If you are using a different Linux distribution, the concepts should be same, but the exact commands and files may be different. Note that Chapter 6 describes tools that automate many of the following steps; we are describing them here to provide an understanding of the steps involved in setting up a cluster network.

Our example cluster consists of eight nodes. As in our previous examples, to avoid using IP addresses that may belong to an existing domain, we place the nodes of our cluster on a private network with a network address of `192.168.13.0` and a netmask of `255.255.255.0`. The gateway address to our router is `192.168.13.254`,

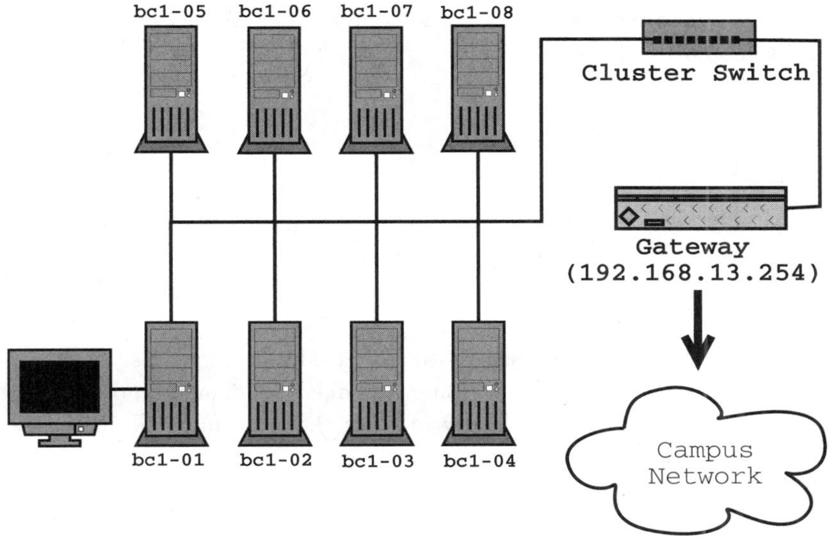

Figure 5.2: Diagram showing the configuration of our simple example cluster.

the domain is `phy.myu.edu`, and our nodes are named `bc1-01` through `bc1-08`. The cluster configuration is depicted in Figure 5.2.

When installing Red Hat Linux 9 on each of the eight nodes, we used the standard "Workstation" install with one exception. We included the NIS server package `ypserv` on the first node. Later, we will run a NIS server on `bc1-01` for the purposes of propagating system information like accounts and hostname to IP address mappings. Although the NIS hosts map is used for resolving names local to our cluster, we assume that a DNS server exists at `192.168.1.1` to obtain information about hosts outside of our cluster network. In addition to NIS, we will also run a NFS server on `bc1-01` to provide each user access to a common home directory accessible from all of the nodes.

5.4.1 Hostname and gateway address

We begin by setting the hostname and gateway address on each of the machines. These parameters may have been set during the installation of the operating system; in which case, we need only verify that they are correct. Both of these parameters are set in '/etc/sysconfig/network'. The contents of this file for the first node of our cluster should be as follows.

```
NETWORKING=yes
HOSTNAME=bc1-01.phy.myu.edu
GATEWAY=192.168.13.254
```

Alterations made to this file do not take effect immediately; however, the changes should be realized the next time the system is rebooted. If you had to make changes, it is recommended that you reboot now. This can be accomplished by executing `shutdown -r now`.

Notice that the long name is used in the `HOSTNAME` setting. Use of the short name for this setting is discouraged as doing so makes it difficult, if not impossible, for applications and libraries to properly identify the local machine in the global namespace. This can cause some programs to behave incorrectly or fail altogether.

5.4.2 Network interface configuration

Next, we need to configure the IP settings for the network interface on each of the nodes. The network interface settings can be changed using two different methods. The first is to use a program like `netconf`; the second is to edit the configuration file directly. We will edit the configuration file, '/etc/sysconf/network-scripts/ifcfg-eth0', so the exact location of the settings is clear. The contents of the configuration file for the first node of our cluster should be as follows.

```
DEVICE=eth0
ONBOOT=yes
BOOTPROTO=static
IPADDR=192.168.13.1
NETMASK=255.255.255.0
NETWORK=192.168.13.0
BROADCAST=192.168.13.255
```

The settings on the other nodes are largely the same. Only the `IPADDR` setting needs to be adjusted.

Alterations to the network interface configuration file should only be made when the interface is disabled, accomplished by running `ifdown eth0`. Once the changes are complete, `ifup eth0` can be run to re-enable the interface with the new settings.

5.4.3 Name resolution

For our cluster, the hostname to IP address mappings are as follows.

```
127.0.0.1       localhost.phy.myu.edu  localhost
192.168.13.1    bc1-01.phy.myu.edu     bc1-01
192.168.13.2    bc1-02.phy.myu.edu     bc1-02
192.168.13.3    bc1-03.phy.myu.edu     bc1-03
192.168.13.4    bc1-04.phy.myu.edu     bc1-04
192.168.13.5    bc1-05.phy.myu.edu     bc1-05
192.168.13.6    bc1-06.phy.myu.edu     bc1-06
192.168.13.7    bc1-07.phy.myu.edu     bc1-07
192.168.13.8    bc1-08.phy.myu.edu     bc1-08
192.168.13.254  bc1-gw.phy.myu.edu     bc1-gw
```

To avoid a substantial amount of repetitive typing, the complete set of mappings need only be entered into the '/etc/hosts' file on bc1-01. Later, in Section 5.4.7, we will configure NIS to provide this information to the other seven nodes. The '/etc/hosts' file on the remaining nodes should consist only of the following entry.

```
127.0.0.1       localhost.phy.myu.edu  localhost
```

In addition to the hosts file, we need to configure the service that resolves names (the resolver for short) on each node of the cluster. The configuration file, '/etc/resolv.conf', must contain the following.

```
nameserver 192.168.1.1
search phy.myu.edu
```

The resolver configuration file contains two important pieces of information. The first is the IP address of the DNS server used to resolve names not found in the hosts file or the NIS hosts map; the second is the search list for hostname lookup. If a short or incomplete hostname is supplied, entries in the search list are individually appended to the hostname. For example, if the system were attempting to resolve the hostname foo, it would append phy.myu.edu and then perform a DNS query for foo.phy.myu.edu.

5.4.4 Accounts

At this time, we need to create accounts for the users of our cluster. It is recommended that each user have his own account, including the system administrator(s). While the administrator already has access to the root account, that account should only be used to perform administrative tasks. Use of the root account for non-administrative tasks is frowned upon because that account is unchecked, allowing for unintentional damage to the operating system. For more details on account management, see Section 13.6.

Users may be added to the system with the `adduser` program. Running `adduser <username>` creates an entry for the user in the account information and shadow password files, '`/etc/passwd`' and '`/etc/shadow`' respectively. The `adduser` program also adds a group for the user in '`/etc/group`' and creates a home directory for that user in '`/home/<username>`'. Usage information about the `adduser` program can be obtained by running `man adduser`.

The creation of user accounts and home directories across all of the nodes in the cluster could be handled by running `adduser` on each node for each user. However, this repetition is tedious and requires care so that the user and group identifiers are consistent across all nodes. Alternatively, we could create a script which uses `scp` to replicate the appropriate system files and `ssh` create the necessary home directories on each node. Instead, since we are already using NIS to provide the host map, we will configure NIS to also provide account and group information to the other seven nodes. Additionally, we will use NFS to make the '`/home`' directory on `bc1-01` accessible to the remaining nodes. NIS will be configured in Section 5.4.7 and NFS in Section 5.4.8.

By default, `adduser` creates the account with a bogus password entry; thus effectively disabling the account. To enable the account, run `passwd <username>` to set an initial password for the account. Usage information about the `passwd` program can be obtained by running `man passwd`.

Unlike normal user accounts, NIS does not publish account information for the root user, and NFS is not configured to export the root user's home directory, '`/root`'. Doing either is considered a security risk as it may allow a malicious user to obtain privileged information and compromise one or more nodes of the cluster. Instead the root user has a separate entry in '`/etc/passwd`' and '`/etc/shadow`' and a separate home directory on each cluster node. While these restrictions affect the ease with which the root user can change its password or share files between machines, the security of the cluster as a whole is improved.

5.4.5 Packet filtering

As a security measure, the Linux kernel has the ability to filter IP packets. Among other things, packet filtering allows the system administrator to control access to services running on a machine. By default, Red Hat Linux 9 uses packet filtering to block remote access to most services including SSH, NFS and NIS. This default configuration presents a problem for a cluster environment where remote execution, file sharing and collective system administration are critical.

To allow SSH, NIS and NFS to function, we must add a few new packet filtering rules to each node of our cluster, allowing SSH, NFS and NIS to function. For Red Hat Linux 9, packet filtering rules are specified in the file '`/etc/sysconfig/iptables`'. Into this file, we insert the following rules before the first line that starts with `-A INPUT`.

```
-A INPUT -p tcp -m tcp --dport 22 --syn -j ACCEPT
-A INPUT -p tcp -s 192.168.13.0/24 -j ACCEPT
-A INPUT -p udp -s 192.168.13.0/24 -j ACCEPT
```

Once those changes have been made, the following command must be executed so the changes will take effect.

```
/etc/rc.d/init.d/iptables restart
```

The first rule we added tells the packet filter to allow new TCP connection requests made to port 22, the port monitored by `sshd`. With this rule in place, `ssh` and `scp` can be used to access the nodes in our cluster from any other machine on the network, including those not part of the cluster. If we were using routable addresses and our network was Internet accessible, any machine on the Internet could attempt to access our cluster nodes. This accessibility might appear to be a security concern; but, the connecting entity must know the name of an existing account and the associated password to obtain access, both of which SSH encrypts before transmitting them over the network.

The second and third rules tell the packet filter to accept any packets from any machines on the cluster network. These rules allow NFS and NIS to function between nodes in the cluster. The rules may seem unnecessarily liberal because they allow *all* UDP and TCP packets to pass. However, the NIS services and the network status monitoring service used by NFS are dynamically assigned ports by the `portmap` service. Because these port values are not known in advance, they cannot be explicitly specified in our packet filtering rules. In addition, we don't want to prevent applications running across nodes of the cluster from being able to communicate with each other. Therefore, we allow packets to freely flow between machines on the cluster network while still blocking potentially security threatening traffic from the outside.

More information about Linux firewalls and `iptables` can be found in Section 5.6.2.

5.4.6 Secure shell

The OpenSSH package is installed automatically with Red Hat Linux 9, which means the SSH remote access clients like `ssh` and `scp` are available to users immediately. The SSH service `sshd` is also available and started by default. Once the packet filtering rules discussed in Section 5.4.5 have been applied, the root user should be able to remotely access any of the nodes in the cluster. This ability can be tremendously useful when one needs to replicate configuration files across several nodes of the cluster or to restart a service without being at the console of the specific node.

Initially, non-root users will only be able to remotely access `bc1-01`. This restriction is lifted once NIS and NFS have been configured and enabled, thus providing account information and home directories to other nodes in the cluster. The configuration of NIS and NFS are discussed in Section 5.4.7 and Section 5.4.8 respectively.

The first time the `sshd` service is started, authentication keys for the host are generated. The keys for the remote host are used during the establishment of a SSH session, allowing the client (e.g., `ssh`) to validate the identity of the remote host. However, the validation can occur only if the client knows the public key of the remote host to which it is trying to connect. When the public key of the remote host is unknown, the user is notified that the authenticity of the remote host could not be verified. The connection process then continues only if the user explicitly authorizes it. If the user agrees to continue establishing the connection, the client stores the name of the remote host and its public key in '`~/.ssh/known_hosts`' on the local machine. The stored public key is used during the establishment of future connections to validate the authenticity of the remote host.

To prevent the user from being questioned about host authenticity, the system administrator can establish a system-wide list of hosts and their associated public keys. This list is placed in the '`/etc/ssh/ssh_known_hosts`' file on each of the nodes and any other machines that are likely to remotely access the nodes. This approach has one other advantage. If a node is rebuilt and new authentication keys are generated, then the system administrator can update the '`ssh_known_hosts`' files. Such updates can prevent the user from receiving errors about host identification changes and potential man-in-the-middle attacks.

The contents of the '`ssh_known_hosts`' file can be generated automatically using `ssh-keyscan`. To use `ssh-keyscan`, we must first create a file containing a list of our cluster nodes. Each line of this file, which we will call '`hosts`', should contain the primary IP address of a node followed by all of the names and addresses associated with that node.

```
192.168.13.1 bc1-01.phy.myu.edu,bc1-01,192.168.13.1
192.168.13.2 bc1-02.phy.myu.edu,bc1-02,192.168.13.2
192.168.13.3 bc1-03.phy.myu.edu,bc1-03,192.168.13.3
192.168.13.4 bc1-04.phy.myu.edu,bc1-04,192.168.13.4
192.168.13.5 bc1-05.phy.myu.edu,bc1-05,192.168.13.5
192.168.13.6 bc1-06.phy.myu.edu,bc1-06,192.168.13.6
192.168.13.7 bc1-07.phy.myu.edu,bc1-07,192.168.13.7
192.168.13.8 bc1-08.phy.myu.edu,bc1-08,192.168.13.8
```

Once the '`hosts`' file has been created, the following command will obtain the public keys from each of the nodes and generate the '`ssh_known_hosts`' file.

```
ssh-keyscan -t rsa,dsa,rsa1 -f hosts >/etc/ssh/ssh_known_hosts
```

The '`ssh_known_hosts`' file needs to exist on each node of the cluster. While the above command could be executed on each of the nodes, regenerating the contents each time, it is also possible to use `scp` to copy the file to each of the remaining nodes.

At this point, the client tools are able to validate the identity of the remote host. However, the remote host must still authenticate the user before allowing the client access to the remote system. By default, users are prompted for their passwords as a means of authentication. To prevent this from happening when access is from one cluster node to another, host based authentication can be utilized. Host based authentication, as discussed in Section 5.3.5, allows a trusted client host to vouch for the user. The remote host uses the public key of the client host, found in the file we just generated, to verify the identity of the client host. Enabling host based authentication requires a few configuration changes on each of the nodes.

The `sshd` service must be configured to allow host based authentication by changing ,the following parameters in '`/etc/ssh/sshd_config`'.

```
HostbasedAuthentication yes
IgnoreUserKnownHosts yes
IgnoreRhosts no
```

The first parameter enables host based authentication. The second parameter disables the use of the user maintained known host file, '`~/.ssh/known_hosts`', when host based authentication is performed. This change allows the system administrator to maintain strict control over which hosts can be authenticated and thus authorized. The third parameter allows the user maintained authorization file, '`~/ .shosts`', to be used when determining whether or not a remote host is authorized to access the system using host based authentication. This is largely provided for the root user for whom the system maintained file, '`/etc/ssh/shosts.equiv`', is not used. While utilizing user authorization files could be considered a security risk, the change to the `IgnoreUserKnownHosts` parameter prevents the user from authorizing access to any hosts not listed in the system controlled '`/etc/ssh/ssh_known_hosts`' file. But, if host based authentication is not desired for the root user, then the third parameter should be left at its default value of "yes".

Once the `sshd` configuration file has been updated to enable host based authentication, the system authorization file, '`/etc/ssh/shosts.equiv`', must be created. That file simply consists of the hostnames of machines trusted by the local host. For our cluster, the file should contain the following.

```
bc1-01.phy.myu.edu
bc1-02.phy.myu.edu
bc1-03.phy.myu.edu
bc1-04.phy.myu.edu
bc1-05.phy.myu.edu
bc1-06.phy.myu.edu
bc1-07.phy.myu.edu
bc1-08.phy.myu.edu
```

If host based authentication is to be used to allow a client to vouch for the root user, this same list of hostnames must also be placed in the root user's authorization file, '`/root/.shosts`'. Again, `scp` can be employed to push copies of these files to each of the nodes.

Now that the `sshd` service has been configured and the list of authorized hosts properly established, the `sshd` service must be restarted. This is accomplished using the following command.

```
/etc/rc.d/init.d/sshd restart
```

In addition to changing the service configuration file, a small change must be made to the client configuration file, '`/etc/ssh/ssh_config`'. The following line should be added just after the line containing "`Host *`".

```
HostbasedAuthentication yes
```

This option tells the client tools that they should attempt to use host based authentication when connecting to a remote host. By default, they do not.

Users, including the root user, also have the ability to create authentication keys which can be use in place of passwords. Such keys are generated with the command `ssh-keygen -t rsa`. By default, the public and private keys are placed in '`~/.ssh/id_rsa.pub`' and '`~/.ssh/id_rsa`' respectively. The contents of the public key can be added to '`~/.ssh/authorized_keys`' on any machine, allowing remote access to that machine using the authentication keys.

The `ssh-keygen` command will allow keys to be generated without a passphrase to protect the private key. Users often generate unprotected keys simply to avoid having to reenter the passphrase with each remote operation. However, this practice is not recommended as it substantially weakens the security of any machine allowing public key authentication. Instead of using unprotected keys, a SSH agent can be established to manage the private key(s) of the user for the duration of a session. The passphrase need only be typed once when the private key is registered with the agent. Thereafter, remote operations can proceed without the continual reentry of the passphrase; but, the private key is still protected should a malicious user obtain access to the file containing it.

From the shell, the agent is often used in the following manner.

```
[root@bc1-01 root]# ssh-agent $SHELL
[root@bc1-01 root]# ssh-add
Enter passphrase for /root/.ssh/id_rsa:
Identity added: /root/.ssh/id_rsa (/root/.ssh/id_rsa)
[root@bc1-01 root]# <various SSH client commands>
[root@bc1-01 root]# exit
```

The first command starts the agent and then begins a new shell. The second command adds the root user's private key to the set of keys managed by the agent. In this case, only one key is managed by the agent, but more could be added through subsequent invocations of `ssh-add`. After the agent has been started and the private key has been registered, the root user may execute various client commands attempting to access to one or more remote machines. If the user's '`~/.ssh/authorized_keys`' file on the remote host contains root's public key, the client command will proceed without requesting a password or passphrase. The final command, `exit`, causes the shell and thus the agent to terminate.

A general discussion of SSH usage, configuration and protocols can be found in [11], although the details involving OpenSSH are somewhat out of date. Information specific to OpenSSH commands and configuration can be found in the manual pages installed with Red Hat Linux 9 and on the OpenSSH website, `www.openssh.org`. Links to IETF draft documents describing the SSH protocols can also be found on the OpenSSH website.

5.4.7 Network Information Service

Now that the IP packet filter has been configured in a way that allows our services to function, and we have introduced the finer points of SSH, we will proceed with configuring NIS. On each of the nodes, the following line must be added to '/etc/sysconfig/network'.

```
NISDOMAIN=bc1.phy.myu.edu
```

This line tells the NIS services the name of the NIS domain to which our nodes belong. The NIS domain name can be different than the Internet domain in which the nodes reside (phy.myu.edu). The NIS domain name should identify the group of machines the domain is servicing. In our case, this NIS domain is used only by our first Beowulf cluster. Therefore, we use the domain name bc1.phy.myu.edu to avoid conflicts with other NIS domains that might exist on our local network.

Once the NIS domain has been set on each of the nodes, we must prepare bc1-01 to run the NIS server. Before enabling the server to export information, we must secure the server so that only hosts in our cluster can obtain information from it. Entries in the '/var/yp/securenets' file accomplish this. For our cluster, this file (on bc1-01) should contain the following entries.

```
host            127.0.0.1
255.255.255.0   192.168.13.0
```

Now we are ready to configure and run the NIS server. To begin, we edit the '/var/yp/Makefile' file on bc1-01. We need to comment out the existing line that begins with "all:" and add the following line before it.

```
all:  passwd group hosts networks services protocols rpc
```

This line lists the information sources that we desire NIS to export to the client nodes. NIS maintains a set of databases, known as maps, separate from the source files. To build the maps, the following commands must be executed on bc1-01.

```
echo "loopback 127" >>/etc/networks
/etc/rc.d/init.d/ypserv start
/etc/rc.d/init.d/ypxfrd start
/etc/rc.d/init.d/yppasswdd start
cd /var/yp
make
```

Since '/etc/networks' does not exist on Red Hat Linux 9 installations, the first command creates the file, adding the loopback network as an entry. The next three commands start the services needed by a NIS server. And the last two commands build the actual maps.

The previous commands started the necessary NIS services; however, they did not configure the system so the services would be automatically started at boot time. To accomplish this, we must adjust the runlevel associated with the services. The following commands tell the system to automatically start the services when booting the system. Remember, these commands should only be executed on bc1-01, the system running the NIS server.

```
chkconfig --level 345 ypserv on
chkconfig --level 345 ypxfrd on
chkconfig --level 345 yppasswdd on
```

Now that we have a running NIS server, it is time to configure the clients. The NIS client service ypbind will be run on all of the nodes in our cluster, including bc1-01. The following commands start the client service and configure the operating system so the service is started automatically when the system is booted.

```
/etc/rc.d/init.d/ypbind start
chkconfig --add ypbind
chkconfig --level 345 ypbind on
```

To make the operating system use NIS when looking up information, we must update the name service switch configuration file, '/etc/nsswitch.conf', on each of the nodes. The entries that follow should be modified accordingly.

```
passwd:         files nis
group:          files nis
hosts:          files nis dns
networks:       files nis
services:       files nis
protocols:      files nis
rpc:            files nis
```

When the source files on the server are modified, the NIS maps are not automatically updated . Therefore anytime a new account or group is added or the hosts file is updated, the maps need to be rebuilt. To rebuild the maps, the following commands must be run on bc1-01.

```
cd /var/yp
make
```

Once the maps are rebuilt, any updates are available to all nodes in the cluster.

The exception to the maps not being immediately updated is the changing of a user's password. If the password is changed using the yppasswd program, the yppasswdd service immediately updates both the NIS maps and account files on bc1-01, making the updated password immediately available to all nodes in the cluster. yppasswd may be run from any node that is part of the NIS domain.

A small problem exists with regards to the NIS client and the sshd service. If sshd is started before ypbind, as it was in our example, then sshd will not use NIS services to obtain account information. Therefore users will not be able to remotely access bc1-02 through bc1-08 until sshd is restarted. The service may be restarted by executing

```
/etc/rc.d/init.d/sshd restart
```

on each of those nodes. A similar problem will occur if bc1-02 through bc1-08 are rebooted and bc1-01 is not online or is not running the NIS server. The ypbind service will fail causing sshd not to use NIS even if ypbind is started later. So, as a general rule, if ypbind is manually started, sshd should also be restarted.

5.4.8 Network File System

Now that the NIS server and clients are running, the next task is to configure the NFS server and clients, thus allowing users access to their home directories from any of the cluster nodes.

We will begin with configuring the server on bc1-01. To export the user home directories, the following line must be added to the file '/etc/exports'.

```
/home 192.168.13.0/24(rw)
```

This line tells the NFS server that any machine on our cluster network may access the home file system. Once the file has been modified, the NFS service must be enabled and started using the following commands.

```
chkconfig --level 345 nfs on
/etc/rc.d/init.d/nfs start
```

Next we need to configure the other seven nodes to *mount* the '/home' directory on bc1-01. Mounting is the UNIX term for attaching a file system space, whether it be local or remote, into the local directory structure. To express that we wish to have '/home' on bc1-01 be mounted as '/home' in the directory structure present on our remaining cluster nodes, we must add the following line to '/etc/fstab' on all nodes except bc1-01.

```
192.168.13.1:/home /home nfs rw,hard,intr,bg,rsize=8192,wsize=8192 0 0
```

Then we execute the following command on each of those nodes to cause the remote file system to be mounted.

```
/etc/rc.d/init.d/netfs restart
```

You might have noticed that we use the IP address for bc1-01 instead of its hostname when we added the entry to '/etc/fstab'. The reason is that **netfs** is started before before **ypbind** when the operating system is booting. If we were to use bc1-01 in place of the address, hostname resolution would fail causing the mount to fail.

The options for mounting a file system exported by NFS are numerous. The manual pages, obtained by executing **man fstab** and **man nfs**, provide an explanation of the '/etc/fstab' structure and the available options when mounting file systems via NFS. Additional information can also be found in [109].

5.4.9 Scripting it

For small clusters, installing the operating system on each node, and performing the previously mention configuration adjustments might not seem so bad. However, for a larger cluster, the task can be annoyingly repetitive and prone to error. Fortunately, several solutions exist.

The Kickstart system, part of the Red Hat Linux 9 distribution, is one such solution. When Red Hat Linux 9 is installed, a Kickstart configuration file is automatically generated during the installation process and stored as '/root/anaconda-ks.cfg'. Starting with the file on created for bc1-01, we can create a 'ks.cfg' file for the other nodes of the cluster. Below is an example configuration file for bc1-02.

```
install
lang en_US.UTF-8
langsupport --default en_US.UTF-8 en_US.UTF-8
keyboard us
mouse generic3ps/2 --device psaux
skipx
```

```
network --device eth0 --bootproto static --ip 192.168.13.2
        --netmask 255.255.255.0 --gateway 192.168.13.254
        --nameserver 192.168.1.1 --hostname bc1-02.phy.myu.edu
rootpw --iscrypted $1$i0.gt4GF$75mVC3kgB2keUwJVgTZo8.
firewall --medium
authconfig --enableshadow --enablemd5
timezone --utc America/Chicago
bootloader --location=mbr
clearpart --all --drives=sda
part /boot --fstype ext3 --size=100 --ondisk=sda
part / --fstype ext3 --size=1100 --grow --ondisk=sda
part swap --size=96 --grow --maxsize=192 --ondisk=sda

%packages
@ Administration Tools
@ Development Tools
@ Dialup Networking Support
@ Editors
@ Emacs
@ Engineering and Scientific
@ GNOME Desktop Environment
@ GNOME Software Development
@ Games and Entertainment
@ Graphical Internet
@ Graphics
@ Office/Productivity
@ Printing Support
@ Sound and Video
@ Text-based Internet
@ X Software Development
@ X Window System

%post
```

Note: the lines containing the `network` option were broken into three separate lines for printing purposes. The Kickstart system requires that these three lines exist as a single line in the actual '`ks.cfg`' file.

A few changes have been made to the original '`anaconda-ks.cfg`' file in creating a '`ks.cfg`' for `bc1-02`. First, the hostname and IP address, part of the `network` option, have been updated. Second, the disk partitioning options `clearpart` and `part` have been uncommented informing Kickstart to clear and rewrite the disk partition table with an appropriate set of partitions for `bc1-02`. Finally, the `ypserv` package was removed from packages list as `bc1-01` is the only node that needs to run the NIS server.

Now that we have created a '`ks.cfg`' file, we need to place that file on a floppy diskette. Insert a floppy diskette, preferably a blank one, into the floppy drive and execute the following commands.

```
mformat a:
mcopy ks.cfg a:
```

The `mformat` command will destroy any existing files on the diskette, so do not insert a diskette containing files you wish to keep.

Once the '`ks.cfg`' file is on the diskette, you should boot the new node with CD-ROM #1 from the Red Hat Linux 9 distribution. When the Linux boot prompt appears, insert the Kickstart floppy and type the following.

```
linux ks=floppy
```

If the Red Hat Linux 9 installation system has difficulty detecting the graphics chipset or monitor type for your machine, the following may have to be typed instead.

```
linux ks=floppy text
```

Since we are installing from CD-ROM, the Red Hat installer will prompt you to change CD-ROMs as necessary. When the process completes, the operating system has been installed on the new cluster node. However, the adjustments we made throughout this section must still be made. But, the process of answering several pre-installation questions, partitioning the disk, and selecting packages has now been eliminated.

Kickstart has a variety of options, many of which we did not use in our example '`ks.cfg`'. These options can be used to directly adjust some of the settings described earlier in this section. In addition, Kickstart has the ability to run a post installation script. People with knowledge of one or more UNIX scripting environments should be able to create a post install script to automatically perform the configuration adjustments we made throughout this section. The full set of Kickstart options are described in the Kickstart Installations chapter of [93].

In [85], the authors describe a set of tools for rapidly building (or rebuilding) a cluster. These tools consist of a set of Kickstart configuration files and post-processing scripts. Although their post-processing scripts are run separate from Kickstart, their toolkit is an excellent example of a simple yet effective means of automating operating system installation and network configuration in a cluster environment. More sophisticated approaches are described in Chapter 6, including NPACI Rocks, which takes advantage of Kickstart to setup a cluster.

5.5 Improving Performance

The overall performance of a cluster is very difficult to measure because so many disparate resources must be properly tuned for everything to run at peak performance. Also, different applications may require different tuning parameters to achieve optimal behavior. The cluster network is probably the subsystem that most influences the performance of parallel scientific applications.

Many network performance benefits can be gained at the individual node level, but more still can be uncovered at the network and network design level. When deciding on a specific network technology, the designer must think about performance of the system as well as cost and vendor/OS support. In this section we will discuss some high level network design concepts which increase overall performance of the cluster. In addition, we delve into some low level details involving the tuning of specific protocol and network parameters, thereby giving the reader a feeling for the parts of their network that can be modified to potentially improve application performance.

5.5.1 Offloading Services

One simple method for removing service bottlenecks in a cluster is to offload the service to a dedicated system. In our simple cluster case, we had no machines dedicated to specific tasks. For small systems primarily used for compute bound applications, this may work nicely. But as we increase the number of nodes, the number of users and the complexity of the applications, running services on the compute nodes quickly becomes problematic. Imagine a case where one user's application, running on the node providing NFS service, is fully utilizing the compute and I/O capabilities of that machine. Along comes another user, attempting to run a parallel application with moderate NFS requirements. The result is resource contention for the CPU, disk and network on the NFS server, causing both applications to slow down. If there is one node in a system that has multiple tasks to perform while others have only one task, the potential exists for wasted cycles. The obvious, and often implemented, solution is to offload services to a dedicated service machine so that all compute nodes are identical in the resources they provide to applications. This simple optimization leaves us with a pool of compute nodes distinct from the machine devoted to servicing tasks such as user login, compilation, NFS service, DNS service, etc. If bottlenecks still appear, services may be further split across multiple machines, leaving us with several service nodes, each with their own set of balanced tasks. Service offloading is a very important step towards achieving the goal of maximizing the performance of our cluster. However, the cluster can still have bottlenecks within a specific service.

While not specific to cluster environment, the idea of service load balancing remains a very important concept for cluster network designers. Although the idea of load balancing transfers nicely from more traditional UNIX networks, the specific load characteristics of the same services in a cluster environment can be drastically different. For instance, a traditional UNIX network may happily operate with a single NFS server and a large number of clients; whereas, a cluster with the same number of clients could easily overrun the single NFS server because the intensity and frequency of client accesses is radically different. With this disparity in mind, the cluster network designer should be careful to reevaluate their load balancing experiences with traditional UNIX networks before applying that knowledge to balancing their cluster services.

The specifics of service offloading vary depending on the particular service, but the idea remains the same: identify service bottlenecks (where a single service is being overwhelmed by multiple simultaneous requests) and find a way to offload that specific service to multiple servers so no one server is being overwhelmed. For example, if a NFS home file system server is being overwhelmed, a simple but effective way to lighten the burden is to bring up a second NFS server. The home file system can then be split into two volumes with half the homes served by one machine and the other half served by the second machine. While this technique can work for some services, it can not be used for services that require a synchronized, centralized repository of data. These types of services often have their own mechanisms for dealing with load balancing and should be researched thoroughly before attempting to make any adjustments.

Another case where the "splitting data in two" technique fails is when a single job places high demands on a single service, overloading the associated server. For instance, if a user's job places heavy demands on a single NFS server from many nodes, that job can overload the server. Since there is only one canonical data source, we cannot employ our "split into two" method without introducing serious synchronization problems. As it turns out, this case highlights an inherent scalability problem with the NFS service, which is not easily overcome. In such a situation, we may have to employ more powerful, better scaling solutions to the problem. To rectify this situation, we would likely move to a parallel file system,

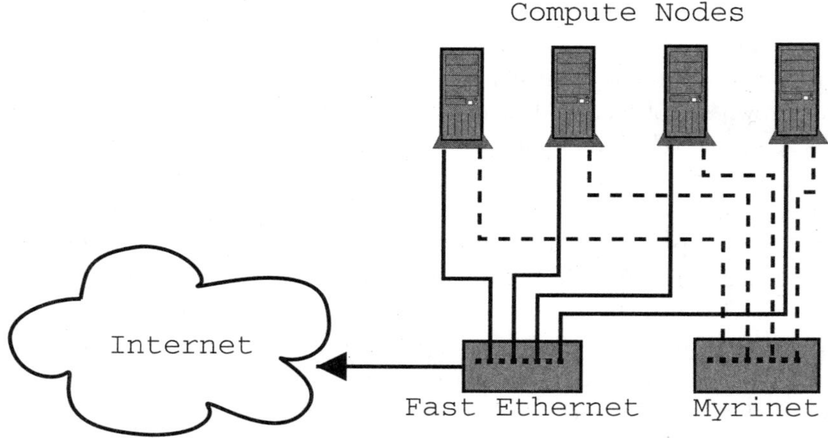

Figure 5.3: Diagram showing compute nodes with multiple interfaces on multiple networks. Notice that the Myrinet network is entirely internal to the cluster, a common design point since the dedicated network is typically much higher performing than networks outside the cluster.

such as PVFS (see Chapter 19), which scales by splitting data requests to multiple servers and therefore eliminates the single server problem with NFS.

5.5.2 Multiple Networks

For a cluster with high performance requirements, a common network design optimization employs multiple networks to separate different classes of network traffic. Examples of network traffic classes are application message passing, NFS traffic, cluster management traffic, etc. If we think about the types of high bandwidth traffic that pass over a cluster network, we can identify times when the network is saturated by one class, thus reducing the performance of the another class. In most cases, both classes would be affected, and the overall performance of the system would suffer. We can imagine the situation where a user's job is simultaneously reading a large file from NFS and attempting to do a collective communication operation, resulting in serious network resource contention.

Application message passing traffic is probably the most sensitive to network resource contention. Since the performance of the cluster is often gauged in terms of application performance, application message passing traffic is usually the class that drives the need for a separate, dedicated network. The concept is fairly straightforward; we would have one network devoted to message passing, and one devoted to all other traffic. While we can sometimes use a duplicate network technology such as fast Ethernet for our dedicated network, the performance may not be sufficient. More often, designers invest in a specialized network technology that will improve network performance for message passing by a large order of magnitude. The drawbacks of installing a specialized dedicated network include increased cost and administrative complexity. The cost of a specialized network, on a per host basis, may double the cost of a node.

5.5.3 Channel Bonding

As we stated earlier, cost plays a role in cluster network design. The highest bandwidth networks tend to be emerging technologies with premium price tags. However, sometimes applications require more capacity than a single channel (link) of a more suitably priced network can provide. One solution is to bind multiple channels together, thus creating a virtual channel of higher capacity.

As you might have guessed, channel bonding is no stranger to Beowulf clusters. In the early days of Beowulf clusters, 10Mb Ethernet was commonplace, but 100Mb Ethernet was still emerging and quite costly. Cluster designers wishing to obtain additional bandwidth, but unable to afford 100Mb Ethernet, would place multiple 10Mb Ethernet cards in each node and bond them together so they appeared as a single higher capacity link. The same thing occurred when 100Mb Ethernet became readily available and gigabit Ethernet was still being sold at a premium price. Now, as the price of gigabit Ethernet hardware drops and 10Gb Ethernet begins to emerge, we are starting to see the bonding of multiple gigabit Ethernet channels appear in Beowulf clusters.

While channel bonding can be an attractive solution to a bandwidth problem, it is not without its difficulties. For example, channel bonding may require additional switches, one for each channel, if the switch itself does not support bonding. Also, the configuration process is somewhat more complex than for a single network interface. More information on channel bonding can be found in the Linux Ethernet Bonding Driver mini-howto, '`/usr/src/linux/Documentation/networking/bonding.txt`', as well as in the mailing list archives on `Beowulf.org`.

5.5.4 Jumbo Frames

Often techniques for improving network performance spawn directly from the specific network technology deployed. The cluster designer is encouraged to research their own choice of network technology to determine how best to tune their network. While many technology specific solutions exist, we focus on one technology in particular, gigabit Ethernet using jumbo frames, as it has gained a degree of support within the network vendor and user communities.

Historically, the Ethernet standard has specified a frame size of 1518 bytes. Drivers commonly set the MTU (Maximum Transfer Unit) of the interface to 1500 bytes, leaving space for Ethernet header information in the frame. While this frame size was appropriate for 10Mb and even 100Mb Ethernet, the introduction of 1000Mb Ethernet (gigabit Ethernet) has caused a great deal of controversy surrounding the initial choice to stay with 1500/1518 byte MTU/frame sizes. Because gigabit Ethernet network adapters, running at 1000Mb/s, can transmit far more frames per time unit than before, many modern computer architectures are having difficulty keeping up with the number of frames, and hence interrupts, that must be serviced from the network. Increasing the frame size decreases the number of times the network adapter must interrupt the processor, thus freeing CPU cycles for other tasks when performing large network transfers. The commonly chosen size of this increased MTU/frame size, or **jumbo frame**, is approximately 9000 bytes. This size was chosen for its proximity to a base two value (8192) with additional room for headers, while still being small enough to not compromise Ethernet error detection schemes. The choice of an exact MTU greatly depends on the largest size supported by both the gigabit Ethernet adapter and the switch hardware. Unfortunately, increasing the size of MTU creates problems for existing hardware and clients that are configured to use the standard 1500 byte MTU. This disparity can cause hosts communication problems, switch hardware to drop what it considers to be **oversized** frames, and various other problems.

For the sake of simplicity, we will assume that the cluster network is composed entirely of all gigabit Ethernet connected hosts with no external communication requirements. In other words, the network is a dedicated communication network. With this assumption, enabling **jumbo frames** within the cluster just means that we need to set our interface's MTU to 9000 bytes using the following command. If the reader's adapter/hardware configuration supports a different maximum MTU size, they should substitute that value for the 9000 value used below.

```
ifconfig eth0 mtu 9000 up
```

This command can be placed in the startup scripts of each node to ensure that the setting will persist across reboots. On Red Hat systems, we can insert the following line into the '`/etc/sysconfig/network-scripts/ifcfg-eth0`' file to automatically set the MTU for device `eth0` on boot.

```
MTU=9000
```

When configured correctly, we should see lower CPU utilization when network transfers are active, and higher bandwidth due to the removal of potential bottlenecks.

5.5.5 Interrupt Coalescing

The primary advantage of jumbo frames is the reduction in the number of interrupts, and thus the CPU utilization, required to process incoming data. As an alternative, some network cards can be configured to delay interrupting the host until multiple packets have been sent or received. On the receive side, the interrupt is typically delayed until a specific number of packets have been received or a specified amount of time has elapsed since the first packet was received after the last interrupt. A similar thing occurs on the send side. The exact use of packet counts or delay times depends on implementation of the network card. Regardless of the mechanism causing the interrupt delay, the effect is the coalescing of interrupts.

Network cards that support interrupt coalescing generally have tunable parameters that can be modified when the driver is loaded. Care must be taken when adjusting these parameters. Increasing the maximum delay or packet count threshold too high can have negative effects. On the send side, too long of a delay can result in all of the send descriptors being depleted, thus causing a stall. A stall translates into wasted bandwidth. On the receive side, too long of a delay can result in all of the receive descriptors being depleted, thus causing incoming packets to be dropped. For TCP, dropped packets means retransmission, wasting bandwidth and delaying data reception. Frequent retransmission causes the TCP implementation to decide the link is oversubscribed and to apply its congestion control algorithms. The net effect is a further reduction in available bandwidth for the application(s) attempting to send data. (For details on TCP congestion control see [28, 110].)

Assuming the parameters are set to values preventing descriptor depletion, interrupt coalescing still impacts performance in interesting ways. The obvious positive impact is the decrease in the amount of CPU time spent entering and exiting the interrupt handling code, freeing the CPU to spend more time executing other user or kernel codes. If prior to enabling interrupt coalescing the CPU was saturated with interrupts, the application may not have been receiving enough cycles to keep the send buffer sufficiently full or the receive buffer sufficiently empty. Enabling interrupt coalescing may be just what a bandwidth starved application needs to obtain maximal performance. On the other hand, any delay in triggering the receive interrupt directly affects latency as the kernel has no knowledge of a packet's arrival until the interrupt occurs. This delay could have a negative effect on latency sensitive applications.

As you can see, interrupt coalescing has tradeoffs and requires careful tuning to obtain maximal bandwidth while also achieving a minimal impact on latency. But, when jumbo frames are not an available option, interrupt coalescing may prove important to meeting the performance needs of your applications.

5.5.6 Socket Buffers

For TCP communication, the size of the send socket buffer determines the maximum window size at the sender. As mentioned in Section 5.2, the send window controls the amount of unacknowledged data that can be outstanding, thereby affecting the actual bandwidth achieved over the connection. Your first instinct might be to make the send socket buffer as big as possible; however, this would unnecessarily consume a shared resource, thus possibly depriving other connections of suitable buffer space. Additionally, excessively large buffers can result in less than optimal performance. The trick is to determine a suitably sized buffer that maximizes bandwidth while minimizing the consumption of shared resources. The bandwidth-delay product is used to compute the minimum necessary buffer size.

For the bandwidth-delay product, bandwidth is defined to be the maximum bandwidth obtainable over the connection. In other words, it is the maximum possible bandwidth of the slowest network involved in the connection. On most clusters, intra-cluster communication travels over a system area network for which the bandwidth is generally known, so obtaining the bandwidth figure should not be difficult.

Delay is measured as the time it takes for the sender to send a packet to the receiver, the receiver to receive the packet and to send an acknowledge back to the sender (possibly piggybacked on a data packet), and the sender to receive that acknowledgment. This delay is traditionally known as the round trip time (RTT). RTT is frequently measured using the `ping` program. Although `ping` does not use the same protocol nor have the same processing overheads as TCP, the `ping` RTT is usually sufficiently close to the TCP RTT. The best results can be obtained if the size of the packet transmitted by `ping` is equal to the MTU of the underlying network. Fortunately, the version of `ping` provided with most Linux distributions allows the data size to be specified. For Ethernet, a data size of 1472 bytes plus the ICMP and IP headers will result in the desired MTU of 1500 bytes.

The size of the receive socket buffer determines the amount of data that can be buffered by the receiver while it is waiting for the application to consume the data. The receive buffer size also impacts how much data the sender may send before being notified that more buffer space is available on the receiving end. This notification is sent by the receiver along with acknowledgment and data packets and is therefore impacted by the round trip delay we have already discussed. The implication is that the receive buffer should be at least as big as the send buffer if maximum bandwidth is to be achieved.

Unfortunately, for high bandwidth, low latency links like those used for a cluster network, the bandwidth-delay product only computes the lower bound of the needed buffer space. Other factors in the network hardware and software layers, for which the delay measurements do not account, affect the amount of buffer space required to achieve the maximum obtainable bandwidth. In fact, even the communication characteristics of the application can affect the buffer sizes required to obtain optimal performance.

The application itself (or a kernel of it) is a the best tool for determining the appropriate socket buffer sizes needed to obtain high communication performance from that application. Sophisticated applications allow the send and receive buffer sizes to be specified, either as command line options or through environment variables. Unfortunately, not all applications which use sockets and TCP to communicate include this ability. And, even if they were included, many users are either unaware of the options or lack the understanding to set them. Therefore, programs like iperf [59] and NetPIPE [104] must be used by the system administrator to determine reasonable defaults.

Linux provides a mechanism for the system administrator to manipulate the default socket buffer sizes. The '`/proc`' file system entries '`/proc/sys/net/core/wmem_default`' and '`/proc/sys/net/core/rmem_default`' correspond to the default send and receive buffer sizes respectively. The current defaults can be obtained by executing the following commands.

```
cat /proc/sys/net/core/wmem_default
cat /proc/sys/net/core/rmem_default
```

New defaults can be set by writing the desired buffer sizes to those same '`/proc`' entries. For example, if send and receive buffer sizes of 256KB were determined to be appropriate, the following commands could be executed to set those buffer sizes.

```
echo 256000 >/proc/sys/net/core/wmem_default
echo 256000 >/proc/sys/net/core/rmem_default
```

To automatically apply the settings when then system reboots, the above commands can be added to '`/etc/rc.d/rc.local`'.

The system administrator also has control over the maximum buffer sizes, preventing applications from allocating excessive amounts of buffer space. The maximum send and receive buffer sizes are set by writing the desired sizes to '/proc/sys/net/core/wmem_max' and '/proc/sys/net/core/wmem_max' respectively. As before, the current settings can be obtained by reading those same entries. The maximum buffer sizes should be set so they are at least as large as the defaults. Again, commands to set these parameters when the system boots may be added to '/etc/rc.d/rc.local'.

5.6 Protecting Your Cluster

One of the most important issues that face the cluster network designer is that of cluster security. This is not only one of the most obvious concerns, but security decisions are far reaching and can potentially interfere with the usability and performance of the system.

In this section we discuss security concerns and delve into the details of techniques that cluster designers can employ to find the optimal security solution for their own unique requirements.

Briefly, we define 'Protecting Your Cluster' as a series of techniques that range from minimizing a cluster's susceptibility to outsider attacks to making a hackers life difficult even if they somehow gain login access to internal cluster machines. We will not be addressing the securing/validation of application or user data via encryption or digital signature techniques.

We approach the concept of security by breaking the realm into two distinct phases: stopping unwanted network packets before they reach a computer and stopping unwanted network packets once they reach a computer. It should be noted that some cluster network design schemes will require attention in one or the other phases, but all schemes should probably pay attention to both. Although this may seem oversimplified, we believe that by thinking of security in this way we can capture the major issues surrounding cluster network security.

5.6.1 Phase 1: Once the Packets Get There

Since the simplest cluster network design case is one where all machines are openly connected to the Internet, we will first consider security from the standpoint of how to make sure that individual systems are safeguarded against malicious network packets once they arrive at the machine. We can imagine this case analogous to a case where a castle is being attacked by an invading army. Once the invaders have breached the outer defenses, the castle is still far from lost as it could have internal safeguards to keep the attacking forces at bay. While boiling oil and sharpened sticks will not help us in securing a compute cluster (generally), we can still use common node securing techniques to keep intruders from damaging the integrity of our systems once they have breached outer security systems (if such outer security systems exist).

Locking down individual node software

One simple concept, and one that should probably be understood and implemented regardless of a chosen network design, is that of securing individual machines on a local level. History has shown us that Operating Systems are often times initially installed with insecure parameters. The reasons for this truth vary, but are most often the cause of the wide range of users that are installing from a single version of OS media. In our case, the version of Linux we will be installing on nodes was most likely not meant to be a secure, high performance, optimized for scientific computing, cluster node OS. It was probably designed to be an out of the box small business server OS or home desktop OS. The default settings, therefore, may not be properly tuned for our specific application of the OS and must therefore be reconfigured to fit our needs.

Disabling unnecessary services

As a first step towards locking down our systems, we should first take a look at what is running on our systems when nobody is logged in. Is a web server running? An NFS server? Other various network daemons that we don't necessarily need? Ideally, our clusters would be running only what is necessary for compute jobs to run. In reality, this is very little, and is mostly software that does not need to be running with an open port on the system. Historically, popular Linux distributions have been attacked by security experts because the default OS configuration had almost every conceivable UNIX service process enabled. Although these services had no known exploits at the time of distribution rollout, malicious entities across the world are continually looking for service exploits, and inevitably some of the default services were found to be insecure, allowing remote attackers to gain super-user access to machines. This situation gave rise to many Linux machines being installed that were immediately insecure. Although the situation has recently improved a great deal (Linux distributions now focus on simple service configuration tools, but have most of them disabled by default) the lesson is still an important one.

The first step to disabling unnecessary service is to first realize which services are running on the system. As discussed in Section 3.2.3, this information can be gathered using simple `ps` and `netstat` commands to examine what processes are running and what network ports they are listening on respectively. See the man pages of these tools for more information. Another common tool for examining which network ports a machine is listening on is the `nmap` tool which is used to show the network ports that are open on a remote machine.

The second step is to understand the service startup scheme of your systems. This varies from distribution to distribution, but is usually fairly straightforward using bundled GUI tools or command line interaction.

The last step in shutting off unwanted services, once they have been identified and the process for disabling them is understood, is insuring that all systems in the cluster have identical configurations. The specifics of synchronizing configuration across machines in your cluster is beyond the scope of this chapter, but can usually be accomplished via bundled cluster software or simple shell scripts.

Although it would be generally grand to disable *all* services that can be remotely exploited, there will inevitably be some services that must be enabled for proper cluster operation. This being said, since we can't disable the service, we must do our best to make sure that each enabled service is secure as possible. First, since these network services typically accept remote queries, we should enumerate the remote entities that need to be able to make connections to our local hosts. By default, most services will allow connections from any machine on the Internet, a behavior which is most likely more flexible than it needs to be for Linux cluster services (does a machine in Egypt really need to be able to connect to our local print spool?). For each service, the cluster designer should be able to enumerate domains that should be able to connect to that service, often times to the IP level. The cluster operator should make a table of necessary services, and which groups of external machines need to have access to the service. Table 5.1 summarizes some of the important services.

Once we have a clear notion of which remote entities should be able to connect to each of our services, we must identify the mechanism by which these services restrict access. Most services have their own mechanism for access control, while others may rely on a uniform access control system. Following is an example of how we use the '`/etc/exports`' file to control access to an NFS server process.

```
[root@host.myu.edu /root]# cat /etc/exports
/exports/rootnfs        *.myu.edu(rw,no_root_squash)
/exports/stage          *.myu.edu(rw)
```

Service	Description	Allowed
ssh	Allows remote users to log into machine securely	Entire Internet
nfsd	Allows remote machines to share file system volumes over the network	Internal cluster nodes
named	DNS server, serves name/IP mapping information	Internal site machines
httpd	Web server, serves cluster information documents, files	Internal site machines
scheduler	Batch job scheduler	Login nodes only

Table 5.1: Some example services with descriptions and category of external systems that should have access to them.

```
/exports/my              *.myu.edu(rw)
/exports/scratch100      192.168.1.100(rw)
[root@host.myu.edu /root]#
```

In this example, we are granting access to all machines in the domain `myu.edu` to the first three file systems, and only to the machine which is bound to the IP address `192.168.1.100` for the last file system.

Now that we've disabled unneeded processes and secured everything else as much as possible, it may seem that on a local level, we have gone as far as possible. However, the one dimension that most frequently creates security problems for UNIX machine administrators is that of time. Generally, services are not written to be insecure (hopefully) and are not installed on systems with known security holes. The problem is that over time, flaws are first found, shortly afterwards they are exploited. An attentive cluster administrator needs to notice when flaws are found by the Internet security community and act to update installed software in the short time interval between when the flaw is found and when the flaw is exploited. To do this, an administrator must regularly watch the security websites and mailing lists for the uncovering of exploits, as well as watching the distribution vendors security pages for notification of updates. Some examples of established and useful security websites are [101] and [23]. The former has shown to be very fast to respond to new vulnerabilities and often includes proof of concept exploit code in addition to descriptions fixes to security problems. CERT is a very complete index of vendor supplied problems/patches to security problems but is sometimes slower to respond to new vulnerabilities.

5.6.2 Phase 2: Before the Packets Get There

In the previous section, we assumed that an attacker has breached a first line of defense and had the ability to make attacks on individual machine entities in the cluster. To return to our analogy of a castle being attacked, the previous situation implied that our outer walls had fallen or that we didn't have an outer wall at all. While this is sometimes considered sufficient security, we can use outer walls in conjunction with local security measures to provide an even safer system.

Previously, we made sure that our local services were configured to reject connections from sources that we knew were not supposed to be able to access that service but this rejection implicitly assumes that our service is operating properly with regards to its decisions about incoming traffic. There are cases, however, where a service may have such a serious flaw that a remote attacker can introduce a service failure to the point where the service is unable to operate properly anymore, making our hard work of configuring access rules at the service level obsolete. The only way of preventing this from happening is by making sure malicious network traffic never reaches our systems, a task that firewalls can help us with.

In this section we describe some very simple techniques that can be applied to prohibit unwanted network traffic from ever reaching individual cluster machines in the form of software and hardware firewalls.

Firewalls Clarified

A firewall, simply put, is some mechanism that allows for the inspection of individual network packets combined with some set of decisions to make based on where packets originated and where they are destined. Firewalls take many forms, ranging from hardware devices that sit between a site's uplink to the Internet and all internal machines to kernel level software layers that are active on each individual machines. Regardless of how a specific firewall is implemented, its job is essentially the same as any other firewall; inspect a network packet for source and destination information, and decide what to do about it—let it through, divert it to somewhere else, or throw it away.

By using firewalls, we can very efficiently block network packets from ever reaching nodes that we are certain never will need to accept said packets. The first decision we must make, however, is that of where to put our firewall in the network chain of events. The two extremes, as mentioned above, are between a site's uplink

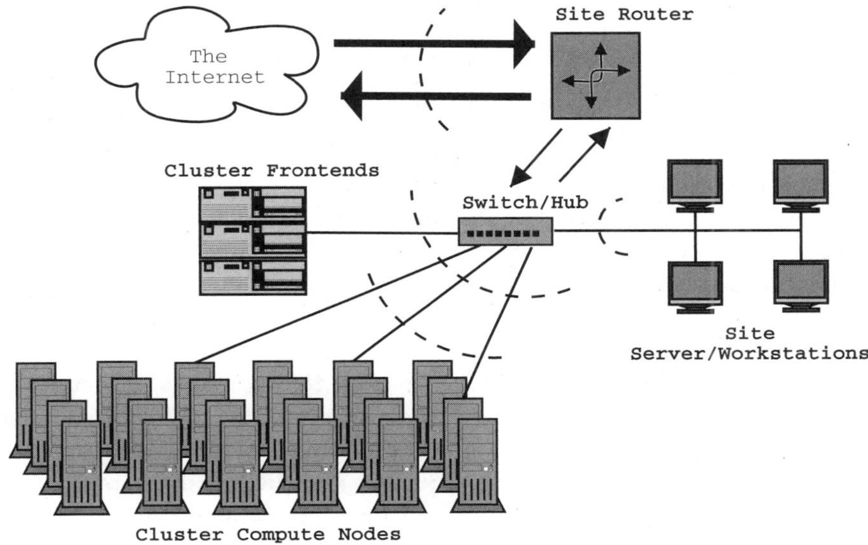

Figure 5.4: Above are shown some possible locations one may wish to place a firewall, denoted by the curved dotted lines.

and all internal machines, and one firewall per machine. Both extremes are most likely not ideal for a Linux cluster scenario. Since a cluster will comprise some subset of all machines at a site, policies for the cluster nodes will not mirror policies for general site machines. This prohibits the use of one site firewall that can handle all cases. On the other extreme, we would have to maintain one firewall per machine, which can be a potential source of unneeded complexity. Most likely, the cluster designer would want to place a firewall in front of logical partitions of their cluster, whether it be the entire cluster, compute nodes only, management nodes only, server nodes only, or some combination of the above.

Where a firewall is placed is entirely dependent on the policies set up by the cluster designer, but for simplicity we will assume one firewall between the cluster uplink and the rest of the Internet (including other site machines). This is to say, all packets that are destined for any machine inside the cluster must past through our firewall, and any packet originating from the Linux cluster must also pass through the firewall.

Linux provides a very powerful suite of firewalling software, which we will cover in detail. Later we will briefly explore various hardware solutions to the same problem.

Linux software firewalling using iptables

The Linux operating system, as of the time of this writing (Linux version 2.4.X), provides a very complete packet filtering and mangling system that can be used as, among other things, a software firewall. All packet inspection/alteration activity is done via a kernel subsystem known as **netfilter** and is controlled by a userspace utility known as `iptables`. The scenario in which these subsystems are applicable in our case is when we're using a Linux machine as a network router. Say our cluster machines exist in the `192.168.13.0/24` address range. We have one Linux machine with two network interfaces (one interface on the `192.168.13.0/24` network and the other on a network that is routed to the rest of the site). We can run routing software (refer to `routed` or `gated` documentation) to cause our machine to forward packets from one interface to the other, thereby creating an site gateway for our cluster nodes. If one's cluster was using an Internet routable network, the same router setups applies except the router would now be acting as an Internet gateway instead of a simple gateway between one unroutable site network and the unroutable cluster network. Once we have set up this routing Linux machine, we can configure it as a very powerful firewall.

The iptables/netfilter subsystem is best understood when considering the path a network packet takes when traveling through a Linux machine that is acting as a router. Along this path, there are certain predefined inspection points where we can define sets of tests that the packet must endure. Based on the outcome of the tests, we may allow the packet to continue, we may jump to a different set of tests, we may alter the packet, or we may throw the packet away forever.

To understand how we might use such a system, we can start by considering two of the predefined checkpoints, or chains in `iptables` terminology. One chain is encountered after a packet arrives at the Linux router and the router decides to forward the packet on to its destination (box 1 in Figure 5.5). The other chain is reached by a packet when a Linux machine (router or otherwise) decides that the packet is destined for itself (box 2 in Figure 5.5), and moves the packet up into userspace where a waiting process can handle it. The former, in netfilter terminology is referred to as the FORWARD chain and the latter is the INPUT chain. Each of these chains contain rules that are of the logical form "if the packet matches `<X>` then perform action `<Y>`". For a given chain, a packet starts at the first rule and continues through the conditionals (assuming it does not match the

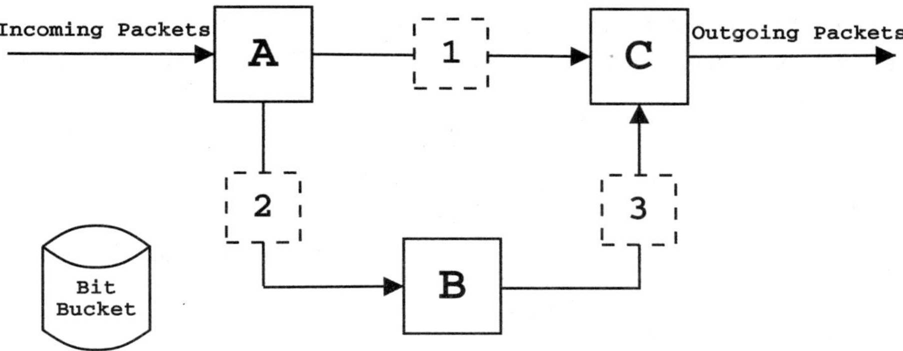

Figure 5.5: Above are shown some of the interesting points through the Linux kernel where network packets are affected. The letters are points in kernel space where routing decisions are made. Numbered locations are some of the places where netfilters exist that will determine the fate of packets passing through. A.) incoming packet routing decision. B.) local machine process space. C.) postrouting decision. 1.) FORWARD netfilter table. 2.) INPUT netfilter table. 3.) OUTPUT netfilter table.

`<X>` criteria) until it reaches the very end. If a packet does match the `<X>` criteria, a common `<Y>` action to take would be to accept the packet (let it continue on past the chain). Each chain has a policy set on what to do once a packet makes it through all the rules in the chain.

With this basic knowledge of what is happening to a inspected packet, we can start to think about how to use this system to provide reasonable security for our cluster. An old but useful paradigm in firewall policies is to start by blocking all network traffic, then start allowing only what needs to make it through. For us, this would mean that by default, we would want to set the chain policy (remember this is the decision that is made when a packet passes through all the rules without matching any of them) to drop the packet, and then insert rules that look for only the packets we would like to let through and allow them to pass. Generally, we can expect to be able to set up rules that look at a packets source, its destination, protocol (TCP/UDP), and its service type based on the port of its destination process. In this way, we can makes rules based on who is sending the packet, who the packet is supposed to go to, and what service (`sshd`, `httpd`, etc) the packet is supposed to be a part of. Following is an example of how we would set up a simple firewall that all incoming traffic except for that destined for the **sshd** and **httpd** processes on cluster nodes. We do this by using a Linux router that is sitting between our cluster and the Internet.

First we show how to inspect the current state of the default chains (checkpoints).

```
[root@host.myu.edu tmp]# iptables -L
Chain INPUT (policy ACCEPT)
target     prot opt source               destination

Chain FORWARD (policy ACCEPT)
target     prot opt source               destination

Chain OUTPUT (policy ACCEPT)
target     prot opt source               destination
[root@host.myu.edu tmp]#
```

We can see that there are no rules defined.

Next we set the policy on the FORWARD chain to DROP, thus insuring that any packet that does not match one of our to be determined rules will be immediately dropped instead of forwarded on.

```
[root@host.myu.edu root]# iptables -P FORWARD DROP
```

Since our DROP policy will drop packets coming from and heading to the internal cluster machines, we set up a simple rule to let all traffic originating from the cluster through. In the following, where we needed to continue an input line, we used a backslash at the end of the line.

```
[root@host.myu.edu root]# iptables -A FORWARD \
     -s 192.168.13.0/24 -d 0.0.0.0 -j ACCEPT
```

Finally we can set up some rules for allowing packets destined for **sshd** (port 22) or **httpd** (port 80) to pass from the outside network to our internal network.

```
[root@host.myu.edu root]# iptables -A FORWARD -s 0.0.0.0 \
    --protocol tcp --dport 22 -d 192.168.13.0/24 -j ACCEPT

[root@host.myu.edu root]# iptables -A FORWARD -s 0.0.0.0 \
    --protocol tcp --dport 80 -d 192.168.13.0/24 -j ACCEPT
```

Once again, we use the -L flag to view our new firewall setup.

```
[root@host.myu.edu root]# iptables -L
Chain INPUT (policy ACCEPT)
target  prot opt source            destination

Chain FORWARD (policy DROP)
target  prot opt source            destination
ACCEPT  all  --  192.168.13.0/24    0.0.0.0
ACCEPT  tcp  --  0.0.0.0           192.168.13.0/24 tcp dpt:22
ACCEPT  tcp  --  0.0.0.0           192.168.13.0/24 tcp dpt:www

Chain OUTPUT (policy ACCEPT)
target  prot opt source            destination
[root@host.myu.edu root]#
```

If we wanted to set up rules to block packets arriving at the local machine, we would perform the same style of operations but instead add rules to the INPUT chain instead of the FORWARD chain.

Setting up a complete firewall will take many rules, and will be different for every site. For more information regarding Linux firewalls, the reader may wish to consult one of the many books written on the topic, for instance [127].

Hardware firewalls

An alternative to using a Linux machine as a router/firewall between protected machines and the Internet is to use any number of specialized hardware devices which essentially do the same thing. Many companies have provided embedded systems that are easy to configure/manage and quite robust. The benefit of these systems are they're relative ease of use (no `iptables` commands to learn) and the fact that they have vendor support. The drawbacks are the slower response times to security hole fixes and of course cost.

5.7 Troubleshooting

Although cluster networks are typically rather robust, they are still sometimes responsible for unexpected behavior in one's cluster. Some of these problems can be caused by hardware failures, but are more often the result of improper software configuration or corrupted data in the system. Since the cluster network is not always easily identifiable as the cause of problems, we have chosen to present some simple techniques which cluster administrators can employ while tracking down various cluster network related problems. We also wish to illustrate the use of popular network troubleshooting tools by walking the reader through some common failure/recovery scenarios. For a more complete network troubleshooting handbook, the reader may refer to one of many such books devoted to the topic [103]. This section is designed to bring some potential pitfalls to the attention of the reader but is more intended as a starting point for administrators attempting to track down various bugs in the system.

In order to diagnose a cluster network problem, we first must understand the various levels of the cluster and how they might cause a problem. It is usually good practice to start at the application level, and work our way down through the kernel and logical network, and finish by checking hardware. An example of an application problem may be a user using an incorrect hostname or port in their application. OS level problems, which range from service configuration to driver problems, offer a wide variety of debugging challenges. Logical network problems can be improper firewall rules or routing configurations, and hardware issues range from bad switch ports to damaged cables. Attacking problems from the top of this chain, we can eliminate higher level problems before getting lost in lower level details that may not have anything to do with the original problem.

Before we begin the failure scenarios along with solutions, we first need to have a toolkit of utilities that we can use to help us determine the source of the problem.

- `ping`. The faithful UNIX command `ping` has proven to be one of the most useful utilities in UNIX history. It uses a property of the ICMP protocol that specifies that when an echo request packet is sent to a remote machine or gateway, the remote machine sends back an echo response packet along with some timing metadata. Essentially we will use `ping` to give us a first impression of whether a host is alive on the network.

- `netstat`. Linux provides a utility `netstat` which allows us to inspect the current network connection status of our machine. We use it to see which ports our machine has open, which remote machines are currently connected to us, what state our TCP connections are in, etc.

- `Iperf`. The `iperf` utility is a very complete network performance testing software suite. Being a modern utility for testing network bandwidth, it supports all standard protocols, includes support for multicast performance testing, and has IPv6 support.

- `nmap`. The `nmap` utility is used to probe the network accessibility of a remote machine. It can be used to essentially "map" a network by finding which machines are alive on the network and what ports they currently have open.
- telnet. Although the use of the `telnet` remote login service is most likely disabled on any reasonable modern OS (or should be), the client program, `telnet`, has other useful applications. To `telnet` we can specify a hostname and a port to connect to, at which point the client makes a straightforward TCP connection to the remote host/port and allows us to send and receive character streams to/from the remote host. This usage model can be quite helpful when testing basic machine connectivity.
- User applications. Often times, one of the best tools for finding problems, and sometimes solving them, is the actual application codes being run on the system. After all, if our users are having no problems, are there actually any problems?

Now that we have some useful tools in our toolbox, we can examine some problem scenarios and see how we can diagnose, then attempt to solve them. The reader should bare in mind that real life problems will not mirror our examples exactly, and our procedures are only meant to illustrate a general process, not a specific solution.

When I try to rsh/ssh to a remote machines, it fails.

Most often this problem is caused by improper software configuration. First, following our own advice, we should quickly check the `sshd/rsh` configuration files to see if anything is obviously misconfigured. If the services appear to be configured correctly, we step down to the OS/network level. For the `ssh/rsh` tools to function properly, the two machines in question must be visible to each other on the network (connected), and they must be able to correctly identify each other when a connection is attempted. We use `ping` and `telnet` to determine if both above conditions are satisfied.

- log into source machine
- ping destination machine
- log into destination machine
- ping source machine

This process will give us a very crude notion of whether the machines can contact each other over the network. If the above process fails, skip down to the next scenario **ping doesn't seem to be working** to try resolving the problem, then return to this scenario if there is still a problem with `rsh/ssh`.

Both `ssh` and `rsh` use TCP to start up an initial connection. We can test simple TCP connectivity using the `telnet` command. Start by logging into the source machine. If a connection is established, one should see the following form of output.

```
source.myu.edu % telnet remote.myu.edu 514
Trying 192.168.13.7...
Connected to remote.myu.edu.
Escape character is '^]'.
Connection closed by foreign host.
source.myu.edu %
```

For `ssh`, replace the port number of `rshd` (514 in the above example) with `sshd`'s port, 22. Current port assignments should be verified by looking in the machine's '`/etc/services`' file. If for some reason the two machines we able to ping one another but not send TCP traffic to specified ports, we would expect the session to look similar to the following.

```
source.myu.edu % telnet remote.myu.edu 514
Trying 192.168.13.7...
telnet: connect to address 192.168.13.7: Connection refused
source.myu.edu %
```

If this occurs, our problem may be related to a routing or firewall problem, refer to the problem situation below entitled "ssh works, but ... does not" for more details on how to track this down.

If we can ping our remote machine and `telnet` to the port in question, our problem is most likely a simple configuration file problem (we're most likely to see an error message reporting a permission problem or similar). Check the utility's documentation to learn more on how to set up the servers (`sshd` for `ssh` problems, `inetd/xinetd` for rsh problems) to accept remote logins/commands.

ping doesn't seem to be working.

If our simple ping procedure is failing, either the machines are not properly configured for the network they're connected to, our name resolution configuration is incorrect, our firewall is improperly configured, or we are having hardware problems.

To confirm that our machines are properly configured to have a presence on their networks, we can attempt to ping *some* external machine (the gateway perhaps, some internal web site, etc). If one or the other cannot ping any external machine, there is most likely a problem with the way the network interface is configured on the machine (see Section 5.4.2) or with bad hardware/cables. If they are both alive and able to ping a common third machine, then we should try to ping with an IP address as opposed to using hostnames. Using the `ifconfig` utility, we can acquire both machine's IP addresses which can then be used instead of hostnames by a repeat of our ping procedure. If this fails, please refer to the problem scenario below entitled **ssh works, but . . . does not.**. Now if pinging with IP addresses works, but pinging with hostnames does not, then we know we have a problem with the way our machines are resolving hostname mappings (or vice versa). We should consider how our systems are supposed to resolve these mappings ('`/etc/hosts`', NIS, DNS, all three) and check the appropriate configuration files to make sure both sides are properly set up to resolve hostnames (refer to Section 5.4.3 for details).

ssh works, but ping/rsh/application/etc does not.

If one finds that some specific application is functioning properly, while others are failing, the problem usually lies in the misconfiguration of the failing application(s). Great care should be first put into determining if the cause of the failure is specific to an application. If the failure continues when all configurations appear correct, we should turn our attention to router/firewall based causes. Remember that just as we can configure a firewall to only allow certain traffic, we can also configure it to deny certain traffic. We should check to make sure our firewall isn't explicitly denying our service traffic. Another possibility would be that we have forgotten to include a rule in our firewall that fully allows a service's network requirements to be fulfilled. Often times services require only one port for an initial connection to be made by a client, but use other ports upon successful connections, and we must allow connections on all needed ports in order for such services to operate. Note that commonly we only need to allow a single open port in one direction, but many ports must be unblocked in the other direction. The firewall must be configured to manage this types of service behaviors.

The user's application is running, but seems like the network is slowing it down.

If everything appears functionally to be operating, but is simply performing poorly or is performance is wildly varying, we can usually use `iperf` to quantify the problem. Below is an example of running the simplest test (TCP bandwidth, default window size) on a set of machines.

```
# This is the server command
remote.myu.edu % iperf -s

# This is the client command
source.myu.edu % iperf -c remote.myu.edu
```

Both processes will show that a test has started and after a few seconds each will report the number of seconds taken, size of total transfer, and calculated bandwidth of the connection. Try running this benchmark a few times, checking to see that whether your network is supplying the expected performance. On an unloaded system, one should expect to see approximately 95 percent of total link bandwidth to be reported by `iperf`, the remaining bandwidth being used by headers and other control traffic. If `iperf` is giving you expected measurements, there may be something wrong with the application that is showing poor network performance. Otherwise, the problem could be a bad port, cable, or even network card driver.

Nothing works!

A good rule of thumb to follow when nothing seems to be working is to follow the chain of commands that should be apparent from this section. We have application errors, local host service configuration, local name resolution configuration, logical network failures (firewalls), and hardware failures. Most problems that appear in a cluster network lie in one or many of these steps, and careful consideration at each step before moving to the next should flush out the problem.

6 Setting Up Clusters

Philip Papadopoulos

Your day is starting off well—many boxes of the fastest-ever cluster nodes have arrived on your shipping dock and you are ready to tear them open, set them up, and start running your favorite code just as soon as you can. The space is planned out, you know what kinds of nodes you need in terms of login, storage, compute and other types of devices, the electricians finished putting in the plugs yesterday, and the cooling has been upgraded to keep your cluster nicely chilled. It then dawns up you, you are looking at literally hundreds of components—computers, power distribution units, networking switches, racks (or tables, or shelves), disks, and a monitor or two. You need to have a plan for how to layout and organize your cluster for the physical buildout. The harder part is really deciding on how you are going to get the operating system onto each one of the nodes so that you can get started computing in the shortest time possible. There isn't a "right way" or a "wrong way" to do this. And, in reality, how you provision your nodes has quite a bit to do with personal taste and administrative style. There are, however, are two broad issues to keep in mind—scalability and reproducibility.

Initial setup is closely aligned with management of the cluster (see Chapter 13). Setup is not a one-time task for a few reasons. First, nodes do break and replacement nodes need to be turned on and provisioned with the latest software. Second, clusters often incrementally expand requiring you to provision new (and sometimes physically different) nodes over the lifetime of a the machine. Third, Linux moves quite rapidly—with 3 package updates every two days on the current release of Redhat—at some point, patching simply won't work and a wholesale re-installation is needed to make the cluster stable and consistent. A real plan is needed for both management and setup. These two aspects support each other.

This chapter is organized as follows: the challenges of cluster setup are introduced first, some simple but effective tips for physically organizing your system, an overview of general approaches to cluster setup is given, and finally some detail is given about two popular approaches to cluster setup: NPACI Rocks's description-based installation, and OSCAR's image-based setup. This chapter is not meant to be a step-by-step instruction manual for any particular method, but has the primary purpose of giving the reader some comparisons and motivation for why different teams choose very different approaches.

Before launching into the deep details it is worth noting that this chapter covers traditional Beowulfs where each node has a disk and contains a local copy of the operating system. Single system image toolkits like Scyld and SCore have their own custom installers. In particular, Scyld's setup and management are given in Chapter 18. Diskless systems are not covered in this section.

After reading this chapter, the reader should have a good overview of how different provisioning methodologies work. Setup and ongoing management are intimately connected, and an administrator's style often dictates how a system is provisioned. In the end, instantiated clusters, whether built with Rocks, OSCAR, SCE, or even other lesser-known systems toolkits, have very similar functionality. Afterall, each has a basic Linux OS, a queueing system, monitoring, message passing, and I/O subsystems. The key to evaluating each of these systems for your own use is how does a particular approach reduce *your* time for administrative issues and increase your time for actually using the cluster.

6.1 Challenges

Initial setup of a cluster is not trivial, but neither is it untenable. Suppose that 68 brand new computers have just arrived. 64 are slated as compute nodes, two function as login and job launching nodes, and two are dedicated to providing I/O services, often using plain old NFS. The hardware related challenges revolve around selecting your network setup (see Chapter 5), laying out the systems in an organized fashion, physically wiring, and getting your electricians to believe just how much power the cluster will actually consume. For the moment, let's assume that the cluster has been physically constructed and sitting with power turned off and no software on any system (frontend, storage, compute, etc). It's raw hardware just waiting to be unleashed.

6.1.1 Software Provisioning Challenges—There are No Homogeneous Clusters

This subsection starts with a bold proposition—"There are no homogeneous clusters". Standard Beowulfs have at least two types of nodes: login and compute, so homogeneity of function is already split. As clusters get larger, some nodes take on specialized service roles to handle the aggregate load—system logging nodes, dedicated I/O nodes, additional public login nodes, and dedicated installation nodes are just a few personalities that might need to be supported. In a tale of two clusters (Chapter 20), one can see the various node types that make up a real cluster. It's more than just head node and compute. Role specialization isn't the only way that a model of homogeneity can break—differences in hardware is also quite common at design time and throughout the life of the cluster. Even though many clusters may start out with compute nodes being of a homogeneous hardware type, they often don't stay that way. Hardware is simply moving too quickly to expect that future expansions of a cluster could be identical to current nodes. Equipment breaks and the replacement parts might have different memory types, updated processors or a different network adapter. Even when all nodes are purchased at the same time in an attempt to insure hardware homogeneity, small differencess still can get in the way.

Some years ago, the author worked with NT-based clusters. Our team had purchased 64 9.1 GB SCSI drives, all with the same part number, all with the same specifications. They differed slightly—some had 980 cylinders and some had 981. From the manufacturers perspective, both provided the advertised space. The problem occurred in the imaging program (ImageCast, in this case). An image was taken from the 981 cylinder drive. Attempts to re-image the 980 cylinder drives failed beeause of the single cylinder difference. Image-based programs have certainly improved since then, but these types of small differences can cause many lost hours. We solved the problem by building the model node on the 980 cylinder disk that just happened to work on the larger drive. We were lucky, we might have been forced to have two images just because of a one cylinder difference in the local hard drive. The reality is that in commodity components, small low-level differences exist. Your setup and management methodology must be able to handle these subtle differences without administrative intervention.

The previous example makes clusters sound ominous, impossible to provision, disorganized and the reader may feel that it is a hopeless cause to build a real, functioning and stable cluster. That somehow small differences can wreak havoc on the provisioning stage. Fear not. Clusters are everywhere. They include some of the fastest machines in the world, are stable and can be provisioned easily to meet the configuration challenges to manage the inhomegeneity at the functional and hardware levels.

Differentiation along Functional Lines

Commonly, several types of functionality are needed to build a working cluster. As clusters grow in the number of nodes, specialization of particular nodes to perform specific tasks becomes much more prevalent. In the largest clusters, functional specialization of nodes is a necessity. The specialization is a direct outcome of needing to scale certain services. On a small cluster, the head node can "do it all"—system logging, ganglia monitoring, function as an installation server, compilation, login, and serve out home areas. As the cluster grows, these services need to be spread across physical machines so that each can handle the load.

Any node in the cluster is differentiated by the types of services and software that are configured on it. Nodes can change their logical functionality just by deploying and configuring a different software stack. A common differentiation in mid-sized clusters has nodes of the following types (we will henceforth call these *appliances*):

- *Head Node/Frontend Node*—This node is the public persona of the cluster. This is where users log in, compile, and submit jobs.
- *Compute Node*— Where most of the work happens
- *I/O server*—Often an NFS server, but aggressive systems like PVFS can be used
- *Web server*
- *System logging server*
- *Installation server*
- *Grid gateway node*
- *Batch Scheduler and cluster-wide monitoring*

When setting up a cluster, decisions are made as to how many I/O servers, how many system logging servers, and how many installation servers are needed to support a given number of compute nodes. For small- to mid-sized clusters (perhaps up to 128 nodes), the services are all hosted by a single (or small number) of front-end or head nodes, so no real decision has to be made. However, even in mid-sized clusters, special attention is often paid to improving file handling capability by provisioning a sub-cluster of nodes dedicated to I/O. Chiba City at Argonne, for example, has different "towns"—visualization, storage, and compute—that clearly define functional differences.

In common cluster construction, one builds a head node, a set of I/O nodes (collectively, an I/O cluster), and a set of compute nodes. This chapter assumes that these types of "appliance" classifications have already been made by the cluster designer, but that at this point, nothing is installed or set up.

6.1.2 System Software Consistency Across the Cluster

The issue that overshadows all others in cluster setup and management is creating and maintaining a software environment that is consistent across all nodes and node types. Small anomolies such as different versions of the standard C library can cause performance and correctness of operations problems. Progamming clusters is challenging enough without users needing to figure out that nodes are behaving differently because of software version "skew" across the cluster. It is for this reason that cluster installation and setup is so intimately tied to ongoing management. It simply does no good to install a new node (either expansion or replacement of a failed node) that differs in software versions or configuration from the running cluster. The new node must be brought into parity with the rest of cluster. Two popular open-source clustering toolkits, NPACI Rocks and OSCAR, take radically different approaches to provisioning and management. Both toolkits' perspective on installation will described in some detail in this chapter.

It is worth noting that diskless clusters often have fewer issues with software skew because all nodes mount a common root file system over NFS. Even so, diskless clusters are significantly less popular because of the scaling problems of serving all system software from a central NFS server. Chapters 3 and 20 cover some of the advantages and disadvantages of diskless nodes.

6.2 Hardware Provisioning Challenges and Best Practices

Chapters 2 and 4 describe the critical hardware choices that one has to make when constructing a cluster. In this section, we describe a few "tricks of the trade" that, down the road, can make a huge difference in terms of neatness, maintainability, and, ultimately, reliability. The watchword is *organization.* Neat cables aren't just to look pretty, they can significantly improve your ability to debug some types of problems on the cluster. Labeling cables and nodes is always helpful, but having a regular layout is essential. For obvious reasons, powers of two (and/or multiples of 8) are natural quantities to deal with in the computing world, and clusters are no different. There are four key areas to focus on in hardware provisioning

- Layout of nodes—Rackmount vs. Workstation Towers vs. Blades
- Cable management
- Airflow management
- Power Management

Paying attention to these issues for that pile of boxes in the corner will make your cluster last longer and be more stable. Building a cluster is fun and rewarding, take the small amount of time to plan out your physical layout.

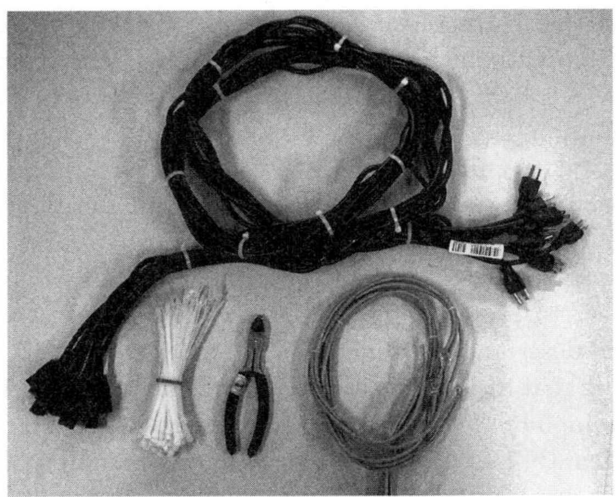

Figure 6.1: Cable bundles. Wire ties make 8 power cables into a neat and managable group

Node Layout and Cable Management

Rackmount systems are perhaps the most convenient way to stack nodes into a small space. in Figure 6.2, one can see the front side and back side of a typical racking system. Cluster nodes themselves are defined in terms of a standard rack unit or "U". One Rack Unit is 1.75" (4.45cm) and standard height (2 Meter tall) racks have 42U of available space. Rackmount nodes are typically called servers, but there are plenty of hardware chassis that are rack mountable and take standard motherboards. As one gets more densely packed such as in a tower full of 1U servers, CAP (Cable, Airflow, and Power) becomes of paramount importance. We will take some time to detail out these issues for rack-based systems and then make comments on how these can be carried over to shelves of desktops and newer blade servers.

In cable management, groups of four (4) and eight (8) are the tickets to success. In Figure 6.1, one can see 8 power cables in one bundle and 4 ethernet cables in another bundle using wire ties available from the local home improvement store. To prebundle the cables, just lay them out on the floor, and wrap a wire tie every 6–12 inches (15–30 cm). Clip off the excess from each wire tie and you have taken just a few minutes to create nice, tidy packages. Do this with all of your cables. You will soon discover that a 128 node cluster can be wired with 16 power bundles and 16 ethernet bundles. A bit of pre-planning cable lengths is needed, especially in the case of workstation towers. In this case you might prebundle a set of cables that contains two each of 5,6,7 and 8 foot long ethernet cables. At one end the cables are even so that they plug easily into the ethernet switch, the others are of the correct length to plug into a specific server that are sitting in a line next to each other in a shelf configuration. If towers are 6 inches wide, then the 8th tower is about four feet (about 1 meter) further away than the first one. If on the other hand, you have rackmounted 2U servers then the top server in a "bank" of 8 is only about 15 inches (40cm) away from the first one. In this case, cabling 8 ethernet cables of the same length often works well.

The power cables are also grouped and bundled. It turns out that power cables are actually quite a headache. They are big, bulky, heavy and rarely are close to the correct length. What you decide to do with the power cables can have a significant impact on cooling. Figure 6.2 illustrates how cables are pulled to the sides of the rack allowing for unrestricted airflow. This is really one of the compelling reasons to bundle cables—neatness improves the ability of the chassis to cool themselves by getting the cables out of the airflow. Heat kills clusters and blocking the airflow is a common mistake. High-end nodes often dissipate 150–200 Watts, so a rack of 32 such servers is equivalent to 4 hair dryers running at high. As processor speeds improve, power consumption always goes up before it comes back down as the semiconductor process is improved.

Power consumption of needs means power planning in the number circuits, and the number of power distribution units. In reality, power is just another network. Take the power consumption seriously—there are many cases of overloaded power strips melting, or worse, catching fire. There are many rules of thumb for how many machines can go on single circuit. The critical observation is to not get too close to the max current of your circuit and to use thick enough power cabling. Standard power distribution units (PDUs) are significantly better than the $2.00 power strip from the clearance table at the local hardware store. PDUs run about $10.00/outlet and have quality cabling that won't overheat even as the current load increases. Remember, a Beowulf cluster is a personal supercomputer, it has the electricty appetite to match. Network controlled PDUs generally run at about $50/outlet, and these enable you to cycle power remotely. This is a very nice convenience for large installations.

Figure 6.2: The back of a rack, showing the clean organization of the cables. Note that the fans are unobstructed.

6.3 Different Types of Installation Management

As discussed in the introduction, setup and management of clusters can come down to a personal style choice. However, there are technical and practical reasons to choose one type of installation method over another. We will describe the trade-offs of each type of installation. Popular open-source management systems include: NPACI Rocks, OSCAR, SCore, Scyld, and XCAT. The Linux space is enormous and cluster toolkit designers have to make some decisions on what types of generalizations are the most important. In particular, authors have to determine if and how they will scale across distributions and how they will support different kinds of hardware. None of these toolkits covers the complete space of $distributions \times hardware$.

The Linux distribution space is a moving target and includes (as of this writing) a number of players: RedHat, SuSE, Mandrake, Debian, United Linux, and more. Each distribution has it's own style, file layout, package format, package definitions, and support for a variety of hardware. Small differences such as using shadow passwords (or not), using `xinetd` or `inetd`, and SysV-compatible startup differentiate distributions. For cluster software service designers (e.g., PBS, MPICH, Sun Grid Engine, Ganglia), differences in packaging definitions can cause more headaches, especially in resolving dependencies. Redhat packages, for example, are put together differently than similarly named SuSE packages. Debian uses `dpkg` and `apt-get`. For the cluster toolkit designer, supporting all these variations is an impossibly large task. As a would-be cluster builder, you have to choose the distribution and the toolkit. Do pick a toolkit as a starting point for your cluster and become involved in its improvement. Don't roll your own installation and management from the ground up, as this just becomes a waste of your time in retreading old ground. You have more important things to do with your time—*using* your new cluster.

Each of the commercial Linux distributions must do hardware detection to automatically install the right device drivers on the widest variety of hardware possible. Distributions that don't detect the most common hardware (and support the quickly changing network device world), simply are discarded by the user community in a classic case of "survival of the fittest." This last point is of significant importance to cluster builders because of the desire to use the best, fastest, newest, and cheapest. No judgment is made here as to which distribution is superior—rather it is the fact that these differences exist that is important.

The hardware space gets more complicated each day. Beowulf clusters used to be only IDE disks. Today, IDE (EIDE, UltraATA, Serial ATA), SCSI, Integrated Drive Arrays, and Storage Area Network (SAN) adapters are *de rigeur* for cluster builders. High-speed interconnects including Scali, Myrinet, Quadrics, and Infiniband need to be supported by cluster toolkits. Motherboards, specialized chipsets, variants of x86, Itanium, and Opteron add more to the hardware mix. Again, none of the toolkits covers all of this hardware space. You may asking yourself, "What's the problem? Why don't the cluster toolkits support all of these?". It comes down to practical issues of time, money and resource. Each of the cluster toolkits tests a release on as much hardware as possible—that collection of hardware is simply too small to cover most cases that users see in the field. The toolkit designers and implementers must decide on "which disributions" and "what hardware" is supported. Another way to ask the question is

> Should the toolkit scale across Linux distributions? *or* Should the toolkit scale across hardware?

Scaling across both, the obvious answer, is simply not something that the toolkit designers are able to practically accomplish.

The tradeoffs are simple—if you choose to scale across (support) multiple distributions, then one is practically forced to make some generalizations to fit all the various distributions. The generalization uniformly selected by toolkits that scale across distributions is to take over the base installation and hardware detection piece from the vendors and make these core pieces of the cluster toolkit. These approaches don't leverage the installer supplied by the distribution. Instead, they build their own customized installation programs that can handle a number of different distributions. The advantage is that users have more choice of specific distributions. The drawback here is that the hardware space is large, and it is quite a job to manage the hardware detection and customized kernel modules for lots of hardware.

If you choose a single distribution, then you can leverage the installation and hardware detection of the commericial vendor and worry only about extensions to specific pieces of hardware, such as Myrinet. The clear drawback is that if the distribution does a poor job of this, then the toolkit suffers the same fate.

What we see in the cluster toolkit space is a dichotomy of approaches—disk imaging and description methods. Disk imaging was described in the first edition of this book as the practical way to clone a system onto your cluster nodes. Commercial and open-source tools image-based programs are popular and include: Norton Ghost, PowerQuest Drive Image, SystemImager, Chiba City Imager, and PowerCockpit. Complete clustering toolkits that use imaging include OSCAR, Chiba City, and CLIC. Description-based installers, on the other hand, use text files to provide a list of packages and instructions needed to completely configure a node. Text-based installers are distribution-specific: Redhat Kickstart, SuSE YaST, and Debian Fully Automatic Installation (FAI). Most of have their genesis (or, at least, inspiration) from Sun's Jumpstart installer. The text-based installation captures disk partitioning, package listing, and software configuration. The advantage here is that a reasonably general text description can work on many different variants of hardware because the distribution's installer is handling all the low-level details of hardware detection. One popular description-based cluster toolkit is NPACI Rocks. But other examples exist like IBMs partially-open source XCAT, and the European Data Grid's LCFG.

6.4 The Basic Steps

Before you select a toolkit to build your cluster, one needs to understand the basic high-level steps that are required to install your basic Beowulf. At this point, we assume that the hardware has been physically assembled, cabled, and is ready for power up. The steps are:

1. Install Head Node
2. Configure Cluster Services on Head Node
3. Define Configuration of a Compute Node
4. For each compute node—repeat
   (a) Detect Ethernet Hardware Address of New Node
   (b) Install complete OS onto new node
   (c) Complete Configuration of new node
5. Restart Services on head node that are cluster-aware (e.g. PBS, Sun Grid Engine)

Sounds simple enough, and it is. Let's examine the first steps of installation and cluster services on the head node. Some toolkits, like OSCAR, require the user to set up the Linux configuration separately from installing the cluster toolkit. Others, like Rocks, combine these two steps into one.

The next step (define configuration of a cluster node) is perhaps where the differences between disk imaging and description methods are most keenly felt. For disk imaging, a *golden node* needs to be installed and configured by a savvy administrator. OSCAR's System Installation Suite (SIS), which is a combination of the Linux Utility for Installation and System Imager (originally from VA Linux), uses a package list and an elaborate set of GUI's to create a golden image without actually first installing a node and represents a significant improvement over older methods. (More details on OSCAR Installation will be given in Section 6.6). Rocks uses an automatically generated text-description of a compute node "appliance" that is quite general across a wide variety of harware types. (More details about Rocks installation and design will given in Section 6.5).

Once the basic configuration of compute node has either been created by a golden image or defined through a text description, one must map where nodes are in the cluster. All ethernet interfaces have a unique MAC (Media Access Control) address,

00:50:8B:D3:47:A5 is an example) and this is used by all tookits to identify particular nodes. When a node boots, it needs network configuration parameters and usually gets this through a DHCP (Dynamic Host Configration Protocol) request. The node presents the DHCP server with its MAC address and the server returns IP, Netmask, routing, node name, and other useful components. (Chapters 2, 18 and 20 give further examples and details) Nearly all toolkits have some function or program to help detect new MAC addresses (and hence new nodes). Rocks, for example, probes the '/var/log/messages' file for the appearance of DHCPDISCOVER requests and checks these against a database. If an unknown address appears, the node is added. OSCAR uses tcpdump to ascertain the same information. Not only do these detect the new addresses, but new node names are automatically assigned. Once the detection is complete for a node, it does not have to be repeated, and the assigned IP address is (almost always) permanent.

Installing the OS onto each node is another place where decription and image-based sytems differ. Image-based systems download the golden image, make some adjustments for differences in disk geometry, IP address and other limited changes, and then install the image on the compute node disk. Description-based methods download a text-based node description (which already contains customization information) and use the native installer to drive the installation automatically. The description will partition the disk, download packages, and perform post configuration of packages. The packages themselves are downloaded from a distribution server instead of being contained inside of disk image.

It is critical to understand that disk image methods put the bulk of configuration information into the creation of the golden image. Description-based methods, on the other hand, put configuration information into the text description, which is then applied at installation time. It is often a matter of style as to which an administrator prefers. But, certain scenarios favor one method over another.

The final step of node installation is to complete node configuration. Until recently, this was something that had to be done explicitly by the system administrator after the base images were installed. Current toolkits completely automate this step.

The last step in complete cluster configuration is simply reconfiguring and restarting cluster-wide services like schedulers and monitors to reflect an updated cluster configuration. Modern toolkits automate this for you.

In the next two sections we describe in some detail the NPACI Rocks Toolkit and the OSCAR Toolkit as two exemplars of description-based and image-based methods. These sections do not take the place of howto's or installation instructions, but rather describe the underlying mechanisms for installation and configuration.

6.5 NPACI Rocks

NPACI Rocks clustering software leverages RedHat's Kickstart utility to manage the software and configuration of all nodes. It fundamentally enables the notion that reals clusters have many node types (hereafter referred to as "appliance types" or "appliances"). Rocks decomposes the configuration of each appliance into several small single-purpose package and configuration modules. Further, all site- and machine-specific information is managed in an SQL (MySQL) database as a single "oracle" of cluster-wide information.

The Rocks configuration modules can be easily shared between cluster nodes and, more importantly, cluster sites. For example, a single module is used to describe the software components and configuration of the `ssh` service. Cluster appliance types which require `ssh` are built with this module. The configuration is completely transferrable, as is, to all Rocks clusters.

In Rocks, a single object-oriented framework is used to build the configuration/installation module hierarchy, resulting in multiple cluster appliances being constructed from the same core software and configuration description. This framework is composed of XML files and a Python engine to convert component descriptions of an appliance into a Redhat-compliant Kickstart file.

Anaconda is RedHat's installer that interprets *Kickstart* files. The Kickstart file describes what must be done from disk partitioning, to package installation, and finally post- or site-configuration to create a completely functional node. Figure 6.3 presents a sample Kickstart file. It has three sections: *command*, *package*, and *post*. The *command* section contains almost all the answers posed by an interactive installation (e.g., location of the distribution, disk partitioning parameters and language support). The *packages* section lists the names of Redhat packages (RPMs) to be installed on the machine. Finally, the *post* section contains scripts which are run during the installation to further configure installed packages. The *post* section is the most complicated because this is where site-specific customization is done. Rocks, for example, does not repackage available software—it simply has a mechanism to easily provide the needed post-configuration.

While a Kickstart file is a text-based description of all the software packages and software configuration to be deployed on a node, it is both static and monolithic. At best, this requires separate files for each appliance type. At worst, this requires a separate file for each host. The overwhelming advantage of Kickstart is that it provides a *de facto* standard for installing software, performing the system probing required to install and configure the correct device drivers, and automating the selection of these drivers on a per machine basis. A Kickstart file is quite generic in

```
url --url http://10.1.1.1/install/i386
zerombr yes
clearpart --all
part / --size 4096
lang en_US
keyboard us
mouse genericps/2
timezone --utc GMT
skipx
install
reboot

%packages
@Base
pdksh

%post
cat > /etc/motd  << 'EOF'
Kickstarted on `date`
EOF
```

Figure 6.3: Basic RedHat Kickstart file. The RedHat Installer, Anaconda, interprets the contents of the kickstart file to build a node

that references to specific versions of packages are not needed. Neither is specific identification of ethernet, disk, video, memory, motherboard, or other hardware devices needed.

Because the Kickstart file does not contain package versions, resolution of specific version information must be held somewhere. For RedHat, this information is kept in a distribution tree. The distribution is simply a collection of RedHat Packages (RPMS) in particular directory structure and a RedHat-specific index file that maps a generic package name to its fully-qualified version. In this way, the Kickstart file may list an `openssh-clients` package, but the Anaconda installer will resolve this to the full name `openssh-clients-3.1p1-6.i386.rpm` by referencing the distribution's index file. Rocks provides some critical software (`rocks-dist`) that greatly simplifies the creation of custom distributions. Multiple distributions can sit on a single server and end-users can easily integrate site-specific software. In addition, distribution can be built with the latest update of packages so that when a Rocks appliance installs itself, it can apply completely updated software in a single step. This eliminates an install-then-patch scenario.

It is important to understand that the distribution contains all possible packages that might be installed on a cluster appliance node. The Kickstart file describes exactly which of these will be installed and how each software subsystem will be configured to make a particular appliance. Rocks allows a head node to serve out multiple distributions. This facilitates testing of nodes against new software simply by pointing the installer to new distribution. See Chapter 20 and the Jazz cluster for a real world experience on the necessity of having test hardware.

Description mechanisms for other distributions and operating systems exist and include SuSE's YaST (and YaST2), Debian FAI (Fully Automatic Installer), and Sun Solaris Jumpstart. The structure of each of the text descriptions are actually quite similar as the same problems of hardware probing, software installation, and software post-configuration must be done. The specifics of package naming, partitioning commmands and other details are quite different among these methods.

6.5.1 Component-based configuration

The key functionality missing from Kickstart to make it the only installation tool needed for clusters is the lack of macro language and a framework for code re-use. A macro language would improve the programmability of Kickstart and code reuse significantly ameliorates the problems of software skew across appliances by having shared configuration among appiance types be truly shared (instead of being copies that require vigilance to keep in sync).

Rocks uses the concept of package and configuration *modules* as building blocks for creating entire appliances. Rocks modules are small XML files that encapsulate package names and post-configuration into logical "chunks" of functionality. XML is used by Rocks because of *de facto* standard software for parsing data.

Once the functionality of a system is broken into small single-purpose modules, a framework describing the inheritance model is used to derive the full functionality of complete systems, each of which shares common base configuration. Figure 6.4 is a representation of such a framework which describes the configuration of all appliances in a Rocks cluster. The framework is a directed graph—each vertex represents the configuration for a specific service (software package(s), service configuration, local machine configuration, etc.) Relationships between services are represented with edges. At the top of the graph there are four vertexes which indicate the configuration of a "laptop", "desktop", "frontend", and "compute" cluster appliance.

When a node is built using Rocks, the Kickstart file for a particular node is generated and customized on-the-fly by starting at an appliance entry node and traversing the graph. The modules (XML Files) are parsed, and customization data is read from the Rocks SQL database. Figure 6.5 shows some detail of the

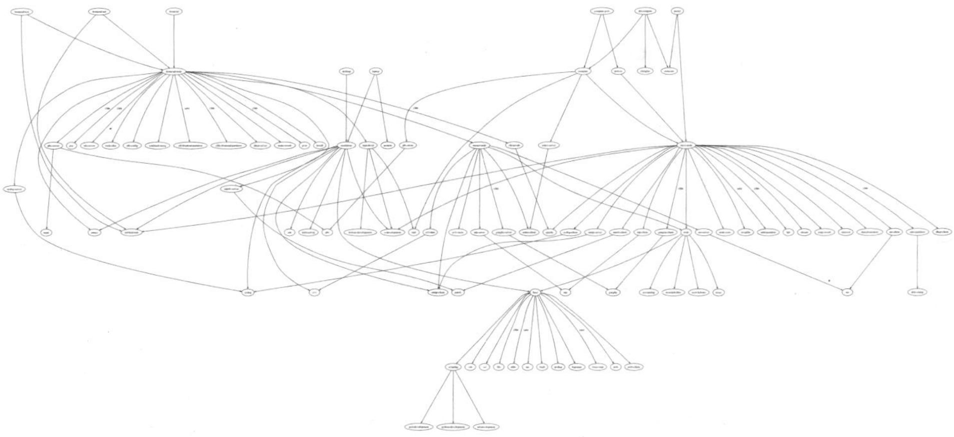

Figure 6.4: Description (Kickstart) Graph. This graph completely describes *all* of the appliances of a Rocks Cluster.

configuration graph. Two appliance types are illustrated here—`standalone` and `node`. Both share everything that is contained in the `base` module and hence will be indentically installed and configured for everything in `base` and modules below. In this example, a module called `c-development` is only attached to `standalone`. With this type of construction it is quite easy to see (and therefore focus on) the differences between appliances.

It is interesting to note that the interconnection graph is a different file from the modules themselves. This means that if a user desires to have the `c-development` module as part of the base installation, one simply makes that change in the graph file and attaches `c-development` to the `base` module. Also in Figure 6.5, edges can be annotated with architecture type (`i386` and `ia64` in this example). This allows the same generic structure to describe appliances across significant architectural boundaries. Real differences, such as the `grub` (for ia32) and `elilo` (for ia64) boot loaders can be teased out without completely replicating all of the configuration.

6.5.2 Graph Components

In an earlier section, it was stated that image-based systems put the bulk of their configuration into creating an image, while description methods put the bulk of

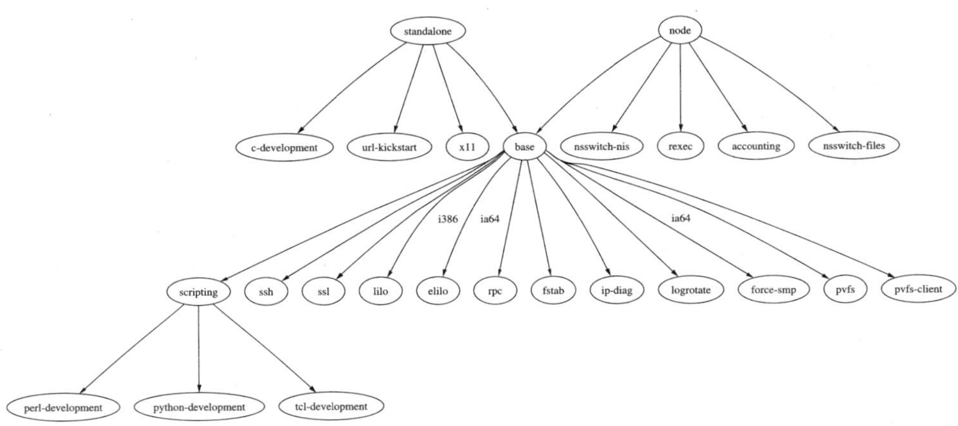

Figure 6.5: Description Graph Detail. This illustrates how two modules '`standalone.xml`' and '`base.xml`' share base configuration and also differ in other specifics

their configuration into the description (e.g. Kickstart) file. In Rocks, the modules are small XML files with simple structures as illustrated in Figures 6.6 and 6.7.

Figure 6.6 shows the XML file for an "ssh" module in the graph. The single purpose of this module is to describe the packages and configuration associated with the installation of the ssh service and client on a machine. The *package* and *post* XML tags map directly to Kickstart keywords. Figure 6.7 shows how global operations such as the root password and mouse selection similarly can be described. Rocks also contains options on partitioning hard drives that ranges from a fully-automated scheme (which works on IDE, SCSI, and RAID Arrays) to completely manual (adminstrator-controlled). The real advantage here is that `ssh` configuration policy is done once instead of being replicated across all appliance types.

6.5.3 Putting it all together

Rocks uses a graph structure to create decription files for appliances. In the background is a mySQL database that holds cluster-wide configuration information. When a node requests an IP address, a dhcp server on the head node replies with a `filename` tag that contains a URL for the node's kickstart file. The node contacts

```
<?xml version="1.0" standalone="no"?>
<!DOCTYPE kickstart SYSTEM "dtds/node.dtd"
[<!ENTITY ssh "openssh">]>
<kickstart>

  <package>&ssh;</package>
  <package>&ssh;-clients</package>
  <package>&ssh;-server</package>
  <package>&ssh;-askpass</package>

  <!-- Required for X11 Forwarding -->
  <package>XFree86</package>
  <package>XFree86-libs</package>

<post>
<!-- default client setup -->
cat &gt; /etc/ssh/ssh_config &lt;&lt; 'EOF'
Host *
        CheckHostIP             no
        ForwardX11              yes
        ForwardAgent            yes
        StrictHostKeyChecking   no
        UsePrivilegedPort       no
        FallBackToRsh           no
        Protocol                1,2
EOF
</post>

</kickstart>
```

Figure 6.6: The ssh.xml module includes the ssh packages and configures the service in the Kickstart post section.

```
<?xml version="1.0" standalone="no"?>
<!DOCTYPE kickstart SYSTEM "dtds/node.dtd">
<kickstart>
  <main>
    <lang><var name="Kickstart_Lang"/></lang>
    <keyboard><var name="Kickstart_Keyboard"/></keyboard>
    <mouse><var name="Kickstart_Mouse"/></mouse>
    <timezone><var name="Kickstart_Timezone"/></timezone>
    <rootpw>--iscrypted <var name="RootPassword"/></rootpw>
    <install/>
    <reboot/>
  </main>
</kickstart>
```

Figure 6.7: The '`base.xml`' module configures the main section of the Kickstart file.

the web server and a CGI script is run that 1) looks up the node and appliance type in the database, and 2) traverses and expands the graph for that appliance and node type to dynamically create the Kickstart file. Once the decscription is downloaded, the native installer takes over and downloads packages from the location specified in the kickstart file, installs packages, performs the post installation tasks specified, and then reboots. Rocks also uses the same structure to bootstrap a head node, except that the kickstart generation framework and Linux distribution is held on the local boot CD and interactive screens gather the local information. In summary, we annotate the installation steps with the steps that Rocks takes:

1. Install Head Node—*Boot Rocks-augmented CD*
2. Configure Cluster Services on Head Node—*automatically done in step 1*
3. Define Configuration of a Compute Node—*Basic setup installed. Can edit graph or nodes to customize further*
4. For each compute node—repeat
   (a) Detect Ethernet Hardware Address of New Node *use* `insert-ethers` *tool*
   (b) Install complete OS onto new node—*Kickstart*
   (c) Complete Configuration of new node—*already described in Kickstart file*
5. Restart Services on head node that are cluster-aware (e.g. PBS, Sun Grid Engine)—*part of* `insert-ethers`

The key features of Rocks are that it is RedHat-specific, uses descriptions to build appliances, leverages the Redhat Installer to do hardware detection, and will take hardware with no installed OS to an operating cluster in a short period of time. The description files are almost completely hardware independent allowing the construction of Beowulfs with different physical nodes to be handled as easily as homogeneous nodes.

6.6 The OSCAR Toolkit

The Open Source Cluster Application Resource (OSCAR) uses imaging as its primary method of installing the operating system on compute nodes of a cluster. Because it is image-based, OSCAR supports a wider array of Linux distributions (Redhat 7.2, 7.3 and Mandrake 8.0 as of this writing) with the with the same cluster tool stack, but is more limited in its hardware support. The more limited hardware support juxtaposed to supporting more distributions seems to be an oxymoron. One has to examine exactly how image-based installers actually work to see why this is the case.

6.6.1 How Image-based Installers Work

The most primitive image program is the venerable Unix `dd` command. With `dd`, one can save, bit-for-bit, a disk partition or entire disk and store it as a file. The problem is that restoring such an image in a naive way requires that the new hardware be in everyway identical. For disks, this level of identity is down to the geometry and cylinder count. Modern image-based installers take this basic capability, but then add some critical features to significantly increase their utility across hardware.

The first key insight on how imaging works is to treat a disk (or partition) image as file system. Let's digress with an example. Suppose you have a Linux system with a root partition in '`/dev/hda1`' and a separate partition (e.g. scratch) with enough free space to hold a complete image of the root. Then try the following sequence (as root):

- `# dd if=/dev/hda1 of=/scratch/root.image`
- `# mkdir /mnt/root`
- `# mount /scratch/root.image /mnt/root -o loop`
- `# ls -l /mnt/root`

As you make changes to the '`/mnt/root`', the contents of '`/scratch/root.image`' are updated. When you unmount the file system, those changes are saved in the original image file. So it is really straightforward to take an image of system, save it, update the image by using standard tools and tricks. Because the entire root file system is available in an image, there are no limits on what could done to it. Files (like '`fstab`', '`hosts`', IP configuration, and more) can added, edited or deleted. In fact, because it is the raw file system, it theoretically doesn't matter if the distribution is Redhat, Mandrake, Debian, or any of the 100's of Linux distributions that are out there. Practically, the installer most know something about the file layout to be efficient and therefore only a small subset of distributions is actually supported by any image-based installer. The one key feature that many admins like about image based techniques is that they can *handcraft* a configuration and then take a snaphot. Image-based installers help with the replication of this snapshot.

The second critical piece of image-based management is the customized installer. The installer must download an image from a server, customize some portions of it for the target node, and then install the updated image on the particular hardware of the node, taking into account small differences in hardware. An example of necessary customization is changing the network configuration file which must be be updated to a new node's IP address. If this isn't done properly, then nodes would be are identical in everyway—even to their IP address—which obviously leads to an unusable cluster. The installer, like System Imager used in OSCAR can make several changes based upon differences in node hardware. It supports the most common adjustments without intervention by the administrator: changes in the ethernet driver, changes in disk drive geometry (but not in disk type), and memory size differences. Because the installer itself is designed to handle a variety of distributions, the onus of basic hardware detection (e.g. disk geometry, network driver) is in the installer and not on the distribution. Resource constraints in supporting the imaging software leads to the reality that only a subset of hardware can be supported. In OSCAR, for example, IDE and SCSI devices are supported by the installer, but IDE and SCSI hardware RAID (e.g. HP Proliant's Integrated Drive Array, '`/dev/ida/`') is not understood by the installer and hence not supported. A further constraint is the the installer itself is a specialized program that runs a customized Linux kernel. The kernel may not have the complete set of device drivers needed to run your hardware, even if the distribution natively supports your hardware. OSCAR allows users to build customized installation kernels to handle the case where an administrator can identify manually the needed driver. Even though the above dd-based example is straightforward, installing and customizing images is actually quite complex: to make configuration changes, the installer must understand the file system, layout, and location of config files to do localization. Small differences, like choosing `inetd` over `xinetd`, must be dealt with to manage across distributions.

6.6.2 Bootstrapping and Configuration

OSCAR assumes a working head node—which generally is installed "by hand" using the tools of the base distribution (Mandrake or Redhat). The OSCAR toolset is then installed afterwards and requires additional configuration steps. The core of OSCAR is a set of tools, all driven by the OSCAR install wizard, to define the set of packages and resources that are needed to create a disk image. Resources include drive partitioning installation, which MPI libararies to install, and other OSCAR-specific tools. Once the set of base software (stored as RPMs), is selected a *client image* is created. If further customization is needed, then the image can be "edited" using SIS (System Installation Suite) tools. If one wants to create other types of nodes (e.g. an NFS server instead of compute node) or if nodes of the same type haven't different disk subsytems (IDE and SCSI) the entire process is started again with a different image name. The case of homogeneous hardware (and node function type) is handled easily by this setup. If your cluster has heterogenous node types and/or different appliance types, then description-based methods generally provide a simpler solution.

Once the OSCAR image is built, the wizard will guide you to start integrating new nodes. OSCAR uses a `tcpdump` to detect DHCP requests—when a new node is seen, a new name is automatically assigned. The SIS installer kernel starts the process of downloading the correct image from the server and at this point takes over, doing node customization by looking up node-specific information in the SIS database. In summary, we annotate the installation steps with the steps that OSCAR takes:

1. Install Head Node—*Hand installation. Usually using Distro installer*
2. Configure Cluster Services on Head Node—*Follow installer setup script*
3. Define Configuration of a Compute Node—*Use The OSCAR wizard to define a client image*
4. For each compute node—repeat
   (a) Detect Ethernet Hardware Address of New Node *use OSCAR Wizard*
   (b) Install complete OS onto new node—*SIS disk image downloaded and installed*
   (c) Complete Configuration of new node—*Most customization already done in the image*
5. Restart Services on head node that are cluster-aware (e.g. PBS, Sun Grid Engine)—*part of the OSCAR install wizard*

The key features of OSCAR is that it uses disk images and supports multiple distributions, it uses a configuration wizard to create a client image without first installing a golden client, and supports cluster nodes with no previously installed OS. The images have some hardware independence, but differences in disk subsystem type require different images.

6.7 Other Important Toolkits

There are a number of other toolkits that might be used. In this section, we give a non-exhaustive description of some of the more popular kits

6.7.1 SCore

SCore is a single system image abstraction that has traditionally focused on extreme performance. SCore was initially designed as system for high-performance systems research and the well-known PM messaging layer is one of it's key technologies. PM works on Myrinet and other low-latency networks (some of which are being developed by the Japanese Consortium that now maintains and advances SCore). SCore uses a multicast-based image installer to put software onto each of the nodes. Multicast is used to improve the speed of installation by broadcasting the image to a number of clients. The installer is itself a custom piece of software and must manage making the multicast transport reliable

6.7.2 LCFG

LFCG is a description-based installer. It differs from Rocks in that inheritance is supported in LCFG through file inclusion (e.g., `#include`). LCFG also employs a proprietary configuration language for their source files and they provide a custom *profile* compiler to combine the source files into single XML profile. LCFG doesn't use kickstart to install the operating environment. Rather it uses its own boot environment to configure the machine (e.g., to detect the hardware, partition the disk, install RPMs).

6.7.3 XCat

XCat uses descriptions to create Kickstart files and just recently has added limited support for SuSE Linux YaST. XCat is quasi open-source and its specific license is limited for use only on IBM hardware. The generation of descriptions must be generated beforehand by the system administrator and each node must have it's own install file. XCat provides some structure in creating the description files, but there is quite a bit of scripting needed to define different node types, add resources and the like. XCat's strength lies in its integration with IBM's proprietary management processor—allowing administrators to handles BIOS updates, remote power cycling, and more through remote console access and custom scripts.

6.7.4 Chiba City Toolkit

Chiba City Toolkit is an unsupported collection of tools from Argonne National Laboratory. Chiba, described more fully in Chapter 20, uses an image-based installer and was designed to help US Department Energy researchers investigate systems problems. The model of operation for system developers is that complete (serial) console access is available to a user so they can install any operating system image—including Windows. They have developed an image-based installer and a set of tools to interact with each serial console to tell each node how to boot (e.g. from local hard drive or to download a particular image). Like the SIS suite included in OSCAR, administrators can edit an image on a server and then push out changes or entire images to a node. Like all image-based systems, the variation of hardware that the installer supports is limited.

6.8 When Things go Wrong

For cluster installation there are literally hundreds of small items that can be show-stoppers in getting an installation to work over the network. In this section, we'll describe some the of common problems that users might encounter. There are many email and web resources to check if you run into an installation problem including toolkit-specific discussion lists and the general Beowulf users list. The key thing that makes clusters different is that one relies on a network to enable installation (whether image or decription).

- **MAC addresses of new nodes are never detected.**There a few things to check here. First, make sure on motherboards with dual interfaces that you have plugged into the interface that will be labeled `eth0`. If you are using PXE, make certain that it is enabled

  on this interface. It is non-standard as to which interface is eth0 and sometimes the fix is as simple is switching the cable. If you are still not seeing `DHCPDISCOVER` messages on the frontend, attach the frontend to the node with a standard ethernet cross-over cable. If you do see the `DHCPDISCOVER` message in the logs (make sure `dhcpd` is running), then you have narrowed things down to the network itself. For today's managed switches, you will need to make certain that broadcast is enabled on the switch itself.

- **During download of image or packages, the node just freezes**. There generally are two possibilities. The device driver for your network card is buggy or unreliable (this is actually usual when new NICs are introduced) or your node hardware is simply bad (memory, processor, disk, or more). If the problem affects all nodes, then look for something that is common (like the network driver). It is also possible that either an image or a package is corrupted on the server itself. For RPM-based installations, the installer will often tell you on what package things have failed and using RPM to verify the package on the server is an easy remedy.

- **My network card isn't supported.** This problem is much more common than you might think. NIC manufacturers use a number of variants of a standard interface (the Intel e1000 has over 6 hardware variants)—and the Linux driver may not have caught up to the latest versions. You first have to determine exactly what the interface is—if you can hand-install a version of Linux on the node, you can use `lspci` to find all about the devices on your PCI bus. Ethernet controllers will be listed that way and you can look at the specifics of the PCI ID and the text description in the PCI record. A look at the source code will determine if that variant of a known device is supported. If is is supported, then you have to work to get a custom installation kernel, boot floppy, or PXE image constructed. This is toolkit specific and is quite deep into the specifics of a toolkit.

6.9 Summary

This section has described description-based and image based installers. In particular the Rocks and OSCAR toolkits were discussed in some detail. Readers should recall the physical planning of cluster layout and trunking of cables leads to a more reliable physical design. Also, real clusters are never homogeneous in function and rarely are they homogeneous in hardware configuration. Finally, setup and installation is never done just once and is intimately tied to the style of management of the administrator. Having a solid setup and initial software provisioning plan will allow you to get the more interesting part of clusters—using them for productive work.

II PARALLEL PROGRAMMING

7 An Introduction to Writing Parallel Programs for Clusters

Ewing Lusk, William Gropp, and Ralph Butler

There are two common kinds of parallelism. The first, the master-worker approach, is the simplest and easiest to implement. It relies on being able to break the computation into independent tasks. A master then coordinates the solution of these independent tasks by worker processes. This kind of parallelism is discussed in detail in this Chapter, starting with Section 7.1. This part of the chapter has three goals:

- To present some of the ways parallelism can be introduced into an application.
- To describe how to express parallelism using functions built into the operating system. Depending on your target application, this information may be all you need, and we will show how to access these functions from several different application-development languages.
- To provide some realistic examples of applications illustrating this approach. We include string matching with applications to computational biology.

The first task in creating a parallel program is to express concurrent work. Section 7.1 then focuses on *task parallelism.* Section 7.2 describes the use of Linux system calls for task parallelism. Section 7.4 then outlines an example from computational biology to illustrate the use of task parallelism to carry out a large computation.

The second kind of parallelism is for computations that cannot (or cannot easily) be broken into independent tasks. In this kind of parallelism, the computation is broken down into communicating, interdependent tasks. One example of this kind of parallelism was introduced in Section 1.3.6. These parallel programs are more difficult to write, and a number of programming models have been developed to support this kind of parallel program. The most common, and the one most appropriate for Beowulf clusters, is *message passing*. The two most common message-passing systems are MPI (Message Passing Interface) and PVM (Parallel Virtual Machine), covered in Chapters 8–11. In this chapter, Section 7.5 introduces some of the techniques used in dividing programs into communicating, interdependent parts. Expressing these ideas as programs is left for the following chapters.

7.1 Creating Task Parallelism

The essence of task parallelism is that the task to be accomplished can be executed in parallel. Since we assume that the tasks are not *completely* independent (otherwise they are just a collection of ordinary sequential jobs), some sort of coordinating mechanism must exist. We will call this process the *manager*, and the processes that carry out the subtasks the *workers*. (The manager could even be the human user, who manages the worker processes "by hand," but we will assume that the manager is a single program that the user causes to be started.) Manager/worker algorithms and execution mechanisms have many variations, which we survey in the next section; but as we use the term, "task parallelism" always involves the following steps.

1. Divide the task into independent or nearly independent subtasks. By "independent" we mean that while communication of some sort occurs between the manager and the workers, there is no direct communication between any two workers.

2. Start the workers. We assume that each worker is represented by an operating system process. In Section 7.2 we will describe Unix processes and how to start them. (Use of threads for workers is atypical for a Beowulf cluster and will not be described.)

3. Communicate subtask specifications from the manager to the workers.

4. Communicate results from the workers to the manager.

5. Ensure that all results have been collected and that the workers have been shut down.

7.1.1 Variations on Task Parallelism

The scheme just described had many variations; we will discuss a few of them here, and then in the following section we will illustrate some of these with concrete examples. The variations involve the scheduling algorithm by which the manager assigns subtasks to the workers, the ways in which the worker processes are started and managed, and the communication mechanism between manager and workers.

Variations in How Work Is Assigned

For an efficient manager/worker parallel program, the workers should be kept working as much of the total time as possible. If the total work to be done can be easily divided into arbitrarily sized subtasks, then the scheduling job is easy: if there are n workers, then divide the work up into n pieces, each of which will take the same amount of time, and give one piece to each worker. This is called *static scheduling*.

```
manager:
for (i=0; i<n; i++) {
    start new process
    send work
}
while (not done) {
    wait for msg from any worker
    receive results
    if (work left) {
        send new work to worker
    }
    else {
        send exit msg to worker
    }
}
```

```
worker:
receive msg from manager
while (not exit msg) {
    do work
    send results
    receive next message
}
exit
```

Figure 7.1: Schematic of a general manager-worker system

Although sometimes such scheduling can be done, breaking up the total amount of work into subtasks typically results in subtasks of widely differing sizes, more subtasks than there are workers, or both. In all of these cases, the manager must organize the assignment of work to workers more carefully in order to keep the workers working. If some workers are idle when there is still more work to do, a *load balancing problem* occurs. Fortunately the general manager/worker algorithms can be used to overcome this problem when there are substantially more subtasks than there are workers. The idea is for the manager to make an initial assignment of subtasks to workers and then wait for subtask completion by any worker. At that point the worker can be assigned another subtask. In this way the master does not need to know ahead of time how much time each subtask will take; it just keeps all the workers as busy as possible.

Figure 7.1 shows a high-level framework for the manager and worker in a manager/worker system. In this example, n processes (workers) are started and then each process is sent the data for each task to perform. New processes are started once rather than for each task, because starting a new process is often a time-consuming operation.

We note a few points about this algorithm.

- A load balancing problem will inevitably occur near the end of the job, as some workers become idle but there is no more work to be assigned, because all the work that is not done is being worked on by other workers.

- To make this period of load imbalance as small as possible, it is a good idea to make the subtasks small. If the manager can estimate the sizes of the subtasks, then it should assign the larger tasks first and the smaller ones near the end.

- If the subtasks are *too* small, then the overhead of communication between manager and worker will take up too much of the total time.

Therefore one needs to give some thought to just exactly how to divide up the work. A technique that is sometimes used is to further subdivide the work units during the computation. In some algorithms, the workers subdivide their own tasks and return the new subsubtasks to the manager for redistribution to the other workers. An example is the Mandelbrot program described in Chapter 5 of [48].

Variations in Implementation Mechanisms

Processes can be started in a variety of ways, including shell commands, Unix system calls, remote shell commands of different kinds, parallel process management systems, and the use of daemons of various kinds. Even Web browsers can be used to launch remote tasks. We will discuss process startup in Section 7.2, after we have established a deeper understanding of operating system processes.

Similarly, the communication between manager and worker can be carried out in many ways. One way is to use the file system as a communication device. This is particularly convenient if all of the workers have access to the same file system. (See Chapter 19 for a discussion of shared file systems.) This mechanism is often used when the manager is programmed as a shell script.

A more flexible and powerful approach to communication among processes uses *sockets*. Sockets and how to use them in several programming languages are covered in Section 7.2.5. The use of higher-level communication libraries (MPI and PVM) is covered in later chapters.

7.2 Operating System Support for Parallelism

Although parallel programs can be quite complex, many applications can be made parallel in a simple way to take advantage of the power of Beowulf clusters. In this section we describe how to write simple programs using features of the Linux operating system that you are probably already familiar with. We begin with a discussion of processes themselves (the primary unit of parallelism) and the ways they can be created in Unix environments such as Linux. A good reference on this material is [111].

7.2.1 Programs and Processes

First we review terminology. A *program* is a set of computer instructions. A computer fetches from its memory the instruction at the address contained in its *program counter* and executing that instruction. Execution of the instruction sets the program counter for the next instruction. This is the basic von Neumann model of computation. A *process* consists of a program, an area of computer memory called an *address space*, and a program counter. (If there are multiple program counters for a single address space, the process is called a *multithreaded* process.) Processes are isolated from one another in the sense that no single instruction from the program associated with one process can access the address space of another process. Data can be moved from the address space of one process to that of another process by methods that we will describe in this and succeeding chapters. For the sake of simplicity, we will discuss single-threaded processes here, so we may think of a process as an (address space, program, program counter) triple.

7.2.2 Local Processes

Where do processes come from? In Unix-based operating systems such as Linux, new processes are created by the `fork` system call. This is an efficient and lightweight mechanism that duplicates the process by copying the address space and creating a new process with the same program. The only difference between the process that executed the `fork` (called the *parent* process) and the new process (called the *child* process) is that the `fork` call returns 0 in the child and the process id in the parent. Based on this different return code from `fork`, the parent and child processes, now executing independently, can do different things.

One thing the child process often does is an `exec` system call. This call changes the program for the process, sets the program counter to the beginning of the program, and reinitializes the address space. The `fork-exec` combination, therefore, is the mechanism by a process create a new, completely different one. The new process is executing on the same machine and competing for CPU cycles with the original process through the process scheduler in the machine's operating system.

You have experienced this mechanism many times. When you are logged into a Unix system, you are interacting with a *shell*, which is just a normal Unix process that prompts you, reads your input commands, and processes them. The default program for this process is `/bin/bash`; but depending on the shell specified for your user name in '/etc/passwd', you may be using another shell. Whenever you run a Unix command, such as grep, the shell forks and execs the program associated with the command. The command ps shows you all the processes you are running under the current shell, including the ps process itself (strictly speaking, the process executing the ps program).

Normally, when you execute a command from the shell, the shell process waits for the child process to complete before prompting you for another command, so that only one process of yours at a time is actually executing. By "executing" we mean that it is in the list of processes that the operating system will schedule for execution according to its time-slicing algorithm. If your machine has ony one CPU, of course only one instruction from one process can be executing at a time. By time-slicing the CPU among processes, however, the illusion of simultaneously executing process on a single machine, even a single CPU, is presented.

The easiest way to cause multiple processes to be scheduled for execution at the same time is to append the '&' character to a command that you execute in the shell. When you do this, the shell starts the new process (using the fork-exec mechanism) but then immediately prompts for another command without waiting for the new one to complete. This is called "running a process in the background." Multiple background processes can be executing at the same time. This situation provides us with our first example of parallel processes.

To determine whether a file contains a specific string, you can use the Unix command grep. To look in a directory containing mail files in order to find a message about the Boyer-Moore string-matching algorithm, you can cd to that directory and do

```
grep Boyer *
```

If your mail is divided into directories by year, you can consider search all those directories in parallel. You can use background processes to do this search in a shell script:

```
!# /bin/bash
echo searching for $1
for i in 20* ;
    do ( cd $i; grep $1 * > $1.out & ) ;
done
wait
cat 20*/$1.out > $1.all
```

and invoke this with `Boyer` as an argument.

This simple parallel program matches our definition of a manager/worker algorithm, in which the master process executes this script and the worker processes execute `grep`. We can compare its properties with the list in Section 7.1:

1. The subtasks, each of which is to run `grep` over all the files in one directory, are independent.

2. The workers are started by this shell script, which acts as the master.

3. The subtask specifications (arguments to `grep`) are communicated to the workers on their respective command lines.

4. The results are written to the file system, one result file in each directory.

5. The `wait` causes the shell script to wait for all background processes to finish, so that the results can be collected by the manager (using `cat`) into one place.

One can make a few further observations about this example:

- The first line of the script tells the system which program to use to interpret the script. Here we have used the default shell for Linux systems, called `bash`. Other shells may be installed on your system, such as `csh`, `tcsh`, or `zsh`. Each of these has a slightly different syntax and different advanced features, but for the most part they provide the same basic functionality.

- We could have made the size of the subtask smaller by running each invocation of `grep` on a single file. This would have led to more parallelism, but it is of dubious value on a single machine, and we would have been creating potentially thousands of processes at once.

- We could time this script by putting `date` commands at the beginning and end, or by running it under the shell's `time` command:

  ```
  time grepmail boyer
  ```

  where `grepmail` is the name of this script and `boyer` is the argument.

7.2.3 Remote Processes

Recall that the way a process is created on a Unix system is with the `fork` mechanism. Only one process is not `fork`ed by another process, namely the single `init` process that is the root of the tree of all processes running at any one time.

Thus, if we want to create a new process on another machine, we must contact some existing process and cause it to fork our new process for us. There are many ways to do this, but all of them use this same basic mechanism. They differ only in which program they contact to make a fork request to. The contact is usually made over a TCP socket. We describe sockets in detail in Section 7.2.5.

rsh

The `rsh` command contacts the `rshd` process if it is running on the remote machine and asks it to execute a program or script. To see the contents of the '`/tmp`' directory on the machine `foo.bar.edu`, you would do

```
rsh foo.bar.edu ls /tmp
```

The standard input and output of the remote command are routed through the standard input and output of the `rsh` command, so that the output of the `ls` comes back to the user on the local machine. Chapter 5 describes how to set up `rsh` on your cluster.

ssh

The `ssh` (secure shell) program behaves much like `rsh` but has a more secure authentication mechanism based on public key encryption and encrypts all traffic between the local and remote host. It is now the most commonly used mechanism for starting remote processes. Nevertheless, `rsh` is substantially faster than `ssh`, and is used when security is not a critical issue. A common example of this situation occurs when the cluster is behind a firewall and `rsh` is enabled just within the cluster. Setting up `ssh` is described in Chapter 5, and a book on `ssh` has recently appeared [11].

Here is a simple example. Suppose that we have a file called '`hosts`' with the names of all the hosts in our cluster. We want to run a command (in parallel) on all those hosts. We can do so with a simple shell script as follows:

```
#! /bin/bash
for i in `cat hosts` ;
    do (ssh -x $i hostname & ) ;
done
```

If everything is working correctly and **ssh** has been configured so that it does not require a password on every invocation, then we should get back the names of the hosts in our cluster, although not necessarily in the same order as they appear in the file.

(What is that `-x` doing there? In this example, since the remotely executed program (hostname) does not use any X windowing facilities, we turn off X forwarding by using the `-x` option. To run a program that does use X, the X option must be turned on by the **sshd** server at each remote machine and the user should set the `DISPLAY` environment variable. Then, the connection to the X display is automatically forwarded in such a way that any X programs started from the shell will go through the encrypted channel, and the connection to the real X server will be made from the local machine. We note that if you run several X programs at several different hosts, they will each create a file named '`.Xauthority`' in your home directory on each of the machines. If the machines all have the same home directory, for example mounted via NFS, the '`.Xauthority`' files will conflict with each other.)

Other Process Managers

Programs such as the ones `rsh` and `ssh` contact to fork processes on their behalf are often called *daemons*. These processes are started when the system is booted and run forever, waiting for connections. You can see whether the `ssh` daemon is installed and running on a particular host by logging into that host and doing `ps auxw | grep sshd`. Other daemons, either run as root by the system or run by a particular user, can be used to start processes. Two examples are the daemons used to start processes in resource managers and the `mpd`'s that can be used to start MPI jobs quickly (see Chapter 8).

7.2.4 Files

Having discussed how processes are started, we next tunr to the topic of remote *files*, files that are local to a remote machine. Often we need to move files from one host to another, to prepare for remote execution, to communicate results, or even to notify remote processes of events.

Moving files is not always necessary, of course. On some clusters, certain file systems are accessible on all the hosts through a system like NFS (Network File System) or PVFS (Parallel Virtual File System). (Chapter 19 describes PVFS in detail.) However, direct remote access can sometimes be slower than local access. In this section we discuss some mechanisms for moving files from one host to another, on the assumption that the programs and at least some of the files they use are desired to be staged to a local file system on each host, such as '`/tmp`'.

rcp

The simplest mechanism is the remote copy command `rcp`. It has the same syntax as the standard local file copy command `cp` but can accept user name and host information from the file name arguments. For example,

```
rcp thisfile jeeves.uw.edu:/home/jones/thatfile
```

copies a local file to a specific location on the host specified by the prefix before the '`:`'. A remote user can also be added:

```
rcp smith@jeeves.uw.edu:/home/jones/thatfile .
```

The `rcp` command uses the same authentication mechanism as `rsh` does, so it will either ask for a password or not depending on how `rsh` has been set up. Indeed, `rcp` can be thought of as a companion program to `rsh`. The `rcp` command can handle "third party" transfers, in which neither the source nor destination file is on the local machine.

scp

Just as `ssh` is replacing `rsh` for security reasons, `scp` is replacing `rcp`. The `scp` command is the `ssh` version of `rcp` and has a number of other convenient features, such as a progress indicator, which is handy when large files are being transferred.

The syntax of `scp` is similar to that for `rcp`. For example,

```
scp jones@fronk.cs.jx.edu:bazz .
```

will log in to machine `fronk.cs.jx.edu` as user `jones` (prompting for a password for `jones` if necessary) and then copy the file '`bazz`' in user `jones`'s home directory to the file '`bazz`' in the current directory on the local machine.

ftp and sftp

Both `ftp` and `sftp` are interactive programs, usually used to browse directories and transfer files from "very" remote hosts rather than within a cluster. If you are not already familiar with `ftp`, the `man` page will teach you how to work this basic program. The `sftp` program is the more secure, `ssh`-based version of `ftp`.

rdist

One can use `rdist` to maintain identical copies of a set of files across a set of hosts. A flexible '`distfile`' controls exactly what files are updated. This is a useful utility when one wants to update a master copy and then have the changes reflected in local copies on other hosts in a cluster. Either `rsh`-style (the default) or `ssh`-style security can be specified.

rsync

An efficient replacement for `rcp` is `rsync`, particularly when an earlier version of a file or directory to be copied already exists on the remote machine. The idea is to detect the differences between the files and then just transfer the differences over the network. This is especially effective for backing up large directory trees; the whole directory is specified in the command, but only (portions of) the changed files are actually copied.

7.2.5 Interprocess Communication with Sockets

The most common and flexible way for two processes on different hosts in a cluster to communicate is through *sockets*. A socket between two processes is a bidirectional channel that is accessed by the processes using the same `read` and `write` functions that processes use for file I/O. In this section we show how a process connects to another process, establishing a socket, and then uses it for communication. An excellent reference for the deep topic of sockets and TCP/IP in general is [111]. Here we just scratch the surface, but the examples we present here should enable you to write some useful programs using sockets. Since sockets are typically accessed from programming and scripting languages, we give examples in C, Perl, and Python, all of which are common languages for programming clusters.

Although once a socket is established, it is symmetric in the sense that communication is bidirectional, the initial setup process is asymmetric: one process connects; the other one "listens" for a connection and then accepts it. Because this situation occurs in many client/server applications, we call the process that waits for a connection the *server* and the process that connects to it the *client*, even though they may play different roles after the socket has been established.

We present essentially the same example in three languages. In the example, the server runs forever in the background, waiting for a socket connection. It advertises its location by announcing its host and "port" (more on ports below), on which it can be contacted. Then any client program that knows the host and port can set up a connection with the server. In our simple example, when the server gets the connection request, it accepts the request, reads and processes the message that the client sends it, and then sends a reply.

Client and Server in C

The server is shown in Figure 7.2. Let us walk through this example, which may appear more complex than it really is. Most of the complexity surrounds the `sockaddr_in` data structure, which is used for two-way communication with the kernel.

First, we acquire a socket with the `socket` system call. Note that we use the word "socket" both for the connection between the two processes, as we have used it up to now, and for a single "end" of the socket as it appears inside a program, as here. Here a socket is a small integer, a file descriptor just like the ones used to represent open files. Our call creates an Internet (`AF_INET`) stream (`SOCK_STREAM`) socket, which is how one specifies a TCP socket. (The third argument is relevant only to "raw" sockets, which we are not interested in here. It is usually set to zero.) This is our "listening socket," on which we will receive connection requests. We then initialize the `sockaddr_in` data structure, setting its field `sin_port` to `0` to indicate that we want the system to select a port for us. A *port* is an operating system resource that can be made visible to other hosts on the network. We *bind* our listening socket to this port with the `bind` system call and notify the kernel that we wish it to accept incoming connections from clients on this port with the `listen` call. (The second argument to `listen` is the number of queued connection requests we want the kernel to maintain for us. In most Unix systems this will be 5.) At this point clients can connect to this port but not yet to our actual server process. Also, at this point no one knows what port we have been assigned.

We now publish the address of the port on which we can be contacted. Many standard daemons listen on "well known" ports, but we have not asked for a specific port, so our listening socket has been assigned a port number that no one yet knows. We ourselves find out what it is with the `getsockname` system call and, in this case, just print it on `stdout`.

```
#include <stdio.h>
#include <sys/types.h>
#include <sys/socket.h>
#include <netinet/in.h>

main(int argc,char *argv[])
{
    int rc, n, len, listen_socket, talk_socket;
    char buf[1024];
    struct sockaddr_in sin, from;

    listen_socket = socket(AF_INET, SOCK_STREAM, 0);

    bzero(&sin, sizeof(sin));
    sin.sin_family = AF_INET;
    sin.sin_addr.s_addr = INADDR_ANY;
    sin.sin_port = htons(0);

    bind(listen_socket, (struct sockaddr *) &sin ,sizeof(sin));
    listen(listen_socket, 5);

    getsockname(listen_socket, (struct sockaddr *) &sin, &len);
    printf("listening on port = %d\n", ntohs(sin.sin_port));

    while (1) {
        talk_socket = accept(listen_socket,
                             (struct sockaddr *) &from, &len);
        n = read(talk_socket, buf, 1024);
        write(talk_socket, buf, n);    /* echo */
        close(talk_socket);
    }
}
```

Figure 7.2: A simple server in C

At this point we enter an infinite loop, waiting for connections. The `accept` system call blocks until there is a connection request from a client. Then it returns a *new* socket on which we are connected to the client, so that it can continue listening on the original socket. Our server simply reads some data from the client on the new socket (`talk_socket`), echoes it back to the client, closes the new socket,

```
#include <stdio.h>
#include <sys/types.h>
#include <sys/socket.h>
#include <netdb.h>
#include <netinet/in.h>

main(int argc,char *argv[])
{
    int rc, n, talk_socket;
    char buf[1024] = "test msg";
    struct sockaddr_in sin;
    struct hostent *hp;

    talk_socket = socket(AF_INET, SOCK_STREAM, 0);

    hp = gethostbyname(argv[1]);
    bzero((void *)&sin, sizeof(sin));
    bcopy((void *) hp->h_addr, (void *) &sin.sin_addr, hp->h_length);
    sin.sin_family = hp->h_addrtype;
    sin.sin_port = htons(atoi(argv[2]));

    connect(talk_socket,(struct sockaddr *) &sin, sizeof(sin));

    n = write(talk_socket, buf, strlen(buf)+1);
    buf[0] = '\0';     /* empty the buffer */
    n = read(talk_socket, buf, 1024);
    printf("received from server: %s \n",buf);
}
```

Figure 7.3: A simple client in C

and goes back to listening for another connection.

This example is extremely simple. We have not checked for failures of any kind (by checking the return codes from our system calls), and of course our server does not provide much service. However, this example does illustrate how to code a common sequence of system calls (the socket-bind-listen sequence) that is used in nearly all socket setup code.

The corresponding client is shown in Figure 7.3. In order to connect to the server, it must know the name of the host where the server is running and the number of the port on which it is listening. We supply these here as command-line arguments.

Again we acquire a socket with the `socket` system call. We then fill in the `sockaddr_in` structure with the host and port (first calling `gethostbyname` to fill in the `hostent` structure needed to be placed in `sin`). Next we call `connect` to create the socket. When `connect` returns, the `accept` has taken place in the server, and we can write to and read from the socket as a way of communicating with the server. Here we send a message and read a response, which we print.

Client and Server in Python

Python is an object-oriented scripting language. Implementations exist for Unix and Windows; see `www.python.org` for details. It provides an extensive set of modules for interfacing with the operating system. One interesting feature of Python is that the block structure of the code is given by the indentation of the code, rather than explicit "begin"/"end" or enclosing braces.

Much of the complexity of dealing with sockets has to do with properly managing the `sockaddr` data structure. Higher-level languages like Python and Perl make socket programming more convenient by hiding this data structure. A number of good books on Python exist that include details of the `socket` module; see, for example, [14] and [70]. Python uses an exception handling model (not illustrated here) for error conditions, leading to very clean code that does not ignore errors. The Python version of the server code is shown in Figure 7.4. Here we use the "well-known port" approach: rather than ask for a port, we specify the one we want to use. One can see the same socket-bind-listen sequence as in the C example, where now a socket object (`s`) is returned by the `socket` call and `bind`, `listen`, and `accept` are methods belonging to the socket object. The `accept` method returns two objects, a socket (`conn`) and information (`addr`) on the host and port on the other (connecting) end of the socket. The methods `send` and `recv` are methods on the socket object `conn`, and so this server accomplishes the same thing as the one in Figure 7.2.

The Python code for the corresponding client is shown in Figure 7.5. It has simply hard-coded the well-known location of the server.

Client and Server in Perl

Perl [124] is a powerful and popular scripting language. Versions exist for Unix and for Windows; see `www.perl.com` for more information. Perl provides a powerful set of string matching and manipulation operations, combined with access to many of the fundamental system calls. The man page `perlipc` has samples of clients and servers that use sockets for communication.

```
#! /usr/bin/env python
#echo server program
from socket import *
HOST = ''                    # symbolic name for local host
PORT = 50007                 # arbibrary port
s = socket(AF_INET, SOCK_STREAM)
s.bind((HOST, PORT))
s.listen(1)
conn, addr = s.accept()
print 'connected to by', addr
while 1:
  data = conn.recv(1024)
  if not data:
    break
  conn.send(data)
conn.close()
```

Figure 7.4: A simple server in Python

```
#!/usr/bin/env python
# Echo client program
from socket import *
HOST = 'donner.mcs.anl.gov'     # the remote host
PORT = 50007
s = socket(AF_INET, SOCK_STREAM)
s.connect((HOST, PORT))
s.send('Hello, world')
data = s.recv(1024)
s.close()
print 'Received', `data`
```

Figure 7.5: A simple client in Python

The code for a "time server" in Perl is shown in Figure 7.6. It follows the same pattern as our other servers. The code for the corresponding client is shown in Figure 7.7.

7.2.6 Managing Multiple Sockets with Select

So far our example socket code has involved only one socket open by the server at a time (not counting the listening socket). Further, the connections have been

```
#!/usr/bin/perl

use strict;
use Socket;
use FileHandle;

my $port  = shift || 12345;
my $proto = getprotobyname('tcp');
socket(SOCK, PF_INET, SOCK_STREAM, $proto)
    || die "socket: $!";
SOCK->autoflush();
setsockopt(SOCK, SOL_SOCKET, SO_REUSEADDR, pack("l", 1))
    || die "setsockopt: $! ";
bind(SOCK, sockaddr_in($port, INADDR_ANY))
    || die "bind: $!";
listen(SOCK,SOMAXCONN)
    || die "listen: $!";

print "server started on port $port\n";

while (1)
{
    my $paddr = accept(CLIENT,SOCK);
    CLIENT->autoflush();
    my $msg = <CLIENT>;
    print "server: recvd from client: $msg \n";
    print CLIENT "Hello there, it's now ", scalar localtime, "\n";
    close(CLIENT);
}
```

Figure 7.6: A simple server in Perl

short lived: after accepting a connection request, the server handled that request and then terminated the connection. This is a typical pattern for a classical server but may not be efficient for manager/worker algorithms in which we might want to keep the connections to the workers open rather than reestablish them each time. Unlike the clients in the examples above, the workers are persistent, so it makes sense to make their connections persistent as well.

What is needed by the manager in this case is a mechanism to wait for communication from any of a set of workers simultaneously. Unix provides this capability

```
#!/usr/bin/perl -w

use strict;
use Socket;
use FileHandle;

my ($host,$port, $iaddr, $paddr, $proto, $line);

$host = shift || 'localhost';
$port = shift || 12345;

$iaddr = inet_aton($host)
    || die "no valid host specified: $host";
$paddr = sockaddr_in($port, $iaddr);  # packed addr

$proto = getprotobyname('tcp');
socket(SOCK, PF_INET, SOCK_STREAM, $proto)
    || die "socket failed: $!";
SOCK->autoflush();  # from FileHandle
connect(SOCK, $paddr)
    || die "connect failed: $!";
print SOCK "hello from client\n";
$line = <SOCK>;
print "client: recvd from server: $line \n";
```

Figure 7.7: A simple client in Perl

with the `select` system call. The use of `select` allows a process to block, waiting for a change of state on any of a set of sockets. It then "wakes up" the process and presents it with a list of sockets on which there is activity, such as a connection request or a message to be read. We will not cover all of the many aspects of `select` here, but the code in Figure 7.8 illustrates the features most needed for manager/worker algorithms. For compactness, we show this in Python. A C version would have the same logic. See the `select` man page or [111] for the details of how to use `select` in C. It is also available, of course, in Perl.

The first part of the code in Figure 7.8 is familiar. We acquire a socket, bind it to a port, and listen on it. Then, instead of doing an `accept` on this socket directly, we put it into a list (`sockets`). Initially it is the only member of this list, but eventually the list will grow. Then we call `select`. The arguments to select are three lists of sockets we are interested in for reading, writing, or other events.

```
#!/usr/bin/env python

from socket import socket, AF_INET, SOCK_STREAM
from select import select

lsock = socket(AF_INET,SOCK_STREAM)
lsock.bind(('',0)) # this host, anonymous port
lsock.listen(5)
lport = lsock.getsockname()[1]
print 'listening on port =', lport

sockets = [lsock]
while 1:
    (inReadySockets, None, None) = select(sockets, [], [])
    for sock in inReadySockets:
        if sock == lsock:
            (tsock,taddr) = lsock.accept()
            sockets.append(tsock)
        else:
            msg = sock.recv(1024)
            if msg:
                print 'recvd msg=', msg
            else:
                sockets.remove(sock)
                sock.close()
```

Figure 7.8: A Python server that uses `select`

The `select` call blocks until activity occurs on one of the sockets we have given to it. When `select` returns, it returns three lists, each a sublist of the corresponding input lists. Each of the returned sockets has changed state, and one can take some action on it with the knowledge that the action will not block.

In our case, we loop through the returned sockets, which are now active. We process activity on the listening socket by accepting the connection request and then adding the new connection to the list of sockets we are interested in. Otherwise we read and print the message that the client has sent us. If our read attempt yields an empty message, we interpret this as meaning that the worker has closed its end of the socket (or exited, which will close the socket), and we remove this socket from the list.

We can test this server with the client in Figure 7.9.

```
#!/usr/bin/env python

from sys    import argv, stdin
from socket import socket, AF_INET, SOCK_STREAM

sock = socket(AF_INET,SOCK_STREAM)
sock.connect((argv[1],int(argv[2])))

print 'sock=', sock
while 1:
    print 'enter something:'
    msg = stdin.readline()
    if msg:
        sock.sendall(msg.strip())  # strip nl
    else:
        break
```

Figure 7.9: A Python client

7.3 Parameter Studies

One straightforward application of task parallelism is the “parameter study”, in which the same sequential program is run multiple times with different sets of input parameters. Since the program to be run is sequential, there is no communication among the workers, and the manager can be a simple script that communicates with the workers by means of the arguments to the sequential program and its standard output. We can start the workers with `ssh` and collect the output by using the `popen` system call, which returns a file descriptor we can `select` on and read the remote process's `stdout` from.

Although both the algorithm we use and its implementation are general, we present here a concrete example. We explore the parameter space of compiler options for the default Linux C compiler `gcc`. The `man` page for `gcc` conveniently lists in one place all the options that can be passed to `gcc` to cause it to produce faster machine code. Here is an excerpt from the `man` page:

```
Optimization Options
    -fcaller-saves -fcse-follow-jumps -fcse-skip-blocks
    -fdelayed-branch -felide-constructors
    -fexpensive-optimizations -ffast-math -ffloat-store
    -fforce-addr -fforce-mem -finline-functions
```

```
-fkeep-inline-functions -fmemoize-lookups
-fno-default-inline -fno-defer-pop
-fno-function-cse -fno-inline -fno-peephole
-fomit-frame-pointer -frerun-cse-after-loop
-fschedule-insns -fschedule-insns2
-fstrength-reduce -fthread-jumps -funroll-all-loops
-funroll-loops -O -O2 -O3
```

For the matrix-matrix multiply program we are going to test with, which has no function calls, only some of these look useful. Here is a subset of the above list containing optimization flags that might have an effect on the speed of the program:

```
-fexpensive-optimizations
-ffast-math
-ffloat-store
-fno-peephole
-fschedule-insns
-fschedule-insns2
-fstrength-reduce
-funroll-all-loops
-funroll-loops
-O
-O2
-O3
```

Since there are twelve switches that can be either present or absent, there are 2^{12} possible combinations. These are not completely independent, since some switch settings imply others, especially the three `-O` flags, but we will ignore thus fact for the sake of simplifying our example, and just try all 4096 combinations, Indeed, which switch settings are redundant in the presence of others should be deducible from our results!

Our plan will be to take a simple test program and compile it with all possible switch combinations and run it, reporting back the times. Since we have 4096 jobs to run, the use of a cluster will make a big difference, even if the individual tasks are short.

For our test program, we will use a straightforward matrix-matrix multiply program, shown in Figure 7.10. It multiples two 300 $\times$ 300 matrices, timing the calculation. this may not be the highest performing way to do this, but it will do for our purposes. The program echoes its command line arguments, which it does

```
#include <stdio.h>
#include <sys/time.h>
#include <unistd.h>
#define SIZE 300

main(int argc, char *argv[])
{
    double a[SIZE][SIZE], b[SIZE][SIZE], c[SIZE][SIZE];
    int i, j, k;
    struct timeval tv;
    double starttime, endtime;

    for (i = 0; i < SIZE; i++)
        for (j = 0; j < SIZE; j++)
            a[i][j] = (double) (i + j);
    for (i = 0; i < SIZE; i++)
        for (j = 0; j < SIZE; j++)
            b[i][j] = (double) i - j;
    for (i = 0; i < SIZE; i++)
        for (j = 0; j < SIZE; j++)
            c[i][j] = 0.0;

    gettimeofday( &tv, ( struct timezone * ) 0 );
    starttime = tv.tv_sec + (tv.tv_usec / 1000000.0);
    for (i = 0; i < SIZE; i++) {
        for (j = 0; j < SIZE; j++) {
            for (k = 0; k < SIZE; k++) {
                c[i][j] = c[i][j] + a[i][k] * b[k][j];
            }
        }
    }
    gettimeofday( &tv, ( struct timezone * ) 0 );
    endtime = tv.tv_sec + (tv.tv_usec / 1000000.0);
    printf("%f seconds for", endtime - starttime);
    for (i = 1; i < argc; i++)
        printf(" %s", argv[i]);
    printf("\n");
}
```

Figure 7.10: Matrix-matrix multiply program

not otherwise use; we will use them to help us record the arguments used to compile the program.

Our worker programs will just be the sequence

```
gcc <flags> -o matmult matmult.c
matmult
```

and the manager will start them with **ssh**, on hosts whose names are in a file. The other argument to our manager is a file of possible arguments. It contains exactly the twelve lines listed above. The manager just steps through the numbers from 0 up to the total number of runs (in our case 4096) treating each number as a binary number where a 1 bit represent the presence of the compiler switch corresponding to that position in the binary number. Thus we will run through all possible combinations.

The overall plan is to loop through the parameter space represented by the binary numbers represented by the binary numbers from 0 to 2^{12}. If there is a free host (no worker is working there) we assign it the next task; if not we `select` on the sockets that are open to currently working workers. When one of them reports back, we add it back to the list of free hosts. At the end, after all the work has been assigned, we still have to wait for the last tasks to complete.

Let us step through the code in Figure 7.11 in detail. First we read in the list of hosts (initial value of the list `freeHosts`) and the list of possible arguments (`parmList`). We initialize the set of sockets to select on to empty since there are no workers yet, and create an empty Python dictionary (`fd2host`) where we will keep track of busy hosts and the connections to them. We set `numParmSets` to the number of subtasks, which we can calculate from the number of possible compiler flags in the input file. Then we enter the main loop, which runs until we have assigned all the work and there are no outstanding workers working. If there is a subtask still to do and a free host to do it on, we construct the parameter list corresponding to the next task (in `ParmSet`), and pick the first host from the list of free hosts, temporarily removing it from the list. We then build a string containing the specification of the subtask. The `Popen3` command forks a process that runs the `ssh` program locally, which runs the `gcc-matmult` sequence remotely. The `ssh`'s, and therefore the remote processes, run in parallel.

We set `runfd` to the `stdout` of the `ssh`, which collects the `stdout` from the `matmult`. Each line of `stdout` will contain the time followed by the compiler flags used. Then we add this `fd` to the list of sockets available for selecting on and enter into the list `fd2host` the host attached to that `fd`.

If there are no free hosts or we have already assigned all the subtasks, then we select on the sockets connected to busy workers. When one those sockets becomes active, it means that the associated worker has set us a line of output. We read it and print it, or if the read fails (the worker exited, which sends an `EOF` on the

```
#!/usr/bin/python

from sys    import argv
from popen2 import Popen3
from select import select, error

hostFile = open(argv[1])
parmsFile = open(argv[2])
freeHosts = [ line.strip() for line in hostFile.readlines() ]
parmList = [ line.strip() for line in parmsFile.readlines() ]
lenParmList = len(parmList)
socketsToSelect = []
fd2host = {}
numParmSets = 2 ** lenParmList
pcnt = 0
while pcnt < numParmSets  or  socketsToSelect:
    if pcnt < numParmSets  and  freeHosts:
        parmSet = []
        for i in range(0,lenParmList):
            bit = 1 << i
            if bit & pcnt:
                parmSet.append(parmList[lenParmList-i-1])
        host = freeHosts[0]
        freeHosts.remove(host)
        cmd = ("ssh -l lusk -x -n %s 'gcc %s -o matmult matmult.c; " +
               "matmult %s'") % (host,' '.join(parmSet),' '.join(parmSet))
        runner = Popen3(cmd)
        runfd = runner.fromchild
        socketsToSelect.append(runfd)
        fd2host[runfd] = host
        pcnt += 1
    else:
        readyFDs = 0
        (readyFDs,None,None) = select(socketsToSelect,[],[],30)
        for fd in readyFDs:
            line = fd.readline()
            if line:
                print '%s on %s' % (line.strip(),fd2host[fd])
            else:
                freeHosts.append(fd2host[fd])
                socketsToSelect.remove(fd)
                fd.close()
```

Figure 7.11: Manager for parameter study

socket), we close that socket, take it out of the list of sockets to select on, and add the corresponding host to the list of free hosts, since it can mow be assigned another subtask.

The manager exits once all the subtasks have been done and all the workers have completed. If we run this with

```
parmstudy.py hostfile parmfile | sort -n
```

then we will get the best combinations at the top of the list. Try it!

7.4 Sequence Matching in Computational Biology

One of the most exciting application areas for clusters is bioinformatics. An enormous amount of fundamental data is becoming available in the form of sequences: either nucleotide sequences (RNA and DNA) or amino acid sequences (proteins). In both cases the data comes encoded in the form of long strings of characters. Important biological information can be extracted from this data by matching, either exactly or inexactly, single strings of characters against other strings, or, more commonly, against large databases of strings in order to find similarities. The process is like a glorified `grep`.

7.4.1 BLAST

Widely distributed (sequential) tools exist for matching a string, or a small file of strings, against a database of other strings. One of the most widely used is a program called BLAST [2]. BLAST can deal with both nucleotide and amino acid sequences. Here we will focus on amino acid sequences, which describe the structure of proteins. BLAST, together with many other tools, uses FASTA format. Here is a single protein in FASTA format. Each letter in the sequence represents a single amino acid.

```
>sp|P28469 Alcohol dehydrogenase alpha chain (ADH).
 - Macaca mulatta
MSTAGKVIKCKAAVLWEVMKPFSIEDVEVAPPKAYEVRIKMVTVGICGTDDH
VVSGTMVTPLPVILGHEAAGIVESVGEGVTTVEPGDKVIPLALPQCGKCRI
CKTPERNYCLKNDVSNPRGTLQDGTSRFTCRGKPIHHFLGVSTFSQYTVVD
ENAVAKIDAASPMEKVCLIGCGFSTGYGSAVKVAKVTPGSTCAVFGLGGVG
LSAVMGCKAAGAARIIAVDINKDKFAKAKELGATECINPQDYKKPIQEVLK
EMTDGGVDFSFEVIGRLDTMMASLLCCHEACGTSVIVGVPPDSQNLSINPM
LLLTGRTWKGAVYGGFKSKEDIPKLVADFMAKKFSLDALITHVLPFEKINE
```

```
GFDLLRSGKSIRTILTF
```

Files containing proteins in FASTA format are fed into a program called `formatdb` to create an indexed database, consisting of three files, that is structured to facilitate searching for matches. Suppose we have constructed a small database of proteins and we wish to search for substring similarities between our protein above (P28469) and the proteins in our database (the three files produced from the file '`homodimer.faa`' by `formatdb`). Then we put our protein in a file that we might call '`homodimerstest.faa`' and do:

```
blastall -i homodimerstest.faa
         -d homodimer.faa
         -p blastp
```

The last parameter specifies the standard protein-protein matching algorithm. We get the following output, which lists the proteins that are similar in some way, sorted in decreasing order of similarity.

```
Query= sp|P28469 Alcohol dehydrogenase alpha chain  (ADH).
- Macaca mulatta  (375 letters)

Database: homodimer.faa
           30 sequences; 10,597 total letters

Searching.done
                                                                Score    E
Sequences producing significant alignments:                    (bits) Value

sp|P28469 Alcohol dehydrogenase alpha chain  (ADH). ...         721   0.0
sp|P14139 Alcohol dehydrogenase  (ADH). - Papio hama...         682   0.0
sp|Q03505 Alcohol dehydrogenase alpha chain  (ADH). ...         623   0.0
sp|Q64415 Alcohol dehydrogenase A chain . - Geomys k...         568   e-165
sp|Q64413 Alcohol dehydrogenase A chain . - Geomys b...         568   e-165
sp|P19631 Alcohol dehydrogenase alpha chain  (ADH3)....         538   e-156
sp|P80338 Alcohol dehydrogenase I . - Struthio camelus          536   e-155
sp|P49645 Alcohol dehydrogenase I . - Apteryx australis         533   e-155
...
```

We also get details about just exactly what the similarities were.

```
>sp|P14139 Alcohol dehydrogenase  (ADH). - Papio hamadryas
          Length = 375
```

```
 Score =  682 bits (1761), Expect = 0.0
 Identities = 336/375 (89%), Positives = 346/375 (92%)

Query: 1    MSTAGKVIKCKAAVLWEVMKPFSIEDVEVAPPKAYEVRIKMVTVGICGTDDHVVSGTMVT 60
            MSTAGKVIKCKAAVLWEV KPFSIEDVEVAPPKAYEVRIKMV VGIC TDDHVVSG +V+
Sbjct: 1    MSTAGKVIKCKAAVLWEVKKPFSIEDVEVAPPKAYEVRIKMVAVGICRTDDHVVSGNLVS 60

Query: 61   PLPVILGHEAAXXXXXXXXXXXXXXXXDKVIPLALPQCGKCRICKTPERNYCLKNDVSNP 120
            PLP ILGHEAA                DKVIPL  PQCGKCR+CK+PE NYC+KND+SNP
Sbjct: 61   PLPAILGHEAAGIVESVGEGVTTVKPGDKVIPLFTPQCGKCRVCKSPEGNYCVKNDLSNP 120

...
```

7.4.2 Running BLAST in Parallel

A single machine is sufficient for running small BLAST jobs, but some of the most important information is extracted by running jobs involving large numbers of sequences. One widely used database contains roughly 1.4 million sequences. Suppose we want to compare all the sequences in the database against one another. This is in some sense the largest possible BLAST job, but many other smaller BLAST jobs are still large.

Fortunately, parallelism abounds. Clusters are popular platforms in computational biology precisely because there is so much parallelism in many biologically significant computations. Moreover, most of them fit the manager/worker structure we have been discussing in this chapter. Here we will describe one way to carry out a large BLAST computation.

The plan is to use the manager/worker scheme described in the previous section with a number of changes.

1. The database will be distributed ahead of time to all the nodes of the cluster using either `rsync` or `rdist`.

2. The workers will run `blastall` with an input file consisting of some subset of the large number of input sequences, defined by the manager and referred to here as a *chunk* of input sequences. Each chunk will be sent to a worker by the manager over a socket connected to the worker.

3. Each subtask will consist of running `blastall` with a chunk of input sequences against the database.

4. The workers will be persistent. That is, instead of a new process being started by `ssh` for each subtask, each worker will remain running, exchanging messages over a socket with the manager, until the end of the job.

5. When a worker finishes a chunk, the output of the BLAST run will be copied to a directory of output files using `scp`.

6. The manager is not responsible for starting the workers. The manager will start off selecting only on his "listening" socket; as new workers are started (by whatever means) they connect to the manager and their sockets are added to the "select" list. Thus workers can come and go independently.

7. Individual worker processes can die, or nodes crash altogether, with no impact on the job as long as the manager keeps running. If a worker dies, it can be replaced by another one, which just connects to the manager on the manager's advertised listening port and joins the worker pool.

8. The manager keeps track of the chunks that have been assigned to workers, those that have been completed, and those that have not yet been assigned. Every time this information changes, the manager writes it to a file. Thus, the whole job can be restarted if the system crashes.

The code is not given here, but can be constructed using the Python code we used in Section 7.2.6.

The combination of allowing the pool of workers to vary in size and keeping track of exactly what work has been done contributes to the *fault tolerance* of this scheme: if workers or the machines they are running on fail, they can be replaced; and even if the manager dies or must be halted due to scheduling constraints, it can be restarted and pick up again where it left off.

We note that a number of useful tools for dealing with FASTA format in Python, and other Python-based tools for computational biology, can be found at `www.biopython.org`.

7.5 Decomposing Programs Into Communicating Processes

Not all problems can be divided into independent tasks. As we saw in Section 1.3.6, some applications are too large, in terms of their memory or compute needs, for a single processor or even a single SMP node. Solving these problems requires breaking the task into communicating (rather than independent) processes. In this section we will introduce two examples of decomposing a single task into multiple communicating processes. Because these programs are usually written using a message-passing programming model such as MPI or PVM, the details of implementing these examples are left to the chapters on these programming models.

7.5.1 Domain Decomposition

Many problems, such as the 3-dimensional partial differential equation (PDE) introduced in Section 1.3.6, are described by an approximation on a mesh of values. This mesh can be structured (also called regular) or unstructured. These meshes can be very large (as in the example in Chapter 1) and require more memory and computer power than a single processor or node can supply. Fortunately, the

For simplicity, we consider a two-dimensional example. A simple PDE is the Poisson equation,

$$\begin{aligned} \nabla^2 u &= f \text{ in the interior,} \\ u &= 0 \text{ on the boundary} \end{aligned}$$

where f is a given function and the problem is to find u. To further simplify the problem, we have chosen Dirichlet boundary conditions, which just means that the value of u along the boundary is zero. Finally, the domain is the unit square $[0,1] \times [0,1]$. A very simple discretization of this problem uses a finite difference approximation to the derivatives, yielding the approximation

$$\begin{aligned} \frac{u(x+h,y) - 2u(x,y) + u(x-h,y)}{h^2} & + \\ \frac{u(x,y+h) - 2u(x,y) + u(x,y-h)}{h^2} & = f(x,y) \end{aligned}$$

Defining a mesh of points $(x_i, y_j) = (i \times h, j \times h)$ with $h = 1/n$, and using the $u_{i,j}$ to represent the approximation of $u(x_i, y_j)$, we get

$$\begin{aligned} \frac{u_{i+1,j} - 2u_{i,j} + u_{i-1,j}}{h^2} & + \\ \frac{u_{i,j+1} - 2u_{i,j} + u_{i,j-1}}{h^2} & = f_{i,j} \end{aligned} \tag{7.1}$$

We can now represent this using two dimensional arrays. We'll use Fortran because Fortran has some features that will make these examples easier to write. We will use `U(i,j)` as our computed value for $u_{i,j}$.

To solve this approximation for the Poisson problem, we need to find the the values of `U`. This is harder than it may seem at first, because Equation 7.1 must be satisified at all points on the mesh (i.e., all values of i and j) simultaneously. In fact, this equation leads to a system of simultaneous linear equations. Excellent software exists to solve this problem (see Chapter 12), but we will use a very simple approach to illustrate how this problem can be parallelized. The first step is to write this problem as an iterative process

$$\begin{aligned} 4u_{i,j}^{new} &= u_{i+1,j} + u_{i-1,j} + u_{i,j+1} + u_{i,j-1} - h^2 f_{i,j} \\ &\text{or} \\ u_{i,j}^{new} &= \frac{1}{4}\left(u_{i+1,j} + u_{i-1,j} + u_{i,j+1} + u_{i,j-1} - h^2 f_{i,j}\right) \end{aligned}$$

This is the Jacobi iteration, and can be written in Fortran as

```
real UNEW(0:n,0:n), U(0:n,0:n), F(1:n-1,1:n-1)
... code to initialize U and F
do iter=1,itermax
    do j=1,n-1
        do i=1,n-1
            UNEW(i,j) = 0.25 * (U(i+1,j)+U(i-1,j) +     &
                                U(i,j+1)+U(i,j-1) - F(i,j))
        enddo
    enddo
    ... code to determine if the iteration has converged
enddo
```

At this point, we can see how to divide this problem across multiple processors. The simplest approach is to divide the mesh into small pieces, giving each piece to a separate processor. For example, we could divide the original mesh (`U(0:n,0:n)` in the code) into two parts: `U(0:n,0:n/2)` and (`U(0:n,n/2+1:n)`. This approach is called *domain decomposition*, and is based on using the decompositions of the physical domain (the unit square in this case) to create parallelism.

Applying this approach for two processors, we have the two code fragments shown in Figure 7.12. Note that each process now has only half of the data because each array is declared with only the data "owned" by that processor. This also shows why we used Fortran; the ability to specify the range of the indices for the arrays in Fortran makes these codes very easy to write.

However, unlike the decompositions into independent tasks in the first part of this chapter, this decomposition does not produce indepentent tasks. Consider the case of `j=n/2` in the original code. Process zero in Figure 7.12 computes the values of `UNEW(i,n/2)`. However, to do this, it needs the values of `U(i,n/2+1)`. This data

Code for process zero

```
real UNEW(0:n,0:n/2), U(0:n,0:n/2), F(1:n-1,1:n/2)
... code to initialize u and f
do iter=1,itermax
    do j=1,n/2
        do i=1,n-1
            UNEW(i,j) = 0.25 * (U(i+1,j)+U(i-1,j) +      &
                                U(i,j+1)+U(i,j-1) - F(i,j))
        enddo
    enddo
    ... code to determine if the iteration has converged
enddo
```

Code for process one

```
real UNEW(0:n,n/2+1:n), U(0:n,n/2+1:n), F(1:n-1,n/2+1:n-1)
... code to initialize u and f
do iter=1,itermax
    do j=n/2+1,n-1
        do i=1,n-1
            UNEW(i,j) = 0.25 * (U(i+1,j)+U(i-1,j) +      &
                                U(i,j+1)+U(i,j-1) - F(i,j))
        enddo
    enddo
    ... code to determine if the iteration has converged
enddo
```

Figure 7.12: Two code fragments for parallelizing the Poisson problem with the Jacobi iteration

is owned by processor one. In order to make this code work, we must communicate the data owned by processor one (the values of `U(i,n/2+1)` for `i=1,...,n-1`) to processor zero. We must also allocate another row of storage to hold these values; this extra row is often called a *ghost points* or a *halo*. The resulting code is shown in Figure 7.13.

Note also that although both processes have variables named `UNEW` and `i`, these are different variables. This kind of parallel programming model is sometimes called a *shared-nothing* model because no data (variables or instructions) are shared between the processes. Instead, explicit communication is required to move data

Code for process zero

```
real UNEW(0:n,0:n/2+1), U(0:n,0:n/2+1), F(1:n-1,1:n/2)
... code to initialize u and f
do iter=1,itermax
    ... code to Get u(i,n/2+1) from process one
    do j=1,n/2
        do i=1,n-1
            UNEW(i,j) = 0.25 * (U(i+1,j)+U(i-1,j) +     &
                                U(i,j+1)+U(i,j-1) - F(i,j))
        enddo
    enddo
    ... code to determine if the iteration has converged
enddo
```

Code for process one

```
real UNEW(0:n,n/2:n), U(0:n,n/2:n), F(1:n-1,n/2+1:n-1)
... code to initialize u and f
do iter=1,itermax
    ... code to Get u(i,n/2) from process zero
    do j=n/2+1,n-1
        do i=1,n-1
            UNEW(i,j) = 0.25 * (U(i+1,j)+U(i-1,j) +     &
                                U(i,j+1)+U(i,j-1) - F(i,j))
        enddo
    enddo
    ... code to determine if the iteration has converged
enddo
```

Figure 7.13: Two code fragments for parallelizing the Poisson problem with the Jacobi iteration, including the communication of ghost points. Note the changes in the declarations for `U` and `UNEW`.

from one process to another. Section 8.3 discusses this example in detail, using the Message Passing Interface (MPI) to implement the communication of data between the processors, using code written in C.

There are more complex and powerful domain decomposition techniques, but they all start from dividing the domain (usually the physical domain of the problem) into a number of separate pieces. These pieces must communicate along their edges at each step of the computation. As described in Section 1.3.6, a decomposition into squares (in two-dimensions) or cubes (in three dimensions) reduces the amount of data that must be communicated because those shapes maximize the volume to surface area ratio for rectangular solids.

7.5.2 Data Structure Decomposition

Not all problems have an obvious decomposition in terms of a physical domain. For these problems, a related approach that decomposes the data-structures in the application can be applied. An example of this kind of application is the solution of a system of linear equations $Ax = b$, where the equations are said to be *dense*. This simply means that most of the elements of the matrix describing the problem are non-zero. A good algorihm for solving this problem is called *LU* factorization, because it involves first computing a lower trianular matrix L and an upper triangular matrix U such that the original matrix A is given by the product LU. Because an lower (resp. upper) triangular matrix has only zero elements below (resp. above) the diagonal, it is easy to find the solution x once L and U are known. This is the algorithm used in the LINPACK [34] benchmark. A parallel verison of this is used in the High-Performance Linpack benchmark, and this section will sketch out some of the steps used in parallelizing this kind of problem.

The LU factorization algorithm looks something like the code shown in Figure 7.14, an $n \times n$ matrix A represented by the Fortran array `a(n,n)`.

An obvious way to decompose this problem, following the domain decomposition discussion, is to divide the matrix into groups of rows (or groups of columns):

$$A = \left(\begin{array}{c} \text{P0} \\ \hline \text{P1} \\ \hline \text{P2} \\ \hline \text{P3} \end{array} \right)$$

However, this will yield an inefficient program. Because of the outer-loop over the rows of the matrix (the loop over `i`), once `i` reaches `n/4` in the case of four processors, processor zero has no work left to do. As the computation proceeds, fewer and fewer processors can help with the computation. For this reason, more complex decompositions are used. For example, the ScaLAPACK library uses the two-dimensional block-cyclic distribution shown here:

$$A = \left(\begin{array}{c|c|c|c} \text{P0} & \text{P1} & \text{P0} & \text{P1} \\ \hline \text{P2} & \text{P3} & \text{P2} & \text{P3} \\ \hline \text{P0} & \text{P1} & \text{P0} & \text{P1} \\ \hline \text{P2} & \text{P3} & \text{P2} & \text{P3} \end{array} \right)$$

```
real a(n,n)
do i=i, n
   do k=1,i-1
       sum = 0
       do j=1,k-1
           sum = sum + a(i,j)*a(j,k)
       enddo
       a(i,k) = (a(i,k) - sum) / a(k,k)
   enddo
   do k=1,i
       sum = 0
       do j=1,k-1
           sum = sum + a(k,j)*a(j,i)
       enddo
       a(k,i) = a(k,i) - sum
   enddo
enddo
```

Figure 7.14: LU Factorization code. The factors L and U are computed in-place; that is, they are stored over the input matrix `a`.

This decomposition ensures that most processors are in use until the very end of the algorithm.

Just as in the domain decomposition example, communication is required to move data from one processor to another. In this example, data from the `i`th row must be communicated from the processors that hold that data to the processors holding the data needed for the computations (the loops over `j`). We do not show the communication here; see the literature on solving dense linear systems in parallel for details on these algorithms.

The technique of dividing the data structure among processors is a general one. Chosing the decomposition to use requires balancing the issues of load balance, communication, and algorithm complexity. Addressing these may suggest algorithmic modifications to provide better parallel performance. For example, certain variations of the LU factorization method described above may perform the floating-point operations in a different order. Because floating-point arithmetic is not associative, small differences in the results may occur. Other variations may produce answers that are equally valid as approximations but give results that are slightly different. Care must be exercised here, however, because some approximations are better behaved than others. Before changing the algorithm, make sure that you understand the consequences of any change. Consult with a numerical analysist or read about stability and well-posedness in any textbook on numerical computing.

7.5.3 Other Approaches

There are many techniques for creating parallel algorithms. Most involve dividing the problem into separate tasks that may need to communicate. For an effective decomposition for a Beowulf cluster, the amount of computation must be large relative to the amount of communication. Examples of these kinds of problems include sophisticated search and planning algorithms, where the results of some tests are used to speed up other tests (for example, a computation may discover that a subproblem has already been solved.).

Some computations are implemented as master/worker applications, where each worker is itself a parallel program (e.g., because of the memory needs or the requirement that the computation finish within a certain amount of time, such as overnight). Master/worker algorithms can also be made more sophisticated, guiding the choice and order of worker tasks by previous results returned by the workers.

8 Parallel Programming with MPI

William Gropp and Ewing Lusk

Chapter 7 described how parallel computation on a Beowulf is accomplished by dividing a computation into parts, making use of multiple processes and executing each on a separate processor. Sometimes an ordinary program can be used by all the processes, but with distinct input files or parameters. In such a situation, no communication occurs among the separate tasks. When the power of a parallel computer is needed to attack a large problem with a more complex structure, however, such communication is necessary.

One of the most straightforward approaches to communication is to have the processes coordinate their activities by sending and receiving messages, much as a group of people might cooperate to perform a complex task. This approach to achieving parallelism is called *message passing*.

In this chapter and the next, we show how to write parallel programs using MPI, the Message Passing Interface. MPI is a message-passing library specification. All three parts of the following description are significant.

- MPI addresses the message-passing model of parallel computation, in which processes with separate address spaces synchronize with one another and move data from the address space of one process to that of another by sending and receiving messages.[1]

- MPI specifies a library interface, that is, a collection of subroutines and their arguments. It is not a language; rather, MPI routines are called from programs written in conventional languages such as Fortran, C, and C++.

- MPI is a specification, not a particular implementation. The specification was created by the MPI Forum, a group of parallel computer vendors, computer scientists, and users who came together to cooperatively work out a community standard. The first phase of meetings resulted in a release of the standard in 1994 that is sometimes referred to as MPI-1. Once the standard was implemented and in wide use a second series of meetings resulted in a set of extensions, referred to as MPI-2. MPI refers to both MPI-1 and MPI-2.

As a specification, MPI is defined by a standards document, the way C, Fortran, or POSIX are defined. The MPI standards documents are available at `www.mpi-forum.org` and may be freely downloaded. The MPI-1 and MPI-2 standards are available as journal issues [72, 73] and in annotated form as books in

[1] Processes may be single threaded, with one program counter, or multithreaded, with multiple program counters. MPI is for communication among processes rather than threads. Signal handlers can be thought of as executing in a separate thread.

```
#include "mpi.h"
#include <stdio.h>

int main( int argc, char *argv[] )
{
    MPI_Init( &argc, &argv );
    printf( "Hello World\n" );
    MPI_Finalize();
    return 0;
}
```

Figure 8.1: Simple “Hello World” program in MPI.

this series [105, 46]. Implementations of MPI are available for almost all parallel computers, from clusters to the largest and most powerful parallel computers in the world. In Section 8.9 we summarizes the most popular cluster implementations.

A goal of the MPI Forum was to create a powerful, flexible library that could be implemented efficiently on the largest computers and provide a tool to attack the most difficult problems in parallel computing. It does not always do the simplest tasks in the simplest way but comes into its own as more complex functionality is needed. As a result, many tools and libraries have been built on top of MPI (see Table 9.1 and Chapter 12). To get the flavor of MPI programming, in this chapter and the next we work through a set of examples, starting with the simplest.

8.1 Hello World in MPI

To see what an MPI program looks like, we start with the classic “hello world” program. MPI specifies only the library calls to be used in a C, Fortran, or C++ program; consequently, all of the capabilities of the language are available. The simplest “Hello World” program is shown in Figure 8.1.

All MPI programs must contain one call to `MPI_Init` (or `MPI_Init_thread`, described in Section 9.9) and one to `MPI_Finalize`. All other[2] MPI routines must be called after `MPI_Init` and before `MPI_Finalize`. All C and C++ programs must also include the file '`mpi.h`'; Fortran programs must either `use` the `MPI` module or include `mpif.h`.

[2]There are a few exceptions, including `MPI_Initialized`.

```
#include "mpi.h"
#include <stdio.h>

int main( int argc, char *argv[] )
{
    int rank, size;

    MPI_Init( &argc, &argv );
    MPI_Comm_rank( MPI_COMM_WORLD, &rank );
    MPI_Comm_size( MPI_COMM_WORLD, &size );
    printf( "Hello World from process %d of %d\n", rank, size );
    MPI_Finalize();
    return 0;
}
```

Figure 8.2: A more interesting version of "Hello World".

The simple program in Figure 8.1 is not very interesting. In particular, all processes print the same text. A more interesting version has each process identify itself. This version, shown in Figure 8.2, illustrates several important points. Of particular note are the variables `rank` and `size`. Because MPI programs are made up of communicating processes, each process has its own set of variables. In this case, each process has its own address space containing its own variables `rank` and `size` (and `argc`, `argv`, etc.). The routine `MPI_Comm_size` returns the number of processes in the MPI job in the second argument. Each of the MPI processes is identified by a number, called the *rank*, ranging from zero to the value of `size` minus one. The routine `MPI_Comm_rank` returns in the second argument the rank of the process. The output of this program might look something like the following:

```
Hello World from process 0 of 4
Hello World from process 2 of 4
Hello World from process 3 of 4
Hello World from process 1 of 4
```

Note that the output is not ordered from processes 0 to 3. MPI does not specify the behavior of other routines or language statements such as `printf`; in particular, it does not specify the order of output from print statements. However, there are tools, built using MPI, that can provide ordered output of messages.

8.1.1 Compiling and Running MPI Programs

The MPI standard does not specify how to compile and link programs (neither do C or Fortran). However, most MPI implementations provide tools to compile and link programs.

For example, one popular implementation, MPICH, provides scripts to ensure that the correct include directories are specified and that the correct libraries are linked. The script `mpicc` can be used just like `cc` to compile and link C programs. Similarly, the scripts `mpif77`, `mpif90`, and `mpicxx` may be used to compile and link Fortran 77, Fortran, and C++ programs.

If you prefer not to use these scripts, you need only ensure that the correct paths and libraries are provided. The MPICH implementation provides the switch `-show` for `mpicc` that shows the command lines used with the C compiler and is an easy way to find the paths. Note that the name of the MPI library may be '`libmpich.a`', '`libmpi.a`', or something similar and that additional libraries, such as '`libsocket.a`' or '`libgm.a`', may be required. The include path may refer to a specific installation of MPI, such as '`/usr/include/local/mpich2-1.0/include`'.

Running an MPI program (in most implementations) also requires a special program, particularly when parallel programs are started by a batch system as described in Chapter 14. Many implementations provide a program `mpirun` that can be used to start MPI programs. For example, the command

```
mpirun -np 4 helloworld
```

runs the program `helloworld` using four processes.

The name and command-line arguments of the program that starts MPI programs were not specified by the original MPI standard, just as the C standard does not specify how to start C programs. However, the MPI Forum did recommend, as part of the MPI-2 standard, an `mpiexec` command and standard command-line arguments to be used in starting MPI programs. A number of MPI implementations including the all-new version of MPICH, called MPICH2, now provide `mpiexec`. The name `mpiexec` was selected because no MPI implementation was using it (many are using `mpirun`, but with incompatible arguments). The syntax is almost the same as for the MPICH version of `mpirun`; instead of using `-np` to specify the number of processes, the switch `-n` is used:

```
mpiexec -n 4 helloworld
```

The MPI standard defines additional switches for `mpiexec`; for more details, see Section 4.1, "Portable MPI Process Startup," in the MPI-2 standard. For greatest portability, we recommend that the `mpiexec` form be used; if your preferred implementation does not support **mpiexec**, point the maintainers to the MPI-2 standard.

Most MPI implementations will attempt to run each process on a different processor; most MPI implementations provide a way to select particular processors for each MPI process.

8.1.2 Adding Communication to Hello World

The code in Figure 8.2 does not guarantee that the output will be printed in any particular order. To force a particular order for the output, and to illustrate how data is communicated between processes, we add communication to the "Hello World" program. The revised program implements the following algorithm:

```
Find the name of the processor that is running the process
If the process has rank > 0, then
    send the name of the processor to the process with rank 0
Else
    print the name of this processor
    for each rank,
        receive the name of the processor and print it
Endif
```

This program is shown in Figure 8.3. The new MPI calls are to `MPI_Send` and `MPI_Recv` and to `MPI_Get_processor_name`. The latter is a convenient way to get the name of the processor on which a process is running. `MPI_Send` and `MPI_Recv` can be understood by stepping back and considering the two requirements that must be satisfied to communicate data between two processes:

1. Describe the data to be sent or the location in which to receive the data
2. Describe the destination (for a send) or the source (for a receive) of the data.

In addition, MPI provides a way to tag messages and to discover information about the size and source of the message. We will discuss each of these in turn.

Describing the Data Buffer

A data buffer typically is described by an address and a length, such as "`a,100`," where `a` is a pointer to 100 bytes of data. For example, the Unix `write` call describes the data to be written with an address and length (along with a file descriptor). MPI generalizes this to provide two additional capabilities: describing

```
#include "mpi.h"
#include <stdio.h>

int main( int argc, char *argv[] )
{
    int  numprocs, myrank, namelen, i;
    char processor_name[MPI_MAX_PROCESSOR_NAME];
    char greeting[MPI_MAX_PROCESSOR_NAME + 80];
    MPI_Status status;

    MPI_Init( &argc, &argv );
    MPI_Comm_size( MPI_COMM_WORLD, &numprocs );
    MPI_Comm_rank( MPI_COMM_WORLD, &myrank );
    MPI_Get_processor_name( processor_name, &namelen );

    sprintf( greeting, "Hello, world, from process %d of %d on %s",
             myrank, numprocs, processor_name );

    if ( myrank == 0 ) {
        printf( "%s\n", greeting );
        for ( i = 1; i < numprocs; i++ ) {
            MPI_Recv( greeting, sizeof( greeting ), MPI_CHAR,
                      i, 1, MPI_COMM_WORLD, &status );
            printf( "%s\n", greeting );
        }
    }
    else {
        MPI_Send( greeting, strlen( greeting ) + 1, MPI_CHAR,
                  0, 1, MPI_COMM_WORLD );
    }

    MPI_Finalize( );
    return 0;
}
```

Figure 8.3: A more complex "Hello World" program in MPI. Only process 0 writes to stdout; each process sends a message to process 0.

noncontiguous regions of data and describing data so that it can be communicated between processors with different data representations. To do this, MPI uses three values to describe a data buffer: the address, the (MPI) datatype, and the number or *count* of the items of that datatype. For example, a buffer `a` containing four C `ints` is described by the triple "`a, 4, MPI_INT`." There are predefined MPI datatypes for all of the basic datatypes defined in C, Fortran, and C++. The most common datatypes are shown in Table 8.1.

C		Fortran	
	MPI type		MPI type
int	`MPI_INT`	INTEGER	`MPI_INTEGER`
double	`MPI_DOUBLE`	DOUBLE PRECISION	`MPI_DOUBLE_PRECISION`
float	`MPI_FLOAT`	REAL	`MPI_REAL`
long	`MPI_LONG`		
char	`MPI_CHAR`	CHARACTER	`MPI_CHARACTER`
		LOGICAL	`MPI_LOGICAL`
—	`MPI_BYTE`	—	`MPI_BYTE`
—	`MPI_PACKED`	—	`MPI_PACKED`

Table 8.1: The most common MPI datatypes. C and Fortran types on the same row are often but not always the same type. The type `MPI_BYTE` is used for raw data bytes and does not correspond to any particular datatype. The type `MPI_PACKED` is used for data that was incrementally packed with the routine `MPI_Pack`. The C++ MPI datatypes have the same name as the C datatypes but without the `MPI_` prefix, for example, `MPI::INT`.

Describing the Destination or Source

The destination or source is specified by using the rank of the process. MPI generalizes the notion of destination and source rank by making the rank relative to a group of processes. This group may be a subset of the original group of processes. Allowing subsets of processes and using relative ranks make it easier to use MPI to write component-oriented software (more on this in Section 9.4). The MPI object that defines a group of processes (and a special communication context that will be discussed in Section 9.4) is called a *communicator*. Thus, sources and destinations are given by two parameters: a rank and a communicator. The communicator `MPI_COMM_WORLD` is predefined and contains all of the processes started by `mpirun` or `mpiexec`. As a source, the special value `MPI_ANY_SOURCE` may be used to indicate that the message may be received from any rank of the MPI processes in this MPI program.

Selecting among Messages

The "extra" argument for `MPI_Send` is a nonnegative integer *tag* value. This tag allows a program to send one extra number with the data. `MPI_Recv` can use this value either to select which message to receive (by specifying a specific tag value) or to use the tag to convey extra data (by specifying the *wild card* value `MPI_ANY_TAG`). In the latter case, the tag value of the received message is stored in the `status` argument (this is the last parameter to `MPI_Recv` in the C binding). This is a structure in C, an integer array in Fortran, and a class in C++. The tag and rank of the sending process can be accessed by referring to the appropriate element of `status` as shown in Table 8.2.

C	Fortran	C++
`status.MPI_SOURCE`	`status(MPI_SOURCE)`	`status.Get_source()`
`status.MPI_TAG`	`status(MPI_TAG)`	`status.Get_tag()`

Table 8.2: Accessing the source and tag after an `MPI_Recv`.

Determining the Amount of Data Received

The amount of data received can be found by using the routine `MPI_Get_count`. For example,

```
MPI_Get_count( &status, MPI_CHAR, &num_chars );
```

returns in `num_chars` the number of characters sent. The second argument should be the same MPI datatype that was used to receive the message. (Since many applications do not need this information, the use of a routine allows the implementation to avoid computing `num_chars` unless the user needs the value.)

Our example provides a maximum-sized buffer in the receive. It is also possible to find the amount of memory needed to receive a message by using `MPI_Probe`, as shown in Figure 8.4.

MPI guarantees that messages are ordered, that is, that messages sent from one process to another arrive in the same order in which they were sent and that an `MPI_Recv` after an `MPI_Probe` will receive the message that the probe returned

```
char *greeting;
int num_chars, src;
MPI_Status status;
...
MPI_Probe( MPI_ANY_SOURCE, 1, MPI_COMM_WORLD, &status );
MPI_Get_count( &status, MPI_CHAR, &num_chars );
greeting = (char *)malloc( num_chars );
src      = status.MPI_SOURCE;
MPI_Recv( greeting, num_chars, MPI_CHAR,
          src, 1, MPI_COMM_WORLD, &status );
```

Figure 8.4: Using `MPI_Probe` to find the size of a message before receiving it.

information on as long as the same message selection criteria (source rank, communicator, and message tag) are used. Note that in this example, the source for the `MPI_Recv` is specified as `status.MPI_SOURCE`, not `MPI_ANY_SOURCE`, to ensure that the message received is the same as the one about which `MPI_Probe` returned information.

8.2 Manager/Worker Example

We now begin a series of examples illustrating approaches to parallel computations that accomplish useful work. While each parallel application is unique, a number of paradigms have emerged as widely applicable, and many parallel algorithms are variations on these patterns.

One of the most universal is the "manager/worker" or "task parallelism" approach. The idea is that the work that needs to be done can be divided by a "manager" into separate pieces and the pieces can be assigned to individual "worker" processes. Thus the manager executes a different algorithm from that of the workers, but all of the workers execute the same algorithm. Most implementations of MPI (including MPICH2) allow MPI processes to be running different programs (executable files), but it is often convenient (and in some cases required) to combine the manager and worker code into a single program with the structure shown in Figure 8.5.

Sometimes the work can be evenly divided into exactly as many pieces as there are workers, but a more flexible approach is to have the manager keep a pool of units of work larger than the number of workers and assign new work dynamically to workers as they complete their tasks and send their results back to the manager.

```
#include "mpi.h"

int main( int argc, char *argv[] )
{
    int numprocs, myrank;

    MPI_Init( &argc, &argv );
    MPI_Comm_size( MPI_COMM_WORLD, &numprocs );
    MPI_Comm_rank( MPI_COMM_WORLD, &myrank );

    if ( myrank == 0 )          /* manager process */
        manager_code ( numprocs );
    else                        /* worker process */
        worker_code ( );
    MPI_Finalize( );
    return 0;
}
```

Figure 8.5: Framework of the matrix-vector multiply program.

This approach, called *self-scheduling*, works well in the presence of tasks of varying sizes or workers of varying speeds.

We illustrate this technique with a parallel program to multiply a matrix by a vector. (A Fortran version of this same program can be found in [48].) This program is not a particularly good way to carry out this operation, but it illustrates the approach and is simple enough to be shown in its entirety. The program multiplies a square matrix `a` by a vector `b` and stores the result in `c`. The units of work are the individual dot products of the rows of `a` with the vector `b`. Thus the manager, code for which is shown in Figure 8.6, starts by initializing `a`. The manager then sends out initial units of work, one row to each worker. We use the MPI tag on each such message to encode the row number we are sending. Since row numbers start at 0 but we wish to reserve 0 as a tag with the special meaning of "no more work to do," we set the tag to one greater than the row number. When a worker sends back a dot product, we store it in the appropriate place in `c` and send that worker another row to work on. Once all the rows have been assigned, workers completing a task are sent a "no more work" message, indicated by a message with tag 0.

The code for the worker part of the program is shown in Figure 8.7. A worker initializes `b`, receives a row of `a` in a message, computes the dot product of that

```
#define SIZE 1000
#define MIN( x, y ) ((x) < (y) ? x : y)

void manager_code( int numprocs )
{
    double a[SIZE][SIZE], c[SIZE];

    int i, j, sender, row, numsent = 0;
    double dotp;
    MPI_Status status;

    /* (arbitrary) initialization of a */
    for (i = 0; i < SIZE; i++ )
        for ( j = 0; j < SIZE; j++ )
            a[i][j] = ( double ) j;

    for ( i = 1; i < MIN( numprocs, SIZE ); i++ ) {
        MPI_Send( a[i-1], SIZE, MPI_DOUBLE, i, i, MPI_COMM_WORLD );
        numsent++;
    }
    /* receive dot products back from workers */
    for ( i = 0; i < SIZE; i++ ) {
        MPI_Recv( &dotp, 1, MPI_DOUBLE, MPI_ANY_SOURCE, MPI_ANY_TAG,
                  MPI_COMM_WORLD, &status );
        sender = status.MPI_SOURCE;
        row    = status.MPI_TAG - 1;
        c[row] = dotp;
        /* send another row back to this worker if there is one */
        if ( numsent < SIZE ) {
            MPI_Send( a[numsent], SIZE, MPI_DOUBLE, sender,
                      numsent + 1, MPI_COMM_WORLD );
            numsent++;
        }
        else                        /* no more work */
            MPI_Send( MPI_BOTTOM, 0, MPI_DOUBLE, sender, 0,
                      MPI_COMM_WORLD );
    }
}
```

Figure 8.6: The matrix-vector multiply program, manager code.

```
void worker_code( void )
{
    double b[SIZE], c[SIZE];
    int i, row, myrank;
    double dotp;
    MPI_Status status;

    for ( i = 0; i < SIZE; i++ ) /* (arbitrary) b initialization */
        b[i] = 1.0;

    MPI_Comm_rank( MPI_COMM_WORLD, &myrank );
    if ( myrank <= SIZE ) {
        MPI_Recv( c, SIZE, MPI_DOUBLE, 0, MPI_ANY_TAG,
                  MPI_COMM_WORLD, &status );
        while ( status.MPI_TAG > 0 ) {
            row = status.MPI_TAG - 1;
            dotp = 0.0;
            for ( i = 0; i < SIZE; i++ )
                dotp += c[i] * b[i];
            MPI_Send( &dotp, 1, MPI_DOUBLE, 0, row + 1,
                      MPI_COMM_WORLD );
            MPI_Recv( c, SIZE, MPI_DOUBLE, 0, MPI_ANY_TAG,
                      MPI_COMM_WORLD, &status );
        }
    }
}
```

Figure 8.7: The matrix-vector multiply program, worker code.

row and the vector b, and then returns the answer to the manager, again using the tag to identify the row. A worker repeats this until it receives the "no more work" message, identified by its tag of 0.

This program requires at least two processes to run: one manager and one worker. Unfortunately, adding more workers is unlikely to make the job go faster. We can analyze the cost of computation and communication mathematically and see what happens as we increase the number of workers. Increasing the number of workers will decrease the amount of computation done by each worker, and since they work in parallel, this should decrease total elapsed time. On the other hand, more workers mean more communication, and the cost of communicating a number is usually much greater than the cost of an arithmetical operation on it. The study of how the total time for a parallel algorithm is affected by changes in the number of processes, the problem size, and the speed of the processor and communication network is called *scalability analysis*. We analyze the matrix-vector program as a simple example.

First, let us compute the number of floating-point operations. For a matrix of size n, we have to compute n dot products, each of which requires n multiplications and $n-1$ additions. Thus the number of floating-point operations is $n \times (n+(n-1)) = n \times (2n-1) = 2n^2-n$. If T_{calc} is the time it takes a processor to do one floating-point operation,[3] then the total computation time is $(2n^2-n) \times T_{calc}$. Next, we compute the number of communications, defined as sending one floating-point number. (We ignore for this simple analysis the effect of message lengths; following Section 1.3, we could model these as $s+rn$, where $T_{comm} \approx r$.) Leaving aside the cost of communicating `b` (perhaps it is computed locally in a preceding step), we have to send each row of `a` and receive back one dot product answer. So the number of floating-point numbers communicated is $(n \times n)+n = n^2+n$. If T_{comm} is the time to communicate one number, we get $(n^2+n) \times T_{comm}$ for the total communication time. Thus the ratio of communication time to computation time is

$$\left(\frac{n^2+n}{2n^2-n}\right) \times \left(\frac{T_{comm}}{T_{calc}}\right).$$

In many computations the ratio of communication to computation can be reduced almost to 0 by making the problem size larger. Our analysis shows that this is not the case here. As n gets larger, the term on the left approaches $\frac{1}{2}$. Thus we can expect communication costs to prevent this algorithm from showing good speedups, even on large problem sizes.

The situation is better in the case of matrix-*matrix* multiplication, which could be carried out by a similar algorithm. We would replace the vectors `b` and `c` by matrices, send the entire matrix `b` to the workers at the beginning of the computation, and then hand out the rows of `a` as work units, just as before. The workers would compute an entire row of the product, consisting of the dot products of the row of `a` with all of the column of `b`, and then return a row of `c` to the manager.

Let us now do the scalability analysis for the matrix-matrix multiplication. Again we ignore the initial communication of `b`. The number of operations for one dot product is $n+(n+1)$ as before, and the total number of dot products calculated is

[3] The symbol f was used in Section 1.3; we use T_{calc} here because of the more prominent role of floating point in this analysis.

n^2. Thus the total number of operations is $n^2 \times (2n-1) = 2n^3 - n^2$. The number of numbers communicated has gone up to $(n \times n) + (n \times n) = 2n^2$. So the ratio of communication time to computation time has become

$$\left(\frac{2n^2}{2n^3 - n^2}\right) \times \left(\frac{T_{comm}}{T_{calc}}\right),$$

which does tend to 0 as n gets larger. Thus, for large matrices the communication costs play less of a role.

Two other difficulties with this algorithm might occur as we increase the size of the problem and the number of workers. The first is that as messages get longer, the workers waste more time waiting for the next row to arrive. A solution to this problem is to "double buffer" the distribution of work, having the manager send two rows to each worker to begin with, so that a worker always has some work to do while waiting for the next row to arrive.

Another difficulty for larger numbers of processes can be that the manager can become overloaded so that it cannot assign work in a timely manner. This problem can most easily be addressed by increasing the size of the work unit, but in some cases it is necessary to parallelize the manager task itself, with multiple managers handling subpools of work units.

A more subtle problem has to do with *fairness*: ensuring that all worker processes are fairly serviced by the manager. MPI provides several ways to ensure fairness; see [48, Section 7.1.4].

8.3 Two-Dimensional Jacobi Example with One-Dimensional Decomposition

A common use of parallel computers in scientific computation is to approximate the solution of a partial differential equation (PDE). One of the most common PDEs, at least in textbooks, is the Poisson equation (here shown in two dimensions):

$$\frac{\partial^2 u}{\partial x^2} + \frac{\partial^2 u}{\partial y^2} = f(x, y) \text{ in } \Gamma \tag{8.1}$$

$$u = g(x, y) \text{ on } \partial\Gamma \tag{8.2}$$

This equation is used to describe many physical phenomena, including fluid flow and electrostatics. The equation has two parts: a differential equation applied everywhere within a domain Γ (8.1) and a specification of the value of the unknown u along the boundary of Γ (the notation $\partial\Gamma$ means "the boundary of Γ"). For example, if this equation is used to model the equilibrium distribution of temperature

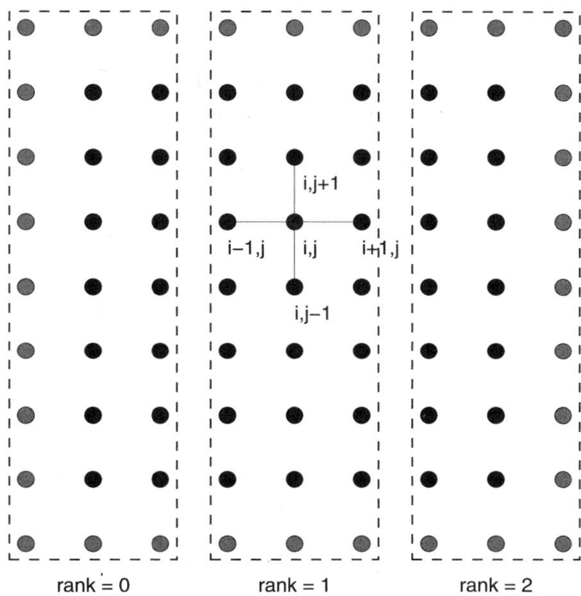

Figure 8.8: Domain and 9×9 computational mesh for approximating the solution to the Poisson problem.

inside a region, the boundary condition $g(x, y)$ specifies the applied temperature along the boundary, $f(x, y)$ is zero, and $u(x, y)$ is the temperature within the region. To simplify the rest of this example, we will consider only a simple domain Γ consisting of a square (see Figure 8.8).

To compute an approximation to $u(x, y)$, we must first reduce the problem to finite size. We cannot determine the value of u everywhere; instead, we will approximate u at a finite number of points (x_i, y_j) in the domain, where $x_i = i \times h$ and $y_j = j \times h$. (Of course, we can define a value for u at other points in the domain by interpolating from these values that we determine, but the approximation is defined by the value of u at the points (x_i, y_j).) These points are shown as black disks in Figure 8.8. Because of this regular spacing, the points are said to make up a *regular mesh*. At each of these points, we approximate the partial derivatives with finite differences. For example,

$$\frac{\partial^2 u}{\partial x^2}(x_i, y_j) \approx \frac{u(x_{i+1}, y_j) - 2u(x_i, y_j) + u(x_{i-1}, y_j)}{h^2}.$$

If we now let $u_{i,j}$ stand for our approximation to solution of Equation 8.1 at the point (x_i, y_j), we have the following set of simultaneous linear equations for the values of u:

$$\frac{u_{i+1,j} - 2u_{i,j} + u_{i-1,j}}{h^2} + \frac{u_{i,j+1} - 2u_{i,j} + u_{i,j-1}}{h^2} = f(x_i, y_j). \tag{8.3}$$

For values of u along the boundary (e.g., at $x = 0$ or $y = 1$), the value of the boundary condition g is used. If $h = 1/(n+1)$ (so there are $n \times n$ points in the interior of the mesh), this gives us n^2 simultaneous linear equations to solve.

Many methods can be used to solve these equations. In fact, if you have this particular problem, you should use one of the numerical libraries described in Section 12.2. In this section, we describe a very simple (and inefficient) algorithm because, from a parallel computing perspective, it illustrates how to program more effective and general methods. The method that we use is called the *Jacobi* method for solving systems of linear equations. The Jacobi method computes successive approximations to the solution of Equation 8.3 by rewriting the equation as follows:

$$\begin{aligned} u_{i+1,j} &- 2u_{i,j} + u_{i-1,j} + u_{i,j+1} - 2u_{i,j} + u_{i,j-1} = h^2 f(x_i, y_j) \\ u_{i,j} &= \frac{1}{4}(u_{i+1,j} + u_{i-1,j} + u_{i,j+1} + u_{i,j-1} - h^2 f_{i,j}). \end{aligned} \tag{8.4}$$

Each step in the Jacobi iteration computes a new approximation to $u_{i,j}^{N+1}$ in terms of the surrounding values of u^N:

$$u_{i,j}^{N+1} = \frac{1}{4}(u_{i+1,j}^N + u_{i-1,j}^N + u_{i,j+1}^N + u_{i,j-1}^N - h^2 f_{i,j}). \tag{8.5}$$

This is our algorithm for computing the approximation to the solution of the Poisson problem. We emphasize that the Jacobi method is a poor numerical method but that the same communication patterns apply to many finite difference, volume, or element discretizations solved by iterative techniques.

In the uniprocessor version of this algorithm, the solution u is represented by a two-dimensional array `u[max_n][max_n]`, and the iteration is written as follows:

```
double u[NX+2][NY+2], u_new[NX+2][NY+2], f[NX+2][NY+2];
int    i, j;
...
for (i=1;i<=NX;i++)
   for (j=1;j<=NY;j++)
      u_new[i][j] = 0.25 * (u[i+1][j] + u[i-1][j] +
                            u[i][j+1] + u[i][j-1] - h*h*f[i][j]);
```

Here, we let u[0][j], u[n+1][j], u[i][0], and u[i][n+1] hold the values of the boundary conditions g (these correspond to $u(0, y)$, $u(1, y)$, $u(x, 0)$, and $u(x, 1)$ in Equation 8.1). To parallelize this method, we must first decide how to decompose the data structure u and u_new across the processes. Many possible decompositions exist. One of the simplest is to divide the domain into strips as shown in Figure 8.8.

Let the local representation of the array u be ulocal; that is, each process declares an array ulocal that contains the part of u held by that process. No process has all of u; the data structure representing u is *decomposed* among all of the processes. The code that is used on each process to implement the Jacobi method is

```
double ulocal_new[NLOCAL][NY+2];
...
for (i=i_start;i<=i_end;i++)
  for (j=1;j<=NY;j++)
    ulocal_new[i-i_start][j] =
       0.25 * (ulocal[i-i_start+1][j] + ulocal[i-i_start-1][j] +
               ulocal[i-i_start][j+1] + ulocal[i-i_start][j-1] -
               h*h*flocal[i-i_start][j]);
```

where i_start and i_end describe the strip on this process (in practice, the loop would be from zero to i_end-i_start; we use this formulation to maintain the correspondence with the uniprocessor code). We have defined ulocal so that ulocal[0][j] corresponds to u[i_start][j] in the uniprocessor version of this code. Using variable names such as ulocal that make it obvious which variables are part of a distributed data structure is often a good idea.

From this code, we can see what data we need to communicate. For i=i_start we need the values of u[i_start-1][j] for j between 1 and NY, and for i=i_end we need u[i_end+1][j] for the same range of j. These values belong to the adjacent processes and must be communicated. In addition, we need a location in which to store these values. We could use a separate array, but for regular meshes the most common approach is to use *ghost* or *halo* cells, where extra space is set aside in the ulocal array to hold the values from neighboring processes. In this case, we need only a single column of neighboring data, so we will let u_local[1][j] correspond to u[i_start][j]. This changes the code for a single iteration of the loop to

```
exchange_nbrs( ulocal, i_start, i_end, left, right );
for (i_local=1; i_local<=i_end-i_start+1; i_local++)
  for (j=1; j<=NY; j++)
```

```
void exchange_nbrs( double ulocal[][NY+2], int i_start, int i_end,
                    int left, int right )
{
    MPI_Status status;
    int c;

    /* Send and receive from the left neighbor */
    MPI_Send( &ulocal[1][1], NY, MPI_DOUBLE, left, 0,
              MPI_COMM_WORLD );
    MPI_Recv( &ulocal[0][1], NY, MPI_DOUBLE, left, 0,
              MPI_COMM_WORLD, &status );

    /* Send and receive from the right neighbor */
    c = i_end - i_start + 1;
    MPI_Send( &ulocal[c][1], NY, MPI_DOUBLE, right, 0,
              MPI_COMM_WORLD );
    MPI_Recv( &ulocal[c+1][1], NY, MPI_DOUBLE, right, 0,
              MPI_COMM_WORLD, &status );
}
```

Figure 8.9: A simple version of the neighbor exchange code. See the text for a discussion of the limitations of this routine.

```
      ulocal_new[i_local][j] =
         0.25 * (ulocal[i_local+1][j] + ulocal[i_local-1][j] +
                 ulocal[i_local][j+1] + ulocal[i_local][j-1] -
                 h*h*flocal[i_local][j]);
```

where we have converted the `i` index to be relative to the start of `ulocal` rather than `u`. All that is left is to describe the routine `exchange_nbrs` that exchanges data between the neighboring processes. A very simple routine is shown in Figure 8.9.

We note that ISO/ANSI C (unlike Fortran) does not allow runtime dimensioning of multidimensional arrays. To keep these examples simple in C, we use compile-time dimensioning of the arrays. An alternative in C is to pass the arrays as one-dimensional arrays and compute the appropriate offsets.

The values `left` and `right` are used for the ranks of the left and right neighbors, respectively. These can be computed simply by using the following:

```
int rank, size, left, right;
...
```

```
/* Better exchange code.  */
void exchange_nbrs( double ulocal[][NY+2], int i_start, int i_end,
                    int left, int right )
{
    MPI_Status status;
    int c;

    /* Send and receive from the left neighbor */
    MPI_Sendrecv( &ulocal[1][1], NY, MPI_DOUBLE, left, 0,
                  &ulocal[0][1], NY, MPI_DOUBLE, left, 0,
                  MPI_COMM_WORLD, &status );

    /* Send and receive from the right neighbor */
    c = i_end - i_start + 1;
    MPI_Sendrecv( &ulocal[c][1], NY, MPI_DOUBLE, right, 0,
                  &ulocal[c+1][1], NY, MPI_DOUBLE, right, 0,
                  MPI_COMM_WORLD, &status );
}
```

Figure 8.10: A better version of the neighbor exchange code.

```
    MPI_Comm_rank( MPI_COMM_WORLD, &rank );
    MPI_Comm_size( MPI_COMM_WORLD, &size );
    left  = rank - 1;
    right = rank + 1;
    if (left < 0)       left  = MPI_PROC_NULL;
    if (right >= size) right = MPI_PROC_NULL;
```

The special rank MPI_PROC_NULL indicates the edges of the mesh. If MPI_PROC_NULL is used as the source or destination rank in an MPI communication call, the operation is ignored. MPI also provides routines to compute the neighbors in a regular mesh of arbitrary dimension and to help an application choose a decomposition that is efficient for the parallel computer.

The code in exchange_nbrs will work with most MPI implementations for small values of n but, as described in Section 9.3, is not good practice (and will fail for values of NY greater than an implementation-defined threshold). A better approach in MPI is to use the MPI_Sendrecv routine when exchanging data between two processes, as shown in Figure 8.10.

In Sections 9.3 and 9.7, we discuss other implementations of the exchange routine that can provide higher performance. MPI support for more scalable decompositions of the data is described in Section 9.3.2.

8.4 Collective Operations

A *collective* operation is an MPI function that is called by all processes belonging to a communicator. (If the communicator is `MPI_COMM_WORLD`, this means all processes, but MPI allows collective operations on other sets of processes as well.) Collective operations involve communication and also sometimes computation, but since they describe particular patterns of communication and computation, the MPI implementation may be able to optimize them beyond what is possible by expressing them in terms of MPI point-to-point operations such as `MPI_Send` and `MPI_Recv`. The patterns are also easier to express with collective operations.

Here we introduce two of the most commonly used collective operations and show how the communication in a parallel program can be expressed entirely in terms of collective operations with no individual `MPI_Sends` or `MPI_Recvs` at all. The program shown in Figure 8.11 computes the value of π by numerical integration. Since

$$\int_0^1 \frac{1}{1+x^2}dx = \arctan(x)|_0^1 = \arctan(1) - \arctan(0) = \arctan(1) = \frac{\pi}{4},$$

we can compute π by integrating the function $f(x) = 4/(1 + x^2)$ from 0 to 1. We compute an approximation by dividing the interval [0,1] into some number of subintervals and then computing the total area of these rectangles by having each process compute the areas of some subset. We could do this with a manager/worker algorithm, but here we preassign the work. In fact, each worker can compute its set of tasks, and so the "manager" can be a worker, too, instead of just managing the pool of work. The more rectangles there are, the more work there is to do and the more accurate the resulting approximation of π is. To experiment, let us make the number of subintervals a command-line argument. (Although the MPI standard does not guarantee that any process receive command-line arguments, in most implementations, especially for Beowulf clusters, one can assume that at least the process with rank 0 can use `argc` and `argv`, although they may not be meaningful until after `MPI_Init` is called.) In our example, process 0 sets n, the number of subintervals, to `argv[1]`. Once a process knows n, it can claim approximately $\frac{1}{n}$ of the work by claiming every nth rectangle, starting with the one numbered by its

```
#include "mpi.h"
#include <stdio.h>
#include <math.h>
double f(double a) { return (4.0 / (1.0 + a*a)); }

int main(int argc,char *argv[])
{
  int  n, myid, numprocs, i;
  double PI25DT = 3.141592653589793238462643;
  double mypi, pi, h, sum, x;
  double startwtime = 0.0, endwtime;

  MPI_Init(&argc,&argv);
  MPI_Comm_size(MPI_COMM_WORLD,&numprocs);
  MPI_Comm_rank(MPI_COMM_WORLD,&myid);
  if (myid == 0) {
      startwtime = MPI_Wtime();
      n = atoi(argv[1]);
  }
  MPI_Bcast(&n, 1, MPI_INT, 0, MPI_COMM_WORLD);
  h   = 1.0 / (double) n;
  sum = 0.0;
  for (i = myid + 1; i <= n; i += numprocs) {
      x = h * ((double)i - 0.5);
      sum += f(x);
  }
  mypi = h * sum;
  MPI_Reduce(&mypi, &pi, 1, MPI_DOUBLE, MPI_SUM, 0, MPI_COMM_WORLD);
  if (myid == 0) {
      endwtime = MPI_Wtime();
      printf("pi is approximately %.16f, Error is %.16f\n",
             pi, fabs(pi - PI25DT));
      printf("wall clock time = %f\n", endwtime-startwtime);
  }
  MPI_Finalize();
  return 0;
}
```

Figure 8.11: Computing π using collective operations.

own rank. Thus, process j computes the areas of rectangles j , $j + n$, $j + 2n$, and so on.

Not all MPI implementations make the command-line arguments available to *all* processes, however, so we start by having process 0 send n to each of the other processes. We could have a simple loop, sending n to each of the other processes one at a time, but this is inefficient. If we know that the same message is to be delivered to all the other processes, we can ask the MPI implementation to do this in a more efficient way than with a series of `MPI_Send`s and `MPI_Recv`s.

Broadcast (`MPI_Bcast`) is an example of an MPI *collective* operation. A collective operation must be called by all processes in a communicator. This allows an implementation to arrange the communication and computation specified by a collective operation in a special way. In the case of `MPI_Bcast`, an implementation is likely to use a tree of communication, sometimes called a spanning tree, in which process 0 sends its message to a second process, then both processes send to two more, and so forth. In this way most communication takes place in parallel, and all the messages have been delivered in $\log_2 n$ steps.

The precise semantics of `MPI_Bcast` is sometimes confusing. The first three arguments specify a message with (address, count, datatype) as usual. The fourth argument (called the *root* of the broadcast) specifies which of the processes owns the data that is being sent to the other processes. In our case it is process 0. `MPI_Bcast` acts like an `MPI_Send` on the root process and like an `MPI_Recv` on all the other processes, but the call itself looks the same on each process. The last argument is the communicator that the collective call is *over*. All processes in the communicator must make this same call. Before the call, n is valid only at the root; after `MPI_Bcast` has returned, all processes have a copy of the value of n.

Next, each process, including process 0, adds up the areas of its rectangles into the local variable `mypi`. Instead of sending these values to one process and having that process add them up, however, we use another collective operation, `MPI_Reduce`. `MPI_Reduce` performs not only collective communication but also collective computation. In the call

```
MPI_Reduce( &mypi, &pi, 1, MPI_DOUBLE, MPI_SUM, 0,
            MPI_COMM_WORLD);
```

the sixth argument is again the root. All processes call `MPI_Reduce`, and the root process gets back a result in the second argument. The result comes from performing an arithmetic operation, in this case summation (specified by the fifth argument), on the data items on all processes specified by the first, third, and fourth arguments.

Process 0 concludes by printing out the answer, the difference between this approximation and a previously computed accurate value of π, and the time it took to compute it. This illustrates the use of `MPI_Wtime`.

`MPI_Wtime` returns a double-precision floating-point number of seconds. This value has no meaning in itself, but the *difference* between two such values is the wall-clock time between the two calls. Note that calls on two different processes are not guaranteed to have any relationship to one another, unless the MPI implementation promises that the clocks on different processes are synchronized (see `MPI_WTIME_IS_GLOBAL` in any of the MPI books).

The routine `MPI_Allreduce` computes the same result as `MPI_Reduce` but returns the result to all processes, not just the root process. For example, in the Jacobi iteration, it is common to use the two-norm of the difference between two successive iterations as a measure of the convergence of the solution.

```
...
norm2local = 0.0;
for (ii=1; ii<i_end-i_start+1; ii++)
    for (jj=1; jj<NY; jj++)
        norm2local += ulocal[ii][jj] * ulocal[ii][jj];
MPI_Allreduce( &norm2local, &norm2, 1, MPI_DOUBLE,
               MPI_COMM_WORLD, MPI_SUM );
norm2 = sqrt( norm2 );
```

Note that `MPI_Allreduce` is not a routine for computing the norm of a vector. It merely combines values contributed from each process in the communicator.

8.5 Parallel Monte Carlo Computation

One of the types of computation that is easiest to parallelize is the *Monte Carlo* family of algorithms. In such computations, a random number generator is used to create a number of independent trials. Statistics done with the outcomes of the trials provide a solution to the problem.

We illustrate this technique with another computation of the value of π. If we select points at random in the unit square $[0, 1] \times [0, 1]$ and compute the percentage of them that lies inside the quarter circle of radius 1, then we will be approximating $\frac{\pi}{4}$. (See [48] for a more detailed discussion together with an approach that does not use a parallel random number generator.) We use the SPRNG parallel random number generator (`sprng.cs.fsu.edu`). The code is shown in Figure 8.12.

```
#include "mpi.h"
#include <stdio.h>
#define SIMPLE_SPRNG                /* simple interface  */
#define USE_MPI                     /* use MPI           */
#include "sprng.h"                  /* SPRNG header file */
#define BATCHSIZE 1000000

int main( int argc, char *argv[] )
{
    int i, j, numin = 0, totalin, total, numbatches, rank, numprocs;
    double x, y, approx, pi = 3.141592653589793238462643;

    MPI_Init( &argc, &argv );
    MPI_Comm_size( MPI_COMM_WORLD, &numprocs );
    MPI_Comm_rank( MPI_COMM_WORLD, &rank );
    if ( rank == 0 ) {
        numbatches = atoi( argv[1] );
    }
    MPI_Bcast( &numbatches, 1, MPI_INT, 0, MPI_COMM_WORLD );
    for ( i = 0; i < numbatches; i++ ) {
        for ( j = 0; j < BATCHSIZE; j++ ) {
            x = sprng( ); y = sprng( );
            if ( x * x + y * y  < 1.0 )
                numin++;
        }
        MPI_Reduce( &numin, &totalin, 1, MPI_INT, MPI_SUM, 0,
                    MPI_COMM_WORLD );
        if ( rank == 0 ) {
            total = BATCHSIZE * ( i + 1 ) * numprocs;
            approx = 4.0 * ( (double) totalin / total );
            printf( "pi = %.16f; error = %.16f, points = %d\n",
                    approx, pi - approx, total );
        }
    }
    MPI_Finalize( );
    return 0;
}
```

Figure 8.12: Computing π using the Monte Carlo method.

The defaults in SPRNG make it extremely easy to use. Calls to the `sprng` function return a random number between 0.0 and 1.0, and the stream of random numbers on the different processes is independent. We control the *grain size* of the parallelism by the constant `BATCHSIZE`, which determines how much computation is done before the processes communicate. Here a million points are generated, tested, and counted before we collect the results to print them. We use `MPI_-Bcast` to distribute the command-line argument specifying the number of batches, and we use `MPI_Reduce` to collect at the end of each batch the number of points that fell inside the quarter circle, so that we can print the increasingly accurate approximations to π.

8.6 MPI Programming without MPI

One of the major strengths of MPI is the support that MPI provides for building libraries of useful software. These libraries often eliminate the need for explicit programming in MPI; in cases where no suitable library exists, MPI's design encourages the use of modern software engineering techniques in creating application-specific support libraries. Some of the available libraries are shown in Table 9.1; Chapter 12 discusses some of the more important libraries in more detail. To illustrate the power of libraries in MPI, this section shows several programs that solve partial differential equations without the explicit use of MPI. These are still MPI programs, however, and must be run using `mpiexec` just like other MPI programs.

8.6.1 A Poisson Solver

Section 8.3 presented an MPI code that implemented the Jacobi method for solving a simple partial differential equation. This example provided a good introduction to MPI but is not meant as an example of how to solve differential equations in parallel with MPI. For that task, one or more parallel libraries should be used. Figure 8.13 shows a short code for solving two-dimentional Poisson problems on a regular mesh. This code makes very heavy use of two libraries:

- PETSc [9, 10, 8] is a library designed to solve in parallel linear and nonlinear equations that arise from PDEs. PETSc uses MPI.
- "regmesh" is an application-specific library written to simplify the use of PETSc for regular mesh discritizations of elliptic partial differential equations. This library makes no explicit MPI calls; instead, all parallelism is handled through PETSc.

```
#include <math.h>
#include "petsc.h"
#include "regmesh.h"

/* This function is used to define the right-hand side of the
   Poisson equation to be solved */
double func( double x, double y )
{
    return sin(x)*sin(y);
}

int main( int argc, char *argv[] )
{
    SLES    sles;
    RegMesh g;
    Mat     m;
    Vec     b, x;
    Viewer  viewer;
    int     its;

    PetscInitialize( &argc, &argv, 0, 0 );

    g = Create2dDistributedArray( n, n, 0.0, 1.0, 0.0, 1.0 );
    m = ApplyStencilTo2dDistributedArray( g, REGMESH_LAPLACIAN );
    b = SetVectorFromFunction( g, (RegMeshFunc)func );
    VecDuplicate( b, &x );
    SLESCreate( PETSC_COMM_WORLD, &sles );
    SLESSetOperators( sles, m, m, DIFFERENT_NONZERO_PATTERN);
    SLESSetFromOptions( sles );
    SLESSolve( sles, b, x, &its );
    PetscViewerNetcdfOpen( PETSC_COMM_WORLD, "solution.nc",
                           PETSC_NETCDF_CREATE, &viewer );
    MeshDAView( g, viewer );
    RegMeshDestroy( g ); MatDestroy( m ); VecDestroy( b ); VecDestroy( x );
    SLESDestroy( sles );
    PetscFinalize( );
    return 0;
}
```

Figure 8.13: A parallel Poisson solver that exploits two libraries written with MPI.

The routines in this example perform the following operations:

`PetscInitialize` — Initialize the PETSc library

`Create2dDistributedArray` — Create a handle (g) to a structure that defines a two-dimensional mesh of size $n \times n$ on the unit square. This mesh is distributed across all processes. This routine is from regmesh.

`ApplyStencilTo2dDistributedArray` — Create the sparse matrix (returned as the value `m`) by applying a disretization stencil to the mesh `g`. The discretization is predefined and is the same one described in Section 8.3. This routine is from regmesh but returns a handle to a PETSc matrix.

`SetVectorFromFunction` — Return the vector representing the right-hand side of the problem by applying a function `func` to the mesh `g`. This routine is from regmesh but returns a handle to a PETSc vector.

`SLESCreate` — Create a PETSc *context* for solving a linear system of equations. This is a handle for the internal structure that PETSc uses to hold all of the information, such as the choice of algorithm, used to solve a linear system of equations.

`SLESSetOperators` — Define the linear system to solve by specifying the matrices. This routine allows several variations of specification; this example uses the most common.

`SLESSetFromOptions` — Set the various parameter choices from the command line and a defaults file. This lets the user choose the iterative method and preconditioner at run time by using command-line arguments.

`SLESSolve` — Solve the linear system $Ax = b$, returning the solution in the PETSc vector `x`. This is a PETSc routine.

`PetscViewerNetcdfOpen` — Create a "viewer" by which a PETSc vector can be written to a file (here '`solution.nc`') using the community-standard NetCDF format [95]. This is a PETSc routine.

`MeshDAView` — Output the solution using the viewer. This makes use of the PETSc "distributed array" structure as well as other data from the regmesh `g`.

xxxDestroy — Free the space used by the mesh, vector, and matrix structures, as well as the linear equation solver.

An advantage of this approach to writing parallel programs is that it allows the application programmer to take advantage of the best numerical algorithms and parallel tools. For example, the command-line

```
mpiexec -n 64 poisson -pc_type=ilu -ksp_type=gmres
```

runs this example on 64 processors, using the GMRES iterative method with a block incomplete factorization preconditioner. Changing the choice of iterative method or preconditioner is accomplished by simply changing the command-line arguments.

In addition, this example includes output of the solution, using parallel I/O into a file (when supported by a parallel file system such as PVFS, described in Chapter 19). Further, this file is written in a standard format called NetCDF; a wide variety of tools exist for postprocessing this file, including programs to display the contents graphically.

Regmesh is a specialized library designed to simplify the creation of parallel programs that work with regular meshes. More importantly, Regmesh is an example of structuring an application so that the important operations are organized into logical units.

8.6.2 Solving a Nonlinear Partial Differential Equation

To further illustrate the power of MPI libraries, Figure 8.14 shows the main program for solving the problem

$$\begin{aligned} \nabla^2 u &= -\lambda e^u \text{ on } \Omega = [0,1] \times [0,1] \\ u &= 0 \text{ on the boundary of } \Omega. \end{aligned}$$

This problem is the *Bratu* problem. This code uses only PETSc and, as a result, is somewhat longer. Not included in this figure are some of the routines for computing the Jacobian elements, evaluating the function, setting the initial guess, or checking for errors. A complete version of this example is included as '`src/snes/examples/tutorials/ex5.c`' in the PETSc distribution. Even this program is only a few hundred lines, including extensive comments.

These two examples show that tools are available that make writing parallel programs using MPI relatively easy, as long as high-quality libraries are available for the operations needed by an application. Fortunately, in many areas of science and engineering, such libraries are available, and more are added all the time.

8.7 Installing MPICH2 under Linux

The MPICH implementation of MPI [47] is one of the most popular versions of MPI. Recently, MPICH was completely rewritten; the new version is called MPICH2 and includes all of MPI, both MPI-1 and MPI-2. In this section we describe how to

```
#include "petsc.h"
/* User-defined data describing the problem */
typedef struct {
   DA           da;             /* distributed array data structure */
   double       param;          /* test problem parameter */
} AppCtx;
extern int FormFunctionLocal(DALocalInfo*,double**,double**,AppCtx*);
extern int FormJacobianLocal(DALocalInfo*,double**,Mat,AppCtx*);
int main(int argc,char *argv[])
{
  SNES      snes;      /* nonlinear solver */
  Vec       x,r;       /* solution, residual vectors */
  Mat       A,J;       /* Jacobian matrix */
  AppCtx    user;      /* user-defined work context */
  int       its;       /* iterations for convergence */

  PetscInitialize(&argc,&argv,(char *)0,help);
  user.param = 6.0;
  SNESCreate(PETSC_COMM_WORLD,&snes);
  DACreate2d(PETSC_COMM_WORLD,DA_NONPERIODIC,DA_STENCIL_STAR,
                  -4,-4,PETSC_DECIDE,PETSC_DECIDE,
                  1,1,PETSC_NULL,PETSC_NULL,&user.da);
  DACreateGlobalVector(user.da,&x);
  VecDuplicate(x,&r);
  DASetLocalFunction(user.da,(DALocalFunction1)FormFunctionLocal);
  DASetLocalJacobian(user.da,(DALocalFunction1)FormJacobianLocal);
  SNESSetFunction(snes,r,SNESDAFormFunction,&user);
  DAGetMatrix(user.da,MATMPIAIJ,&J);
  A    = J;
  SNESSetJacobian(snes,A,J,SNESDAComputeJacobian,&user);
  SNESSetFromOptions(snes);
  FormInitialGuess(&user,x);
  SNESSolve(snes,x,&its);
  PetscPrintf(PETSC_COMM_WORLD,"Number of Newton iterations = %d\n",its);

  MatDestroy(J); VecDestroy(x); VecDestroy(r); SNESDestroy(snes);
  DADestroy(user.da);
  PetscFinalize();
  return 0;
}
```

Figure 8.14: The main program in a high-level program to solve a nonlinear partial differential equation using PETSc.

obtain, build, and install MPICH2 on a Beowulf cluster. We then describe how to set up an MPICH2 environment in which MPI programs can be compiled, executed, and debugged. We recommend MPICH2 for all Beowulf clusters. Original MPICH is still available but is no longer being developed.

8.7.1 Obtaining and Installing MPICH2

The current version of MPICH2 is available at `www.mcs.anl.gov/mpi/mpich`.[4] From there one can download a `gzip`ped tar file containing the complete MPICH2 distribution, which contains

- all source code for MPICH2;
- configure scripts for building MPICH2 on a wide variety of environments, including Linux clusters;
- simple example programs like the ones in this chapter;
- MPI compliance test programs; and
- the MPD parallel process management system.

MPICH2 is architected so that a number of communication infrastructures can be used. These are called "devices." The device that is most relevant for the Beowulf environment is the channel device (also called "ch3" because it is the third version of the channel approach for implementing MPICH); this supports a variety of communication methods and can be built to support the use of both TCP over sockets and shared memory. In addition, MPICH2 uses a portable interface to process management systems, providing access both to external process managers (allowing the process managers direct control over starting and running the MPI processes) and to the `MPD` scalable process manager that is included with MPICH2.

To run your first MPI program, carry out the following steps (assuming a C-shell):

1. Download `mpich2.tar.gz` from `www.mcs.anl.gov/mpi/mpich` or from `ftp://ftp.mcs.anl.gov/pub/mpi/mpich2.tar.gz`
2. `tar xvfz mpich2.tar.gz ; cd mpich2-1.0`
3. `configure <configure options> >& configure.log`. Most users should specify a `prefix` for the installation path when configuring:

[4] As this chapter is being written, the current version of MPICH2 is 0.93, and the current verison of MPICH is 1.2.5.

```
configure --prefix=/usr/local/mpich2-1.0 >& configure.log
```

By default, this creates the `channel` device for communication with TCP over sockets.

4. `make >& make.log`
5. `make install >& install.log`
6. Add the '`<prefix>/bin`' directory to your path; for example, for `tcsh`, do

   ```
   setenv PATH <prefix>/bin:$PATH
   rehash
   ```

7. `cd examples`
8. `make cpi`
9. Before running your first program, you must start the `mpd` process manager. To run on a single node, you need only do `mpd -d &`. See Section 8.7.3 for details on starting `mpd` on multiple nodes.
10. `mpiexec -n 4 cpi` (if '.' is not in your path, you will need to use `mpiexec -n 4 ./cpi`).

8.7.2 Building MPICH2 for SMP Clusters

To build MPICH2 to support SMP clusters and to use shared-memory to communicate data between processes on the same node, configure MPICH2 with the additional option `--with-device=ch3:ssm`, as in

```
configure --with-device=ch3:ssm --prefix=/usr/local/mpich2-1.0
```

In a system that contains both SMP nodes and uniprocessor nodes, or if you want an executable that can run on both kinds of nodes, use this version of the ch3 device.

8.7.3 Starting and Managing MPD

Running MPI programs with the MPD process manager assumes that the `mpd` daemon is running on each machine in your cluster. In this section we describe how to start and manage these daemons. The `mpd` and related executables are built when you build and install MPICH2 with the default process manager. The code for the MPD demons are found in '`<prefix-directory>/bin`', which you should ensure is in your path. A set of MPD daemons can be started with the command

```
mpichboot <file> <num>
```

where `file` is the name of a file containing the host names of your cluster and `num` is the number of daemons you want to start. The startup script uses `ssh` to start the daemons, but if it is more convenient, they can be started in other ways. The first one can be started with `mpd -t`. The first daemon, started in this way, will print out the port it is listening on for new `mpd`s to connect to it. Each subsequent `mpd` is given a host and port to connect to. The `mpichboot` script automates this process. At any time you can see what `mpd`s are running by using `mpdtrace`.

An `mpd` is identified by its host and a port. A number of commands are used to manage the ring of `mpd`s:

`mpdhelp` prints a short description of the available `mpd` commands.

`mpdcleanup` cleans up `mpd` if a problem occurred. For example, it can repair the local Unix socket that is used to communicate with the MPD system if the MPD ring crashed.

`mpdtrace` causes each `mpd` in the ring to respond with a message identifying itself and its neighbors.

`mpdallexit` causes all `mpd`s to exit gracefully.

`mpdlistjobs` lists active jobs for the user managed by `mpd`s in ring. With the command-line option `-a` or `--all`, lists the jobs for all user4s.

`mpdkilljob job_id` kills all of the processes of the specified job.

`mpdsigjob sigtype job_id` delivers the specified signal to the specified job. Signals are specified using the name of the signal, e.g., `SIGSTOP`.

Several options control the behavior of the daemons, allowing them to be run either by individual users or by `root` without conflicts. The most important is

`-d` background or "daemonize"; this is used to start an `mpd` daemon that will run without being connected to a terminal session.

8.7.4 Running MPICH2 Jobs under MPD

MPICH2 jobs are run under the MPD process manager by using the `mpiexec` command. MPD's `mpiexec` is consistent with the specification in the MPI standard and also offers a few extensions, such as passing of environment variables to individual MPI processes. An example of the simplest way to run an MPI program is

```
mpiexec -n 32 cpi
```

which runs the MPI program `cpi` with 32 processes and lets the MPD process manager choose which hosts to run the processes on. Specific hosts and separate executables can be specified:

```
mpiexec -n 1 -host node0 manager : -n 1 -host node1 worker
```

A configuration file can be used when a command line in the above format would be too long:

```
mpiexec -configfile multiblast.cfg
```

where the file '`multiblast.cfg`' contains

```
-n 1 -host node0 blastmanager
-n 1 -host node1 blastworker
...
-n 1 -host node31 blastworker
```

One can use

```
mpiexec -help
```

to discover all the possible command-line arguments for `mpiexec`.

The program `mpiexec` runs in a separate (non-MPI) process that starts the MPI processes running the specified executable. It serves as a single-process representative of the parallel MPI processes in that signals sent to it, such as `^Z` and `^C` are conveyed by the MPD system to all the processes. The output streams `stdout` and `stderr` from the MPI processes are routed back to the `stdout` and `stderr` of `mpiexec`. As in most MPI implementations, `mpirun`'s `stdin` is routed to the `stdin` of the MPI process with rank 0.

8.7.5 Debugging MPI Programs

Debugging parallel programs is notoriously difficult. Parallel programs are subject not only to the usual kinds of bugs but also to new kinds having to do with timing and synchronization errors. Often, the program "hangs," for example when a process is waiting for a message to arrive that is never sent or is sent with the wrong tag. Parallel bugs often disappear precisely when you add code to try to identify the bug, a particularly frustrating situation. In this section we discuss three approaches to parallel debugging.

The `printf` Approach

Just as in sequential debugging, you often wish to trace interesting events in the program by printing trace messages. Usually you wish to identify a message by the rank of the process emitting it. This can be done explicitly by putting the rank in the trace message. As noted above, using the "line labels" option (`-l`) with `mpirun` in the `ch_p4mpd` device in MPICH adds the rank automatically.

Using a Commercial Debugger

The TotalView© debugger from Etnus, Ltd. [119] runs on a variety of platforms and interacts with many vendor implementations of MPI, including MPICH on Linux clusters. For the `ch_p4` device you invoke TotalView with

```
mpirun -tv <other arguments>
```

and with the `ch_p4mpd` device you use

```
totalview mpirun <other arguments>
```

That is, again `mpirun` represents the parallel job as a whole. TotalView has special commands to display the message queues of an MPI process. It is possible to attach TotalView to a collection of processes that are already running in parallel; it is also possible to attach to just one of those processes.

Check the documentation on how to use Totalview with `mpiexec` in MPICH2, or with other implementations of MPI.

8.7.6 Other Compilers

MPI implementations are usually configured and built by using a particular set of compilers. For example, the `configure` script in the MPICH implementation determines many of the characteristics of the compiler and the associated runtime libraries. As a result, it can be difficult to use a different C or Fortran compiler with a particular MPI implementation. This can be a problem for Beowulf clusters because several different compilers are commonly used.

The compilation scripts (e.g., `mpicc`) accept an argument to select a different compiler. For example, if MPICH is configured with `gcc` but you want to use `pgcc` to compile and build an MPI program, you can use

```
mpicc -cc=pgcc -o hellow hellow.c
mpif77 -fc=pgf77 -o hellowf hellowf.f
```

This works as long as both compilers have similar capabilities and properties. For example, they must use the same lengths for the basic datatypes, and their runtime libraries must provide the functions that the MPI implementation requires. If the compilers are similar in nature but require slightly different libraries or compiler options, then a *configuration file* can be provided with the `-config=name` option:

```
mpicc -config=pgcc -o hellow hellow.c
```

Details on the format of the configuration files can be found in the MPICH installation manual.

The same approach can be used with Fortran as for C. If, however, the Fortran compilers are not compatible (for example, they use different values for Fortran `.true.` and `.false.`), then you must build new libraries. MPICH2 provides a way to build just the necessary Fortran support. See the MPICH2 installation manual for details.

8.8 Tools for MPI Programs

A number of tools are available for developing, testing, and tuning MPI programs. In this section, we describe some of the tools that are available from `www.mcs.anl.gov/mpi`. These tools work with most MPI implementations, not just MPICH2.

8.8.1 Profiling Libraries

The MPI Forum decided not to standardize any particular tool but rather to provide a general mechanism for intercepting calls to MPI functions, which is the sort of capability that tools need. The MPI standard requires that any MPI implementation provide two entry points for each MPI function: its normal `MPI_` name and a corresponding `PMPI` version. This strategy allows a user to write a custom

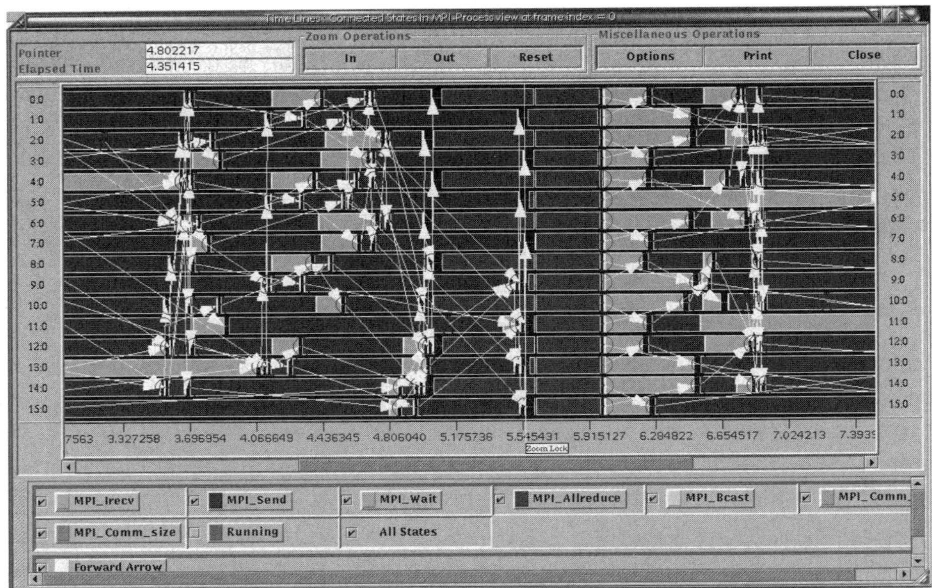

Figure 8.15: Jumpshot displaying message traffic.

version of `MPI_Send`, for example, that carries out whatever extra functions might be desired, calling `PMPI_Send` to perform the usual operations of `MPI_Send`. When the user's custom versions of MPI functions are placed in a library and the library precedes the usual MPI library in the link path, the user's custom code will be invoked around all MPI functions that have been replaced.

Three such "profiling libraries" and some tools for creating more are provided in the MPE tools. MPE is available at `ftp://ftp.mcs.anl.gov/pub/mpi/mpe.tar.gz`.

8.8.2 Visualizing Parallel Program Behavior

The detailed behavior of a parallel program is surprisingly difficult to predict. It is often useful to examine a graphical display that shows the exact sequence of states that each process went through and what messages were exchanged at what times and in what order. The data for such a tool can be collected by means of a profiling library. One tool for looking at such log files is Jumpshot [126]. A screenshot of Jumpshot in action is shown in Figure 8.15.

The horizontal axis represents time, and there is a horizontal line for each process. The states that processes are in during a particular time interval are represented by colored rectangles. Messages are represented by arrows. It is possible to zoom in for microsecond-level resolution in time.

8.9 MPI Implementations for Clusters

Many implementations of MPI are available for clusters; Table 8.3 lists some of the available implementations. These range from commercially supported software to supported, freely available software to distributed research project software.

Name	URL
BeoMPI	`www.scyld.com`
LAM/MPI	`www.lam-mpi.org`
MPICH	`www.mcs.anl.gov/mpi/mpich`
MPICH-GM	`www.myricom.com`
MPICH-G2	`www.niu.edu/mpi`
MPICH-Madeleine	`dept-info.labri.u-bordeaux.fr/~mercier/mpi.html`
MPICH-V	`www.lri.fr/~gk/MPICH-V/`
MPI/GAMMA	`www.disi.unige.it/project/gamma/mpigamma/`
MPI/Pro	`www.mpi-softtech.com`
MP-MPICH	`www.lfbs.rwth-aachen.de/mp-mpich/`
MVABICH	`nowlab.cis.ohio-state.edu/projects/mpi-iba/`
MVICH	`www.nersc.gov/research/ftg/mvich/`
ScaMPI	`www.scali.com`

Table 8.3: Some MPI implementations for Linux.

9 Advanced Topics in MPI Programming

William Gropp and Ewing Lusk

In this chapter we continue our exploration of parallel programming with MPI. We describe capabilities that are more specific to MPI than to part of the message-passing programming model in general. We cover the more advanced features of MPI, such as dynamic process management, parallel I/O, and remote memory access. These features are often described as MPI-2 because they were added to the MPI standard in a second round of specification; however, MPI means both the original (MPI-1) and new (MPI-2) features. We will use the term "MPI-2" to emphasize that a feature was added to MPI in the second round.

9.1 Dynamic Process Management in MPI

A new feature of MPI is the ability of an MPI program to create new MPI processes and communicate with them. (In the original MPI specification, the number of processes was fixed at startup.) MPI calls this capability (together with related capabilities such as connecting two independently started MPI jobs) *dynamic process management*. Three main issues are introduced by this collection of features:

- maintaining simplicity and flexibility;
- interacting with the operating system, a parallel process manager, and perhaps a job scheduler; and
- avoiding race conditions that could compromise correctness.

The key to avoiding race conditions is to make creation of new processes a collective operation, over both the processes creating the new processes and the new processes being created. Using a collective operation in creating new processes also provides scalability and addresses these other issues.

9.1.1 Intercommunicators

Recall that an MPI communicator consists of a group of processes together with a communication context. Strictly speaking, the communicators we have dealt with so far are *intracommunicators*. There is another kind of communicator, called an *intercommunicator*. An intercommunicator binds together a communication context and *two* groups of processes, called (from the point of view of a particular process) the *local* group and the *remote* group. Processes are identified by rank in group, but ranks in an intercommunicator always refer to the processes in the remote group. That is, an `MPI_Send` using an intercommunicator sends a message to the process with the destination rank in the *remote* group of the intercommunicator. Collective operations are also defined for intercommunicators; see [50, Chapter 7] for details.

9.1.2 Spawning New MPI Processes

We are now in a position to explain exactly how new MPI processes are created by an already running MPI program. The MPI function that creates these processes is `MPI_Comm_spawn`. Its key features are the following.

- It is collective over the communicator of processes initiating the operation (called the *parents*) and also collective with the calls to `MPI_Init` in the processes being created (called the *children*). That is, `MPI_Comm_spawn` does not return in the parents until it has been called in all the parents and `MPI_Init` has been called in all the children.
- It returns an intercommunicator in which the local group contains the parents and the remote group contains the children.
- The new processes, which must call `MPI_Init`, have their own `MPI_COMM_WORLD`, consisting of all the processes created by this one collective call to `MPI_Comm_spawn`.
- The function `MPI_Comm_get_parent`, called by the children, returns an intercommunicator with the children in the local group and the parents in the remote group.
- The collective function `MPI_Intercomm_merge` may be called by parents and children to create a normal (intra)communicator containing all the processes, both old and new, but for many communication patterns this is not necessary.

9.1.3 Revisiting Matrix-Vector Multiplication

Here we illustrate the use of `MPI_Comm_spawn` by revisiting the matrix-vector multiply program of Section 8.2. Instead of starting with a fixed number of processes, we compile separate executables for the manager and worker programs, start the manager with

```
mpiexec -n 1 manager <number-of-workers>
```

and then let the manager create the worker processes dynamically. We assume that only the manager has the matrix `a` and the vector `b` and broadcasts them to

```
#include "mpi.h"
#include <stdio.h>
#define SIZE 10000

int main( int argc, char *argv[] )
{
    double a[SIZE][SIZE], b[SIZE], c[SIZE];
    int i, j, row, numworkers;
    MPI_Status status;
    MPI_Comm workercomm;

    MPI_Init( &argc, &argv );
    if ( argc != 2 || !isnumeric( argv[1] ))
        printf( "usage: %s <number of workers>\n", argv[0] );
    else
        numworkers = atoi( argv[1] );

    MPI_Comm_spawn( "worker", MPI_ARGV_NULL, numworkers,
                    MPI_INFO_NULL,
                    0, MPI_COMM_SELF, &workercomm, MPI_ERRCODES_IGNORE );
    ...
    /* initialize a and b */
    ...
    /* send b to each worker */
    MPI_Bcast( b, SIZE, MPI_DOUBLE, MPI_ROOT, workercomm );
    ...
    /* then normal manager code as before*/
    ...
    MPI_Finalize();
    return 0;
}
```

Figure 9.1: Dynamic process matrix-vector multiply program, manager part.

the workers after the workers have been created. The program for the manager is shown in Figure 9.1 and the code for the workers is shown in Figure 9.2.

Let us consider in detail the call in the manager that creates the worker processes.

```
MPI_Comm_spawn( "worker", MPI_ARGV_NULL, numworkers,
            MPI_INFO_NULL,
            0, MPI_COMM_SELF, &workercomm, MPI_ERRCODES_IGNORE );
```

It has eight arguments. The first is the name of the executable to be run by the new processes. The second is the null-terminated argument vector to be passed to all of the new processes; here we are passing no arguments at all, so we specify the special value MPI_ARGV_NULL. Next is the number of new processes to create. The fourth argument is an MPI "Info" object, which can be used to specify special environment- and/or implementation-dependent parameters, such as the names of the nodes to start the new processes on. In our case we leave this decision to the MPI implementation or local process manager, and we pass the special value MPI_INFO_NULL. The next argument is the "root" process for this call to MPI_-Comm_spawn; it specifies which process in the communicator given in the following argument is supplying the valid arguments for this call. The communicator we are using consists here of just the one manager process, so we pass MPI_COMM_SELF. Next is the address of the new intercommunicator to be filled in, and finally an array of error codes for examining possible problems in starting the new processes. Here we use MPI_ERRCODES_IGNORE to indicate that we will not be looking at these error codes.

Code for the worker processes that are spawned is shown in Figure 9.2. It is essentially the same as the worker subroutine in the preceding chapter but is an MPI program in itself. Note the use of intercommunicator broadcast in order to receive the vector b from the parents. We free the parent intercommunicator with MPI_Comm_free before exiting.

9.1.4 More on Dynamic Process Management

For more complex examples of the use of MPI_Comm_spawn, including how to start processes with different executables or different argument lists, see [50, Chapter 7]. MPI_Comm_spawn is the most basic of the functions provided in MPI for dealing with a dynamic MPI environment. By querying the attribute MPI_UNIVERSE_SIZE, you can find out how many processes can be usefully created. Separately started MPI computations can find each other and connect with MPI_Comm_connect and MPI_Comm_accept. Processes can exploit non-MPI connections to "bootstrap" MPI communication. These features are explained in detail in [50].

```
#include "mpi.h"

int main( int argc, char *argv[] )
{
    int numprocs, myrank;
    double b[SIZE], c[SIZE];
    int i, row, myrank;
    double dotp;
    MPI_Status status;
    MPI_Comm parentcomm;

    MPI_Init( &argc, &argv );
    MPI_Comm_size( MPI_COMM_WORLD, &numprocs );
    MPI_Comm_rank( MPI_COMM_WORLD, &myrank );

    MPI_Comm_get_parent( &parentcomm );

    MPI_Bcast( b, SIZE, MPI_DOUBLE, 0, parentcomm );

    ...
    /* same as worker code from original matrix-vector multiply */
    ...

    MPI_Comm_free( &parentcomm );
    MPI_Finalize( );
    return 0;
}
```

Figure 9.2: Dynamic process matrix-vector multiply program, worker part.

9.2 Fault Tolerance

Communicators are a fundamental concept in MPI. Their sizes are fixed at the time they are created, and the efficiency and correctness of collective operations rely on this fact. Users sometimes conclude from the fixed size of communicators that MPI provides no mechanism for writing fault-tolerant programs. Now that we have introduced intercommunicators, however, we are in a position to discuss how this topic might be addressed and how you might write a manager-worker program with MPI in such a way that it would be fault tolerant. In this context we mean

```
/* highly incomplete */

MPI_Comm worker_comms[MAX_WORKERS];
int last_row_sent[MAX_WORKERS];

rc = MPI_Send( a[numsent], SIZE, MPI_DOUBLE, 0, numsent+1,
               worker_comms[sender] );
if ( rc != MPI_SUCCESS ) {
    /* Check that error class is one we can recover from */
    ...
    MPI_Comm_spawn( "worker" , ... );
```

Figure 9.3: Fault-tolerant manager.

that if one of the worker processes terminates abnormally, instead of terminating the job you will be able to carry on the computation with fewer workers, or perhaps dynamically replace the lost worker.

The key idea is to create a separate (inter)communicator for each worker and use it for communications with that worker rather than use a communicator that contains all of the workers. If an implementation returns "invalid communicator" from an `MPI_Send` or `MPI_Recv` call, then the manager has lost contact only with one worker and can still communicate with the other workers through the other, still-intact communicators. Since the manager will be using separate communicators rather than separate ranks in a larger communicator to send and receive message from the workers, it might be convenient to maintain an array of communicators and a parallel array to remember which row has been last sent to a worker, so that if that worker disappears, the same row can be assigned to a different worker. Figure 9.3 shows these arrays and how they might be used. What we are doing with this approach is recognizing that two-party communication can be made fault tolerant, since one party can recognize the failure of the other and take appropriate action. A normal MPI communicator is not a two-party system and cannot be made fault tolerant without changing the semantics of MPI communication. If, however, the communication in an MPI program can be expressed in terms of intercommunicators, which are inherently two-party (the local group and the remote group), then fault tolerance can be achieved.

Note that while the MPI standard, through the use of intercommunicators, makes it possible to write an implementation of MPI that encourages fault-tolerant programming, the MPI standard itself does not require MPI implementations to continue past an error. This is a "quality of implementation" issue and allows the MPI implementor to trade performance for the ability to continue after a fault. As this section makes clear, however, nothing in the MPI standard stands in the way of fault tolerance, and the two primary MPI implementations for Beowulf clusters, MPICH2 and LAM/MPI, both endeavor to support some style of fault tolerance for applications.

9.3 Revisiting Mesh Exchanges

The discussion of the mesh exchanges for the Jacobi problem in Section 8.3 concentrated on the algorithm and data structures, particularly the ghost-cell exchange. In this section, we return to that example and cover two other important issues: blocking and nonblocking communications and communicating noncontiguous data.

9.3.1 Blocking and Nonblocking Communication

Consider the following simple code (note that this is similar to the simple version of `exchange_nbrs` in Section 8.3):

```
if (rank == 0) {
    MPI_Send( sbuf, n, MPI_INT, 1, 0, MPI_COMM_WORLD );
    MPI_Recv( rbuf, n, MPI_INT, 1, 0, MPI_COMM_WORLD, &status );
}
else if (rank == 1) {
    MPI_Send( sbuf, n, MPI_INT, 0, 0, MPI_COMM_WORLD );
    MPI_Recv( rbuf, n, MPI_INT, 0, 0, MPI_COMM_WORLD, &status );
}
```

What happens with this code? It looks like process 0 is sending a message to process 1 and that process 1 is sending a message to process 0. But more is going on here. Consider the steps that the MPI implementation must take to make this code work:

1. Copy the data from the `MPI_Send` into a temporary, system-managed buffer.
2. Once the `MPI_Send` completes (on each process), start the `MPI_Recv`. The data that was previously copied into a system buffer by the `MPI_Send` operation can now be delivered into the user's buffer (`rbuf` in this case).

This approach presents two problems, both related to the fact that data must be copied into a system buffer to allow the `MPI_Send` to complete. The first problem is obvious: any data motion takes time and reduces the performance of the code. The second problem is more subtle and important: the amount of available system buffer space always has a limit. For values of `n` in the above example that exceed the available buffer space, the above code will *hang*: neither `MPI_Send` will complete, and the code will wait forever for the other process to start an `MPI_Recv`. This is true for *any* message-passing system, not just MPI. The amount of buffer space available for buffering a message varies among MPI implementations, ranging from many megabytes to as little as 128 bytes.

How can we write code that sends data among several processes and that does not rely on the availability of system buffers? One approach is to carefully order the send and receive operations so that each send is guaranteed to have a matching receive. For example, we can swap the order of the `MPI_Send` and `MPI_Recv` in the code for process 1:

```
if (rank == 0) {
    MPI_Send( sbuf, n, MPI_INT, 1, 0, MPI_COMM_WORLD );
    MPI_Recv( rbuf, n, MPI_INT, 1, 0, MPI_COMM_WORLD, &status );
}
else if (rank == 1) {
    MPI_Recv( rbuf, n, MPI_INT, 0, 0, MPI_COMM_WORLD, &status );
    MPI_Send( sbuf, n, MPI_INT, 0, 0, MPI_COMM_WORLD );
}
```

This can be awkward to implement, however, particularly for more complex communication patterns; in addition, it does not address the extra copy that may be performed by `MPI_Send`.

The approach used by MPI, following earlier message-passing systems as well as nonblocking sockets (see [48, Chapter 9]), is to split the send and receive operations into two steps: one to initiate the operation and one to complete the operation. Other operations, including other communication operations, can be issued between the two steps. For example, an MPI receive operation can be initiated by a call to `MPI_Irecv` and completed with a call to `MPI_Wait`. Because the routines that initiate these operations do not wait for them to complete, they are called *nonblocking* operations. The "I" in the routine name stands for "immediate"; this indicates that the routine may return immediately without completing the operation. The arguments to `MPI_Irecv` are the same as for `MPI_Recv` except for the last (`status`) argument. This is replaced by an `MPI_Request` value; it is a *handle* that is used to identify an initiated operation. To complete a nonblocking operation, the request is given to `MPI_Wait`, along with a `status` argument; the `status` argument serves the same purpose as `status` for an `MPI_Recv`. Similarly, the nonblocking counterpart to `MPI_Send` is `MPI_Isend`; this has the same arguments as `MPI_Send` with the addition of an `MPI_Request` as the last argument (in C). Using these routines, our example becomes the following:

```
if (rank == 0) {
    MPI_Request req1, req2;
    MPI_Isend( sbuf, n, MPI_INT, 1, 0, MPI_COMM_WORLD, &req1 );
    MPI_Irecv( rbuf, n, MPI_INT, 1, 0, MPI_COMM_WORLD, &req2 );
    MPI_Wait( &req1, &status );
    MPI_Wait( &req2, &status );
}
else if (rank == 1) {
    MPI_Request req1, req2;
    MPI_Irecv( rbuf, n, MPI_INT, 0, 0, MPI_COMM_WORLD, &req1 );
    MPI_Isend( sbuf, n, MPI_INT, 0, 0, MPI_COMM_WORLD, &req2 );
    MPI_Wait( &req1, &status );
    MPI_Wait( &req2, &status );
}
```

The buffer `sbuf` provided to `MPI_Isend` must not be modified until the operation is completed with `MPI_Wait`. Similarly, the buffer `rbuf` provided to `MPI_Irecv` must not be modified or read until the `MPI_Irecv` is completed.

The nonblocking communication routines allow the MPI implementation to wait until the message can be sent directly from one user buffer to another (e.g., from `sbuf` to `rbuf`) without requiring any copy or using any system buffer space.

Because it is common to start multiple nonblocking operations, MPI provides routines to test or wait for completion of any one, all, or some of the requests. For example, `MPI_Waitall` waits for all requests in an array of requests to complete. Figure 9.4 shows the use of nonblocking communication routines for the Jacobi example.[1]

MPI nonblocking operations are not the same as asynchronous operations. The MPI standard does not require that the data transfers overlap computation with communication. MPI specifies only the semantics of the operations, not the details of the implementation choices. The MPI nonblocking routines are provided primarily for correctness (avoiding the limitations of system buffers) and performance (avoiding copies).

[1]On many systems, calling `MPI_Isend` before `MPI_Irecv` will improve performance.

```
void exchange_nbrs( double ulocal[][NY+2], int i_start, int i_end,
                    int left, int right )
{
    MPI_Status  statuses[4];
    MPI_Request requests[4];
    int c;

    /* Begin send and receive from the left neighbor */
    MPI_Isend( &ulocal[1][1], NY, MPI_DOUBLE, left, 0,
               MPI_COMM_WORLD, &requests[0] );
    MPI_Irecv( &ulocal[0][1], NY, MPI_DOUBLE, left, 0,
               MPI_COMM_WORLD, &requests[1] );

    /* Begin send and receive from the right neighbor */
    c = i_end - i_start + 1;
    MPI_Isend( &ulocal[c][1], NY, MPI_DOUBLE, right, 0,
               MPI_COMM_WORLD, &requests[2] );
    MPI_Irecv( &ulocal[c+1][1], NY, MPI_DOUBLE, right, 0,
               MPI_COMM_WORLD, &requests[3] );

    /* Wait for all communications to complete */
    MPI_Waitall( 4, requests, statuses );
}
```

Figure 9.4: Nonblocking exchange code for the Jacobi example.

9.3.2 Communicating Noncontiguous Data in MPI

The one-dimensional decomposition used in the Jacobi example (Section 8.3) is simple but does not scale well and can lead to performance problems. We can analyze the performance of the Jacobi following the discussion in Section 8.2. Let the time to communicate n bytes be

$$T_{comm} = s + rn,$$

where s is the *latency* and r is the (additional) time to communicate one byte. The time to compute one step of the Jacobi method, using the one-dimensional decomposition in Section 8.3, is

$$\frac{5n}{p} f + 2(s + rn),$$

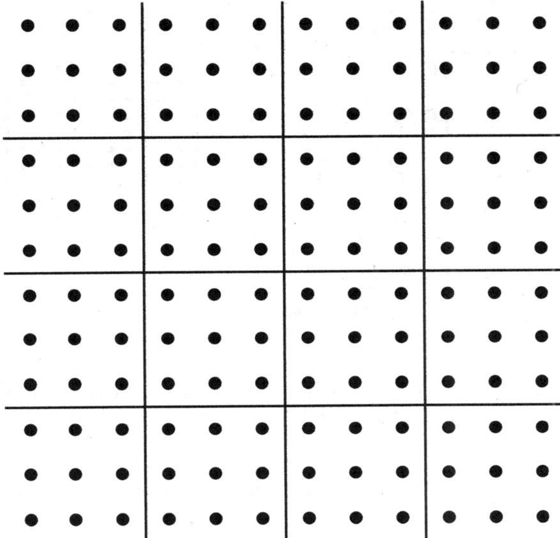

Figure 9.5: A 12×12 computational mesh, divided into 4×4 domains, for approximating the solution to the Poisson problem using a two-dimensional decomposition.

where f is the time to perform a floating-point operation and p is the number of processes. Note that the cost of communication is independent of the number of processes; eventually, this cost will dominate the calculation. Hence, a better approach is to use a two-dimensional decomposition, as shown in Figure 9.5.

The time for one step of the Jacobi method with a two-dimensional decomposition is just

$$\frac{5n}{p} f + 4\left(s + r\frac{n}{\sqrt{p}}\right).$$

This is faster than the one-dimensional decomposition as long as

$$n > \frac{2}{1 - 4/\sqrt{p}} \frac{s}{r}$$

(assuming $p \geq 16$). To implement this decomposition, we need to communicate data to four neighbors, as shown in Figure 9.6.

The left and right edges can be sent and received by using the same code as for the one-dimensional case. The top and bottom edges have noncontiguous data.

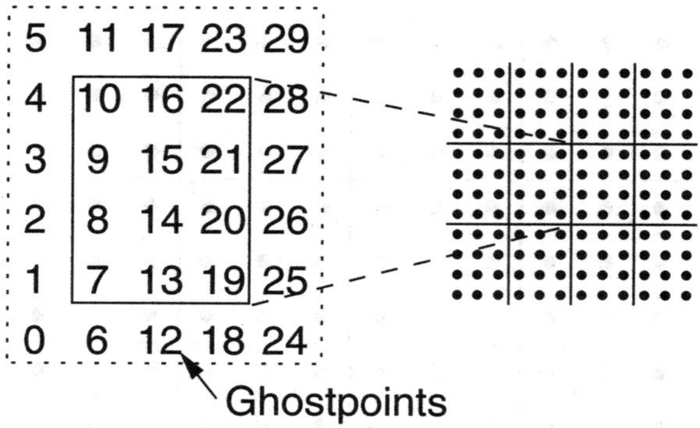

Figure 9.6: Locations of mesh points in `ulocal` for a two-dimensional decomposition.

For example, the top edge needs to send the tenth, sixteenth, and twenty-second element. There are four ways to move this data:

1. Each value can be sent separately. Because of the high latency of message passing, this approach is inefficient and normally should not be used.

2. The data can be copied into a temporary buffer by using a simple loop, for example,

```
for (i=0; i<3; i++) {
    tmp[i] = u_local[i][6];
}
MPI_Send( tmp, 3, MPI_DOUBLE, ..  );
```

   This is a common approach and, for some systems and MPI implementations, may be the most efficient.

3. MPI provides two routines to pack and unpack a buffer. These routines are `MPI_Pack` and `MPI_Unpack`. A buffer created with these routines should be sent and received with MPI datatype `MPI_PACKED`. We note, however, that these routines are most useful for complex data layouts that change frequently within a program.

4. MPI provides a way to construct new datatypes representing any data layout. These routines can be optimized by the MPI implementation, in principle providing better performance than the user can achieve using a simple loop [120].

In addition, using these datatypes is crucial to achieving high performance with parallel I/O.

MPI provides several routines to create datatypes representing common patterns of memory. These new datatypes are called *derived* datatypes. For this case, `MPI_Type_vector` is what is needed to create a new MPI datatype representing data values separated by a constant *stride*. In this case, the stride is `NY+2`, and the number of elements is `i_end-i_start+1`.

```
MPI_Type_vector( i_end - i_start + 1, 1, NY+2,
                 MPI_DOUBLE, &vectype );
MPI_Type_commit( &vectype );
```

The second argument is a *block count* and is the number of the basic datatype items (`MPI_DOUBLE` in this case); this is useful particularly in multicomponent PDE problems. The routine `MPI_Type_commit` must be called to *commit* the MPI datatype; this call allows the MPI implementation to optimize the datatype (the optimization is not included as part of the routines that create MPI datatypes because some complex datatypes are created recursively from other derived datatypes).

Using an MPI derived datatype representing a strided data pattern, we can write a version of `exchange_nbr` for a two-dimensional decomposition of the mesh; the code is shown in Figure 9.7. Note that we use the same derived datatype `vectype` for the sends and receives at the top and bottom by specifying the first element into which data is moved in the array `u_local` in the MPI calls.

When a derived datatype is no longer needed, it should be freed with `MPI_Type_free`. Many other routines are available for creating datatypes; for example, `MPI_Type_indexed` is useful for scatter-gather patterns, and `MPI_Type_create_struct` can be used for an arbitrary collection of memory locations.

Early implementations of derived datatypes did not achieve good performance, trading simplicity of implementation for performance. More recent implementations provide better performance, sometimes greater than is possible with straightforward user code. See [49, 120, 20] for some examples.

9.4 Motivation for Communicators

Communicators in MPI serve two purposes. The most obvious purpose is to describe a collection of processes. This feature allows collective routines, such as `MPI_Bcast` or `MPI_Allreduce`, to be used with any collection of processes. This capability is particularly important for hierarchical algorithms. It also facilitates dividing a

```
void exchange_nbrs2d( double ulocal[][NY+2],
                      int i_start, int i_end, int j_start, int j_end,
                      int left, int right, int top, int bottom,
                      MPI_Datatype vectype )
{
    MPI_Status  statuses[8];
    MPI_Request requests[8];
    int c;

    /* Begin send and receive from the left neighbor */
    MPI_Isend( &ulocal[1][1], NY, MPI_DOUBLE, left, 0,
               MPI_COMM_WORLD, &requests[0] );
    MPI_Irecv( &ulocal[0][1], NY, MPI_DOUBLE, left, 0,
               MPI_COMM_WORLD, &requests[1] );

    /* Begin send and receive from the right neighbor */
    c = i_end - i_start + 1;
    MPI_Isend( &ulocal[c][1], NY, MPI_DOUBLE, right, 0,
               MPI_COMM_WORLD, &requests[2] );
    MPI_Irecv( &ulocal[c+1][1], NY, MPI_DOUBLE, right, 0,
               MPI_COMM_WORLD, &requests[3] );

    /* Begin send and receive from the top neighbor */
    MPI_Isend( &ulocal[1][NY], 1, vectype, top, 0,
               MPI_COMM_WORLD, &requests[4] );
    MPI_Irecv( &ulocal[1][NY+1], 1, vectype, top, 0,
               MPI_COMM_WORLD, &requests[5] );

    /* Begin send and receive from the bottom neighbor */
    MPI_Isend( &ulocal[1][1], 1, vectype, bottom, 0,
               MPI_COMM_WORLD, &requests[6] );
    MPI_Irecv( &ulocal[1][0], 1, vectype, bottom, 0,
               MPI_COMM_WORLD, &requests[7] );

    /* Wait for all communications to complete */
    MPI_Waitall( 8, requests, statuses );
}
```

Figure 9.7: Nonblocking exchange code for the Jacobi problem for a two-dimensional decomposition of the mesh.

computation into subtasks, each of which has its own collection of processes. For example, in the manager-worker example in Section 8.2, it may be appropriate to divide each task among a small collection of processes, particularly if this causes the problem description to reside only in the fast memory cache. MPI communicators are perfect for this; the MPI routine `MPI_Comm_split` is the only routine needed when creating new communicators. Using ranks relative to a communicator for specifying the source and destination of messages also facilitates dividing parallel tasks among smaller but still parallel subtasks, each with its own communicator.

A more subtle but equally important purpose of the MPI communicator involves the *communication context* that each communicator contains. This context is essential for writing software libraries that can be safely and robustly combined with other code, both other libraries and user-specific application code, to build complete applications. Used properly, the communication context guarantees that messages are received by appropriate routines *even if other routines are not so careful.* Consider the example in Figure 9.8 (taken from [48, Section 6.1.2]). In this example, two routines are provided by separate libraries or software modules. One, `SendRight`, sends a message to the right neighbor and receives from the left. The other, `SendEnd`, sends a message from process 0 (the leftmost) to the last process (the rightmost). Both of these routines use `MPI_ANY_SOURCE` instead of a particular source in the `MPI_Recv` call. As Figure 9.8 shows, the messages can be confused, causing the program to receive the wrong data. How can we prevent this situation? Several approaches will *not* work. One is to avoid the use of `MPI_ANY_SOURCE`. This fixes the example, but only if both `SendRight` and `SendEnd` follow this rule. The approach may be adequate (though fragile) for code written by a single person or team, but it isn't adequate for libraries. For example, if `SendEnd` was written by a commercial vendor and did not use `MPI_ANY_SOURCE`, but `SendRight`, written by a different vendor or an inexperienced programmer, did use `MPI_ANY_SOURCE`, then the program would still fail, and it would look like `SendEnd` was at fault (because the message from `SendEnd` was received first).

Another approach that does not work is to use message tags to separate messages. Again, this can work if one group writes all of the code and is very careful about allocating message tags to different software modules. However, using `MPI_ANY_TAG` in an MPI receive call can still bypass this approach. Further, as shown in Figure 6.5 in [48], even if `MPI_ANY_SOURCE` and `MPI_ANY_TAG` are not used, separate code modules still can receive the wrong message.

The communication context in an MPI communicator provides a solution to these problems. The routine `MPI_Comm_dup` creates a new communicator from an input communicator that contains the same processes (in the same rank order) but with a

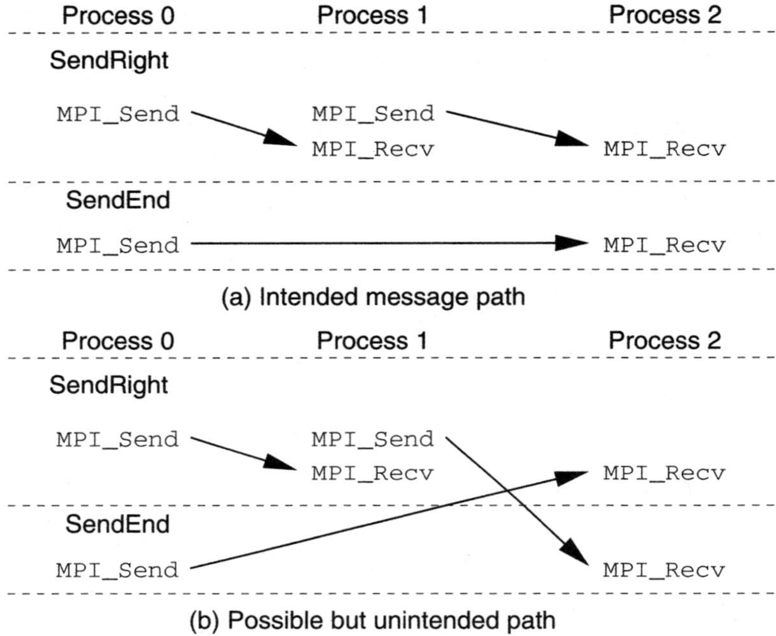

Figure 9.8: Two possible message-matching patterns when `MPI_ANY_SOURCE` is used in the `MPI_Recv` calls (from [48]).

new communication context. MPI messages sent in one communication context can be received only in that context. Thus, any software module or library that wants to ensure that all of its messages will be seen only within that library needs only to call `MPI_Comm_dup` at the beginning to get a new communicator. All well-written libraries that use MPI create a private communicator used only within that library.

Enabling the development of libraries was one of the design goals of MPI. In that respect MPI has been very successful. Many libraries and applications now use MPI, and, because of MPI's portability, most of these run on Beowulf clusters. Table 9.1 provides a partial list of libraries that use MPI to provide parallelism. More complete descriptions and lists are available at `www.mcs.anl.gov/mpi/libraries` and at `sal.kachinatech.com/C/3`. Chapter 12 discusses software, including MPI libraries and programs, in more detail.

Library	Description	URL
PETSc	Linear and nonlinear solvers for PDEs	www.mcs.anl.gov/petsc
Aztec	Parallel iterative solution of sparse linear systems	www.cs.sandia.gov/CRF/aztec1.html
Cactus	Framework for PDE solutions	www.cactuscode.org
FFTW	Parallel FFT	www.fftw.org
PPFPrint	Parallel print	www.llnl.gov/CASC/ppf/
HDF	Parallel I/O for Hierarchical Data Format (HDF) files	hdf.ncsa.uiuc.edu/Parallel_HDF
NAG	Numerical library	www.nag.co.uk/numeric/fd/FDdescription.asp
ScaLAPACK	Parallel linear algebra	www.netlib.org/scalapack
SPRNG	Scalable pseudorandom number generator	sprng.cs.fsu.edu

Table 9.1: A sampling of libraries that use MPI. See Chapter 12 for a more thorough list.

9.5 More on Collective Operations

One of the strengths of MPI is its collection of scalable collective communication and computation routines. Figure 9.9 shows the capabilities of some of the most important collective communication routines. To illustrate their utility, we consider a simple example.

Suppose we want to gather the names of all of the nodes that our program is running on, and we want all MPI processes to have this list of names. This is an easy task with `MPI_Allgather`:

```
char my_hostname[MAX_LEN], all_names[MAX_PROCS][MAX_LEN];
MPI_Allgather( my_hostname, MAX_LEN, MPI_CHAR,
               all_names, MAX_LEN, MPI_CHAR, MPI_COMM_WORLD );
```

This code assumes that no hostname is longer than `MAX_LEN` characters (including the trailing null). A better code would check this fact:

```
char my_hostname[MAX_LEN], all_names[MAX_PROCS][MAX_LEN];
int my_name_len, max_name_len;
...
my_name_len = strlen(my_hostname) + 1;
```

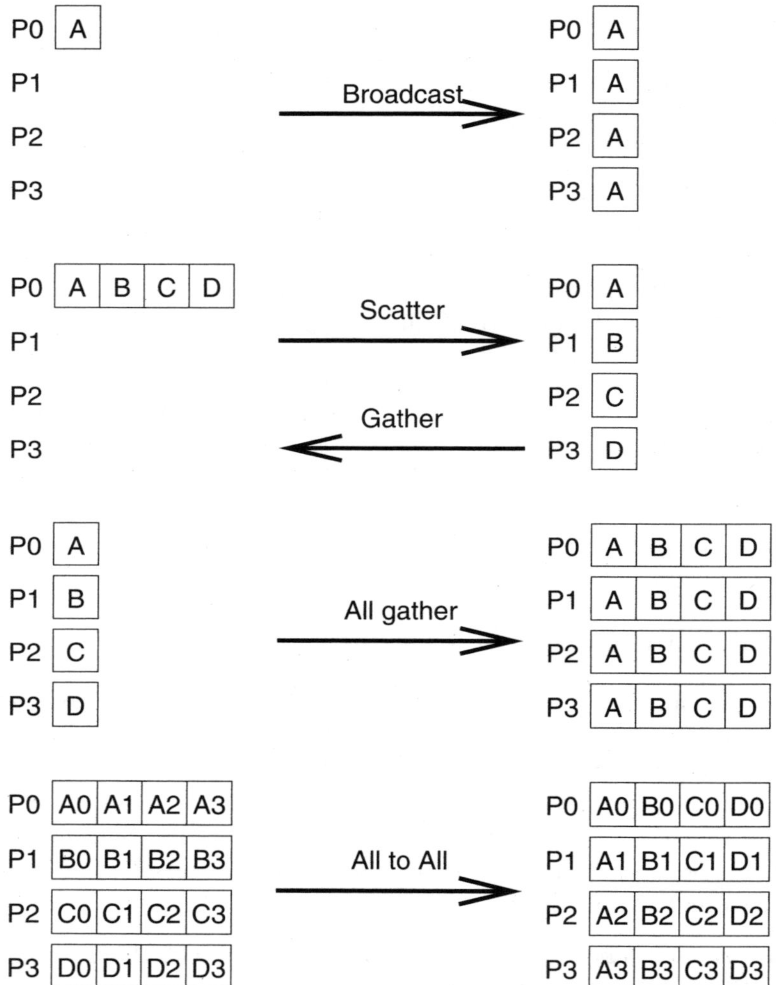

Figure 9.9: Schematic representation of collective data movement in MPI.

```
MPI_Allreduce( &my_name_len, &max_name_len, 1, MPI_INT, MPI_MAX,
               MPI_COMM_WORLD );
if (max_name_len > MAX_LEN) {
    printf( "Error: names too long (%d)\n", max_name_len );
```

```
int all_lens[MAX_PROCS], displs[MAX_PROCS], totlen;
char all_names[MAX_NAMES];
...
/* Gather the names lengths from all of the processes */
mylen = strlen(my_hostname) + 1;  /* Include the trailing null */
MPI_Allgather( &mylen, 1, MPI_INT, all_lens, 1, MPI_INT,
               MPI_COMM_WORLD );
/* Compute the displacement (displs) of each string in the
   result array all_names and total length of all strings */
totlen = all_lens[size-1];
for (i=0; i<size-1; i++) {
    displs[i+1] = displs[i] + all_lens[i];
    totlen      += all_lens[i];
}
all_names = (char *)malloc( totlen );
if (!all_names) MPI_Abort( MPI_COMM_WORLD, 1 );
/* Gather the names from each process, where the name from
   process i is all_lens[i] long and is placed into
   all_names[displs[i]] */
MPI_Allgatherv( my_hostname, mylen, MPI_CHAR,
                all_names, all_lens, displs, MPI_CHAR,
                MPI_COMM_WORLD );
/* Hostname for the jth process is &all_names[displs[j]] */
```

Figure 9.10: Using `MPI_Allgather` and `MPI_Allgatherv`.

```
}
MPI_Allgather( my_hostname, MAX_LEN, MPI_CHAR,
               all_names, MAX_LEN, MPI_CHAR, MPI_COMM_WORLD );
```

Both of these approaches move more data than necessary, however. An even better approach is to first gather the size of each processor's name and then gather exactly the number of characters needed from each processor. This uses the "v" (for vector) version of the allgather routine, `MPI_Allgatherv`, as shown in Figure 9.10. The array `all_lens` is used to hold the length of the name of the process with rank `i` in the $\texttt{i}^{\text{th}}$ location. From this information, the array `displs` is calculated, where the $\texttt{i}^{\text{th}}$ element is the offset into the character array `all_names` where the name for the process with rank `i` begins.

This example provides a different way to accomplish the action of the example in Section 8.3. Many parallel codes can be written with MPI collective routines instead of MPI point-to-point communication; such codes often have a simpler logical structure and can benefit from scalable implementations of the collective communications routines.

9.6 Parallel I/O

MPI provides a wide variety of parallel I/O operations, more than we have space to cover here. See [50, Chapter 3] for a more thorough discussion of I/O in MPI. These operations are most useful when combined with a high-performance parallel file system, such as PVFS, described in Chapter 19.

The fundamental idea in MPI's approach to parallel I/O is that a file is opened collectively by a set of processes that are all given access to the same file. MPI thus associates a communicator with the file, allowing a flexible set of both individual and collective operations on the file.

This approach can be used directly by the application programmer, as described below. An alternative is to use libraries that are designed to provide efficient and flexible access to files, described in a standard format. Two such libraries are parallel NetCDF [66] and HDF5 [25].

9.6.1 A Simple Example

We first provide a simple example of how processes write contiguous blocks of data into the same file in parallel. Then we give a more complex example, in which the data in each process is not contiguous but can be described by an MPI datatype.

For our first example, let us suppose that after solving the Poisson equation as we did in Section 8.3, we wish to write the solution to a file. We do not need the values of the ghost cells, and in the one-dimensional decomposition the set of rows in each process makes up a contiguous area in memory, which greatly simplifies the program. The I/O part of the program is shown in Figure 9.11.

Recall that the data to be written from each process, not counting ghost cells but including the boundary data, is in the array `ulocal[i][j]` for `i=i_start` to `i_end` and `j=0` to `NY+1`.

Note that the type of an MPI file object is `MPI_File`. Such file objects are opened and closed much the way normal files are opened and closed. The most significant difference is that opening a file is a collective operation over a group of processes specified by the communicator in the first argument of `MPI_File_open`. A single process can open a file by specifying the single-process communicator

```
MPI_File outfile;
size = NX * (NY + 2);
MPI_File_open( MPI_COMM_WORLD, "solutionfile",
               MPI_MODE_CREATE | MPI_MODE_WRONLY,
               MPI_INFO_NULL, &outfile );
MPI_File_set_view( outfile,
              rank * (NY+2) * (i_end - i_start) * sizeof(double),
              MPI_DOUBLE, MPI_DOUBLE, "native", MPI_INFO_NULL );
MPI_File_write( outfile, &ulocal[1][0], size, MPI_DOUBLE,
               MPI_STATUS_IGNORE );
MPI_File_close( &outfile );
```

Figure 9.11: Parallel I/O of Jacobi solution. Note that this choice of file view works only for a single output step; if output of multiple steps of the Jacobi method are needed, the arguments to `MPI_File_set_view` must be modified.

`MPI_COMM_SELF`. Here we want all of the processes to share the file, and so we use `MPI_COMM_WORLD`.

In our discussion of dynamic process management, we mentioned `MPI_Info` objects. An MPI info object is a collection of `key=value` pairs that can be used to encapsulate a variety of special-purpose information that may not be applicable to all MPI implementations. In this section we will use `MPI_INFO_NULL` whenever this type of argument is required, since we have no special information to convey. For details about `MPI_Info`, see [50, Chapter 2].

The part of the file that will be seen by each process is called the file *view* and is set for each process by a call to `MPI_File_set_view`. In our example the call is

```
MPI_File_set_view( outfile, rank * (NY+2) * ( ... ),
                   MPI_DOUBLE, MPI_DOUBLE, "native", MPI_INFO_NULL )
```

The first argument identifies the file; the second is the displacement (in bytes) into the file of where the process's view of the file is to start. Here we simply multiply the size of the data to be written by the process's rank, so that each process's view starts at the appropriate place in the file. The type of this argument is `MPI_Offset`, which can be expected to be a 64-bit integer on systems that support large files.

The next argument is called the *etype* of the view; it specifies the unit of data in the file. Here it is just `MPI_DOUBLE`, since we will be writing some number of doubles. The next argument is called the *filetype*; it is a flexible way of describing noncontiguous views in the file. In our case, with no noncontiguous units to be written, we can just use the etype, `MPI_DOUBLE`. In general, any MPI predefined or derived datatype can be used for both etypes and filetypes. We explore this use in more detail in the next example.

The next argument is a string defining the *data representation* to be used. The native representation says to represent data on disk exactly as it is in memory, which provides the fastest I/O performance, at the possible expense of portability. We specify that we have no extra information by providing `MPI_INFO_NULL` for the final argument.

The call to `MPI_File_write` is then straightforward. The data to be written is a contiguous array of doubles, even though it consists of several rows of the (distributed) matrix. On each process it starts at `&ulocal[0][1]` so the data is described in (address, count, datatype) form, just as it would be for an MPI message. We ignore the status by passing `MPI_STATUS_IGNORE`. Finally we (collectively) close the file with `MPI_File_close`.

9.6.2 A More Complex Example

Parallel I/O requires more than just calling `MPI_File_write` instead of write. The key idea is to identify the object (across processes), rather than the contribution from each process. We illustrate this with an example of a regular distributed array.

The code in Figure 9.12 writes out an array that is distributed among processes with a two-dimensional decomposition. To illustrate the expressiveness of the MPI interface, we show a complex case where, as in the Jacobi example, the distributed array is surrounded by ghost cells. This example is covered in more depth in Chapter 3 of *Using MPI-2* [50], including the simpler case of a distributed array without ghost cells.

This example may look complex, but each step is relatively simple.

1. Set up a communicator that represents a virtual array of processes that matches the way that the distributed array is distributed. This approach uses the `MPI_Cart_create` routine and uses `MPI_Cart_coords` to find the coordinates of the calling process in this array of processes. This particular choice of process ordering is important because it matches the ordering required by `MPI_Type_create_subarray`.

2. Create a *file view* that describes the part of the file that this process will write to. The MPI routine `MPI_Type_create_subarray` makes it easy to construct the MPI datatype that describes this region of the file. The arguments to this routine specify the dimensionality of the array (two in our case), the

```
/* no. of processes in vertical and horizontal dimensions
   of process grid */
dims[0] = 2;    dims[1] = 3;
periods[0] = periods[1] = 1;
MPI_Cart_create(MPI_COMM_WORLD, 2, dims, periods, 0, &comm);
MPI_Comm_rank(comm, &rank);
MPI_Cart_coords(comm, rank, 2, coords);
/* global indices of the first element of the local array */

/* no. of rows and columns in global array*/
gsizes[0] = m;    gsizes[1] = n;

lsizes[0] = m/dims[0];    /* no. of rows in local array */
lsizes[1] = n/dims[1];    /* no. of columns in local array */

start_indices[0] = coords[0] * lsizes[0];
start_indices[1] = coords[1] * lsizes[1];
MPI_Type_create_subarray(2, gsizes, lsizes, start_indices,
                         MPI_ORDER_C, MPI_FLOAT, &filetype);
MPI_Type_commit(&filetype);

MPI_File_open(comm, "/pfs/datafile",
              MPI_MODE_CREATE | MPI_MODE_WRONLY,
              MPI_INFO_NULL, &fh);
MPI_File_set_view(fh, 0, MPI_FLOAT, filetype, "native",
                  MPI_INFO_NULL);

/* create a derived datatype that describes the layout of the local
   array in the memory buffer that includes the ghost area. This is
   another subarray datatype! */
memsizes[0] = lsizes[0] + 8; /* no. of rows in allocated array */
memsizes[1] = lsizes[1] + 8; /* no. of columns in allocated array */
start_indices[0] = start_indices[1] = 4;
/* indices of the first element of the local array in the
   allocated array */
MPI_Type_create_subarray(2, memsizes, lsizes, start_indices,
                         MPI_ORDER_C, MPI_FLOAT, &memtype);
MPI_Type_commit(&memtype);
MPI_File_write_all(fh, local_array, 1, memtype, &status);
MPI_File_close(&fh);
```

Figure 9.12: C program for writing a distributed array that is also noncontiguous in memory because of a ghost area (derived from an example in [50]).

global size of the array, the local size (that is, the size of the part of the array on the calling process), the location of the local part (`start_indices`), the ordering of indices (column major is `MPI_ORDER_FORTRAN`, and row major is `MPI_ORDER_C`), and the basic datatype.

3. Open the file for writing (`MPI_MODE_WRONLY`), and set the file view with the datatype we have just constructed.

4. Create a datatype that describes the data to be written. We can use `MPI_Type_create_subarray` here as well to define the part of the local array that does *not* include the ghost points. If there were no ghost points, we could instead use `MPI_FLOAT` as the datatype with a count of `lsizes[0]*lsizes[1]` in the call to `MPI_File_write_all`.

5. Perform a collective write to the file with `MPI_File_write_all`, and close the file.

By using MPI datatypes to describe both the data to be written and the destination of the data in the file with a collective file write operation, the MPI implementation can make the best use of the I/O system. The result is that file I/O operations performed with MPI I/O can achieve hundredfold improvements in performance over using individual Unix I/O operations [116].

9.7 Remote Memory Access

The message-passing programming model requires that both the sender and the receiver (or all members of a communicator in a collective operation) participate in moving data between two processes. An alternative model where one process controls the communication, called one-sided communication, can offer better performance and in some cases a simpler programming model. MPI-2 provides support for this one-sided approach. The MPI-2 model was inspired by the work on the bulk synchronous programming (BSP) model [54] and the Cray SHMEM library used on the massively parallel Cray T3D and T3E computers [30].

In one-sided communication, one process may *put* data directly into the memory of another process, without that process using an explicit receive call. For this reason, this is also called *remote memory access* (RMA).

Using RMA involves four steps:

1. Describe the memory into which data may be put.

2. Allow access to the memory.

3. Begin put operations (e.g., with `MPI_Put`).

4. Complete all pending RMA operations.

The first step is to describe the region of memory into which data may be placed by an `MPI_Put` operation (also accessed by `MPI_Get` or updated by `MPI_Accumulate`). This is done with the routine `MPI_Win_create`:

```
MPI_Win win;
double ulocal[MAX_NX][NY+2];

MPI_Win_create( ulocal, (NY+2)*(i_end-i_start+3)*sizeof(double),
                sizeof(double), MPI_INFO_NULL, MPI_COMM_WORLD, &win );
```

The input arguments are, in order, the array `ulocal`, the size of the array in bytes, the size of a basic unit of the array (`sizeof(double)` in this case), a "hint" object, and the communicator that specifies which processes may use RMA to access the array. `MPI_Win_create` is a collective call over the communicator. The output is an MPI *window object* `win`. When a window object is no longer needed, it should be freed with `MPI_Win_free`.

RMA operations take place between two sentinels. One begins a period where access is allowed to a window object, and one ends that period. These periods are called *epochs*.[2] The easiest routine to use to begin and end epochs is `MPI_Win_fence`. This routine is collective over the processes that created the window object and both ends the previous epoch and starts a new one. The routine is called a "fence" because all RMA operations before the fence complete before the fence returns, and any RMA operation initiated by another process (in the epoch begun by the matching fence on that process) does not start until the fence returns. This may seem complex, but it is easy to use. In practice, `MPI_Win_fence` is needed only to separate RMA operations into groups. This model closely follows the BSP and Cray SHMEM models, though with the added ability to work with any subset of processes.

Three routines are available for initiating the transfer of data in RMA. These are `MPI_Put`, `MPI_Get`, and `MPI_Accumulate`. All are nonblocking in the same sense MPI point-to-point communication is nonblocking (Section 9.3.1). They complete at the end of the epoch that they start in, for example, at the closing `MPI_Win_fence`. Because these routines specify both the source and destination of data,

[2] MPI has two kinds of epochs for RMA: an *access epoch* and an *exposure epoch*. For the example used here, the epochs occur together, and we refer to both of them as just epochs.

they have more arguments than do the point-to-point communication routines. The arguments can be easily understood by taking them a few at a time.

1. The first three arguments describe the *origin* data, that is, the data on the calling process. These are the usual "buffer, count, datatype" arguments.

2. The next argument is the rank of the *target* process. This serves the same function as the destination of an `MPI_Send`. The rank is relative to the communicator used when creating the MPI window object.

3. The next three arguments describe the destination buffer. The `count` and `datatype` arguments have the same meaning as for an `MPI_Recv`, but the buffer location is specified as an offset from the beginning of the memory specified to `MPI_Win_create` on the target process. This offset is in units of the displacement argument of the `MPI_Win_create` and is usually the size of the basic datatype.

4. The last argument is the MPI window object.

Note that there are no MPI requests; the `MPI_Win_fence` completes all preceding RMA operations. `MPI_Win_fence` provides a collective synchronization model for RMA operations in which all processes participate. This is called *active target* synchronization.

With these routines, we can create a version of the mesh exchange that uses RMA instead of point-to-point communication. Figure 9.13 shows one possible implementation.

Another form of access requires no MPI calls (not even a fence) at the target process. This is called *passive target* synchronization. The origin process uses `MPI_Win_lock` to begin an access epoch and `MPI_Win_unlock` to end the access epoch.[3] Because of the passive nature of this type of RMA, the local memory (passed as the first argument to `MPI_Win_create`) should be allocated with `MPI_Alloc_mem` and freed with `MPI_Free_mem`. For more information on passive target RMA operations, see [50, Chapter 6]. Also note that as of 2003, not all MPI implementations support passive target RMA operation. Check that your implementation fully implements passive target RMA operations before using them.

A more complete discussion of remote memory access can be found in [50, Chapters 5 and 6]. Note that MPI implementations are just beginning to provide the

[3]The names `MPI_Win_lock` and `MPI_Win_unlock` are really misnomers; think of them as begin-RMA and end-RMA.

```
void exchang_nbrs( double u_local[][NY+2], int i_start, int i_end,
                   int left, int right, MPI_Win win )
{
    MPI_Aint left_ghost_disp, right_ghost_disp;
    int      c;

    MPI_Win_fence( 0, win );
    /* Put the left edge into the left neighbors rightmost
       ghost cells.  See text about right_ghost_disp */
    right_ghost_disp = 1 + (NY+2) * (i_end-i-start+2);
    MPI_Put( &u_local[1][1], NY, MPI_DOUBLE,
            left, right_ghost_disp, NY, MPI_DOUBLE, win );
    /* Put the right edge into the right neighbors leftmost ghost
       cells */
    left_ghost_disp = 1;
    c = i_end - i_start + 1;
    MPI_Put( &u_local[c][1], NY, MPI_DOUBLE,
             right, left_ghost_disp, NY, MPI_DOUBLE, win );

    MPI_Win_fence( 0, win )
}
```

Figure 9.13: Neighbor exchange using MPI remote memory access.

RMA routines described in this section. Most current RMA implementations emphasize functionality over performance. As implementations mature, however, the performance of RMA operations will also improve.

9.8 Using C++ and Fortran 90

MPI-1 defined bindings to C and Fortran 77. These bindings were very similar; the only major difference was the handling of the error code (returned in C, set through the last argument in Fortran 77). In MPI-2, a binding was added for C++, and an MPI module was defined for Fortran 90.

The C++ binding provides a lightweight model that is more than just a C++ version of the C binding but not a no-holds-barred object-oriented model. MPI objects are defined in the `MPI` namespace. Most MPI objects have corresponding classes, such as `Datatype` for `MPI_Datatype`. Communicators and requests are slightly different. There is an abstract base class `Comm` for general communica-

```
#include "mpi.h"
#include <iostream.h>

int main( int argc, char *argv[] )
{
    int data;
    MPI::Init();

    if (MPI::COMM_WORLD.Get_rank() == 0) {
        // Broadcast data from process 0 to all others
        cout << "Enter an int" << endl;
        data << cin;
    }
    MPI::COMM_WORLD.Bcast( data, 1, MPI::INT, 0 );

    MPI::Finalize();
    return 0;
}
```

Figure 9.14: Simple MPI program in C++.

tors with four derived classes: `Intracomm`, `Intercomm`, `Graphcomm`, and `Cartcomm`. Most communicators are `Intracomms`; `GraphComm` and `CartComm` are derived from `Intracomm`. Requests have two derived classes: `Prequest` for persistent requests and `Grequest` for generalized requests (new in MPI-2). Most MPI operations are methods on the appropriate objects; for example, most point-to-point and collective communications are methods on the communicator. A few routines, such as `Init` and `Finalize`, stand alone. A simple MPI program in C++ is shown in Figure 9.14.

The C++ binding for MPI has a few quirks. One is the C++ analogue to `MPI_Comm_dup`. In the C++ binding, `MPI::Comm` is an abstract base class (ABC). Since it is impossible to create an instance of an abstract base class, there can be no general "dup" function that returns a new `MPI::Comm`. Since it is possible in C++ to create a reference to an ABC, however, MPI defines the routine (available only in the C++ binding) `MPI::Clone` that returns a reference to a new communicator.

Two levels of Fortran 90 support are provided in MPI. The basic support provides an '`mpif.h`' include file. The extended support provides an `MPI` module. The module makes it easy to detect the two most common errors in Fortran MPI programs: forgetting to provide the variable for the error return value and forgetting to declare status as an array of size `MPI_STATUS_SIZE`. There are a few drawbacks. Fortran derived datatypes cannot be directly supported (the Fortran 90 language provides no way to handle an arbitrary type). Often, you can use the first element of the Fortran 90 derived type. Array sections should not be used in receive operations, particularly nonblocking communication (see Section 10.2.2 in the MPI-2 standard for more information). Another problem is that while Fortran 90 enables the user to define MPI interfaces in the MPI module, a different Fortran 90 interface file must be used for each combination of Fortran datatype and array dimension (scalars are different from arrays of dimension one, etc.). This leads to a Fortran 90 MPI module library that is often (depending on the Fortran 90 compiler) far larger than the entire MPI library. However, particularly during program development, the MPI module can be very helpful.

9.9 MPI, OpenMP, and Threads

The MPI standard was carefully written to be a thread-safe specification. That means that the design of MPI doesn't include concepts such as "last message" or "current pack buffer" that are not well defined when multiple threads are present. MPI implementations can choose whether to provide thread-safe *implementations*. Allowing this choice is particularly important because thread safety usually comes at the price of performance due to the extra overhead required to ensure that internal data structures are not modified inconsistently by two different threads. Most early MPI implementations were not thread safe.

MPI-2 introduced four levels of thread safety that an MPI implementation could provide. The lowest level, `MPI_THREAD_SINGLE`, allows only single threaded programs. The next level, `MPI_THREAD_FUNNELED`, allows multiple threads provided that all MPI calls are made in a single thread; most MPI implementations provide `MPI_THREAD_FUNNELED`. The next level, `MPI_THREAD_SERIALIZED`, allows many user threads to make MPI calls, but only one thread at a time. The highest level of support, `MPI_THREAD_MULTIPLE`, allows any thread to call any MPI routine. The level of thread support can be requested by using the routine `MPI_Init_thread`; this routine returns the level of thread support that is available.

Understanding the level of thread support is important when combining MPI with approaches to thread-based parallelism. OpenMP [83] is a popular and powerful language for specifying thread-based parallelism. While OpenMP provides some tools for general threaded parallelism, one of the most common uses is to parallelize a loop. If the loop contains no MPI calls, then OpenMP may be combined with

MPI. For example, in the Jacobi example, OpenMP can be used to parallelize the loop computation:

```
exchange_nbrs( u_local, i_start, i_end, left, right );
#pragma omp for
for (i_local=1; i<=i_end-i_start+1; i++)
  for (j=1; j<=NY; j++)
    ulocal_new[i_local][j] =
       0.25 * (ulocal[i_local+1][j] + ulocal[i_local-1][j] +
               ulocal[i_local][j+1] + ulocal[i_local][j-1] -
               h*h*flocal[i_local][j]);
```

This exploits the fact that MPI was designed to work well with other tools, leveraging improvements in compilers and threaded parallelism.

9.10 Measuring MPI Performance

Many tools have been developed for measuring performance. The best test is always your own application, but a number of tests are available that can give a more general overview of the performance of MPI on a cluster. Measuring communication performance is actually quite tricky; see [51] for a discussion of some of the issues in making reproducible measurements of performance. That paper describes the methods used in the `mpptest` program for measuring MPI performance.

9.10.1 mpptest

The `mpptest` program allows you to measure many aspects of the performance of any MPI implementation. The most common MPI performance test is the Ping-Pong test; this test measures the time it takes to send a message from one process to another and then back. The `mpptest` program provides Ping-Pong tests for the different MPI communication modes, as well as providing a variety of tests for collective operations and for more realistic variations on point-to-point communication, such as halo communication (like that in Section 8.3) and communication that does not reuse the same memory locations (thus benefiting from using data that is already in memory cache). The `mpptest` program can also test the performance of some MPI-2 functions, including `MPI_Put` and `MPI_Get`.

Using mpptest

The `mpptest` program is distributed with MPICH and MPICH2 in the directory '`examples/perftest`'. You can also download it separately from `www.mcs.anl.gov/mpi/perftest`. Building and using `mpptest` is very simple:

```
% tar zxf perftest.tar.gz
% cd perftest-1.2.1
% ./configure --with-mpich
% make
% mpiexec -n 2 ./mpptest -logscale
% mpiexec -n 16 ./mpptest -bisect
% mpiexec -n 2 ./mpptest -auto
```

To run with LAM/MPI, simply configure with the option `--with-lammpi`. The '`README`' file contains instructions for building with other MPI implementations.

9.10.2 SKaMPI

The SKaMPI test suite [94] is a comprehensive test of MPI performance, covering virtually all of the MPI-1 communication functions.

One interesting feature of the SKaMPI benchmarks is the online tables showing the performance of MPI implementations on various parallel computers, ranging from Beowulf clusters to parallel vector supercomputers.

9.10.3 High Performance LINPACK

Perhaps the best-known benchmark in technical computing is the LINPACK benchmark. The version of this benchmark that is appropriate for clusters is the High Performance LINPACK (HPL). Obtaining and running this benchmark are relatively easy, though getting good performance can require a significant amount of effort. In addition, while the LINPACK benchmark is widely known, it tends to significantly overestimate the achieveable performance for many applications because it involves n^3 computation on n^2 data and is thus relatively insensitive to the performance of the node memory system.

The HPL benchmark depends on another library, the basic linear algebra subroutines (BLAS), for much of the computation. Thus, to get good performance on the HPL benchmark, you must have a high-quality implementation of the BLAS. Fortunately, several sources of these routines are available. You can often get implementations of the BLAS from the CPU vendor directly, sometimes at no cost. Another possibility is to use the ATLAS implementation of the BLAS.

ATLAS

ATLAS is available from `math-atlas.sourceforge.net`. If prebuilt binaries fit your system, you should use those. Note that ATLAS is tuned for specific system characteristics including clock speed and cache sizes; if you have any doubts about whether your configuration matches that of a prebuilt version, you should build ATLAS yourself.

To build ATLAS, first download ATLAS from the Web site and then extract it. This will create an '`ATLAS`' directory into which the libraries will be built, so extract this where you want the libraries to reside. A directory on a local disk (such as '`/tmp`') rather than on on an NFS-mounted disk can help speedup ATLAS.

```
% cd /tmp
% tar zxf atlas3.4.1.tgz
% cd ATLAS
```

Check the '`errata.html`' file at `math-atlas.sourceforge.net/errata.html` for updates. You may need to edit various files (no patches are supplied for ATLAS). Pay particular attention to the items that describe various possible ways that the install step may fail; you may choose to update values such as `ATL_nkflop` before running ATLAS. Next, have ATLAS configure itself. Select a compiler; note that you should not use the Portland Group compiler here.

```
% make config CC=gcc
```

Answer `yes` to most questions, including threaded and express setup, and accept the suggested architecture name. Next, make ATLAS. Here, we assume that the architecture name was `Linux-PIIISSE2`:

```
% make install arch=Linux-PIIISSE2 >&make.log
```

Note that this is not an "install" in the usual sense; the ATLAS libraries are not copied to '`/usr/local/lib`' and the like by the install. This step may take as long as several hours, unless ATLAS finds a precomputed set of parameters that fits your machine. ATLAS is also sensitive to variations in runtimes, so try to use a machine that has no other users. Make sure that it is the exact same type of machine as your nodes (e.g., if you have login nodes that are different from your compute nodes, make sure that you run ATLAS on the compute nodes).

At the end of the "make install" step, the BLAS are in '`ATLAS/lib/Linux-PIIISSE2`'. You are ready for the next step.

HPL

Download and unpack the HPL package from `www.netlib.org/benchmark/hpl`:

```
% tar zxf hpl.tgz
% cd hpl
```

Create a '`Make.<archname>`' in the '`hpl`' directory. Consider an `archname` like `Linux_PIII_CBLAS_gm` for a Linux system on Pentium III processors, using the C version of the BLAS constructed by ATLAS, and using the `gm` device from the MPICH implementation of MPI. To create this file, look at the samples in the '`hpl/setup`' directory, for example,

```
% cp setup/Make.Linux_PII_CBLAS_gm Make.Linux_PIII_CBLAS_gm
```

Edit this file, changing `ARCH` to the name you selected (e.g., `Linux_PIII_CBLAS_gm`), and set `LAdir` to the location of the ATLAS libraries. Then do the following:

```
% make arch=<thename>
% cd bin/<thename>
% mpiexec -n 4 ./xhpl
```

Check the output to make sure that you have the right answer. The file '`HPL.dat`' controls the actual test parameters. The version of '`HPL.dat`' that comes with the `hpl` package is appropriate for testing `hpl`. To run `hpl` for performance requires modifying '`HPL.dat`'. The file '`hpl/TUNING`' contains some hints on setting the values in this file for performance. Here are a few of the most important:

1. Change the problem size to a large value. Don't make it too large, however, since the total computational work grows as the cube of the problem size (doubling the problem size increases the amount of work by a factor of eight). Problem sizes of around 5,000–10,000 are reasonable.

2. Change the block size to a modest size. A block size of around 64 is a good place to start.

3. Change the processor decomposition and number of nodes to match your configuration. In most cases, you should try to keep the decomposition close to square (e.g., P and Q should be about the same value), with $P \geq Q$.

4. Experiment with different values for `RFACT` and `PFACT`. On some systems, these parameters can have a significant effect on performance. For one large cluster, setting both to `right` was preferable.

9.11 MPI-2 Status

MPI-2 is a significant extension of the MPI-1 standard. Unlike the MPI-1 standard, where complete implementations of the entire standard were available when the standard was released, complete implementations of all of MPI-2 have been slow in coming. As of June 2003, few complete implementations of MPI-2 exist for Beowulf clusters. Most MPI implementations include the MPI-IO routines, in large part because of the ROMIO implementation of these routines, and at least some of the RMA routines (typically the active-target operations `MPI_Put` and `MPI_Get`, along with `MPI_Win_fence`). Progress continues in both the completeness and performance of MPI-2 implementations, and we expect more full MPI-2 implementations to appear by the end of 2003. One of these is the MPICH2 implementation of MPI.

10 Parallel Virtual Machine

Al Geist

PVM (Parallel Virtual Machine) was first released in the early 1990s as an outgrowth of an ongoing computing research project involving Oak Ridge National Laboratory, the University of Tennessee, and Emory University. The general goals of this project are to investigate issues in, and develop solutions for, heterogeneous distributed computing. PVM was one of the solutions. PVM was designed to be able to combine computers having different operating systems, different data representations (both number of bits and byte order), different architectures (multiprocessor, single processor, and even supercomputers), different languages, and different networks and have them all work together on a single computational problem.

PVM existed before Beowulf clusters were invented and in fact was the software used to run applications on the first Beowulf clusters. Today, both PVM and MPICH are often included in software distributions for Beowulf clusters.

The basic idea behind PVM was to create a simple software package that could be loaded onto any collection of computers that would make the collection appear to be a single, large, distributed-memory parallel computer. PVM provides a way for aggregating the power and memory of distributed compute resources. Today this is called Grid computing. In the early 1990s PVM was used to do a number of early Grid experiments, including creating the first international Grid by combining supercomputers in the United Kingdom with supercomputers in the United States, creating a Grid that combined 53 Cray supercomputers across the United States into a single super-supercomputer, and connecting the two largest parallel computers in the world into a 4,000-processor system to solve a nanotechnology problem that eventually led to the high-capacity hard drives used in today's PCs. In 1990 PVM was used for an application in high-temperature superconductivity; the application won a Gordon Bell Prize in supercomputing—the first of many Gordon Bell prizes won by researchers using PVM.

But PVM's real contribution to science and computing is not in supercomputing. PVM's reliability and ease of use made this software package very popular for hooking together a network of workstations or a pile of PCs into a virtual parallel computer that gave PVM users several times more power than they would have otherwise. With tens of thousands of users, PVM was so popular that it became a de facto standard for heterogeneous distributed computing worldwide.

PVM still remains popular, particularly for applications that require fault tolerance. For example, PVM is used to provide fault tolerance to the Globus Toolkit Grid Information Services for the DOE Science Grid. PVM is also used on clusters running the Genomics Integrated Supercomputer Toolkit to provide 24/7 availability despite faults in the clusters.

The tiny 1.5 Mbyte PVM software package is an integrated set of software tools and libraries that emulates a general-purpose, dynamic, heterogeneous parallel computing environment on a set of computers that are connected by a network. The network can be the Internet (Grid computing) or a dedicated local network (cluster). One use of PVM today is to combine multiple Beowulf clusters at a site into a Grid of clusters as shown in Figure 10.1.

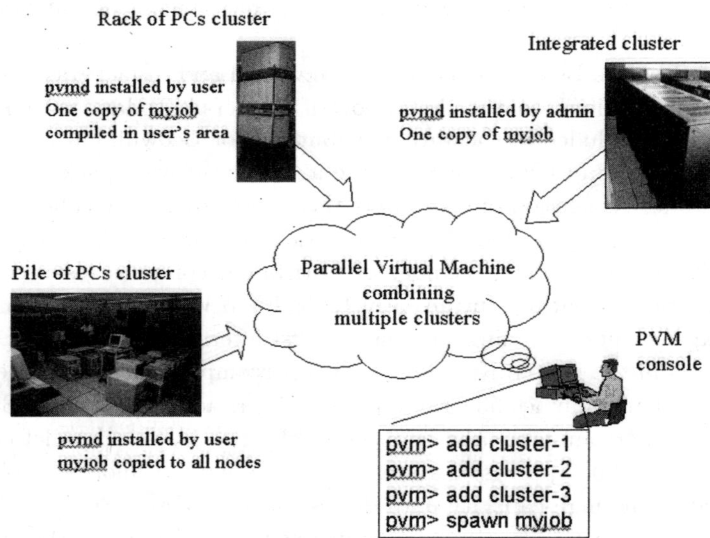

Figure 10.1: PVM used to create a Grid of clusters.

The PVM library includes functions to add computers to the parallel virtual machine, spawn tasks on these computers, and exchange data between tasks through message passing. This chapter provides detailed descriptions and examples of the basic concepts and methodologies involved in using PVM on clusters as well as its use as a means to combine multiple clusters into a Grid of clusters. The next chapter details the special functions in PVM for use in fault tolerant and dynamic environments.

10.1 The PVM System

The PVM system is composed of two parts. The first part is a daemon, called `pvmd3` and sometimes abbreviated `pvmd`, that must be installed on all the computers making up the virtual machine. (An example of a daemon program is the mail program that runs in the background and handles all the incoming and outgoing electronic mail on a computer.) The daemon `pvmd3` is designed so any user with a valid login can install this daemon on a machine. To run a PVM application, you first create a virtual machine by starting up PVM (Section 10.3.2 details how this is done). Multiple users can configure virtual machines that overlap the same cluster nodes, and each user can execute several applications simultaneously on his own virtual machine.

The second part of the system is a library of PVM interface routines. It contains a functionally complete repertoire of primitives that are needed for cooperation between tasks of an application. This library contains user-callable routines for fault detection, message passing, spawning processes, coordinating tasks, and modifying the virtual machine.

The Parallel Virtual Machine computing environment is based on the following concepts:

- **User-configured host pool:** The application's parallel tasks execute on a set of machines that are selected by the user for a given run of the PVM program. The host pool may be altered by adding and deleting machines at any time (an important feature for fault tolerance). When PVM is used on Beowulf clusters, the nodes within a cluster and/or nodes spanning multiple clusters make up the host pool. There is no restriction on the number of parallel tasks that can exist in a given virtual machine. If the number of tasks exceeds the number of processors in the cluster, then PVM will run multiple tasks per processor.

- **Translucent access to hardware:** Application programs may view the hardware environment as a transparent computing resource or may exploit the capabilities of specific machines in the host pool by positioning certain tasks on the most appropriate computers. On large clusters, for example, I/O nodes may run the monitoring tasks and compute nodes may get the bulk of the computing load.

- **Explicit message-passing:** PVM provides basic blocking and nonblocking send, receive, and collective communication operations. For performance,

PVM uses the native message-passing facilities on multiprocessors to take advantage of the underlying hardware. For example, on the IBM SP, PVM transparently uses IBM's MPI to move data. On the SGI multiprocessor, PVM uses shared memory to move data. On Linux clusters PVM typically uses a mixture of UDP and TCP/IP to move data.

- **Dynamic program model:** The PVM system supports a dynamic programming model where hosts and tasks can come and go at any time. PVM tasks are dynamic. New ones can be spawned and existing ones killed at any time by the application or manually from any host in the virtual machine. The virtual machine monitors its state and automatically adapts to such changes.
- **Dynamic Groups:** In some applications it is natural to think of a *group* of tasks. And there are cases where you would like to identify your tasks by the numbers 0 to $(p - 1)$, where p is the number of tasks. PVM includes the concept of user-named groups. When a task joins a group, it is assigned a unique "instance" number in that group. Instance numbers start at 0 and count up (similar to an MPI "rank"). In keeping with the dynamic programming model in PVM , the group functions are designed to be very general and transparent to the user. For example, any PVM task can join or leave any group at any time without having to inform any other task in the affected groups, groups can overlap, and tasks can broadcast messages to groups of which they are not a member. To use any of the group functions, a program must be linked with '`libgpvm3.a`'.

10.2 Writing PVM Applications

The PVM system currently supports many languages. C, C++, and Fortran languages are supported in the standard distribution. Third-party groups have created freely available Java, Perl, Python, S, Matlab, TCL/TK, and IDL interfaces to PVM. All these are downloadable from the PVM Web site (`www.csm.ornl.gov/pvm`). PVM is designed so that an application can be composed of tasks written in any mixture of these languages and the tasks will still be able to exchange data and to synchronize with each other.

The general paradigm for application programming with PVM is as follows. You write one or more sequential programs that contain embedded calls to the PVM library. Each program corresponds to a task making up the application. These programs are compiled for each architecture in the host pool, and the resulting object files are placed at a location accessible from machines in the host pool.

To execute an application, you typically start one copy of one task (typically the "manager" or "initiating" task) by hand from a machine within the host pool. This process subsequently spawns other PVM tasks, eventually resulting in a collection of active tasks that then compute on the cluster and exchange messages with each other to solve the problem.

The C and C++ language bindings for the PVM user interface library are implemented as functions, following the general conventions used by most C systems. To elaborate, function arguments are a combination of value parameters and pointers as appropriate, and function result values indicate the outcome of the call. In addition, macro definitions are used for system constants, and global variables such as `errno` and `pvm_errno` are the mechanism for discriminating between multiple possible outcomes. Application programs written in C and C++ access PVM library functions by linking against an archival library ('`libpvm3.a`') that is part of the standard distribution.

Fortran language bindings are implemented as subroutines rather than as functions. This approach was taken because some compilers on the supported architectures would not reliably interface Fortran functions with C functions. One immediate implication of this is that an additional argument is introduced into each PVM library call for status results to be returned to the invoking program. Moreover, library routines for the placement and retrieval of typed data in message buffers are unified, with an additional parameter indicating the datatype. Apart from these differences (and the standard naming prefixes `pvm_` for C, and `pvmf` for Fortran), a one-to-one correspondence exists between the two language bindings. Fortran interfaces to PVM are implemented as library stubs that in turn invoke the corresponding C routines, after casting and/or dereferencing arguments as appropriate. Thus, Fortran applications are required to link against the stubs library ('`libfpvm3.a`') as well as the C library.

All PVM tasks are identified by an integer task identifier *tid.* Messages are sent to tids and received from tids. Since tids must be unique across the entire virtual machine, they are supplied by the local pvmd and are not user chosen. Although PVM encodes information into each tid to improve performance, the user is expected to treat the tids as opaque integer identifiers. PVM contains several routines that return tid values so that the user application can identify other tasks in the system.

As mentioned earlier, tasks interact through explicit message passing, identifying each other with a system-assigned, opaque tid.

Shown in Figure 10.2 is the body of the PVM program '`hello.c`', a simple example that illustrates the basic concepts of PVM programming. This program

```
#include "pvm3.h"

main()
{
        int cc, tid, msgtag;
        char buf[100];

        printf("i'm t%x\n", pvm_mytid());

        cc = pvm_spawn("hello_other", (char**)0, 0, "", 1, &tid);

        if (cc == 1) {
                msgtag = 1;
                pvm_recv(tid, msgtag);
                pvm_upkstr(buf);
                printf("from t%x: %s\n", tid, buf);
        } else
                printf("can't start hello_other\n");

        pvm_exit();
}
```

Figure 10.2: PVM program '`hello.c`'.

is intended to be invoked manually; after printing its task id (obtained with `pvm_mytid()`), it initiates a copy of another program called '`hello_other.c`' using the `pvm_spawn()` function. A successful spawn causes the program to execute a blocking receive using `pvm_recv`. After the message is received, it is unpacked into a format the receiving computer understands using `pvm_upkstr`. Then the program prints the message as well its task id. The final `pvm_exit` call dissociates the program from the PVM system.

Figure 10.3 is a listing of the hello_other program. Its first PVM action is to obtain the task id of its parent using the `pvm_parent` call. This program then obtains its hostname and transmits it to the parent using the three-call sequence: `pvm_initsend` to initialize the (transparent) send buffer; `pvm_pkstr` to place a string in a strongly typed and architecture-independent manner into the send buffer; and `pvm_send` to transmit it to the destination process specified by *ptid*, "tagging" the message with the number 1.

Message tags are user-defined identifiers put on a message by the sender so that

```
#include "pvm3.h"

main()
{
        int ptid, msgtag;
        char buf[100];

        ptid = pvm_parent();

        strcpy(buf, "hello, world from ");
        gethostname(buf + strlen(buf), 64);
        msgtag = 1;
        pvm_initsend(PvmDataDefault);
        pvm_pkstr(buf);
        pvm_send(ptid, msgtag);

        pvm_exit();
}
```

Figure 10.3: PVM program '`hello_other.c`'.

the receiving task can selectively get a particular message from the many that may have arrived. The receiver does not have to, nor may it be able to, know the tag put on a message. It is possible in PVM to probe for what tags have arrived so far. It is also possible to ignore the tag and simply receive the messages in the order they arrive at the receiving task. Message tags will become necessary as we explore more complicated PVM examples.

The next example, '`forkjoin.c`', demonstrates spawning a parallel application from one cluster node. We then show PVM used in a Fortran dot product program PSDOT.F and a matrix multiply example that demonstrates the use of groups. Lastly, we show an example of a master/worker PVM application that calculates heat diffusion through a wire.

10.2.1 fork/join

The fork/join example demonstrates how to spawn off PVM tasks and synchronize with them. The program spawns the number of tasks specified by the user during startup. The children then synchronize by sending a message to their parent task.

The parent receives a message from each of the spawned tasks and prints out information about the message from the child tasks.

This program contains the code for both the parent and the child tasks. Let's examine it in more detail. The first action the program takes is to call `pvm_mytid()`. In fork/join we check the value of `mytid`; if it is negative, indicating an error, we call `pvm_perror()` and exit the program. The `pvm_perror()` call will print a message indicating what went wrong with the last PVM call. In this case the last call was `pvm_mytid()`, so `pvm_perror()` might print a message indicating that PVM hasn't been started on this machine. The argument to `pvm_perror()` is a string that will be prepended to any error message printed by `pvm_perror()`. In this case we pass `argv[0]`, which is the name of the program as it was typed on the command-line. The `pvm_perror()` function is modeled after the Unix `perror()` function.

Assuming we obtained a valid result for `mytid`, we now call `pvm_parent()`. The `pvm_parent()` function will return the tid of the task that spawned the calling task. Since we run the initial `forkjoin` program from a command prompt, this initial task will not have a parent; it will not have been spawned by some other PVM task but will have been started manually by the user. For the initial fork/join task the result of `pvm_parent()` will not be any particular task id but an error code, `PvmNoParent`. Thus we can distinguish the parent fork/join task from the children by checking whether the result of the `pvm_parent()` call is equal to `PvmNoParent`. If this task is the parent, then it must spawn the children. If it is not the parent, then it must send a message to the parent.

Let's examine the code executed by the parent task. The number of tasks is taken from the command-line as `argv[1]`. If the number of tasks is not legal, then we exit the program, calling `pvm_exit()` and then returning. The call to `pvm_exit()` is important because it tells PVM this program will no longer be using any of the PVM facilities. (In this case the task exits and PVM will deduce that the dead task no longer needs its services. Regardless, it is good style to exit cleanly.) If the number of tasks is valid, fork/join will then attempt to spawn the children.

The `pvm_spawn()` call tells PVM to start `ntask` tasks named `argv[0]`. The second parameter is the argument list given to the spawned tasks. In this case we don't care to give the children any particular command-line arguments, so this value is null. The third parameter to spawn, `PvmTaskDefault`, is a flag telling PVM to spawn the tasks in the default method. The default method is to distribute the tasks round robin to all the cluster nodes in the virtual machine. Had we been interested in placing the children on a specific machine or a machine of a particular architecture, we would have used `PvmTaskHost` or `PvmTaskArch` for this flag and specified the host or architecture as the fourth parameter. Since we don't care where the tasks execute, we use `PvmTaskDefault` for the flag and `null` for the fourth parameter. Finally, `ntask` tells `spawn` how many tasks to start, and the integer array `child` will hold the task ids of the newly spawned children. The return value of `pvm_spawn()` indicates how many tasks were successfully spawned. If `info` is not equal to `ntask`, then some error occurred during the spawn. In case of an error, the error code is placed in the task id array, child, instead of the actual task id; `forkjoin` loops over this array and prints the task ids or any error codes. If no tasks were successfully spawned, then the program exits.

For each child task, the parent receives a message and prints out information about that message. The `pvm_recv()` call receives a message from any task as long as the tag for that message is `JOINTAG`. The return value of `pvm_recv()` is an integer indicating a message buffer. This integer can be used to find out information about message buffers. The subsequent call to `pvm_bufinfo()` does just this; it gets the length, tag, and task id of the sending process for the message indicated by `buf`. In `forkjoin` the messages sent by the children contain a single integer value, the task id of the child task. The `pvm_upkint()` call unpacks the integer from the message into the `mydata` variable. As a sanity check, `forkjoin` tests the value of `mydata` and the task id returned by `pvm_bufinfo()`. If the values differ, the program has a bug, and an error message is printed. Finally, the information about the message is printed, and the parent program exits.

The last segment of code in `forkjoin` will be executed by the child tasks. Before data is placed in a message buffer, the buffer must be initialized by calling `pvm_initsend()`. The parameter `PvmDataDefault` indicates that PVM should do whatever data conversion is needed to ensure that the data arrives in the correct format on the destination processor. In some cases this may result in unnecessary data conversions. If you are sure no data conversion will be needed because the destination machine uses the same data format, then you can use `PvmDataRaw` as a parameter to `pvm_initsend()`. The `pvm_pkint()` call places a single integer, `mytid`, into the message buffer. It is important to make sure the corresponding unpack call exactly matches the pack call. Packing an integer and unpacking it as a float is an error. There should be a one-to-one correspondence between pack and unpack calls. Finally, the message is sent to the parent task using a message tag of `JOINTAG`.

```
/*
    Fork Join Example
    Demonstrates how to spawn processes and exchange messages
*/
```

```
/* defines and prototypes for the PVM library */
#include <pvm3.h>

/* Maximum number of children this program will spawn */
#define MAXNCHILD   20
/* Tag to use for the joing message */
#define JOINTAG     11

int
main(int argc, char* argv[])
{

    /* number of tasks to spawn, use 3 as the default */
    int ntask = 3;
    /* return code from pvm calls */
    int info;
    /* my task id */
    int mytid;
    /* my parents task id */
    int myparent;
    /* children task id array */
    int child[MAXNCHILD];
    int i, mydata, buf, len, tag, tid;

    /* find out my task id number */
    mytid = pvm_mytid();

    /* check for error */
    if (mytid < 0) {
        /* print out the error */
        pvm_perror(argv[0]);
        /* exit the program */
        return -1;
        }
    /* find my parent's task id number */
    myparent = pvm_parent();

    /* exit if there is some error other than PvmNoParent */
    if ((myparent < 0) && (myparent != PvmNoParent)
         && (myparent != PvmParentNotSet)) {
        pvm_perror(argv[0]);
        pvm_exit();
        return -1;
        }
```

```
    /* if i don't have a parent then i am the parent */
    if (myparent == PvmNoParent || myparent == PvmParentNotSet) {
        /* find out how many tasks to spawn */
        if (argc == 2) ntask = atoi(argv[1]);

        /* make sure ntask is legal */
        if ((ntask < 1) || (ntask > MAXNCHILD)) { pvm_exit(); return 0; }

        /* spawn the child tasks */
        info = pvm_spawn(argv[0], (char**)0, PvmTaskDefault, (char*)0,
            ntask, child);
        /* print out the task ids */
        for (i = 0; i < ntask; i++)
            if (child[i] < 0) /* print the error code in decimal*/
                printf(" %d", child[i]);
            else  /* print the task id in hex */
                printf("t%x\t", child[i]);
        putchar('\n');

        /* make sure spawn succeeded */
        if (info == 0) { pvm_exit(); return -1; }

        /* only expect responses from those spawned correctly */
        ntask = info;

        for (i = 0; i < ntask; i++) {
            /* recv a message from any child process */
            buf = pvm_recv(-1, JOINTAG);
            if (buf < 0) pvm_perror("calling recv");
            info = pvm_bufinfo(buf, &len, &tag, &tid);
            if (info < 0) pvm_perror("calling pvm_bufinfo");
            info = pvm_upkint(&mydata, 1, 1);
            if (info < 0) pvm_perror("calling pvm_upkint");
            if (mydata != tid) printf("This should not happen!\n");
            printf("Length %d, Tag %d, Tid t%x\n", len, tag, tid);
            }
        pvm_exit();
        return 0;
        }

   /* i'm a child */
   info = pvm_initsend(PvmDataDefault);
   if (info < 0) {
```

```
% forkjoin
t10001c t40149  tc0037
Length 4, Tag 11, Tid t40149
Length 4, Tag 11, Tid tc0037
Length 4, Tag 11, Tid t10001c
% forkjoin 4
t10001e t10001d t4014b  tc0038
Length 4, Tag 11, Tid t4014b
Length 4, Tag 11, Tid tc0038
Length 4, Tag 11, Tid t10001d
Length 4, Tag 11, Tid t10001e
```

Figure 10.4: Output of fork/join program.

```
      pvm_perror("calling pvm_initsend"); pvm_exit(); return -1;
      }
   info = pvm_pkint(&mytid, 1, 1);
   if (info < 0) {
      pvm_perror("calling pvm_pkint"); pvm_exit(); return -1;
      }
   info = pvm_send(myparent, JOINTAG);
   if (info < 0) {
      pvm_perror("calling pvm_send"); pvm_exit(); return -1;
      }
   pvm_exit();
   return 0;
}
```

Figure 10.4 shows the output of running fork/join. Notice that the order the messages were received is nondeterministic. Since the main loop of the parent processes messages on a first-come first-served basis, the order of the prints are determined simply by the time it takes messages to travel from the child tasks to the parent.

10.2.2 Dot Product

Here we show a simple Fortran program, PSDOT, for computing a dot product. The program computes the dot product of two arrays, X and Y. First `PSDOT` calls `PVMFMYTID()` and `PVMFPARENT()`. The `PVMFPARENT` call will return `PVMNOPARENT` if the task wasn't spawned by another PVM task. If this is the case, then `PSDOT` task is the master and must spawn the other worker copies of `PSDOT`. `PSDOT` then asks the user for the number of processes to use and the length of vectors to compute. Each spawned process will receive $n/nproc$ elements of X and Y, where n is the length of the vectors and *nproc* is the number of processes being used in the computation. If *nproc* does not divide n evenly, then the master will compute the dot product on the extra elements. The subroutine `SGENMAT` randomly generates values for X and Y. `PSDOT` then spawns $nproc-1$ copies of itself and sends each new task a part of the X and Y arrays. The message contains the length of the subarrays in the message and the subarrays themselves. After the master spawns the worker processes and sends out the subvectors, the master then computes the dot product on its portion of X and Y. The master process then receives the other local dot products from the worker processes. Notice that the `PVMFRECV` call uses a wild card (-1) for the task id parameter. This indicates that a message from *any* task will satisfy the receive. Using the wild card in this manner results in a race condition. In this case the race condition does not cause a problem because addition is commutative; in other words, it doesn't matter in which order we add up the partial sums from the workers. However, unless one is certain that the race will not affect the program adversely, race conditions should be avoided.

Once the master receives all the local dot products and sums them into a global dot product, it then calculates the entire dot product locally. These two results are then subtracted, and the difference between the two values is printed. A small difference can be expected because of the variation in floating-point roundoff errors.

If the `PSDOT` program is a worker, then it receives a message from the master process containing subarrays of X and Y. It calculates the dot product of these subarrays and sends the result back to the master process. In the interests of brevity we do not include the `SGENMAT` and `SDOT` subroutines.

```
      PROGRAM PSDOT
*
*  PSDOT performs a parallel inner (or dot) product, where the vectors
*  X and Y start out on a master node, which then sets up the virtual
*  machine, farms out the data and work, and sums up the local pieces
*  to get a global inner product.
*
*     .. External Subroutines ..
      EXTERNAL PVMFMYTID, PVMFPARENT, PVMFSPAWN, PVMFEXIT, PVMFINITSEND
      EXTERNAL PVMFPACK, PVMFSEND, PVMFRECV, PVMFUNPACK, SGENMAT
*
*     .. External Functions ..
      INTEGER ISAMAX
      REAL SDOT
```

```
      EXTERNAL ISAMAX, SDOT
*
*     .. Intrinsic Functions ..
      INTRINSIC MOD
*
*     .. Parameters ..
      INTEGER MAXN
      PARAMETER ( MAXN = 8000 )
      INCLUDE 'fpvm3.h'
*
*     .. Scalars ..
      INTEGER N, LN, MYTID, NPROCS, IBUF, IERR
      INTEGER I, J, K
      REAL LDOT, GDOT
*
*     .. Arrays ..
      INTEGER TIDS(0:63)
      REAL X(MAXN), Y(MAXN)
*
*     Enroll in PVM and get my and the master process' task ID number
*
      CALL PVMFMYTID( MYTID )
      CALL PVMFPARENT( TIDS(0) )
*
*     If I need to spawn other processes (I am master process)
*
      IF ( TIDS(0) .EQ. PVMNOPARENT ) THEN
*
*        Get starting information
*
         WRITE(*,*) 'How many processes should participate (1-64)?'
         READ(*,*) NPROCS
         WRITE(*,2000) MAXN
         READ(*,*) N
         TIDS(0) = MYTID
         IF ( N .GT. MAXN ) THEN
            WRITE(*,*) 'N too large.  Increase parameter MAXN to run'//
     $                 'this case.'
            STOP
         END IF
*
*        LN is the number of elements of the dot product to do
*        locally.  Everyone has the same number, with the master
*        getting any left over elements.  J stores the number of
```

```
*       elements rest of procs do.
*
        J = N / NPROCS
        LN = J + MOD(N, NPROCS)
        I = LN + 1
*
*       Randomly generate X and Y
*       Note: SGENMAT() routine is not provided here
*
        CALL SGENMAT( N, 1, X, N, MYTID, NPROCS, MAXN, J )
        CALL SGENMAT( N, 1, Y, N, I, N, LN, NPROCS )
*
*       Loop over all worker processes
*
        DO 10 K = 1, NPROCS-1
*
*          Spawn process and check for error
*
           CALL PVMFSPAWN( 'psdot', 0, 'anywhere', 1, TIDS(K), IERR )
           IF (IERR .NE. 1) THEN
              WRITE(*,*) 'ERROR, could not spawn process #',K,
     $                   '. Dying . . .'
              CALL PVMFEXIT( IERR )
              STOP
           END IF
*
*          Send out startup info
*
           CALL PVMFINITSEND( PVMDEFAULT, IBUF )
           CALL PVMFPACK( INTEGER4, J, 1, 1, IERR )
           CALL PVMFPACK( REAL4, X(I), J, 1, IERR )
           CALL PVMFPACK( REAL4, Y(I), J, 1, IERR )
           CALL PVMFSEND( TIDS(K), 0, IERR )
           I = I + J
   10   CONTINUE
*
*       Figure master's part of dot product
*       SDOT() is part of the BLAS Library (compile with -lblas)
*
        GDOT = SDOT( LN, X, 1, Y, 1 )
*
*       Receive the local dot products, and
*       add to get the global dot product
*
```

```
         DO 20 K = 1, NPROCS-1
            CALL PVMFRECV( -1, 1, IBUF )
            CALL PVMFUNPACK( REAL4, LDOT, 1, 1, IERR )
            GDOT = GDOT + LDOT
   20    CONTINUE
*
*        Print out result
*
         WRITE(*,*) '  '
         WRITE(*,*) '<x,y> = ',GDOT
*
*        Do sequential dot product and subtract from
*        distributed dot product to get desired error estimate
*
         LDOT = SDOT( N, X, 1, Y, 1 )
         WRITE(*,*) '<x,y> : sequential dot product.  <x,y>^ : '//
     $              'distributed dot product.'
         WRITE(*,*) '| <x,y> - <x,y>^ | = ',ABS(GDOT - LDOT)
         WRITE(*,*) 'Run completed.'
*
*     If I am a worker process (i.e. spawned by master process)
*
      ELSE
*
*        Receive startup info
*
         CALL PVMFRECV( TIDS(0), 0, IBUF )
         CALL PVMFUNPACK( INTEGER4, LN, 1, 1, IERR )
         CALL PVMFUNPACK( REAL4, X, LN, 1, IERR )
         CALL PVMFUNPACK( REAL4, Y, LN, 1, IERR )
*
*        Figure local dot product and send it in to master
*
         LDOT = SDOT( LN, X, 1, Y, 1 )
         CALL PVMFINITSEND( PVMDEFAULT, IBUF )
         CALL PVMFPACK( REAL4, LDOT, 1, 1, IERR )
         CALL PVMFSEND( TIDS(0), 1, IERR )
      END IF
*
      CALL PVMFEXIT( 0 )
*
1000  FORMAT(I10,' Successfully spawned process #',I2,', TID =',I10)
2000  FORMAT('Enter the length of vectors to multiply (1 -',I7,'):')
      STOP
```

```
*
*     End program PSDOT
*
      END
```

10.2.3 Matrix Multiply

In this example we program a matrix multiply algorithm described by Fox et al. in [39]. The `mmult` program can be found at the end of this section. The `mmult` program will calculate $C = AB$ where C, A, and B are all square matrices. For simplicity we assume that $m \times m$ tasks are used to calculate the solution. Each task calculates a subblock of the resulting matrix C. The block size and the value of m are given as a command-line argument to the program. The matrices A and B are also stored as blocks distributed over the m^2 tasks. Before delving into the details of the program, let us first describe the algorithm at a high level.

In our grid of $m \times m$ tasks, each task (t_{ij}, where $0 \leq i, j < m$), initially contains blocks C_{ij}, A_{ij}, and B_{ij}. In the first step of the algorithm the tasks on the diagonal (t_{ij} where $i = j$) send their block A_{ii} to all the other tasks in row i. After the transmission of A_{ii}, all tasks calculate $A_{ii} \times B_{ij}$ and add the result into C_{ij}. In the next step, the column blocks of B are rotated. That is, t_{ij} sends its block of B to $t_{(i-1)j}$. (Task t_{0j} sends its B block to $t_{(m-1)j}$.) The tasks now return to the first step, $A_{i(i+1)}$ is multicast to all other tasks in row i, and the algorithm continues. After m iterations, the C matrix contains $A \times B$, and the B matrix has been rotated back into place.

Let us now go over the matrix multiply as it is programmed in PVM. In PVM there is no restriction on which tasks may communicate with which other tasks. However, for this program we would like to think of the tasks as a two-dimensional conceptual torus. In order to enumerate the tasks, each task joins the group `mmult`. Group ids are used to map tasks to our torus. The first task to join a group is given the group id of zero. In the `mmult` program, the task with group id zero spawns the other tasks and sends the parameters for the matrix multiply to those tasks. The parameters are m and *bklsize*, the square root of the number of blocks and the size of a block, respectively. After all the tasks have been spawned and the parameters transmitted, `pvm_barrier()` is called to make sure all the tasks have joined the group. If the barrier is not performed, later calls to `pvm_gettid()` might fail because a task may not have yet joined the group.

After the barrier, the task ids for the other tasks are stored in the `row` in the array `myrow`. Specifically, the program calculates group ids for all the tasks in the row, and we ask PVM for the task id for the corresponding group id. Next the program allocates the blocks for the matrices using `malloc()`. (In an actual application program we would expect that the matrices would already be allocated.) Then the program calculates the row and column of the block of C it will be computing; this calculation is based on the value of the group id. The group ids range from 0 to $m-1$ inclusive. Thus, the integer division of $(mygid/m)$ will give the task's row and $(mygid \bmod m)$ will give the column if we assume a row major mapping of group ids to tasks. Using a similar mapping, we calculate the group id of the task directly *above* and *below* in the torus and store their task ids in `up` and `down`, respectively.

Next the blocks are initialized by calling `InitBlock()`. This function simply initializes A to random values, B to the identity matrix, and C to zeros. This will allow us to verify the computation at the end of the program by checking that $A = C$.

Finally we enter the main loop to calculate the matrix multiply. First the tasks on the diagonal multicast their block of A to the other tasks in their row. Note that the array `myrow` actually contains the task id of the task doing the multicast. Recall that `pvm_mcast()` will send to all the tasks in the tasks array except the calling task. This approach works well in the case of `mmult` because we don't want to have to needlessly handle the extra message coming into the multicasting task with an extra `pvm_recv()`. Both the multicasting task and the tasks receiving the block calculate the AB for the diagonal block and the block of B residing in the task.

After the subblocks have been multiplied and added into the C block, we now shift the B blocks vertically. Specifically, the block of B is packed into a message and sent to the `up` task id; then a new B block is received from the `down` task id.

Note that we use different message tags for sending the A blocks and the B blocks as well as for different iterations of the loop. We also fully specify the task ids when doing a `pvm_recv()`. It's tempting to use wild cards for the fields of `pvm_recv()`; however, such use can be dangerous. For instance, had we incorrectly calculated the value for `up` and used a wild card for the `pvm_recv()` instead of `down`, we would be sending messages to the wrong tasks without knowing it. In this example we fully specify messages, thereby reducing the possibility of receiving a message from the wrong task or the wrong phase of the algorithm.

Once the computation is complete, we check to see that $A = C$, just to verify that the matrix multiply correctly calculated the values of C. This step would not be done in a matrix-multiply library routine, for example.

You do not have to call `pvm_lvgroup()` because PVM will automatically detect that the task has exited and will remove it from the group. It is good form, however, to leave the group before calling `pvm_exit()`. The reset command from the PVM console will reset all the PVM groups. The `pvm_gstat` command will print the status of any groups that currently exist.

```
/*
    Matrix Multiply
*/

/* defines and prototypes for the PVM library */
#include <pvm3.h>
#include <stdio.h>

/* Maximum number of children this program will spawn */
#define MAXNTIDS    100
#define MAXROW      10

/* Message tags */
#define ATAG        2
#define BTAG        3
#define DIMTAG      5

void
InitBlock(float *a, float *b, float *c, int blk, int row, int col)
{
    int len, ind;
    int i,j;

    srand(pvm_mytid());
    len = blk*blk;
    for (ind = 0; ind < len; ind++)
        { a[ind] = (float)(rand()%1000)/100.0; c[ind] = 0.0; }
    for (i = 0; i < blk; i++) {
        for (j = 0; j < blk; j++) {
            if (row == col)
                b[j*blk+i] = (i==j)? 1.0 : 0.0;
            else
                b[j*blk+i] = 0.0;
            }
        }
}

void
BlockMult(float* c, float* a, float* b, int blk)
{
    int i,j,k;
```

```
    for (i = 0; i < blk; i++)
        for (j = 0; j < blk; j ++)
            for (k = 0; k < blk; k++)
                c[i*blk+j] += (a[i*blk+k] * b[k*blk+j]);
}

int
main(int argc, char* argv[])
{

    /* number of tasks to spawn, use 3 as the default */
    int ntask = 2;
    /* return code from pvm calls */
    int info;
    /* my task and group id */
    int mytid, mygid;
    /* children task id array */
    int child[MAXNTIDS-1];
    int i, m, blksize;
    /* array of the tids in my row */
    int myrow[MAXROW];
    float *a, *b, *c, *atmp;
    int row, col, up, down;

    /* find out my task id number */
    mytid = pvm_mytid();
    pvm_setopt(PvmRoute, PvmRouteDirect);

    /* check for error */
    if (mytid < 0) {
        /* print out the error */
        pvm_perror(argv[0]);
        /* exit the program */
        return -1;
        }

    /* join the mmult group */
    mygid = pvm_joingroup("mmult");
    if (mygid < 0) {
        pvm_perror(argv[0]); pvm_exit(); return -1;
        }

    /* if my group id is 0 then I must spawn the other tasks */
```

```
if (mygid == 0) {
    /* find out how many tasks to spawn */
    if (argc == 3) {
        m = atoi(argv[1]);
        blksize = atoi(argv[2]);
        }
    if (argc < 3) {
        fprintf(stderr, "usage: mmult m blk\n");
        pvm_lvgroup("mmult"); pvm_exit(); return -1;
        }

    /* make sure ntask is legal */
    ntask = m*m;
    if ((ntask < 1) || (ntask >= MAXNTIDS)) {
        fprintf(stderr, "ntask = %d not valid.\n", ntask);
        pvm_lvgroup("mmult"); pvm_exit(); return -1;
        }
    /* if there is more than one task spawn them*/
    if (ntask > 1) {

        /* spawn the child tasks */
        info = pvm_spawn("mmult", (char**)0, PvmTaskDefault, (char*)0,
        ntask-1, child);

        /* make sure spawn succeeded */
        if (info != ntask-1) {
            pvm_lvgroup("mmult"); pvm_exit(); return -1;
            }

        /* send the matrix dimension */
        pvm_initsend(PvmDataDefault);
        pvm_pkint(&m, 1, 1);
        pvm_pkint(&blksize, 1, 1);
        pvm_mcast(child, ntask-1, DIMTAG);
        }
    }
else {
    /* recv the matrix dimension */
    pvm_recv(pvm_gettid("mmult", 0), DIMTAG);
    pvm_upkint(&m, 1, 1);
    pvm_upkint(&blksize, 1, 1);
    ntask = m*m;
    }
```

```
/* make sure all tasks have joined the group */

info = pvm_barrier("mmult",ntask);
if (info < 0) pvm_perror(argv[0]);

/* find the tids in my row */
for (i = 0; i < m; i++)
    myrow[i] = pvm_gettid("mmult", (mygid/m)*m + i);

/* allocate the memory for the local blocks */
a = (float*)malloc(sizeof(float)*blksize*blksize);
b = (float*)malloc(sizeof(float)*blksize*blksize);
c = (float*)malloc(sizeof(float)*blksize*blksize);
atmp = (float*)malloc(sizeof(float)*blksize*blksize);
/* check for valid pointers */
if (!(a && b && c && atmp)) {
    fprintf(stderr, "%s: out of memory!\n", argv[0]);
    free(a); free(b); free(c); free(atmp);
    pvm_lvgroup("mmult"); pvm_exit(); return -1;
    }

/* find my block's row and column */
row = mygid/m; col = mygid % m;
/* calculate the neighbor's above and below */
up = pvm_gettid("mmult", ((row)?(row-1):(m-1))*m+col);
down = pvm_gettid("mmult", ((row == (m-1))?col:(row+1)*m+col));

/* initialize the blocks */
InitBlock(a, b, c, blksize, row, col);

/* do the matrix multiply */
for (i = 0; i < m; i++) {
    /* mcast the block of matrix A */
    if (col == (row + i)%m) {
        pvm_initsend(PvmDataDefault);
        pvm_pkfloat(a, blksize*blksize, 1);
        pvm_mcast(myrow, m, (i+1)*ATAG);
        BlockMult(c,a,b,blksize);
        }
    else {
        pvm_recv(pvm_gettid("mmult", row*m + (row +i)%m), (i+1)*ATAG);
        pvm_upkfloat(atmp, blksize*blksize, 1);
        BlockMult(c,atmp,b,blksize);
        }
```

```
        /* rotate the columns of B */
        pvm_initsend(PvmDataDefault);
        pvm_pkfloat(b, blksize*blksize, 1);
        pvm_send(up, (i+1)*BTAG);
        pvm_recv(down, (i+1)*BTAG);
        pvm_upkfloat(b, blksize*blksize, 1);
        }

    /* check it */
    for (i = 0 ; i < blksize*blksize; i++)
        if (a[i] != c[i])
            printf("Error a[%d] (%g) != c[%d] (%g) \n", i, a[i],i,c[i]);

    printf("Done.\n");
    free(a); free(b); free(c); free(atmp);
    pvm_lvgroup("mmult");
    pvm_exit();
    return 0;
}
```

10.2.4 One-Dimensional Heat Equation

Here we present a PVM program that calculates heat diffusion through a substrate, in this case a wire. Consider the one-dimensional heat equation on a thin wire,

$$\frac{\partial A}{\partial t} = \frac{\partial^2 A}{\partial x^2}, \tag{10.1}$$

and a discretization of the form

$$\frac{A_{i+1,j} - A_{i,j}}{\triangle t} = \frac{A_{i,j+1} - 2A_{i,j} + A_{i,j-1}}{\triangle x^2}, \tag{10.2}$$

giving the explicit formula

$$A_{i+1,j} = A_{i,j} + \frac{\triangle t}{\triangle x^2}(A_{i,j+1} - 2A_{i,j} + A_{i,j-1}). \tag{10.3}$$

The initial and boundary conditions are

$A(t,0) = 0$, $A(t,1) = 0$ for all t
$A(0,x) = \sin(\pi x)$ for $0 \leq x \leq 1$.

The pseudocode for this computation is as follows:

```
for i = 1:tsteps-1;
    t = t+dt;
    a(i+1,1)=0;
    a(i+1,n+2)=0;
    for j = 2:n+1;
        a(i+1,j)=a(i,j) + mu*(a(i,j+1)-2*a(i,j)+a(i,j-1));
    end;
end
```

For this example we use a master/worker programming model. The master, '`heat.c`', spawns five copies of the program `heatslv`. The workers compute the heat diffusion for subsections of the wire in parallel. At each time step the workers exchange boundary information, in this case the temperature of the wire at the boundaries between processors.

Let's take a closer look at the code. In '`heat.c`' the array `solution` will hold the solution for the heat diffusion equation at each time step. First the `heatslv` tasks are spawned. Next, the initial dataset is computed. Notice that the ends of the wires are given initial temperature values of zero.

The main part of the program is then executed four times, each with a different value for Δt. A timer is used to compute the elapsed time of each compute phase. The initial datasets are sent to the `heatslv` tasks. The left and right neighbor task ids are sent along with the initial dataset. The `heatslv` tasks use these to communicate boundary information. Alternatively, we could have used the PVM group calls to map tasks to segments of the wire. By using that approach we would have avoided explicitly communicating the task ids to the slave processes.

After sending the initial data, the master process waits for results. When the results arrive, they are integrated into the solution matrix, the elapsed time is calculated, and the solution is written to the output file.

Once the data for all four phases have been computed and stored, the master program prints out the elapsed times and kills the slave processes.

```
/*
heat.c

  Use PVM to solve a simple heat diffusion differential equation,
  using 1 master program and 5 slaves.

  The master program sets up the data, communicates it to the slaves
  and waits for the results to be sent from the slaves.
  Produces xgraph ready files of the results.
```

```
*/

#include "pvm3.h"
#include <stdio.h>
#include <math.h>
#include <time.h>
#define SLAVENAME "heatslv"
#define NPROC 5
#define TIMESTEP 100
#define PLOTINC 10
#define SIZE 1000

int num_data = SIZE/NPROC;

main()
{   int mytid, task_ids[NPROC], i, j;
    int left, right, k, l;
    int step = TIMESTEP;
    int info;

    double init[SIZE], solution[TIMESTEP][SIZE];
    double result[TIMESTEP*SIZE/NPROC], deltax2;
    FILE *filenum;
    char *filename[4][7];
    double deltat[4];
    time_t t0;
    int etime[4];

    filename[0][0] = "graph1";
    filename[1][0] = "graph2";
    filename[2][0] = "graph3";
    filename[3][0] = "graph4";

    deltat[0] = 5.0e-1;
    deltat[1] = 5.0e-3;
    deltat[2] = 5.0e-6;
    deltat[3] = 5.0e-9;

/* enroll in pvm */
    mytid = pvm_mytid();

/* spawn the slave tasks */
    info = pvm_spawn(SLAVENAME,(char **)0,PvmTaskDefault,"",
```

```
        NPROC,task_ids);
/* create the initial data set */
    for (i = 0; i < SIZE; i++)
        init[i] = sin(M_PI * ( (double)i / (double)(SIZE-1) ));
    init[0] = 0.0;
    init[SIZE-1] = 0.0;

/* run the problem 4 times for different values of delta t */
    for (l = 0; l < 4; l++) {
        deltax2 = (deltat[l]/pow(1.0/(double)SIZE,2.0));
        /* start timing for this run */
        time(&t0);
        etime[l] = t0;
/* send the initial data to the slaves. */
/* include neighbor info for exchanging boundary data */
        for (i = 0; i < NPROC; i++) {
            pvm_initsend(PvmDataDefault);
            left = (i == 0) ? 0 : task_ids[i-1];
            pvm_pkint(&left, 1, 1);
            right = (i == (NPROC-1)) ? 0 : task_ids[i+1];
            pvm_pkint(&right, 1, 1);
            pvm_pkint(&step, 1, 1);
            pvm_pkdouble(&deltax2, 1, 1);
            pvm_pkint(&num_data, 1, 1);
            pvm_pkdouble(&init[num_data*i], num_data, 1);
            pvm_send(task_ids[i], 4);
            }

/* wait for the results */
        for (i = 0; i < NPROC; i++) {
            pvm_recv(task_ids[i], 7);
            pvm_upkdouble(&result[0], num_data*TIMESTEP, 1);
/* update the solution */
            for (j = 0; j < TIMESTEP; j++)
                for (k = 0; k < num_data; k++)
                    solution[j][num_data*i+k] = result[wh(j,k)];
            }

/* stop timing */
        time(&t0);
        etime[l] = t0 - etime[l];

/* produce the output */
        filenum = fopen(filename[l][0], "w");
```

```
        fprintf(filenum,"TitleText: Wire Heat over Delta Time: %e\n",
            deltat[l]);
        fprintf(filenum,"XUnitText: Distance\nYUnitText: Heat\n");
        for (i = 0; i < TIMESTEP; i = i + PLOTINC) {
            fprintf(filenum,"\"Time index: %d\n",i);
            for (j = 0; j < SIZE; j++)
                fprintf(filenum,"%d %e\n",j, solution[i][j]);
            fprintf(filenum,"\n");
            }
        fclose (filenum);
    }

/* print the timing information */
    printf("Problem size: %d\n",SIZE);
    for (i = 0; i < 4; i++)
        printf("Time for run %d: %d sec\n",i,etime[i]);

/* kill the slave processes */
    for (i = 0; i < NPROC; i++) pvm_kill(task_ids[i]);
    pvm_exit();
}

int wh(x, y)
int x, y;
{
    return(x*num_data+y);
}
```

The `heatslv` programs do the actual computation of the heat diffusion through the wire. The worker program consists of an infinite loop that receives an initial dataset, iteratively computes a solution based on this dataset (exchanging boundary information with neighbors on each iteration), and sends the resulting partial solution back to the master process. As an alternative to using an infinite loop in the worker tasks, we could send a special message to the worker ordering it to exit. Instead, we simply use the infinite loop in the worker tasks and kill them off from the master program. A third option would be to have the workers execute only once, exiting after processing a single dataset from the master. This would require placing the master's spawn call inside the main `for` loop of '`heat.c`'. While this option would work, it would needlessly add overhead to the overall computation.

For each time step and before each compute phase, the boundary values of the temperature matrix are exchanged. The left-hand boundary elements are first sent to the left neighbor task and received from the right neighbor task. Symmetrically, the right-hand boundary elements are sent to the right neighbor and then received from the left neighbor. The task ids for the neighbors are checked to make sure no attempt is made to send or receive messages to nonexistent tasks.

```
/*

heatslv.c

    The slaves receive the initial data from the host,
    exchange boundary information with neighbors,
    and calculate the heat change in the wire.
    This is done for a number of iterations, sent by the master.

*/

#include "pvm3.h"
#include <stdio.h>

int num_data;

main()
{
    int mytid, left, right, i, j, master;
    int timestep;

    double *init, *A;
    double leftdata, rightdata, delta, leftside, rightside;

/* enroll in pvm */
    mytid = pvm_mytid();
    master = pvm_parent();

/* receive my data from the master program */
  while(1) {
    pvm_recv(master, 4);
    pvm_upkint(&left, 1, 1);
    pvm_upkint(&right, 1, 1);
    pvm_upkint(&timestep, 1, 1);
    pvm_upkdouble(&delta, 1, 1);
    pvm_upkint(&num_data, 1, 1);
    init = (double *) malloc(num_data*sizeof(double));
    pvm_upkdouble(init, num_data, 1);

/* copy the initial data into my working array */
```

```
    A = (double *) malloc(num_data * timestep * sizeof(double));
    for (i = 0; i < num_data; i++) A[i] = init[i];

/* perform the calculation */

  for (i = 0; i < timestep-1; i++) {
    /* trade boundary info with my neighbors */
    /*  send left, receive right    */
    if (left != 0) {
        pvm_initsend(PvmDataDefault);
        pvm_pkdouble(&A[wh(i,0)],1,1);
        pvm_send(left, 5);
        }
    if (right != 0) {
        pvm_recv(right, 5);
        pvm_upkdouble(&rightdata, 1, 1);
    /* send right, receive left */
        pvm_initsend(PvmDataDefault);
        pvm_pkdouble(&A[wh(i,num_data-1)],1,1);
        pvm_send(right, 6);
        }
    if (left != 0) {
        pvm_recv(left, 6);
        pvm_upkdouble(&leftdata,1,1);
        }

/* do the calculations for this iteration */

    for (j = 0; j < num_data; j++) {
        leftside = (j == 0) ? leftdata : A[wh(i,j-1)];
        rightside = (j == (num_data-1)) ? rightdata : A[wh(i,j+1)];
        if ((j==0)&&(left==0))
            A[wh(i+1,j)] = 0.0;
        else if ((j==(num_data-1))&&(right==0))
            A[wh(i+1,j)] = 0.0;
        else
            A[wh(i+1,j)]=
                A[wh(i,j)]+delta*(rightside-2*A[wh(i,j)]+leftside);
        }
  }

/* send the results back to the master program */

    pvm_initsend(PvmDataDefault);
```

```
    pvm_pkdouble(&A[0],num_data*timestep,1);
    pvm_send(master,7);
  }

/* just for good measure */
  pvm_exit();
}

int wh(x, y)
int x, y;
{
    return(x*num_data+y);
}
```

In this section we have given a variety of example programs written in both Fortran and C. These examples demonstrate various ways of writing PVM programs. Some divide the application into two separate programs, while others use a single program with conditionals to handle spawning and computing phases. These examples show different styles of communication, both among worker tasks and between worker and master tasks. In some cases messages are used for synchronization, and in others the master processes simply kill off the workers when they are no longer needed.

10.3 Installing PVM

This section describes how to set up the PVM software package, how to configure a simple virtual machine, and how to compile and run the example programs supplied with PVM. The first part describes the straightforward use of PVM and the most common problems in setting up and running PVM. The latter part describes some of the more advanced options available for customizing your PVM environment.

10.3.1 Setting Up PVM

One of the reasons for PVM's popularity is that PVM is simple to set up and use. It does not require special privileges to be installed. Anyone with a valid login on the hosts can do so. In addition, only one person at an organization needs to get and install PVM for everyone at that organization to use it.

PVM uses two environment variables when starting and running. Each PVM user needs to set these two variables to use PVM. The first variable is `PVM_ROOT`, which is set to the location of the installed `pvm3` directory. The second variable is

PVM_ARCH, which tells PVM the architecture of this host and thus what executables to pick from the PVM_ROOT directory.

Because of security concerns many sites no longer allow any of their computers, including those in clusters, to use rsh, which is what PVM uses by default to add hosts to a virtual machine. It is easy to configure PVM to use ssh instead. Just edit the file 'PVM_ROOT/conf/PVM_ARCH.def' and replace rsh with ssh then recompile PVM and your applications.

If PVM is already installed at your site, you can skip ahead to "Creating Your Personal PVM." The PVM source comes with directories and makefiles for Linux and most architectures you are likely to have in your cluster. Building for each architecture type is done automatically by logging on to a host, going into the PVM_ROOT directory, and typing make. The 'makefile' will automatically determine which architecture it is being executed on, create appropriate subdirectories, and build pvmd3, libpvm3.a, and libfpvm3.a, pvmgs, and libgpvm3.a. It places all these files in 'PVM_ROOT/lib/PVM_ARCH' with the exception of pvmgs, which is placed in 'PVM_ROOT/bin/PVM_ARCH'.

Setup Summary

- Set PVM_ROOT and PVM_ARCH in your '.cshrc' file.
- Build PVM for each architecture type.
- Create an '.rhosts' file on each host listing all the hosts.
- Create a '$HOME/.xpvm_hosts' file listing all the hosts prepended by an "&".

10.3.2 Creating Your Personal PVM

Before we go over the steps to compile and run parallel PVM programs, you should be sure you can start up PVM and configure a virtual machine. On any host on which PVM has been installed you can type

```
% pvm
```

and you should get back a PVM console prompt signifying that PVM is now running on this host. You can add hosts to your virtual machine by typing at the console prompt

```
pvm> add hostname
```

You also can delete hosts (except the one you are on) from your virtual machine by typing

```
pvm> delete hostname
```

If you get the message "Can't Start `pvmd`," PVM will run autodiagnostics and report the reason found.

To see what the present virtual machine looks like, you can type

```
pvm> conf
```

To see what PVM tasks are running on the virtual machine, you can type

```
pvm> ps -a
```

Of course, you don't have any tasks running yet. If you type "quit" at the console prompt, the console will quit, but your virtual machine and tasks will continue to run. At any command prompt on any host in the virtual machine, you can type

```
% pvm
```

and you will get the message "pvm already running" and the console prompt. When you are finished with the virtual machine you should type

```
pvm> halt
```

This command kills any PVM tasks, shuts down the virtual machine, and exits the console. This is the recommended method to stop PVM because it makes sure that the virtual machine shuts down cleanly.

You should practice starting and stopping and adding hosts to PVM until you are comfortable with the PVM console. A full description of the PVM console and its many command options is given in the documentation that comes with the PVM software.

If you don't wish to type in a bunch of hostnames each time, there is a hostfile option. You can list the hostnames in a file one per line and then type

```
% pvm hostfile
```

PVM will then add all the listed hosts simultaneously before the console prompt appears. Several options can be specified on a per host basis in the hostfile, if you wish to customize your virtual machine for a particular application or environment.

PVM may also be started in other ways. The functions of the console and a performance monitor have been combined in a graphical user interface called XPVM, which is available from the PVM Web site. If XPVM has been installed at your site, then it can be used to start PVM. To start PVM with this interface, type

```
% xpvm
```

The menu button labeled "hosts" will pull down a list of hosts you can add. If you click on a hostname, it is added, and an icon of the machine appears in an animation of the virtual machine. A host is deleted if you click on a hostname that is already in the virtual machine. On startup XPVM reads the file '`$HOME/.xpvm_hosts`', which is a list of hosts to display in this menu. Hosts without leading "&" are added all at once at startup.

The quit and halt buttons work just like the PVM console. If you quit XPVM and then restart it, XPVM will automatically display what the running virtual machine looks like. Practice starting and stopping and adding hosts with XPVM. If any errors occur, they should appear in the window where you started XPVM.

10.3.3 Running PVM Programs

This section describes how to compile and run the example programs supplied with the PVM software. These example programs make useful templates on which to base your own PVM programs.

The first step is to copy the example programs into your own area:

```
% cp -r $PVM_ROOT/examples $HOME/pvm3/examples
% cd $HOME/pvm3/examples
```

The examples directory contains a '`Makefile.aimk`' and '`Readme`' file that describe how to build the examples. PVM supplies an architecture-independent make, `aimk`, that automatically determines `PVM_ARCH` and links any operating system–specific libraries to your application. when you placed the '`cshrc.stub`' in your '`.cshrc`' file, `aimk` was automatically added to your `$PATH`. Using `aimk` allows you to leave the source code and makefile unchanged as you compile across different architectures.

The master/worker programming model is the most popular model used in cluster computing. To compile the master/slave C example, type

```
% aimk master slave
```

If you prefer to work with Fortran, compile the Fortran version with

```
% aimk fmaster fslave
```

Depending on the location of `PVM_ROOT`, the `INCLUDE` statement at the top of the Fortran examples may need to be changed. If `PVM_ROOT` is not '`HOME/pvm3`', then change the include to point to '`$PVM_ROOT/include/fpvm3.h`'. Note that `PVM_ROOT` is not expanded inside the Fortran, so you must insert the actual path.

The makefile moves the executables to '$HOME/pvm3/bin/PVM_ARCH', which is the default location where PVM will look for them on all hosts. If your file system is not common across all your cluster nodes, then you will have to copy these executables on all your nodes.

From one window start up PVM and configure some hosts. These examples are designed to run on any number of hosts, including one. In another window, cd to the location of the PVM executables and type

```
% master
```

The program will ask about the number of tasks. This number does not have to match the number of hosts in these examples. Try several combinations.

The first example illustrates the ability to run a PVM program from a prompt on any host in the virtual machine. This is how you would run a serial a.out program on a front console of a cluster. The next example, which is also a master/slave model called codehitc, shows how to spawn PVM jobs from the PVM console and also from XPVM.

The model hitc illustrates dynamic load balancing using the pool of tasks paradigm. In this paradigm, the master program manages a large queue of tasks, always sending idle slave programs more work to do until the queue is empty. This paradigm is effective in situations where the hosts have very different computational powers because the least-loaded or more powerful hosts do more of the work and all the hosts stay busy until the end of the problem. To compile hitc, type

```
% aimk hitc hitc_slave
```

Since hitc does not require any user input, it can be spawned directly from the PVM console. Start the PVM console, and add some cluster nodes. At the PVM console prompt, type

```
pvm> spawn -> hitc
```

The "->" spawn option causes all the print statements in hitc and in the slaves to appear in the console window. This can be a useful feature when debugging your first few PVM programs. You may wish to experiment with this option by placing print statements in 'hitc.f' and 'hitc_slave.f' and recompiling.

10.3.4 PVM Console Details

The PVM console, called pvm, is a standalone PVM task that allows you to interactively start, query, and modify the virtual machine. The console may be started and stopped multiple times on any of the hosts in the virtual machine without affecting PVM or any applications that may be running.

When the console is started, pvm determines whether PVM is already running and, if not, automatically executes pvmd on this host, passing pvmd the command-line options and hostfile. Thus, PVM need not be running to start the console.

```
pvm [-n<hostname>] [hostfile]
```

The -n option is useful for specifying another name for the master pvmd (in case hostname doesn't match the IP address you want). This feature becomes very useful with Beowulf clusters because the nodes of the cluster sometime are on their own network. In this case the front-end node will have two hostnames: one for the cluster and one for the external network. The -n option lets you specify the cluster name directly during PVM startup.

Once started, the console prints the prompt

```
pvm>
```

and accepts commands from standard input. The available commands are as follows:

add followed by one or more hostnames (cluster nodes), adds these hosts to the virtual machine.

alias defines or lists command aliases.

conf lists the configuration of the virtual machine including hostname, pvmd task ID, architecture type, and a relative speed rating.

delete followed by one or more hostnames, deletes these hosts from the virtual machine. PVM processes still running on these hosts are lost .

echo echoes arguments.

halt kills all PVM processes including console and then shuts down PVM. All daemons exit.

help can be used to get information about any of the interactive commands. The help command may be followed by a command name that will list options and flags available for this command.

id prints console task id.

jobs lists running jobs.

kill can be used to terminate any PVM process.

mstat shows status of specified hosts.

ps -a lists all processes currently on the virtual machine, their locations, their task IDs, and their parents' task IDs.

pstat shows status of a single PVM process.

quit exits the console, leaving daemons and PVM jobs running.

reset kills all PVM processes except consoles, and resets all the internal PVM tables and message queues. The daemons are left in an idle state.

setenv displays or sets environment variables.

sig followed by a signal number and tid, sends the signal to the task.

spawn starts a PVM application. Options include the following:

- **-count** shows the number of tasks; default is 1
- **-(host)** spawn on host; default is any
- **-(PVM_ARCH)** spawn of hosts of type PVM_ARCH
- **-?** enable debugging
- -> redirect task output to console
- ->**file** redirect task output to file
- ->>**file** redirect task output append to file
- **-@** trace job; display output on console
- **-@file** trace job; output to file

unalias undefines command alias.

version prints version of PVM being used.

PVM supports the use of multiple consoles. It is possible to run a console on any host in an existing virtual machine and even multiple consoles on the same machine. It is possible to start up a console in the middle of a PVM application and check on its progress.

11 Fault-Tolerant and Adaptive Programs with PVM

Al Geist and Jim Kohl

A number of factors must be considered when you are developing applications for Beowulf clusters. In the preceding chapters the basic methods of message passing were illustrated so that you could create your own parallel programs. This chapter describes the issues and common methods for making parallel programs that are fault tolerant and adaptive.

Fault tolerance is the ability of an application to continue to run or make progress even if a hardware or software problem causes a node in the cluster to fail. It is also the ability to tolerate failures within the application itself. For example, one task inside a parallel application may get an error and abort, but the rest of the tasks are able to carry on the calculation. Because Beowulf clusters are built from commodity components that are designed for the desktop rather than heavy-duty computing, failures of components inside a cluster are higher than in a more expensive multiprocessor system that has an integrated RAS (Reliability, Availability, Serviceability) system.

While fault-tolerant programs can be thought of as adaptive, the term "adaptive programs" is used here more generally to mean parallel (or serial) programs that dynamically change their characteristics to better match the application's needs and the available resources. Examples include an application that adapts by adding or releasing nodes of the cluster according to its present computational needs and an application that creates and kills tasks based on what the computation needs.

In later chapters you will learn about Condor and other resource management tools that automatically provide some measure of fault tolerance and adaptability to jobs submitted to them. This chapter teaches the basics of how to write such tools yourself.

PVM is based on a dynamic computing model in which cluster nodes can be added and deleted from the computation on the fly and parallel tasks can be spawned or killed during the computation. PVM doesn't have nearly as rich a set of message-passing features as MPI; but, being a virtual machine model, PVM has a number of features that make it attractive for creating dynamic parallel programs. For this reason, PVM will be used to illustrate the concepts of fault tolerance and adaptability in this chapter.

11.1 Considerations for Fault Tolerance

A computational biologist at Oak Ridge National Laboratory wants to write an parallel application that runs 24/7 on his Beowulf cluster. The application involves analysis of the human genome and is driven by a constant stream of new data arriving from researchers all around the world. The data is not independent because new data helps refine and extend previously calculated sequences. How can he write such a program?

A company wants to write an application to process a constant stream of sales orders coming in from the Web. The program needs to be robust because down time costs not only the lost revenue stream but also wages of workers who are idle. The company has recently purchased a Beowulf cluster to provide a reliable, cost-effective solution. But how does a company write the fault-tolerant parallel program to run on the cluster?

When you are developing algorithms that must be reliable the first consideration is the hardware. The bad news is that your Beowulf cluster will have failures; it will need maintenance. It is not a matter of *whether* some node in the cluster will fail but *when*. Experience has shown that the more nodes the cluster has, the more likely one will fail within a given time.

How often a hardware failure occurs varies widely between clusters. It depends on the quality of the components used by the manufacturer. It depends on the room the cluster is set up in. Is it adequately cooled? Is ventilation good? It is possible to have a cool room but have the cluster nodes stacked so close together that the inner nodes get hot and begin to have component failures. It is possible to have the hot air from one node blow into the cool air intake of another node. Hardware failure also depends on the applications being run on the nodes. Some parallel applications do intense sustained calculations that cause the floating point chips to generate much more heat. Other applications read and write intensely to memory, thereby increasing the probability of having a memory fault.

Some clusters have failures every week; others run for months. It is not uncommon for several nodes to fail at about the same time with similar hardware problems. Evaluate your particular cluster under a simulated load for a couple of weeks to get data on expected mean time between failures (MTBF). If the MTBF is many times longer than your average application run time, then it may not make sense to restructure the application to be fault tolerant. In most cases it is more efficient simply to rerun a failed application if it has a short run time.

The second consideration is the fault tolerance of the underlying software environment. If the runtime system is not robust, then the hardware is the least of your problems. The PVM system sits between the operating system and the application and, among other things, monitors the state of the virtual machine. The PVM runtime system is designed to be fault tolerant and to reconfigure itself automatically when a failure is detected. (It doesn't help your fault-tolerant application if the underlying failure detection system crashes during a failure!) The

PVM failure detection system is responsible for detecting problems and notifying running applications about the problem. The PVM runtime system keeps track of and automatically reconfigures itself around failed nodes and tasks. It makes no attempt to recover a parallel application automatically.

The third consideration is the application. Not every parallel application can recover from a failure; recovery depends on the design of the application and the nature of the failure. For example, in the manager/worker programs of the preceding chapters, if the node that fails was running a worker, then recovery is possible; but if the node was running the manager, then key data may be lost that can't be recovered.

At the least, any parallel program can be made fault tolerant by restarting it automatically from the beginning if a failure in detected. The most common form of fault tolerance in use today is a variation of this approach, called checkpoint/restart. Instead of starting from the beginning, an application periodically stops calculating and sending messages and writes out its partial results to disk as a checkpoint. When a failure occurs, the runtime system kills the parallel application and automatically restarts it from the last checkpoint. The time lost in this technique is the time from the last checkpoint and the time it takes to write out all the checkpoints during the entire run.

This technique works for MPI, PVM, shared-memory paradigms, and most other programming paradigms. The application developer has to write two routines. One collects and writes out the checkpoint information from all the parallel tasks. The other checks whether the application is restarting, reads in the checkpoint data, and distributes the data to the parallel tasks. While writing these two routines is not trivial, failure recovery without stopping the application can get much more complicated.

On-the-fly recovery of parallel programs is complicated because data in messages may be in flight when the recovery begins. Hence, a race condition arises. If the data does not arrive, then it will need to be resent as part of the recovery. But if the data manages to be received just before the recovery, then there isn't an outstanding receive call, and the data shouldn't be resent.

File I/O is another problem that complicates recovery. File pointers may need to be reset to the last checkpoint to avoid getting a repeated set of output data in the file.

Despite all these issues, a few common methods can be used to improve the fault tolerance of many parallel applications.

11.2 Building Fault-Tolerant Parallel Applications

From the application's view, three steps must be performed for fault tolerance: detection, notification, and recovery.

The first step is being able to detect that something has gone wrong. Detection is typically the job of the runtime environment; but when the runtime envoronment does not provide this capability, application developers can create their own set of monitoring tasks to oversee an application.

The PVM runtime system has a monitoring and notification capability built into it. Any or all tasks in an application can ask to be notified of specific events. These events include the failure of a task, the failure of a cluster node, or the availability of new nodes into the application.

The second step in building fault-tolerant applications is notification. The PVM task(s) requesting notification can specify a particular task or set of tasks to be monitored. Or it can ask to be notified if *any* task within the application fails. The notification message contains the ID of the task that failed.

Unlike many detection systems, PVM's monitoring system is not based on the detection of a broken communication channel between the monitored and notifed task. Thus there is no need for the notified task and the failed task ever to have communicated in order to detect the failure. This approach provides more robustness in the first step of detection.

The failure or deletion of a node in the cluster is another notify event that can be requested. Again the requesting application task can specify a particular node, set of nodes, or all nodes. And, as before, the notification message returns the ID of the failed node(s).

The addition of one or more cluster nodes to the application's computational environment is also an event that PVM can notify an application about. In this case no ID can be specified, and the notification message returns the ID of the new node(s).

```
int info = pvm_notify( int EventType, int msgtag, int cnt, int *ids )
```

The `EventType` options are `PvmTaskExit`, `PvmHostDelete`, or `PvmHostAdd`. A separate notify call must be made for each event type that the application wishes to be notified about. The `msgtag` argument specifies what message tag the task will be using to listen for events. The `cnt` argument is the number of tasks or node IDs in the ids list for which notification is requested.

Given the flexibility of the `pvm_notify` command, there are several options for how the application can be designed to receive notification from the PVM system.

The first option is designing a separate watcher task. One or more of these watcher tasks are spawned across the cluster and often have the additional responsibility of managing the recovery phase of the application. The advantage of this approach is that the application code can remain cleaner. Note that in the manager/worker scheme the manager often assumes the additional duty as watcher.

A second option is for the application tasks to watch each other. A common method is to have each task watch its neighbor in a logical ring. Thus each task just watches one or two other tasks. Another common, but not particularly efficient, method is to have every task watch all the other tasks. Remember that the PVM system is doing the monitoring, not the application tasks. So the monitoring overhead is the same with all these options. The difference is the number of notification messages that get sent in the event of a failure.

Recovery is the final step in building fault-tolerant programs. Recovery depends heavily on the type of parallel algorithm used in the application. The most commonly used options are restart from the beginning, roll back to the last checkpoint, or reassign the work of a failed task.

The first option is the simplest to implement but the most expensive in the amount of calculation that must be redone. This option is used by many batch systems because it requires no knowledge of the application. It guarantees that the application will complete even if failures occur, although it does not guarantee how long this will take. On average the time is less than twice the normal run time. For short-running applications this is the best option.

For longer-running applications, checkpointing is a commonly used option. With this option you must understand the parallel application and modify it so that the application can restart from an input data file. You then have to modify the application to write out such a data file periodically. In the event of a failure, only computations from the last checkpoint are lost. The application restarts itself from the last successful data file written out. How often checkpoints are written out depends on the size of the restart file and how long the application is going to run. For large, scientific applications that run for days, checkpointing is typically done every few hours.

Note that if a failure is caused by the loss of a cluster node, then the application cannot be restarted until the node is repaired or is replaced by another node in the cluster. The restart file is almost always written out assuming that the same number of nodes is available during the restart.

In the special case where an application is based on a manager/worker scheme, it is often possible to reassign the job sent to the failed worker to another worker or to spawn a replacement worker to take its place. Manager/worker is a very popular parallel programming scheme for Beowulf clusters, so this special case arises often. Below is an example of a fault-tolerant manager/worker program.

```
/* Fault Tolerant Manager / Worker Example
 * using notification and task spawning.
 * example1.c
 */

#include <stdio.h>
#include <math.h>
#include <pvm3.h>

#define NWORK        4
#define NPROB        10000
#define MSGTAG       123

int main()
{
    double sum = 0.0, result, input = 1.0;
    int tids[NWORK], numt, probs[NPROB], sent=0, recvd=0;
    int aok=0, cc, bufid, done=0, i, j, marker, next, src;

    /* If I am a Manager Task */
    if ( (cc = pvm_parent()) == PvmNoParent || cc == PvmParentNotSet ) {

        /* Spawn NWORK Worker Tasks */
        numt = pvm_spawn( "example1", (char **) NULL, PvmTaskDefault,
                (char *) NULL, NWORK, tids );

        /* Set Up Notify for Spawned Tasks */
        pvm_notify( PvmTaskExit, MSGTAG, numt, tids );

        /* Send Problem to Spawned Workers */
        for ( i=0 ; i < NPROB ; i++ ) probs[i] = -1;
        for ( i=0 ; i < numt ; i++ ) {
            pvm_initsend( PvmDataDefault );
            pvm_pkint( &aok, 1, 1 );  /* Valid Problem Marker */
            input = (double) (i + 1);
            pvm_pkdouble( &input, 1, 1 );
            pvm_send( tids[i], MSGTAG );
            probs[i] = i;  sent++;  /* Next Problem */
        }

        /* Collect Results / Handle Failures */
        do {
```

```
/* Receive Result */
bufid = pvm_recv( -1, MSGTAG );
pvm_upkint( &marker, 1, 1 );

/* Handle Notify */
if ( marker > 0 ) {
    /* Find Failed Task Index */
    for ( i=0, next = -1 ; i < numt ; i++ )
        if ( tids[i] == marker )
            /* Find Last Problem Sent to Task */
            for ( j=(sent-1) ; j > 0 ; j-- )
                if ( probs[j] == i ) {
                    /* Spawn Replacement Task */
                    if ( pvm_spawn( "example1", (char **) NULL,
                            PvmTaskDefault, (char *) NULL, 1,
                            &(tids[i]) ) == 1 ) {
                        pvm_notify( PvmTaskExit, MSGTAG, 1,
                                &(tids[i]) );
                        next = i;  sent--;
                    }
                    probs[j] = -1; /* Reinsert Prob */
                    break;
                }
} else {
    /* Get Source Task & Accumulate Solution */
    pvm_upkdouble( &result, 1, 1 );
    sum += result;
    recvd++;
    /* Get Task Index */
    pvm_bufinfo( bufid, (int *) NULL, (int *) NULL, &src );
    for ( i=0 ; i < numt ; i++ )
        if ( tids[i] == src ) next = i;
}

/* Send Another Problem */
if ( next >= 0 ) {
    for ( i=0, input = -1.0 ; i < NPROB ; i++ )
        if ( probs[i] < 0 ) {
            input = (double) (i + 1);
            probs[i] = next;  sent++;  /* Next Problem */
            break;
        }
    pvm_initsend( PvmDataDefault );
    pvm_pkint( &aok, 1, 1 );  /* Valid Problem Marker */
```

```
                pvm_pkdouble( &input, 1, 1 );
                pvm_send( tids[next], MSGTAG );
                if ( input < 0.0 ) tids[next] = -1;
            }

        } while ( recvd < sent );

        printf( "Sum = %lf\n", sum );
    }

    /* If I am a Worker Task */
    else if ( cc > 0 ) {
        /* Notify Me If Manager Fails */
        pvm_notify( PvmTaskExit, MSGTAG, 1, &cc );
        /* Solve Problems Until Done */
        do {
            /* Get Problem from Master */
            pvm_recv( -1, MSGTAG );
            pvm_upkint( &aok, 1, 1 );
            if ( aok > 0 )  /* Master Died */
                break;
            pvm_upkdouble( &input, 1, 1 );
            if ( input > 0.0 ) {
                /* Compute Result */
                result = sqrt( ( 2.0 * input ) - 1.0 );
                /* Send Result to Master */
                pvm_initsend( PvmDataDefault );
                pvm_pkint( &aok, 1, 1 );    /* Ask for more... */
                pvm_pkdouble( &result, 1, 1 );
                pvm_send( cc, MSGTAG );
            } else
                done = 1;
        } while ( !done );
    }

    pvm_exit();

    return( 0 );
}
```

This example illustrates another useful function: pvm_spawn(). The ability to spawn a replacement task is a powerful capability in fault tolerance. It is also a key function in adaptive programs, as we will see in the next section.

```
int numt = pvm_spawn( char *task, char **argv, int flag,
                      char *node, int ntasks, int *tids )
```

The routine `pvm_spawn()` starts up `ntasks` copies of an executable file `task` on the virtual machine. The PVM virtual machine is assumed to be running on the Beowulf cluster. Here `argv` is a pointer to an array of arguments to `task` with the end of the array specified by NULL. If task takes no arguments, then `argv` is NULL. The `flag` argument is used to specify options and is a sum of the following options:

`PvmTaskDefault`: has PVM choose where to spawn processes

`PvmTaskHost`: uses a `where` argument to specify a particular host or cluster node to spawn on

`PvmTaskArch`: uses a `where` argument to specify an architecture class to spawn on

`PvmTaskDebug`: starts up these processes under debugger

`PvmTaskTrace`: uses PVM calls to generate trace data

`PvmMppFront`: starts process on MPP front-end/service node

`PvmHostComp`: starts process on complementary host set

For example, `flag = PvmTaskHost + PvmHostCompl` spawns tasks on every node but the specified node (which may be the manager, for instance).

On return, `numt` is set to the number of tasks successfully spawned or an error code if no tasks could be started. If tasks were started, then `pvm_spawn()` returns a vector of the spawned tasks' `tids`. If some tasks could not be started, the corresponding error codes are placed in the last $(ntask - numt)$ positions of the vector.

In the example above, `pvm_spawn()` is used by the manager to start all the worker tasks and also is used to replace workers who fail during the computation. This type of fault-tolerant method is useful for applications that run continuously with a steady stream of new work coming in, as was the case in our two initial examples. Both used a variation on the above PVM example code for their solution.

11.3 Adaptive Programs

In this section, we use some more of the PVM virtual machine functions to illustrate how cluster programs can be extended to adapt not only to faults but also to many other metrics and circumstances. The first example demonstrates a parallel application that dynamically adapts the size of the virtual machine through adding and releasing nodes based on the computational needs of the application. Such a feature is used every day on a 128-processor Beowulf cluster at Oak Ridge National Laboratory that is shared by three research groups.

```
int numh = pvm_addhosts( char **hosts, int nhost, int *infos)
int numh = pvm_delhosts( char **hosts, int nhost, int *infos)
```

The PVM `addhosts` and `delhosts` routines add or delete a set of `hosts` in the virtual machine. In a Beowulf cluster this corresponds to adding or deleting nodes from the computation; `numh` is returned as the number of nodes successfully added or deleted. The argument `infos` is an array of length `nhost` that contains the status code for each individual node being added or deleted. This allows you to check whether only one of a set of hosts caused a problem, rather than trying to add or delete the entire set of hosts again.

```
/*
 * Adaptive Host Allocation Example adds and removes cluster nodes
 * from computation on the fly for different computational phases
 */

#include <stdio.h>
#include <pvm3.h>

static char *host_set_A[] = { "node1", "node2", "node3" };
static int nhosts_A = sizeof( host_set_A ) / sizeof( char ** );

static char *host_set_B[] = { "node10", "node12" };
static int nhosts_B = sizeof( host_set_B ) / sizeof( char ** );

#define MAX_HOSTS    255
#define MSGTAG        123

double phase1( int prob ) {
    return( (prob == 1) ? 1 : ((double) prob * phase1( prob - 1 )) ); }

double phase2( int prob ) {
```

```
    return( (prob == 1) ? 1 : ((double) prob + phase2( prob - 1 )) ); }

int main( int argc, char **argv )
{
    double sum1 = 0.0, sum2 = 0.0, result;
    int status[MAX_HOSTS], prob, cc, i;
    char *args[3], input[16];

    /* If I am the Manager Task */
    if ( (cc = pvm_parent()) == PvmNoParent || cc == PvmParentNotSet ) {

        /* Phase #1 of computation - Use Host Set A */
        pvm_addhosts( host_set_A, nhosts_A, status );

        /* Spawn Worker Tasks - One Per Host */
        args[0] = "phase1";  args[1] = input;  args[2] = (char *) NULL;
        for ( i=0, prob=0 ; i < nhosts_A ; i++ )
            if ( status[i] > 0 ) {  /* Successful Host Add */
                sprintf( input, "%d", prob++ );
                pvm_spawn( "example2", args, PvmTaskDefault | PvmTaskHost,
                        host_set_A[i], 1, (int *) NULL );
            }
        /* Collect Results */
        for ( i=0 ; i < prob ; i++ ) {
            pvm_recv( -1, MSGTAG );
            pvm_upkdouble( &result, 1, 1 );
            sum1 += result;
        }

        /* Remove Host Set A after Phase #1 */
        for ( i=0 ; i < nhosts_A ; i++ )
            if ( status[i] > 0 )  /* Only Delete Successful Hosts */
                pvm_delhosts( &(host_set_A[i]), 1, (int *) NULL );

        /* Phase #2 of Computation - Use Host Set B */
        pvm_addhosts( host_set_B, nhosts_B, status );

        /* Spawn Worker Tasks - One Per Host (None Locally) */
        args[0] = "phase2";
        for ( i=0, prob=0 ; i < nhosts_B ; i++ )
            if ( status[i] > 0 ) {  /* Successful Host Add */
                sprintf( input, "%d", prob++ );
                pvm_spawn( "example2", args, PvmTaskDefault | PvmTaskHost,
                        host_set_B[i], 1, (int *) NULL );
```

```
        }
        /* Collect Results */
        for ( i=0 ; i < prob ; i++ ) {
            pvm_recv( -1, MSGTAG );
            pvm_upkdouble( &result, 1, 1 );
            sum2 += result;
        }

        /* Remove Host Set B from Phase #2 */
        for ( i=0 ; i < nhosts_B ; i++ )
            if ( status[i] > 0 )  /* Only Delete Successful Hosts */
                pvm_delhosts( &(host_set_B[i]), 1, (int *) NULL );

        /* Done */
        printf( "sum1 (%lf) / sum2 (%lf) = %lf\n", sum1, sum2, sum1/sum2);
    }

    /* If I am a Worker Task */
    else if ( cc > 0 ) {
        /* Compute Result */
        prob = atoi( argv[2] );
        if ( !strcmp( argv[1], "phase1" ) )
            result = phase1( prob + 1 );
        else if ( !strcmp( argv[1], "phase2" ) )
            result = phase2( 100 * ( prob + 1 ) );
        /* Send Result to Master */
        pvm_initsend( PvmDataDefault );
        pvm_pkdouble( &result, 1, 1 );
        pvm_send( cc, MSGTAG );
    }

    pvm_exit();

    return( 0 );
}
```

One of the main difficulties of writing libraries for message-passing applications is that messages sent inside the application may get intercepted by the message-passing calls inside the library. The same problem occurs when two applications want to cooperate, for example, a performance monitor and a scientific application or an airframe stress application coupled with an aerodynamic flow application. Whenever two or more programmers are writing different parts of the overall message-passing application, there is the potential that a message will be inadvertently received by the wrong part of the application. The solution to this problem is communication context. As described earlier in the MPI chapters, communication context in MPI is handled cleanly through the MPI communicator.

In PVM 3.4, `pvm_recv()` requests a message from a particular source with a user-chosen message tag (either or both of these fields can be set to accept anything). In addition, communication context is a third field that a receive must match on before accepting a message; the context cannot be specified by a wild card. By default a base context is predefined, which is similar to the default `MPI_COMM_WORLD` communicator in MPI.

PVM has four routines to manage communication contexts.

```
new_context = pvm_newcontext()
old_context = pvm_setcontext( new_context )
info        = pvm_freecontext( context )
context     = pvm_getcontext()
```

`Pvm_newcontext()` returns a systemwide unique context tag generated by the local daemon (in a way similar to the way the local daemon generates systemwide unique task IDs). Since it is a local operation, `pvm_newcontext` is very fast. The returned context can then be broadcast to all the tasks that are cooperating on this part of the application. Each of the tasks calls `pvm_setcontext`, which switches the active context and returns the old context tag so that it can be restored at the end of the module by another call to `pvm_setcontext`. `Pvm_freecontext` and `pvm_getcontext` are used to free memory associated with a context tag and to get the value of the active context tag, respectively.

Spawned tasks inherit the context of their parent. Thus, if you wish to add context to an existing parallel routine already written in PVM, you need to add only four lines to the source:

```
int mycxt, oldcxt;
/* near the beginning of the routine set a new context */
mycxt = pvm_newcontext();
oldcxt = pvm_setcontext( mycxt );

/* spawn slave tasks to help */
/* slave tasks require no source code change */
/* leave all the PVM calls in master unchanged */

/* just before exiting the routine restore previous context */
```

```
    mycxt = pvm_setcontext( oldcxt );
    pvm_freecontext( mycxt );

    return;
```

PVM has always had message handlers internally, which were used for controlling the virtual machine. In PVM 3.4 the ability to define and delete message handlers was raised to the user level so that parallel programs can be written that can add new features while the program is running.

The two new message handler functions are

```
    mhid = pvm_addmhf( src, tag, context, *function );
           pvm_delmhf( mhid );
```

Once a message handler has been added by a task, whenever a message arrives at this task with the specified source, message tag, and communication context, the specified function is executed. The function is passed the message so that it may unpack the message if desired. PVM places no restrictions on the complexity of the function, which is free to make system calls or other PVM calls. A message handler ID is returned by the add routine, which is used in the delete message handler routine.

There is no limit on the number of handlers you can set up, and handlers can be added and deleted dynamically by each application task independently.

By setting up message handlers, you can now write programs that can dynamically change the features of the underlying virtual machine. For example, message handlers can be added that implement active messages; the application then can use this form of communication rather than the typical send/receive. Similar opportunities exist for almost every feature of the virtual machine.

The ability of the application to adapt features of the virtual machine to meet its present needs is a powerful capability that has yet to be fully exploited in Beowulf clusters.

```
/* Adapting available Virtual Machine features with
 * user redefined message handlers.
 */
#include <stdio.h>
#include <pvm3.h>

#define NWORK           4
#define MAIN_MSGTAG   123
#define CNTR_MSGTAG   124
```

```
int counter = 0;

int handler( int mid ) {
    int ack, incr, src;

    /* Increment Counter */
    pvm_upkint( &incr, 1, 1 );
    counter += incr;
    printf( "counter = %d\n", counter );

    /* Acknowledge Counter Task */
    pvm_bufinfo( mid, (int *) NULL, (int *) NULL, &src );
    pvm_initsend( PvmDataDefault );
    ack = ( counter > 1000 ) ? -1 : 1;
    pvm_pkint( &ack, 1, 1 );
    pvm_send( src, CNTR_MSGTAG );

    return( 0 );
}

int main( int argc, char **argv )
{
    int ack, cc, ctx, bufid, incr=1, iter=1, max, numt, old, value=1, src;
    char *args[2];

    /* If I am a Manager Task */
    if ( (cc = pvm_parent()) == PvmNoParent || cc == PvmParentNotSet ) {

        /* Generate New Message Context for Counter Task messages */
        ctx = pvm_newcontext();

        /* Register Message Handler Function for Independent Counter */
        pvm_addmhf( -1, CNTR_MSGTAG, ctx, handler );

        /* Spawn 1 Counter Task */
        args[0] = "counter";  args[1] = (char *) NULL;
        old = pvm_setcontext( ctx );  /* Set Message Context for Task */
        if ( pvm_spawn( "example3", args, PvmTaskDefault,
                (char *) NULL, 1, (int *) NULL ) != 1 )
            counter = 1001;  /* Counter Failed to Spawn, Trigger Exit */
        pvm_setcontext( old );  /* Reset to Base Message Context */

        /* Spawn NWORK Worker Tasks */
```

```
    args[0] = "worker";
    numt = pvm_spawn( "example3", args, PvmTaskDefault,
            (char *) NULL, NWORK, (int *) NULL );

    /* Increment & Return Worker Values */
    do {
        /* Get Value */
        bufid = pvm_recv( -1, MAIN_MSGTAG );
        pvm_upkint( &value, 1, 1 );
        max = ( value > max ) ? value : max;
        printf( "recvd value = %d\n", value );

        /* Send Reply */
        pvm_bufinfo( bufid, (int *) NULL, (int *) NULL, &src );
        if ( counter <= 1000 ) value += iter++;
            else { value = -1; numt--; }  /* Tell Workers to Exit */
        pvm_initsend( PvmDataDefault );
        pvm_pkint( &value, 1, 1 );
        pvm_send( src, MAIN_MSGTAG );
    } while ( numt > 0 );

    printf( "Max Value = %d\n", max );
}

/* If I am a Worker Task */
else if ( cc > 0 && !strcmp( argv[1], "worker" ) ) {
    /* Grow Values Until Done */
    do {
        /* Send Value to Master */
        value *= 2;
        pvm_initsend( PvmDataDefault );
        pvm_pkint( &value, 1, 1 );
        pvm_send( cc, MAIN_MSGTAG );
        /* Get Incremented Value from Master */
        pvm_recv( cc, MAIN_MSGTAG );
        pvm_upkint( &value, 1, 1 );
    } while ( value > 0 );
}

/* If I am a Counter Task */
else if ( cc > 0 && !strcmp( argv[1], "counter" ) ) {
    /* Grow Values Until Done */
    do {
        /* Send Counter Increment to Master */
```

```
            pvm_initsend( PvmDataDefault );
            pvm_pkint( &incr, 1, 1 );
            pvm_send( cc, CNTR_MSGTAG );
            incr *= 2;
            /* Check Ack from Master */
            pvm_recv( cc, CNTR_MSGTAG );
            pvm_upkint( &ack, 1, 1 );
        } while ( ack > 0 );
    }

    pvm_exit();

    return( 0 );
}
```

In a typical message-passing system, messages are transient, and the focus is on making their existence as brief as possible by decreasing latency and increasing bandwidth. But in a growing number of situations in the parallel applications seen today, programming would be much easier if one could have persistent messages. This is the purpose of the *Message Box* feature in PVM.

The Message Box is an simple key/value database in the virtual machine. The key is a user-specified name, and the value is any valid PVM message. Given that there are no restrictions on the complexity or size of a PVM message, the database is simple, but remarkably flexible.

Four functions make up the Message Box:

```
index = pvm_putinfo( name, msgbuf, flag )
        pvm_recvinfo( name, index, flag )
        pvm_delinfo( name, index, flag )
        pvm_getmboxinfo( pattern, matching_names, info )
```

Tasks can use regular PVM pack routines to create an arbitrary message and then use pvm_putinfo() to place this message into the Message Box with an associated name. Copies of this message can be retrieved by any PVM task that knows the name. If the name is unknown or is changing dynamically, then pvm_getmboxinfo() can be used to find the list of names active in the Message Box. The flag defines the properties of the stored message, such as who is allowed to delete this message, whether this name allows multiple instances of messages, and whether a *put* to the same name can overwrite the message.

The Message Box has been used for many other purposes. For example, the dynamic group functionality in PVM is implemented in the new Message Box functions; the Cumulvs computational steering tool uses the Message Box to query for the instructions on how to attach to a remote distributed simulation; and performance monitors leave their findings in the Message Box for other tools to use.

The capability to have persistent messages in parallel computing opens up many new application possibilities not only in high-performance computing but also in collaborative technologies.

```
/* Example using persistent messages to adapt to change
 * Monitor tasks are created and killed as needed
 * Information is exchanged between these tasks using persistent messages
 */

#include <stdio.h>
#include <sys/time.h>
#include <pvm3.h>

#define MSGBOX          "load_stats"

int main()
{
    int cc, elapsed, i, index, load, num;
    struct timeval start, end;
    double value;

    /* If I am a Manager Task */
    if ( (cc = pvm_parent()) == PvmNoParent || cc == PvmParentNotSet ) {

        /* Periodically Spawn Load Monitor, Check Current System Load */
        do {
            /* Spawn Load Monitor Task */
            if ( pvm_spawn( "example4", (char **) NULL, PvmTaskDefault,
                    (char *) NULL, 1, (int *) NULL ) != 1 ) {
                perror( "spawning load monitor" );  break;
            }
            sleep( 1 );

            /* Check System Load (Microseconds Per Megaflop) */
            for ( i=0, load=0.0, num=0 ; i < 11 ; i++ )
                if ( pvm_recvinfo( MSGBOX, i, PvmMboxDefault ) >= 0 ) {
                    pvm_upkint( &elapsed, 1, 1 );
                    load += elapsed;  num++;
                }
            if ( num )
                printf( "Load Avg = %lf usec/Mflop\n",
                        (double) load / (double) num );
```

```
            sleep( 5 );
        } while ( 1 );
    }

    /* If I am a Load Monitor Task */
    else if ( cc > 0 ) {
        /* Time Simple Computation */
        gettimeofday( &start, (struct timezone *) NULL );
        for ( i=0, value=1.0 ; i < 1000000 ; i++ )
            value *= 1.2345678;
        gettimeofday( &end, (struct timezone *) NULL );
        elapsed = (end.tv_usec - start.tv_usec)
                + 1000000 * (end.tv_sec - start.tv_sec);

        /* Dump Into Next Available Message Mbox */
        pvm_initsend( PvmDataDefault );
        pvm_pkint( &elapsed, 1, 1 );
        index = pvm_putinfo( MSGBOX, pvm_getsbuf(),
                PvmMboxDefault | PvmMboxPersistent
                    | PvmMboxMultiInstance | PvmMboxOverWritable );

        /* Free Next Mbox Index for Next Instance (Only Save 10) */
        pvm_delinfo( MSGBOX, (index + 1) % 11, PvmMboxDefault );
    }

    pvm_exit();

    return( 0 );
}
```

12 Numerical and Scientific Software for Clusters

Victor Eijkhout and Jack Dongarra

In this chapter we discuss numerical software for clusters. We focus on some of the most common numerical operations: linear system solving, eigenvalue computations, and fast Fourier transform.

Numerical operations such as linear system solving and eigenvalue calculations can be applied to two different kinds of matrix: dense and sparse. In dense systems, essentially every matrix element is nonzero; in sparse systems, a sufficiently large number of matrix elements is zero that a specialized storage scheme is warranted; for an introduction to sparse storage, see [12]. Because the two classes are so different, usually different numerical libraries apply to them. For dense systems, we discuss ScaLAPACK and PLAPACK as the choices for both system solving and eigenvalue computations. For sparse systems, we discuss Arpack for eigenvalue problems. There exist two classes of algorithms for solving sparse linear systems: direct methods and iterative methods. We will discuss SuperLU as an example of a direct solver and PETSc and Aztec as examples of iterative solvers.

Fast Fourier transforms (FFTs) typically are applied many times to different data. For FFTs we discuss the FFTW package (Section 12.4), which is probably better optimized than any other free FFT package.

In addition to numerical software operations, we discuss the issue of load balancing. We focus on two software packages, ParMetis and Chaco, which can be used in the above-mentioned sparse packages.

We conclude this chapter with a brief list of some popular science applications that run on Linux clusters, as well as a list of software for linear algebra that is freely available on the Web.

A practical point. Some of these packages are written in Fortran, some in C. While calling a Fortran package from C is relatively easy by observing linker naming conventions, the reverse direction can be difficult unless the package was designed to be called from Fortran. We will remark on the implementation language of each package, and the ease with which it can be interfaced to other languages.

12.1 Dense Linear System Solving

The problem in solving linear systems is: Given a square matrix A and a vector b, find a vector x such that $Ax = b$. In the most general case, the matrix is stored as a distributed array, and the system is solved by Gaussian elimination. This is the basic algorithm in ScaLAPACK and PLAPACK, the two packages we discuss for solving a linear system with a distributed dense coefficient matrix. (Sparse systems are discussed in Section 12.2.)

On a single processor, the algorithm for dense linear system solving is fairly obvious, although a good deal of optimization is needed for high performance (see Section 12.6.) In a distributed context, achieving high performance—especially performance that scales up with increasing processor numbers—requires radical rethinking about the basic data structures. Both ScaLAPACK and PLAPACK use block-cyclic data distributions. In Section 11.2.1, we focus on how to specify data in this distribution in ScaLAPACK, since it is the more widely used package; we then briefly compare PLAPACK's calling style.

12.1.1 ScaLAPACK

ScaLAPACK is a parallel version of LAPACK, both in function and in software design. Like the earlier package, ScaLAPACK targets linear system solution and eigenvalue calculation for dense and banded matrices. Note that, while sparse matrices are often of banded form, use of the band storage is usually not an efficient way of dealing with sparse systems; other software packages are better suited to that. In particular, one should use SuperLU (section 12.2.1) for sparse linear systems and Arpack (section 12.3.2) for eigenvalue computations.

In a way, ScaLAPACK is the culmination of a line of linear algebra packages that started with LINPACK and EISPACK. The coding of those packages was fairly straightforward, using at most Basic Linear Algebra Subprograms (BLAS) Level-1 operations as an abstraction level. LAPACK [4, 63] attains high efficiency on a single processor (or a small number of shared-memory processors) through the introduction of blocked algorithms and the concomitant use of BLAS Level-3 operations. ScaLAPACK uses these blocked algorithms in a parallel context to attain scalably high performance on parallel computers.

The seemingly contradictory demands of portability and efficiency are realized in ScaLAPACK through confining the relevant parts of the code to two subroutine libraries: the BLAS for the computational kernels and the BLACS (Basic Linear Algebra Communication Subprograms) for communication kernels. While the BLACS come with ScaLAPACK, the user is to supply the BLAS library; see Section 12.6.

ScaLAPACK is written in Fortran, as are the examples in this section. The distribution has no C prototypes, but interfacing to a C program is simple, observing the usual name conversion conventions.

ScaLAPACK Parallel Initialization

ScaLAPACK relies for its communications on the BLACS, (Basic Linear Algebra Communication Subprograms) (Basic Linear Algebra Communication Subprograms) which offers an abstraction layer over MPI. Its main feature is the ability to communicate submatrices, rather than arrays, and of both rectangular and trapezoidal shape. The latter is of obvious value in factorization algorithms. We will not go into the details of the BLACS here; instead, we focus on the aspects that come into play in the program initialization phase.

Suppose you have divided your cluster into an approximately square grid of `nprows` by `npcols` processors. The following two calls set up a BLACS processor grid – its handle is returned as `ictxt` – and return the current processor number (by row and column) in it:

```
call sl_init(ictxt,nprows,npcols)
call blacs_gridinfo(ictxt,nprows,npcols,myprow,mypcol)
```

Correspondingly, at the end of your code you need to release the grid by

```
call blacs_gridexit(ictxt)
```

ScaLAPACK Data Format

Creating a matrix in ScaLAPACK is, unfortunately, not simple, even though none of the indirect addressing problems of sparse storage concern us here. The difficulty lies in the fact that for scalably high performance on factorization algorithms, a storage mode called "two-dimensional block-cyclic" storage is used. The blocking is what enables the use of BLAS Level-3 routines; the cyclic storage is needed for scalable parallelism.

Specifically, the block-cyclic storage implies that a global (i, j) coordinate in the matrix gets mapped to a triplet of (p, l, x) for both the i and the j directions, where p is the processor number, l the block, and x the offset inside the block.

The block size has to be decided by the user; 64 is usually a safe bet. For generality, let us assume that block sizes `bs_i` and `bs_j` have been chosen. First we determine how much storage is needed for the local part of the matrix:

```
mlocal = numroc(mglobal,bs_i,myprow,0,nprows)
nlocal = numroc(nglobal,bs_j,mypcol,0,npcols)
```

where `numroc` is a library function. (The m and n sizes of the matrix need not be equal, since ScaLAPACK also has routines for QR factorization and such.)

Filling in a matrix requires the conversion from (i, j) coordinates to (p, l, x) coordinates. It is best to use conversion functions

```
p_of_i(i,bs,p) = mod(int((i-1)/bs),p)
l_of_i(i,bs,p) = int((i-1)/(p*bs))
x_of_i(i,bs,p) = mod(i-1,bs)+1
```

that take i or j as input, as well as the block size and the number of processors in that direction. The global matrix element (i, j) is then mapped to

```
pi = p_of_i(i,bs_i,nprows)
li = l_of_i(i,bs_i,nprows)
xi = x_of_i(i,bs_i,nprows)

pj = p_of_i(j,bs_j,npcols)
lj = l_of_i(j,bs_j,npcols)
xj = x_of_i(j,bs_j,npcols)

mat(li*bs_i+xi,lj*bs_j+xj) = mat_global(i,j)
```

if the current processor is (p_i, p_j).

Calling ScaLAPACK Routines

ScaLAPACK routines adhere to the LAPACK naming scheme: PXYYZZZ, where P indicates parallel; X is the "precision," meaning single or double, real or complex; YY is the shape, with GE for rectangular and TR for triangular; and ZZZ denotes the function.

For most functions there is a "simple driver" (for instance, SV for system solving), which makes the routine name in our example PDGESV for double precision, as well as an "expert driver," which has X attached to the name, PDGESVX in this example. The expert driver usually has more input options and usually returns more diagnostic information.

In the call to a ScaLAPACK routine, information about the matrix has to be passed by way of a descriptor:

```
      integer desca(9)
      call descinit(desca,
     >     mglobal,nglobal, bs_i,bs_j, 0,0,ictxt,lda,ierr)
      call pdgesv(nglobal,1, mat_local,1,1, desca,ipiv,
     >     rhs_local,1,1, descb, ierr)
```

where `lda>mlocal` is the allocated first dimension of `a`.

Linear System Solution Routines

ScaLAPACK linear solver routines support dense and banded matrices. The drivers for solving a linear system are `PxyySV`, where `yy=GE` or `GB` for dense and band, respectively. We do not discuss here other cases such as positive definite band, nor do we discuss band matrices, which are stored by using a variant of the scheme described above. The reader is referred to the *ScaLAPACK Users' Guide* [15] for details. The input matrix A of the system is on output overwritten with the LU factorization, and the right-hand side B is overwritten with the solution. Temporary storage is needed only for the (integer) pivot locations.

12.1.2 PLAPACK

PLAPACK [86] is a package with functionality similar to that of ScaLACK but with a different calling style. It also relies on optimized BLAS routines and is therefore able to achieve a high performance. Whereas ScaLAPACK uses a calling style that is similar to Fortran, to stay close to its LAPACK roots PLAPACK uses a more object-oriented style. Its interface is similar in philosophy to that of the PETSc package (discussed later in this chapter).

As an illustration of this object-oriented handling of matrices and vectors, here are matrix-vector multiply and triangular system solve calls:

```
PLA_Gemv( PLA_NO_TRANS, one, A, x, zero, b );
PLA_Trsv( PLA_LOWER_TRIANGULAR, PLA_NO_TRANSPOSE,
          PLA_UNIT_DIAG, A, b );
```

The distribution of the matrix over the processors is induced as a "distribution template" declared by the user and is passed to the matrix creation call:

```
PLA_Matrix_create(  datatype, size, size,
                    templ, PLA_ALIGN_FIRST, PLA_ALIGN_FIRST, &A );
```

PLAPACK wins over ScaLAPACK in user-friendliness in filling in the matrix. As in PETSc, matrix elements can be specified anywhere; and instead of being written directly into the data structure, they are passed by a `PLA_API_axpy_matrix_to_-global` call. On the other hand, PLAPACK lacks ScaLAPACK's sophistication of simple and expert drivers and pays less attention to the issue of numerical stability.

12.2 Sparse Linear System Solving

For sparse matrices, more economical storage can be used, but the most foolproof algorithm is still Gaussian elimination. This is the principle behind SuperLU (Section 12.2.1). In certain applications, especially physics-based ones, the matrix has favorable properties that allow so-called iterative solution methods, which can be much more efficient than Gaussian elimination. The Aztec and PETSc packages are built around such iterative methods (Sections 12.2.2 and 12.2.3).

12.2.1 SuperLU

SuperLU [67, 112] is one of the foremost direct solvers for sparse linear system. It is available in single-processor, multithreaded, and parallel versions.

One of the aims of SuperLU is obtaining a high computational efficiency. To this end it finds cliques in the matrix graph. Eliminating these reduces the cost of the graph algorithms used; and since cliques lead to dense submatrices, it enables the use of higher-level BLAS routines.

The sequential and threaded versions of SuperLU use partial pivoting for numerical stability. Partial pivoting is avoided in the parallel version, however, because it would lead to large numbers of small messages. Instead, "static pivoting" is used, with repair of zero pivots during run time. To compensate for these numerically suboptimal strategies, the solution process uses iterative refinement to obtain the full available precision.

Like ScaLAPACK, SuperLU has both simple drivers and expert drivers; the latter give the user opportunity for further steering, return more detailed information, and are more sophisticated in terms of numerical precision.

While SuperLU accepts the user's matrix data structure (it must be in compressed column format), this is not a critical feature as it is in our discussion of the relative merits of PETSc (Section 12.2.3) and Aztec (Section 12.2.2), for the following reason. SuperLU, being a direct method, generates large amounts of data for the factorization, making the savings from reusing the user data and the extra matrix storage in the parallel case relatively unimportant.

ScaLAPACK accepts two input modes: one where the matrix is distributed and the other where the matrix is replicated on every processor. The former mode is less efficient because it requires more data redistribution.

SuperLU is written in C and cannot easily be used from Fortran. The standard installation comes with its own collection of BLAS routines; one can edit the makefile to ensure that an optimized version of the BLAS library is used.

12.2.2 Aztec and Trilinos

The Aztec package [57, 6] has as its main focus linear system solving. While it is not so sophisticated as PETSc, it has two advantages:

- It has far fewer routines, so the learning curve is conceivably shorter.
- It uses the user's matrix data structure and thus is easier to integrate in existing applications and to avoid duplication of storage. (See Section 12.2.3 for a discussion of this issue in PETSc.)

Thus, Aztec is an attractive choice for supplying matrix-vector product and linear system solution routines for use in Arpack (Section 12.3.2).

Aztec is written in C but supports a full set of Fortran interfaces.

Aztec supports a few parallel sparse matrix formats, in particular a parallel form of compressed row storage. The user first partitions the matrix over the parallel processors using the global numbering for the element indices; Aztec then transforms the matrix to a local (on-processor) indexing scheme.

The following code illustrates the gist of an Aztec iterative solution program:

```
AZ_transform(proc_config,&external, idx,mat_el,update,
             &update_index,&extern_index,&data_org, n_update,
             index,bpntr,rpntr,&cpntr,AZ_MSR_MATRIX);
AZ_defaults(options,params);
options[AZ_conv] = AZ_r0;
params[AZ_tol] = rtol;
options[AZ_solver] = AZ_bicgstab;
options[AZ_precond] = AZ_Jacobi;
options[AZ_max_iter] = maxit;
AZ_reorder_vec(invec,data_org,update_index,rpntr);
AZ_solve(outvec,invec, options,params,
         index,idx,rpntr,cpntr,bpntr,mat_el,data_org,
         status,proc_config);
iterations  = status[AZ_its];
convergence = (status[AZ_why]==AZ_normal);
```

Aztec is no longer under development but has been incorporated in a larger Sandia project, Trilinos [122],[1] that includes linear and nonlinear solvers, with time-stepping methods and eigensolvers planned.

[1]As of this writing, a first public release of Trilinos is scheduled for the second half of 2003.

Trilinos is based on an object-oriented design with matrix/vector classes and an abstract solver interface that are specified pure virtual. A linear algebra library called Epetra implements this interface, but the user can write a matrix and vector class, thereby using the Trilinos algorithms on the user data structures.

Apart from the Epetra lower layer, Trilinos contains the algorithms of Aztec, plus (among others) Belos (a block Krylov package), IFPACK (which has Schwarz preconditioners with local ILU), and the ML algebraic multilevel package.

12.2.3 PETSc

PETSc is a library for the solution of partial differential equations. It features tools for manipulating sparse matrix data structures, a sizable repertoire of iterative linear system solvers and preconditioners, and nonlinear solvers and time-stepping methods. Although it is written in C, it includes Fortran and F90 interfaces.

PETSc differs from other libraries in a few aspects. First, it is usable as a tool box: many low-level routines can be used to implement new methods. In particular, PETSc provides tools for parallel computation (`VecScatter` objects) that offer an abstraction layer over straight MPI communication.

Second, PETSc's approach to parallelism is very flexible. Many routines operate on local matrices as easily as on distributed ones. Impressively, during the construction of a matrix any processor can specify the value of any matrix element. This approach, for instance, facilitates writing parallel FEM codes because, along processor boundaries, elements belonging to different processors will contribute to the value of the same matrix element.

A third difference between PETSc and other packages (often counted as a disadvantage) is that its data structures are internal and not explicitly documented. Unlike Aztec (Section 12.2.2), which accepts the user's matrix, PETSc has its own data structure, built up by passing matrix elements through function calls.

```
MatCreate(comm,...,&A);
for (i=... )
  for (j=... )
    MatSetValue(A,...,i,j,value,...);
```

Thus, the user faces the choice of maintaining duplicate matrices (one in the native user format and one in PETSc format) with the resulting storage overhead or of using PETSc throughout the code. However, because PETSc provides a large set of operations, many applications can be written using PETSc for all matrix operations. In this case, there is no duplicate storage because the only storage is within the

PETSc routines. In addition, PETSc provides a way, though what are called "shell" objects, to make direct use of application data structures. This provides a modular alternative to the "reverse communication" approach used by Arpack.

Once PETSc data objects have been built, they are used in an object-oriented manner, where the contents and the exact nature of the object are no longer visible:

```
MatMult(A,X,Y);
```

Likewise, parameters to the various objects are kept internal:

```
PCSetType(pc,PCJACOBI);
```

Of particular relevance in the current context is that after the initial creation of an object, its parallel status is largely irrelevant.

12.3 Eigenvalue Problems

Eigenvalue problems involve the following: Given a matrix A, find the numbers λ and vectors x such that $Ax = \lambda x$, or more generally, $Ax = \lambda Mx$, where M is another matrix. The distinction between sparse and dense matrices does not play so large a role as it does in systems solving; for eigenvalues the main distinction is whether one wants all the possible λ values and attendant x vectors, or just a subset, typically the few largest or smallest. ScaLAPACK and PLAPACK are packages that start with a dense matrix to calculate all or potentially part of the spectrum (Section 12.3.1), while Arpack (Section 12.3.2) is preferable when only part of the spectrum is wanted; since it uses reverse communication, Arpack can handle matrices in sparse format.

12.3.1 Eigenvalue Computations in ScaLAPACK and PLAPACK

In addition to the linear system solvers mentioned above, ScaLAPACK has eigenvalue routines. For the symmetric eigenvalue problem there are driver routines; for the nonsymmetric (non-Hermitian) problem, you need to call individual computational routines.

- For the single- and double-precision real symmetric eigenvalue problem, there are simple drivers `PSSYEV` and `PDSYEV`, respectively, as well as expert drivers with `X` appended.

- For the complex Hermitian problem there are only expert drivers: `PCHEEVX` and `PZHEEVX` for single and double precision, respectively.

- The nonsymmetric eigenvalue problem is tackled in two steps: reduction to upper Hessenberg form by `PxGEHERD`, followed by reduction of the Hessenberg matrix to Schur form by `PxLAHQR`.
- ScaLAPACK has routines for the generalized eigenvalue problem only in the symmetric (Hermitian) definite case: `PxSYGST` (with `x=S,D`), and `PxHEGST` (with `x=C,Z`).

PLAPACK version 3.2 (announced for release in late 2003) contains an implementation of the "Holy Grail" eigensolver, which is also present in LAPACK. The functionality of the PLAPACK eigensolvers is twofold. First, there is a parallel eigensolver for tridiagonal symmetric matrices extending the algorithm presented by Dhillon and Parlett [32]; this routine allows the computation of all or a subset of the eigenvalues and eigenvectors with a given number of processors. This is claimed to be the fastest parallel tridiagonal eigensolver available. Second, the tridiagonal eigensolver is merged with a routine to reduce a dense symmetric matrix to tridiagonal form and with a routine for the backtransformation, thus obtaining a dense eigensolver for symmetric matrices. Large problems ($n > 100,000$) can be tackled with this routine on a 256-processor machine.

12.3.2 Eigenvalue Computations in Arpack

Often, in eigenvalue computations, not all eigenvalues or eigenvectors are needed. In such cases One is typically interested in the largest or smallest eigenvalues of the spectrum, or eigenvalues clustered around a certain value.

While ScaLAPACK has routines that can compute a full spectrum, Arpack focuses on the computation of a small number of eigenvalues and corresponding eigenvectors. It is based on the Arnoldi method.[2]

The Arnoldi method is unsuitable for finding eigenvalues in the interior of the spectrum, so such eigenvalues are found by "shift-invert": Given some σ close to the eigenvalues being sought, one solves the eigenvalue equation $(A - \sigma)^{-1}x = \mu x$, since eigenvalues of A close to σ will become the largest eigenvalues of $(A - \sigma)^{-1}$.

Reverse Communication Program Structure

The Arnoldi method has the attractive property of accessing the matrix only through the matrix-vector product operation. However, finding eigenvalues other

[2] In fact, the pure Arnoldi method would have prohibitive memory demands; what is used here is the "implicitly restarted Arnoldi method" [106].

than the largest requires solving linear systems with the given matrix or one derived from it.

Since the Arnoldi method can be formulated in terms of the matrix-vector product operation, Arpack (strictly speaking) never needs access to individual matrix elements. To take advantage of this fact, Arpack uses a technique called "reverse communication," which dispenses with the need for the user to pass the matrix to the library routines. Thus, Arpack can work with any user data structure or even with matrices that are only operatively defined.

With reverse communication, whenever a matrix operation is needed, control is passed back to the user program, with a return parameter indicating what operation is being requested. The user then satisfies this request, with input and output in arrays that are passed to the library, and calls the library routine again, indicating that the operation has been performed.

Thus, the structure of a routine using Arpack will be along the following lines:

```
      ido = 0
10    continue
      call dsaupd( ido, .... )
      if (ido.eq.-1 .or. ido.eq.1) then
C        perform matrix vector product
         goto 10
      end if
```

For the case of shift-invert or the generalized eigenvalue problem, the conditional has more clauses, but the structure stays the same.

Arpack can be used in a number of different modes, covering the regular and generalized eigenvalue problem, symmetry of the matrix A (and possibly M), and various parts of the spectrum to be computed. Rather than explaining these modes, we refer the reader to the excellent example drivers provided in the Arpack distribution.

Practical Aspects of Using Arpack

Arpack is written in Fortran. No C prototypes are given, but the package is easily interfaced to a C code, observing the usual linker naming conventions for Fortran and C routines. The parallel version of Arpack, PArpack, can be based on either MPI or the BLACS, the communication layer of Scalapack; see Section 12.1.1. Arpack uses LAPACK and, unfortunately, relies on an older version than the current. While this version is included in the distribution, it cannot easily be replaced by a vendor-optimized version.

The flip side of the data independence obtained by reverse communication is that the user must provide a matrix-vector product, a task that—especially in the parallel case—is not trivial. Also, in the shift-invert case the user must provide a linear system solver. We recommend the use of a package such as Aztec [57] (see Section 12.2.2), or PETSc [8] (see Section 12.2.3).

12.4 FFTW

FFTW [40, 37], the "Faster Fourier Transform in the West," is arguably the best public-domain FFT package available. It features both real and complex multi-dimensional transforms and is available in sequential, multithreaded, and parallel versions.[3] FFTW uses runtime optimization of the desired transform to adapt to the runtime platform. Furthermore, it claims that the optimizer will become more sophisticated over time.

Since Fourier transforms are typically executed many times on different data, FFTW has separate create/destroy and execute calls. A notable feature of the create call is a flag with values **`FFTW_ESTIMATE`** and **`FFTW_MEASURE`**, which determines the dynamic choice of a suitable implementation of the desired transform. With the former value, the package picks an implementation at essentially no cost, but probably with suboptimal performance. The latter value instructs FFTW to run and measure the execution time of several FFTs in order to find the best way to compute the desired transform. This process may take several seconds, depending on the platform and the size of the transform. Further flags **`FFTW_PATIENT`** and **`FFTW_EXHAUSTIVE`** can give even "more optimal" performance. Transform implementations found through this search mechanism are stored in a datatype **`fftw_plan`**; plans can be exported and imported between runs in a mechanism called "wisdom."

Also influencing the speed of FFTW is the fact that it can take advantage of SIMD instructions, such as SSE/SSE2 (Intel), 3DNow! (AMD), and Altivec (PowerPC). The user must align data correctly, as described in the manual.

FFTW is written in C, but wrapper code is provided to facilitate an interface to Fortran.

[3] As of this writing, version 3 of the package does not yet support MPI parallelism, but version 2 does. The two versions have slightly different calling conventions.

12.5 Load Balancing

Many applications can be distributed in more than one way over a parallel architecture. Even if one distribution is the natural result of one component of the computation (for instance, setup of a grid and generation of the matrix), a subsequent component (for instance, an eigenvalue calculation) may be so labor intensive that the cost of a full data redistribution may be outweighed by resulting gains in parallel efficiency.

In this section we discuss two packages for graph partitioning: ParMetis and Chaco. These packages aim at finding a partitioning of a graph that assigns roughly equally sized subgraphs to processors, thereby balancing the work load, while minimizing the size of the separators and the consequent communication cost.

12.5.1 ParMetis

ParMetis [99, 84] is a parallel package for mesh or graph partitioning for parallel load balancing. It is based on a three-step coarsening/partitioning/uncoarsening algorithm that the authors claim is faster than multiway spectral bisection. It can be used in several modes, for instance, repartitioning graphs from adaptively refined meshes or partitioning graphs from multiphysics simulations.

The input format of ParMetis, in its serial form, is a variant on compressed matrix storage. The adjacency of each element is stored consecutively (excluding the diagonal, but for each pair u, v storing both (u, v) and (v, u)), with a pointer array indicating where each element's data starts and ends. Both vertex and edge weights can be specified optionally. The parallel version of the graph input format takes blocks of consecutive nodes and allocates these to subsequent processors. An array that is identical on each processor then indicates which range of variables each processor owns. The distributed format uses global numbering of the nodes.

The output of ParMetis is a mapping of node numbers to processors. No actual redistribution is performed.

12.5.2 Chaco

The Chaco [24] package comprises several algorithms for graph partitioning, including inertial, spectral, Kernighan-Lin, and multilevel algorithms. It can be used in two modes:

stand-alone In this mode, input and output are done through files.

library Chaco can be linked to C or Fortran codes, and all data is passed through arrays.

Unlike ParMetis, Chaco runs only sequentially.

Zoltan [128] is a package for dynamic load balancing that builds on top of Chaco. Thanks to an object-oriented design, it is data structure neutral, so it can be interfaced by using existing user data structures.

12.6 Support Libraries

The packages in this chapter rely on two very common support libraries: MPI and BLAS. Since you are reading this book, we assume that you have an MPI library somewhere.

The Basic Linear Algebra Subprograms [64] are fairly simple linear algebra kernels that you can easily code yourself in a few lines. You can also download the source and compile the library [16]. Doing so, however, is unlikely to give good performance, no matter the level of sophistication of your compiler. The recommended way is to use vendor libraries that are available on a number of platforms, for instance, in the ESSL library on IBM machines and the mkl on Intel. On platforms without such vendor libraries (or sometimes even if they are present) we recommend that you install the ATLAS [125] (for Automatically Tuned Linear Algebra Software) package, which gives a library tuned to your specific machine. In a nutshell, ATLAS has a search algorithm that generates many implementations of each kernel, saving the one with the highest performance. This will far outperform anything you can write by hand.

12.7 Scientific Applications

In the preceding sections we described numerical libraries, that is, software that can be linked to application programs that you write. In this section we list some stand-alone scientific applications that can run on Linux clusters. Such applications typically take an input file of model parameters and specifications and output another file containing the results of the calculation. The following list is obviously incomplete: for each application area there are several applications with similar functionality, and more applications are released all the time.

Gaussian [42] is a connected system of programs for performing semi-empirical and ab initio molecular orbital quantum chemical calculations. It can be used to study molecules and reactions under a wide range of conditions, including both stable species and compounds that are difficult or impossible to observe experimentally, such as short-lived intermediates and transition structures. It is currently available for Unix/Linux, MS Windows, and Mac OS X platforms.

Fluent [38] is a computational fluid dynamics package, used for such applications as environmental control systems, rotor-airframe interactions, propulsion, reactor modeling, airflow around buildings, rotating cavities, fan noise modeling, and vortex shedding. It is available for Unix/Linux and MS Windows clusters.

MSC/Nastran [77] is a computer aided engineering / structural finite element application developed by NASA. It is available for Unix/Linux platforms, MS Windows, and vector machines such as Fujitsu and NEC.

LS-DYNA [69] is a general-purpose transient dynamic finite element program. LS-DYNA is optimized for shared- and distributed-memory Unix, Linux, and Windows-based platforms. LS-DYNA Applications include crashworthiness, occupant safety, metal forming, biomedical, fluid-structure interaction, and earthquake engineering.

NAMD [76] is a molecular dynamics code, available for workstation clusters with Unix/Linux, MS Windows, or Mac OS X.

NWChem [81] provides many methods to compute the properties of molecular and periodic systems using standard quantum mechanical descriptions of the electronic wavefunction or density. In addition, NWChem can perform classical molecular dynamics and free energy simulations. It is available free of charge (certain countries embargoed), with support for various Unix/Linux clusters, MS Windows, and vector computers such as the Fujitsu VPP.

12.8 Freely Available Software for Linear Algebra on the Web

Tables 12.1–12.5 present a list of freely available software for the solution of linear algebra problems. The interest is in software for high-performance computers that is available in "open source" form on the web for solving problems in numerical linear algebra, specifically dense, sparse direct and iterative systems and sparse iterative eigenvalue problems.

Additional pointers to software can be found at:
`www.nhse.org/rib/repositories/nhse/catalog/\hyper@hash{}Numerical_`

`Programs_and_Routines`. A survey of Iterative Linear System Solver Packages can be found at: `www.netlib.org/utk/papers/iterative-survey`.

Notes for Tables 12.1–12.5:

Type: Real for Real arithmetic and Complex for Complex arithmetic

Support: An email address where you can send questions and bug reports.

Language: f77(may also mean Fortran 95), C, C++

Mode: **Seq** for Sequential, vector and/or SMP/multithreaded versions
Dist for distributed memory message passing (M = MPI, P = PVM)

Dense: Dense, triangular, banded, tridiagonal matrices

Sparse: A sparse matrix representation is used to contain the data.

Direct: A direct approach is used to factor and solve the system.

SPD: The matrix is symmetric and positive definite

Gen: The matrix is general

Iterative: An iterative method is used to solve the system.

P: when used in a column labeled "Sparse Iterative," indicates preconditioners

Sparse eigenvalue: An iterative method is used to find some of the eigenvalues

Sym: The matrix is symmetric (Hermitian in the complex case)

Package	Support	Type		Language			Mode		Dense	Sparse Direct		Sparse Iterative	
		Real	Complex	f77	c	c++	Seq	Dist		SPD	Gen	SPD	Gen
ATLAS	yes	X	X	X	X		X		X				
BLAS	yes	X	X	X	X		X		X				
FLAME	yes	X	X	X	X		X		X				
LINALG *	?												
MTL	yes	X				X	X		X				
NETMAT	yes	X				X	X		X				
NIST S-BLAS	yes	X	X	X	X		X			X	X	X	X
PSBLAS	yes	X	X	X	X		X	M		X	X	X	X
SparseLib++	yes	X	X		X	X	X			X	X	X	X

Table 12.1: Support routines for numerical linear algebra. LINALG is a collection of software that is available but too varied to describe.

Package	Support	Type		Language			Mode		Dense	Sparse Iterative		Sparse Eigenvalue	
		Real	Complex	f77	c	c++	Seq	Dist		SPD	Gen	Sym	Gen
LAPACK	yes	X	X	X	X		X		X				
LAPACK95	yes	X	X	95			X		X				
NAPACK	yes	X		X			X		X	X		X	
PLAPACK	yes	X	X	X	X			M	X				
PRISM	yes	X		X			X	M	X				
ScaLAPACK	yes	X	X	X	X			M/P	X				

Table 12.2: Direct solvers for systems of linear equations.

Package	Support	Type		Language			Mode		Dense	Sparse Direct		Sparse Iterative	
		Real	Complex	f77	c	c++	Seq	Dist		SPD	Gen	SPD	Gen
HSL	yes	X	X	X			X			X	X		
MFACT	yes	X			X		X			X			
MP_SOLVE	yes	X	X		X			M			X		
MUMPS	yes	X	X	X	X		X	M		X	X		
PSPASES	yes	X		X	X			M		X			
SPARSE	yes	X	X		X		X			X	X		
SPARSEQR	yes	X			X	X	X			X	X		
SPOOLES	yes	X	X		X		X	M		X	X	X	X
SuperLU	yes	X	X	X	X		X	M		X	X		
TAUCS	yes	X	X		X		X			X	X	X	X
UMFPACK	yes	X	X	X			X			X	X		
Y12M	?	X		X			X			X	X		

Table 12.3: Sparse direct solvers.

Package	Support	Type		Language			Mode		Sparse Eigenvalue	
		Real	Complex	f77	c	c++	Seq	Dist	Sym	Gen
LZPACK	yes	X	X	X			X	M/P	X	
LASO	?	X		X			X		X	
P_ARPACK	yes	X	X	X	X	X	X	M/P	X	X
PLANSO	yes	X		X			X	M	X	
TRLAN	yes	X		X			X	M	X	

Table 12.4: Sparse eigenvalue solvers.

Package	Support	Type		Language			Mode		Sparse Direct		Sparse Iterative		Sparse Eigenvalue	
		Real	Complex	f77	c	c++	Seq	Dist	SPD	Gen	SPD	Gen	Sym	Gen
AZTEC	yes	X			X		X	M			X	X		
BILUM	yes	X		X			X				X	X		
BlockSolve95	?	X		X	X	X		M			X	X		
BPKIT	yes	X		X	X	X					P	P		
CERFACS	yes	X	X	X			X				X	X		
HYPRE	yes	X		X	X		X	M			P	P		
IML++	?	X		X	X	X	X				X	X		
ISIS++	yes	X				X		M			X	X		
ITL	yes	X				X	X				X	X		
ITPACK	?	X		X			X				X	X		
LASPack	yes	X			X		X				X	X		
LSQR	yes	X		X	X		X					X		
pARMS	yes	X		X	X		X	M			X	X		
PARPRE	yes	X			X			M			P	P		
PCG	yes	X		X	X	X		P			X			
PETSc	yes	X	X	X	X		X	M			X	X		
P-SparsLIB	yes	X		X				M				X		
PSPASES	yes	X		X	X		X	M	X					
QMRPACK	?	X	X	X			X				X	X	X	X
SLAP	?	X		X							X	X		
SPAI	yes	X			X		X	M			X	X		
SPLIB	?	X		X			X				X	X		
SPOOLES	?	X	X		X		X	M	X	X	X	X		
SYMMLQ	yes	X		X			X				X	X		
Templates	yes	X		X	X		X				X	X		

Table 12.5: Sparse iterative solvers.

Reading List

Linear systems. The literature on linear system solving, like the research in this topic, is mostly split along the lines of direct versus iterative solvers. An introduction that covers both (as well as eigenvalue methods) is the book by Dongarra et al. [35]. A very practical book about linear system solving by iterative methods is the *Templates* book [12], which in addition to the mathematical details contains sections on sparse data storage and other practical matters. More in depth and less software oriented is the book by Saad [98].

Eigensystems. Along the lines of the *Templates* book for linear systems is a similar book for eigenvalues problems [7].

III MANAGING CLUSTERS

13 Cluster Management

J. P. Navarro

In Section I we covered the enabling technologies that make up a cluster's hardware and software components. As we presented node hardware (Chapter 2), the Linux kernel (Chapter 3), cluster networks (Chapter 4), network configuration and tuning (Chapter 5), and cluster setup (Chapter 6) we presented the most significant concepts to consider in selecting cluster hardware and the major operating system installation and configuration activities necessary to deploy a cluster.

After completing basic hardware and operating system installation a cluster administrator will configure cluster wide file systems, install and configure scheduling and resource management software, and install compilers, application libraries, and other software packages needed by cluster users.

With these activities complete a cluster should be ready for productive use. From this point forward cluster management will include activities focused on: 1) detecting, investigating, and recovering from hardware and software failures; and 2) adapting to changing requirements that drive changes to cluster hardware, software, and usage patterns.

This chapter is organized around these two major aspects of cluster management. First we will cover monitoring, logging, backups, configuration management, and the broader set of activities that surround detecting and recovering from failures. Second we will discuss activities like software upgrades and account management that are primarily driven by changing cluster requirements.

We will finally wrap up by discussing the differences between systems management and cluster management which constitute the most significant cluster management challenges.

After making a cluster available to users it will not take long for someone to report a failure. Perhaps a hardware component like a hard disk, node memory, or an interconnect adapter that had passed initial functionality tests during installation will fail under real application load, or perhaps a software library or service that appeared to work initially will fail when used by a real user or application. These are but two of the many possible reasons why a cluster component can fail.

Investigating a failure to determine a root cause can be a challenge. Problems may be clearly hardware related, software related, or in some cases not clearly either. In the following sections we will discuss cluster management activities used by cluster administrators to investigate failures, find the root cause of those failures, and ensure a smooth return to a functional state.

13.1 Logging

Logging is the process by which almost every aspect of machine and cluster operation can be recorded for future reference. In a cluster, just like in a stand-alone Linux machine, the operating system and system services will normally be configured to log significant event information. At a higher level, workload management software, application libraries, and even user applications can and often do generate logging information.

Many techniques are available for logging, but in the Linux environment a service called `syslog`, and its associated library functions (see the `syslog` man page) is the standard way used by system logging services. While logging performed using `syslog` may be the most common, any application or service can use any technique it wishes for logging. The most simple logging technique is opening a file and writing textual event or error messages to it.

Just as logging techniques can be very different, log file locations can also vary. The most common location where Linux distributions place log files is in the '`/var/log`' directory.

Managing clusters, and especially reviewing activity and failures, requires in-depth knowledge of all the available log files and the information commonly stored in them. The following sections describe the major types of logging that cluster administrators should be familiar with.

13.1.1 Kernel logging

The Linux kernel records log messages to a special memory location called the ring buffer. Two major categories of information logged to the ring buffer are kernel and driver initialization information and significant and unrecoverable hardware failures or other unexpected kernel state information..

The kernel provides its own logging capability using this in-memory ring buffer because it needs to have logging capability independent of any other system services. To view the ring buffer use the `dmesg` command.

```
Linux version 2.4.18-3smp (bhcompile@daffy.perf.redhat.com) (gcc version 2.96
20000731 (Red Hat Linux 7.3 2.96-110)) #1 SMP Thu Apr 18 07:27:31 EDT 2002
BIOS-provided physical RAM map:
 BIOS-e820: 0000000000000000 - 000000000009f400 (usable)
 BIOS-e820: 000000000009f400 - 00000000000a0000 (reserved)
 BIOS-e820: 00000000000d8000 - 00000000000e0000 (reserved)
 BIOS-e820: 00000000000e4000 - 0000000000100000 (reserved)
 BIOS-e820: 0000000000100000 - 000000003fef0000 (usable)
 BIOS-e820: 000000003fef0000 - 000000003fefc000 (ACPI data)
```

```
 BIOS-e820: 000000003fefc000 - 000000003ff00000 (ACPI NVS)
 BIOS-e820: 000000003ff00000 - 000000003ff80000 (usable)
 BIOS-e820: 000000003ff80000 - 0000000040000000 (reserved)
 BIOS-e820: 00000000fec00000 - 00000000fec10000 (reserved)
 BIOS-e820: 00000000fee00000 - 00000000fee01000 (reserved)
 BIOS-e820: 00000000ff800000 - 00000000ffc00000 (reserved)
 BIOS-e820: 00000000fff00000 - 0000000100000000 (reserved)
127MB HIGHMEM available.
found SMP MP-table at 000f6760
hm, page 000f6000 reserved twice.
hm, page 000f7000 reserved twice.
hm, page 0009f000 reserved twice.
hm, page 000a0000 reserved twice.
On node 0 totalpages: 262016
zone(0): 4096 pages.
zone(1): 225280 pages.
zone(2): 32640 pages.
...
```

With some Linux distributions ring buffer contents are saved to the file '`/var/log/dmesg`' at boot time, in effect preserving all the kernel initialization log information. This is valuable because, as the name implies, the ring buffer is circular. When this fixed-size buffer fills up, messages wrap around to the beginning and start overwriting the oldest messages. If you are concerned about preserving all ring buffer messages you should configure a regular `cron` job to write ring buffer contents to a '`/var/log`' file.

If you ever suspect a kernel-related issue the first place to look is in `dmesg` output or in files containing *dmesg* output in the '`/var/log/`' directory.

The following is an example of a kernel crash (also called an "oops") that would be logged to the ring buffer. The line starting with the label "`Process`" identifies the active process when the kernel crash occured.

```
Oops: 0000
CPU:    0
EIP:    0010:[journal_dirty_metadata+98/368]    Not tainted
EIP:    0010:[<c015fcc2>]    Not tainted
EFLAGS: 00010206
eax: 0a60c4ed   ebx: 00000000   ecx: 00000bb8   edx: dfc32a40
esi: d53ccd40   edi: dfee4800   ebp: c8c2b8e0   esp: dfc35c4c
ds: 0018   es: 0018   ss: 0018
Process nfsd (pid: 727, stackpage=dfc35000)
Stack: dfb31480 dfc32a40 00000001 c8c2b8e0 c0158ff
...
```

13.1.2 System service logging

Most of the useful facilities on a machine are provided by system services or daemons. Examples include, `sshd`, the `ssh` server daemon, `xinetd/inetd`, the extended Internet service daemons, `cron` for executing scheduled commands, and others. These and most other system services log using the `syslog` facility to files in the '`/var/log`' directory.

The most common and useful system service log files that a cluster administrator should be familiar with are:

File	Contents
'`/var/log/messages`'	Many common system service messages like `sshd`, `automount`, `ntp`, and some kernel messages
'`/var/log/auth.log`'	security and authorization messages
'`/var/log/kern.log`'	kernel boot time messages (`dmesg`)
'`/var/log/daemon.log`'	system service messages

Table 13.1: Most useful system log files.

13.1.3 Workload Logging

Whether you are running PBS, Maui, Condor, or any other scheduling or resource management software, you will probably have log files produced by these software packages. OpenPBS or PBSPro, for example, default to logging in the '`/var/spool/pbs`' (or '`/var/spool/PBS`'). You should check the documentation of your workload management software for information on logfile locations and become familiar with the contents of those files.

13.1.4 Syslog capabilities and limitations

The `syslog` utility has the ability to both record events to the log files described earlier and to forward the events to other machines. In a cluster environment a common and recommended practice is to designate a central machine where the most commonly referenced log messages get collected and to configure this machine to receive and log `syslog` messages from other machines.

If you have configured a central `syslog` server you will encounter a significant architectural limitation from the standard `syslog` software. Because it uses unreliable data network packets (UDP), under high `syslog` traffic `syslog` messages may be lost. Fortunately where there is a need there is an open-source tool to address

the need. One useful tool that overcomes this scalability challenge is `syslog-ng`. For additional information and to download `syslog-ng` visit:
`http://www.balabit.com/products/syslog_ng/`.

When a machine stays up for a long time the contents of the '`/var/log`' directory can grow large. This is especially true on the central machine where you collect logging for the entire cluster. Many Linux distribution automatically run log rotation `cron` jobs that periodically rename and compress the contents of '`/var/log`' files. Log rotation often also includes automatic deletion of the oldest rotated log files. Whether your distribution has pre-configured `logrotate` capability or not you should review all the logging files generated by system services and scheduling and resource management services to ensure that log files are rotated, compressed, and retained based on your particular requirements.

13.1.5 Tools to Monitor Log Files

When failures happen you will often need to investigate them using log files. As you become more familiar with the most frequent failures and the log entries than accompany them you may find yourself wanting to take automated corrective action, or at a minimum wanting automated e-mail notification that the failure occured. Both of these are possible thanks to a class of tools called *log watchers* that can constantly watch log files for configurable log entry strings and take configurable action.

The following are several examples of log-watching tools:

- LogCheck, `http://www.psionic.com/abacus/logcheck/`
- swatch, `http://swatch.sourceforge.net/`
- LogSentry, `http://www.linux-sxs.org/files/psionic/`
- LogDog, `http://caspian.dotconf.net/menu/Software/LogDog/`

13.2 Monitoring, or Measuring Cluster Health

Monitoring involves watching the many performance and operational variables that establish whether a cluster is running correctly and as efficiently as possible. Correct operation involves looking at all hardware and software components and determining that they are available and operating as expected.

For example, to establish that all the expected hardware components are available one would need to ensure that all the CPUs, memory, disks, and network interfaces were detected by the operating system at boot time, and that all the other devices in a cluster that aren't part of a host, such as network devices, power controllers, terminal servers, and network storage devices are detected by the components that use them.

Similarly one can monitor the collection of software services than need to be running correctly for a cluster to be operational. Services such as schedulers, resource managers, and node monitoring daemons themselves need to be up and operational for the various user or operational activities on a cluster to function.

Sometimes, even though hardware and software components are detected and operational they may be operating in a degraded state, affecting efficient operation of the a cluster. Monitoring for degraded operation is often neglected; strictly speaking, applications may work correctly, but not at the expected level of performance. Monitoring for degraded performance can sometimes help predict components that are likely to fail completely in the near future. Some examples are network cables that may be producing packet loss, a disk that is very close to full, or system processes with higher-than-expected memory consumption, indicating a probable memory leak bug.

When you combine all of possible hardware and software monitoring elements and multiply them by the number of components you may find yourself needing to monitor 1000s of operational elements just to answer the basic question of to what degree a cluster is running normally.

13.2.1 Monitoring Tools

Fortunately, monitoring has been an important element of systems management so a plethora of both commercial and open-source products are available to assist with this task. Whether you want to monitor systems, networks, or both, and whether you want to use protocols like `SNMP` or not, many tools are useful for monitoring clusters. Some of the most common non-commercial cluster monitoring tools are:

- Big Brother, `http://bb4.com/`
- Cluemon, `http://clumon.ncsa.uiuc.edu/`
- Ganglia, `http://ganglia.sourceforge.net/`
- Nagios (was NetSaint), `http://www.nagios.org/`
- PARMON, `http://www.cs.mu.oz.au/~raj//parmon/`
- Performance Co-Pilot, `http://oss.sgi.com/projects/pcp/`

- Supermon, `http://www.acl.lanl.gov/supermon/`

We do not discuss these and other monitoring tools here, since many articles, papers, and discussions on cluster monitoring are available. Our main point is that these tools can be useful for measuring cluster health and summarizing cluster operational status.

13.2.2 What to Monitor

Monitoring Workload

Most workload management tools, including the Condor, Maui, and PBS discussed in this book, offer monitoring capability. Cluster managers should be very familiar with the monitoring capabilities in these tools as they summarize the most visible cluster state information: whether the nodes used by applications appear to be functional from a workload perspective, how active or busy is the cluster currently, and what the workload backlog looks like.

From a monitoring perspective, the node state information offered by workload management tools is an excellent indicator of overall cluster state and health since it indicates both that the workload management services are running and reachable on each node, and that basic monitoring implemented by these workload management services do not detect any type of node fault.

Monitoring for Degraded Performance

Both monitoring tools and logging files may at times detect or record failure situations. If you don't want to constantly have to look at these log files you can use tools designed to detect trigger strings that represent failures and report them via e-mail or other methods.

Resource Usage Monitoring

When cluster resources, such as file system space, machine memory and swap, and network or file I/O bandwidth are exhausted the entire cluster may be affected. One possible effect is the literal failure of a component, for example a machine with exhausted memory and swap is likely to crash or terminate the application exhausting memory. Another and more difficult-to-detect effect is degraded performance.

13.3 Hardware Failure and Recovery

One of the most burdensome responsibilities in cluster management is dealing with the consequences of hardware failures. The impact of hardware failures can vary drastically based on how much of the cluster depends on the failing component.

Of highest impact are failures like the loss of the file-servers serving user file-systems or the loss of infrastructure components like management nodes, nodes where scheduling and resource management services run, and the loss of commodity networking or interconnect components like switches and routers. If any of these components fails, the entire cluster may be unusable.

At the opposite end of the impact spectrum are failures that do not affect any other cluster component, for example the loss of a single compute node. When a single compute node fails, only the users active on that node will be affected and other activities on other nodes may proceed unaffected.

Given the broad impact spectrum that a particular failure can have and that the failing component can be as minor as a single disk or as major as an entire cluster network one can't write a single procedure for recovering from hardware failures. In a general sense though, the following outline should be used. Recovery from a hardware failure involves:

1. Isolating the failed component to make sure no additional cluster activities are impacted.

2. If the failure has a major impact you may want to find existing hardware that can temporarily be used to fill in for the failing component so you can recover immediately. For example, if you lose a disk, controller, or server serving critical file-systems, and you have some other server with available capacity, you can start immediate recovery to an alternate server.

3. Getting the hardware serviced.

4. And finally, fixed hardware must be integrated back into the cluster. If the failed component included data, like a disk containing the operating system or user data the recovery will involve recovering the required contents to the new disk.

13.4 Software Failure

Although software failures may be similar to hardware failures in their ability to bring an entire machine down, they are also quite different in several respects.

Software failures sometimes do not have a fix. If nobody has detected the failure or bug then a new version or patch may not be available. When this happens the only solution is to avoid the conditions that trigger the fault, report the failure to software supplier, and either wait for the fix or try to fix the problem yourself.

Regardless of what type of software failure you are dealing with, kernel, distribution, scheduling and resource management, or application support library, the best practices for avoiding software failures are:

- Keep an eye out for new software versions and bug fixes.
- Perform careful testing and verification prior to upgrading to new software versions.
- Whenever possible give yourself a way to return to previous software in case an upgrade has major problems.
- Maintain good records of unresolved failures, such as the ones that disappear after a reboot.

13.5 File System Failure and Recovery

If a hardware component or software service fails, the most a user will normally lose is the intermediate results from running applications. The user will normally lose a few hours of work at most and can easily recover by restarting jobs. If, on the other hand, a home file system containing months of work results is lost, the impact on users from data loss could be huge.

For this reason, no cluster component is more critical than the storage and file systems that hold users' applications and data.

Regardless of hardware or software used to provide home file systems the first line of defense consists of regularly scheduled backups. Backups also offer the added advantage that they can be used to recover data lost through human error.

Besides backups the following hardware and software options offer improved protection from hardware and software failures.

- Use of RAID 0, 3, or 5 file systems that protect from individual disk failures.
- Use of journaled file systems that protect from file system corruption and provide fast recovery in the case of crashes.

- Use of parallel file systems that protect from the loss of a file server by providing access to the file system through multiple machines. Commercial file systems in this category include GPFS from IBM, GFS from Systina, and PolyServe.

Adapting to Changing Requirements

In previous sections of this chapter we focused on cluster management activities surrounding investigating and recovering from failures. Sometimes the recovery process will drive a change in the base hardware or software configuration. The most common example is upgrading a software package in order to fix a bug in an older version.

Even when a cluster is fully functional, the world around it is constantly evolving. Application developers enhance their code to use new compiler or library features, new users need to use the cluster, potential security vulnerabilities are revealed that if not fixed could make a cluster susceptible. These are just some examples of the changes that surround a cluster. All of these make it necessary to iterate through a careful change-management process.

Examples of changes driven by changing requirements include:

- Adding more disk to expand storage capacity
- Upgrading the RAM or processors in nodes to increase throughput
- Applying security updates to system services
- Upgrading to new and improved compilers or application libraries
- New user account requests
- Workload management

In the following sections we will discuss cluster management activities driven by changes like these. Many factors can influence a change of requirements, but the most common are the evolving needs of existing users, the needs of new users, hardware changes driven by failures or changing capacity requirements, and the software life cycle. Collectively these changes alter the base state of a cluster and the definition of operational.

13.6 Account Management

The Linux environment offers many techniques for maintaining a coherent set of accounts across a collection of machines. The most common and easiest to administer involve the use of network based account management services. When these techniques are employed, individual machines query a central authorization and authentication service of account information. These techniques are easier to manage because maintenance of account and authorization information is maintained in a central location. Examples include `NIS` and `LDAP`.

Using NIS involves maintenance of a central copy of password, group, and other security related files in a `ypserver`. Individual machine needing to reference these security files are configured as `yp` clients and automatically query a `ypserver` for data from the security files.

Another technique for maintaining security information involves updating security information on the machines in a cluster through a distributed push, pull, or update. The primary advantages of using this technique are performance and reliability of authorization and authentication queries. The main disadvantages include the need to initiate distributed security update procedures. Updates can become complicated if a machine is down during the update process. To overcome this a combination of push, pull, and boot time and in between job refresh must be used.

13.7 Workload Management

The next several chapters introduce cluster workload management concepts and present in detail three specific software packages, Condor, Maui, and PBS, which are commonly used to manage the workload on Beowulf clusters.

Managing the workload on a Beowulf cluster is one of the most visible cluster management activities since its purpose is to run user applications. The following are examples of workload management activities that are critical to cluster management:

- Managing node availability
- Configuring node attributes important to the workload
- Managing user/group/project fair usage quotas
- Configuring and tuning scheduling policy
- Managing dedicated or maintenance reservations

- Tracking user/group/project usage history

After selecting and installing workload management software, a cluster administrator will perform these activities to ensure that a cluster usage is consistent with its goals.

Every cluster has a different set of goals, and how to implement an appropriate workload management policy for those goals depends on the software packages in use. You should consult Condor, Maui, PBS, or other workload management software documentation for details on options available to implement the policies you need.

Regardless of what workload management tools you use you should try to find out how to perform the following activities to assist in failure investigation and recovery.

1. Taking a node off line so it is not considered for future jobs.

2. Placing a system or individual user or project reservation on a node so the node is not available to everyone but still available for investigating a hardware or software failure.

3. Modifying the properties or attributes of a node to reflect a change in the availability of a failing component (like the interconnect), or to reflect that it has a test operating system or collection of software.

4. Adding or removing individual nodes from the list of known nodes.

5. Suspending all job execution without losing previously queued jobs.

6. Canceling running jobs.

7. Placing a hold on a queued job to ensure that it doesn't run and trigger some type of harmful failure.

13.8 Software upgrades

Whoever coined the saying that only death and taxes are certain was definitely not a system or cluster administrator. As certain as death and taxes are software upgrades. How many software packages that continue to be useful don't change? Even when a package is stable, the environment around it constantly changes, making new versions necessary to fix new issues derived from this evolving environment.

The scope of the impact of a software upgrade can vary tremendously. At the low end are upgrades that do not affect other software packages on the system, such as the version of a particular numerical library. At the high-impact end are distribution upgrades that change the version of `libc`, the standard C library, which can have a ripple effect through many of the software packages on a system, and a large set of in-between upgrades that can affect a varying number of users and applications.

Upgrading software on an individual cluster machine is similar to upgrading software on non-cluster machines. In many respects clusters should be managed like non-cluster machines. If you are dealing with a production cluster that servers a large user community, then all the standard practices should be followed, such as pre-change testing and a carefully planned and communicated migration path.

One of the most critical reasons to upgrade cluster software is to address security vulnerabilities. If your cluster is reachable by the world at large or by potential hackers you should keep a close eye out for security advisories for your kernel, system services, and any other software component that could be used to compromise a system. Some of the most useful resources to keep an eye on for software vulnerability and fix information are:

1. the vendor supplying the kernel and distribution you use,
2. the U.S. Department of Energy Computer Incident Advisory Capability, also known as *CIAC*, which can be found at `http://www.ciac.org/ciac/`, and
3. the *CERT* Coordination Center: a federally funded Internet security research and development center which can be found at `http://www.cert.org/`.

13.9 Configuration Management

Configuring management refers to the activities performed on a machine that adapt it to a particular organization, its network services, security policies, management policies, access policy, etc. In other words, it is the set of activities that integrate a machine into the cluster and organization.

Why would configuration management need to be mentioned in the context of Beowulf clusters? First, because it's a critical aspect of making a Beowulf cluster functional, and secondly because it can be a challenge if one doesn't follow a carefully designed configuration management process.

Most Beowulf clusters have a variety of machine configurations that share many common characteristics, but also vary in important ways. For example, management nodes, login nodes, file-servers, and computer nodes all may need to be configured similarly to set and maintain accurate clocks, but they all have a slightly different access policy and collection of configured and available software services.

Describing configuration information and propagating it to machines is often performed by the cluster installation software. Chapter 6 describes cluster setup using various tools. Each of these cluster installation tools provides some type of configuration management capability. In some cases the capability is the basic capability you would use on stand-alone machines.

Regardless of which tool you use, an important aspect of cluster management is maintaining a central repository of the configuration information used in a cluster. Without this information, whenever a machine fails and needs to be rebuilt, determining what configuration information was applied to make the machine functional may be difficult to ascertain. Every time you rebuild a compute node you would rather not have to look at other compute nodes to remember which files contain important configuration information that must be applied to the rebuilt machine, and then go through a `diff` process comparing it to other nodes to make sure you remembered everything.

The important point to remember is that the most effective way to deal with configuration management is to maintain some type of central repository from which you push configuration changes. If this repository can be organized by node types or some other organizational approach, all the better. That way when you need to change something on all compute nodes, or all login nodes, or every node on the cluster, you don't have to update a centrally managed file for every node, but just the files from the appropriate classes of nodes.

If you need additional functionality in this respect that is not a part of your cluster distribution or installation suite you may find one of the following tools helpful:

- cfengine, `http://www.cfengine.org/`
- sanity/cfg, `http://www-unix.mcs.anl.gov/systems/software/msys/`
- and various proprietary vendor solutions

Administration Challenges Unique to Clusters

One appealing way to think of cluster management is as management of a collection of individual machines. This approach is appealing since it sidesteps the complexity of the whole by focusing on the management of the individual components. Although managing a cluster this way may work at a basic level, it isn't very effective and doesn't consider the intended architecture and usage model of a cluster.

The Linux cluster's claim to fame is in its ability to produce supercomputer class results at a fraction of the cost. This means, among other things, that the collection of components at a practical level needs to be usable by applications and manageable by administrators as a single machine.

This is where the cluster management challenge begins. To overcome this challenge, cluster administrators must approach cluster management at the cluster level and therefore need tools for logging, monitoring, build and configuration management, workload management, and so forth that are aware of, and operate at, the cluster level.

Today we have many cluster management tools that make it easier to work with the entire cluster. But there is still significant room for improvement. One example is in the area of fault detection, analysis, and recovery. The major supercomputer vendors have worked for decades to make their machines fault tolerant. By contrast, today's cluster management tools for the most part ignore the issue of fault detection and recovery. This deficiency undoubtedly constitutes the greatest cluster management challenge.

An approach used to bridge the gap between cluster level management and machine specific administration tools is scripting or automation. The premise behind this approach is to make scriptable interfaces to all the actions performed at the machine level and to use cluster-level tools to automatically iterate the same action over many components or machines. While this concept sounds simple and achievable, it is unfortunately not always possible since hardware and software at the machine level is often not designed for complete hands-off administration.

One of the most basic and useful tools for invoking a scriptable command on a group of machines is the "parallel distributed shell" or `pdsh`. This tool is the cluster aware equivalent of `rsh` or `ssh`. With it you can define various sets of nodes and perform operation on those collections in parallel. For example, to verify the uptime and load across an entire cluster with pdsh use the command:

```
pdsh -a uptime
```

For download or learn about `pdsh` visit:
`http://www.llnl.gov/linux/pdsh/pdsh.html`

13.10 Conclusion

Cluster management, although based on many of the same procedures and practices used to manage individual machines, is strongly influenced by the unique challenges derived from administering a group of machines that need to operate as a single entity for the application and user.

Cluster management is fundamentally about keeping a machine running. For cluster administrators to do this effectively they must use a set of tools and techniques that operate at the cluster level. In this chapter we have discussed both basic system administration tools and the techniques available to administrators to help them effectively manage the cluster at the cluster level.

14 Cluster Workload Management

James Patton Jones, David Lifka, Bill Nitzberg, and Todd Tannenbaum

A Beowulf cluster is a powerful (and attractive) tool. But managing the workload can present significant challenges. It is not uncommon to run hundreds or thousands of jobs or to share the cluster among many users. Some jobs may run only on certain nodes because not all the nodes in the cluster are identical; for instance, some nodes have more memory than others. Some nodes temporarily may not be functioning correctly. Certain users may require priority access to part or all of the cluster. Certain jobs may have to be run at certain times of the day or only after other jobs have completed. Even in the simplest environment, keeping track of all these activities and resource specifics while managing the ever-increasing web of priorities is a complex problem. Workload management software attacks this problem by providing a way to monitor and manage the flow of work through the system, allowing the *best* use of cluster resources as defined by a supplied policy.

Basically, workload management software maximizes the delivery of resources to jobs, given competing user requirements and local policy restrictions. Users package their work into sets of jobs, while the administrator (or system owner) describes local use policies (e.g., Tom's jobs always go first). The software monitors the state of the cluster, schedules work, enforces policy, and tracks usage.

A quick note on terminology: Many terms have been used to describe this area of management software. All of the following topics are related to workload management: distributed resource management, batch queuing, job scheduling, and resource and task scheduling.

14.1 Goal of Workload Management Software

The goal of workload management software is to make certain the submitted jobs ultimately run to completion by utilizing cluster resources according to a supplied policy. But in order to achieve this goal, workload management systems usually must perform some or all of the following activities:

- Queuing
- Scheduling
- Monitoring
- Resource management
- Accounting

The typical relationship between users, resources, and these workload management activities is depicted in Figure 14.1. As shown in this figure, workload management software sits between the cluster users and the cluster resources. First, users submit jobs to a queue in order to specify the work to be performed. (Once a job has been submitted, the user can request status information about that job at any time.) The jobs then wait in the queue until they are scheduled to start on the cluster. The specifics of the scheduling process are defined by the policy rules. At this point, resource management mechanisms handle the details of properly launching the job and perhaps cleaning up any mess left behind after the job either completes or is aborted. While all this is going on, the workload management system is monitoring the status of system resources and accounting for which users are using what resources.

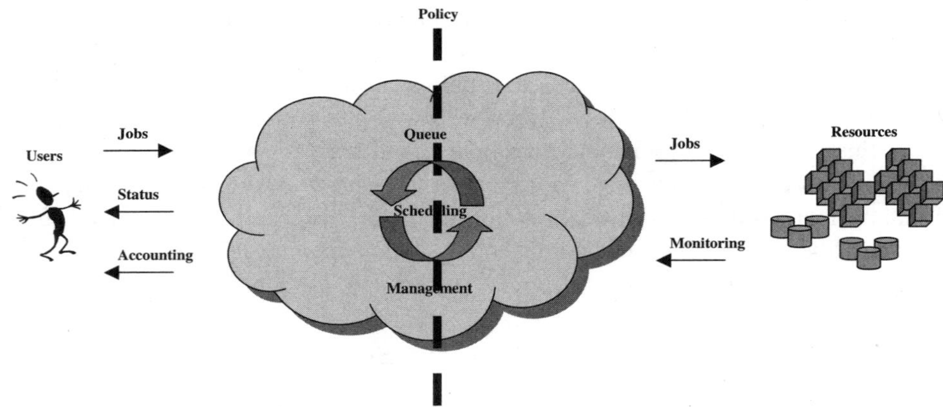

Figure 14.1: Activities performed by a workload management system.

14.2 Workload Management Activities

Now let us take a look in more detail at each of the major activities performed by a cluster workload management system.

14.2.1 Queueing

The first of the five aspects of workload management is *queuing*, or the process of collecting together "work" to be executed on a set of resources. This is also the portion most visible to the user.

The tasks the user wishes to have the computer perform, the work, is submitted to the workload management system in a container called a "batch job." The batch job consists of two primary parts: a set of resource directives (such as the amount of memory or number of CPUs needed) and a description of the task to be executed. This description contains all the information the workload management system needs in order to start a user's job when the time comes. For instance, the job description may contain information such as the name of the file to execute, a list of data files required by the job, and environment variables or command-line arguments to pass to the executable.

Once submitted to the workload management system, the batch jobs are held in a "queue" until the matching resources (e.g., the right kind of computers with the right amount of memory or number of CPUs) become available. Examples of real-life queues are lines at the bank or grocery store. Sometimes you get lucky and there's no wait, but usually you have to stand in line for a few minutes. And on days when the resources (clerks) are in high demand (like payday), the wait is substantially longer.

The same applies to computers and batch jobs. Sometimes the wait is very short, and the jobs run immediately. But more often (and thus the need for the workload management system) resources are oversubscribed, and so the jobs have to wait.

One important aspect of queues is that limits can be set that restrict access to the queue. This allows the cluster manager greater control over the usage policy of the cluster. For example, it may be desirable to have a queue available for short jobs only, analogous to the "ten items or fewer express lane" at the grocery store, providing a shorter wait for "quick tasks."

Each of the different workload management systems discussed later in this volume offers a rich variety of queue limits and attributes.

14.2.2 Scheduling

The second area of workload management is scheduling, which is simply the process of choosing the *best* job to run. Unlike in our real-life examples of the bank and grocery store (which employ a simple first-come, first-served model of deciding who's next), workload management systems offer a variety of ways by which the *best* job is identified.

As we have discussed earlier, however, *best* can be a tricky goal. It depends on the usage policy set by local management, the available workload, the type and availability of cluster resources, and the types of application being run on the cluster. In general, however, scheduling can be broken into two primary activities: *policy enforcement* and *resource optimization.*

Policy encapsulates how the cluster resources are to be used, addressing such issues as priorities, traffic control, and capability vs. high throughput. Scheduling is then the act of enforcing the policy in the selection of jobs, ensuring that priorities are met and policy goals are achieved.

While implementing and enforcing the policy, the scheduler has a second set of goals. These are resource optimization goals, such as "pack jobs efficiently" or "exploit underused resources."

The difficult part of scheduling, then, is balancing policy enforcement with resource optimization in order to pick the *best* job to run.

Logically speaking, one can think of a scheduler as performing the following loop:

1. Select the best job to run, according to policy and available resources.

2. Start the job.

3. Stop the job and/or clean up after a completed job.

4. Repeat.

The nuts and bolts of scheduling is, of course, choosing and tuning the policy to meet your needs. Although different workload management systems each have their own idiosyncrasies, they typically all provide ways in which their scheduling policy can be customized. Subsequent chapters of this book discuss the various scheduling policy mechanisms available in several popular workload management systems.

14.2.3 Monitoring

Resource monitoring is the third part of any cluster workload management system. It provides necessary information to administrators, users and the scheduling system itself on the status of jobs and resources. Resource monitoring comes into play in three critical times:

1. When nodes are idle, to verify that they are in working order before starting another job on them.

2. When nodes are busy running a job. Users and administrators may want to check memory, CPU, network, I/O, and utilization of other system resources. Such checks often are useful in parallel programming when users wish to verify

that they have balanced their workload correctly and are effectively using all the nodes they've been allocated.

3. When a job completes. Here, resource monitoring is used to ensure that no processes remain from the completed job and that the node is still in working order before starting another job on it.

Workload management systems query the compute resources at these times and use the information to make informed decisions about running jobs. Much of the information is cached so that it can be reported quickly in answer to status requests. Some information is saved for historical analysis purposes. Still other information is used in the enforcement of local policy. The method of collection may differ in different workload management systems, but the general purposes are the same.

14.2.4 Resource Management

The fourth area, resource management, is essentially responsible for the starting, stopping, and cleaning up after jobs that are run on cluster nodes. In a batch system resource management involves running a job for a user, under the identity of the user, on the resources the user was allocated, in such a way that the user need not be present at that time.

Many cluster workload management systems provide mechanisms to ensure the successful startup and cleanup of jobs and to maintain node status data internally, so that jobs are started only on nodes that are available and functioning correctly.

In addition, limits may need to be placed on the job and enforced by the workload management system. These limits are yet another aspect of policy enforcement, in addition to the limits on queues and those enacted by the scheduling component.

Resource management also includes removing or adding compute resources to the available pool of systems. Clusters are rarely static; systems go down, or new nodes are added. The "registration" of new nodes and the marking of nodes as unavailable are both additional aspects of resource management.

14.2.5 Accounting

The fifth aspect of workload management is accounting and reporting. Workload accounting is the process of collecting resource usage data for the batch jobs that run on the cluster. Such data includes the job owner, resources requested by the job, and total amount of resources consumed by the job. Other data about the job may also be available, depending on the specific workload managment system in use.

Cluster workload accounting data can used for a variety of purposes, such as

- producing weekly system usage reports,
- preparing monthly per user usage reports,
- enforcing per project allocations,
- tuning the scheduling policy,
- calculating future resource allocations,
- anticipating future computer component requirements, and
- determining areas of improvement within the computer system.

The data for these purposes may be collected as part of the resource monitoring tasks or may be gathered separately. In either case, data is pulled from the available sources in order to meet the objectives of workload accounting.

14.3 Conclusions

Workload management is all about utilizing cluster resources according to a supplied policy. The five activies of workload management—queueing, scheduling, monitoring, resource manangement, and accounting—interact to produce the system usage results desired by the site.

The next few chapters of this book discuss in detail two complete workload management systems (Condor and PBS) and the Maui job scheduler. Details of using the features of each system are provided in the specific chapters. In addition to the systems discussed in this book, there are several others that are popular with Beowulf clusters. One that has recently become popular is the Sun Grid Engine (SGE) `wwws.sun.com/software/gridware/sge.html`. Another system that contains aspects of a workload management system is Scyld, discussed in Chapter 18.

15 Condor: A Distributed Job Scheduler

Todd Tannenbaum, Derek Wright, Karen Miller, Erik Paulson, and Miron Livny

Condor is a sophisticated and unique distributed job scheduler developed by the Condor research project at the University of Wisconsin-Madison Department of Computer Sciences.

Condor is open-source software, under the very liberal Condor Public License. The program binaries, documentation, and source code may all be found on the Condor project's Web site at `www.cs.wisc.edu/condor`. Support contracts are available from several different sources; for additional information see `www.cs.wisc.edu/condor/condor-support`. The Condor Public License permits installation, use, reproduction, display, modification and redistribution of Condor, with or without modification, in source and binary forms.

This chapter introduces all aspects of Condor, from its ability to satisfy the needs and desires of both submitters and resource owners, to the management of Condor on clusters. Following an overview of Condor and Condor's ClassAd mechanism is a description of Condor from the user's perspective. The architecture of the software is presented along with overviews of installation and management. The chapter ends with configuration scenarios specific to clusters.

15.1 Introduction to Condor

Condor is a specialized workload management system for compute-intensive jobs. Like other full-featured batch systems, Condor provides a job queuing mechanism, scheduling policy, priority scheme, resource monitoring, and resource management. Users submit their jobs to Condor, and Condor places them into a queue, chooses when and where to run them based upon a policy, monitors their progress, and ultimately informs the user upon completion.

While providing functionality similar to that of a more traditional batch queuing system, Condor's novel architecture allows it to succeed in areas where traditional scheduling systems fail. Condor can be used to manage a cluster of dedicated Beowulf nodes. In addition, several unique mechanisms enable Condor to effectively harness wasted CPU power from otherwise idle desktop workstations. Condor can be used to seamlessly combine all of your organization's computational power into one resource.

Condor is the product of the Condor Research Project at the University of Wisconsin-Madison (UW-Madison) and was first installed as a production system in the UW-Madison Department of Computer Sciences nearly ten years ago. This Condor installation has since served as a major source of computing cycles to UW-Madison faculty and students. Today, just in our department alone, Condor manages more than one thousand workstations, including the department's 500-CPU Linux Beowulf cluster. On a typical day, Condor delivers more than 650 CPU-*days* to UW researchers. Additional Condor installations have been established over the years across our campus and the world. Hundreds of organizations in industry, government, and academia have used Condor to establish compute environments ranging in size from a handful to hundreds of workstations.

15.1.1 Features of Condor

Condor's features are extensive. Condor provides great flexibility for both the user submitting jobs and for the owner of a machine that provides CPU time toward running jobs. The following list summarizes some of Condor's capabilities.

ClassAds: The ClassAd mechanism in Condor provides an extremely flexible and expressive framework for matching resource requests (jobs) with resource offers (machines). Jobs can easily state both job requirements and job preferences. Likewise, machines can specify requirements and preferences about the jobs they are willing to run. These requirements and preferences can be described in powerful expressions, resulting in Condor's adaptation to nearly any desired policy.

Distributed submission: There is no single, centralized submission machine. Instead, Condor allows jobs to be submitted from many machines, and each machine contains its own job queue. Users may submit to a cluster from their own desktop machines.

User priorities: Administrators may assign priorities to users using a flexible mechanism that enables a policy of fair share, strict ordering, fractional ordering, or a combination of policies.

Job priorities: Users can assign priorities to their submitted jobs in order to control the execution order of the jobs. A "nice-user" mechanism requests the use of only those machines that would have otherwise been idle.

Job dependency: Some sets of jobs require an ordering because of dependencies between jobs. "Start job X only after jobs Y and Z successfully complete" is an example of a dependency. Enforcing dependencies is easily handled.

Support for multiple job models: Condor handles both serial jobs and parallel jobs incorporating PVM, dynamic PVM, and MPI.

Job checkpoint and migration: With certain types of jobs, Condor can transparently take a checkpoint and subsequently resume the application. A checkpoint is a snapshot of a job's complete state. Given a checkpoint, the job can later continue its execution from where it left off at the time of the checkpoint. A checkpoint also enables the transparent migration of a job from one machine to another machine. Condor will take a checkpoint of a job when it schedules the resource to a different job or the resource returns to the owner. Condor will also periodically produce a checkpoint for a job. This provides a form of fault tolerance and safeguards the accumulated computation time of a job. It reduces the loss in the event of a system failure such as the machine being shut down or hardware failure.

Job suspend and resume: Based on policy rules, Condor can ask the operating system to suspend and later resume a job.

Remote system calls: Despite running jobs on remote machines, Condor can often preserve the local execution environment via remote system calls. Users do not need to make data files available or even obtain a login account on remote workstations before Condor executes their programs there. The program behaves under Condor as if it were running as the user that submitted the job on the workstation where it was originally submitted, regardless of where it really executes.

Authentication and authorization: Administrators have fine-grained control of access permissions, and Condor can perform strong network authentication using a variety of mechanisms including Kerberos and X.509 public key certificates.

Heterogeneous platforms: In addition to Linux, Condor has been ported to most of the other primary flavors of Unix as well as Windows NT. A single pool can contain multiple platforms. Jobs to be executed under one platform may be submitted from a different platform. As an example, an executable that runs under Windows 2000 may be submitted from a machine running Linux.

Pools of machines working together: *Flocking* allows jobs to be scheduled across multiple Condor pools. It can be done across pools of machines owned by different organizations that impose their own policies.

Grid computing: Condor incorporates many of the emerging grid-based computing methodologies and protocols. Condor can submit jobs into resources managed via other scheduling systems such as PBS using the Globus Toolkit. Condor also includes all of the necessary software to receive jobs from other sites using the Globus Toolkit.

15.1.2 Understanding Condor ClassAds

The ClassAd is a flexible representation of the characteristics and constraints of both machines and jobs in the Condor system. *Matchmaking* is the mechanism by which Condor matches an idle job with an available machine. Understanding this unique framework is the key to harness the full flexibility of the Condor system. ClassAds are employed by users to specify which machines should service their jobs. Administrators use them to customize scheduling policy.

Conceptualizing Condor ClassAds: Just Like the Newspaper

Condor's ClassAds are analogous to the classified advertising section of the newspaper. Sellers advertise specifics about what they have to sell, hoping to attract a buyer. Buyers may advertise specifics about what they wish to purchase. Both buyers and sellers list constraints that must be satisfied. For instance, a buyer has a maximum spending limit, and a seller requires a minimum purchase price. Furthermore, both want to rank requests to their own advantage. Certainly a seller would rank one offer of $50 higher than a different offer of $25. In Condor, users submitting jobs can be thought of as buyers of compute resources and machine owners are sellers.

All machines in a Condor pool advertise their attributes, such as available RAM memory, CPU type and speed, virtual memory size, current load average, current time and date, and other static and dynamic properties. This machine ClassAd also advertises under what conditions it is willing to run a Condor job and what type of job it prefers. These policy attributes can reflect the individual terms and preferences by which the different owners have allowed their machines to participate in the Condor pool.

After a job is submitted to Condor, a job ClassAd is created. This ClassAd includes attributes about the job, such as the amount of memory the job uses, the name of the program to run, the user who submitted the job, and the time it was submitted. The job can also specify requirements and preferences (or *rank*) for the machine that will run the job. For instance, perhaps you are looking for the fastest floating-point performance available. You want Condor to rank available machines based on floating-point performance. Perhaps you care only that the machine has a minimum of 256 MBytes of RAM. Or, perhaps you will take any machine you can get! These job attributes and requirements are bundled up into a job ClassAd.

Condor plays the role of matchmaker by continuously reading all the job ClassAds and all the machine ClassAds, matching and ranking job ads with machine ads. Condor ensures that the requirements in both ClassAds are satisfied.

Structure of a ClassAd

A ClassAd is a set of uniquely named expressions. Each named expression is called an *attribute*. Each attribute has an *attribute name* and an *attribute value*. The attribute value can be a simple integer, string, or floating-point value, such as

```
Memory = 512
OpSys = "LINUX"
NetworkLatency = 7.5
```

An attribute value can also consist of a logical expression that will evaluate to TRUE, FALSE, or UNDEFINED. The syntax and operators allowed in these expressions are similar to those in C or Java, that is, `==` for equals, `!=` for not equals, `&&` for logical **and**, `||` for logical **or**, and so on. Furthermore, ClassAd expressions can incorporate attribute names to refer to other attribute values. For instance, consider the following small sample ClassAd:

```
MemoryInMegs = 512
MemoryInBytes = MemoryInMegs * 1024 * 1024
Cpus = 4
BigMachine = (MemoryInMegs > 256) && (Cpus >= 4)
VeryBigMachine = (MemoryInMegs > 512) && (Cpus >= 8)
FastMachine = BigMachine && SpeedRating
```

In this example, `BigMachine` evaluates to TRUE and `VeryBigMachine` evaluates to FALSE. But, because attribute `SpeedRating` is not specified, `FastMachine` would evaluate to UNDEFINED.

Condor provides *meta-operators* that allow you to explicitly compare with the UNDEFINED value by testing both the type and value of the operands. If both the types and values match, the two operands are considered *identical*; `=?=` is used for meta-equals (or, is-identical-to) and `=!=` is used for meta-not-equals (or, is-not-identical-to). These operators always return TRUE or FALSE and therefore enable Condor administrators to specify explicit policies given incomplete information.

A complete description of ClassAd semantics and syntax is documented in the Condor manual.

Matching ClassAds

ClassAds can be matched with one another. This is the fundamental mechanism by which Condor matches jobs with machines. Figure 15.1 displays a ClassAd from Condor representing a machine and another representing a queued job. Each ClassAd contains a `MyType` attribute, describing what type of resource the ad represents, and a `TargetType` attribute. The `TargetType` specifies the type of resource desired in a match. Job ads want to be matched with machine ads and vice versa.

Job ClassAd

MyType = "Job"
TargetType = "Machine"
Requirements = ((Arch=="INTEL" && OpSys=="LINUX") && Disk > DiskUsage)
Rank = (Memory * 10000) + KFlops
Args = "-ini ./ies.ini"
ClusterId = 680
Cmd = "/home/tannenba/bin/sim-exe"
Department = "CompSci"
DiskUsage = 465
StdErr = "sim.err"
ExitStatus = 0
FileReadBytes = 0.000000
FileWriteBytes = 0.000000
ImageSize = 465
StdIn = "/dev/null"
Iwd = "/home/tannenba/sim-m/run_55"
JobPrio = 0
JobStartDate = 971403010
JobStatus = 2
StdOut = "sim.out"
Owner = "tannenba"
ProcId = 64
QDate = 971377131
RemoteSysCpu = 0.000000
RemoteUserCpu = 0.000000
RemoteWallClockTime = 2401399.000000
TransferFiles = "NEVER"
WantCheckpoint = FALSE
WantRemoteSyscalls = FALSE
⋮

Machine ClassAd

MyType = "Machine"
TargetType = "Job"
Requirements = Start
Rank = TARGET.Department==MY.Department
Activity = "Idle"
Arch = "INTEL"
ClockDay = 0
ClockMin = 614
CondorLoadAvg = 0.000000
Cpus = 1
CurrentRank = 0.000000
Department = "CompSci"
Disk = 3076076
EnteredCurrentActivity = 990371564
EnteredCurrentState = 990330615
FileSystemDomain = "cs.wisc.edu"
IsInstructional = FALSE
KeyboardIdle = 15
KFlops = 145811
LoadAvg = 0.220000
Machine = "nostos.cs.wisc.edu"
Memory = 511
Mips = 732
OpSys = "LINUX"
Start = (LoadAvg <= 0.300000) && (KeyboardIdle > (15 * 60))
State = "Unclaimed"
Subnet = "128.105.165"
TotalVirtualMemory = 787144
⋮

Figure 15.1: Examples of ClassAds in Condor.

Each ClassAd engaged in matchmaking specifies a `Requirements` and a `Rank` attribute. In order for two ClassAds to match, the `Requirements` expression in both ads must evaluate to TRUE. An important component of matchmaking is the `Requirements` and `Rank` expression can refer not only to attributes in their own ad but also to attributes in the candidate matching ad. For instance, the

Requirements expression for the job ad specified in Figure 15.1 refers to Arch, OpSys, and Disk, which are all attributes found in the machine ad.

What happens if Condor finds more than one machine ClassAd that satisfies the constraints specified by Requirements? That is where the Rank expression comes into play. The Rank expression specifies the desirability of the match (where higher numbers mean better matches). For example, the job ad in Figure 15.1 specifies

```
Requirements = ((Arch=="INTEL" && OpSys=="LINUX") && Disk > DiskUsage)
Rank         = (Memory * 100000) + KFlops
```

In this case, the job requires a computer running the Linux operating system and more local disk space than it will use. Among all such computers, the user prefers those with large physical memories and fast floating-point CPUs (KFlops is a metric of floating-point performance). Since the Rank is a user-specified metric, *any* expression may be used to specify the perceived desirability of the match. Condor's matchmaking algorithms deliver the best resource (as defined by the Rank expression) while satisfying other criteria.

15.2 Using Condor

The road to using Condor effectively is a short one. The basics are quickly and easily learned.

15.2.1 Roadmap to Using Condor

The following steps are involved in running jobs using Condor:

Prepare the Job to Run Unattended. An application run under Condor must be able to execute as a batch job. Condor runs the program unattended and in the background. A program that runs in the background will not be able to perform interactive input and output. Condor can redirect console output (stdout and stderr) and keyboard input (stdin) to and from files. You should create any needed files that contain the proper keystrokes needed for program input. You should also make certain the program will run correctly with the files.

Select the Condor Universe. Condor has five runtime environments from which to choose. Each runtime environment is called a *Universe*. Usually the Universe you choose is determined by the type of application you are asking Condor to run. There are six job Universes in total: two for serial jobs

(Standard and Vanilla), one for parallel PVM jobs (PVM), one for parallel MPI jobs (Parallel), one for Grid applications (Globus), and one for meta-schedulers (Scheduler). Section 15.2.4 provides more information on each of these Universes.

Create a Submit Description File. The details of a job submission are defined in a *submit description* file. This file contains information about the job such as what executable to run, which Universe to use, the files to use for `stdin`, `stdout`, and `stderr`, requirements and preferences about the machine which should run the program, and where to send e-mail when the job completes. You can also tell Condor how many times to run a program; it is simple to run the same program multiple times with different data sets.

Submit the Job. Submit the program to Condor with the `condor_submit` command.

Once a job has been submitted, Condor handles all aspects of running the job. You can subsequently monitor the job's progress with the `condor_q` and `condor_status` commands. You may use `condor_prio` to modify the order in which Condor will run your jobs. If desired, Condor can also record what is being done with your job at every stage in its lifecycle, through the use of a log file specified during submission.

When the program completes, Condor notifies the owner (by e-mail, the user-specified log file, or both) the exit status, along with various statistics including time used and I/O performed. You can remove a job from the queue at any time with `condor_rm`.

15.2.2 Submitting a Job

To submit a job for execution to Condor, you use the `condor_submit` command. This command takes as an argument the name of the submit description file, which contains commands and keywords to direct the queuing of jobs. In the submit description file, you define everything Condor needs to execute the job. Items such as the name of the executable to run, the initial working directory, and command-line arguments to the program all go into the submit description file. The `condor_submit` command creates a job ClassAd based on the information, and Condor schedules the job.

The contents of a submit description file can save you considerable time when you are using Condor. It is easy to submit multiple runs of a program to Condor.

To run the same program 500 times on 500 different input data sets, the data files are arranged such that each run reads its own input, and each run writes its own output. Every individual run may have its own initial working directory, **stdin**, **stdout**, **stderr**, command-line arguments, and shell environment.

The following examples illustrate the flexibility of using Condor. We assume that the jobs submitted are serial jobs intended for a cluster that has a shared file system across all nodes. Therefore, all jobs use the Vanilla Universe, the simplest one for running serial jobs. The other Condor Universes are explored later.

Example 1

Example 1 is the simplest submit description file possible. It queues up one copy of the program 'foo' for execution by Condor. A log file called 'foo.log' is generated by Condor. The log file contains events pertaining to the job while it runs inside of Condor. When the job finishes, its exit conditions are noted in the log file. We recommend that you always have a log file so you know what happened to your jobs. The *queue* statement in the submit description file tells Condor to use all the information specified so far to create a job ClassAd and place the job into the queue. Lines that begin with a pound character (#) are comments and are ignored by condor_submit.

```
# Example 1 : Simple submit file
universe = vanilla
executable = foo
log = foo.log
queue
```

Example 2

Example 2 queues two copies of the program '**mathematica**'. The first copy runs in directory '**run_1**', and the second runs in directory '**run_2**'. For both queued copies, '**stdin**' will be '**test.data**', '**stdout**' will be '**loop.out**', and '**stderr**' will be '**loop.error**'. Two sets of files will be written, since the files are each written to their own directories. This is a convenient way to organize data for a large group of Condor jobs.

```
# Example 2: demonstrate use of multiple
# directories for data organization.
universe = vanilla
executable = mathematica
# Give some command line args, remap stdio
```

```
arguments = -solver matrix
input = test.data
output = loop.out
error = loop.error
log = loop.log

initialdir = run_1
queue
initialdir = run_2
queue
```

Example 3

The submit description file for Example 3 queues 150 runs of program '`foo`'. This job requires Condor to run the program on machines that have greater than 128 megabytes of physical memory, and it further requires that the job not be scheduled to run on a specific node. Of the machines that meet the requirements, the job prefers to run on the fastest floating-point nodes currently available to accept the job. It also advises Condor that the job will use up to 180 megabytes of memory when running. Each of the 150 runs of the program is given its own process number, starting with process number 0. Several built-in macros can be used in a submit description file; one of them is the *$(Process)* macro which Condor expands to be the process number in the job cluster. This causes files '`stdin`', '`stdout`', and '`stderr`' to be '`in.0`', '`out.0`', and '`err.0`' for the first run of the program, '`in.1`', '`out.1`', and '`err.1`' for the second run of the program, and so forth. A single log file will list events for all 150 jobs in this job cluster.

```
# Example 3: Submit lots of runs and use the
# pre-defined $(Process) macro.
universe = vanilla
executable = foo
requirements = Memory > 128  && Machine != "server-node.cluster.edu"
rank = KFlops
image_size = 180

Error   = err.$(Process)
Input   = in.$(Process)
Output  = out.$(Process)
Log = foo.log

queue 150
```

Note that the `requirements` and `rank` entries in the submit description file will become the requirements and rank attributes of the subsequently created ClassAd for this job. These are arbitrary expressions that can reference any attributes of either the machine or the job; see Section 15.1.2 for more on requirements and rank expressions in ClassAds.

15.2.3 Overview of User Commands

Once you have jobs submitted to Condor, you can manage them and monitor their progress. Table 15.1 shows several commands available to the Condor user to view the job queue, check the status of nodes in the pool, and perform several other activities. Most of these commands have many command-line options; see the Command Reference chapter of the Condor manual for complete documentation. To provide an introduction from a user perspective, we give here a quick tour showing several of these commands in action.

Command	Description
`condor_analyze`	Troubleshoot jobs that are not being matched
`condor_checkpoint`	Checkpoint jobs running on the specified hosts
`condor_compile`	Create a relinked executable for submission to the Standard Universe
`condor_glidein`	Add a Globus resource to a Condor pool
`condor_history`	View log of Condor jobs completed to date
`condor_hold`	Put jobs in the queue in hold state
`condor_prio`	Change priority of jobs in the queue
`condor_qedit`	Modify attributes of a previously submitted job
`condor_q`	Display information about jobs in the queue
`condor_release`	Release held jobs in the queue
`condor_reschedule`	Update scheduling information to the central manager
`condor_rm`	Remove jobs from the queue
`condor_run`	Submit a shell command-line as a Condor job
`condor_status`	Display status of the Condor pool
`condor_submit_dag`	Manage and queue jobs within a specified DAG for interjob dependencies.
`condor_submit`	Queue jobs for execution
`condor_userlog`	Display and summarize job statistics from job log files
`condor_version`	Display version number of installed software

Table 15.1: List of user commands.

When jobs are submitted, Condor will attempt to find resources to service the jobs. A list of all users with jobs submitted may be obtained through **condor_status** with the *-submitters* option. An example of this would yield output similar to the following:

```
% condor_status -submitters

Name                 Machine      Running IdleJobs HeldJobs

ballard@cs.wisc.edu  bluebird.c         0       11        0
nice-user.condor@cs. cardinal.c         6      504        0
wright@cs.wisc.edu   finch.cs.w         1        1        0
jbasney@cs.wisc.edu  perdita.cs         0        0        5

                           RunningJobs           IdleJobs           HeldJobs

 ballard@cs.wisc.edu                 0                 11                  0
 jbasney@cs.wisc.edu                 0                  0                  5
nice-user.condor@cs.                 6                504                  0
  wright@cs.wisc.edu                 1                  1                  0

               Total                 7                516                  5
```

Checking on the Progress of Jobs

The condor_q command displays the status of all jobs in the queue. An example of the output from condor_q is

```
% condor_q

-- Schedd: uug.cs.wisc.edu : <128.115.121.12:33102>
 ID       OWNER           SUBMITTED     RUN_TIME ST PRI SIZE CMD
 55574.0  jane           6/23 11:33   4+03:35:28 R  0   25.7 seycplex seymour.d
 55575.0  jane           6/23 11:44   0+23:24:40 R  0   26.8 seycplexpseudo sey
 83193.0  jane           3/28 15:11  48+15:50:55 R  0   17.5 cplexmip test1.mp
 83196.0  jane           3/29 08:32  48+03:16:44 R  0   83.1 cplexmip test3.mps
 83212.0  jane           4/13 16:31  41+18:44:40 R  0   39.7 cplexmip test2.mps

 5 jobs; 0 idle, 5 running, 0 held
```

This output contains many columns of information about the queued jobs. The ST column (for status) shows the status of current jobs in the queue. An R in the status column means the the job is currently running. An I stands for idle. The status H is the hold state. In the hold state, the job will not be scheduled to run until it is released (via the `condor_release` command). The `RUN_TIME` time reported for a job is the time that job has been allocated to a machine as DAYS+HOURS+MINS+SECS.

Another useful method of tracking the progress of jobs is through the user log. If you have specified a `log` command in your submit file, the progress of the job may be followed by viewing the log file. Various events such as execution commencement, checkpoint, eviction, and termination are logged in the file along with the time at which the event occurred. Here is a sample snippet from a user log file

```
000 (8135.000.000) 05/25 19:10:03 Job submitted from host: <128.105.146.14:1816>
...
001 (8135.000.000) 05/25 19:12:17 Job executing on host: <128.105.165.131:1026>
...
005 (8135.000.000) 05/25 19:13:06 Job terminated.
        (1) Normal termination (return value 0)
                Usr 0 00:00:37, Sys 0 00:00:00  -  Run Remote Usage
                Usr 0 00:00:00, Sys 0 00:00:05  -  Run Local Usage
                Usr 0 00:00:37, Sys 0 00:00:00  -  Total Remote Usage
                Usr 0 00:00:00, Sys 0 00:00:05  -  Total Local Usage
        9624  -  Run Bytes Sent By Job
        7146159  -  Run Bytes Received By Job
        9624  -  Total Bytes Sent By Job
        7146159  -  Total Bytes Received By Job
...
```

The `condor_jobmonitor` tool parses the events in a user log file and can use the information to graphically display the progress of your jobs. Figure 15.2 contains a screenshot of `condor_jobmonitor` in action.

You can locate all the machines that are running your job with the `condor_status` command. For example, to find all the machines that are running jobs submitted by `breach@cs.wisc.edu`, type

```
% condor_status -constraint 'RemoteUser == "breach@cs.wisc.edu"'

Name        Arch     OpSys       State     Activity   LoadAv Mem   ActvtyTime

alfred.cs.  INTEL    LINUX       Claimed   Busy       0.980  64    0+07:10:02
biron.cs.w  INTEL    LINUX       Claimed   Busy       1.000  128   0+01:10:00
cambridge.  INTEL    LINUX       Claimed   Busy       0.988  64    0+00:15:00
falcons.cs  INTEL    LINUX       Claimed   Busy       0.996  32    0+02:05:03
happy.cs.w  INTEL    LINUX       Claimed   Busy       0.988  128   0+03:05:00
istat03.st  INTEL    LINUX       Claimed   Busy       0.883  64    0+06:45:01
istat04.st  INTEL    LINUX       Claimed   Busy       0.988  64    0+00:10:00
istat09.st  INTEL    LINUX       Claimed   Busy       0.301  64    0+03:45:00
...
```

To find all the machines that are running any job at all, type

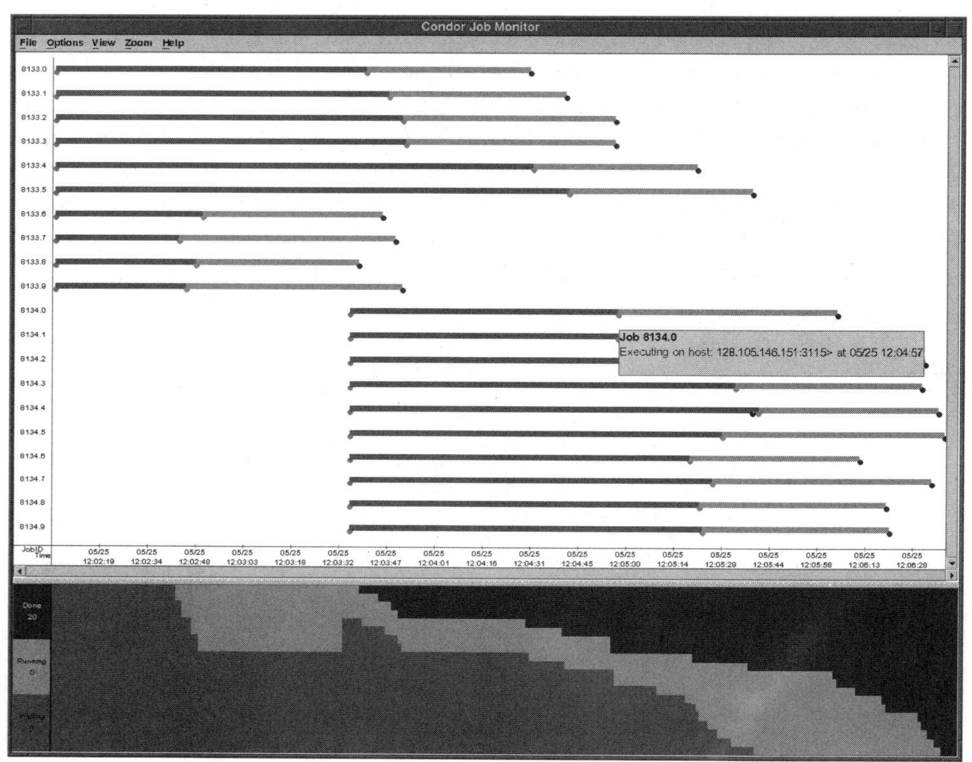

Figure 15.2: Condor jobmonitor tool.

```
% condor_status -run

Name        Arch     OpSys          LoadAv RemoteUser           ClientMachine

adriana.cs INTEL     LINUX          0.980  hepcon@cs.wisc.edu    chevre.cs.wisc.
alfred.cs. INTEL     LINUX          0.980  breach@cs.wisc.edu    neufchatel.cs.w
amul.cs.wi INTEL     LINUX          1.000  nice-user.condor@cs. chevre.cs.wisc.
anfrom.cs. INTEL     LINUX          1.023  ashoks@jules.ncsa.ui jules.ncsa.uiuc
astro.cs.w INTEL     LINUX          1.000  nice-user.condor@cs. chevre.cs.wisc.
aura.cs.wi INTEL     LINUX          0.996  nice-user.condor@cs. chevre.cs.wisc.
balder.cs. INTEL     LINUX          1.000  nice-user.condor@cs. chevre.cs.wisc.
bamba.cs.w INTEL     LINUX          1.574  dmarino@cs.wisc.edu   riola.cs.wisc.e
bardolph.c INTEL     LINUX          1.000  nice-user.condor@cs. chevre.cs.wisc.
...
```

Removing a Job from the Queue

You can remove a job from the queue at any time using the `condor_rm` command. If the job that is being removed is currently running, the job is killed without a checkpoint, and its queue entry is removed. The following example shows the queue of jobs before and after a job is removed.

```
%  condor_q

-- Submitter: froth.cs.wisc.edu : <128.105.73.44:33847> : froth.cs.wisc.edu
 ID      OWNER            SUBMITTED     RUN_TIME ST PRI SIZE CMD
 125.0   jbasney         4/10 15:35   0+00:00:00 I  -10 1.2  hello.remote
 132.0   raman           4/11 16:57   0+00:00:00 R  0   1.4  hello

2 jobs; 1 idle, 1 running, 0 held

%  condor_rm 132.0
Job 132.0 removed.

%  condor_q

-- Submitter: froth.cs.wisc.edu : <128.105.73.44:33847> : froth.cs.wisc.edu
 ID      OWNER            SUBMITTED     RUN_TIME ST PRI SIZE CMD
 125.0   jbasney         4/10 15:35   0+00:00:00 I  -10 1.2  hello.remote

1 jobs; 1 idle, 0 running, 0 held
```

Changing the Priority of Jobs

In addition to the priorities assigned to each user, Condor provides users with the capability of assigning priorities to any submitted job. These job priorities are local to each queue and range from -20 to $+20$, with higher values meaning better priority.

The default priority of a job is 0. Job priorities can be modified using the `condor_prio` command. For example, to change the priority of a job to -15, type

```
%  condor_q raman

-- Submitter: froth.cs.wisc.edu : <128.105.73.44:33847> : froth.cs.wisc.edu
 ID      OWNER            SUBMITTED     RUN_TIME ST PRI SIZE CMD
 126.0   raman           4/11 15:06   0+00:00:00 I  0   0.3  hello

1 jobs; 1 idle, 0 running, 0 held
```

```
%  condor_prio -p -15 126.0

%  condor_q raman

-- Submitter: froth.cs.wisc.edu : <128.105.73.44:33847> : froth.cs.wisc.edu
 ID      OWNER            SUBMITTED     RUN_TIME  ST PRI SIZE CMD
 126.0   raman           4/11 15:06   0+00:00:00 I  -15 0.3  hello

1 jobs; 1 idle, 0 running, 0 held
```

We emphasize that these *job* priorities are completely different from the *user* priorities assigned by Condor. Job priorities control only which one of *your* jobs should run next; there is no effect whatsoever on whether your jobs will run before another user's jobs.

Determining Why a Job Does Not Run

A specific job may not run for several reasons. These reasons include failed job or machine constraints, bias due to preferences, insufficient priority, and the preemption throttle that is implemented by the `condor_negotiator` to prevent thrashing. Many of these reasons can be diagnosed by using the *-analyze* option of `condor_q`. For example, the following job submitted by user jbasney had not run for several days.

```
% condor_q

-- Submitter: froth.cs.wisc.edu : <128.105.73.44:33847> : froth.cs.wisc.edu
 ID      OWNER            SUBMITTED     RUN_TIME  ST PRI SIZE CMD
 125.0   jbasney         4/10 15:35   0+00:00:00 I  -10 1.2  hello.remote

1 jobs; 1 idle, 0 running, 0 held
```

Running `condor_q`'s analyzer provided the following information:

```
%  condor_q 125.0 -analyze

-- Submitter: froth.cs.wisc.edu : <128.105.73.44:33847> : froth.cs.wisc.edu
---
125.000:  Run analysis summary.  Of 323 resource offers,
          323 do not satisfy the request's constraints
            0 resource offer constraints are not satisfied by this request
            0 are serving equal or higher priority customers
```

```
            0 are serving more preferred customers
            0 cannot preempt because preemption has been held
            0 are available to service your request

WARNING:  Be advised:
   No resources matched request's constraints
   Check the Requirements expression below:

Requirements = Arch == "INTEL" && OpSys == "IRIX6" &&
  Disk >= ExecutableSize && VirtualMemory >= ImageSize
```

The `Requirements` expression for this job specifies a platform that does not exist. Therefore, the expression always evaluates to FALSE.

While the analyzer can diagnose most common problems, there are some situations that it cannot reliably detect because of the instantaneous and local nature of the information it uses to detect the problem. The analyzer may report that resources are available to service the request, but the job still does not run. In most of these situations, the delay is transient, and the job will run during the next negotiation cycle.

If the problem persists and the analyzer is unable to detect the situation, the job may begin to run but immediately terminates and return to the idle state. Viewing the job's error and log files (specified in the submit command file) and Condor's `SHADOW_LOG` file may assist in tracking down the problem. If the cause is still unclear, you should contact your system administrator.

Job Completion

When a Condor job completes (either through normal means or abnormal means), Condor will remove it from the job queue (therefore, it will no longer appear in the output of `condor_q`) and insert it into the job history file. You can examine the job history file with the `condor_history` command. If you specified a log file in your submit description file, then the job exit status will be recorded there as well.

By default, Condor will send you an e-mail message when your job completes. You can modify this behavior with the `condor_submit` "notification" command. The message will include the exit status of your job or notification that your job terminated abnormally.

Job Policy

Condor provides several expressions to control your job while it is in the queue. Condor periodically evaluates these expressions and may perform actions on your behalf, reducing the tedium of managing running jobs.

Condor provides five of these expressions: `periodic_hold`, `periodic_release`, `periodic_remove`, `on_exit_hold`, and `on_exit_remove`. The periodic expressions are evaluated every 20 seconds, and the on_exit expressions are evaluated when your job completes, but before the job is removed from the queue. The periodic expressions take precedence over the on_exit requirements, and the hold expressions take precedence over the remove expressions. The periodic expressions are ClassAd expressions, just like the requirements expression introduced in Section 15.1.2. They are added to the job ClassAd via the submit file.

You can use these expressions to automate many common actions. For example, suppose you know that your job will never run for more than an hour, and if it is running for more than an hour, something is probably wrong and will need investigating. Instead leaving your job running on the cluster needlessly, Condor can place your job on hold with the following added to the submit file:

```
periodic_hold = (ServerStartTime - JobStartDate) > 3600
```

Or suppose you have a job that occasionally segfaults but you know if you run it again on the same data, chances are it will finish successfully. You can get this behavior by adding this line to the submit file:

```
on_exit_remove = (ExitBySignal == True) && (ExitSignal != 11)
```

The above expression will not let the job leave the queue if it exited by a signal and that signal number was 11(representing segmentation fault). In any other case of the job exting, it will leave the queue.

15.2.4 Submitting Different Types of Jobs: Choosing a Universe

A Universe in Condor defines an execution environment. Condor supports the following Universes on Linux:

- Vanilla
- Parallel
- PVM

- Globus
- Scheduler
- Java
- Standard

The `Universe` attribute is specified in the submit description file. If the Universe is not specified, it will default to Standard.

Vanilla Universe

The Vanilla Universe is used to run serial (nonparallel) jobs. The examples provided in the preceding section use the Vanilla Universe. Most Condor users prefer to use the Standard Universe to submit serial jobs because of several helpful features of the Standard Universe. However, the Standard Universe has several restrictions on the types of serial jobs supported. The Vanilla Universe, on the other hand, has no such restrictions. Any program that runs outside of Condor will run in the Vanilla Universe. Binary executables as well as scripts are welcome in the Vanilla Universe.

A typical Vanilla Universe job relies on a shared file system between the submit machine and all the nodes in order to allow jobs to access their data. However, if a shared file system is not available, Condor can transfer the files needed by the job to and from the execute machine. See Section 15.2.5 for more details on this.

Parallel Universe

The Parallel Universe allows parallel programs written with MPI to be managed by Condor. To submit an MPI program to Condor, specify the number of nodes to be used in the parallel job. Use the `machine_count` attribute in the submit description file to specify the number of resources to claim, as in the following example:

```
# Submit file for an MPI job which needs 8 large memory nodes
universe = parallel
executable = my-parallel-job
requirements = Memory >= 512
machine_count = 8
queue
```

Further options in the submit description file allow a variety of parameters, such as the job requirements or the executable to use across the different nodes.

The start up of parallel jobs can be a complicated procedure, and each parallel library is different. The Condor parallel universe tries to provide enough flexibility to allow jobs linked with any parallel library to be scheduled and launched. Jobs under the parallel universe are allowed to run a script before a process is started on any node, and Condor provides tools to start processes on other nodes. Condor includes all the necessary scripts to support the most common MPI implementations, such as MPICH, MPICH2 and LAM. By default, Condor expects a parallel job to be linked with the MPICH implementation of MPI configured with the `ch_p4` device. For other parallel libraries, the Condor manual contains directions on how to write the necessary scripts.

If your Condor pool consists of both dedicated compute machines (that is, Beowulf cluster nodes) and opportunistic machines (that is, desktop workstations), by default Condor will schedule MPI jobs to run on the dedicated resources only.

PVM Universe

Several different parallel programming paradigms exist. One of the more common is the "master/worker" or "pool of tasks" arrangement. In a master/worker program model, one node acts as the controlling master for the parallel application and sends out pieces of work to worker nodes. The worker node does some computation and sends the result back to the master node. The master has a pool of work that needs to be done, and it assigns the next piece of work out to the next worker that becomes available.

The PVM Universe allows master/worker style parallel programs written for the Parallel Virtual Machine interface (see Chapter 10) to be used with Condor. Condor runs the master application on the machine where the job was submitted and will not preempt the master application. Workers are pulled in from the Condor pool as they become available.

Specifically, in the PVM Universe, Condor acts as the resource manager for the PVM daemon. Whenever a PVM program asks for nodes via a `pvm_addhosts()` call, the request is forwarded to Condor. Using ClassAd matching mechanisms, Condor finds a machine in the Condor pool and adds it to the virtual machine. If a machine needs to leave the pool, the PVM program is notified by normal PVM mechanisms, for example, the `pvm_notify()` call.

A unique aspect of the PVM Universe is that PVM jobs submitted to Condor can harness both dedicated and nondedicated (opportunistic) workstations throughout the pool by dynamically adding machines to and removing machines from the parallel virtual machine as machines become available.

Writing a PVM program that deals with Condor's opportunistic environment can be a tricky task. For that reason, the MW framework has been created. MW is a tool for making master-worker style applications in Condor's PVM Universe. For more information, see the MW Home page online at `www.cs.wisc.edu/condor/mw`.

Submitting to the PVM Universe is similar to submitting to the MPI Universe, except that the syntax for `machine_count` is different to reflect the dynamic nature of the PVM Universe. Here is a simple sample submit description file:

```
# Require Condor to give us one node before starting
# the job, but we'll use up to 75 nodes if they are
# available.
universe = pvm
executable = master.exe
machine_count = 1..75
queue
```

By using `machine_count = <min>..<max>`, the submit description file tells Condor that before the PVM master is started, there should be at least `<min>` number of machines given to the job. It also asks Condor to give it as many as `<max>` machines.

More detailed information on the PVM Universe is available in the Condor manual as well as on the Condor-PVM home page at URL `www.cs.wisc.edu/condor/pvm`.

Globus Universe

The Globus Toolkit® is available from `www.globus.org` and is the most popular (although not the only) collection of middleware to build computational grids. The Globus universe in Condor is intended to provide the standard Condor interface to users who wish to submit jobs to machines being managed by Globus. Instead of the jobs executing in the Condor pool, jobs in the Globus universe specify which resource the user wants and has authorization to use. The benefits for running Globus jobs in Condor are that all the Condor job management, such as persistent logging, file management, and the DAGMan (15.2.6) meta-scheduler are available.

The Globus universe is not the only way to share resources in Condor. The Condor manual has a section entitled "Grid Computing" that describes Condor Flocking, Condor Glide-in, and the Globus universe in much more detail.

Scheduler Universe

The Scheduler Universe is used to submit a job that will immediately run on the *submit* machine, as opposed to a remote execution machine. The purpose is to provide a facility for job *meta-schedulers* that desire to manage the submission and removal of jobs into a Condor queue. Condor includes one such meta-scheduler that utilizes the Scheduler Universe: the DAGMan scheduler, which can be used to specify complex interdependencies between jobs. See Section 15.2.6 for more on DAGMan.

Java Universe

There is growing interest in writing scientific programs in Java, and Condor provides special support for running Java programs in a pool. Java programs are not loaded directly by the operating system and run on the processor. Instead, they are loaded by the Java Virtual Machine(JVM) and interpreted. This allows the same Java program to run on any operating system and hardware combination at the cost of reduced performance.

One inelegant way to run Java programs in a Condor pool is to submit the JVM to the Standard or Vanilla universe, and give the Java program to be run as an argument. This is deficient in two ways. For one, it puts considerable burdens on users who want to take advantage the platform independence that Java provides. Additionally, it is difficult to determine the cause of errors when a job fails, as the error may be from the JVM or from the Java program running on the JVM.

The Java Universe changes the abstraction of a remote resource from a Linux machine to a Java environment. If a resource has a JVM installed, Condor advertises facts about the JVM such as versions and performance benchmarks. When a Java universe job is matched with a resource, Condor assumes responsibility of running the Java program. This allows specialized JVMs to be deployed by the resource administrator and removes the burden of providing a suitable execution environment from the submitter. If an error occurs, Condor can detect if the error occurred in the job or in the JVM. If the error is from the JVM, Condor automatically retries the job. If the error is from the job, Condor can report directly into the job logfile what the exception was and where it occurred. A sample Java submit file appears in Figure 15.3.

Standard Universe

The Standard Universe requires minimal extra effort on the part of the user but provides a serial job with the following highly desirable services:

- Transparent process *checkpoint* and *restart*
- Transparent process migration

```
# Submit file for an Java job which prefers the fastest JVM in the pool
universe = java
executable = my-java-sim.class
jar_files = simulation_library.jar
arguments = -x 100 -y 100
output = simulation.out
log =    simulation.log
rank = JavaMFlops * 100
queue
```

Figure 15.3: A sample Java submit file.

- Remote system calls
- Configurable file I/O buffering
- On-the-fly file compression/inflation

Process Checkpointing in the Standard Universe

A checkpoint of an executing program is a snapshot of the program's current state. It provides a way for the program to be continued from that state at a later time. Using checkpoints gives Condor the freedom to reconsider scheduling decisions through preemptive-resume scheduling. If the scheduler decides to rescind a machine that is running a Condor job (for example, when the owner of that machine returns and reclaims it or when a higher-priority user desires the same machine), the scheduler can take a checkpoint of the job and preempt the job without losing the work the job has already accomplished. The job can then be resumed later when the Condor scheduler allocates it a new machine. Additionally, periodic checkpoints provide fault tolerance. Normally, when performing long-running computations, if a machine crashes or must be rebooted for an administrative task, all the work that has been done is lost. The job must be restarted from the beginning, which can mean days, weeks, or even months of wasted computation time. With checkpoints, Condor ensures that progress is always made on jobs and that only the computation done since the last checkpoint is lost. Condor can be take checkpoints periodically, and after an interruption in service, the program can continue from the most recent snapshot.

To enable taking checkpoints, you do not need to change the program's source code. Instead, the program must be relinked with the Condor system call library (see below). Taking the checkpoint of a process is implemented in the Condor system call library as a signal handler. When Condor sends a checkpoint signal to a process linked with this library, the provided signal handler writes the state of the process out to a file or a network socket. This state includes the contents of the process's stack and data segments, all CPU state (including register values), the state of all open files, and any signal handlers and pending signals. When a job is to be continued using a checkpoint, Condor reads this state from the file or network socket, restoring the stack, shared library and data segments, file state, signal handlers, and pending signals. The checkpoint signal handler then restores the CPU state and returns to the user code, which continues from where it left off when the checkpoint signal arrived. Condor jobs submitted to the Standard Universe will automatically perform a checkpoint when preempted from a machine. When a suitable replacement execution machine is found (of the same architecture and operating system), the process is restored on this new machine from the checkpoint, and computation is resumed from where it left off.

By default, a checkpoint is written to a file on the local disk of the submit machine. A Condor checkpoint server is also available to serve as a repository for checkpoints.

Remote System Calls in the Standard Universe

One hurdle to overcome when placing an job on a remote execution workstation is data access. In order to utilize the remote resources, the job must be able to read from and write to files on its submit machine. A requirement that the remote execution machine be able to access these files via NFS, AFS, or any other network file system may significantly limit the number of eligible workstations and therefore hinder the ability of an environment to achieve high throughput. Therefore, in order to maximize throughput, Condor strives to be able to run any application on any remote workstation of a given platform without relying upon a common administrative setup. The enabling technology that permits this is Condor's Remote System Calls mechanism. This mechanism provides the benefit that Condor does not require a user to possess a login account on the execute workstation.

When a Unix process needs to access a file, it calls a file I/O system function such as `open()`, `read()`, or `write()`. These functions are typically handled by the standard C library, which consists primarily of stubs that generate a corresponding system call to the local kernel. Condor users link their applications with an enhanced standard C library via the `condor_compile` command. This library does not duplicate any code in the standard C library; instead, it augments certain system call stubs (such as the ones that handle file I/O) into remote system call stubs. The remote system call stubs package the system call number and arguments into a message that is sent over the network to a `condor_shadow` process that runs on the submit machine. Whenever Condor starts a Standard Universe job, it also starts a corresponding shadow process on the initiating host where the user originally submitted the job (see Figure 15.4). This shadow process acts as an agent for the remotely executing program in performing system calls. The shadow then executes the system call on behalf of the remotely running job in the normal way. The shadow packages up the results of the system call in a message and sends it back to the remote system call stub in the Condor library on the remote machine. The remote system call stub returns its result to the calling procedure, which is unaware that the call was done remotely rather than locally. In this fashion, calls in the user's program to `open()`, `read()`, `write()`, `close()`, and all other file I/O calls transparently take place on the machine that submitted the job instead of on the remote execution machine.

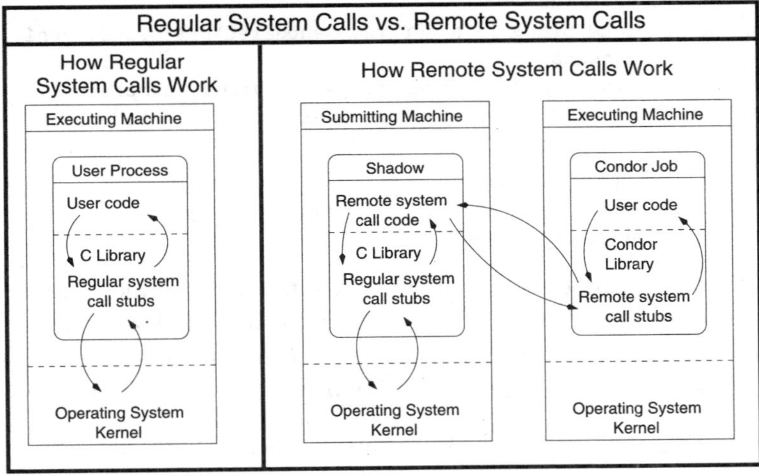

Figure 15.4: Remote System calls in the Standard Universe.

Relinking and Submitting for the Standard Universe

To convert a program into a Standard Universe job, use the `condor_compile` command to relink with the Condor libraries. Place `condor_compile` in front of your usual link command. You do not need to modify the program's source code, but you do need access to its unlinked object files. A commercial program that is packaged as a single executable file cannot be converted into a Standard Universe job.

For example, if you normally link your job by executing

```
% cc main.o tools.o -o program
```

You can relink your job for Condor with

```
% condor_compile cc main.o tools.o -o program
```

After you have relinked your job, you can submit it. A submit description file for the Standard Universe is similar to one for the Vanilla Universe. However, several additional submit directives are available to perform activities such as on-the-fly compression of data files. Here is an example:

```
# Submit 100 runs of my-program to the Standard Universe
universe = standard
executable = my-program.exe
# Each run should take place in a separate subdirectory: run0, run1, ...
initialdir = run$(Process)
# Ask the Condor remote syscall layer to automatically compress
# on-the-fly any writes done by my-program.exe to file data.output
compress_files = data.output
queue 100
```

Standard Universe Limitations

Condor performs its process checkpoint and migration routines strictly in user mode; there are no kernel drivers with Condor. Because Condor is not operating at the kernel level, there are limitations on what process state it is able to checkpoint. As a result, the following restrictions are imposed upon Standard Universe jobs:

1. Multiprocess jobs are not allowed. This includes system calls such as `fork()`, `exec()`, and `system()`.

2. Interprocess communication is not allowed. This includes pipes, semaphores, and shared memory.

3. Network communication must be brief. A job *may* make network connections using system calls such as `socket()`, but a network connection left open for long periods will delay checkpoints and migration.

4. Multiple kernel-level threads are not allowed. However, multiple user-level threads (green threads) *are* allowed.

5. All files should be accessed read-only or write-only. A file that is both read and written to can cause trouble if a job must be rolled back to an old checkpoint image.

6. On Linux, your job must be statically linked. Dynamic linking is allowed in the Standard Universe on some other platforms supported by Condor, and perhaps this restriction on Linux will be removed in a future Condor release.

15.2.5 Giving Your Job Access to Its Data Files

Once your job starts on a machine in your pool, how does it access its data files? Condor provides several choices.

If the job is a Standard Universe job, then Condor solves the problem of data access automatically using the Remote System call mechanism described above. Whenever the job tries to open, read, or write to a file, the I/O will actually take place on the submit machine, whether or not a shared file system is in place.

Condor can use a shared file system, if one is available and permanently mounted across the machines in the pool. This is usually the case in a Beowulf cluster. But what if your Condor pool includes nondedicated (desktop) machines as well? You could specify a `Requirements` expression in your submit description file to require that jobs run only on machines that actually do have access to a common, shared file system. Or, you could request in the submit description file that Condor transfer your job's data files using the Condor File Transfer mechanism.

When Condor finds a machine willing to execute your job, it can create a temporary subdirectory for your job on the execute machine. The Condor File Transfer mechanism will then send via TCP the job executable(s) and input files from the submitting machine into this temporary directory on the execute machine. After the input files have been transferred, the execute machine will start running the job with the temporary directory as the job's current working directory. When the job completes or is kicked off, Condor File Transfer will automatically send back to the submit machine any output files created or modified by the job. After the files have been sent back successfully, the temporary working directory on the execute machine is deleted.

Condor's File Transfer mechanism has several features to ensure data integrity in a nondedicated environment. For instance, transfers of multiple files are performed atomically.

Condor File Transfer behavior is specified at job submission time using the submit description file and `condor_submit`. Along with all the other job submit description parameters, you can use the following File Transfer commands in the submit description file:

transfer_input_files = < file1, file2, file... >: Use this parameter to list all the files that should be transferred into the working directory for the job before the job is started.

transfer_output_files = < file1, file2, file... >: Use this parameter to explicitly list which output files to transfer back from the temporary working directory on the execute machine to the submit machine. Most of the time, however, there is no need to use this parameter. If `transfer_output_files` is not specified, Condor will automatically transfer in the job's temporary working directory all files that have been modified or created by the job.

transfer_files = <ONEXIT | ALWAYS | NEVER>: If `transfer_files` is set to `ONEXIT`, Condor will transfer the job's output files back to the submitting machine only when the job completes (exits). Specifying `ALWAYS` tells Condor to transfer back the output files when the job completes *or* when Condor kicks off the job (preempts) from a machine prior to job completion. The `ALWAYS` option is specifically intended for fault-tolerant jobs that periodically write out their state to disk and can restart where they left off. Any output files transferred back to the submit machine when Condor preempts a job will automatically be sent back out again as input files when the job restarts.

15.2.6 The DAGMan Scheduler

The DAGMan scheduler within Condor allows the specification of dependencies between a set of programs. A directed acyclic graph (DAG) can be used to represent a set of programs where the input, output, or execution of one or more programs is dependent on one or more other programs. The programs are nodes (vertices) in the graph, and the edges (arcs) identify the dependencies. Each program within the DAG becomes a job submitted to Condor. The DAGMan scheduler enforces the dependencies of the DAG.

An input file to DAGMan identifies the nodes of the graph, as well as how to submit each job (node) to Condor. It also specifies the graph's dependencies and describes any extra processing that is involved with the nodes of the graph and must take place just before or just after the job is run.

A simple diamond-shaped DAG with four nodes is given in Figure 15.5.

A simple input file to DAGMan for this diamond-shaped DAG may be

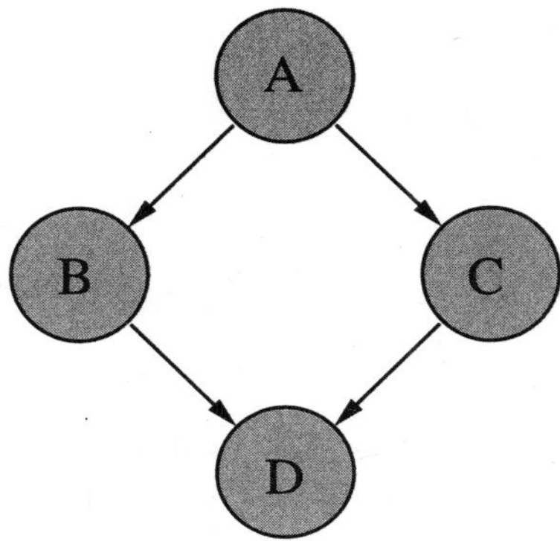

Figure 15.5: A directed acyclic graph with four nodes.

```
# file name: diamond.dag
Job  A  A.condor
Job  B  B.condor
Job  C  C.condor
Job  D  D.condor
PARENT A CHILD B C
PARENT B C CHILD D
```

The four nodes are named `A`, `B`, `C`, and `D`. Lines beginning with the keyword `Job` identify each node by giving it a name, and they also specify a file to be used as a submit description file for submission as a Condor job. Lines with the keyword `PARENT` identify the dependencies of the graph. Just like regular Condor submit description files, lines with a leading pound character (`#`) are comments.

The DAGMan scheduler uses the graph to order the submission of jobs to Condor. The submission of a child node will not take place until the parent node has successfully completed. No ordering of siblings is imposed by the graph, and therefore DAGMan does not impose an ordering when submitting the jobs to Condor. For the diamond-shaped example, nodes `B` and `C` will be submitted to Condor in parallel.

Each job in the example graph uses a different submit description file. An example submit description file for job `A` may be

```
# file name: A.condor
executable   = nodeA.exe
```

```
output      = A.out
error       = A.err
log         = diamond.log
universe    = vanilla
queue
```

An important restriction for submit description files of a DAG is that each node of the graph use the same log file. DAGMan uses the log file in enforcing the graph's dependencies.

The graph for execution under Condor is submitted by using the Condor tool `condor_submit_dag`. For the diamond-shaped example, submission would use the command

```
condor_submit_dag diamond.dag
```

15.3 Condor Architecture

A Condor pool comprises a single machine that serves as the *central manager* and an arbitrary number of other machines that have joined the pool. Conceptually, the pool is a collection of resources (machines) and resource requests (jobs). The role of Condor is to match waiting requests with available resources. Every part of Condor sends periodic updates to the central manager, the centralized repository of information about the state of the pool. The central manager periodically assesses the current state of the pool and tries to match pending requests with the appropriate resources.

15.3.1 The Condor Daemons

In this subsection we describe all the daemons (background server processes) in Condor and the role each plays in the system.

`condor_master`: This daemon's role is to simplify system administration. It is responsible for keeping the rest of the Condor daemons running on each machine in a pool. The master spawns the other daemons and periodically checks the timestamps on the binaries of the daemons it is managing. If it finds new binaries, the master will restart the affected daemons. This allows Condor to be upgraded easily. In addition, if any other Condor daemon on the machine exits abnormally, the `condor_master` will send e-mail to the system administrator with information about the problem and then automatically restart the affected daemon. The condor_master also supports various administrative commands to start, stop, or reconfigure daemons remotely. The condor_master runs on every machine in your Condor pool.

condor_startd: This daemon represents a machine to the Condor pool. It advertises a machine ClassAd that contains attributes about the machine's capabilities and policies. Running the startd enables a machine to execute jobs. The condor_startd is responsible for enforcing the policy under which remote jobs will be started, suspended, resumed, vacated, or killed. When the startd is ready to execute a Condor job, it spawns the condor_starter, described below.

condor_starter: This program is the entity that spawns the remote Condor job on a given machine. It sets up the execution environment and monitors the job once it is running. The starter detects job completion, sends back status information to the submitting machine, and exits.

condor_schedd: This daemon represents jobs to the Condor pool. Any machine that allows users to submit jobs needs to have a condor_schedd running. Users submit jobs to the condor_schedd, where they are stored in the *job queue*. The various tools to view and manipulate the job queue (such as condor_submit, condor_q, or condor_rm) connect to the condor_schedd to do their work.

condor_shadow: This program runs on the machine where a job was submitted whenever that job is executing. The shadow serves requests for files to transfer, logs the job's progress, and reports statistics when the job completes. Jobs that are linked for Condor's Standard Universe, which perform remote system calls, do so via the condor_shadow. Any system call performed on the remote execute machine is sent over the network to the condor_shadow. The shadow performs the system call (such as file I/O) on the submit machine and the result is sent back over the network to the remote job.

condor_collector: This daemon is responsible for collecting all the information about the status of a Condor pool. All other daemons periodically send ClassAd updates to the collector. These ClassAds contain all the information about the state of the daemons, the resources they represent, or resource requests in the pool (such as jobs that have been submitted to a given condor_schedd). The condor_collector can be thought of as a dynamic database of ClassAds. The condor_status command can be used to query the collector for specific information about various parts of Condor. The Condor daemons also query the collector for important information, such as what address to use for sending commands to a remote machine. The `condor_collector` runs on the machine designated as the central manager.

`condor_negotiator`: This daemon is responsible for all the matchmaking within the Condor system. The negotiator is also responsible for enforcing user priorities in the system.

15.3.2 The Condor Daemons in Action

Within a given Condor installation, one machine will serve as the pool's central manager. In addition to the `condor_master` daemon that runs on every machine in a Condor pool, the central manager runs the `condor_collector` and the `condor_negotiator` daemons. Any machine in the installation that should be capable of running jobs should run the `condor_startd`, and any machine that should maintain a job queue and therefore allow users on that machine to submit jobs should run a `condor_schedd`.

Condor allows any machine simultaneously to execute jobs and serve as a submission point by running both a `condor_startd` and a `condor_schedd`. Figure 15.6 displays a Condor pool in which every machine in the pool can both submit and run jobs, including the central manager.

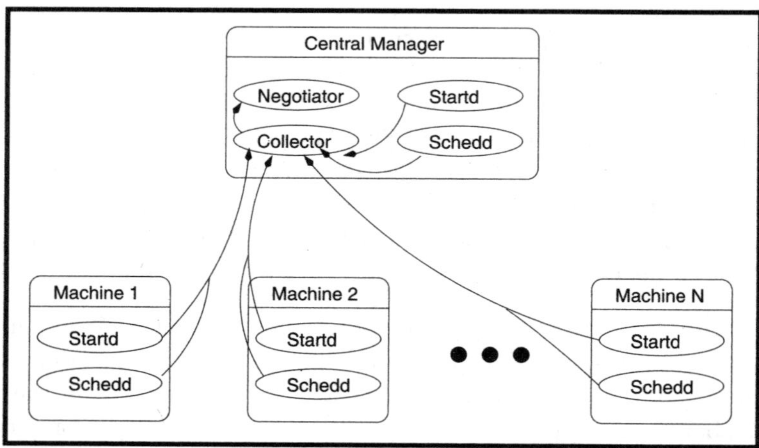

Figure 15.6: Daemon layout of an idle Condor pool.

The interface for adding a job to the Condor system is `condor_submit`, which reads a job description file, creates a job ClassAd, and gives that ClassAd to the `condor_schedd` managing the local job queue. This triggers a *negotiation cycle.* During a negotiation cycle, the `condor_negotiator` queries the `condor_collector` to discover all machines that are willing to perform work and all users with idle jobs. The `condor_negotiator` communicates *in user priority order* with each `condor_schedd` that has idle jobs in its queue, and performs matchmaking to match jobs with machines such that both job and machine ClassAd requirements are satisfied and preferences (rank) are honored.

Once the `condor_negotiator` makes a match, the `condor_schedd` claims the corresponding machine and is allowed to make subsequent scheduling decisions about the order in which jobs run. This hierarchical, distributed scheduling architecture enhances Condor's scalability and flexibility.

When the `condor_schedd` starts a job, it spawns a `condor_shadow` process on the submit machine, and the `condor_startd` spawns a `condor_starter` process on the corresponding execute machine (see Figure 15.7). The shadow transfers the job ClassAd and any data files required to the starter, which spawns the user's application.

If the job is a Standard Universe job, the shadow will begin to service remote system calls originating from the user job, allowing the job to transparently access data files on the submitting host.

When the job completes or is aborted, the `condor_starter` removes every process spawned by the user job, and frees any temporary scratch disk space used by the job. This ensures that the execute machine is left in a clean state and that resources (such as processes or disk space) are not being leaked.

15.4 Configuring Condor

This section describes how to configure and customize Condor for your site. It discusses the configuration files used by Condor, describes how to configure the policy for starting and stopping jobs in your pool, and recommends settings for using Condor on a cluster.

A number of configuration files facilitate different levels of control over how Condor is configured on each machine in a pool. The top-level or global configuration file is shared by all machines in the pool. For ease of administration, this file should be located on a shared file system. In addition, each machine may have multiple local configuration files allowing the local settings to override the global settings.

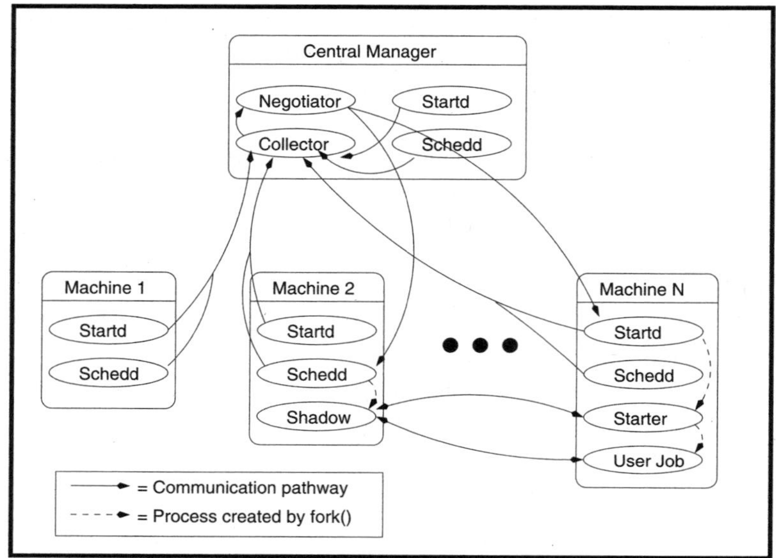

Figure 15.7: Daemon layout when a job submitted from Machine 2 is running.

Hence, each machine may have different daemons running, different policies for when to start and stop Condor jobs, and so on.

All of Condor's configuration files should be owned and writable only by root. It is important to maintain strict control over these files because they contain security-sensitive settings.

The Condor project's website at `www.cs.wisc.edu/condor` has detailed installation instructions. For some Linux distributions, Condor is available in the native packaging format. For Linux distributions that Condor is not natively packaged for, it is available as a tarfile. A perl script is included to help install Condor and customize the configuration.

15.4.1 Location of Condor's Configuration Files

Condor has a default set of locations it uses to try to find its top-level configuration file. The locations are checked in the following order:

1. The file specified in the `CONDOR_CONFIG` environment variable.

2. '`/etc/condor/condor_config`', if it exists.

3. If user condor exists on your system, the 'condor_config' file in this user's home directory.

If a Condor daemon or tool cannot find its global configuration file when it starts, it will print an error message and immediately exit. Once the global configuration file has been read by Condor, however, any other local configuration files can be specified with the LOCAL_CONFIG_FILE macro.

This macro can contain a single entry if you want only two levels of configuration (global and local). If you need a more complex division of configuration values (for example, if you have machines of different platforms in the same pool and desire separate files for platform-specific settings), LOCAL_CONFIG_FILE can contain a list of files.

Condor provides other macros to help you easily define the location of the local configuration files for each machine in your pool. Most of these are special macros that evaluate to different values depending on which host is reading the global configuration file:

- HOSTNAME: The hostname of the local host.
- FULL_HOSTNAME: The fully qualified hostname of the local host.
- TILDE: The home directory of the user condor on the local host.
- OPSYS: The operating system of the local host, such as "LINUX," "WINNT4" (for Windows NT), or "WINNT5" (for Windows 2000). This is primarily useful in heterogeneous clusters with multiple platforms.
- RELEASE_DIR: The directory where Condor is installed on each host. This macro is defined in the global configuration file and is set by Condor's installation program.

By default, the local configuration file is defined as

```
LOCAL_CONFIG_FILE = $(TILDE)/condor_config.local
```

15.4.2 Recommended Configuration File Layout for a Cluster

Ease of administration is an important consideration in a cluster, particularly if you have a large number of nodes. To make Condor easy to configure, we highly recommend that you install all of your Condor configuration files, even the per-node local configuration files, on a shared file system. That way, you can easily make changes in one place.

You should use a subdirectory in your release directory for holding all of the local configuration files. By default, Condor's release directory contains an '`etc`' directory for this purpose.

You should create separate files for each node in your cluster, using the hostname as the first half of the filename, and ".local" as the end. For example, if your cluster nodes are named "n01," "n02," and so on, the files should be called '`n01.local`', '`n02.local`', and so on. These files should all be placed in your '`etc`' directory.

In your global configuration file, you should use the following setting to describe the location of your local configuration files:

```
LOCAL_CONFIG_FILE = $(RELEASE_DIR)/etc/$(HOSTNAME).local
```

The central manager of your pool needs special settings in its local configuration file. These attributes are set automatically by the Condor installation program. The rest of the local configuration files can be left empty at first.

Having your configuration files laid out in this way will help you more easily customize Condor's behavior on your cluster. We discuss other possible configuration scenarios at the end of this chapter.

Note: We recommend that you store all of your Condor configuration files under a version control system, such as CVS. While this is not required, it will help you keep track of the changes you make to your configuration, who made them, when they occurred, and why. In general, it is a good idea to store configuration files under a version control system, since none of the above concerns are specific to Condor.

15.4.3 Configuring Security in Condor

Condor has a rich and highly-configurable security implementation. Condor separates security into two parts: *Authentication* and *Authorization.* Authentication identifies the client requesting an action, and does not pass judgment on if that client is allowed to perform that action. Condor can use many different methods for authentication, including Kerberos, X.509 Public/Private keys, and TCP/IP hostnames. Authentication levels and methods are automatically negotiated by Condor. Authentication can be *Required*, *Preferred*, *Optional*, or *Never.* Given the distributed nature of the daemons that implement Condor, access to these daemons is naturally host based, and is currently the default. However, host-based security is fairly easy to defeat. In any sort of untrusted environment, we strongly recommend using a more sophisticated authentication method such as X.509.

Authorization builds on top of authentication by specifying who is allowed to do what. There are four different classes of access levels: *Read*, *Write*, *Administrator*, and *Config*. Each level may require a different strength of authentication, and have a different set of clients who are allowed to perform that action. For example, it is very common to allow anyone who can authenticate as being from a local subnet to read information about Condor resources and jobs. At the same time, only a few people be might allowed to administer a machine, and these people may be required to identify themselves using Kerberos. The four access levels are described below:

Read: allows a client to obtain information from Condor. Examples of information that may be read are the status of the pool and the contents of the job queue.

Write: allows a client to provide information to Condor, such as submit a job or join the pool. Note that Write access does not imply Read access.

Administrator: allows a client to affect privileged operations such as changing a user's priority level or starting and stopping the Condor system from running.

Config: allows a client to change Condor's configuration settings remotely using the `condor_config_val` tool's *-set* and *-rset* options. This has very serious security implications, so we recommend that you not enable Config access to any hosts.

The defaults during installation give all machines in the pool read and write access. The central manager is also given administrator access. You will probably wish to change these defaults for your site. Read the Condor Administrator's Manual for details on authentication and authorization in Condor and how to customize it for your site.

15.4.4 Customizing Condor's Policy Expressions

Certain configuration expressions are used to control Condor's policy for executing, suspending, and evicting jobs. Their interaction can be somewhat complex. Defining an inappropriate policy impacts the throughput of your cluster and the happiness of its users. If you are interested in creating a specialized policy for your pool, we recommend that you read the Condor Administrator's Manual. Only a basic introduction follows.

All policy expressions are ClassAd expressions and are defined in Condor's configuration files. Policies are usually poolwide and are therefore defined in the global configuration file. If individual nodes in your pool require their own policy, however, the appropriate expressions can be placed in local configuration files.

The policy expressions are treated by the `condor_startd` as part of its machine ClassAd (along with all the attributes you can view with `condor_status -long`). They are always evaluated against a job ClassAd, either by the `condor_negotiator` when trying to find a match or by the `condor_startd` when it is deciding what to do with the job that is currently running. Therefore, all policy expressions can reference attributes of a job, such as the memory usage or owner, in addition to attributes of the machine, such as keyboard idle time or CPU load.

Most policy expressions are ClassAd Boolean expressions, so they evaluate to TRUE, FALSE, or UNDEFINED. UNDEFINED occurs when an expression references a ClassAd attribute that is not found in either the machine's ClassAd or the ClassAd of the job under consideration. For some expressions, this is treated as a fatal error, so you should be sure to use the ClassAd meta-operators, described in Section 15.1.2 when referring to attributes which might not be present in all ClassAds.

An explanation of policy expressions requires an understanding of the different stages that a job can go through from initially executing until the job completes or is evicted from the machine. Each policy expression is then described in terms of the step in the progression that it controls.

The Lifespan of a Job Executing in Condor

When a job is submitted to Condor, the `condor_negotiator` performs matchmaking to find a suitable resource to use for the computation. This process involves satisfying both the job and the machine's requirements for each other. The machine can define the exact conditions under which it is willing to be considered available for running jobs. The job can define exactly what kind of machine it is willing to use.

Once a job has been matched with a given machine, there are four states the job can be in: running, suspended, graceful shutdown, and quick shutdown. As soon as the match is made, the job sets up its execution environment and begins running.

While it is executing, a job can be suspended (for example, because of other activity on the machine where it is running). Once it has been suspended, the job can resume execution or can move on to preemption or eviction.

All Condor jobs have two methods for preemption: graceful and quick. Standard Universe jobs are given a chance to produce a checkpoint with graceful preemption. For the other universes, graceful implies that the program is told to get off the system, but it is given time to clean up after itself. On all flavors of Unix, a SIGTERM is sent during graceful shutdown by default, although users can override this default when they submit their job. A quick shutdown involves rapidly killing all processes associated with a job, without giving them any time to execute their own cleanup procedures. The Condor system performs checks to ensure that processes are not left behind once a job is evicted from a given node.

Condor Policy Expressions

Various expressions are used to control the policy for starting, suspending, resuming, and preempting jobs.

`START`: when the `condor_startd` is willing to start executing a job.

`RANK`: how much the `condor_startd` prefers each type of job running on it. The `RANK` expression is a floating-point instead of a Boolean value. `condor_startd` will preempt the job it is currently running if there is another job in the system that yields a higher value for this expression.

`WANT_SUSPEND`: controls whether the `condor_startd` should even consider suspending this job or not. In effect, it determines which expression, `SUSPEND` or `PREEMPT`, should be evaluated while the job is running. `WANT_SUSPEND` does not control when the job is actually suspended; for that purpose, you should use the `SUSPEND` expression.

`SUSPEND`: when the `condor_startd` should suspend the currently running job. If `WANT_SUSPEND` evaluates to TRUE, `SUSPEND` is periodically evaluated whenever a job is executing on a machine. If `SUSPEND` becomes TRUE, the job will be suspended.

`CONTINUE`: if and when the `condor_startd` should resume a suspended job. The `CONTINUE` expression is evaluated only while a job is suspended. If it evaluates to TRUE, the job will be resumed, and the `condor_startd` will go back to the Claimed/Busy state.

`PREEMPT`: when the `condor_startd` should preempt the currently running job. This expression is evaluated whenever a job has been suspended. If `WANT_SUSPEND` evaluates to FALSE, `PREEMPT` is checked while the job is executing.

`WANT_VACATE`: whether the job should be evicted gracefully or quickly if Condor is preempting a job (because the `PREEMPT` expression evaluates to TRUE).

If WANT_VACATE is FALSE, the condor_startd will immediately kill the job and all of its child processes whenever it must evict the application. If WANT_VACATE is TRUE, the condor_startd performs a graceful shutdown, instead.

KILL: when the condor_startd should give up on a graceful preemption and move directly to the quick shutdown.

PREEMPTION_REQUIREMENTS: used by the condor_negotiator when it is performing matchmaking, not by the condor_startd. While trying to schedule jobs on resources in your pool, the condor_negotiator considers the priorities of the various users in the system (see Section 15.5.3 for more details). If a user with a better priority has jobs waiting in the queue and no resources are currently idle, the matchmaker will consider preempting another user's jobs and giving those resources to the user with the better priority. This process is known as *priority preemption*. The PREEMPTION_REQUIREMENTS expression must evaluate to TRUE for such a preemption to take place.

PREEMPTION_RANK: a floating-point value evaluated by the condor_negotiator. If the matchmaker decides it must preempt a job due to user priorities, the macro PREEMPTION_RANK determines which resource to preempt. Among the set of all resources that make the PREEMPTION_REQUIREMENTS expression evaluate to TRUE, the one with the highest value for PREEMPTION_RANK is evicted.

15.4.5 Customizing Condor's Other Configuration Settings

In addition to the policy expressions, you will need to modify other settings to customize Condor for your cluster.

DAEMON_LIST: the comma-separated list of daemons that should be spawned by the condor_master. As described in Section 15.3.1 discussing the architecture of Condor, each host in your pool can play different roles depending on which daemons are started on it. You define these roles using the DAEMON_LIST in the appropriate configuration files to enable or disable the various Condor daemons on each host.

DedicatedScheduler: the name of the dedicated scheduler for your cluster. This setting must have the form

```
DedicatedScheduler = "DedicatedScheduler@full.host.name.here"
```

15.5 Administration Tools

Condor has a rich set of tools for the administrator. Table 15.2 gives an overview of the Condor commands typically used solely by the system administrator. Of course, many of the "user-level" Condor tools summarized in Table 15.2 can be helpful for cluster administration as well. For instance, the condor_status tool can easily display the status for all nodes in the cluster, including dynamic information such as current load average and free virtual memory.

Command	Description
condor_checkpoint	Checkpoint jobs running on the specified hosts
condor_config_val	Query or set a given Condor configuration variable
condor_fetch_log	Retrieve daemon logs from a remote machine
condor_master_off	Shut down Condor and the condor_master
condor_off	Shut down Condor daemons
condor_on	Start up Condor daemons
condor_reconfig	Reconfigure Condor daemons
condor_restart	Restart the condor_master
condor_stats	Display historical information about the Condor pool
condor_userprio	Display and manage user priorities
condor_vacate	Vacate jobs that are running on the specified hosts

Table 15.2: Commands reserved for the administrator.

15.5.1 Remote Configuration and Control

All machines in a Condor pool can be remotely managed from a centralized location. Condor can be enabled, disabled, or restarted remotely using the condor_on, condor_off, and condor_restart commands, respectively. Additionally, any aspect of Condor's configuration file on a node can be queried or changed remotely via the condor_config_val command. Of course, not everyone is allowed to change your Condor configuration remotely. Doing so requires proper authorization, which is set up at installation time.

Many aspects of Condor's configuration, including its scheduling policy, can be changed on the fly without requiring the pool to be shut down and restarted. This is accomplished by using the condor_reconfig command, which asks the Condor daemons on a specified host to reread the Condor configuration files and take appropriate action—on the fly if possible.

15.5.2 Accounting and Logging

Condor keeps many statistics about what is happening in the pool. Each daemon can be asked to keep a detailed log of its activities; Condor will automatically rotate these log files when they reach a maximum size as specified by the administrator.

In addition to the `condor_history` command, which allows users to view job ClassAds for jobs that have previously completed, the `condor_stats` tool can be used to query for historical usage statistics from a poolwide accounting database. This database contains information about how many jobs were being serviced for each user at regular intervals, as well as how many machines were busy. For instance, `condor_stats` could be asked to display the total number of jobs running at five-minute intervals for a specified user between January 15 and January 30.

The `condor_view` tool takes the raw information obtainable with `condor_stats` and converts it into HTML, complete with interactive charts. Figure 15.8 shows a sample display of the output from `condor_view` in a Web browser. The site administrator, using `condor_view`, can quickly put detailed, real-time usage statistics about the Condor pool onto a Web site.

15.5.3 User Priorities in Condor

The job queues in Condor are not strictly first-in, first-out. Instead, Condor implements *priority queuing*. Different users will get different-sized allocations of machines depending on their current user priority, regardless of how many jobs from a competing user are "ahead" of them in the queue. Condor can also be configured to perform *priority preemption* if desired. For instance, suppose user A is using all the nodes in a cluster, when suddenly a user with a superior priority submits jobs. With priority preemption enabled, Condor will preempt the jobs of the lower-priority user in order to immediately start the jobs submitted by the higher-priority user.

Starvation of the lower-priority users is prevented by a fair-share algorithm, which attempts to give all users the same amount of machine allocation time over a specified interval. In addition, the priority calculations in Condor are based on *ratios* instead of absolutes. For example, if Bill has a priority that is twice as good as that of Fred, Condor will not starve Fred by allocating all machines to Bill. Instead, Bill will get, on average, twice as many machines as will Fred because Bill's priority is twice as good.

The `condor_userprio` command can be used by the administrator to view or edit a user's priority. It can also be used to override Condor's default fair-share policy and explicitly assign users a better or worse priority in relation to other users.

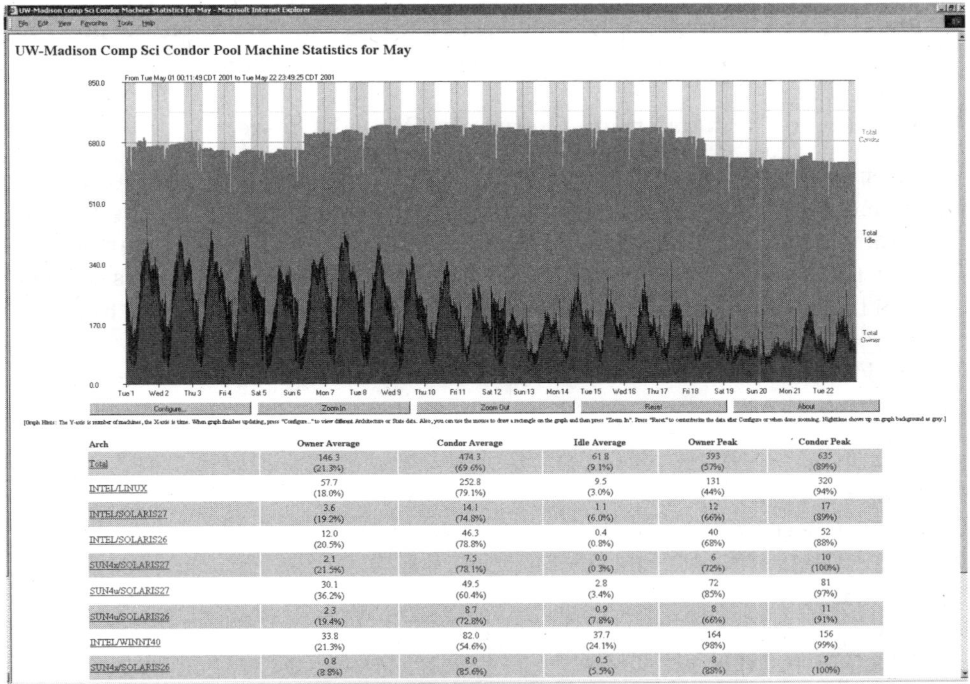

Arch	Owner Average	Condor Average	Idle Average	Owner Peak	Condor Peak
Total	146.3 (21.3%)	474.3 (69.6%)	61.8 (9.1%)	393 (57%)	635 (89%)
INTEL/LINUX	57.7 (18.0%)	252.8 (79.1%)	9.5 (3.0%)	131 (44%)	320 (94%)
INTEL/SOLARIS27	3.6 (19.2%)	14.1 (74.8%)	1.1 (6.0%)	12 (66%)	17 (89%)
INTEL/SOLARIS26	12.0 (20.5%)	46.3 (78.8%)	0.4 (0.8%)	40 (68%)	52 (88%)
SUN4x/SOLARIS27	2.1 (21.5%)	7.5 (78.1%)	0.0 (0.3%)	6 (72%)	10 (100%)
SUN4u/SOLARIS27	30.1 (36.2%)	49.5 (60.4%)	2.8 (3.4%)	72 (85%)	81 (97%)
SUN4u/SOLARIS26	2.3 (19.4%)	8.7 (72.8%)	0.9 (7.8%)	8 (66%)	11 (91%)
INTEL/WINNT40	33.8 (21.3%)	82.0 (54.6%)	37.7 (24.1%)	164 (98%)	156 (99%)
SUN4x/SOLARIS26	0.8 (8.8%)	8.0 (85.6%)	0.5 (5.5%)	8 (88%)	9 (100%)

Figure 15.8: CondorView displaying machine usage.

15.6 Cluster Setup Scenarios

This section explores different scenarios for how to configure your cluster. Five scenarios are presented, along with a basic idea of what configuration settings you will need to modify or what steps you will need to take for each scenario:

1. A uniformly owned, dedicated compute cluster, with a single front-end node for submission, and support for MPI applications.

2. A cluster of multiprocessor nodes.

3. A cluster of distributively owned nodes. Each node prefers to run jobs submitted by its owner.

4. Desktop submission to the cluster.

5. Expanding the cluster to nondedicated (desktop) computing resources.

Most of these scenarios can be combined. Each scenario builds on the previous one to add further functionality to the basic cluster configuration.

15.6.1 Basic Configuration: Uniformly Owned Cluster

The most basic scenario involves a cluster where all resources are owned by a single entity and all compute nodes enforce the same policy for starting and stopping jobs. All compute nodes are dedicated, meaning that they will always start an idle job and they will never preempt or suspend until completion. There is a single front-end node for submitting jobs, and dedicated MPI jobs are enabled from this host.

In order to enable this basic policy, your global configuration file must contain these settings:

```
START = True
SUSPEND = False
CONTINUE = False
PREEMPT = False
KILL = False
WANT_SUSPEND = True
WANT_VACATE = True
RANK = Scheduler =?= $(DedicatedScheduler)
DAEMON_LIST = MASTER, STARTD
```

The final entry listed here specifies that the default role for nodes in your pool is execute-only. The `DAEMON_LIST` on your front-end node must also enable the `condor_schedd`. This front-end node's local configuration file will be

```
DAEMON_LIST = MASTER, STARTD, SCHEDD
```

15.6.2 Using Multiprocessor Compute Nodes

If any node in your Condor pool is a symmetric multiprocessor machine, Condor will represent that node as multiple virtual machines (VMs), one for each CPU. By default, each VM will have a single CPU and an even share of all shared system resources, such as RAM and swap space. If this behavior satisfies your needs, you do not need to make any configuration changes for SMP nodes to work properly with Condor.

Some sites might want different behavior of their SMP nodes. For example, assume your cluster was composed of dual-processor machines with 1 gigabyte of

RAM, and one of your users was submitting jobs with a memory footprint of 700 megabytes. With the default setting, all VMs in your pool would only have 500 megabytes of RAM, and your user's jobs would never run. In this case, you would want to unevenly divide RAM between the two CPUs, to give half of your VMs 750 megabytes of RAM. The other half of the VMs would be left with 250 megabytes of RAM.

There is more than one way to divide shared resources on an SMP machine with Condor, all of which are discussed in detail in the Condor Administrator's Manual. The most basic method is as follows. To divide shared resources on an SMP unevenly, you must define different *virtual machine types* and tell the `condor_startd` how many virtual machines of each type to advertise. The simplest method to define a virtual machine type is to specify what fraction of all shared resources each type should receive.

For example, if you wanted to divide a two-node machine where one CPU received one-quarter of the shared resources, and the other CPU received the other three-quarters, you would use the following settings:

```
VIRTUAL_MACHINE_TYPE_1 = 1/4
VIRTUAL_MACHINE_TYPE_2 = 3/4
NUM_VIRTUAL_MACHINES_TYPE_1 = 1
NUM_VIRTUAL_MACHINES_TYPE_2 = 1
```

If you want to divide certain resources unevenly but split the rest evenly, you can specify separate fractions for each shared resource. This is described in detail in the Condor Administrator's Manual.

15.6.3 Scheduling a Distributively Owned Cluster

Many clusters are owned by more than one entity. Two or more smaller groups might pool their resources to buy a single, larger cluster. In these situations, the group that paid for a portion of the nodes should get priority to run on those nodes.

Each resource in a Condor pool can define its own `RANK` expression, which specifies the kinds of jobs it would prefer to execute. If a cluster is owned by multiple entities, you can divide the cluster's nodes up into groups, based on ownership. Each node would set `Rank` such that jobs coming from the group that owned it would have the highest priority.

Assume there is a 60-node compute cluster at a university, shared by three departments: astronomy, math, and physics. Each department contributed the funds for 20 nodes. Each group of 20 nodes would define its own Rank expression. The astronomy department's settings, for example, would be

```
Rank = Department == "Astronomy"
```

The users from each department would also add a Department attribute to all of their job ClassAds. The administrators could configure Condor to add this attribute automatically to all job ads from each site (see the Condor Administrator's Manual for details).

If the entire cluster was idle and a physics user submitted 40 jobs, she would see all 40 of her jobs start running. If, however, a user in math submitted 60 jobs and a user in astronomy submitted 20 jobs, 20 of the physicist's jobs would be preempted, and each group would get 20 machines out of the cluster.

If all of the astronomy department's jobs completed, the astronomy nodes would go back to serving math and physics jobs. The astronomy nodes would continue to run math or physics jobs until either some astronomy jobs were submitted, or all the jobs in the system completed.

15.6.4 Submitting to the Cluster from Desktop Workstations

Most organizations that install a compute cluster have other workstations at their site. It is usually desirable to allow these machines to act as front-end nodes for the cluster, so users can submit their jobs from their own machines and have the applications execute on the cluster. Even if there is no shared file system between the cluster and the rest of the computers, Condor's remote system calls and file transfer functionality can enable jobs to migrate between the two and still access their data (see Section 15.2.5 for details on accessing data files).

To enable a machine to submit into your cluster, run the Condor installation program and specify that you want to setup a *submit-only* node. This will set the DAEMON_LIST on the new node to be

```
DAEMON_LIST = MASTER, SCHEDD
```

The installation program will also create all the directories and files needed by Condor.

Note that you can have only one node configured as the dedicated scheduler for your pool. Do not attempt to add a second submit node for MPI jobs.

15.6.5 Expanding the Cluster to Nondedicated (Desktop) Computing Resources

One of the most powerful features in Condor is the ability to combine dedicated and opportunistic scheduling within a single system. *Opportunistic scheduling* involves placing jobs on nondedicated resources under the assumption that the resources might not be available for the entire duration of the jobs. Opportunistic scheduling is used for all jobs in Condor with the exception of dedicated MPI applications.

If your site has a combination of jobs and uses applications other than MPI, you should strongly consider adding all of your computing resources, even desktop workstations, to your Condor pool. With checkpointing and process migration, suspend and resume capabilities, opportunistic scheduling and matchmaking, Condor can harness the idle CPU cycles of any machine and put them to good use.

To add other computing resources to your pool, run the Condor installation program and specify that you want to configure a node that can both submit and execute jobs. The default installation sets up a node with a policy for starting, suspending, and preempting jobs based on the activity of the machine (for example, keyboard idle time and CPU load). These nodes will not run dedicated MPI jobs, but they will run jobs from any other universe, including PVM.

15.7 Conclusion

Condor is a powerful tool for scheduling jobs across platforms, both within and beyond the boundaries of your Beowulf clusters. Through its unique combination of both dedicated and opportunistic scheduling, Condor provides a unified framework for high-throughput computing.

16 Maui Scheduler: A High Performance Cluster Scheduler

David B. Jackson

In this chapter we describe the Maui scheduler, a job-scheduling component that coordinates activities among Grid scheduling, resource management, and allocation management services, which can provide advanced scheduling services for most major resource managers.

16.1 Overview

Over the years, Maui has become the standard in high-performance cluster job scheduling. It is capable of operating with and extending the functionality of virtually all major resource management systems, including OpenPBS, PBSPro, SGE, LSF, Loadleveler, SSS, and BProc. From its origins, Maui has been designed to empower a given site to maximize the use of the cluster. It does this by allowing *translation* of local mission policies into scheduling behavior, optimizing scheduling decisions, and intelligently minimizing resource contention. In doing so, it allows sites not only to gain greater return on investment from their cluster but also to improve end-user satisfaction and reduce administrative overhead required to manage the cluster.

At a high level, the role of a job scheduler is to direct the actions of the resource manager, indicating when, where, and how jobs are to be started, preempted, canceled, and otherwise managed. It is also responsible for coordinating actions with other systems such as a Grid scheduler, allocation manager, or information service. In fulfilling these roles, Maui adds a unique suite of scheduling services including advance reservations, backfill, fairshare, dynamic job prioritization, quality of service support, and metascheduling.

Maui's design allows sites to maintain consistently high levels of cluster performance and support for advanced scheduling features regardless of the local resource manager used. With Maui, sites are not locked into a single resource manager but may freely select and interchange resource managers according to need. Further, Maui allows end users the choice of using the command and GUI interfaces of Maui or the commands of the underlying resource manager. Thus, sites can roll Maui in and out with no end-user training; end users can continue using familiar job management commands, GUIs, and job submission languages. If sites wish to introduce end users to new advanced Maui features and commands, they can. If not, the users can operate successfully without even knowing Maui is installed on the system.

16.2 Installation and Initial Configuration

The Maui scheduler is available in the most popular cluster-building toolkits, including *OSCAR* and *Rocks*. The most recent versions of Maui can also be downloaded from the Maui home page at `http://supercluster.org/maui`. This site contains online documentation, FAQs, links to the Maui users mailing list, other standard open source utilities, and contact information for obtaining support and other services. Building the code consists of the standard `configure`, `make`, and `make install` process.

16.2.1 Basic Configuration

The `configure` script will set up the basic build environment and initial configuration files including the master config file, '`maui.cfg`'. This master config file is a *flat text* file that includes information regarding resource manager interface configuration, scheduling optimizations, usage limits, and cluster usage objectives. In most cases, the initial configuration done by the `configure` command is adequate to allow Maui to be used immediately with no further changes. Maui is extremely configurable, with hundreds of parameters available. Rarely, however, do sites need to use more than a fraction of the available services to meet their specific needs. Maui's highly modularized design allows sites to accept the initial defaults and focus only on configuring those aspect of scheduling pertinent to their environment.

Among the parameters detected and set by the `configure` script are `RMCFG`, `SCHEDCFG`, and `ADMIN`. The initial settings of these values can be checked and modified by editing the '`maui.cfg`' file. Alternatively, once the scheduler is running, Maui can be configured dynamically by using text- or GUI-based commands. For text-based configuration, the `schedctl` command can be used with the '`-l`' flag to *list* the value of any parameter whether explicitly set or not, while the '`-m`' flag can be used to dynamically *modify* parameter values. The online `parameters` documentation provides details about all Maui parameters, including format, default values, usage, examples, and links to related sections of the admin manual.

16.2.2 Simulation and Testing

Often, after the initial configuration is verified, sites choose to test the scheduler to become familiar with its capabilities and to verify basic functionality. Maui can be run in a completely *safe* manner by setting the `MODE` attribute of the `SCHEDCFG` parameter to `TEST`, that is, `SCHEDCFG[orion] MODE=TEST PORT=40559`. In *test* mode, Maui contacts the resource manager to obtain up-to-date configuration, node, and job information; however, in this mode, Maui's ability to start or modify these jobs is disabled. Once the needed parameter changes have been made, Maui can be started by issuing the command `maui`. At this point, commands such as `showq`, `showstate`, and `checknode` may be used to verify proper scheduler-resource manager communication and scheduler functionality. Details on the full suite of Maui commands are available online or in the *man-page* documentation included with the distribution.

16.2.3 Production Scheduling

Once evaluation is complete, the scheduler can be placed in production mode by disabling the default resource manager scheduler and setting the scheduler `MODE` attribute to `NORMAL`. Information on disabling the default resource manager scheduler is provided in the resource manager's documentation and in the online Maui *migration guides* located at `http://supercluster.org/documentation/maui`. Running in *normal* mode allows Maui to start, modify, and cancel jobs according to the specified scheduling policies. The default configuration of Maui enables basic scheduling services, providing first-in, first-out scheduling with backfill.

16.3 Advanced Configuration

Maui's real power is unleashed when the defaults are replaced with more advanced configuration. Specifically, sites can map mission objectives into scheduling policies: selecting how resources are to be used, how users are to be treated, and how jobs are to be scheduled. To this end, Maui can be thought of as an integrated scheduling toolkit providing a number of capabilities that may be used individually or in concert to obtain the desired system behavior. These capabilities include

- job prioritization,
- node allocation policies,
- throttling policies,
- fairshare,
- reservations,
- allocation management,
- quality of service,

- backfill,
- node sets, and
- preemption policies.

Most capabilities are disabled by default; thus, a site need configure only the features of interest. In the following subsections, we describe each of these capabilities. While our description will be adequate for configuring these capabilities, the online Maui Administrators Manual should be consulted for full details.

16.3.1 Assigning Value: Job Prioritization and Node Allocation

In general, prioritization is the process of determining which of many options best fulfills overall goals. In the case of scheduling, a site often has multiple, independent goals such as maximizing system utilization, giving preference to users in specific projects, or making certain that no job sits in the queue for more than a given period of time. The most common approach to representing a multifaceted set of site goals is to assign to each objective an overall weight (value or priority) that can be associated with each potential scheduling decision. With the jobs prioritized, the scheduler can roughly fulfill site objectives by starting the jobs in priority order.

Maui allows component and subcomponent weights to be associated with many aspects of a job. In order to realize this fine-grained control, a simple priority-weighting hierarchy is used in which the contribution of priority components is calculated as `PRIORITY-FACTOR-VALUE * SUBFACTORWEIGHT * FACTORWEIGHT`. Component and subcomponent weights are listed in Table 16.1. Values for all weights may be set in the '`maui.cfg`' file by using the associated component-weight parameter specified as the name of the weight followed by the string `WEIGHT` (e.g., `SERVICEWEIGHT` or `PROCWEIGHT`).

By default, Maui prioritizes jobs exclusively on their submission time. By using priority components, however, a site can incorporate additional information, such as current level of service, quality of service targets, resources requested, and historical usage. The contribution of any single component can be limited by specifying a priority component *cap*, such as `RESCAP`, which prevents the contribution of a single component from exceeding the specified value. In the end, a job's priority is equivalent to the sum of all enabled priority components.

Each component or subcomponent may be used for different purposes. For example, `WALLTIME` can be used to favor (or disfavor) jobs based on their duration; `ACCOUNT` can be used to favor jobs associated with a particular project; `QUEUETIME`

Component	Subcomponent
SERVICE (Level of Service)	QUEUETIME (Current queue time in minutes) XFACTOR (Current expansion factor) BYPASS (Number of times jobs were bypassed via backfill)
TARGET (Proximity to Service Target - Exponential)	TARGETQUEUETIME (Delta to queue-time target in minutes) TARGETXFACTOR (Delta to Xfactor target)
RESOURCE (Resources Requested)	PROC (Processors) MEM (Requested memory in MBytes) SWAP (Requested virtual memory in MBytes) DISK (Requested local disk in MBytes) NODE (Requested number of nodes) WALLTIME (Requested wall time in seconds) PS (Requested processor-seconds) PE (Requested processor-equivalents)
FS (Fairshare)	FSUSER (User fairshare percentage) FSGROUP (Group fairshare percentage) FSACCOUNT (Account fairshare percentage) FSCLASS (Class fairshare percentage) FSQOS (QoS fairshare percentage)
CRED (Credential)	USER (User priority) GROUP (Group priority) ACCOUNT (Account priority) CLASS (Class priority) QOS (QoS priority)

Table 16.1: Maui priority components.

can be used to favor those jobs that have been waiting the longest. By mixing and matching priority weights, sites can obtain the desired job-start behavior. To aid in *tuning* job priority, Maui provides the `diagnose -p` command, which summarizes the impact of the current priority-weight settings on idle jobs.

While most subcomponents are metric based (i.e., number of seconds queued or number of nodes requested), the credential subcomponents are based on priorities specified by the administrator. Maui allows use of the `*CFG` parameters to rank jobs by individual job credentials. For example, to favor jobs submitted by users `bob` and `john` and members of the group `staff`, a site might specify the following:

```
USERCFG[bob]        PRIORITY=100
USERCFG[john]       PRIORITY=500
```

```
GROUPWEIGHT[staff] PRIORITY=1000
USERWEIGHT         1
GROUPWEIGHT        1
CREDWEIGHT         1
```

Note that both component and subcomponent weights are specified to enable these credential priorities to take effect. Further details about the use of these component factors, as well as anecdotal usage information, are available in the Maui Administrators Manual.

Complementing the specification of job prioritization is that of node allocation. When the scheduler selects a job to run, it must also determine which resources to allocate to the job. Depending on the use of the cluster, different allocation policies can be specified using NODEALLOCATIONPOLICY. Parameter values include the following:

- MINRESOURCE: This algorithm selects the nodes with the minimum configured resources that still meet the requirements of the job. The algorithm leaves more richly endowed nodes available for other jobs that may specifically request these additional resources.

- LASTAVAILABLE: This algorithm is particularly useful when making reservations for backfill. It determines the earliest time a job can run and then selects the resources available at a time such that, whenever possible, currently idle resources are left unreserved and are thus available for backfilling.

- PRIORITY: This policy allows a site to create its own node allocation prioritization scheme, taking into account issues such as installed software, jobs currently running on the node, available processors, or other local node configurations. This allocation policy requires specification of the PRIORITYF attribute of the NODECFG parameter. For example, to base node allocation priority on available node memory load, historical utilization, and machine speed, a site may specify something like NODECFG[DEFAULT] PRIORITYF='AMEM - 10*USAGE + SPEED'.

- CPULOAD: This policy attempts to allocate the most lightly loaded nodes first.

16.3.2 Fairness: Throttling Policies and Fairshare

The next issue often confronting sites is the management of *fairness*. At first glance, fairness seems like a simple concept, but in actual practice it can be very difficult to map onto a cluster. Should all users get to run the same number of jobs or use the same number of nodes? Do these usage constraints cover the present time only or a specified time frame? If historical information is used, what is the metric of consumption? What is the time frame? Does fair consumption necessarily mean equal consumption? How should resources be allocated if user X bought two-thirds of the nodes and user Y purchased the other third? Is fairness based on a static metric, or is it conditional on current resource demand?

While Maui is not able to address all these issues, it does provide some flexible tools that help with 90 percent of the battle. Specifically, these tools are *throttling policies* and *fairshare* used to control immediate and historical usage, respectively.

Throttling Policies

The term "throttling policies" is collectively applied to a set of policies that constrain real-time resource consumption. Maui supports limits on the number of processors, nodes, proc-seconds, jobs, and processor equivalents allowed at any given time. Limits may be applied on a per user, group, account, QoS, or queue basis via the `*CFG` set of parameters. For example, specifying `USERCFG[bob] MAXJOB=3 MAXPROC=32` will constrain user `bob` to running no more than 3 jobs and 32 total processors at any given time. Specifying `GROUPCFG[DEFAULT] MAXNODE=64` will limit each group to using no more than 64 nodes simultaneously unless overriding limits for a particular group are specified. `ACCOUNTCFG`, `QOSCFG`, and `CLASSCFG` round out the *CFG family of parameters providing a means to throttle instantaneous use on accounts, QoS's, and classes, respectively.

With each of the parameters, *hard* and *soft* limits can be used to apply a form of *demand*-sensitive limits. While hard limits cannot be violated under any conditions, soft limits may be violated if no other jobs can run. For example, specifying `USERCFG[DEFAULT] MAXNODE=16,24` will allow each user to cumulatively allocate up to 16 nodes while jobs from other users can use available resources. If no other jobs can use these resources, a user may run on up to 24 nodes simultaneously.

Throttling policies are effective in preventing cluster "hogging" by an individual user or group. They also provide a simple mechanism of fairness and cycle distribution. Such policies may lead to lower overall system utilization, however. For instance, resources might go unused if these policies prevent all queued jobs from running. When possible, throttling policies should be set to the highest feasible level, and the cycle distribution should be managed by tools such as fairshare, allocation management systems, and QoS-based prioritization.

Fairshare

Fairshare algorithms attempt to distribute resources over time according to specified usage targets. As noted earlier, however, this general statement leaves much to interpretation, including the distribution usage metric and the monitored time frame.

The Maui parameter FSPOLICY specifies the usage metric allowing sites to determine how resource distribution is to be measured. The parameters FSINTERVAL, FSDEPTH, and FSDECAY control how historical usage information is to be weighted.

To control resource distribution, Maui uses fairshare targets that can be applied to users, groups, accounts, queues, and QoS mechanisms with both default and specific targets available. Each target may be one of four different types: *target*, *floor*, *ceiling*, or *cap*. In most cases, Maui adjusts job priorities to meet fairshare targets. With the standard target, Maui attempts to adjust priorities at all times in an attempt to meet the target. In the case of floors, Maui will increase job priority only to maintain *at least* the targeted usage. With ceilings, the converse occurs. Finally, with fairshare caps, job eligibility rather than job priority is adjusted to prevent jobs from running if the cap is exceeded during the specified fairshare interval.

The example below shows a possible fairshare configuration.

```
# maui.cfg
FSPOLICY   DEDICATEDPS
FSDEPTH    7
FSINTERVAL 24:00:00
FSDECAY    0.80

USERCFG[DEFAULT]  FSTARGET=10.0
USERCFG[john]     FSTARGET=25.0+
GROUPCFG[staff]   FSTARGET=20.0-
```

In this case, fairshare usage will track delivered system *processor seconds* over a seven-day period with a 0.8 decay factor. All users will have a fairshare *target* of 10 percent of these processor seconds—with the exception of john, who will have a *floor* of 25 percent. Also, the group staff will have a fairshare *ceiling* of 20 percent. At any time, the status of fairshare can be examined by using the diagnose -f command.

16.3.3 Managing Resource Access: Reservations, Allocation Managers, and Quality of Service

In managing any cluster system, half of the administrative effort involves configuring it to handle the *steady-state* situation. The other half encompasses the handling of the vast array of special *one-time* requests. Maui provides two features, advance reservations and QoS, which greatly ease the handling of these special requests.

Advance Reservations

Reservations allow a site to set aside a block of resources for various purposes such as cluster maintenance, special user projects, or benchmarking nodes. In general, a reservation consists of time frame, and resource lists, and an access control list. The time frame can be specified as a simple start and end time while the resource list can consist of either a list of specific hosts or a general resource description. The access control list indicates who or what will be allowed to use the specified resources during the reservation time frame. Reservations can be created dynamically by scheduler administrators using the `setres` command or managed directly by Maui via config file parameters.

For example, to reserve `nodeA` and `nodeB` for a four-hour maintenance window starting at 2:30 P.M., one could issue the following command:

```
> setres -s 14:30 -d 4:00:00 'node[AB]'
```

For reservations requesting allocation of a given quantity of resources, the `TASK` keyword can be used in the resource description. For example, the following reservation allocates 20 processors with the feature `fast` to users `john` and `sam` starting on April 14 at 5:00 P.M.

```
> setres -u john:sam -f fast -s 17:00_04/14 TASKS==20
```

With no duration or end time specified, this reservation will default to an infinite length and will remain in place until removed by a scheduler administrator using the `releaseres` command.

Access to reservations is controlled by an access control list (ACL). Reservation access is based on job credentials, such as user or group, and job attributes, such as wall time requested. Reservation ACLs can include multiple access types and individuals. For example, a reservation might reserve resources for users A and B, jobs in class C, and jobs that request less than 30 minutes of wall time. Reservations may also overlap each other if desired, in which case access is granted only if the job meets the access policies of all active reservations.

At many sites, reservations are used on a permanent or periodic basis. In such cases, it is best to use *standing* reservations. Standing reservations allow a site to apply reservations as an ongoing part of cluster policies. The attributes of the `SRCFG` parameter are used to configure standing reservations. For example, to specify the *periodicity* of a given reservation, the `SRCFG PERIOD` attribute can be set to `DAY`, `WEEK`, or `INFINITE`. Additional parameter attributes are available to determine what time of the day or week the reservation should be enabled. To demonstrate, the following configuration can be used to create a reservation named `development` that, during primetime hours, will set aside 16 nodes for exclusive use by jobs requiring less than 30 minutes.

```
SRCFG[development]          PERIOD=DAY DAYS=MON,TUE,WED,THU,FRI
SRCFG[development]          STARTTIME=8:00:00 ENDTIME=17:00:00
SRCFG[development]          TASKCOUNT=16 TIMELIMIT=00:30:00
```

Occasionally, a site may want to allow access to a set of resources only if there are no other resources available. Maui enables this conditional usage through reservation *affinity*. When any reservation access list is specified, each access value can be associated with positive, negative, or neutral affinity by using the "+", "-", or "=" characters. If nothing is specified, positive affinity is assumed. For example, consider the following reservation line:

```
SRUSERLIST[special]  bob john steve= bill-
```

With this specification, `bob`'s and `john`'s jobs receive the default positive affinity and are essentially *attracted* to the reservation. For these jobs, Maui will attempt to use resources in the `special` reservation first, before considering any other resources. Jobs belonging to `steve`, on the other hand, can use these resources but are not attracted to them. Finally, `bill`'s jobs will use resources in the `special` reservation only if no other resources are available. Detailed information about reservations can be obtained by using the `showres` and `diagnose -r` commands.

Allocation Managers

Allocation management systems allow a site to control total resource access in real time. While interfaces to support other systems exist, the allocation management system most commonly used with the Maui scheduler is QBank [92], provided by Pacific Northwest National Laboratory. This system and others like it allow sites to provide distinct resource allocations much like the creation of a bank account.

As jobs run, the resources used are translated into a charge and debited from the appropriate account. In the case of QBank, expiration dates may be associated with allocations, private and shared accounts maintained, per machine allocations created, and so forth.

Within Maui, the allocation manager interface is controlled through the AMCFG parameter such as in the example below:

```
AMCFG[qbank] TYPE=QBANK  HOST=bank.univ.edu
AMCFG[qbank] CHARGEPOLICY=DEBITSUCCESSFULWC  DEFERJOBONFAILURE=TRUE
AMCFG[qbank] FALLBACKACCOUNT=freecycle
```

This configuration enables a connection to an allocation manager located on bank.univ.edu using the QBank interface. The unit of charge is configured to be *dedicated processor-seconds*, and users are charged only if their job completes successfully. If the job does not have adequate allocations in the specified account, Maui will attempt to redirect the job to use allocations in the freecycle account. In many cases, a *fallback* account is configured so as to be associated with lower priorities and/or additional limitations. If the job is not approved by the allocation manager, Maui will defer the job for a period of time and try it again later.

Quality of Service

Maui's Quality of Service (QoS) feature allows sites to control access to special functions, resources, and service levels. Each QoS consists of an access control list controlling which users, groups, accounts, and job queues can access the QoS privileges. Associated with each QoS are special service-related priority weights and service targets. Additionally, each QoS can be configured to span resource partitions, preempt other jobs, and the like.

Maui also enables a site to charge a premium rate for the use of some QoS services. For example, the following configuration will cause user john's jobs to use QoS hiprio by default and allow members of the group bio to access it by request:

```
USERCFG[john] QLIST=hiprio:normal QDEF=hiprio
GROUPCFG[bio] QLIST=hiprio:medprio:development QDEF=medprio
QOSCFG[hiprio] PRIORITY=50 QTTARGET=30 FLAGS=PREEMPTOR
QOSCFG[hiprio] OMAXJOB=20 MAXPROC=150
```

Jobs using QoS hiprio receive the following privileges and constraints:

- A priority boost of 50 * QOSWEIGHT * CREDWEIGHT

- A queue-time target of 30 minutes
- The ability to preempt lower-priority `PREEMPTEE` jobs
- The ability to override `MAXJOB` policy limits defined elsewhere
- A cumulative limit of 150 processors allocated to QoS `hiprio` jobs

A site may have dozens of QoS objects described and may allow users access to any number of these. Depending on the type of service desired, users may then choose the QoS that best meets their needs.

16.3.4 Optimizing Usage: Backfill, Node Sets, and Preemption

The Maui scheduler provides several features to optimize performance in terms of system utilization, job throughput, and average job turnaround time.

Backfill

Backfill is a now common method used to improve both system utilization and average job turnaround time by running jobs out of order. Backfill, simply put, enables the scheduler to run any job so long as it does not delay the start of jobs of higher priority. Generally, the algorithm prevents delay of high-priority jobs through some form of reservation. Backfill can be thought of as a process of filling in the resource *holes* left by the high priority jobs. Since holes are being filled, it makes sense that the jobs most commonly backfilled are the ones requiring the least time and/or resources. With backfill enabled, sites typically report system utilization improvements of 10 to 25% and slight improvement in average job response time.

At installation, backfill scheduling is enabled in Maui, but this is configurable with the parameter `BACKFILLPOLICY`. While the default configuration generally is adequate, sites may want to adjust the job selection policy, the reservation policy, the depth of reservations, or other aspects of backfill scheduling. The online documentation indicates the general effects of changing the backfill algorithm or any of the associated backfill parameters.

Allocation Based on Node Set

While backfill can improve the scheduler's performance in terms of job selection, other facilities can be used to further optimize scheduling decisions. At a high level, the efficiency of a cluster, in terms of actual work accomplished, is a function of both scheduling performance and individual job efficiency. In many clusters, job efficiency can vary widely based on the two key factors, node selection, and node mix. Node selection reflects the impact of how well a single task of a job executes on a single node while node mix accounts for performance changes resulting from communication issues or disparities in node performance.

Since most parallel jobs written in popular languages such as MPI or PVM do not internally load balance their workload, they often run only as fast as the slowest node allocated. Consequently, these jobs run most effectively on homogeneous sets of nodes. While many clusters start out as homogeneous, they quickly evolve as new generations of compute nodes are integrated into the system. Research has shown that this integration, while improving scheduling performance because of increased scheduler selection, can actually decrease average job efficiency.

A feature called *node sets* allows jobs to request sets of common resources without specifying exactly what resources are required. Node set policy can be specified globally or on a per job basis and can be based on node processor speed, memory, network interfaces, or locally defined node attributes. In addition to forcing jobs onto homogeneous nodes, these policies may also be used to guide jobs to one or more types of nodes on which a particular job performs best, similar to job preferences available in other systems. For example, an I/O-intensive job may run best on a certain range of processor speeds, running slower on slower nodes while wasting cycles on faster nodes. A job may specify `ANYOF:PROCSPEED:450:500:650` to request nodes with processors speeds in the range of 450 to 650 MHz. Alternatively, if a simple procspeed-homogeneous node set is desired, `ONEOF:PROCSPEED` may be specified. On the other hand, a communication-sensitive job may request a network-based node set with the configuration `ONEOF:NETWORK:VIA:MYRINET:ETHERNET`, in which case Maui will first attempt to locate adequate nodes where all nodes contain VIA network interfaces. If such a set cannot be found, Maui will look for sets of nodes containing the other specified network interfaces. In highly heterogeneous clusters, the use of node sets has been found to improve job throughput by 10 to 15 percent.

Preemption

Many sites possess workloads of varying importance. While some jobs may required resources immediately, other jobs are less time sensitive but have an insatiable hunger for compute cycles. These latter jobs often have turnaround times on the order of weeks or months. The concept of *cycle stealing*, popularized by systems such as Condor, handles such situations well and enables systems to run low-priority preemptible jobs whenever something more pressing is not running. These other systems are often employed on compute farms of desktops where the jobs must vacate whenever interactive system use is detected.

Maui's QoS-based preemption system allows a dedicated, noninteractive cluster to be used in much the same way. Certain QoS objects may be marked with the flag `PREEMPTOR` and others with the flag `PREEMPTEE`. With this configuration, low-priority "preemptee" jobs can be started whenever idle resources are available. These jobs will be allowed to run until a "preemptor" job arrives, at which point the preemptee job will be checkpointed if possible and vacated. This strategy allows almost immediate resource access for the preemptor job. Using this approach, a cluster can maintain nearly 100 percent system utilization while still delivering excellent turnaround time to the jobs of greatest value.

Use of the preemption system is not be limited to controlling low-priority jobs. Site can use this feature to support optimistic backfill scheduling, enable deadline based scheduling, and provide QoS guarantees.

16.3.5 Evaluating System Performance: Diagnostics, Profiling, Testing, and Simulation

High-performance computing clusters are complicated. First, such clusters have an immense array of attributes that affect overall system performance, including processor speed, memory, networks, I/O systems, enterprise services, and application and system software. Second, each of these attributes is evolving over time, as is the usage pattern of the system's users. Third, sites are presented with an equally immense array of buttons, knobs, and levers which they can push, pull, kick, and otherwise manipulate. How does one evaluate the success of a current configuration? And how does one establish a causal effect between pushing one of the many provided buttons and improved system performance when the system is constantly changing in multiple simultaneous dimensions?

To help alleviate this problem, Maui offers several useful features.

Diagnostics

Maui possesses many internal diagnostic functions that both locate problems and present system state information. For example, the *priority* diagnostic aggregates priority relevant information, presenting configuration settings and their impact on the current idle workload; administrators can see the contribution associated with each priority factor on a per job and systemwide average basis. The *node* diagnostic presents significant node-relevant information together with messages regarding any unexpected conditions. Other diagnostics are available for jobs, reservations, QoS, fairshare, priorities, fairness policies, users, groups, and accounts.

Profiling Current and Historical Usage

Maui maintains internal statistics and records detailed information about each job as it completes. The `showstats` command provides detailed usage information for users, groups, accounts, nodes, and the system as a whole. The `showgrid` command presents scheduler performance statistics in a job size/duration matrix to aid in analyzing the effectiveness of current policies.

The completed job statistics are maintained in a flat file located in the '`stats`' directory. These statistics are useful for two primary purposes: driving simulations (described later) and profiling actual system usage. The `profiler` command allows the processing of these historical scheduler statistics and generation of usage reports for specific time frames or for selected users, groups, accounts, or types of jobs.

Testing

Maui supports a scheduling mode called *test*. In this mode, the scheduler initializes, contacts the resource manager and other peer services, and conducts scheduling cycles exactly as it would if running in `NORMAL` or production mode. Job are prioritized, reservations created, policies and limits enforced, and admin and end-user commands enabled. Using the fact that *test* mode disables Maui's ability to impact the system, a site can safely verify scheduler operation and validate new policies and constraints. In fact, Maui can be run in *test* mode on a production system while another scheduler or even another version of Maui is running on the same system. This unique ability can allow new versions and configurations to be fully tested without any exposure to potential failures and with no cluster downtime.

To run Maui in *test* mode, simply set the `MODE` attribute of the `SCHEDCFG` parameter to `TEST` and start Maui. Normal scheduler commands can be used to evaluate configuration and performance. Diagnostic commands can be used to look for any potential issues. Further, the Maui log file can be used to determine which jobs Maui attempted to start and which resources Maui attempted to allocate.

In addition to *test* mode, Maui supports a mode known as *interactive*. This mode also allows for evaluation of new versions and configurations using a different approach. Instead of disabling all resource and job control functions, however, Maui sends the desired change request to the screen and *asks* for permission to complete it. The administrator must specifically accept each command request before Maui will execute it.

If another instance of Maui is running in production mode and a site wishes to evaluate a different configuration or new version using one of the above *evaluation* modes, this is easily done, but care should be taken to avoid conflicts with the primary scheduler. Potential conflicts include statistics files, logs, checkpoint files, and user interface ports. One of the easiest ways to avoid these conflicts is to create a new "test" directory with its own log and stats subdirectories. The new '`maui.cfg`' file can be created from scratch or based on the existing '`maui.cfg`' file already in use. In either case, make certain that the `SCHEDCFG PORT` attribute parameter differs from that used by the production scheduler. If testing is being done with the production binary executable, the `MAUIHOMEDIR` environment variable should be set to point to the new test directory in order to prevent Maui from loading the production '`maui.cfg`' file.

Simulation

The Maui simulation facility allows a site to evaluate cluster performance in an almost arbitrary environment. This is done by creating a *resource* and *workload* tracefile to specify the desired cluster and workload to be evaluated. These traces, specified via the `SIMWORKLOADTRACEFILE` and `SIMRESOURCETRACEFILE`, can accurately and reproducibly replicate the workload and resources recorded at the site or may represent an entirely new cluster and workload. In order to run a simulation, an adjusted '`maui.cfg`' file is created with the policies of interest in place and the `MODE` attribute of the `SCHEDCFG` parameter set to `SIMULATION`. Once started, Maui can be stepped through simulated time using the `schedctl -S` command. In the simulation, all Maui commands continue to function as before, allowing interactive querying of status, adjustment of parameters, or even submission or cancellation of jobs.

This feature enables sites to analyze the impact of different scheduling policies on their own workload and system configuration. The effects of new reservations or job prioritizations can be evaluated in a *zero-exposure* environment, allowing sites to determine ideal policies without experimenting on a production system. Sites can also evaluate the impact of additional or modified workloads or changes in available resources. What impact will removing a block of resources for maintenance have on average queue time? How much benefit will a new reservation dedicated exclusively to development jobs have on development job turnaround time? How much pain will it cause nondevelopment jobs? Using simulation makes it easier and safer to obtain answers to such questions.

This same simulation feature can also be used to test a new algorithm against workload and resource traces from various supercomputing centers. Moreover, with the simulator, sites can create and plug in modules to emulate the behavior of various job types on different hardware platforms, across bottlenecking networks, or under various data migration conditions.

Further information on the capabilities and use of simulation is given in the Maui Administrators Manual.

16.4 Steering Workload and Improving Quality of Information

A good scheduler can improve the use of a cluster significantly, but its effectiveness is limited by the scheduling environment in which it must operate and the quality of information it receives. Often, a cluster is underutilized because users overestimate a job's resource requirements. Other times, inefficiencies crop up when users request job constraints in terms of job duration or processors required that are not easily packed onto the cluster. Maui provides tools to allow fine tuning of job resource requirement information and steering of cluster workload so as to allow maximum utilization of the system.

One such tool is the *feedback* interface, which allows a site to report detailed job usage statistics to users. This interface provides information about the resources requested and those actually used. With the FEEDBACKPROGRAM parameter, local scripts can be executed that use this information to help users improve resource requirement estimates. For example, a site with nodes of various memory configurations may choose to create a script such as the following that automates the mailing of notices at job completion:

```
Job 1371 completed successfully.  Note that it requested nodes
with 512 MBytes of RAM yet used  only 112 MBytes.  Had the job provided a
more accurate estimate, it would have, on average, started 02:27:16
earlier.
```

While such notices can be used to improve memory, disk, processor, and wall-time estimates, they may be freely ignored by the end user. A more forceful approach is to use the allocation manager charge policy so as to charge users for requested resources rather than used resources. This approach quickly motivates end users to evaluate their true job needs and adjust their job requests accordingly.

Another realm of feedback involves steering jobs to use currently available resources. The showbf command is designed to help users tailor jobs to request resources that are free for immediate use. This command allows users to incorporate specific information about what they need and who needs it, allowing all scheduling policies and resource availability information to be integrated into the response. Users may specify details about the prospective job including user, group, queue, and memory requirements, and the command returns information regarding the quantity of available nodes and the duration of their availability.

A third area of user feedback is job scaling. Often, users will submit parallel jobs that only moderately scale, hoping that by requesting more processors, their job will run faster and provide results sooner. A job's completion time is simply the sum of its queue time plus its execution time. Users often fail to realize that a larger job may be more difficult to schedule, resulting in a longer queue time, and may run less efficiently, with a *sublinear* speedup. The increased queue-time delay, together with the limitations in execution time improvements, generally results in larger jobs having a greater average turnaround time than smaller jobs performing the same work. Maui commands such as `showgrid` can provide real-time job efficiency and average queue-time statistics correlated to job attributes such as job size. The output of the `mprof` command can also be used to provide per user job efficiency and average queue time correlated by job size and can alert administrators and users to this problem.

16.5 Troubleshooting

Maui's diagnostic commands provide a good start for troubleshooting any scheduling issues. The `diagnose` command together with `checknode` and `checkjob` provides detailed state information about the scheduler, including its various facilities, nodes, and jobs. In addition to state information, these commands can also trigger extensive internal sanity checks for the scheduling realm of interest. For example, if the job priorities do not appear to properly reflect site objectives, the `diagnose -p` command can be used to display the priorities of all jobs and the contributions of the various priority components and subcomponents. This command will also look for invalid priority values and summarize overall priority contributions of each component. At a glance, it will help administrators determine whether parameters need to be adjusted and, if so, by how much. Other diagnostic commands assist in both problem resolution and system tuning in areas such as throttling policies, reservations, fairshare, Grid scheduling, and job management. If any diagnostic command uncovers a potential problem, the issue is reported in the form of `WARNING` messages appended to the normal command output. Use of these commands typically identifies or resolves the vast majority of all scheduling issues.

If additional information is required, Maui writes out detailed logging information in a logfile specified by the `LOGFILE` parameter (usually in '`log/maui.log`'). The `LOGLEVEL` and `LOGFACILITY` parameters enable control over the verbosity and focus of these logs. Maui's high verbosity levels are very verbose, however, so keeping the LOGLEVEL below 4 or so unless actually tracking problems can help prevent excessing file activity.

These logs contain a number of entries, including the following:

`INFO:` provides status information about normal scheduler operations.

`WARNING:` indicates that an unexpected condition was detected and handled.

`ALERT:` indicates that an unexpected condition occurred that could not be fully handled.

`ERROR:` indicates that problem was detected that prevents Maui from fully operating. This may be a problem with the cluster that is outside of Maui's control or may indicate corrupt internal state information.

`Function header:` indicates when a function is called and what parameters are passed.

A simple `grep` through the log file will usually indicate whether any serious issues have been detected and is of significant value when obtaining support or locally diagnosing problems. If neither commands nor logs point to the source of the problem, the Maui users list (`mauiusers@supercluster.org`) or Supercluster support (`support@supercluster.org`) may be consulted for additional assistance.

16.6 Conclusions

This chapter has introduced some of the key Maui features currently available. With hundreds of sites now using and contributing to this project, Maui is evolving and improving faster than ever. While this chapter was able to address common aspects of scheduler configuration, many features such as Grid scheduling, virtual resources, and dynamic jobs could not be adequately covered. To learn about the latest developments and to obtain more detailed information about the capabilities described above, see the Maui home page at `http://www.supercluster.org/maui`.

17 PBS: Portable Batch System

James Patton Jones

The Portable Batch System (PBS) is a flexible workload management and job scheduling system originally developed to manage aerospace computing resources at NASA. PBS has since become the leader in supercomputer workload management and the *de facto* standard job scheduler for Linux.

Today, growing enterprises often support hundreds of users running thousands of jobs across different types of machines in different geographical locations. In this distributed heterogeneous environment, it can be extremely difficult for administrators to collect detailed, accurate usage data or to set systemwide resource priorities. As a result, many computing resources are left underused, while others are overused. At the same time, users are confronted with an ever-expanding array of operating systems and platforms. Each year, scientists, engineers, designers, and analysts waste countless hours learning the nuances of different computing environments, rather than being able to focus on their core priorities. PBS addresses these problems for computing-intensive industries such as science, engineering, finance, and entertainment.

PBS allows you to unlock the potential in the valuable assets you already have, while at the same time reducing demands on system administrators, freeing them to focus on other activities. PBS can also help you effectively manage growth by tracking use levels across your systems and enhancing effective utilization of future purchases.

17.1 History of PBS

In the past, computers were used in a completely interactive manner. Background jobs were just processes with their input disconnected from the terminal. As the number of processors in computers continued to increase, however, the need to be able to schedule tasks based on available resources rose in importance. The advent of networked compute servers, smaller general systems, and workstations led to the requirement of a networked batch scheduling capability. The first such Unix-based system was the Network Queueing System (NQS) funded by NASA Ames Research Center in 1986. NQS quickly became the *de facto* standard for batch queuing.

Over time, distributed parallel systems began to emerge, and NQS was inadequate to handle the complex scheduling requirements presented by such systems. In addition, computer system managers wanted greater control over their compute resources, and users wanted a single interface to the systems. In the early 1990s NASA needed a solution to this problem, but after finding nothing on the market that adequately addressed their needs, led an international effort to gather requirements for a next-generation resource management system. The requirements and functional specification were later adopted as an IEEE POSIX standard (1003.2d). Next, NASA funded the development of a new resource management system compliant with the standard. Thus the Portable Batch System was born.

PBS was quickly adopted on distributed parallel systems and replaced NQS on traditional supercomputers and server systems. Eventually the entire industry evolved toward distributed parallel systems, taking the form of both special-purpose and commodity clusters. Managers of such systems found that the capabilities of PBS mapped well onto cluster systems.

The PBS story continued when Veridian (the research and development contractor that developed PBS for NASA) released the Portable Batch System Professional Edition (PBS Pro), a complete workload management solution. After three years of commercial success, in March 2003, the PBS technology and associated engineering team was acquired by Altair Engineering, Inc. Altair set up the PBS team as a seperate, subsiderary company (Altair Grid Technologies) focused on continued development of the PBS product line, and created a world-wide PBS support network via the Altair international offices.

The cluster administrator can now choose between two versions of PBS: an older restricted-use Open Source release (Altair OpenPBS); and Altair PBS Pro, the new hardened and enhanced commercial version.

This chapter gives a technical overview of PBS and information on installing, using, and managing both versions of PBS. However, it is not possible to cover all the details of a software system as feature-rich as PBS in a single chapter. Therefore, we limit this discussion to the recommended configuration for Linux clusters, providing references to the various PBS documentation where additional, detailed information is available.

While this chapter describes only single-operating system clusters, the reader should note that PBS Pro is not limited to this configuration. Heterogenous clusters containing UNIX, Linux, and Windows systems are also supported.

17.1.1 Acquiring PBS

While both OpenPBS and PBS Pro are bundled in a variety of cluster kits, the best sources for the most current release of either product are the official Altair PBS Web sites: `www.OpenPBS.org` and `www.PBSpro.com`. Both sites offer downloads of the software and documentation, as well as FAQs, discussion lists, and current PBS news. Hardcopy documentation, media kits, and training classnotes are available from the PBS Online Store, accessed through the PBS Pro Web site.

17.1.2 PBS Features

PBS Pro provides many features and benefits to the cluster administrator. A few of the more important features are the following:

Enterprisewide resource sharing provides transparent job scheduling on any PBS system by any authorized user. Jobs can be submitted from any client system, both local and remote, crossing domains where needed.

Multiple user interfaces provide a graphical user interface for submitting batch and interactive jobs; querying job, queue, and system status; and monitoring job progress. Also provided is a traditional command line interface.

Security and access control lists permit the administrator to allow or deny access to PBS systems on the basis of username, group, host, and/or network domain.

Job accounting offers detailed logs of system activities for charge-back or usage analysis per user, per group, per project, and per compute host.

Automatic file staging provides users with the ability to specify any files that need to be copied onto the execution host before the job runs and any that need to be copied off after the job completes. The job will be scheduled to run only after the required files have been successfully transferred.

Parallel job support works with parallel programming libraries such as MPI, PVM, and HPF. Applications can be scheduled to run within a single multiprocessor computer or across multiple systems.

System monitoring includes a graphical user interface for system monitoring. PBS displays node status, job placement, and resource utilization information for both standalone systems and clusters.

Job interdependency enables the user to define a wide range of interdependencies between jobs. Such dependencies include execution order, synchronization, and execution conditioned on the success or failure of another specific job (or set of jobs).

Computational Grid support provides an enabling technology for meta-computing and computational Grids, including support for the Globus Toolkit.

Comprehensive API includes a complete application programming interface for sites that wish to integrate PBS with other applications or to support unique job-scheduling requirements.

Automatic load-leveling provides numerous ways to distribute the workload across a cluster of machines, based on hardware configuration, resource availability, keyboard activity, and local scheduling policy.

Distributed clustering allows customers to use physically distributed systems and clusters, even across wide area networks.

Common user environment offers users a common view of the job submission, job querying, system status, and job tracking over all systems.

Cross-system scheduling ensures that jobs do not have to be targeted to a specific computer system. Users may submit their job and have it run on the first available system that meets their resource requirements.

Job priority allows users the ability to specify the priority of their jobs; defaults can be provided at both the queue and system level.

Full configurability makes PBS easily tailored to meet the needs of different sites. Much of this flexibility is due to the unique design of the scheduler module, which permits complete customization.

Broad platform availability is achieved through support of Windows 2000 and XP, and every major version of Unix and Linux, from workstations and servers to supercomputers. New platforms are being supported with each new release.

User name mapping provides support for mapping user account names on one system to the appropriate name on remote server systems. This allows PBS to fully function in environments where users do not have a consistent username across all the resources they have access to.

System integration allows PBS to take advantage of vendor-specific enhancements on different systems (such as supporting `cpusets` on SGI systems and interfacing with the global resource manager on the Cray T3E).

For a comparison of the features available in the latest versions of OpenPBS and PBS Pro, visit the PBS Product Comparison web page: `www.OpenPBS.org/product_comparison.html`.

17.1.3 PBS Architecture

PBS consists of two major component types: user-level commands and system daemons. A brief description of each is given here to help you make decisions during the installation process.

PBS supplies both command-line programs that are POSIX 1003.2d conforming and a graphical interface. These are used to submit, monitor, modify, and delete jobs. These *client commands* can be installed on any system type supported by PBS and do not require the local presence of any of the other components of PBS. There are three classifications of commands: user commands that any authorized user can use, operator commands, and manager (or administrator) commands. Operator and manager commands require specific access privileges. (See also the security sections of the PBS Administrator Guide.)

The *job server* daemon is the central focus for PBS, fulfilling the queueing and accounting roles of workload management (see Chapter 16 for details). Within this document, this daemon process is generally referred to as the *Server* or by the execution name `pbs_server`. All commands and the other daemons communicate with the Server via an Internet Protocol (IP) network. The Server's main function is to provide the basic batch services such as receiving or creating a batch job, modifying the job, protecting the job against system crashes, and running the job. Typically, one Server manages a given set of resources.

The *job executor* is the daemon that actually places the job into execution. This daemon, `pbs_mom`, is informally called *MOM* because it is the mother of all executing jobs. (MOM is a reverse-engineered acronym that stands for Machine Oriented Mini-server.) MOM places a job into execution when it receives a copy of the job from a Server. MOM creates a new session as identical to a user login session as possible. For example, if the user's login shell is `csh`, then MOM creates a session in which `.login` is run as well as `.cshrc`. MOM also has the responsibility for returning the job's output to the user when directed to do so by the Server. One MOM daemon runs on each computer that will execute PBS jobs. The MOM daemons, collectively, are responsible for the monitoring and resource management (and part of accounting) roles of workload management.

The *job scheduler* daemon, `pbs_sched`, implements the site's policy controlling when each job is run and on which resources (i.e. fulfiling the scheduling role of workload management). The Scheduler communicates with the various MOMs to query the state of system resources and with the Server to learn about the availability of jobs to execute. The interface to the Server is through the same API (discussed below) as used by the client commands. Note that the Scheduler interfaces with the Server with the same privilege as the PBS manager.

17.2 Using PBS

From the user's perspective, a workload mangement system enables you to make more efficient use of your time by allowing you to specify the tasks you need run on the cluster. The system takes care of running these tasks and returning the results to you. If the cluster is full, then it holds your tasks and runs them when the resources are available.

PBS provides two user interfaces: a command-line interface (CLI) and a graphical user interface (GUI). You can use either to interact with PBS: both interfaces have the same functionality. (The examples below show the command line interface; see the “Using the PBS Graphical User Interface” section below for examples of the GUI.)

Using either interface, you create a *batch job* that you then submit to PBS. A batch job is a shell script containing the set of commands you want run on the cluster. It also contains directives that specify the resource requirements (such as memory or CPU time) that your job needs. Once you create your PBS job, you can reuse it, if you wish, or you can modify it for subsequent runs. Example job scripts are shown below.

PBS also provides a special kind of batch job called *interactive batch.* This job is treated just like a regular batch job (it is queued up and must wait for resources to become available before it can run). But once it is started, the user's terminal input and output are connected to the job in what appears to be an `rlogin` session. It appears that the user is logged into one of the nodes of the cluster, and the resources requested by the job are reserved for that job. Many users find this feature useful for debugging their applications or for computational steering.

17.2.1 Creating a PBS Job

Previously we mentioned that a PBS job is simply a shell script containing resource requirements of the job and the command(s) to be executed. (However, if you use the PBS graphical interface, you do not have to edit any batch files; instead, the GUI provides a point and click interface that creates the batch job script for you.) A sample PBS job might look like the following:

```
#!/bin/sh
#PBS -l walltime=1:00:00
#PBS -l nodes=4
#PBS -j oe

cd ${HOME}/PBS/trial
mpiexec -n 4 myprogram
```

This script would then be submitted to PBS using the *qsub* command.

Let us look at the script for a moment. The first line tells what shell to use to interpret the script. Lines 2–3 are resource directives, specifying arguments to the “resource list” (“`-l`”) option of `qsub`. Note that all PBS directives begin with `#PBS`. These lines tell PBS what to do with your job. Any `qsub` option can also be placed inside the script by using a `#PBS` directive. However, PBS stops parsing directives with the first blank line encountered.

Returning to our example above, we see a request for one hour of wall-clock time and four nodes. The fourth line is a request for PBS to merge the stdout and stderr file streams of the job into a single file. The last two lines are the commands the user wants executed: change directory to a particular location, then execute an MPI program called '`myprogram`'.

This job script could have been created in one of two ways: using a text editor, or using the *xpbs* graphical interface (see below).

17.2.2 Submitting a PBS Job

The command used to submit a job to PBS is `qsub`. For example, say you created a file containing your PBS job called '`myscriptfile`'. The following example shows how to submit the job to PBS:

```
% qsub myscriptfile
12322.sol.pbspro.com
```

The second line in the example is the job identifier returned by the PBS Server. This unique identifier can be used to act on this job in the future (before it completes running). The next section of this chapter discusses using this "job id" in various ways.

The `qsub` command has a number of options that can be specified either on the command-line or in the job script itself. Note that any command-line option will override the same option within the script file.

Table 17.1 lists the most commonly used options to `qsub`. See the PBS User Guide for the complete list and full description of the options.

Option	Purpose
-l list	List of resources needed by job
-q queue	Queue to submit job to
-N name	Name of job
-S shell	Shell to execute job script
-p priority	Priority of job relative to your jobs
-a datetime	Delay job under after datetime
-j oe	Join output and error files
-h	Place a hold on job

Table 17.1: Qsub options.

The "`-l resource_list`" option is used to specify the resources needed by the job. Table 17.2 lists all the resources available to jobs running on clusters.

Resource	Meaning
arch	System architecture needed by job
cput	CPU time required by all processes in job
file	Maximum single file disk space requirements
mem	Total amount of RAM memory required
ncpus	Number of CPUs (processors) required
nice	Requested "nice" (Unix priority) value
nodes	Number and/or type of nodes needed
pcput	Maximum per-process CPU time required
pmem	Maximum per-process memory required
wall time	Total wall-clock time needed
workingset	Total disk space requirements

Table 17.2: PBS resources.

17.2.3 Getting the Status of a PBS Job

Once the job has been submitted to PBS, you can use either the `qstat` or `xpbs` commands to check the job status. If you know the job identifier for your job, you can request the status explicitly. Note that unless you have multiple clusters, you need only specify the sequence number portion of the job identifier:

```
% qstat 12322
Job id         Name         User   Time Use S Queue
-------------- ------------ ------ -------- - -----
12322.sol      myscriptfile jjones 00:06:39 R submit
```

If you run the `qstat` command without specifing a job identifier, then you will receive status on all jobs currently queued and running.

Often users wonder why their job is not running. You can query this information from PBS using the "`-s`" (status) option of `qstat`, for example,

```
% qstat -s 12323
Job id         Name         User   Time Use S Queue
-------------  ------------ ------ -------- - -----
12323.sol      myscriptfile jjones 00:00:00 Q submit
  Requested number of CPUs not currently available.
```

A number of options to `qstat` change what information is displayed. The PBS User Guide gives the complete list.

17.2.4 PBS Command Summary

So far we have seen several of the PBS user commands. Table 17.3 is provided as a quick reference for all the PBS user commands. Details on each can be found in the PBS manual pages and the PBS User Guide.

Command	Purpose
qalter	Alter job(s)
qdel	Delete job(s)
qhold	Hold job(s)
qmsg	Send a message to job(s)
qmove	Move job(s) to another queue
qrls	Release held job(s)
qrerun	Rerun job(s)
qselect	Select a specific subset of jobs
qsig	Send a signal to job(s)
qstat	Show status of job(s)
qsub	Submit job(s)
xpbs	Graphical Interface (GUI) to PBS commands

Table 17.3: PBS user commands.

17.2.5 Using the PBS Graphical User Interface

PBS provides two GUI interfaces: a TCL/TK-based GUI called **xpbs** and an optional Web-based GUI.

The GUI `xpbs` provides a user-friendly point-and-click interface to the PBS commands. To run `xpbs` as a regular, nonprivileged user, type

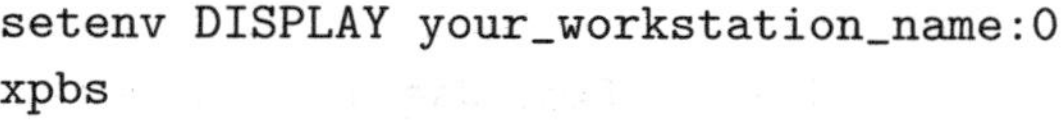

```
setenv DISPLAY your_workstation_name:0
xpbs
```

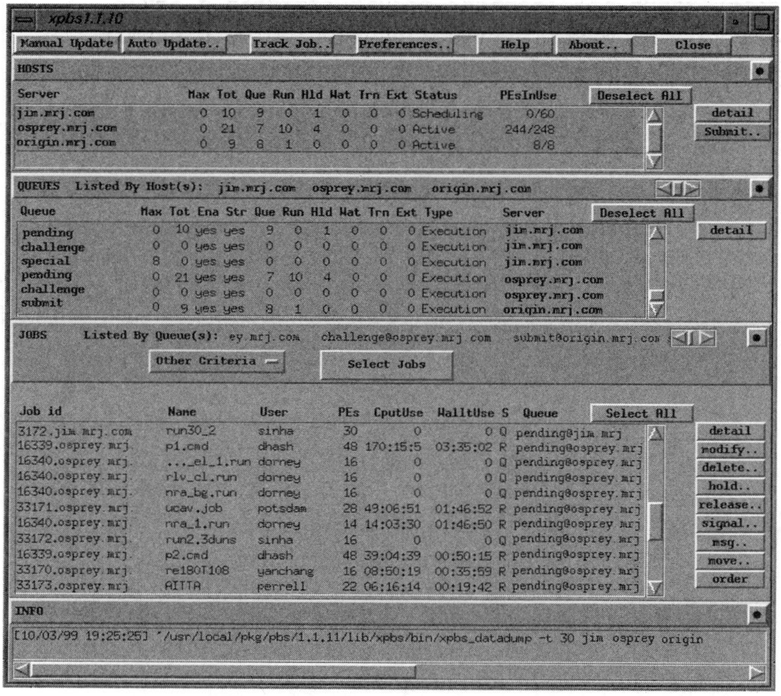

To run xpbs with the additional purpose of terminating PBS Servers, stopping and starting queues, or running or rerunning jobs, type

```
xpbs -admin
```

Note that you must be identified as a PBS operator or manager in order for the additional "-admin" functions to take effect.

From this main xpbs window, you can create and submit jobs, monitor jobs, queues, and servers, as well as perform any of the actions that the command line interface permits you to do.

The optional Web-based user interface provides access to all the functionality of xpbs via almost any Web browser. To access it, you simply type the URL of your PBS Server host into your browser. The layout and usage are similar to those of xpbs.

17.2.6 PBS Application Programming Interface

Part of the PBS package is the PBS Interface Library, or IFL. This library provides a means of building new PBS clients. Any PBS service request can be invoked through calls to the interface library. Users may wish to build a PBS job that will check its status itself or submit new jobs, or they may wish to customize the job status display rather than use the `qstat` command. Administrators may use the interface library to build new control commands.

The IFL provides a user-callable function that corresponds to each PBS client command. There is (approximately) a one-to-one correlation between commands and PBS service requests. Additional routines are provided for network connection management. The user-callable routines are declared in the header file '`PBS_ifl.h`'. Users request service of a batch server by calling the appropriate library routine and passing it the required parameters. The parameters correspond to the options and operands on the commands. The user must ensure that the parameters are in the correct syntax. Each function will return zero upon success and a nonzero error code on failure. These error codes are available in the header file '`PBS_error.h`'. The library routine will accept the parameters and build the corresponding batch request. This request is then passed to the server communication routine. (The PBS API is fully documented in the PBS External Reference Specification.)

17.3 Installing PBS

PBS is able to support a wide range of configurations. It may be installed and used to control jobs on a single system or to load balance jobs on a number of systems. It may be used to allocate nodes of a cluster or parallel system to both serial and parallel jobs. It can also deal with a mix of these situations. However, given the topic of this book, we focus on the recommended configuration for clusters. The PBS Administrator Guide explains other configurations.

When PBS is installed on a cluster, a MOM daemon must be on each execution host, and the Server and Scheduler should be installed on one of the systems or on a front-end system.

For Linux clusters, PBS is packaged in the popular *RPM* format (Red Hat's Package Manager). (See the PBS Administrator Guide for installation instructions on other systems.) PBS RPM packages are provided as a single tar file containing

- the PBS Quick Start Guide in both Postscript and PDF form (PBS Pro only),
- the PBS Administrator Guide in both Postscript and PDF form,

- the PBS User Guide in both Postscript and PDF form (PBS Pro only),
- multiple RPM packages for different components of PBS (see below),
- a full set of Unix-style manual pages, and
- supporting text files: software license, README, release notes, and the like.

When the PBS tar file is extracted, a subtree of directories is created in which all these files are created. The name of the top-level directory of this subtree will reflect the release number and patch level of the version of PBS being installed. For example, the directory for PBS Pro 5.3 will be named 'PBSPro_5_3_0'.

To install PBS Pro, change to the newly created directory, and run the installation program:

```
cd PBSPro_5_3_0
./INSTALL
```

The installation program will prompt you for the names of directories for the different parts of PBS and the type of installation. A "full" installation will install all parts of PBS on the computer (including the PBS daemons/services); the "server-only" is intended for the control node of the cluster; the "execution host only" option is intended for compute-nodes of the cluster. Next, you will be prompted for your software license key(s). (See the "Acquiring PBS" section above if you do not already have your software license key.)

For OpenPBS, there are multiple RPMs corresponding to the different installation possibilities: full installation, execution host only, or client commands only. Select the correct RPM for your installation; then install it manually:

```
cd pbspro_v5.3
rpm -i RPMNAME...
```

Note that in OpenPBS, the RPMs will install into predetermined locations under '/usr/pbs' and '/usr/spool/PBS'.

17.4 Configuring PBS

Now that PBS has been installed, the Server and MOMs can be configured and the scheduling policy selected. Note that further configuration of PBS may not be required since PBS Pro comes preconfigured, and the default configuration may completely meet your needs. However, you are advised to read this section to determine whether the defaults are indeed complete for you or whether any of the optional settings may apply.

17.4.1 Network Addresses and PBS

PBS makes use of fully qualified host names for identifying the jobs and their location. A PBS installation is known by the host name on which the Server is running. The name used by the daemons or used to authenticate messages is the canonical host name. This name is taken from the primary name field, `h_name`, in the structure returned by the library call `gethostbyaddr()`. According to the IETF RFCs, this name must be fully qualified and consistent for any IP address assigned to that host.

17.4.2 The Qmgr Command

The PBS manager command, `qmgr`, provides a command-line administrator interface. The command reads directives from standard input. The syntax of each directive is checked and the appropriate request sent to the Server(s). A `qmgr` directive takes one of the following forms:

```
command server [names] [attr OP value[,...]]
command queue  [names] [attr OP value[,...]]
command node   [names] [attr OP value[,...]]
```

where `command` is the command to perform on an object. The `qmgr` commands are listed in Table 17.4.

Command	Explanation
active	Set the active objects.
create	Create a new object, applies to queues and nodes.
delete	Destroy an existing object (queues or nodes).
set	Define or alter attribute values of the object.
unset	Clear the value of the attributes of the object.
list	List the current attributes and values of the object.
print	Print all the queue and server attributes.

Table 17.4: `qmgr` commands.

The `list` or `print` subcommands of `qmgr` can be executed by the general user. Creating or deleting a queue requires PBS Manager privilege. Setting or unsetting `server` or `queue` attributes requires PBS Operator or Manager privilege.

Here are several examples that illustrate using the **qmgr** command. These and other **qmgr** commands are fully explained below, along with the specific tasks they accomplish.

```
% qmgr
Qmgr: create node mars np=2,ntype=cluster
Qmgr: create node venus properties="inner,moonless"
Qmgr: set node mars properties = inner
Qmgr: set node mars properties += haslife
Qmgr: delete node mars
Qmgr: d n venus
```

Commands can be abbreviated to their minimum unambiguous form (as shown in the last line in the example above). A command is terminated by a new line character or a semicolon. Multiple commands may be entered on a single line. A command may extend across lines by marking the new line character with a backslash. Comments begin with a hash sign ("#") and continue to the end of the line. Comments and blank lines are ignored by **qmgr**. See the **qmgr** section of the PBS Administrator Guide for detailed usage and syntax description.

17.4.3 Nodes

Where jobs will be run is determined by an interaction between the Scheduler and the Server. This interaction is affected by the contents of the PBS '`nodes`' file and the system configuration onto which you are deploying PBS. Without this list of nodes, the Server will not establish a communication stream with the MOM(s), and MOM will be unable to report information about running jobs or to notify the Server when jobs complete. In a cluster configuration, distributing jobs across the various hosts is a matter of the Scheduler determining on which host to place a selected job.

Regardless of the type of execution nodes, each node must be defined to the Server in the PBS nodes file, (the default location of which is '`/usr/spool/PBS/server_priv/nodes`'). This is a simple text file with the specification of a single node per line in the file. The format of each line in the file is

```
node_name[:ts] [attributes]
```

The node name is the network name of the node (host name), it does not have to be fully qualified (in fact, it is best kept as short as possible). The optional ":ts" appended to the name indicates that the node is a timeshared node (i.e. a nodes on which multiple jobs may be run if the required resources are available).

Nodes can have attributes associated with them. Attributes come in three types: properties, `name=value` pairs, and `name.resource=value` pairs. Zero or more properties may be specified. The property is nothing more than a string of alphanumeric characters (first character must be alphabetic) without meaning to PBS. Properties are used to group classes of nodes for allocation to a series of jobs.

Any legal node `name=value` pair may be specified in the node file in the same format as on a `qsub` directive: `attribute.resource=value`. Consider the following example:

```
NodeA resource_available.ncpus=3 max_running=1
```

The expression `np=N` may be used as shorthand for the expression

```
resources_available.ncpus=N
```

which can be added to declare the number of virtual processors (VPs) on the node. This syntax specifies a numeric string, for example, `np=4`. This expression will allow the node to be allocated up to N times to one job or more than one job. If `np=N` is not specified for a cluster node, it is assumed to have one VP.

You may edit the nodes list in one of two ways. If the server is not running, you may directly edit the nodes file with a text editor. If the server is running, you should use `qmgr` to edit the list of nodes.

Each item on the line must be separated by white space. The items may be listed in any order except that the host name must always be first. Comment lines may be included if the first nonwhite space character is the hash sign ("#").

The following is an example of a possible nodes file for a cluster called "planets":

```
# The first set of nodes are cluster nodes.
# Note that the properties are provided to
# logically group certain nodes together.
# The last node is a timeshared node.
#
mercury    inner moonless
venus      inner moonless np=1
earth      inner np=1
mars       inner np=2
jupiter    outer np=18
saturn     outer np=16
```

```
uranus      outer np=14
neptune     outer np=12
pluto:ts
```

17.4.4 Creating or Adding Nodes

After pbs_server is started, the node list may be entered or altered via the qmgr command:

```
create node node_name [attribute=value]
```

where the attributes and their associated possible values are shown in Table 17.5.

Attribute	Value
state	free, down, offline
properties	any alphanumeric string
ntype	cluster, time-shared
resources_available.ncpus (np)	number of virtual processors > 0
resources_available	list of resources available on node
resources_assigned	list of resources in use on node
max_running	maximum number of running jobs
max_user_run	maximum number of running jobs per user
max_group_run	maximum number of running jobs per group
queue	queue name (if any) associated with node
reservations	list of reservations pending on the node
comment	general comment

Table 17.5: PBS node attributes.

Below are several examples of setting node attributes via qmgr:

```
% qmgr
Qmgr: create node mars np=2,ntype=cluster
Qmgr: create node venus properties="inner,moonless"
```

Once a node has been created, its attributes and/or properties can be modified by using the following qmgr syntax:

```
set node node_name [attribute[+|-]=value]
```

where attributes are the same as for create, for example,

```
% qmgr
Qmgr: set node mars properties=inner
Qmgr: set node mars properties+=haslife
```

Nodes can be deleted via `qmgr` as well, using the `delete node` syntax, as the following example shows:

```
% qmgr
Qmgr: delete node mars
Qmgr: delete node pluto
```

Note that the `busy` state is set by the execution daemon, `pbs_mom`, when a load-average threshold is reached on the node. See `max_load` in MOM's config file. The `job-exclusive` and `job-sharing` states are set when jobs are running on the node.

17.4.5 Default Configuration

Server management consist of configuring the Server and establishing queues and their attributes. The default configuration, shown below, sets the minimum server settings and some recommended settings for a typical PBS cluster.

```
% qmgr
Qmgr: print server
# Create queues and set their attributes
#
# Create and define queue workq
#
create queue workq
set queue workq queue_type = Execution
set queue workq enabled = True
set queue workq started = True
#
# Set Server attributes
#
set server scheduling = True
set server default_queue = workq
set server log_events = 511
set server mail_from = adm
set server query_other_jobs = True
set server scheduler_iteration = 600
```

17.4.6 Configuring MOM

The execution server daemons, MOMs, require much less configuration than does the Server. The installation process creates a basic MOM configuration file that contains the minimum entries necessary in order to run PBS jobs. This section describes the MOM configuration file and explains all the options available to customize the PBS installation to your site.

The behavior of MOM is controlled via a configuration file that is read upon daemon initialization (startup) and upon reinitialization (when `pbs_mom` receives a SIGHUP signal). The configuration file provides several types of runtime information to MOM: access control, static resource names and values, external resources provided by a program to be run on request via a shell escape, and values to pass to internal functions at initialization (and reinitialization). Each configuration entry is on a single line, with the component parts separated by white space. If the line starts with a hash sign ("#"), the line is considered to be a comment and is ignored.

A minimal MOM configuration file should contain the following:

```
$logevent 0x1ff
$clienthost server-hostname
```

The first entry, `$logevent`, specifies the level of message logging this daemon should perform. The second entry, `$clienthost`, identifies a host that is permitted to connect to this MOM. You should set the *server-hostname* variable to the name of the host on which you will be running the PBS Server (`pbs_server`). Advanced MOM configuration options are described in the PBS Administrator Guide.

17.4.7 Scheduler Configuration

Now that the Server and MOMs have been configured, we turn our attention to the PBS Scheduler. As mentioned previously, the Scheduler is responsible for implementing the local site policy regarding which jobs are run and on what resources. This section discusses the recommended configuration for a typical cluster. The full list of tunable Scheduler parameters and detailed explanation of each is provided in the PBS Administrator Guide.

The PBS Pro Scheduler provides a wide range of scheduling policies. It provides the ability to sort the jobs in dozens of different ways, including FIFO order. It also can sort on user and group priority. The queues are sorted by queue priority to determine the order in which they are to be considered. As distributed, the Scheduler is configured with the defaults shown in Table 17.6.

Once the Server and Scheduler are configured and running, job scheduling can be initiated by setting the Server attribute scheduling to a value of true:

```
# qmgr -c "set server scheduling=true"
```

Option	Default Value
`round_robin`	`False`
`by_queue`	`True`
`strict_fifo`	`False`
`load_balancing`	`False`
`load_balancing_rr`	`False`
`fair_share`	`False`
`help_starving_jobs`	`True`
`backfill`	`True`
`backfill_prime`	`False`
`sort_queues`	`True`
`sort_by`	`shortest_job_first`
`smp_cluster_dist`	`pack`
`preemptive_sched`	`True`

Table 17.6: Default scheduling policy parameters.

The value of scheduling is retained across Server terminations or starts. After the Server is configured, it may be placed into service.

17.5 Managing PBS

This section is intended for the PBS administrator: it discusses several important aspects of managing PBS on a day-to-day basis.

During the installation of PBS Pro, the file '`/etc/pbs.conf`' was created. This configuration file controls which daemons are to be running on the local system. Each node in a cluster should have its own '`/etc/pbs.conf`' file.

17.5.1 Starting PBS Daemons

The daemon processes (`pbs_server`, `pbs_sched`, and `pbs_mom`) must run with the real and effective `uid` of root. Typically, the daemons are started automatically by the system upon reboot. The boot-time start/stop script for PBS is '`/etc/init.d/pbs`'. This script reads the '`/etc/pbs.conf`' file to determine which daemons should be started.

The startup script can also be run by hand to get status on the PBS daemons, and to start/stop all the PBS daemons on a given host. The command line syntax for the startup script is

```
/etc/init.d/pbs [ status | stop | start ]
```

Alternatively, you can start the individual PBS daemons manually, as discussed in the following sections. Furthermore, you may wish to change the options specified to various daemons, as discussed below.

17.5.2 Monitoring PBS

The node monitoring GUI for PBS is `xpbsmon`. It is used for displaying graphically information about execution hosts in a PBS environment. Its view of a PBS environment consists of a list of sites where each site runs one or more Servers and each Server runs jobs on one or more execution hosts (nodes).

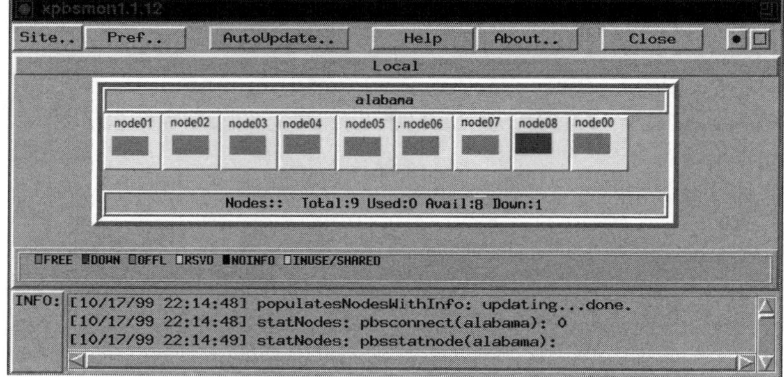

The system administrator needs to define the site's information in a global X resources file, '`PBS_LIB/xpbsmon/xpbsmonrc`', which is read by the GUI if a personal '`.xpbsmonrc`' file is missing. A default '`xpbsmonrc`' file is created during installation defining (under `*sitesInfo` resource) a default site name, the list of Servers that run on the site, the set of nodes (or execution hosts) where jobs on a particular Server run, and the list of queries that are communicated to each node's `pbs_mom`. If node queries have been specified, the host where '`xpbsmon`' is running must have been given explicit permission by the `pbs_mom` daemon to post queries to it; this is done by including a `$restricted` entry in the MOM's config file.

17.5.3 Tracking PBS Jobs

Periodically you (or the user) will want track the status of a job. Or perhaps you want to view all the log file entries for a given job. Several tools allow you to track a job's progress, as Table 17.7 shows. While the job is running, the '`qstat`' command should be used to track the status of a job. However, after the job has completed, then 'tracejob' should be used.

Command	Explanation
qstat	Shows status of jobs, queues, and servers
xpbs	Can alert user when one or more job completes
tracejob	Collates and sorts PBS log entries for specified job

Table 17.7: Job-tracking commands.

17.5.4 PBS Accounting Logs

The PBS Server daemon maintains an accounting log. The log name defaults to '/usr/spool/PBS/server_priv/accounting/yyyymmdd' where yyyymmdd is the date. The file will be closed and a new one opened every day on the first event (write to the file) after midnight.

The accounting log files may be placed elsewhere by specifying the -A option on the pbs_server command line. The option argument is the full (absolute) path name of the file to be used. If a null string is given, for example

```
# pbs_server -A ""
```

then the accounting log will not be opened, and no accounting records will be recorded.

The accounting file is changed according to the same rules as the log files. With either the default file or a file named with the -A option, the Server will close the accounting log and reopen it upon the receipt of a SIGHUP signal. This strategy allows you to rename the old log and start recording anew on an empty file. For example, if the current date is December 1, the Server will be writing in the file '20011201'. The following actions will cause the current accounting file to be renamed 'dec1' and the Server to close the file and starting writing a new '20011201'.

```
# mv 20011201 dec1
# kill -HUP (pbs_server's PID)
```

17.5.5 PBS Accounting Report

The PBS administrator can use the 'pbs-report' command to generate a wide range of system, user, and job usage reports (including statistical analysis of jobs, cluster monitoring reports, etc). The program extracts data from the above-described PBS accounting logs, and performs any necessary calculations to produce the requested report. The PBS Administrator Guide includes detailed examples of the reports this command can produce.

17.6 Troubleshooting

The following is a list of common problems and recommended solutions. Additional information is always available on the PBS Web sites.

17.6.1 Clients Unable to Contact Server

If a client command (such as `qstat` or `qmgr`) is unable to connect to a Server there are several possible errors to check. If the error return is 15034, *No server to connect to*, check (1) that there is indeed a Server running and (2) that the default Server information is set correctly. The client commands will attempt to connect to the Server specified on the command line if given or, if not given, the Server specified in the default server file, '`/usr/spool/PBS/default_server`'.

If the error return is 15007, *No permission*, check for (2) as above. Also check that the executable `pbs_iff` is located in the search path for the client and that it is `setuid` root. Additionally, try running `pbs_iff` by typing

```
pbs_iff server_host 15001
```

where `server_host` is the name of the host on which the Server is running and 15001 is the port to which the Server is listening (if started with a different port number, use that number instead of 15001). The executable `pbs_iff` should print out a string of garbage characters and exit with a status of 0. The garbage is the encrypted credential that would be used by the command to authenticate the client to the Server. If `pbs_iff` fails to print the garbage and/or exits with a nonzero status, either the Server is not running or it was installed with a different encryption system from that used for `pbs_iff`.

17.6.2 Nodes Down

The PBS Server determines the state of nodes (up or down), by communicating with MOM on the node. The state of nodes may be listed by two commands: `qmgr` and `pbsnodes`.

```
% qmgr
Qmgr: list node @active

% pbsnodes -a
Node jupiter
        state = down, state-unknown
        properties = sparc, mine
        ntype = cluster
```

A node in PBS may be marked `down` in one of two substates. For example, the state above of node "jupiter" shows that the Server has not had contact with MOM on that since the Server came up. Check to see whether a MOM is running on the node. If there is a MOM and if the MOM was just started, the Server may have attempted to poll her before she was up. The Server should see her during the next polling cycle in ten minutes. If the node is still marked `down, state-unknown` after ten minutes, either the node name specified in the Server's node file does not map to the real network hostname or there is a network problem between the Server's host and the node.

If the node is listed as

```
% pbsnodes -a
Node jupiter
        state = down
        properties = sparc, mine
        ntype = cluster
```

then the Server has been able to communicate with MOM on the node in the past, but she has not responded recently. The Server will send a `ping` PBS message to every free node each ping cycle (10 minutes). If a node does not acknowledge the ping before the next cycle, the Server will mark the node `down`.

17.6.3 Nondelivery of Output

If the output of a job cannot be delivered to the user, it is saved in a special directory '`/usr/spool/PBS/undelivered`' and mail is sent to the user. The typical causes of nondelivery are the following:

- The destination host is not trusted and the user does not have a .rhost file.

- An improper path was specified.
- A directory in the specified destination path is not writable.
- The user's `.cshrc` on the destination host generates output when executed.

The '`/usr/spool/PBS/spool`' directory on the execution host does not have the correct permissions. This directory must have mode 1777 (`drwxrwxrwxt`).

17.6.4 Job Cannot Be Executed

If a user receives a mail message containing a job identifier and the line "Job cannot be executed," the job was aborted by MOM when she tried to place it into execution. The complete reason can be found in one of two places: MOM's log file or the standard error file of the user's job.

If the second line of the message is "See Administrator for help," then MOM aborted the job before the job's files were set up. The reason will be noted in MOM's log. Typical reasons are a bad user/group account or a system error.

If the second line of the message is "See job standard error file," then MOM had already created the job's file, and additional messages were written to standard error.

18 Scyld Beowulf

Walt Ligon and Dan Stanzione

The first Beowulf developed at NASA Goddard Space Flight Center [107] was billed as a "Giga-ops workstation." The first and most important part being the performance (giga-ops) but the second part being a workstation. In the minds of the creators, a Beowulf was to be a single computer used to solve large problems quickly. The implementation, of course, was quite different. Each node in a Beowulf was, in reality, a distinct computer system with a distinct copy of the operating system running independently of the other nodes. The Beowulf architecture supports the notion of a single computer in that there was one node that was connected to the external network, there was often a network file system to provide a common storage area, and there was software for running programs across the nodes. This software, typically PVM [43] or an implementation of MPI [48], creates a virtual parallel computer that allows the programmer to create and manage processes on the various nodes. This software is not, however integrated with the operating system, it does little or nothing to assist in system configuration and management, and is not well suited to managing processing resources on a system-wide basis. This chapter describes Scyld, a system designed to provide a system-wide view of a Beowulf cluster.

18.1 Introduction

Early on, the ideal was to have a single system image: cooperation between the nodes of a Beowulf at the operating system level that not only eases programming across the nodes, but all aspects of interacting with the machine, including programming, configuration, and management tasks. The first attempts at this were to develop a global process ID space, so that processes running anywhere on the Beowulf could be uniquely identified, and so that the node the process executes on can be determined. This mechanism was implemented for the Linux kernel but proved to be of limited value. A more complete implementation later emerged that extended the process ID space of the master node of the machine, including all aspects of process control and management. The `bproc` process management system included fast creation and migration of processes across nodes, maintained information on remote processes for local reporting, included signal delivery services, and continued the abstraction of the single image process space to processes subsequently created on the remote nodes. Later versions included the ability to control access rights for creating processes on remote nodes.

With bproc process management in place, the next logical step is stripping the nodes down to a bare minimum of processes and services, and letting the master

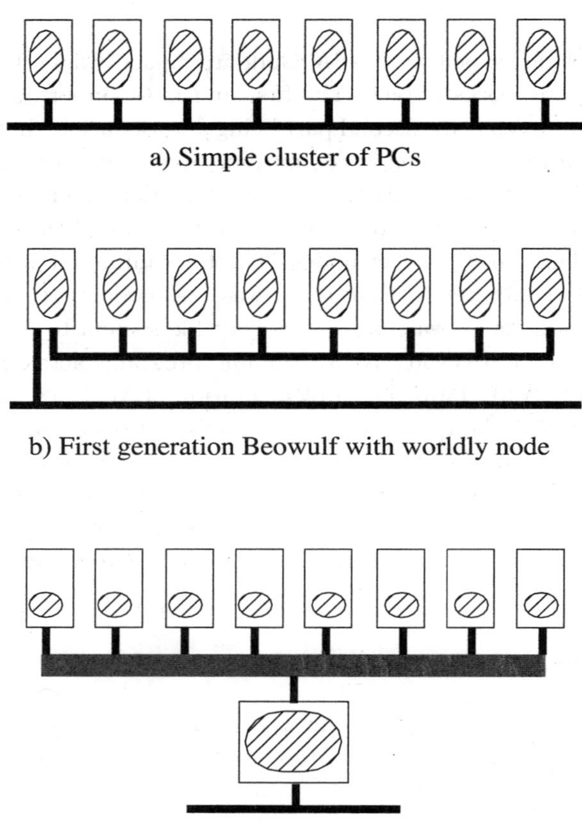

Figure 18.1: Evolution of Beowulf System Image.

node start and manage all other processes using bproc. This quickly reduces the number of actual processes run directly on each compute node to a bproc daemon and a few other key processes. Once this runtime image is reduced, the next and final step is to move the copy of the runtime image off of the node completely so that each node boots from the master. The fact that the runtime image is very small makes this feasible for even a fairly large number of nodes. Finally, the resulting system provides a single system image that allows easy management of the configuration (it is all stored on the master node and loaded to the compute nodes at boot time), of the running system (almost everything is visible from the master node) and programming (uses the same programming model as the original Beowulf).

The resulting single system image approach has been developed and marketed by Scyld Computing, Inc. as Scyld Beowulf. Scyld Beowulf is a complete Linux distribution based on RedHat Linux with modified installation scripts, a Scyld-enabled kernel, and the rest of the tools needed to implement the system. The Scyld CD is booted to install the Master node. Installation scripts configure the private network and set up the services to boot the nodes. Once installed, the Master node can make a CD or floppy that can boot the nodes, or they can boot using PXE boot. Nodes boot a minimal kernel, connect to the server, and then re-boot from the server. Facilities are provided to install a boot area on the local hard disk of each node so that subsequent boots do not require the CD or a floppy. The boot kernel is used only to start the system and thus does not need to be changed even in the event that the desired runtime kernel configuration is changed. The node kernel is updated on the server, the nodes are rebooted, and are ready to go. Utilities are provided to manage the nodes, determine their status, start and monitor processes, and even control access rights to the nodes.

18.1.1 Process Management with Bproc

The heart of Scyld Beowulf is the bproc process management facility. On the surface, bproc is just another facility for starting remote processes such as `rsh` or `ssh`. In reality, bproc is a sophisiticated tool for migrating processes to remote nodes, while maintaining a centralized locus of control. The principle function in bproc is `bproc_move()` which migrates a process from the master to a remote node. This function is built upon the VMADump facility, which is a library for copying and restoring the complete virtual address space of a process. Essentially, VMADump copies the virtual address space on the master node, the copy is sent to the remote node, a new process is started there and then VMADump restores the address space in this new process. The original process does not go away, but becomes a "ghost process." This ghost process stands in on the master node as a placeholder of sorts for the remote process. It is just like a regular process, except that it has no memory space and no open files. In implementation, ghost processes behave like Linux kernel threads, they can sleep or run as needed, they can catch signals (including SIGKILL) and forward them to the running process. They are different than regular threads in that they inherit a number of process statistics

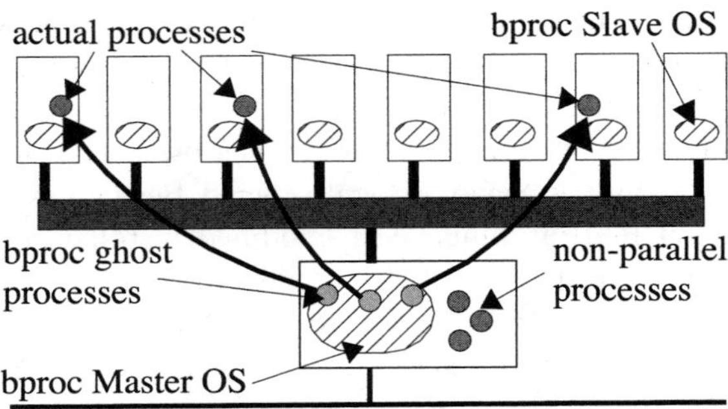

Figure 18.2: Migration of processes using bproc.

like CPU time used from the remote process. For the user on the master node, the ghost process *is* the remote process.

18.1.2 Node Management with Beoboot

The key to managing nodes with Scyld Beowulf lies in the fact that the nodes have no permanent state other than a simple boot loader. All of the node configuration is maintained on the master node and downloaded to the compute nodes when they boot with beoboot. The beoboot utilities, along with the beoserv daemon which runs on the master node, allow the compute node configuration to be tuned as needed. The Scyld Beowulf software allows the kernel to be configured, startup scripts to be adjusted, and very importantly, shared libraries to be managed. Since all processes that are run on the compute nodes of a Scyld Beowulf machine are transferred from the master node, it is important that any libraries used by the executables are either statically linked or present on the compute node. Since this can be a rather extreme requirement, bproc will transfer any shared library linked to a migrated process along with the process itself, if the shared library is not installed on the target compute node. This solves a potential problem with running applications, but may not be as efficient as it could be. Thus, the beoboot system allows the compute nodes to be configured with shared libraries that are highly likely to be used. This increases the size of the boot image, and hence the boot time, but reduces the size of the typical process image and the time to start an application.

18.2 Using Scyld Beowulf

To the typical user of a Scyld Beowulf system, there is little difference between a Scyld and a non-Scyld system. Programs are written with MPI or PVM libraries, and executed interactively or submitted using PBS or some other scheduler. There are small details that may be different, such as how one selects a set of nodes to execute a program or, or how one views a process running on a node. For the most part, these are easier to do. For a system administrator, however, Scyld Beowulf offers a number of features that greatly simplify the configuration and management of a cluster, and in particular, a large cluster.

The ability to boot a machine over a network connection has been available for a long time, and many cluster tool-kits offer mechanisms to simplify cluster installation based on mechanisms such as bootp, dhcp, and similar protocols. Scyld Beowulf also offers a simplified installation procedure for nodes in the form of a boot image that can be installed on a CD or floppy disk. Unlike other systems however, Scyld extends this concept to simplify configuration and management not just at installation time, but every time the cluster boots.

Booting a compute node in a Scyld Beowulf system starts when the node first powers up. A fully installed node will have a boot image installed on the default boot device. This image is responsible for bringing up a minimal running kernel including network services through which the node can broadcast its readiness to boot to the `beoserv` daemon running on the master node. This boot image is extremely generic, it is used only during this first phase of booting, thus it rarely needs to be changed, even if the clusters compute nodes are completely reconfigured. In fact, this image only need be updated if the Scyld beoboot system requires an update, which normally wouldn't occur even if the Scyld software was updated. Only in fairly extreme circumstances requiring extensive changes to the beoboot system would the boot loader be changed. This is a critical point, because updating an on-disk boot loader can be a cumbersome task, though even in the event this is required, the Scyld beoboot system can usually install on-disk boot loaders automatically onto the disk from the master node, making the process much simpler than even a per-node network install.

Once the phase 1 boot loader has contacted the beoserv daemon on the master node, the beoserv daemon sends boot instructions to the node. If the node has been booted before and has a local disk partition with a kernel installed, the daemon can simply instruct the node to boot from the local image. In many cases the node might not have a local boot image. This might be because a decision has been made not to use the local disk to hold the OS. Or it might be that we want to boot a new configuration that the node does not have installed. This could be a kernel upgrade, a distribution upgrade, or a library upgrade. Whatever the reason, the new boot image is transferred over the network to the booting node, where it can either be loaded into a RAM disk or it can be loaded into an available disk partition on the local disk so that future boots can be performed from local disk. Whatever the source, when the beoserv daemon instructs the node to boot a new image an interesting process takes place. A small bit of Scyld code known as "Two-Kernel Monte" loads the new kernel and tricks the old kernel into giving up control to the new image. This bypasses the normal boot process, but effectly switches kernels to the new image.

The beoserv daemon need not instruct a booting node to boot at all. The daemon maintains a database of nodes, their corresponding MAC addresses, and their current disposition in the system. A node that has never been booted before can be placed in a holding pattern to wait for the system administrator to choose to boot it. Even nodes that have been previously booted can be set to stay in the "down" state until such time as the sysadmin decides to bring it "up." In addition, when selecting a node to boot, the sysadmin can specify whether to boot a local disk image or a server image, the logical node number of the node and other configuration information.

Once a node has its boot instructions it loads and initializes its kernel the same way any other Linux computer does. The primary difference at this point lies in the system startup scripts that are part of a Scyld Beowulf image. Put simply, Scyld Beowulf boot nodes do not start any daemons or services that are not needed to bring the node to a running state other than the bproc slave daemon. The bproc slave daemon contacts the bproc master daemon running on the master and enrolls the compute node as a slave to the master. Once this is completed, the master can initiate processes on the node, and all processes, including any service daemons, are started from the master by the beoboot system.

18.2.1 Programming and Debugging

Writing programs for a Scyld Beowulf is generally very straight-forward. Most users of a distributed memory parallel computer will use a message passing library, such as MPI or PVM to write their program. Both MPICH (a popular implementation of MPI) and PVM have configurations for use with Scyld. For the most part, these packages only have to be configured to use `bpsh` rather than `rsh` or its equivalent for starting processes on the nodes. The only other issues comes in naming nodes. Under Scyld, nodes are named `.-1` (the master node), `.0`, `.1`, `.2`, and so on, whereas

Environment Variable	mpirun flag	Description
NP	-np	number of tasks to run
NO_LOCAL	-nolocal	no tasks on master
ALL_LOCAL	-all_local	all tasks on master
ALL_CPUS	-all_cpus	task on every cpu in the system
EXCLUDE	-exclude	exclude nodes
BEOWULF_JOB_MAP	-map	specify node to use for each task

Table 18.1: Environment variables used when starting MPI jobs.

under other Beowulf installation, nodes may be named almost anything. Other than this, the process of creating a socket and establishing a connection are exactly the same as on any other Linux platform. MPICH and PVM are already configured with these issues in mind, and can be used directly for parallel programming.

Running Parallel Programs

When running MPICH, there are a number of features to be aware of. The first of which is that under Scyld, most of the controls for launching a job are controlled with environment variables. Thus, one can launch and MPI job without the traditional `mpirun` command just by setting the various environment variables. For example, the environment variable `NP` specifies the number of tasks to start. The variable `NOLOCAL` specifies not to run any tasks on the master (the default is to run the first task on the master, the rest on the nodes). Table 18.1 lists the environment variables used when starting MPI jobs under Scyld.

Otherwise, writing MPI programs for Scyld is about the same as for any other Beowulf system. On the other hand, things can be a little different when writing more traditional programs or doing things more out of the ordinary within an MPI program. For example, Scyld does not load a copy of shared libraries on the disk of the nodes unless this is specifically done as part of configuration (see the section below on administration of Scyld systems). When a program is launched, all shared libraries referenced by the program and not already loaded on the target node are loaded. On the other hand, shared libraries used by a program but not referenced directly in the calling code (done via a call to `dl_open()` and the path to the library) cannot be loaded by Scyld, and will fail unless the library referenced is already installed on the nodes.

Scyld Libraries

In addition to libraries such as MPI, programmers can take advantage of APIs provided specifically for Scyld systems. Table 18.2 outlines the libraries provided by Scyld. Of these, the bproc, perf, and beostat libraries are the most likely to be of interest to some programmers.

libbeostat	Library for returning compute node status info
libbeomap	Library for finding available (unloaded) nodes
libbpsh	Library for bproc shell-like functions
libbproc	Library for access to Bproc API
libbpslave	Library for compute nodes to receive Bproc requests
perf	Library for access to Pentium Hardware Performance Counters

Table 18.2: Scyld libraries.

The bproc libraries provide access to routines for starting new processes under bproc and for moving existing processes. The perf libraries provide access to performance counters in the Pentium hardware. beostat routines are for gathering node status info. These facilities are most likely to useful to systems programmers rather than applications programmers.

Other libraries such a mathematical codes like lapack or IO packages such as HDF are pretty much independent of Scyld, unless they have library loading issues as described above.

Debugging

Debugging parallel programs can be a complex task. Debugging programs with Scyld Beowulf can in many cases be easier than on a standard Beowulf system because of the bproc process management. Typical debugging techniques for MPI programs involve the use of MPE to generate a log file and tools such as Jumpshot [126] to help in analyzing the data. Using these tools on Scyld Beowulf is no different than on any platform. Similarly, the use if print statements in the program code is relatively straight-forward due to the structure of most MPI implementations.

On the other hand, sometimes these tools are not as effective as we may like for debugging. Other tools such as `strace`, `ltrace`, and `gdb` are standard for debugging sequential programs, but are often difficult to use on a parallel program because the processes are not local, but are distributed among many machines. On a standard Beowulf, the approach is to run all of the processes locally, thus allowing these tools to be used, but on Scyld Beowulf, these tools can be used even if the processes are remote. As an example, `gdb` can be made to attach to a running processes, and once attached can set breakpoints examine and change memory, trace references, and a number of other useful things. On a standard Beowulf, this involves logging in to the remote node the processes is running on, and then running GDB. On Scyld Beowulf, we merely need to identify the process id and attach to it just like any other process.

Overall, debugging is not significantly different under Scyld Beowulf, but in some cases is a little easier and a little more flexible. For more details on these debugging tools see their respective documentation and Section 8.8.

File I/O

A critical issue in an program is I/O. Most programs read at least some data from a file and output results to a file. The I/O may be quite minimal, or it may be hundreds of megabytes. File I/O in any Beowulf system is an issue because there are several distinct ways file I/O can be configured, and these alternatives have very different performance depending on how you use them. There are three major options: local disks on the nodes, Network File System (NFS), or a parallel file system.

Local disks are easy to use, assuming your cluster has local disks. Each task in your program can simply open a file and read and write data from and to that file. The difficulty comes in coordinating the files before and after running your program. If all of your tasks need to read the same data, then you simply copy the file to all of your disks before the program runs. If they all need to ready different parts of a single file, then you must divide the file accordingly and copy the correct part to each node. Similarly, after running the program there are many output files that may need to be reassembled. Sometimes this is a complex enough task as to not be worth the trouble. If your program requires that one task writes a file that is subsequently read by another task, this will not work on local disks, the reading task will only see what was written on that node. If your program runs more than one task on a node, then you must be careful in naming files to prevent a conflict. There are C library routines such as `mktemp()` that make this fairly easy to do.

Another alternative is the use of NFS [109]. With NFS the disk or disks on one machine can be accessed from all of the nodes. This eliminates the need to distribute and gather files before and after execution, and allows the tasks to read and write portions of the same file simultaneously. The Master node can act as an NFS server, which works well for small clusters, or a dedicated server might be set up. This machine can act as a slave, but usually is configured as a full server just like the master, but without acting as bproc master. This prevents traffic related to NFS from bogging down bproc traffic to and from the master. The down side of NFS is performance. The NFS server becomes a bottleneck. Experience has shown that one a machine gets to be the side of 100 nodes or more, the potential for severe performance problems exists. Even for much smaller clusters, if there is a large amount of data read or written during the execution of a job, NFS can become the limiting factor to performance. In other words the processors have to wait on the I/O. Other issues of concern include caching and other matters related to semantics as implemented by NFS. In general NFS was not designed to act as a parallel file system, thus in many cases it does not behave as one would expect.

The last option for file I/O is the use of a parallel file system. Parallel file systems allow program tasks to interact with a shared file just like NFS, but they do it by distributing the data among many servers, and managing the I/O throughput across the network so as the reduce or eliminate the effect of bottlenecks. An example of a parallel file system is PVFS [22], detailed in Chapter 19. Not only do parallel file systems provide high performance access to shared files, they also tend to offer interfaces better suited to parallel processing. As previously mentioned, there are issues of caching and other semantics that should make a parallel file system better suited to parallel computing. The MPI specification includes a parallel I/O standard called MPI-IO as detailed in Chapter 9. As discussed in chapter 19, one implementation of MPI-IO known as ROMIO [115] works with PVFS and MPICH implementation of MPI.

On the down side, some parallel file systems are so tuned for high performance use by parallel programs that they are not particularly well suited to common every day file system use the NFS is. In the end, it is usually best to provide all three forms of storage and let each application make use of the facilities as best it can. User's home file systems and small config files work well in NFS, large data files work well in parallel file systems, and local disks are still useful for certain types of logging and in other applications.

18.3 Administration

One of the primary advantages to the single system image approach is simple system administration. Most administrative work, from simple jobs like adding users to more complex tasks like adding network drivers or kernel modules, can be done simply by manipulating the image, rather than manually configuring each node. Experience has shown that administration of traditional Beowulf systems can be as labor intensive as managing a comparable number of workstations, with as much one

/etc/Beowulf	Directory with Scyld Beowulf configuration files
/etc/Beowulf/config	Main configuration file
/etc/Beowulf/fdisk	Default disk partitioning for nodes
/etc/Beowulf/fdisk.1	Disk passioning for node 1
/etc/Beowulf/fstab	Default fstab for nodes
/etc/Beowulf/fstab.1	Fstab for node 1
/var/Beowulf	Node boot images
/var/log/Beowulf	Node logging
/usr/lib/Beowulf	Scripts and programs

Table 18.3: Common configuration files.

full time administrator required per 128 nodes. While nothing in the Scyld approach makes maintaining the cluster hardware any less labor intensive, managing the OS is substantially simpler. In earlier chapters of this book, such as Chapters 5, 6, and 13, the complexities of managing traditional clusters have been discussed in detail. This section contrasts with that the Scyld approach to some common administrative tasks to provide some insight into the process of administering Scyld clusters versus the more traditional approach.

Most of the administration tasks that will need to be done can be performed using Scyld's `beosetup` program, which provides a GUI interface for performing all common configuation tasks. The system can also be configured and administered using command line programs and by modifying relevant configuration files using a text editor. Table 18.3 lists the major configuration files. The sections below describe common administration tasks, including the configuration files and tools related. Sysadmins new to Scyld should probably try to use `beosetup` rather than using a manual approach until they are familiar with a running system.

While some functions of administering the cluster use the same configuration systems as normal Linux machines (such as user accounts and groups), the Beowulf specific functions require additions to the "normal" set of Linux configuration files. Scyld encapsulates the additional configuration information into a small set of files consistent with the Linux/UNIX administrative philosophy. The '`/etc/beowulf`' directory contains information about cluster configuration and node management. Node boot images and related information are kept in '`/var/beowulf`'. Node logging information is in the directory '`/var/log/beowulf`', and scripts and programs used in booting are in '`/usr/lib/beoboot`'.

The sections below discuss how some of the normal tasks of a cluster administrator are performed using the Scyld Beowulf OS. These tasks are broadly grouped into four categories: managing nodes, system maintenance tasks, failure detection and recovery, and finally node allocation and scheduling.

18.3.1 Managing Nodes

A fairly frequent task for a Beowulf system administrator is the addition, deletion, or customization of the compute nodes. Like most tasks on a Scyld Beowulf, all of these tasks are handled from the head node.

Adding and Deleting Compute Nodes

When a new node is added to the cluster, the phase 1 boot image must be booted on this node. This is the same procedure as discussed previously in the install section, and can be done via floppy, CD, or PXE boot. When the node boots, it will make a RARP request to the head node. When the head node sees this request, it examines the MAC address of the requesting node, then examines it's configuration file, '`/etc/Beowulf/config`' to determine what to do.

If the MAC address of the node does not appear in the configuration file, the request is ignored, and the address is added to the file '`/var/Beowulf/unknown_addresses`'. If the MAC address of the requesting node does appear in the configuration file, there are two possibilities. If the address is labeled in the configuration file as "ignore", the request will simply be ignored. Otherwise, the head node will respond to the compute node's RARP request, and assign it a node number corresponding to the label or position in the configuration file. Nodes can be removed from the cluster by simply marking the corresponding line in the configuration file as "ignore".

This behavior can be modified if the `beosetup` GUI is used when nodes are being added. This GUI includes an option to auto-activate new nodes that appear as unknown addresses. This option is particularly useful when adding large numbers of new nodes to the cluster. `beosetup` also allows you to drag and drop nodes between the unknown and active lists, reorder the node list, and perform many other node setup features as mentioned in the installation section.

Compute Node Disks

One of the components in a Beowulf cluster that is most susceptible to failure is the disk drives. Due to the short product life cycles of commodity hard drives, it is only a matter of time before a Beowulf cluster will be using several different types and sizes of disk drives in the compute nodes. The single system image concept provided by Scyld and the Bproc system make it possible to deal with frequent rebuilds of node file systems. However, it is important that the system image have flexibility in dealing with different disk drives on which the image is to be stored.

The Scyld OS deals with this issue by keeping partition tables for each type of disk in the cluster in the '`/etc/Beowulf`' directory on the head node. These partition tables are indexed by either the geometry and device number of the disk to which they apply. This allows the head node to automatically determine the appropriate partitioning for a given disk drive at boot time. To add a new type of disk drive to a cluster, the administrator can either manually add the new configuration, or take it from a running node. When a new type of disk is installed on a node, the node can initially be booted using a RAM disk. The node's new disk can be partitioned using the standard `fdisk` command via `bpsh`, then this partition table can be read in by the head node in the appropriate format via the `beofdisk` command. `beofdisk` can also be used to propagate this partition table to every other node in the cluster with the same hardware, eliminating the need to manually partition each disk.

Compute Node File systems

The default setting in Scyld Beowulf is for each node to use a RAM disk for it's root file system, and to use NFS to mount the '`/home`' file system from the head. However, it is a simple process for the administrator to customize compute nodes to make use of local disks, or to access any number of network or parallel file systems, either from the head or another accessible server.

In traditional Linux systems, the file systems a node mounts is determined by the '`/etc/fstab`' file. In the Scyld OS, compute node '`fstab`' files are kept in the '`/etc/Beowulf`' directory. A single file may be used to control all nodes, or, if there are differences in node configurations, fstab files may be created for each node. Ideally, a single fstab would suffice for an entire cluster (and frequently does), but sometimes certain nodes may have additional disks to provide additional swap or temporary space, or to serve as I/O servers for a parallel file system. The list of network file systems available to nodes may change to allow only certain nodes to have access to sensitive data.

The syntax for the '`fstab`' files is identical to normal Linux syntax, and allows the use of RAM disks, local disks, NFS file systems, or parallel file systems such as PVFS as described in Chapter 19.

The Scyld OS also provides a number of options for when node file systems should be rebuilt. To maintain a single system image, some users opt to have all local file systems on a node rebuilt each time a node is booted. This option is particularly useful when adding new nodes to the cluster. Some choose to use the local file systems for permanent storage, and never wish to rebuild those images. Still others may choose for performance reasons to only rebuild node file systems when checks on the file system fail, indicating errors. Scyld supports all of these options, and the policy can be changed at any time through the `Beosetup` GUI or by editing the '`/etc/Beowulf/config`' file and sending HUP signals to the associated beoboot and bproc daemons.

Compute Node Shared Libraries

The Bproc system provided with Scyld allows jobs to be migrated quickly to the nodes by not migrating shared library code with the nodes, but rather remapping these libraries within the process after it is migrated. To achieve high performance with this technique, nodes must keep a cache of the shared libraries. Administrators can easily change the list of libraries kept cached on the nodes to achieve good performance on any application. The '`/etc/Beowulf/config`' file contains a keyword `libraries`, after which can be listed individual libraries or whole directories of libraries can be listed. All libraries listed in this line will be moved to the compute nodes when they boot.

18.3.2 System Maintenance

Another group of important tasks involves the overall maintenance of the system, such as controlling the state of the nodes, the boot image and kernel run by the nodes, and account management.

Controlling Node State

Compute nodes can be in any of a number of states, including `up, down, unavailable, boot, reboot, error`, and `pwroff`. As a node powers up, it moves from the down state to the boot state, and, if all goes well, eventually to the up state. The state of a node can also be controlled by the administrator via the `bpctl` command. This command allows the the administrator to set the state (among other things) of all the nodes, individual nodes, or ranges of nodes. `Bpctl` can be used to reboot nodes, shut them down, tag them as unavailable to users or mark them as back up.

Node Boot Images

Periodically, as updates become available or new drivers are added, the administrator may want to change either the phase 1 or phase 2 boot images that are given to the slave nodes. Both images can be recreated through the `beosetup` GUI or via the `beofdisk` command.

The phase 1 image rarely needs to be changed. It consists simply of a small RAM disk image and a minimal kernel, and is designed to fit on a floppy disk or in a 2 megabyte partition at the start of a hard drive. The RAM disk and kernel can also be generated separately for use with a PXE boot server.

The phase 2 image contains the runtime kernel, and may need to be updated more frequently. This image is created in a format suitable for download by a phase 1 image. When the image is created, the head node must be running the same version of the kernel as to be placed in the phase 2 image.

Kernel Maintenance

Periodically, administrators may wish to update kernels on their cluster to take advantage of bug fixes, new features, etc. More frequently, an administrator may wish to add a device driver or new module to the existing kernel, and propagate this change to the slaves. The kernel used in the Scyld system is not quite the standard Linux kernel, so the recommended procedure is to download source for the new kernel from Scyld. If you wish to use a kernel version that is not available from Scyld, you should have some expertise in hacking Linux kernels, and be prepared to add in a number of additional modules for beoboot, bproc, PVFS, etc.

Adding drivers to kernels is a fairly simple task in a Scyld cluster. Most drivers are added via a dynamically loadable module, so recompiling the full kernel is not necessary. In order to add a driver, you will need to compile the module twice, once with options for the kernel on the head node, and a second time with the options for the beoboot kernel on the nodes. The correct options are shown in Table 18.4.

For Uniprocessor kernel on head:	`-D__BOOT_KERNEL_SMP=0` `-D__BOOT_KERNEL_UP=1`

For Uniprocessor kernel for BeoBoot:	`-D__BOOT_KERNEL_SMP=0`
	`-D__BOOT_KERNEL_UP=1`
	`-D__module__beoboot`

Table 18.4: Parameters for building Scyld kernels.

Each compiled version will need to be installed in '/lib/modules' in the appropriate directory for each kernel (the kernel for the head has an _Scyld after the version number, the kernel for the compute nodes has an _Scyldbeoboot extension). Once the modules are created, you will need to update your Beoboot images. If the module is a critical one, such as the module for your compute node's primary network interface, you may need to update both the phase 1 and phase 2 kernel images.

If the new module is to be included in the phase 1 image, the '/etc/Beowulf/config' file must be edited to include this module in the module list and to determine how it is loaded. The bootmodule lines in the configuration file list all the modules to be included in the phase 1 image. Addition of new modules may require the deletion of some old ones if the phase 1 image must still fit on the floppy drive. If you wish the module to always be loaded, you must also add a modprobe to the config file. If you wish it to be loaded only when the corresponding hardware is detected, the system's PCI table must be edited. Finally, the new beoboot images can be created including the new kernel modules using the beoboot command.

Additional Compute Node Boot Commands

System administrators may wish to perform site specific customizations of the compute nodes when they boot, such as starting additional daemons or copying extra files to the nodes. At the end of the node boot cycle, each node runs a script called node_up. During its execution, this script looks in the directory '/etc/beowulf/init.d' and executes any scripts it finds there. This is where administrators can add any additional site-specific commands to be run. Any script run from this directory will have the additional environment variable $NODE defined, which will contain the node number of the node on which the script is being executed. This makes it possible to have the script only act on certain nodes, or act differently on each node if this is desired.

Account Maintenance

Managing user accounts on a Scyld system is just as easy as managing user accounts on a single workstation. All account management is done from the head node, using the normal linux tools, for instance the adduser script or the passwd command, or manual editing of the '/etc/password' file. Compute nodes see exactly the set of user IDs and permissions that are available on the head, and need no passwords.

This removes a number of authentication problems that can exist in traditional Beowulfs. For instance, as seen in Chapter 5, in a traditional Beowulf, user accounts must be added on every node with the same user ID, and passwords must be kept consistent on every node, or some central account management service such as NIS (Network Information Service) must be maintained and accessed via the network by all nodes. Typically, users wish to spawn tasks on compute nodes of the cluster without being prompted for a password. The solution to this problem is usually to maintain a '`hosts.equiv`' or '`.rhosts`' file on every node in the Beowulf, which contains the name or network address of every other node in the Beowulf. This file must be kept to up-to-date each time the cluster's configuration changes.

Managing groups is equally simple. Groups take on an added importance in Scyld clusters. In addition to the traditional use of managing file access, groups can be used to manage access to compute nodes. Groups are defined by the file '`/etc/group`', and can be changed by directly editing the file, or through the standard `usermod`, `groupadd` and `groupdel` commands.

More sophisticated mechanisms to prevent User and Group ID-space conflicts are being built into the newest version of the Scyld OS to allow for clusters with multiple heads, primarily to provide high availability or failover capabilities.

18.3.3 Failure Detection and Recovery

An important issue whenever working with a large number of nodes is detecting their failure and recovering. This includes systems for monitoring the nodes, and strategies for replacing a failed node.

Monitoring Cluster Status

The Bproc and Beoboot packages provide useful libraries for tracking the status of your cluster from a central location. The Scyld Beowulf OS provides a number of tools that take advantage of these libraries to allow administrators to better control their clusters, as well as the APIs for the creation of more sophisticated tools.

Among the tools provided for for cluster monitoring are the tools `beostatus` and `bpstat`, which are designed for direct user interaction, and the `beostat` tool which is more appropriate for embedding in scripts. `beostatus` provides a display of common performance metrics for each node, such as CPU, memory, and network utilization. The output display can be graphical or text based. Bpstat provides a summary of the state and permissions for each node, and can also be used in conjunction with the UNIX `ps` command to list which compute node every bproc process is running on. The beostat tool provides any of the information normally available in the '`/proc`' file system of a Linux machine for any or all of the compute nodes. The '`libbeostat`' library and the bproc kernel module provide a variety of system calls and library functions which make cluster status information easily available to a programmer. These calls can be used for making more sophisticated status reporting tools, or to import status information into load management and other tools. '`libbeostat`' has a library call to report each of the same fields as the `beostat` command line tool, ranging from node status to CPU speed and about twenty other quantities.

Web Based Monitoring

Most of the functionality provided by the `beosetup` configuration tool, the `beostatus` monitor, and the Beowulf batch queue monitor can also be accessed through the web on a Scyld Beowulf cluster. All of these functions are provided as add-ons to the standard `webmin` interface for remote system administration.

Compute Node Failure

Inevitably, nodes will eventually fail. This may be do to software failures somewhere along the boot process, such as file system errors or bad scripts added to the boot sequence, or a variety of hardware failures. In the case of software failures, the node is placed in the error state and a complete log of both the phase 1 and phase 2 boot process is stored on a per node basis in the directory '`/var/log/Beowulf`' in a file named '`node.<nodenumber>`'. This makes debugging possible without having to physically access one of the compute nodes.

In the case of a hardware failure, Scyld provides no additional support beyond simply marking the node as being in the down or error state. A system administrator would be well advised to employ one of the cluster management techniques described in Chapter 13 to debug hardware issues.

In either case, the Scyld OS continues to function in the event of a compute node failure. Processes currently running on a node that fails will be lost, and it is up to the application to provide checkpoints if recovery of the job is possible. However, the system as a whole will continue to function, and the OS will not schedule any new tasks on the node that has failed. Unfortunately, some applications and/or users may hard code node numbers into scripts that run jobs. While this practice should generally be discouraged, system administrators can compensate this by simply reordering the node list such that another node takes the place of the one that has failed. For instance, say a cluster has one spare node available for failover. If node 15 on that cluster fails, the administrator can either use the `beosetup` GUI or edit the configuration file to place the MAC address of the spare node in the 15th position on the node list. If the administrator then boots the spare node, it will come up as node 15. The users will then see the same set of nodes they always see, and service was not interrupted on any other node, though anything on the original node 15 at the time of the failure will be lost.

18.3.4 Node Allocation and Scheduling

One of the primary chores of running a large Beowulf is allocating and scheduling nodes to particular jobs or to particular users. The Scyld/bproc system provides an elegant means for providing access to nodes, and a simple set of tools for allocation and scheduling. These mechanisms can in turn be used as a basis for building more sophisticated tools.

The core of the node allocation mechanism is the Bproc permission model. Nodes are given owners, groups, and permission bits, much like the UNIX file permission system. For nodes, the "read" and "write" bits are meaningless, only the execute bit has importance. Nodes are given an owner and group user ID. The permission bits allow the administrator to define whether a node can be used by the owner, by all members of the group, or by all users. Permissions can be changed on the fly manually by the administrator, or can be set by allocation and scheduling software to restrict node access.

The Beowulf Batch Queue

Scyld Beowulf includes a simple load management system based on the UNIX `at` facility known as `bbq`, the *Beowulf Batch Queue*. The `bbq` system queues jobs submitted by users, and runs them on a first-come, first-served basis to processors deemed available by the `beomap` calls. The number of processors required for a particular job is determined from the users submitted job script. A request for this number of processors is made of `beomap`, which will return a list of processor numbers which have a load average below 0.8. The job is then issued to this list of processors.

The scheduling policy implemented in BBQ can be changed by replacing '`libbeostat`', or by just replacing the call `get_beowulf_job_map()`. *BBQ* is a functional scheduler for simple workloads, but lacks the ability to enforce limits on job time, out-of-order execution, and other features expected in a modern scheduler. If a Beowulf has a fairly complicated workload, the PBS system described in Chapter 17 has also been modified to work with Scyld Beowulf, and may provide a better option.

atd	Beowulf Batch Queue daemon
atrm	Remove jobs from batch queue
batch	Submit job to queue
bbq	Check queue status
bdate	Set the time and date on slave nodes
beoboot	Generate Beowulf boot images
beoboot-install	Install beoboot on compute node drives
beofdisk	Partition slave node disks
beoserv	Beoboot server daemon
beostatus	Interactive status tool
beostat	Display raw data from libbeostat
beowebenable	Activate web access
bpcp	Copy files to compute nodes
bpctl	Set node state and ownership
bpmaster	The bproc server daemon on the head
bpsh	Run programs on compute nodes
bpslave	Bproc client daemon on compute nodes
bpstat	Show node status information
linpack	Run linpack benchmark
mpprun	Launch a non-parallel job on compute nodes
mpirun	Launch an MPI job on compute nodes
node_down	Shutdown compute nodes cleanly
recvstats	Daemon to receive multicast status info for libbeostat
sendstats	Daemon to send multicast status info for libbeostat

Table 18.5: Scyld command line programs.

18.3.5 Scyld Command Summary

The commands listed in Table 18.5 are used to perform all of the Scyld system administration tasks. New administrators should stick to the GUI systems provided, but in some cases these commands can be very useful. Man pages are provided online with all of the details.

18.4 Features in Upcoming Releases

The Scyld Beowulf OS continues to evolve over time, and many new features are planned for upcoming releases, primarily focused on scalability and high reliability. Beowulf clusters are being built with larger and larger numbers of nodes, and are more often now used in production environments. Larger clusters often require substantially different techniques than those used to run 8, 16, or 64 node clusters, and production environments find downtime to deal with hardware failures or upgrades less acceptable.

18.4.1 Failover Head Nodes

One of the most important new features will be support for multi-headed clusters. While a current Scyld cluster can continue to function in the event of a compute node failure, the head node remains a single point of failure. In the upcoming release, a new head node can take over when the original head fails.

This is achieved by adding some extensions to the *bproc* model. *Bproc* is being extended to allow slave processes to detach from the head node that spawned them, and run independently. These tasks can then continue to run to completion on their own, or they can use the slave daemon on the nodes to contact a new master, and insert themselves into the process table of the new head node. This will allow a switch from one head to another without disrupting any ongoing jobs.

18.4.2 Scalable bproc Job Spawning

The `bproc` mechanism provides extremely rapid migration of jobs from the head node to the compute nodes. However, as the number of compute nodes grows to hundreds or even thousands, the total time to launch jobs via bproc can become substantial. Future versions of `bproc` will contain the ability to do a tree-based spawn. In this system, the head node will migrate tasks to nodes at the top of the tree, and these nodes will then migrate the tasks to additional nodes, and so on. This offloads some of the load of spawning tasks from the head, and removes a potential bottleneck. Experimental work at Scyld has shown that this approach begins to become useful as clusters grow past 256 nodes using a single head.

18.5 Conclusion

Scyld Beowulf is a packaged product that makes the installation, management, and use of Beowulf computers easier and more effective. The main tools for doing this are the bproc process management libraries and the beoboot node management tools. Together these tools create an effective single system image that allows all installation and management activities to be performed from a single master node. From the programmer's perspective, a Scyld Beowulf is pretty much the same as any Beowulf system, right down to the use of tools and libraries for parallel programming. Current development of Scyld Beowulf is exploring new ways to use its unique features to provide even better system management for clusters.

19 Parallel I/O and the Parallel Virtual File System

Walt Ligon and Rob Ross

Ever more frequently users of clusters find themselves in an interesting situation: it isn't the processors, communication network, or memory that is limiting their application; it is the storage system. This might force the users to checkpoint less frequently than they would like, might limit the resolution of output visualization data, or might prevent the use of out-of-core solutions needed for the largest of problems. What's worse, the I/O hardware in the system may indeed be adequate for the user's needs but may be being used ineffectively by one of the many software layers involved.

A lot of mystery surrounds I/O solutions in clusters today. For this reason we have rewritten this chapter in the second edition. We begin by covering what we believe are some of the most important issues in parallel I/O systems. These include parallel access patterns, parallel I/O system components and architectures, and consistency semantics. Knowing how parallel I/O systems operate and the issues involved can be useful when performance tuning an application for a particular system or choosing an I/O solution to match expected workloads. This material builds on material in many preceding chapters, including the I/O hardware discussion in Chapter 2, the local and distributed file system discussion in Chapter 3, and the network hardware discussion in Chapter 4.

Following this more general discussion, we delve into PVFS, specifically covering some of the quirks of PVFS, management and tuning, and approaches for narrowing down the source of problems that may crop up. Finally, we discuss some critical issues for parallel file systems and how PVFS2, the next-generation parallel file system being developed by the PVFS team, attempts to address these.

These are very interesting times for parallel file systems on Linux clusters. As we are writing this chapter, the Lustre, PVFS2, and GPFS groups are all bringing new parallel file systems to the Linux cluster environment. The relative success of each of these is not likely to be known for quite some time, but we can certainly hope that at least one of these projects will result in a new, high-performance parallel file system designed to operate on systems with thousands of nodes (and,we hope, more!).

19.1 Parallel I/O Systems

What do we mean by a "parallel I/O system"? At a high level three characteristics are key:

- multiple hardware I/O resources on which data will be stored,

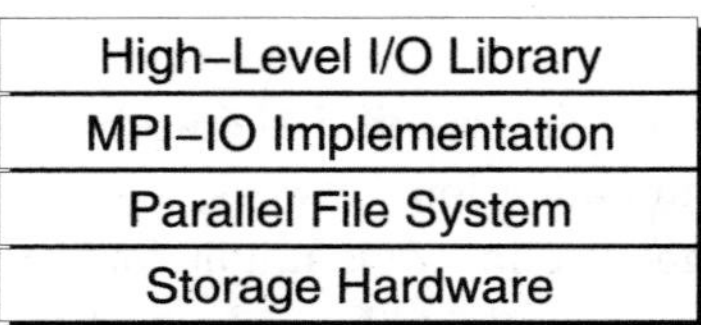

Figure 19.1: Parallel I/O System Components

- multiple connections between these I/O resources and compute resources, and
- high-performance, concurrent access to these I/O resources by numerous compute resources.

Parallel I/O systems get their performance by using multiple I/O resources that are connected to compute resources through multiple I/O paths. Multiple physical I/O devices and paths are required to ensure that the system has enough bandwidth to attain the performance desired. The hardware could consist of nodes with local disks attached via more traditional IP networks, a separate storage area network, or something else entirely; all of these are valid options for parallel I/O systems.

The third characteristic is easily as important as the first two but is considerably more difficult to pin down. Parallel I/O systems should be designed from the bottom up with the assumption that performance is a key attribute and that concurrent access to resources will be commonplace. This characteristic is heavily dependent on the software architecture; the software managing the hardware resources can make or break a parallel I/O system.

Often I/O systems that have multiple connections and hardware devices but don't cater to high-performance concurrent access are called *distributed* file systems. The software in these systems is tailored to other workloads. Chapter 3 discusses distributed file systems such as NFS.

A parallel file system is simply a component of a parallel I/O system that presents a hierarchical (file- and directory-based) view of data stored in the system. In the next section will see where this component fits into the big picture.

19.1.1 Components of a Parallel I/O Stack

A parallel I/O system includes both the hardware and a number of layers of software, as shown in Figure 19.1. While this chapter really focuses on parallel file systems and PVFS in particular, it is important to understand what other components might be involved and how these work together to provide a reasonable solution to a tricky problem.

At the lowest level is the I/O hardware, described briefly in Chapter 2. This layer comprises the disks, controllers, and interconnect across which data is moved. Obviously, this hardware determines the maximum raw bandwidth and the minimum latency of the system. The bisection bandwidth (defined in Chapter 4) of the underlying I/O transport is an important measure for determining the possible aggregate bandwidth of the resulting parallel I/O system, just as it is an important measure for the communication network as seen in Chapter 4. At the hardware level, data is usually accessed at the granularity of blocks, either physical disk blocks or logical blocks spread across multiple physical devices, such as in a RAID array.

Above the hardware is the parallel file system. The role of the parallel file system is to manage the data on the storage hardware, to present this data as a directory hierarchy, and to coordinate access to files and directories in a consistent manner. Later in this chapter we'll talk more about what "consistent manner" means, as this is an interesting topic in itself. At this layer the file system typically provides a UNIX-like interface allowing users to access contiguous regions of files. Additional low-level interfaces may also be provided by the file system for higher-performance access.

While some applications still choose to access I/O resources by using a UNIX-like interface, many parallel scientific applications instead choose to use higher-level interfaces. These higher-level interfaces allow for richer I/O description capabilities that enable application programmers to better describe to the underlying system how the application as a whole wants to access storage resources. Furthermore, these interfaces, especially high-level I/O interfaces, provide data abstractions that better match the way scientific applications view data.

Above the parallel file system layer sits the MPI-IO implementation. The MPI-IO interface [46], part of the MPI-2 interface specification, is the standard parallel I/O interface and exists on most parallel computing platforms today. The role of the MPI-IO implementation, in addition to simply providing the API, is to provide optimizations such as collective I/O that are more effectively implemented at this layer. In some sense the job of MPI-IO is to take accesses presented by the user and translate them, as best as possible, into accesses that can be performed efficiently on the underlying parallel file system. This makes the MPI-IO interface the ideal place to leverage file system-specific interfaces transparently to the user. The MPI-IO API is covered in Chapter 9.

The MPI-IO interface is useful from a performance and portability standpoint, but the interface is relatively low level (basic types stored at offsets in a file), while most scientific applications work with more structured data. For this reason many scientific applications choose to use a higher-level API written on top of MPI-IO (e.g., HDF5 [25] or Parallel netCDF [66]). This allows scientists to work with data sets in terms closer to those used in their applications, such as collections of multidimensional variables. These high-level interfaces often provide the same level of performance as using MPI-IO directly. However, one should be aware that in practice the implementation details of some of these systems do sometimes add significant overhead [96].

19.1.2 Access Patterns and Scientific Applications

Applications exhibit all sorts of different access patterns, and these patterns have a significant effect on overall I/O performance. The `cat` program, for example, accesses blocks of a file starting from beginning to end. This is the ideal pattern of access for most file systems, because many systems can identify this pattern and optimize for it, and the prefetching implemented in many I/O devices also matches with this well. This pattern is seen for a large number of applications, including video and audio streaming, copying of data files, and archiving.

Database systems use I/O resources as another level of memory. In doing so, they tend to access it in very large blocks (contiguous data regions) in an order that the I/O system cannot always predict. However, because the blocks are large and are aligned to match well with the underlying disks, this access pattern can also match well with the I/O system.

Studies tell us that the access patterns seen in scientific applications are significantly different from what we see in these other application domains. Scientific applications are in some sense worst-case scenarios for parallel I/O systems. One such study, the CHARISMA project [79], provides a great deal of insight into the patterns seen in scientific applications. We will extract some of the more important points here.

The CHARISMA project defines *sequential* access as a pattern where each subsequent access begins at a higher file offset than the point at which the previous access ended. Most of the write-only files were written sequentially by a single process. This behavior was likely because in many applications each process would write out its data to a separate file. This may have been an artifact of poor concurrent write performance on the studied platform. Read-only files were accessed sequentially as well, but regions were often skipped over by processes indicating

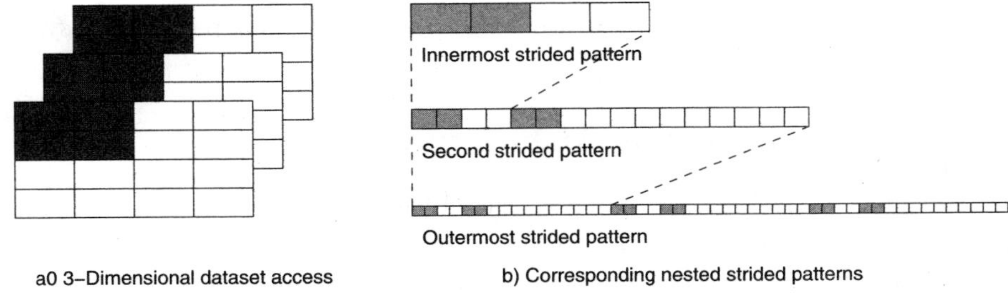

Figure 19.2: Nested-Strided Example

that multiple processes were somehow dividing up the data. About a third of the files were accessed with a single request.

Figure 19.2 shows an example of a nested-strided access, in this case utilizing three strided patterns in order to access a block of a 3D data set. The study noted that strided access patterns were very common in these applications, with both simple (single) strides and nested strides present. A nested-strided pattern is simply the application of multiple simple-strided patterns, allowing the user to build more complex descriptions of stored data. These patterns arise from applications partitioning structured data such as multidimensional arrays. More recent studies, such as an analysis of the FLASH I/O benchmark [96], support these findings, although in this particular case the strided patterns occur in memory rather than in the file (which is written sequentially) and data from all processes is always written to a single file.

What does all this mean to us? First, it indicates that application programmers really can benefit from the descriptive capabilities available in high-level interfaces. Second, it suggests that the layers *below* these high-level interfaces should be capable of operating in terms of structured data as well. As we will see in the next section, some parallel file systems fall short in this area.

Because of the differences in access patterns between various applications, I/O solutions that work well for one application may perform poorly for another. This situation encourages us to consider using multiple file systems in the same cluster to fill particular roles. For example, a very reliable distributed file system that might not handle concurrent writes well could be a very useful file system for storing home directories in a large cluster. For smaller clusters NFS might fill this role. On the other hand, a very fast parallel file system with no fault tolerance capabilities might be perfect for storing application data used at run time that is backed up elsewhere. With this in mind, we will now discuss some typical parallel file system architectures with specific examples.

19.2 Parallel File System Architectures

Numerous parallel I/O systems have been built, although few have seen wide use. If we look at these file systems we do see trends in how the systems are designed. The architecture of these systems, both hardware and software, can have a significant effect on application performance, particularly with the demanding access characteristics of scientific applications.

We discuss the two most common architectures, including the components of the systems and some of the key characteristics. These architectures serve as a starting point for discussion of specific parallel file systems. For each architecture we give three example file systems, all of which have run on Linux at one time or another, and all of which have had an impact on parallel I/O systems of today.

19.2.1 Shared Storage Architectures

File systems relying on a shared storage architecture are the most popular approach for large production systems. The reason rests at least in part on the popularity of storage area networks (SANs) and fibre channel (FC) storage. File systems using shared storage have the common feature of accessing block devices remotely, either through direct attach hardware (such as FC disks) or through intermediate I/O servers that provide a block-oriented interface to disks attached locally to the server. In either case, a key component of these systems is a locking subsystem. The locking subsystem is necessary to coordinate access to these shared resources. While we will not discuss the issue of fault tolerance with respect to the locking subsystems of the example file systems, we note that a significant amount of effort has been put forth to ensure that locks can be recovered from failed nodes. This is a complicated problem, and the cited works discuss the issues in detail.

Some file systems that use shared storage implement a "virtual block device" in order to separate the access of logical blocks of data from their physical representation on storage. This virtual block device provides a mapping from logical blocks to physical storage. A file system component builds on this to provide the directory hierarchy for the file system, just as a local file system builds on a disk or RAID volume. This approach is advantageous from a system management point of view. The virtual block device, because it abstracts away physical data location, can provide facilities for data migration and replication transparent to the upper layers of the system. This approach simplifies the implementation of the upper level components. Further, this virtual block device provides a mechanism for adding and removing hardware while the system runs. Data blocks can be migrated off a device before removal and can later be moved onto a newly installed device. This capability is very valuable in systems that must provide high availability.

The abstraction is, however, limiting in some ways as well. First, all file system accesses must be translated to block accesses before hitting this component. Because scientific applications often have noncontiguous access patterns, this approach can result in read/modify/write patterns that could have been avoided if more fine-grained accesses were allowed. Second, control over physical data locations is lost to the upper layers. While few scientific applications currently try to perform careful block placement for performance reasons, this could be an issue as groups attempt to further push the boundaries of I/O performance. Finally, this additional level of indirection adds overhead in the system, increasing the latency of operations.

A number of systems are available with this architecture. The first two example systems that we cover, Frangipani and GFS, rely on virtual block devices. The last, GPFS, uses a slightly different organization. SGI's CXFS file system, not discussed here, has a similar architecture to GFS.

Frangipani and Petal

The Frangipani and Petal systems, originally developed at Digital Equipment Corporation (DEC), together form a good example of the virtual block device approach. The Petal [65] component implements a virtual block device with replication, snapshotting, and hot swapping of devices. It presents a simple RPC-like API for atomically reading and writing blocks that higher-level components can use to build a file system. The Petal component runs on nodes that have attached storage. Instances of the Petal component communicate to manage these devices, as not all Petal instances can directly access all the devices that make up the virtual block device.

The Frangipani [118] component implements a distributed file system on top of Petal. A distributed locking component is used by Frangipani to manage consistency. Locks are multiple-reader, single-writer and are granted on a per file basis. Locks are "sticky"; clients hold onto locks until asked to release them by the locking subsystem, allowing for read and write caching at the client side. The Frangipani component runs on nodes that access the shared storage region. Instances of the

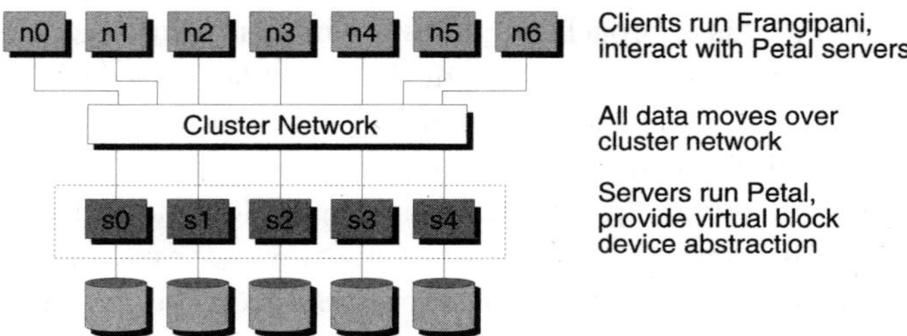

Figure 19.3: Frangipani and Petal File System Architecture

Frangipani component do not communicate with each other, only the locking component and Petal.

This architecture provides us with a good opportunity to introduce a common term in distributed file systems. A system can be considered a *serverless* distributed file system if nodes work together as peers to provide a shared storage region, as opposed to some specific server or servers providing this functionality [5]. When the term was coined back in the mid-1990s, systems weren't particularly large (the referenced paper tested on 32 nodes), and the point was really to distribute both metadata and data across multiple nodes more than to actually use every node as a storage resource.

In any case, it's easy to imagine that the Frangipani and Petal approach could be used in this "serverless" mode with Petal running on all clients, or it could be used in a system with a collection of heavy-duty servers with RAID arrays running Petal, with most nodes running only Frangipani. Without knowing more about a particular architecture, it's not clear which of these would be the right choice.

Frangipani and Petal are an early and well-documented example of this architecture. The Frangipani and Petal code is still around, although obtaining it seems difficult. At the time of writing rumor was that the code has been ported to Linux 2.4 and is floating around at one of the major hardware vendors. Perhaps it will pop up again to compete with some of the currently available systems.

GFS

The Global File System (GFS) was originally developed at Minnesota and is now developed and supported by Sistina [89, 88]. GFS is actively maintained and improved by Sistina. An older version of the source code, originally released under the GPL, is also available under the name OpenGFS. GFS also uses a virtual block

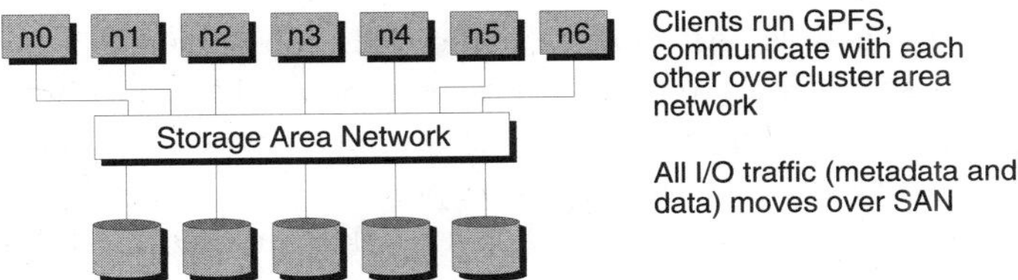
n0
n1
n2
n3
n4
n5
n6
Storage Area Network
Clients run GPFS, communicate with each other over cluster area network
All I/O traffic (metadata and data) moves over SAN

Figure 19.4: GPFS Architecture Using Storage Area Network

device architecture, in this case using LVM (Logical Volume Manager) underneath the GFS file system layer.

GFS currently uses a "Pool" driver to organize storage devices into a logical space. They are investigating the use of LVM [52], a newer system for organizing multiple physical storage devices into "volume groups" and then partitioning these into "logical volumes," which are the virtual equivalent of partitions on a disk. Just as with Petal, the Pool driver (and eventually LVM) provides capabilities for snapshotting and hot swapping of devices. The typical installation of GFS uses some number of nodes connected to shared fibre channel storage, with all nodes running both the LVM and GFS software (making it serverless). Alternatively a GNBD component can be used to provide remote access to a storage device over IP. This is similar to the VSD component in GPFS, which will be discussed in the next section.

GFS stores data as blocks on this virtual block device. A locking subsystem, OmniLock, provides the locking infrastructure necessary to ensure consistency. A number of locking modules are available with OmniLock allowing the locking granularity to be tuned to match expected workloads. Locks are sticky here as well, again allowing for read and write caching of data at the client.

GPFS

The General Parallel File System (GPFS) from IBM grew out of the Tiger Shark multimedia file system [100] and has been widely used on the AIX platform. Unlike the other file systems described, GPFS has no explicit virtual block device component. Instead GPFS simply uses one of two techniques for accessing block devices remotely and manages these devices itself. IBM's Virtual Shared Disk (VSD) component allows storage devices attached to multiple I/O nodes to be accessed remotely. VSD is different from the previous two approaches in that no logical volume management is performed at this level; it just exports an API to allow access to the devices. Alternatively, the VSD component can be avoided by attaching all nodes that wish to access the system to a SAN that gives them direct access to storage devices (Figure 19.4). This can be an expensive solution for large clusters, thus the existence of the VSD component. The newer Linux version of GPFS uses a similar component, called the Network Shared Disk (NSD), to provide remote access to storage devices.

In either case, GPFS operates on a shared storage region using block accesses. Because there is no volume management, however, GPFS sees multiple devices. This approach was a conscious decision on the part of the developers to provide the file system with direct control over striping of data across devices. A side effect of this decision is that volume management and fault tolerance capabilities must be handled outside of the VSD, either below the VSD or in GPFS. RAID devices can be used below the VSD layer (or directly attached via the SAN). In addition to or in place of RAID, GPFS also supports data and metadata replication at the file system layer. If this capability is enabled, GPFS will allocate space for a copy of data on a different disk and keep copies synchronized. In the event of a temporary failure, GPFS will continue to operate and will update the device when it is returned to service. Likewise, functionality for migrating data onto new devices or off bad ones is also implemented within GPFS.

GPFS relies on a distributed locking component to guarantee consistency. Similarly to the other two systems, locks are acquired and kept by clients who then cache data. The granularity of locking in GPFS is at the byte-range level (actually rounded to data blocks), so writes to nonoverlapping data blocks of the same file can proceed concurrently.

GPFS provides as an alternative a consistency management system called *data shipping*. This mode disables the byte-range locks described above. Instead nodes become responsible for particular data blocks, and clients forward data belonging in these blocks to the appropriate node for writing. This approach is similar to the *two-phase I/O* approach often applied to collective I/O operations [113]. It is more effective than the default locking approach when fine-grained sharing is present, and it forms a building-block optimization for MPI-IO implementations.

The GPFS system also recognizes metadata blocks as distinct from data blocks. A single node that is accessing a file is given responsibility for metadata updates for that file. A multiple-reader, multiple-writer system then is applied to metadata that allows concurrent updates in many circumstances.

GPFS is arguably the most successful parallel file system to date. It is in use on a variety of large parallel machines, such as ASCI White, a 512-node Power3-based system. We note that only 16 I/O server nodes (running VSD) are used in that particular instantiation. At this time GPFS has been made available in a limited fashion on IA32 and IA64 Linux systems but has not seen widespread use on these platforms.

19.2.2 Intelligent Server Architectures

The second common approach to parallel file systems is the use of "intelligent" I/O servers. By this we mean that the servers do more than simply export a block-oriented interface to local storage devices. These systems usually communicate with clients in terms of higher-level constructs, such as files (or parts of files) and directories. Specific operations to act on metadata atomically might be included as well, rather than treating them as data operations as in the previous systems. Further these servers have knowledge that the data they are storing corresponds to particular file system entities (e.g., files or directories), not just arbitrary blocks on a storage device. Hence they have the potential to accept more complex, structured requests than are possible with other approaches. This is a particularly useful capability for scientific applications given their structured file accesses.

Designers of systems using this architecture often logically separate the storage of metadata from the storage of file data. This approach allows for flexibility in configuration because they can choose to handle metadata operations with different servers from the I/O traffic. Because providing distributed metadata services is more complicated than placing metadata in a single location, some systems support only a single metadata server while maintaining many I/O servers. On the other hand, using a single metadata server adds a potential bottleneck, so some systems distribute metadata across multiple servers, possibly even all the I/O servers. We will see examples of both of these approaches in upcoming sections.

Groups have been implementing parallel file systems using this approach for quite some time as well. Two of these systems are the Galley parallel file system and the Parallel Virtual File System (PVFS). An emerging parallel file system, Lustre, also has this type of architecture.

Galley

The Galley parallel file system [78] was developed at Dartmouth College in the mid-1990s (Figure 19.5). It was a research file system designed to investigate file structures, application interfaces, and data transfer ordering for parallel I/O systems. As such many things that we expect from a production file system were never implemented, including kernel modules to allow mounting of Galley file systems and administrative tools.

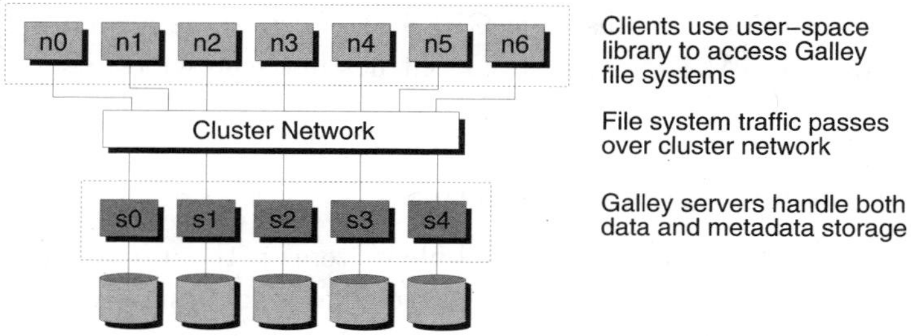
n0
n1
n2
n3
n4
n5
n6
Clients use user–space library to access Galley file systems
Cluster Network
File system traffic passes over cluster network
s0
s1
s2
s3
s4
Galley servers handle both data and metadata storage

Figure 19.5: Galley Architecture

Galley breaks user's files into *subfiles*, which are stored on Galley servers. These subfiles have *forks* that allow for multiple byte streams to be associated with a particular subfile as well and can be used for more complex storage organizations. The client-side code handles placement of file data into appropriate subfiles and forks. Metadata is also stored on all the Galley servers. File names are hashed to find a server on which to store data (a technique also used by the Vesta parallel file system [29], which we will not cover in detail here).

Galley servers understand strided and batch accesses, making the interface quite rich. Many of the application access patterns seen in the CHARISMA study, as well as the patterns seen in the Flash I/O study, could be described with Galley's I/O language as single accesses.

Galley also implements *disk-directed I/O* [62], a method for organizing how data is moved between client and server. In disk-directed I/O, the server calculates a preferable ordering of data transfer based on predicted disk access costs. This ordering is then used when moving data. The method worked well for many access patterns, although the designers of Galley did see low performance due to network flow control problems in some cases. Later work showed that a more general approach of optimizing for the bottleneck resource can be more effective [97].

While Galley never made it into production, it is an excellent example of the intelligent server approach. Further, many of the ideas embodied in this design, in particular rich I/O request capabilities and more complex file representations, are becoming key components of new parallel file system designs. The Galley source code is available online [41].

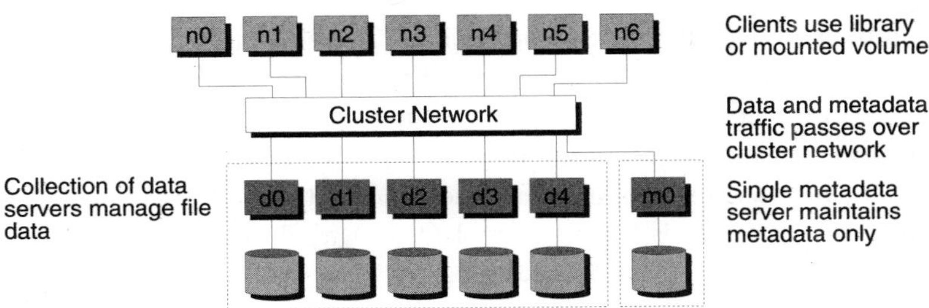

Figure 19.6: PVFS File System Architecture

PVFS

The Parallel Virtual File System (PVFS) [22] was originally developed at Clemson University by the authors of this chapter, starting in the mid-1990s, and is now a joint project between Clemson University and the Mathematics and Computer Science Division at Argonne National Laboratory. PVFS is designed to be used as a high-performance scratch space for parallel applications.

PVFS file systems are maintained by two types of servers (Figure 19.6). A single metadata server, typically called the "mgr" because of the name of the daemon that runs on this server, maintains metadata for all files. For many workloads and configurations this is not seen as a bottleneck, although it is increasingly becoming one as systems grow in numbers of nodes. Separate I/O servers handle storage of file data. File data is distributed in a round-robin fashion across some set of I/O servers using a user-defined stripe size. Thus a simple algorithm can be used to determine the I/O server holding a particular file region. This simplifies the metadata stored on the metadata server and eliminates the need for metadata updates as files are written. I/O servers write to local file systems, so local disk management is managed by the local file system. Likewise, single disk failures can be tolerated by using a RAID to store local file system data at the I/O server.

PVFS uses what the authors term *stream-based I/O* for data movement. PVFS transfers data using TCP, and the stream-based I/O technique leverages this by predefining a data ordering and eliminating all control messages in the data stream. This approach is able to attain very high utilization of TCP bandwidth; however, in many cases PVFS is disk bound, not network bound. The more adaptive approach given in [97] would likely provide better overall performance, but it was not merged into the PVFS source.

PVFS implements simple strided operations. These can be useful for some patterns; however, a more general approach is necessary for implementing MPI-IO operations. More recently a more flexible (but less concise) system was added for accepting arbitrary lists of I/O regions as single operations [27]. Called List I/O, this was first proposed in [115] and has been shown to be of great benefit to some access patterns. Support is provided in ROMIO for leveraging this; the hint to enable this is described in Section 19.4.4.

PVFS has no locking component. Instead, the metadata server supplies atomic metadata operations, eliminating the need for locking when performing metadata operations. Data operations are guaranteed by I/O servers to be consistent for concurrent writes that do not overlap at the byte granularity, but byte-overlapping concurrent writes result in undefined file state. This approach allows for a relatively simple system with no file system state held at clients, but it precludes client-side caching, which makes for very poor performance in a number of cases, particularly uniprocess workloads where systems from the preceding section would perform well.

Further, PVFS does not implement any form of fault tolerance. RAID can be used to tolerate disk failures, but node failures cause the system to be at least temporarily unusable. High-availability (HA) software is being investigated as a solution to this problem.

PVFS is also missing many of the administrative features that file systems such as GPFS offer. This limitation, combined with the lack of fault tolerance, has dissuaded many sites from using PVFS.

Nevertheless, PVFS has made it into production use at a number of sites around the world, mainly as a large, shared scratch space. PVFS is actively developed and supported, and the source for the file system, now commonly referred to as PVFS1 by the developers, is freely available online [90]. Because of its easy installation and source availability, many I/O researchers have chosen to compare their work to PVFS or to use PVFS as the starting point for their own research. We couldn't be happier that so many people have found this work to be so useful!

PVFS1 is showing its age, and a new version is under development to replace it before typical systems scale beyond its capabilities. We discuss this version, PVFS2, later in the chapter.

Lustre

The Lustre file system [17] is being developed by Cluster File Systems. At the time of writing the Lustre file system is under development, but much documentation and early code is available. The Lustre design benefits heavily from previous work in parallel file systems.

One of the key features of Lustre is the use of modules connected by well-defined APIs. This is seen in at least three areas: networking, allowing for multiple underlying transports; metadata storage, allowing for multiple underlying metadata targets; and object (data) storage, allowing for caching and multiple underlying data storage technologies. In the latter two cases modules can be stacked to implement additional functionality. This provides great potential for the reuse of significant portions of the code when porting to new platforms or adding support for new hardware. Lustre uses the Portals API [19] for request processing and data transfer. Portals is a full-featured, reliable transfer layer designed for use in large-scale systems over multiple underlying network technologies.

Lustre breaks the nodes of the system into three types: clients, Object Storage Targets (OSTs), and Metadata Servers (MDSs). Object Storage Targets store objects, similar to inodes, which hold file data. OSTs perform their own block allocation, simplifying the metadata for a file in a manner similar to previous systems [22]. Objects can be stored on a number of back-end resources attached to OSTs, including using raw file system inodes. Alternatively data can be stored on more traditional SAN resources. In this case OSTs would still be in place, but would handle only authentication and block allocation, allowing data to be transferred directly between clients and SAN storage devices. This is similar to the GPFS approach when the VSD component is not used. This configuration could be convenient for sites with a SAN already in place.

Metadata servers store attributes and directory hierarchy information that is used to build the name space for the file system. Lustre's design calls for multiple MDS nodes in order to help balance the load on these systems. The protocol for metadata operations is explicit and transaction based, allowing for the avoidance of locks. An option is provided for using a node as both a MDS and as an OST.

A snapshot capability is also provided in Lustre, similar to the approach seen in [65], except that snapshotting is performed on object volumes (collections of objects) rather than a collection of blocks.

The designers of Lustre also propose a collaborative caching capability, where caching servers aggregate accesses to particular objects so that a single cache can be shared by multiple applications. This is similar in some ways to the data shipping scheme used in GPFS and distributed caches seen in research parallel file systems [55, 123]. However it is of particular note that Lustre is able to provide this functionality in a modular way.

Lustre relies on a distributed locking system for data coherence. Locks are available at different granularity levels to allow for concurrent access to disjoint file regions. Locks are managed by the OST that stores the object. Metadata operations are also performed by using locks to allow for client-side caching. Lustre adds *intent* locks for use in metadata operations. These are special locks that are used to perform some type of atomic operation at lock time. While in many instances an explicit operation to perform the intent could be used instead, this approach may lead to fewer opportunities for races between atomic operations by immediately returning a lock that could be used for a subsequent operation.

Lustre implements full POSIX semantics, but this can be turned off on a per file or per file system basis. An interface similar to the List I/O interface described in [115] is proposed as an optimization as well.

Beta versions of Lustre are available, and development is very active. Also released under the GPL license, Lustre could become the next widely used parallel file system for Linux clusters; license compatibility with the PVFS2 project means that the two projects could share components if appropriate APIs were developed.

19.3 File System Access Semantics

From the user's point of view, two aspects of the file system API should be considered: what types of accesses can be described to the file system, and what happens when multiple processes access a file at the same time. We discussed earlier the importance of structured access descriptions; in this section we will focus on the second aspect, concurrent access semantics.

19.3.1 POSIX I/O Semantics

The most significant barrier to scalable parallel I/O systems today is the POSIX I/O interface and its associated semantics.

The POSIX I/O interface [58] was specified with local file systems in mind. The POSIX I/O interface specifies the `open`, `close`, `read`, `write` interface that we are all accustomed to using. It further specifies that writes through this interface must be performed in a sequentially consistent manner. Writes to the file must also appear as atomic operations to any readers that access the file during the write; the reader will see either all or none of any write. These semantics apply to any processes that access the file from any location.

Internal to a single system, the disadvantages of the POSIX semantics are not so apparent. In the single system, all operations to a file will pass through to a single device, and locks can be used to efficiently manage atomic access to files. However, the semantics of the POSIX interface have broad-reaching implications on any type of distributed or parallel file storage. In stark contrast to the single system, now we have multiple devices that might be accessed by any single operation, and all these devices, plus the clients, are distributed across some type of network. In this situation maintaining the POSIX semantics can be a complicated and communication-intensive process, particularly when many processes access the same resources.

POSIX I/O and Locking

The most common approach to providing these semantics is to use a locking subsystem to manage access to files, and this is in fact the approach applied in all our example systems that implement the POSIX semantics (Frangipani, GFS, GPFS, and Lustre). POSIX semantics require that all accesses be atomic operations. When implemented with locks, this means that before a process can write to a region of a file, it must obtain the lock associated with that region. It can then write, then release the lock. Sophisticated lock caching and forwarding are used to alleviate the overhead of the locking subsystem in systems that expect to see a high degree of concurrent access.

Locks may be applied at the block, file, or extent granularity. The most coarse grained of these is file-based locks. File-based locks associate a single lock with an entire file. No distributed file system employing file-based locks should be seriously considered as part of a parallel I/O system because the contention for locks during concurrent access will ruin the performance of all but the least I/O-bound problems.

The second most coarse grained is block-based locks. This approach is often used in systems that use block-based accesses when communicating between clients and the underlying storage. Block-based locks have the advantage of being much finer grained than are file based locks. For large files, however, this approach can result in a very large number of locks being present in the system. Often these file systems address this by simply increasing the size of blocks. This, however, results in a situation where false sharing of blocks is more likely to occur.

The third, and most flexible, locking approach is extent-based locks. This approach can result in fewer locks in use because large ranges may be described as a single extent. This advantage is lost; however, if accesses are interleaved at a fine granularity. This approach, when coupled with noncontiguous access, can also result in a very large number of locks being processed in the system. Even with these two disadvantages this is the best locking approach for concurrent access under POSIX in use in parallel file systems today.

Scientific access patterns have a great deal of regularity. None of this information is retained in any of these locking approaches, however, leading to all these approaches being relatively inefficient, either in number of locks or in contention for a small number of locks. Approaches like IBM's data shipping can certainly help make lock approaches perform more effectively, especially when accesses are interleaved. We will discuss the similar two-phase I/O approach later in Section 19.4.4.

From this discussion, and the presence of optimizations such as data shipping, it should be clear that the POSIX semantics are known in the community to be a problem. In fact, this problem is very similar to those seen in distributed shared memory (DSM) systems, where hardware and software are used to build globally accessible memory regions [121, 54]. The DSM community has for the most part abandoned the sequential consistency model in favor of more relaxed consistency models, in large part because of the overhead of maintaining such a model as systems scale. Perhaps it is time for the I/O community to follow suit.

19.3.2 NFS Semantics

The Network File System (NFS) protocol [80, 21, 102] is probably the most popular means for accessing remote file systems. Typically, remote file systems are "mounted" via NFS and accessed through the Linux virtual file system (VFS) layer just as local file systems are. What many users don't understand is that these NFS-mounted file systems do not provide the POSIX consistency semantics! The NFS version 3 RFC notes [21]:

> The NFS version 3 protocol does not define a policy for caching on the client or server. In particular, there is no support for strict cache consistency between a client and server, nor between different clients.

The story is a little more complicated for NFS version 4, but the lack of cache consistency on the client side remains.

NFS is an everyday example of relaxing the POSIX I/O consistency semantics in order to gain performance. NFS clients cache file data, checking every now and again to see whether the file has changed. This loosely synchronous consistency model makes for convenient, low-latency access to one's home directory stored on a remote system. Further, the locking systems typically used to implement the POSIX semantics are avoided along with their overheads.

On the other hand, NFS semantics are nearly useless from a parallel computing point of view. Clients can cache data indiscriminately, and tend to do so at arbitrary

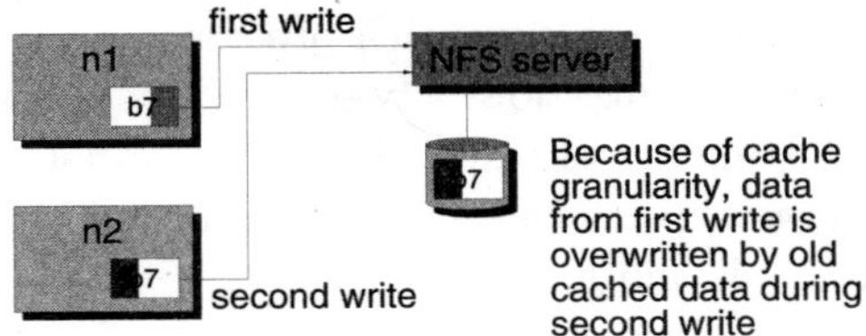

Figure 19.7: Concurrent Writes and NFS

block boundaries. This causes unexpected results when nearby regions are written by processes on different clients; if two processes concurrently write to the same block on different processes, even if they write to different bytes, the result is undefined! Figure 19.7 shows an example of how this happens. Two nodes have cached the same block, and processes have written to different parts. First one block is committed back to storage, then the second. Because of the blocking, and the lack of consistency control, the data from the first write is lost when the second write completes.

Nevertheless, the semantics implemented by most NFS clients are sufficient to provide a usable file system for a number of situations.

19.3.3 MPI-IO Semantics

One could argue that the POSIX semantics are stricter than necessary for use in parallel I/O in that they force I/O systems to implement more consistency control than applications really need. Do scientific application programmers typically write to overlapping regions and let the file system sort it out? Probably not; they have better things to do with the I/O bandwidth! On the other hand, NFS semantics are definitely too loose; the nondeterminism introduced by uncoordinated client-side caching makes NFS semantics troublesome for concurrent writes.

The MPI-IO semantics [46] provide a very precise, but less strict, set of consistency semantics. The *Using MPI-2* [50] book provides a very thorough description of these semantics; they are actually relatively complicated. We touch on the semantics for some common cases here.

First, the scope of the MPI-IO semantics is the MPI communicator used to open the file. MPI says nothing about the semantics of access from different communicators, leaving this coordination to the application programmer. Second, by default MPI-IO does guarantee that concurrent *nonoverlapping* writes will be written correctly (unlike NFS) and that the changes will be immediately visible *to the writing process.* These changes are not visible by other processes in the communicator right away. Instead, explicit synchronization between the processes is necessary. This can be accomplished in a number of ways, all outlined in [50]. Simply closing and reopening the file is one method of synchronization, and the use of explicit file synchronization operations is another.

This model makes a lot of sense for many access modes seen in parallel applications, including checkpointing and of course all read-only modes. More importantly it relaxes the requirements on the underlying I/O components significantly and provides many opportunities for optimization within the MPI-IO implementation. We will discuss two such optimizations later in this chapter in the context of using ROMIO with PVFS.

19.3.4 PVFS Semantics

Noting the increased system complexity and potential overhead in implementing full POSIX I/O semantics (and having limited resources!), the PVFS developers chose to implement a different set of I/O semantics. With PVFS, concurrent nonoverlapping writes are written correctly and are immediately visible to all processes. Note that this approach is stronger than the default MPI-IO semantics. Overlapping writes will leave some undefined combination of the written data in the overlapping file region, and reads that occur concurrently with writes may see pieces of old and new data.

These semantics are adequate for implementing most of MPI-IO and are more than adequate for most access methods while simultaneously simplifying the system significantly: no coordination is needed at write time between clients or servers. The result is a more scalable system, at the cost of POSIX semantics.

19.4 Using PVFS

In the previous edition of this book, the majority of this chapter was dedicated to the specifics of PVFS configuration and use. This information is all available at the PVFS Web site [90], in particular in the User's Guide [91]. Rather than rehash that document, we'll talk a little bit about practical aspects of using PVFS, including implications of the PVFS design on certain types of operations, managing and tuning PVFS file systems, using ROMIO with PVFS, and bug spotting. We hope that this information supplements the online documentation nicely. Section 19.5 describes PVFS2, the next generation of PVFS, which addresses many of the design limitations of PVFS.

19.4.1 Implications of the PVFS Design

The preceding sections have prepared us to discuss the implications of the PVFS design from a practical standpoint. First, PVFS does not perform client-side caching for metadata. Hence, all metadata operations have to travel across the network to the metadata server. For heavy metadata workloads, this design can cause sluggish performance.

Additionally, PVFS does not keep a file size as part of the metadata stored at the metadata server; rather, it calculates this value when it is requested. The advantage is that, during writes, the metadata need not be updated. However, a `stat` on a file requires not only a message to the metadata server to obtain the static metadata but also a sequence of messages to the I/O servers (performed by the metadata server) in order to obtain the partial sizes necessary to fill in the file size. The `ls` program performs this operation on *every* file in a listed directory, which can cause `ls` to be very slow for PVFS file systems. In practice, this makes PVFS a poor performer for small files, too, because users tend to put all the small files in one directory. Then they `ls` the directory and are frustrated by the delay. A `pvfs-ls` utility is provided with PVFS that avoids gathering this metadata, instead just printing directory contents. For users who simply want to see what resides in a directory, this is a much faster option.

PVFS does not cache data at the client side because it has no mechanism for ensuring that cached data is kept synchronized with data in other caches or on I/O servers. Hence, all data reads and writes must cross the network as well. Thus, the size of reads and writes to large files does have a significant impact on performance, especially through the VFS interface, which has particularly high overhead. This design decision makes PVFS perform poorly for benchmarks such as Bonnie [18]. Along these same lines, executing programs stored on a PVFS volume can be quite slow because pages are read one at a time on demand.

Missing Features

Users are occasionally surprised by the fact that some features are missing from PVFS. Here's a list as of version 1.5.8:

- links (both hard and symbolic)
- write-sharing through `mmap`
- `flock` and `fcntl` locks
- fault tolerance (other than using RAID, described later)

That's about it! If a user requires one of these features, perhaps one of the systems described earlier in the chapter will suffice instead.

19.4.2 Managing PVFS File Systems

PVFS allows for many different possible configurations. In this section we'll discuss some of these options.

While PVFS is relatively simple for a parallel file system, it can sometimes be difficult to discover the cause of problems when they occur simply because there are many components that might be the source of trouble. Here we discuss some tools and techniques for finding problem spots.

Monitoring File System Health

The `pvfs-ping` utility is the most useful tool for discovering the status of a PVFS file system and has turned into something of a "Swiss army knife" for PVFS debugging at this point.

A simple example of its use is as follows:

```
# pvfs-ping -h localhost -f /pvfs-meta -p 3000
mgr (localhost:3000) is responding.
iod 0 (127.0.0.1:7000) is responding.
pvfs file system /pvfs-meta is fully operational.
```

In this case the I/O server is dead and needs to be restarted:

```
# pvfs-ping -h localhost -f /pvfs-meta -p 3000
mgr (localhost:3000) is responding.
pvfs-ping: unable to connect to iod at 127.0.0.1:7000.
iod 0 (127.0.0.1:7000) is down.
pvfs file system /pvfs-meta has issues.
```

Using Multiple File Systems

Since PVFS includes no fault tolerance, for large systems it can make sense from a fault tolerance point of view to create multiple PVFS volumes. A single metadata server can serve multiple file systems if desired; however, if multiple file systems are chosen for fault tolerance reasons, it is definitely better to use multiple servers for I/O (one per file system). A single I/O server daemon (`iod`) cannot serve more than one file system. However, more than one daemon may be run on the same server if desired by specifying a different `port` value in the `iod.conf` file used to start the server.

Tolerating Disk Failures

Disk failures can be tolerated by using any of the many available RAID solutions under Linux, including both hardware devices and software RAID. There have been very few reported instances of data loss with PVFS because of software failures. Using RAID to tolerate disk failures is an effective mechanism for increasing the reliability of PVFS.

Increasing Usable File Descriptors

While some improvements have been made in PVFS with respect to file descriptor (FD) utilization, the servers in particular still can end up using all of their available FDs. The I/O servers will print a little message when this is about to happen:

```
NOTICE: exceeded 90 percent of available FDs (1024)!
```

Luckily this is easy to fix. The limits are set in `/etc/security/limits.conf`. Lines are of the following format:

```
<domain> <type> <item> <value>
```

The domain can be "*" for everyone, a userid, or a group using "@group". The type can be soft (setting the default) or hard (setting the maximum). The item parameter controls what limit this affects and can take many values, including nofile (open files). "Value" is the new value to set.

For example, the following lines would set the maximum number of FDs for root to 8192 and the default to 4096:

```
root hard nofile 8192
root default nofile 4096
```

Likewise one can set a new maximum and then use `limit` or `ulimit` as appropriate in the startup script for the servers.

Migrating Metadata

When upgrading to a newer PVFS version, occasionally the format of metadata on disk changes. This is due to oversights in the original design of the metadata format. Tools are now provided that can be used to convert metadata to the new format (assuming you haven't gotten too far behind on updates).

For example, if you are moving from version 1.5.6 to version 1.5.8, a utility called `migrate-1.5.6-to-1.5.8` is provided (there were no changes from 1.5.7 to 1.5.8 in the metadata format). This tool is used in conjunction with `find`:

```
# find /pvfs-meta -type f -not -name .pvfsdir -not \
  -name .iodtab -exec migrate-1.5.6-to-1.5.8 \{\} \;
```

Warning messages will be printed and the process aborted if the utility detects that the metadata is not the correct version. This process should be performed after stopping the mgr.

19.4.3 Tuning PVFS File Systems

We often get questions about how to tune PVFS file systems for the best performance. Truthfully, system hardware varies widely enough that it is difficult for us to supply any single set of parameters that will work best for everyone. Instead, in this section discuss some specific parameters common to all machines and some general techniques for improving overall PVFS file system performance. Chapters 3 and 5 include many tips for improving the overall performance of Linux nodes; all that information certainly applies to PVFS servers as well.

Of course, in addition to tuning the file system itself, many steps can be taken *above* the file system that can make a huge difference. Given the discussion of the PVFS design, many of these are obvious: using large requests rather than small ones, using MPI-IO so PVFS List I/O optimizations can be leveraged, and avoiding lots of metadata operations (opens, closes, and stats). Often such optimizations in application code can make more difference than any tuning within PVFS itself. An in-depth discussion of improving the performance of MPI-IO access can be found in [50].

Adjusting Socket Buffers

PVFS relies heavily on the `select` call and kernel handling of multiple TCP connections for parallelism. For this reason, it is often useful to tune the network-related parameters on the system. Chapter 5 covers this process in some detail; in particular increasing the `wmem_max` and `rmem_max` values is often very helpful.

Once these have been increased, the `socket_buf` option in the I/O server's configuration file (`iod.conf`) can be used to adjust the socket buffer size up to the new maximum.

Enabling DMA for Hard Drives

Chapter 3 describes the `hdparm` tool. It can be used to verify that DMA is turned on for the hard drives that are being used for PVFS storage and to turn this on if it is not enabled. Because PVFS pushes both the network and storage hardware, alleviating any load on the CPU is helpful. Note that DMA isn't reliable on some hardware, so you should check the support of your hardware if this isn't turned on by default.

Improving Space Utilization

Originally we thought that users would want to know where their data was striped so that they could distribute processes to match data locations. Hence, we set up default striping so that data always started on the first I/O server. It turns out that for the most part people don't care about this and rarely use this information. Additionally, when users create lots of small files, this unbalances the distribution of data across the I/O servers.

We have subsequently added a "`-r`" flag that can be passed to the metadata server (`mgr`). This flag will cause the metadata server to choose a random starting I/O server when no server is specified (this can be done through the MPI-IO interface, for example). This will better distribute files and has a particularly large effect in the small files case.

Here we examine the free space on the I/O servers of a PVFS file system using the additional "`-s`" option to `pvfs-ping`:

```
# pvfs-ping -h localhost -f /pvfs-meta -s
mgr (localhost:3000) is responding.
iod 0 (192.168.67.51:7000) is responding.
iod 0 (192.168.67.51:7000): total space = 292825 Mbytes,
 free space = 92912 Mbytes
iod 1 (192.168.67.52:7000) is responding.
iod 1 (192.168.67.52:7000): total space = 307493 Mbytes,
 free space = 121154 Mbytes
iod 2 (192.168.67.53:7000) is responding.
iod 2 (192.168.67.53:7000): total space = 307485 Mbytes,
 free space = 121155 Mbytes
iod 3 (192.168.67.54:7000) is responding.
iod 3 (192.168.67.54:7000): total space = 307493 Mbytes,
 free space = 121199 Mbytes
```

We see that the first I/O server has significantly less free space than the others. This will show up in the df output:

```
Filesystem              Size  Used Avail Use% Mounted on
localhost:/pvfs-meta
                        1.2T  824G  363G  69% /pvfs
```

PVFS calculates the available space returned to the system by the minimum amount available on any single I/O server (in this case 92.9 Gbytes) times the number of I/O servers (in this case 4). Because so much less space is available on the first server, we get a very low reported available space. Using the "-r" manager flag described above will help alleviate this problem.

Testing Aggregate Bandwidth

Since users are mostly interested in PVFS for high performance, obtaining a baseline performance number for a particular configuration is fairly important. The `pvfs-test` tool supplied with PVFS can be used for this purpose. This is an MPI program that opens a file from a large number of processes and writes or reads that file in parallel with each process accessing a different large block of the file. A "-h" option will cause it to list its options. This program can be used as a simple benchmark for testing the effects of configuration changes.

Here's the output of one of our favorite runs, using 80 nodes of Chiba City (see Chapter 20) as clients for PVFS and 128 separate nodes for I/O servers back in April of 2001:

```
mpirun -nolocal -np 80 -machinefile mach.all pvfs-test -s 262144 -f
 /sandbox/pvfs/testfile -b 268435456 -i 1 -u
# Using native pvfs calls.
nr_procs = 80, nr_iter = 1, blk_sz = 268435456, nr_files = 1
# total_size = 21474836480
# Write:  min_t = 3.639028, max_t = 6.166665, mean_t = 4.755538,
 var_t = 0.334923
# Read:  min_t = 6.490499, max_t = 7.171075, mean_t = 6.977580,
 var_t = 0.023353
Write bandwidth = 3482.406857 Mbytes/sec
Read bandwidth = 2994.646755 Mbytes/sec
```

We did not sync after the writes ("-y" option), so the data was at the servers but not necessarily on disk. Nevertheless we were able to create a 20 Gbyte file in just over 6 seconds and read it back in just over 7 seconds. Not too shabby at the time. Note that we found a strip size of 256 Kbytes to be the best for that particular configuration, where a *strip* is the amount of data written to a single server (and a stripe is the amount written across all servers in the round-robin fashion).

Adjusting the Default Strip Size

By default the strip size (the size of the regions distributed in round-robin fashion to I/O servers) is set to 64 Kbytes (as of version 1.5.8). For some systems, particularly ones using large RAID volumes at each I/O server, this is simply too small.

The `pvfs-test` tool can be used to experiment with various strip sizes in order to find a good one for a particular configuration. Using the "`-y`" option will help ensure more accurate results by forcing data to the disk. Once a good value has been found, an additional "`-s ssize`" option can be used with the metadata server in order to provide the new default value (ssize is in bytes).

It is also useful to adjust the I/O server write buffer size to be larger than this size. That value is set in the I/O server configuration file with the `write_buf` option (value is in Kbytes, and the default is 512 Kbytes).

19.4.4 ROMIO and PVFS

MPI-IO implementations provide a number of services over using a local file interface. First and foremost these implementations provide a portable interface to which application programmers can code. The MPI-IO implementation takes MPI-IO operations and translates these into operations that can be performed by the underlying file system. Depending on the underlying file system, the MPI-IO implementation has a number of options with respect to how it translates an MPI-IO read or write operation into file system operations. If the underlying file system supports only POSIX operations, the MPI-IO layer might convert the MPI-IO request into a collection of contiguous operations. For a file system such as PVFS, MPI-IO requests might instead be converted into List I/O operations.

The second service that MPI-IO implementations provide is I/O optimizations. As we have discussed before, the MPI-IO semantics leave some opportunities for performance optimizations that are not available under the POSIX semantics. Further, the information provided by the use of collective I/O calls provides additional opportunities for optimizations. For more information on MPI-IO in general, including examples, see Chapter 9 of this book or [50]. In this section we will touch upon building ROMIO with PVFS support and then discuss in detail the optimizations available within ROMIO that are usable with PVFS.

Building MPICH and ROMIO with PVFS Support

Chapter 8 introduced the MPICH implementation of the MPI standard. ROMIO is included as part of the MPICH package. When configuring MPICH with ROMIO and PVFS support, a few additional parameters are necessary. Particularly we want to tell ROMIO what kinds of file systems to support, link to the PVFS library, and provide the path to PVFS include files.

For example, let us assume that PVFS was previously installed into `/soft/pub/packages/pvfs-1.5.8`, and we want both PVFS and "regular" (UFS) file system support:

```
# ./configure --with-romio="-file_system=pvfs+ufs"
 -lib="-L/soft/pub/packages/pvfs-1.5.8/lib/ -lpvfs"
 -cflags="-I/soft/pub/packages/pvfs-1.5.8/include"
```

The standard MPICH build and installation procedure can be followed from here. Building with LAM is very similar.

If ROMIO is not compiled with PVFS support, it will access files only through the kernel-supported interface (i.e., a mounted PVFS file system). If PVFS support is compiled into ROMIO and you attempt to access a PVFS-mounted volume, the PVFS library will detect that these are PVFS files (if the `pvfstab` file is correct) and use the library calls to avoid the kernel overhead. If PVFS support is compiled into ROMIO and you attempt to access a PVFS file for which there is *no* mounted volume, the file name passed to the MPI-IO call *must* be prefixed with `pvfs:` to indicate that the file is a PVFS file; otherwise ROMIO will not be able to find the file.

ROMIO Optimizations

ROMIO implements a pair of optimizations to address inefficiencies in existing file system interfaces and to leverage additional information provided through the use of collective operations. These optimizations, as well as PVFS options such as striping parameters, are controlled through the use of the MPI_Info system, commonly known as "hints." Much of the information in this section comes from the ROMIO users guide [117]; this guide provides additional information on these topics as well as covering the use of ROMIO on file systems other than PVFS.

ROMIO implements two I/O optimization techniques that in general result in improved performance for applications. The first of these is *data sieving* [114]. Data sieving is a technique for efficiently accessing noncontiguous regions of data in files when noncontiguous accesses are not provided as a file system primitive

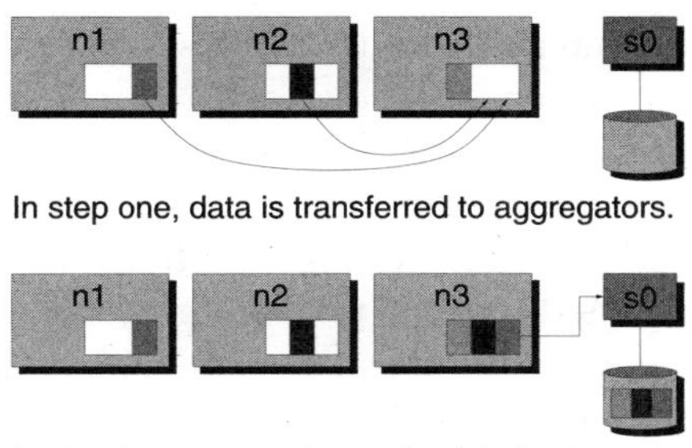
n1
n2
n3
s0
In step one, data is transferred to aggregators.
n1
n2
n3
s0
In step two, aggregators write data to storage.

Figure 19.8: Two-Phase Write Steps

or where the noncontiguous access primitives are inefficient for a certain datatype. In the data sieving technique, a number of noncontiguous regions are accessed by reading a block of data containing all of the regions, including the unwanted data between them (called "holes"). The regions of interest are then extracted from this large block by the client. This technique has the advantage of a single I/O call, but additional data is read from the disk and passed across the network. For file systems with locking the data sieving technique can also be used for writes through the use of a read-modify-write process. Unfortunately, since PVFS does not have file locking of any kind currently, this is not available for PVFS.

Two hints can be used to control the application of data sieving in ROMIO for PVFS:

- `ind_rd_buffer_size` controls the size (in bytes) of the intermediate buffer used by ROMIO when performing data sieving during read operations. Default is `4194304` (4 Mbytes). If data will not all fit into this buffer, multiple reads will be performed.

- `romio_ds_read` determines when ROMIO will choose to perform data sieving. Valid values are `enable`, `disable`, or `automatic`. Default value is `automatic`. In `automatic` mode ROMIO may choose to enable or disable data sieving based on heuristics.

The second optimization is *two-phase I/O* [113]. Two-phase I/O, also called collective buffering, is an optimization that applies only to collective I/O operations. In two-phase I/O, the collection of independent I/O operations that make up the collective operation are analyzed to determine what data regions must be transferred (read or written). These regions are then split up among a set of aggregator processes that will actually interact with the file system. In the case of a read, these aggregators first read their regions from disk and redistribute the data to the final locations; in the case of a write, data is first collected from the processes before being written to disk by the aggregators. Figure 19.8 shows a simple example of the two-phase write using a single aggregator process. In the first phase (step), the two nonaggregator processes pass their data to the aggregator. In the second step the aggregator writes all the data to the storage system. In practice many aggregators are used to help balance the I/O rate of the aggregators to that of the I/O system. Because the MPI semantics specify results of I/O operations only in the context of the processes in the communicator that opened the file, and all these processes are involved in collective operations, two-phase I/O *can* be applied on PVFS files.

Six hints can be used to control the application of two-phase I/O:

- `cb_buffer_size` controls the size (in bytes) of the intermediate buffer used in two-phase collective I/O (both reads and writes). If the amount of data that an aggregator will transfer is larger than this value, then multiple operations are used. The default is `4194304` (4 Mbytes). If the data size exceeds this buffer size, multiple iterations of the two-phase algorithm will be used to accomplish data movement.

- `cb_nodes` controls the maximum number of aggregators to be used. By default this is set to the number of unique hosts in the communicator used when opening the file.

- `romio_cb_read` controls when collective buffering is applied to collective read operations. Valid values are `enable`, `disable`, and `automatic`. Default is `automatic`. When enabled, all collective reads will use collective buffering. When disabled, all collective reads will be serviced with individual operations by each process. When set to `automatic`, ROMIO will use heuristics to determine when to enable the optimization.

- `romio_cb_write` controls when collective buffering is applied to collective write operations. Valid values are `enable`, `disable`, and `automatic`. Default is `automatic`. See the description of `romio_cb_read` for an explanation of the values.

- `romio_no_indep_rw` indicates that no independent read or write operations will be performed. This can be used to limit the number of processes that open the file.

- `cb_config_list` provides explicit control over aggregators, allowing for particular hosts to be used for I/O. See the ROMIO users guide for more information on the use of this hint.

ROMIO Data Placement Hints

Three hints may also be used to control file data placement. These are valid only at open time:

- `striping_factor` controls the number of I/O servers to stripe across. The default is file system dependent, but for PVFS it is `-1`, indicating that the file should be striped across all I/O devices.

- `striping_unit` controls the striping unit (in bytes). For PVFS the default will be the PVFS file system default strip size.

- `start_iodevice` determines what I/O device data will first be written to. This is a number in the range of 0 ... striping_factor - 1.

ROMIO and PVFS List I/O

Two hints are available for controlling the use of list I/O in PVFS:

- `romio_pvfs_listio_read` has valid values `enable`, `disable`, and `automatic`. The default is `disable`. This hint takes precedence over the `romio_ds_read` hint.

- `romio_pvfs_listio_write` has valid values `enable`, `disable`, and `automatic`. The default is `disable`.

Clearly, a wide variety of parameters can be used to control the behavior of ROMIO and PVFS when used together. Because no single set of parameters works best for all applications, experimentation is often necessary to attain the best set of parameters. A study examining some of these parameters has been published [26]; this can serve as a starting point for your own tuning.

19.4.5 Bugs

Users sometimes encounter bugs in PVFS. When they do, we generally guide them through a predictable set of steps to help us discover where the problem lies. This section outlines this process. The purpose is not to discourage users from reporting bugs or asking for help, but to streamline the process. If you have already tried these steps, we can skip a number of email exchanges and get right to the root of the problem!

Checking the List Archives

The very first thing to do is to check the PVFS mailing list archives. These are searchable online and available from the PVFS Web site [90]. Many problems have already been reported, so checking here might provide you with an immediate solution.

Reporting Versions and Logged Output

Bugs should always be reported to the PVFS users mailing list. This is an open list for discussion of many PVFS issues, one of them being bugs. By reporting to the mailing list you reach the maximum number of people that might be able to solve your problem, and you guarantee that an archive of the discussion will be saved.

We will always ask what version of the code you are running, especially if the problem that you report looks like something that has already been fixed. The distribution and kernel version you are using are helpful as well. If the problem is related to compiling, we'll ask for configure output and a log of the make process. If the problem is a runtime one, we'll ask for any information in the logs that might help. This includes `dmesg` output, the `pvfsd` log, the `iod` logs, and the `mgr` log. By default the three types of log files are all placed in `/tmp`, although this can be changed with configure-time options.

Providing this information in your first message is the easiest way to get the bug reporting and fixing process started.

Client Side or Server Side

The most common runtime bugs seen in PVFS at this time concern the Linux kernel module. One of the first things that we do in the case of a runtime problem is try to determine whether the problem is related to the servers themselves or to a particular client. We usually ask the user to look at the state of other clients in order to determine this. For example, one bug that we have seen prevented new files from showing up on certain clients. One client would see the new file while others did not. By looking at the state of multiple clients, the user was able to report this back and help us narrow down the problem.

Simplifying the Scenario

The simpler the set of conditions necessary to cause the problem on your system, the more likely we are to be able to replicate it on some system we have access to. Hacking out portions of a scientific code so that it performs only I/O or writing a script that uncovers a metadata incoherence problem really helps us see what is going on and replicate the problem on our end.

19.5 Parallel I/O in the Future

Machines with tens of thousands of nodes are on the horizon. For a parallel I/O system to efficiently operate at this scale, a number of issues must be addressed.

Adapting to new technologies is critical in this environment. It is not clear what processor, storage, or network technologies will be present in future machines, or even what operating system will run on nodes. Any new parallel file system design should be built with abstract interfaces to allow adoption of new technologies and porting to new operating systems.

Leveraging collective operations, rich I/O request languages, and relaxed consistency semantics will be key to operating efficiently on these machines and exploiting the inherent hierarchy in these systems. Opportunities exist at many levels in the I/O component stack to boost performance.

Management of I/O systems is a growing concern because the systems continue to become more complex. Tools to aid the administrator are key, and self-maintaining solutions would be ideal.

Our next-generation parallel file system, PVFS2, is being designed to tackle just these problems. By the time this book is published, early versions of the next-generation Parallel Virtual File System, PVFS2, should be available online. The core of PVFS2 has been designed to provide

- modular networking and storage subsystems,
- a structured data request format modeled after MPI datatypes,
- flexible and extensible data distribution modules,
- distributed metadata,
- tunable consistency semantics, and
- and support for data redundancy.

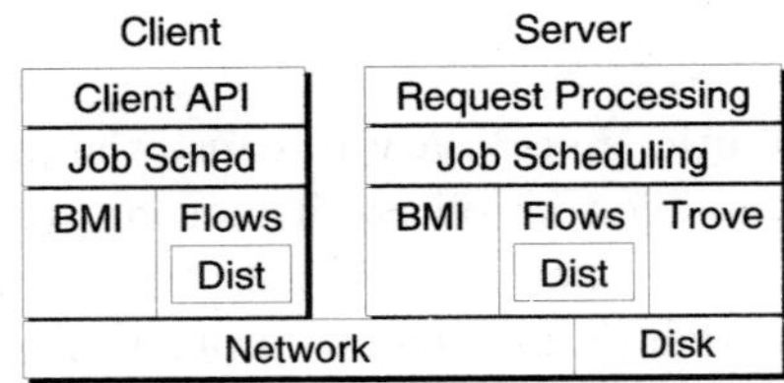

Figure 19.9: PVFS2 Software Architecture

PVFS2 is the culmination of a 3-year effort to redesign PVFS as a production-capable parallel file system based on experience gained in the design and operation of the original PVFS, observations of other parallel file systems, and interactions with the scientific data management community.

In this section we will examine some of the challenges facing parallel I/O systems both today and in the near future. We will use PVFS2 as one example of how these problems might be addressed.

19.5.1 Supporting New Hardware Technologies

While in some sense cluster computing is about using commodity parts, we often see new technologies in use in larger clusters before they hit the commodity market. Networks are a great example of this; we see many interesting network technologies, including Myrinet, Quadrics, and InfiniBand, in use in clusters today. Likewise on the storage side we see locally attached hardware, SANs, and iSCSI as some of the potential mechanisms for storage access. Leveraging these technologies requires appropriate abstractions in the I/O system. In the Lustre design we see a very modular system used to attack just this problem [17].

19.5.2 PVFS2 Abstract Interfaces

PVFS2 also addresses this problem with abstraction layers. The first two of these are BMI, through which client and server messages flow, and Trove, through which storage is accessed. Figure 19.9 shows the overall software architecture of PVFS2; we will discuss the major components here.

The Buffered Messaging Interface (BMI) provides a nonblocking network interface that can be used with a variety of high-performance network fabrics and is tailored for use in file system servers and clients. Currently BMI modules exist for both TCP/IP and GM networks.

The Trove storage interface provides a nonblocking interface that can be used with a number of underlying storage mechanisms. Trove storage objects, called data spaces, consist of both a stream of bytes and a keyword/value pair space, similar in some ways to the data and resource forks available in other local file systems. Keyword/value pairs are convenient for arbitrary metadata storage and directory entries, while the stream of bytes is a natural place to store file data. The current implementation uses Unix files and Berkeley db4, but many other implementations are possible.

The third major abstraction in PVFS2 is Flows. Flows combine the functionality of the network and storage subsystems by providing a mechanism to specify a flow of data between network and storage. Flows also incorporate the request and distribution processing system that allows PVFS2 to handle highly complex access patterns. Finally, Flows provide a point for optimization: specific flow implementations to optimize data movement between a particular network and storage pair can be implemented to exploit fast paths.

Above all these the job scheduling layer provides a common interface for posting BMI, Trove, and Flows and checking on their completion. Within this layer, scheduling decisions are made, and multiple threads are used to manage asynchrony and leverage multiple CPUs. This is tightly integrated with a state machine processing system that is used to track operations in progress. With this layer in place, new underlying components may also be added and integrated with minimal effort. At the highest level within the server, the request processing component handles incoming requests and initializes new state machines to process these requests.

19.5.3 Tolerating Faults

Parallel computing systems continue to grow in numbers of components (nodes, disks, etc.), and because components are becoming no more reliable, the likelihood of component failure is increasing. While application and middleware are beginning to be adapted to handle faults, most users depend on the I/O system to be a reliable and available location for data storage. On the other hand, because providing fault tolerance usually lowers performance, some users will desire to forego fault tolerance at the I/O system level and instead implement it in a more efficient manner at the application level. Doing so allows them to get the highest performance from the I/O system. For a parallel file system to be usable in many domains, the level of redundancy should be configurable. The approach PVFS2 takes to redundancy is much the same as it takes to semantics and other issues involving a trade-off between performance and protection: that is, it provides a choice of various levels of protection, with the requisite loss or gain in performance. Thus PVFS2 aims to allow files to be stored with no redundancy or with varying degrees of redundancy, as needed. Multiple technologies may be leveraged to accomplish this, some built into the file system and others external components.

Redundant Storage

Many tools are available for providing fault tolerance in storage systems. One is the use of local RAID arrays. This is a time-proven approach to handling disk failures, and a RAID provides high-performance I/O with minimal performance degradation when directly accessed by a single I/O server. We encourage this application of RAID with both PVFS1 and PVFS2. RAID like-techniques can also be applied across the devices on a SAN; the file system examples implementing a VSD use this type of approach. Using RAID in this way can incur performance penalties because of the fine-grained locking often used to control concurrent access when multiple nodes have access to the resources.

In PVFS2 we will provide what we term *lazy redundancy* as an option. In this approach writes to files do not update redundant information automatically as they would in a RAID-like approach. Instead redundant information is updated only when clients make explicit calls. These calls can be automatically made within I/O middleware libraries at logical points, such as MPI sync or close operations. By delaying the update to these explicit points we allow the I/O layers the option of aggregating updates to redundant data. Further, in the context of MPI-IO we have control of all the processes accessing the file; we can use these processes to update redundant data in parallel for higher performance. The data distribution component of PVFS allows us to describe where this redundant data is located in a convenient manner, and the approach can be applied on a per file basis. Lazy redundancy can be coupled with server failover to provide an even greater degree of protection.

Failover

High availability (HA) software provides a mechanism for server failover in the case of node failure. Dual-attach storage hardware can be used with this software to tolerate single-node failures by creating pairs of nodes that provide "backup" for each other. This allows systems to run in what is termed *active-active* mode (meaning that neither node sits idle in absence of failure), with somewhat degraded performance in the event that one node fails. Of course, if you don't mind having half your system sitting idle, *active-passive* mode can be used, leaving an extra server for each of the ones in service. More complicated HA solutions are becoming available that allow for a pool of backup servers that can be brought online as needed. In contrast to active-active pairs, this architecture would allow for a small number of extra servers that could fill in without degrading performance. However, these extra servers would need access to many different storage resources; providing this capability could be prohibitively expensive.

Having the hardware and software infrastructure necessary to restart a server on backup hardware is just the first step. A second issue to be considered with respect to failover is shared state. Clients and servers in a *stateless* system do not maintain information about other entities in the system that is necessary for correct operation (i.e., they can cache information for performance reasons, but the system must be able to function without this information). Assuming that a system is stateless and that no file system data is cached in volatile storage, a server restart need not cause the loss of any data. Unfortunately, shared state is used in many parallel file systems; write-back caches are an example, where a client is holding onto the state of blocks (for performance reasons) that a server is in fact responsible for. Servers and clients can checkpoint their state on shared storage if it is available. This is a viable option for systems where clients and servers have access to shared storage, but this connectivity may not be available. Another option is to implement an arbitration process that allows the system as a whole to reclaim resources and synchronize state in the event of a node loss. Handling all the failure cases can be very difficult. PVFS2 servers and clients are stateless in order to simplify the use of failover solutions and minimize complication in failure scenarios.

19.5.4 Aiding Management

Most parallel file systems today (excluding PVFS1) have mechanisms for checking the status of devices involved in the system, migrating data on and off particular resources, checking the consistency of the file system, and adding or removing devices from the file system. Looking beyond this functionality, we can imagine I/O systems that can suggest optimizations based on observed access patterns or, even better, manage themselves. The areas of "autonomic computing" [61] and "autonomous storage" in particular cover just this type of operation. PVFS1 lacked most of the management tools that administrators expect from such a system, and we believe that this discouraged its use in a number of cases. We intend to take management very seriously in PVFS2, and we will discuss some of the basics here.

System Monitoring

The first step in easing the management task is providing tools for system monitoring. These tools should allow for both examining the real-time state of the system and looking at trends over time for optimization purposes. A complicating factor in parallel I/O monitoring is the sheer amount of data available, particularly information on access patterns. This process is similar to gathering logs from parallel programs in that data from many cooperating components must be collected and presented coherently.

The PVFS development team has experimented with instrumentation of the PVFS1 servers and has developed tools to aggregate performance metrics, collect access pattern statistics, and visualize the results. Using the tools and techniques developed for PVFS and looking at other work in the area, we have slated monitoring operations to be an integral part of the suite of operations that PVFS2 supports. These monitoring functions can be used as a starting point for visualization, analysis, and self-management tools.

Data Migration

In PVFS2, file data is distributed to Trove data objects for storage. Trove data objects are referenced by a handle. These data object handles are clustered into logical groups such that all handles within a logical group are managed by a single server. In the simplest case, each server manages a single logical group of Trove handles, and therefore the objects referenced by those handles. These groups can be split and merged if necessary for repartitioning purposes, and servers may be responsible for many of these logical groups. The mapping of handles to the servers where they are stored is a part of system configuration and is easily changed. This not only provides a decoupling from handles to servers but potentially allows storage objects to be moved from server to server by transferring the control of an entire logical group and updating the handle mapping appropriately.

Figure 19.10 shows three servers, each with two logical groups of storage objects referenced by different handle ranges. If resources on the middle server need to be freed (e.g., to replace faulty hardware), the groups of objects stored on the server can be relocated to one or more servers, and requests from the clients can be redirected by updating the mapping of these groups. Because these Trove objects are used to store both metadata and data, metadata can be migrated in the same manner.

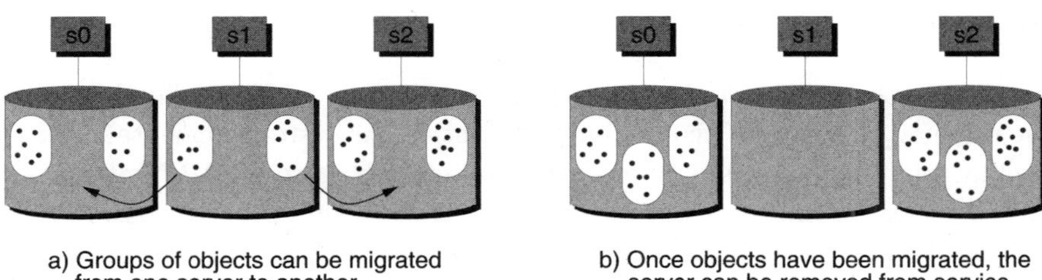
s0
s1
s2
s0
s1
s2
a) Groups of objects can be migrated from one server to another.
b) Once objects have been migrated, the server can be removed from service.

Figure 19.10: Migrating Storage Objects

Automated Management

Ideally, these systems would simply manage themselves! If components fail, data could be migrated appropriately to allow for continued fault tolerance and minimum degradation of performance. Data that is used frequently as input could be replicated so that multiple copies were available for reading or redistributed to match observed access patterns. Infrequently used data could be kept on slower disks or moved to tertiary storage. Caching and scheduling policies could be tuned to match access patterns as well.

We are very interested in this type of system, and we plan to start working in this area once the PVFS2 system matures. The first step is to provide a suite of management operations as part of the server API. With this API in place, an additional set of monitoring processes can interpret the performance monitoring information over time and direct changes to the file system accordingly. Separating these management processes into their own components will maintain the simplicity of the underlying PVFS2 core.

19.5.5 Leveraging I/O Languages and Semantics

Earlier in the chapter we discussed consistency semantics; obviously we feel that experimentation in this area could lead to useful alternative semantics. Equally important is the use of structured I/O descriptions from the highest-level interfaces down as low as possible in the I/O stack. Certainly, parallel file systems should be supporting these operations.

MPI-IO

So far, MPI-IO implementations have been very conservative in their exploitation of the more relaxed MPI-IO consistency semantics. As systems scale, taking further advantage of these semantics allows us to potentially improve I/O system performance using the same hardware as before. During this process, however, some users are likely to experience surprising behavior from the I/O system because of assumptions about what level of consistency MPI-IO will provide. We will do everything possible to minimize the pain experienced by users in order to keep them from abandoning this powerful API.

Caching at the MPI layer is one of the biggest opportunities that has so far been unexploited in production systems. The constrained scope of the MPI-IO semantics, coupled with the explicit synchronization points, makes caching in MPI-IO a straightforward process. This is in stark contrast to the infrastructure necessary to cache under the POSIX interface. File systems such as PVFS2 can benefit greatly from caching at this layer.

Operations such as `MPI_File_open` can be further optimized with appropriate support from the parallel file system. PVFS2 does not keep state regarding open files. Instead, clients essentially find only a file handle during an open call. A scalable implementation of `MPI_File_open` for PVFS2 can have a single process perform the mapping from file name to handle, then broadcast the file handle to the rest of the processes. This type of optimization can be applied in a number of cases where MPI collectives are used.

Configurable Semantics

Earlier in the chapter we discussed the file consistency semantics of a number of interfaces. We noted that for some types of workloads the NFS semantics were acceptable, while for others they were not. It is not difficult for a parallel file system to relax its semantics; usually this is a matter of simply neglecting to perform consistency checks it might have otherwise. This approach should be considered seriously. As a real example, many large physics datasets are being put online today. Files in these datasets are never modified once written. Aggressive caching of these files can be performed because the semantics applied to the dataset by the scientists permit it. We should allow for these optimizations.

Likewise, relaxing the consistency of directory contents provides another potential point of optimization, as could metadata of files and directories (in particular file size). PVFS2 will provide a configurable window of time for which previous metadata values and directory contents are treated as up to date. This allows for

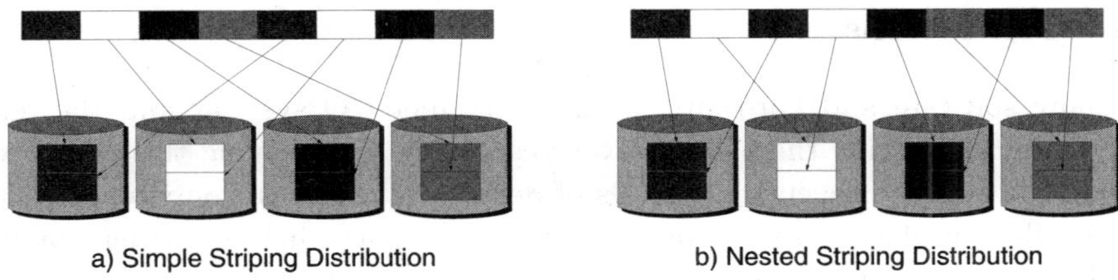

Figure 19.11: Examples of Data Distributions

caching without locks, at the cost of short periods of time where views of the file system on different clients are slightly different. Such an approach might be useful as we attempt to share parallel file system access across wide-area networks.

Describing I/O Operations and Data Distributions

PVFS2 allows for structured I/O requests via a format based directly on MPI datatypes. Currently a set of datatype constructor functions identical in function to the equivalent MPI calls is provided, and the format can readily be translated from existing MPI datatype formats, making it trivial to leverage this functionality within an MPI-IO implementation such as ROMIO. PVFS2 servers directly process this format (in the flow component) to service I/O requests; the type is not converted into a vector before processing.

With structured data sets comes the potential for leveraging more sophisticated data distributions. Most parallel file systems use striping. In PVFS2, however, the distribution mechanism has been abstracted so that different files can be stored with different distributions. PVFS2 relies on an algorithmic mechanism for distribution of data to servers. The functions that define the distribution can now be selected at file creation time, permitting a number of potential data distributions.

One such alternative distribution pattern is nested striping. As shown in Figure 19.11, simple striping distributes data round-robin to all IO nodes used to store the file. Nested striping distributes data round-robin first to one subset of nodes and then to another subset in a round-robin pattern among subsets. This pattern better matches block distributions of multidimensional datasets. Any distribution that can be represented algorithmically can potentially become a PVFS2 distribution scheme.

19.6 Conclusions

The many software and hardware layers of parallel I/O systems and the terminology used to describe them can be very confusing. Underlying this complexity, however, are simple concepts: methods of describing accesses, consistency semantics, distributing data across many resources, and surviving component failures. Armed with knowledge of these concepts, one can both qualitatively assess the appropriateness of a particular system to a given problem and devise tests to measure quantitatively the effectiveness of the system. Many of these I/O systems share common traits, so the example systems presented here can be used as a frame of reference when examining new systems as well.

Parallel I/O continues to grow in importance as a component of clusters. While existing parallel file systems such as PVFS1, GPFS, and GFS are filling existing needs, new systems such as Lustre and PVFS2 are already being built to meet the needs of upcoming systems. These systems build on the successes of the past but also address issues germane to upcoming systems, in particular parallel I/O system portability and increased scale. Even so, additional effort will be necessary to see exciting concepts such as autonomous storage become reality.

As parallel I/O researchers and developers, we definitely have our work cut out for us!

20 A Tale of Two Clusters: Chiba City and Jazz

Rémy Evard

This case study examines and compares two large-scale Linux clusters. The first of these is Chiba City, a 256-node cluster supporting computer science that was installed at Argonne National Laboratory in 1999. The second is Jazz, a 350-node cluster for production computing. Jazz was installed a few feet away from Chiba City in late 2002.

A comparison between the two clusters is instructive. Chiba City is beginning to fade into the half-life of technology, while Jazz is just getting started. Our design choices on Jazz were based on our experiences with Chiba City, on changes in the industry, and the need to support a production computing user base.

We'll first describe Chiba City in some detail, considering the design, configuration, operation and usage. While Chiba City's technology is aging, the cluster architecture itself is still extremely relevant. Then we'll describe Jazz similarly while contrasting it with Chiba City in order to illustrate those aspects of cluster design that change over time.

20.1 Chiba City

With 256 dual-CPU computing nodes, Chiba City is the largest cluster in the Argonne scalable clusters project.

Chiba City was designed with a unique purpose in mind: to support scalable computer science and the development of scalable systems software. We believe that advances in the state of system software for high-performance computing are critical in order to improve the performance and reliability of high-end machines. Yet the developers and researchers who will bring about those advances often find it very difficult to gain access to the largest systems because those computers are dedicated to running large code. With the advent of commodity clusters, the solution to this problem became clear: using relatively inexpensive parts, it was now possible to build a system that could be used to support activities that required development and testing at large scale without the usual large price tag. This was the basis of the idea for Chiba City.

In addition, Chiba City was built to support a wide range of parallel computational science applications. In the Mathematics and Computer Science (MCS) Division of Argonne National Laboratory, we collaborate with hundreds of researchers around the world who use our computing facilities in partnership with the scientists in our division. Chiba City was meant to be used by these scientists in order to tackle real scientific problems while they simultaneously worked with computer scientists to expand the scope of problem that they could address.

In essence, Chiba City is intended to support two distinct goals that are occasionally in conflict: scalable computer science research, which needs a dynamic and interactive testbed, and computational science, which has historically used stable, batch-oriented systems. We believe that Chiba City has achieved a comfortable balance between these two worlds and has helped promote good science in both.

The difference in requirements between experimentation and classic production computing has kept us—Chiba City's designers and administrators—living in two worlds at once, trying to keep the cluster both stable and interesting.

20.1.1 Chiba City Configuration

In this section, we describe the configuration of the Chiba City from multiple perspectives. We cover not only what went into the cluster but why it is there and how it is used.

Node Configuration

Chiba City includes the following computing components (see Figure 20.1):

- 256 computing nodes
- 32 visualization nodes
- 8 storage nodes
- 18 management nodes

Computing Nodes. The 256 computing nodes are the workhorse portion of the cluster. These are the primary nodes that run the user's programs.

CPU. Each computing node has two 550 MHz Pentium III CPUs. This lets us play the game of sometimes referring to the system as a "512-CPU computer" rather than a "256-node computer." (Of course, some people actually include every CPU on the system when they count, not just the ones available to the users. In Chiba's case, this would be 574 CPUs, not including the CPUs in the networking equipment.)

One of the more hotly debated issue throughout the design phase of Chiba was the question of how many CPUs each node should have. From a pure performance viewpoint, it makes the most sense to have only one CPU per system, for several reasons. First, the memory bandwidth on Pentium IIIs is quite limited; thus one

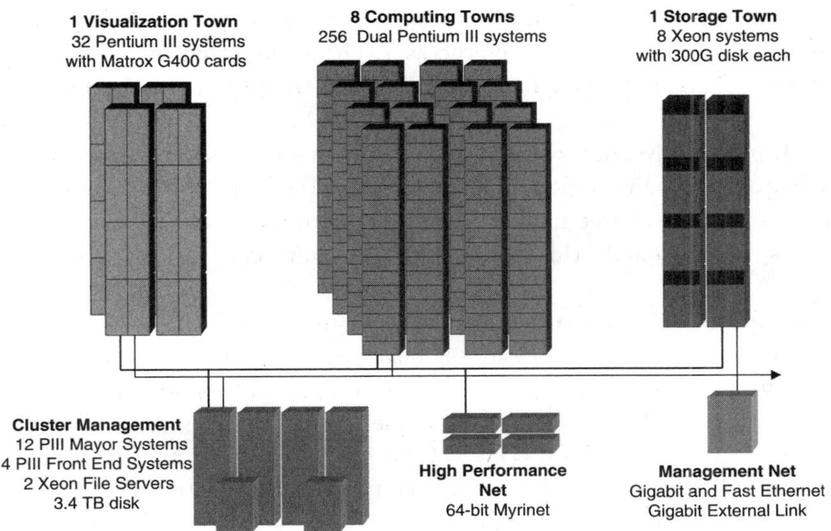

Figure 20.1: Chiba City schematic.

CPU alone can easily saturate the memory bus, making any more than the first one potentially useless. Second, in order to most efficiently use all of the CPUs in the system with an MPI job, the communication between processes must use both network and shared-memory communication, which is difficult. Third, at the time of the installation, Linux didn't run on more than one CPU particularly well.

On the other hand, from a price/performance perspective, it makes much more sense to have multiple CPUs on each node—and in fact, four would have been better than two from this viewpoint. It's typically cheaper to buy a dual-CPU system than to buy two of the same system, each with only one CPU. Furthermore, it's far cheaper to install a network for 256 nodes than for 512 nodes. (On the other hand, if the network is the bottleneck, then some people who use multi-CPU systems end up installing two or more network interfaces per computer.)

On Chiba City, we decided to go with dual-CPUs for flexibility. We wanted to be able to support experiments and development on both types of MPI programming. Those wishing to go for maximal node performance could ignore the second CPU. Alternatively, those wishing to use or experiment with mixed-mode MPI programming would have that option as well.

In retrospect, this is exactly what has happened. Some users find that their code is more efficient if they use only one processor. Others find that two processors work well for them. And developers have needed access to both types of configurations.

Computing Node Memory. Each computing node has 512 megabytes of RAM. We felt that this was a minimum for dual CPUs at the time. We do occasionally see applications run out of free memory and start swapping, particularly when using both CPUs, but in general this has proven to be sufficient.

Computing Node Footprint. The nodes themselves are 2U units. (Equipment that can be housed in computer racks is measured in the unit U, where 1U is 1.75 inches. A standard rack is 42U.) We went with these because they were the smallest system we could find at the time. In fact, the size of the units was a major driver: one of the initial proposals we received from vendors had 3U and 5U units, which would essentially doubled the floor space required for the cluster. We simply didn't have that much space in our machine room.

Ironically, 1U Pentium systems hit the market a few months after we installed Chiba City. We knew they were likely be available around then, but renegotiating the cluster purchase to have 1Us was simply not an option. These days, blade technology and clever mounting schemes allow configurations of less than 1U.

Computing Node Disks. Some cluster builders include disks in all nodes. Others go completely diskless. Diskless nodes have a number of advantages in a cluster. First, it's a little easier to configure the operating systems on the nodes when they're diskless, because those configurations are stored on management nodes. (This advantage can be negated if adequate configuration tools are used to manage diskful nodes.) Also, disks tend to break. If the nodes don't have disks, that's one less thing on each node that may require service. On large clusters, it's a good idea to eliminate any situation that involves touching the nodes.

On Chiba City, we have 9 gigabyte hard drives on each node. We decided to install disks in each node for maximum flexibility. Some applications that the scientists run make extensive use of local disk. We also anticipated that system-software experiments or alternative operating systems might need to use the local disk. It has turned out that, for us, this was the right choice. Many, many uses of the system rely on or take advantage of the local disk. And while we do occasionally have drives that fail, this has been much less of an issue than many other hardware components, particularly the fans.

Other Computing Node Hardware. In addition to the CPUs, the RAM, and the hard drive, each computing node has

- one 32-bit PCI slot that is used for a Myrinet card,
- a 10/100 Ethernet port on the motherboard,
- a floppy drive (because that was included), and
- serial, parallel, keyboard, and the other usual PC ports.

Computing Node Connections. Looking at the back of a node can be instructive. Each connection plugs into another component of the cluster, all of which are described in detail in following sections of this chapter.

- The Myrinet card is a part of the Myrinet network. Each node has one fairly large Myrinet cable that runs under the floor to a Myrinet Clos64 switch.
- The Ethernet port is used for to connect to the Ethernet network. Each node connects to an Ethernet switch in its rack or in a neighboring rack.
- The serial port that Linux uses as the console plugs into a serial concentrator in the rack, which enables remote access to all of the consoles.
- The "management" serial port on each node plugs into a separate serial concentrator, to be used for low-level hardware and management. This is a motherboard-specific management interface, and we've never needed to use it.
- The power cable runs to a Baytech power control unit that allows us to remotely monitor and control the power to each node.
- The keyboard and video ports are left vacant. In rare situations, such as hardware diagnosis or BIOS upgrades, we may plug a keyboard and monitor into them. In an ideal world, we would never use these at all. Other clusters built since Chiba use daisy-chain mechanisms to allow somewhat remote access to the keyboard and video.

Visualization Nodes. The 32 visualization nodes are used by computer scientists for research into cluster-based image synthesis and computer graphics. They are sometimes used as their own independent 32-node cluster and sometimes used in conjunction with the computing nodes as part of one large program.

The primary feature of the visualization nodes is that they include high-end video cards that can be used for graphics and image synthesis. Ideally, these cards can be used in two ways:

- Simply as video cards. In our environment, we have a remote console infrastructure for graphics systems that allows us to connect the display port of graphics systems located in one spot to display systems located in a laboratory. This means that the visualization nodes can be housed in the machine room and still be used to drive the CAVE or our 15-projector Active Mural, both of which are in other rooms.
- As pipelines for generating images.

These video cards typically require an AGP slot. The requirement for the AGP slot drives every other detail of the visualization nodes. For example, computers with AGP slots are usually desktop systems or workstations rather than servers. Our visualization nodes are workstation-style systems that don't fit into racks well and are actually kept on shelves. The systems that were available at the time we purchased Chiba City were 550 MHz Pentium III systems configured with 13 GBytes of disk and 384 MBytes of RAM. We manage them the same way that we do the compute nodes, including remote serial and power control.

The video cards were originally Matrox Millenium 32 MBytes G400Max cards. Since installing Chiba City, we've upgraded the video cards to NVidea GEFORCE3 cards.

Storage Nodes. The eight storage nodes are not accessed directly by most of the users of Chiba City. Instead, they provide file system service to the computing nodes, as described below under "file servers."

Each storage node has a 500 MHz Xeon, 512 MBytes of RAM, and, most important, 300 Gbytes of SCSI-attached disk. So, in aggregate, the storage nodes provide 2.4 TBytes of raw disk space to the computing nodes. This was a lot of disk at the time we installed the cluster.

The storage nodes are a part of the Myrinet network. In some cases, cluster builders will choose to put their storage nodes exclusively on the Ethernet network. This choice is primarily an issue of performance versus cost. With an even order of two number of computing nodes (i.e., 64, 128, 256, etc.), one can often build an interconnect network with a lot less hardware than would be required for those same compute nodes plus a few storage nodes. The difference may be negligible or may be substantial. In our case, getting the storage nodes onto the Myrinet meant that we needed to purchase several additional Myrinet switches. Because I/O performance and experiments are important to our user community, we felt the cost was worth it.

The storage nodes interface with the rest of the cluster in the same way that the rest of nodes on the cluster do. In addition to being available over Myrinet, they're also on the Ethernet. They also have remote power and console control.

Under normal conditions users don't have direct access to the storage nodes. However, scientists working on a project specifically related to I/O research may have access to the I/O servers. In this case, it's possible that their programs will run simultaneously on both the compute nodes and the storage nodes.

Management Nodes and Servers. The nodes used for cluster management come in several different flavors:

- 12 systems used as the cluster "mayors," or monitor systems
- 4 front ends
- 2 file servers

The mayors provide a scalable management mechanism, which is described in greater detail in Section 20.1.1. Most clusters don't need this many mayors because their configuration isn't changed as frequently as Chiba City's.

Mayor systems. Every set of 32 computers in the cluster is associated with a computer, called their "mayor," that monitors and manages them. The mayors are never used as part of any computation or experiment running on the cluster but are instead used to configure the cluster for that experiment and recover from any problems it might cause. Each mayor is system with a single 550 MHz Pentium III, 512 MBytes of RAM, 10/100 Ethernet, Gigabit Ethernet, and 200 GBytes of SCSI disk. Two of the mayor units have special functions. One serves as the "city mayor" and is used to control the other mayors. The other runs the scheduler for the cluster.

Front ends. Chiba City was originally configured with four front ends: systems that users could login to in order to build their programs and launch them onto the compute nodes. Since these systems are identical to the compute nodes, the users' build environment would be the same as program's execution environment. In practice we found that two front ends was sufficient, and we have used the other two nodes as test systems.

File servers. The two file servers provide file systems via NFS to the login nodes and to the mayors. They house all of the user's home file systems and all of the configuration files (kernels, RPMs, config files, and so on) for the nodes. They do not export file systems directly to the nodes—that's the job of the storage nodes. The file servers have exactly the same hardware configuration as the storage nodes. Each has 500 GBytes of disk.

Nodes We Missed. After a few years of running the cluster, we've concluded that the configuration that we put together is almost correct, but we missed a few pieces.

First, we could use more test systems. Linux kernels, file systems, system software, and applications all change rapidly. Having between four and eight test machines for testing individual pieces of code and cluster functions would be extremely helpful. At present, we usually allocate some of the compute nodes in order to test new software. This procedure works okay, but since it reduces the pool of compute nodes the users can access, it tends to be a short-term solution.

Second, we could use a few spare nodes. We always seem to have a small handful of nodes with hardware problems, which makes it difficult to reliably be able to run jobs on all 256 nodes. We would like to have a pool of spare nodes that we would swap in for a node with broken hardware. Then, once that node was repaired, it would go into the pool of spare nodes. Four spare nodes would probably cover most situations.

We actually considered both of these in the original plan, but for financial reasons they were removed. It's difficult to justify between eight and twelve computers that aren't really being used most of the time.

Logical Configuration

Chiba City is conceptually divided into cluster building units which we call "towns." In our definition, a town consists of a set of computers and a single "mayor" node

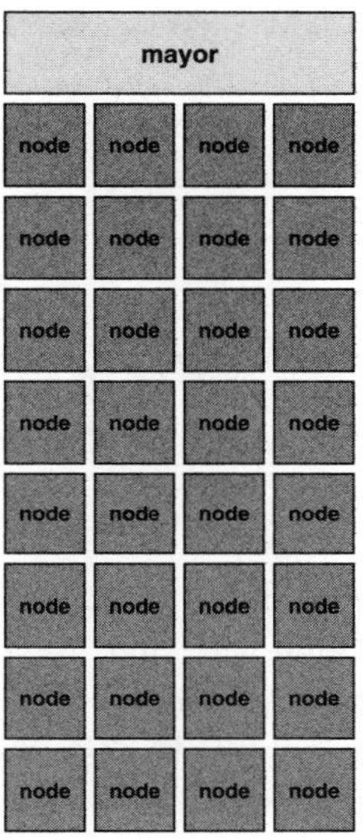

Figure 20.2: A Chiba City town.

that manages them. For example, each of the eight towns of computing nodes in Chiba City includes one mayor and thirty-two computing nodes.

In Chiba City, there are eleven towns:

- 8 computing towns, each with 32 computing nodes
- 1 visualization town of 32 visualization nodes
- 1 storage town with the 8 storage nodes
- 1 server/mayor town with the 10 mayors, login nodes, and file servers

The towns are a mechanism to allow scalable management (see Figure 20.2). From a systems administration perspective, we would like to be able to completely manage every node in a town by interacting with its mayor. So, in order to manage the 256 computing nodes in Chiba, one merely needs to manage the 8 mayors of those computing nodes. To accomplish this, the mayor provides boot service, operating system configuration, console management, and file services to each of the other nodes in its town. It monitors those nodes to make sure that they're running correctly. The mayor performs management functions only and never participates in the computing activity of the nodes, so the users of the cluster never work with the mayors directly.

In most cases on Chiba City, each mayor monitors 32 nodes. In a few cases, such as the storage town, there are fewer nodes in the town. We chose 32 clients for a number of reasons:

- Our tests indicated that NFS performed reasonably with 32 clients. Thus, NFS would be an option within a town if we so chose.
- In a 1024-node cluster, there would be 32 towns of 32 nodes.
- The hardware for a 32-node town fit nearly perfectly into two racks.

The town relationship is hierarchical. A collection of mayors can be managed by a higher-level mayor in the same way that a collection of nodes is managed by a mayor. In Chiba City, we have one node, which we refer to as the City Mayor, that is responsible for managing each of the mayors. This gives us a single point of control from which the entire cluster can be managed.

The concept of building the larger system out of smaller replicated systems, each with their own server, wasn't a new one. Beyond being a classic computer science technique, it was used to some degree in the IBM SP, has been a standard approach for years in the systems administration community, and was demonstrated on clusters by the Sandia National Laboratories CPlant project.

We've made a number of observations about the mayor/town concept while operating the cluster:

- The mayor concept has proven its worth over and over. We could not manage the cluster without some sort of hierarchical approach.
- Some network services already have scalability mechanisms built in, or scale to the size of the cluster. The Dynamic Host Configuration Protocol (DHCP) is one of these. Breaking these down so that it runs on each mayor and supports only the local town isn't worth the time. In other words, some services for the cluster can and should be global.
- The ratio of clients to mayor is highly dependent on what those clients are doing. With 32 nodes, we're comfortable supporting network booting and remote operating system installation. If we were also supporting high-capacity file systems or other services, we might need to scale down. On the other hand, if every node was largely independent except for monitoring and time service, for example, then we could probably shift to 64 nodes per mayor.

We have often been asked why we call the building blocks "towns." In the early design phases of Chiba City, we talked to a lot of people in a lot of companies who had never heard of clusters before. We had trouble explaining that we wanted to build the cluster out of these subclusters that had a monitoring agent, so we started to call them "towns" as a part of the city metaphor. This explanation helped quite a bit even though, of course, real cities aren't made up of towns that look identical—they're made up of neighborhoods that are usually very different. But the metaphor helped explain the concept, and the name stuck.

Network Configuration

Chiba City has two types of networks—Myrinet and Ethernet. In this section, we describe their configuration and their use.

Myrinet. The Myrinet network is used to support high-speed communication between nodes as part of a user's program, usually related to computation or I/O.

On Chiba City, a high-performance network is essential. Many of the jobs that run on the cluster are bound by the performance of the network: the faster the network, the better the performance of their code. Also, a lot of the computer science research on Chiba is related to communication.

We chose to use Myrinet, a product of Myricom, because it was the most cost-effective high-performance networking solution on the market at the time we purchased the cluster. Myrinet has a number of nice characteristics. It can deliver a full bisection bandwith network between all of the nodes of a cluster. The network cards that we installed can support a theoretical 1.28 Gbps transfer rate, with latencies from process to process in the 10–15 microsecond range.

The specific Myrinet hardware on Chiba City includes 4 Myrinet spine switches, 5 CLOS-64 switches, and 320 Lanai 7.2 NICs. The hosts that usually participate on the Myrinet network include the computing nodes, the visualization nodes, the storage nodes, and the login nodes. In other words, everything except the management nodes and the file servers is typically on Myrinet. At different times over the life of the cluster, we have connected the file servers and mayors to support experiments.

It is possible to run IP over Myrinet, and we do. From an IP standpoint, the Myrinet network is a flat IP subnet and is not accessible from outside of the cluster.

Ethernet. The Ethernet network is used for everything that the Myrinet network isn't. For the most part, this means management functions, remote access, and

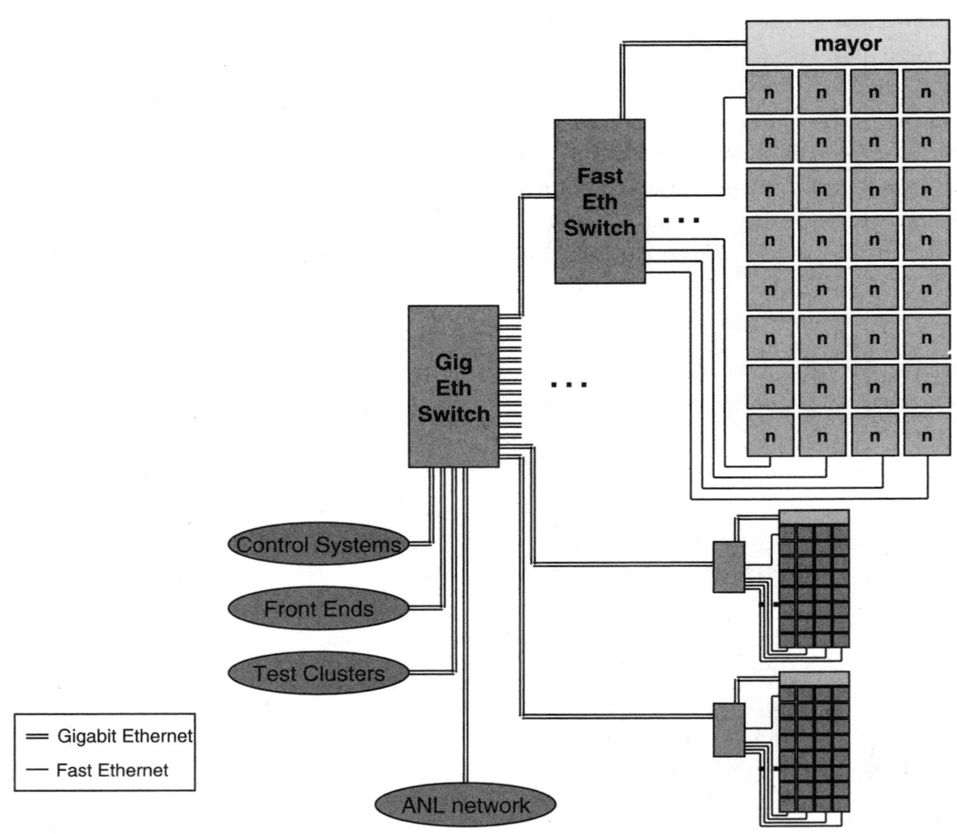

Figure 20.3: The Chiba City Ethernet.

a fallback communications network for applications if the Myrinet network isn't available.

Figure 20.3 is a diagram of the Ethernet network, which is arranged in a simple tree structure. Each computing, visualization, and storage node is connected via Fast Ethernet to an Ethernet switch near that node. There are 10 Cisco Catalyst 4000s distributed around the cluster, each connecting approximately 32 nodes.

A central Gigabit Ethernet switch, a Cisco Catalyst 6509, is connected to each of the Catalyst 4000s with two channel bonded Gigabit Ethernet links. The remaining computers—the front end nodes, the file servers, and the mayors—all connect directly to the Catalyst 6509. Also, Chiba City's link to the outside world comes in through the Catalyst 6509.

In essence, Chiba City has a completely switched Ethernet. The IP network layered on top of this Ethernet is one flat subnet with no routing. Every node in the cluster is at most three Ethernet switch hops away from every other node.

Physical Configuration

The physical layout of a cluster is particularly important if space is limited, as is the case for us. Chiba City occupies twenty-seven standard 19-inch racks arranged into two rows (see Figure 20.4). The racks include

- 16 racks of computing nodes. Each computing town fits precisely into two racks. This include the 32 compute nodes, the mayor and its disk, the serial and power management systems, and the Ethernet switch for the town.
- 4 racks of storage nodes. The storage nodes and their associated disk each take up half of a rack.
- 2 double-layer shelving units for the visualization nodes. Because of cable length limits for the video systems, these are located in another part of our machine room from the rest of Chiba City.
- 3 racks for the Myrinet switches. These racks have the heaviest cable density in Chiba, because every node has a cable that runs to some port in these racks.
- 1 rack for the file servers and their disk.
- 1 rack for the Gigabit Ethernet switch and remaining servers.

20.1.2 Chiba City Timeline

In this section of the case study, we examine the phases of activity that Chiba City has gone through, starting with the early seeds of the idea up through full-time operation. These are similar to the phases that most other clusters go through.

Phase 1: Motivation

As noted at the beginning of this chapter, the primary driver for Chiba City was to create a testbed that could be used to support scalability testing and research

Figure 20.4: One of two rows of Chiba City.

into scalability issues. We believe that this area is the most important aspect of computing to address in order to advance the state of high-performance computing.

Furthermore, we felt that it was important to build a system that could be used for general computer science and development, rather than on applications and simulations, which is typically what large computers are used for.

Before building Chiba City, we had been building and running small clusters for several years, including clusters based on Windows NT, Linux, and FreeBSD. We had used those to support research into communication, visualization, and several other areas of experimentation. But, by fall of 1998, we still had not yet been convinced that the large system in MCS would be a cluster.

However, once we considered the issues of scalability, the need for a computer science testbed, and the price/performance of commodity clusters, it became clear that a large-scale cluster could probably address all of these needs as well as become the next major MCS platform for simulation and computational science.

We originally considered installing a 1024-node system. However, we decided to start with a 256-node system in order to test many of the concepts. Thus, Chiba City was started as the first step toward a thousand-node (or larger) cluster, with a primary goal of supporting scalable computer science and a secondary goal of supporting scientific applications.

Phase 2: Design and Purchase

Having convinced ourselves that a large cluster was the right direction for MCS, we started, in December 1998, to design the system and arrange to purchase it.

We spent the next several months repeating this cycle over and over:

1. Think about what we needed and how we would use it.
2. Talk to vendors, integrators, and the cluster community in order to find out what would be available on our time frame.
3. Consider various funding options and match those with design and availability.

We discovered, among other things, that the traditional set of high-performance computing vendors were all trying to decide what to do about clusters (and what to do about Linux). At the time, it was possible to buy an actual cluster from Compaq and from a number of small integrators, but none of the larger vendors had yet created cluster product lines. No one was selling anything like what we wanted for Chiba City.

Eventually we put together a presentation to use to explain to vendors what we wanted to buy. The presentation explained what clusters were, what the cluster would be used for, how we wanted to operate it, and what we thought the necessary parts might be. As we updated our internal designs for the system software, we updated the purchasing presentation. We talked to a lot of different vendors and then went through the formal purchasing process. Eventually we agreed to buy the system through IBM. IBM arranged to provide subsets of the system from other vendors, including the Ethernet hardware from Cisco, the Myrinet from Myricom, and the 2U compute nodes from VA Linux.

These days, the purchasing phase is a lot easier. Almost every vendor can sell you a small or medium cluster without much thought, and even standard large clusters are relatively simple. However, the very large clusters with focused requirements still require a great deal of interaction with the vendor, as will be described later in this chapter when we discuss Jazz.

Throughout this period, we continued the design of the management infrastructure and system software for Chiba City, developing and testing it on a small cluster. (We called the nodes in the small cluster "the freakies." No one seems to knows why. That small cluster is long gone, but the name continues to live on in code references and machine configurations. Be warned.)

Phase 3: Installation

In October 1999, we installed the cluster.

During the preceding month, truck after truck had backed up to our loading dock and dropped off boxes. We had piles of computers, racks, cables, network boxes, disks, and miscellaneous hardware stacked everywhere. Fortunately we had been through large computer installations before, so we were careful to keep rigorous track of which boxes arrived from which vendor on which truck on which day. Despite this, there were still a few missing boxes that took weeks to locate.

During the purchase phase of the system, we realized that the installation of the cluster would be interesting. While the vendors were willing to provide installation technicians as part of the package, we were the ones who knew how the cluster should be connected. We needed to be actively involved in the installation.

Once we realized this, we decided this was an opportunity rather than a problem. Many of the scientists at Argonne are interested in the details of the computers, and we felt that they would probably enjoy being able to help install the system. We decided to assemble the cluster in the style of an old-fashioned barnraising, inviting everyone to join in. Everyone was enthusiastic about the idea. Over forty people signed up to help.

Before the installation, the MCS Systems Group built one of the computing towns. We took detailed notes on what we did and then put together a twelve-page installation manual. Based on the amount of time it took us and the space to work in the machine room, we estimated that we could build the entire cluster in two days. We spent the day before the barnraising working with technicians from VA to assemble the racks and to put the Ethernet and serial cables under the floor.

The barnraising itself was great fun. We divided the volunteers into teams of four people. Each team was led by a member of the Systems Group or a VA technician. We ran four teams at a time. Each team took half a day to assemble one rack, and each rack was half a town. So, by the end of the first day, four computing towns—half of Chiba City—was assembled.

While the teams worked, lots of other things were going on. IBM engineers assembled the storage nodes. The Chiba development team fine-tuned the software for some initial testing. And, most important, Janet Sayre of the Systems Group created just the right kind of atmosphere by sitting in the middle of all the activity and playing the banjo.

At the end of the second day, we connected all of the towns and booted every node. There were a few minor hardware problems with a few systems, so we weren't able to bring them all up, but we were able to run an MPI job on 248 of the nodes.

A time-lapse video of the barnraising is available on the Chiba City Web page `www.mcs.anl.gov/chiba/barnraising/video.html`.

Phase 4: Final Development

For the next four months, the cluster was primarily in development mode. While we had demonstrated that the nodes were running an operating system and connected to each other at the end of the barnraising, a lot of work had to be completed before the system was ready for users.

Among other things, we needed to finish the cluster environment: to get a cluster schedule installed, arrange for data management, and tune the communications networks. We also had to get the management system working, including the ability to create user accounts, push out node configuration changes, and so on.

During this time, we asked a few users to try various tests on the system, but it was not available to more than three or four users.

Phase 5: Early Users

Starting in March 2000, we opened up the cluster to the first set of early application users. There were around four early users at first, all of whom were trying to use the cluster but were also providing detailed feedback to us so that we could fix problems they found.

Once things were relatively stable for them, we opened up the cluster to a few more users, and then a few more, and so on. By the end of the early user phase, we had around sixty user accounts on the cluster.

The majority of the problems that we had to address during this time were related to the scheduler and to the Myrinet communication libraries.

Phase 6: Full Operation

In June 2000, we felt that we had eliminated most of problems that would impact users of the system, and we opened up the cluster for general use.

From this point on, account requests for Chiba City were handled in the same way that requests are handled for other MCS computing facilities—the account request is approved based on whether the use matches the mission (and therefore the funding) of the system. These decisions are made by a group of MCS scientists who are responsible for the activities on the MCS systems.

Chiba City has been in full operation mode since that point. The nature of the operational load has shifted—initially it was supporting a lot of computational science interspersed with computer science testing. As the cluster aged, however, many computational scientists shifted to faster platforms while the computer scientists begin to carry out more substantial systems software development and deployment. Fortunately, the cluster was able to support both of these kinds of usage without any modification.

In the future, Chiba will no doubt go through the next phase: gradual obsolescense. At one time, we could have upgraded it, but at this point it will likely make more sense to simply replace it.

20.1.3 Chiba City Software Environment

In this section we examine two aspects of the Chiba City software environment: computing and management.

The Computing Environment

The computing environment on Chiba City was, like the rest of the cluster, optimized to support computer science yet intended to support other uses. In this section, we describe the standard computing environment on the cluster as well as the special modifications we've made to support computer science and scalability research.

The Default Node Environment. The "node computing environment" is the set of programs and services available on the user-accessible nodes of the system, that is, the computing nodes, the visualization nodes, and the login nodes.

All machines in the cluster run Linux by default. The original distribution that we started with when building the node operating system was Red Hat 6.2. Over time, we added and removed RPMs, changed much of the default behavior, and added software from all over. The nodes are still vaguely recognizable as Red Hat, but they could just as easily have been another distribution.

The specific kernel installed by default on the computing nodes varies over time. Intially, it varied a bit more than we would like because we kept running into odd problems that forced us to switch kernels to isolate problems. After the first year of operation, this settled down—we found a kernel version that worked and didn't change it without substantial testing.

Twice in the lifetime of the cluster, we have installed a completely new software image on the entire cluster in order to roll out a global update of new kernels, libraries, and software. These images are tested rigorously on a small set of nodes before they become the default environment. Updating the computing nodes has proven to be relatively simple, while updating the mayors and servers is always complex.

The compilers available on the front end include C, C++, and Fortran 90. Some users also program in Java, Perl, Python, and PHP.

The Default Cluster Environment. The software glue that we use to turn the pile of nodes into a functional cluster includes a number of different packages.

Communications libraries. The vast majority of jobs on Chiba City use MPI for communication. Our preferred version of MPI is MPICH. We have multiple versions of MPICH installed in order to allow users to choose their favorite compiler and flavor of network. To use generic messages over Myrinet, you must link with MPICH-GM from Myricom.

The set of MPICH installations on Chiba got so large, in fact, that we built a small tool that lists all of the MPICH installations and allows you to pick the one you will be working with by default. The number of MPICH installations inspired the MPICH group to provide an alternative for handling multiple compilers; see Section 8.7.6.

Scheduling. We use OpenPBS on Chiba City for queue management. (See Chapter 17 for a detailed discussion of PBS.) OpenPBS is the open source fork of the Portable Batch Scheduler (PBS).

OpenPBS wasn't designed for environments as large or distributed as Chiba City and therefore has some scalability issues. Most of the problems that users of the cluster have had are related to OpenPBS. Many of these have been solved by the community over time, while others remain issues. Becaues OpenPBS is not under active development by a focused author or community, it's not clear that these will ever be solved.

OpenPBS can be interfaced with an external scheduler that makes the decisions about which jobs in the queue will run at what time. We use the Maui scheduler for this purpose (see Chapter 16 for a detailed discussion of the Maui scheduler). We've been quite happy with Maui.

Global file systems. A global file system is one that is available on every node of the cluster and presents the same view of the data in the file system. It is not necessarily capable of supporting high-performance use, but at least provides a common name space. This normally is used for home directories, common applications, and so on.

One of the early design decisions on Chiba City was that we would not use NFS as a global file system on the cluster. NFS performs badly and scales worse. We felt that if it were really necessary, NFS could be made to work on the 256+ nodes of Chiba City, perhaps by using an optimized NFS server such as a Network Appliance box. However, Chiba City is meant in part to be a prototype of a much larger cluster of 1024 nodes or more, and at that level we expect NFS to be useless. Therefore, we decided to try to run the cluster without a global NFS file system to see how it worked out.

This has been an experiment with a clear finding: global file systems are very important.

Because there was no plausible file system alternative at the time we built Chiba City, we avoided NFS by simply not having a global file system.

It's fairly easy to survive without a global file system for administration purposes—one simply uses `rdist` or other file synchronization mechanisms. On the user side, though, we've had two primary problems:

- *Job staging.* The user's program, support files, and data must be copied out to that user's nodes at the beginning of their job. After the job has completed, any output files that were created must be staged off the nodes before the nodes can be used by the next user. We've tackled this problem from a number of angles and have a solution in place that works but is not as fast as we would like. We believe that multicast file copying is the right solution to this problem and will be investigating it in the near future.

- *Confusion.* Users tend to expect that the cluster will have a global file system. When they log in to their nodes and look around, they don't see the files they expect in their home file system on that node. Even when the entire environment is explained, it is difficult to use the data transfer tools to copy in the right files and copy out the right files.

Initially, we felt that a global file system would be convenient, but not critical. Based on all the difficulties that the users of the system have had, we now believe that a global file system, even if it performs relatively poorly, is essential.

Parallel file systems. In contrast to a global file system, a parallel file system is specifically meant to provide high-performance access to application data for large parallel jobs. For example, one might store a very large input dataset on a parallel file system and subsequently start an application consisting of a few hundred tasks, all of which simultaneously access portions of this dataset. The parallel file system provides both a single logical space for application processes to look for data files and also the performance necessary for these parallel applications to have timely access to their data.

The only open source parallel file system available on Linux clusters at the time that we installed Chiba City was the Parallel Virtual File System (PVFS), which is described in detail in Chapter 19. PVFS and Chiba have a comfortable relationship, and over the years Chiba has become the primary development platform for PVFS. In this environment PVFS has been proven to scale to hundreds of I/O servers and compute processes, and peak aggregate throughput of over 3 GBytes per second has been shown.

Running at these scales also served to highlight some reliability issues in PVFS that were not evident when running in smaller configurations. As these problems have been addressed and PVFS has begun to stabilize, we have begun to make a PVFS file system available as a full-time resource for the users of Chiba City. This has two benefits for users: it provides a high-performance data storage space for use by applications, and it gives users a single place to store datasets that can be accessed from any node.

Job invocation. Job startup of hundreds of processes using MPICH with its default `ch_p4` device is slow. Especially for interactive jobs, something more scalable is needed. Chiba provided some of the motivation for the `ch_p4mpd` device that made use of an earlier version of the MPD process startup system, described in Section 8.7.3. Chiba City has provided a valuable testbed for the development of the MPD system and the version of MPICH that relies on it for job startup. The MPD daemons can run as root, and we have been using them to run a mix of user jobs.

Parallel Unix commands. Chiba City is also serving as testbed for the Scalable Unix Commands [44], which provide parallel versions of the common Unix commands such as `ps` and `cp`. A new version of these [82] is now available at `www.mcs.anl.gov/sut`. The new version implements these interactive commands as MPI applications, so the fast startup of MPI jobs made possible by MPD is critical. We plan to make these familiar commands available to all users as part of the Chiba environment.

Support for Computer Science. Computer scientists have a few general requirements that conflict with running applications on a system: interactivity, a license to crash the system, and the need to modify the system software.

Interactivity. Computer scientists, as well as developers of all types, often want to use the computer in "interactive" mode. They want to edit code, compile it, and then test it immediately. The test, and even the production run, may last only for a few seconds, but it often needs to use the entire system.

If the computer scientist has to submit a test job in a queue and wait until it can be scheduled, it can take hours or even days to complete a one-minute run. If the scheduler is optimized to allow access to the entire machine quickly, the resulting schedule will have huge numbers of unused node time. Production sites and computers that have real dollars tied to machine utilization simply can't afford to have that type of scheduling policy.

This need for interactivity is not unique to computer scientists, of course. Application developers need interactive test cycles while building code that will eventually run for hours. But many of these developers can get away with testing on a small set of nodes, which is easier to acquire, and computer scientists may never need the entire cluster for more than a few minutes at a time.

On Chiba City, we do run a batch scheduler because we have not yet found a better way to equitably share the system between many users. But we clear the cluster of all jobs every day for a two-hour period, during which time no job longer than five minutes can run. This gives computer scientists a two-hour window every day for quick turnaround. Long-running jobs have to wait until the weekend, when we allow jobs to go from Friday evening until Monday morning.

Also, it's possible to schedule a number of nodes and then simply use them in interactive mode during that timeslot.

License to crash. Some computer scientists and developers work on low-level pieces of code that can have bugs that impact the entire operating system on a node. In some cases, such as in file systems and job managers, they may even crash the entire cluster. It's important to have some kind of facility where code like this can be tested in a real-world environment.

Crashing a node on Chiba, even to the point of requiring a rebuild, is fairly minor. We have remote power control, remote monitoring, and the ability to rebuild a node from scratch. (All of these systems are described in Section 20.1.3.) If a node needs to be rebuilt, we simply set a flag in the City database for that node, and that node's mayor will initiate a rebuild the next time that node reboots. If necessary, the mayor can force the reboot.

Crashing the entire cluster is a bigger problem. Still, we set the expectation that we actively support development of the cluster's system software and that we expect things will occasionally crash. We try to minimize the frequency of these large-scale problems and try to minimize their impact. But in a worst-case situation, we can rebuild all the nodes and reboot in 20–30 minutes.

Modifiable node environment. A small number of developers actually need a completely different node environment. They might be testing a set of device drivers that are unusual, or comparing FreeBSD to Windows XP to Linux. (We actually have run FreeBSD and Windows XP on the computing nodes on Chiba.) In any of these cases, the scientists may need to have root access on their nodes or may want to replace the node operating system entirely for the duration of their job.

We support the ability to arbitrarily modify the node computing environment. The mayors build their nodes from a node "image," where an image is a set of files or binary file system data. The mayor will write that to the node's disk, then boot it.

You can build an image of any operating system desired, as long as it boots. During the time that the nodes are reserved for you by the scheduler, you can do whatever is necessary on those nodes. Once your scheduled time is up, the mayor power cycles the node, catches the booting system, and reinstalls the Chiba City default Linux image on the node. This process is illustrated in Figure 20.5.

Management Environment

Starting with the very first design for the cluster, we put a great deal of emphasis on scalable management of Chiba City. For example, one of our goals was never to have to physically touch a node unless it was having hardware problems.

We emphasized scalable administration because we must. All management functions of a very large system, of which Chiba City is a prototype, must scale for

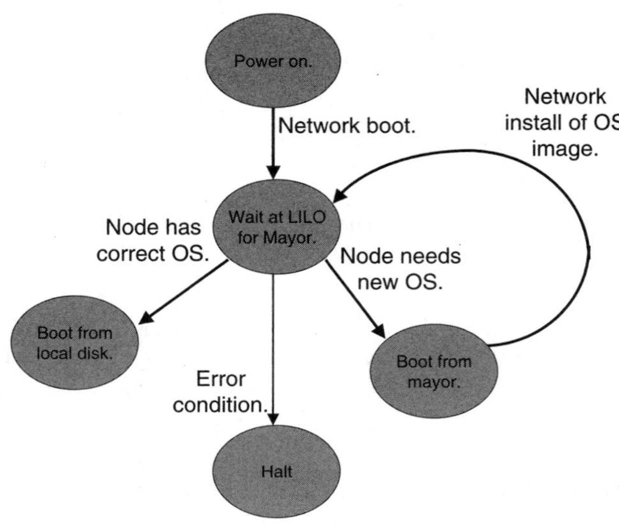

Figure 20.5: Node image management.

obvious reasons. Furthermore, we need scalable management for Chiba itself. The management team for Chiba City consists of three people who are responsible for all aspects of the administration of the cluster, all user support, the development of management tools and system software, involvement in experiments, and other aspects of the MCS computing environment.

The management approach for Chiba City incorporates a number of philosophies:

- Support all the needs of the diverse user community, ranging from stable batch-oriented computing to letting individual users have root access on their nodes.
- Don't change the model too much, because our scientists need to work in the common model to make their tools applicable to others. For example, we couldn't switch over to a shared-memory model of the cluster.
- Manage from a central point. The mayor/town architecture—in which the city mayor presides over the mayors, each of whom manages a set of nodes—is designed to strongly support central management.
- Use open source and existing tools as much as possible. As much as we like to invent cooler wheels, we don't have time.

The remainder of this section describes the individual components of the management environment.

City Database. The city mayor keeps a database of relatively static cluster information. We call this database the City Database or "citydb." The database describes the node/mayor relationship, keeps track of which nodes have what types of hardware, and knows which nodes should have which operating system image at which time.

The City Database is different from the database kept by the scheduler, which is much more dynamic. The dynamic database includes job information, which users own which nodes, and which nodes are currently up. Optimally, both databases would be more closely related, but in practice it has been easier for us to keep the functionality split.

The City Database is authoritative. If the database and reality don't match, then reality must be wrong. Using this philosophy, we can describe the desired cluster configuration in the database and then tell the mayors to make sure the cluster conforms to the configuration. The configuration management tools described below take care of this.

Citydb is built on MySQL using standard SQL.

Configuration Management. At the highest level, the configuration model works this way:

- The configuration for every node is described on the city mayor. Since many nodes are identical, this is not as bad as it might seem.
- The city mayor is the source for all configuration files, images, and RPMs. All mayors keep a mirror image of those files.
- When a configuration change is necessary, the administrator makes a change on the city mayor and then invokes a process to push that change out.
- The nodes themselves are checked at boot up and after user jobs run to make sure that they have the correct configuration.

The primary configuration management tool that we use on Chiba City is a program called `sanity`. The idea behind `sanity` is that it can install RPMs, modify configuration files, and execute scripts. It decides what to do based on a configuration file that can be general or very specific to a node. Once it has established that the node matches the configuration in that file, the node is pronounced sane.

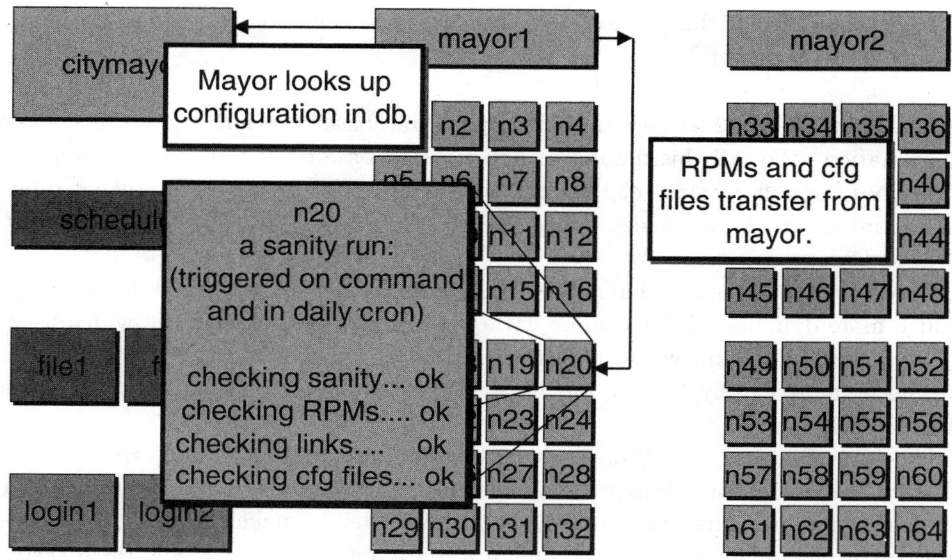

Figure 20.6: OS image management.

The mayors have the ability to invoke `sanity` on each of their nodes. The nodes also run `sanity` when they first boot and after a user job completes. The configuration for `sanity` is an aspect of the image on that node, and the image for each node is recorded in the citydb on the city mayor.

In order to make a change to all of the nodes on the system, one would modify the `sanity` configuration file for the default image, then invoke a global `sanity` push on the city mayor. It tells each mayor to kick off a `sanity` run, and each mayor in turn tells each node to run `sanity`. This process is illustrated in Figure 20.6.

Serial Infrastructure. Another tool in the management arsenal is remote console management. The console of every system in Chiba City is available over the network. The system works in the following way:

- The console port on each node is connected to a serial concentrator for that town.
- The serial concentrator is connected to the mayor.

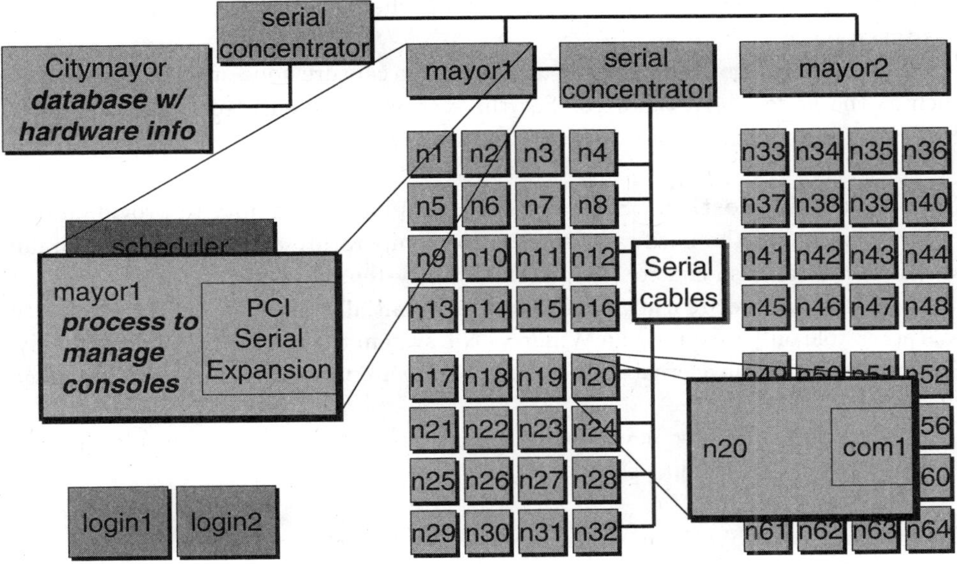

Figure 20.7: Serial infrastructure.

- The mayor runs a daemon called `conserver` that enables remote access to the console from anywhere on the network that has permission. This daemon is an open source tool that is widely used in the system administration community.

- From any point on the MCS network, an administrator can type `console <node>` and get access to the console of that node.

This process is illustrated in Figure 20.7.

In practice, we use this feature only when debugging. Ideally we don't want to actually have to go to all the consoles of all the nodes. Sometimes, though, a node will quit responding for no reason. It's frequently possible to recover the node via the console—or at least get a hint from the console messages what might have gone wrong.

The `conserver` daemon has another feature of console management that is also critical to Chiba City. It can log all of the output of any console to a file or to a process. We wrote a program called `chex` that monitors the output of each console, looking for particular strings. Among other things, this lets us know whether a node is rebooting, whether it has panicked, or whether some other error condition has taken place.

We take advantage of this console monitoring to capture node-specific information such as the node's MAC address. See the section below entitled "The First Boot Process" for an example of why this is useful.

Low-Level Diagnostics. Some motherboards have the ability to provide useful information about the hardware, such as the temperature of the node and the fan speed. Some can also control the power of the system.

The nodes that we are using have this ability. Initially, however, this functionality was accessible only if you used a Windows NT system to monitor the node remotely. Since then, people have created open source software that runs on Linux to manage these ports.

Unfortunately, we have never taken advantage of this system. It would be nice, but we haven't had time to get to it.

Power Control. We do, however, have remote power control for every component of Chiba City. The power control system works as follows:

- Every computer and network box is plugged into a Baytech power unit. There are, on average, five Baytech units per town.
- The Baytech unit is somewhat like a power strip with an Ethernet port. It's possible to telnet to the Baytech and then power on, power off, or query the power status of anything plugged into it.
- We have a simple tool called `city_power` that allows a Chiba City administrator to control the power of any device or set of devices in Chiba City.

The Baytechs are connected to their own network, which is built of very simple Ethernet hubs. We could connect them using the Chiba City Ethernet, but then, if something went wrong with the network, we couldn't access the Baytechs to reset the Ethernet devices. The power network is accessible only via the City Mayor.

The power configuration is shown in detail in Figure 20.8.

The First Boot Process. To explain how the management tools work together, we give an example. One of the more complicated scenarios on a cluster is when a node is booted for the very first time. The cluster software needs to be made

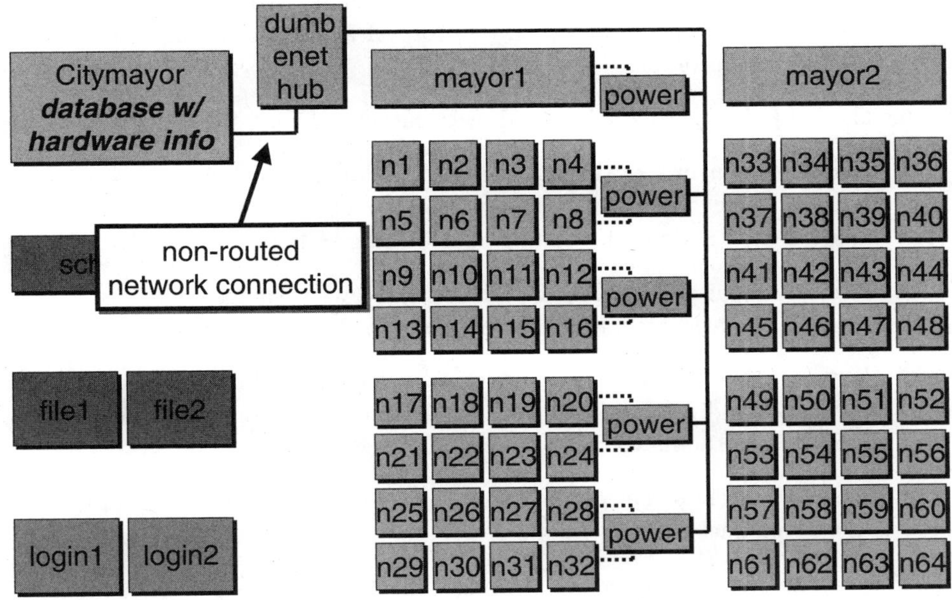

Figure 20.8: Power infrastructure.

aware of that process, and the node needs to get the right operating system. Many people ignore this situation and take care of the details by hand.

Here is what happens on Chiba City when a completely new node is installed in the cluster:

1. We set a flag in the City Database indicating that this is a new node.

2. The node is installed in the correct spot in the rack and cabled appropriately.

3. We install the correct BIOS in the node. This, unfortunately, is still done manually, although we are looking into a boot floppy approach that will do the right thing. Among other things, the BIOS is set to boot using PXE, a type of network booting. This means that on all subsequent power cycles, the node will boot from the network.

4. The node is turned on, and it boots from the network. Some server on the net, usually that node's mayor, responds with the boot image.

5. The boot code is a Linux boot image that includes LILO and a kernel. LILO is configured to launch and then wait forever at its boot prompt, occasionally reissuing the prompt.

6. The LILO boot prompt is issued over the serial line.

7. The node's mayor sees the Boot prompt. It knows which node this is because it knows which serial lines it is watching. Thus, at this point, the mayor knows that it node15 (for example) is waiting to boot.

8. The mayor checks the City Database to see what image should be on that node. It discovers that this is a new node.

9. Based on this information, it issues a boot command over the serial line to the node, handing it a set of boot parameters. This command tells the node to boot from the mayor from the Build Image.

10. The node receives the command and boots the Build Image kernel that was transferred back in Step 4.

11. As a part of booting the Build Image, the setup scripts partition the node's disk and install the correct image files.

12. At the end of the Build Image, the node displays certain relevant pieces of information to its console, including its Ethernet MAC address.

13. The mayor, which is monitoring the console, now knows that this new node has successfully built. Furthermore, it has the MAC address of that node.

14. The mayor updates the DHCP tables on the city mayor with the new MAC address and queues a DHCP restart request.

15. The mayor updates Citydb with a flag saying that the node has the correct image installed.

16. The node waits for a minute and then reboots. Once again, it PXE boots and loads the boot image from the mayor. It issues the LILO boot prompt to the serial console and waits.

17. The mayor checks Citydb and notes that this node has already built the correct image onto its local disk. It issues a "boot from local disk" command to the LILO boot prompt over the serial line.

18. The node boots from the local disk. Among other things, it will send out a DHCP request to get its IP address and will be sent the correct IP address for the node in that spot of the cluster.

19. After rebooting, the node runs `sanity`. It installs any modifications necessary for that operating system image.

20. Finally, the node is ready to run. The scheduler notes that the node is up and adds it to the pool of allocatable resources.

This whole process is long to describe but fast to run. The only slow part is the operating system build in Step 11, when the bits are being installed on the local disk. That can take 10–15 minutes, with the exact time dependent on the size of the image and the activity on the network. Once the node has been installed and the BIOS updated, the process requires no intervention from an administrator.

20.1.4 Chiba City Use

The average user of Chiba City interacts with it just like any other cluster of distributed supercomputer. Consider the following scenario.

A user logs into the front end node using `ssh`. She compiles her code on that system, or perhaps copy in precompiled code. If she wants to test the code on several nodes before submitting a large job, she can choose nodes on the 32 nodes of the cluster that we refer to as the interactive town. This set of nodes is configured in the same way as the standard computing nodes, but is never scheduled. It is always available specifically for testing purposes. It's quite possible that two users' codes will conflict with each other, so it's not useful for performance testing or long-running code. Once she is confident that her code will run successfully, she prepares her code and her job data to be copied out to the nodes that she will eventually be allocated. She does this by putting everything together in a directory. Finally, she submits her job to the PBS queue using the `qsub` command. She can check on the status of her job with `qstat`. Eventually she will be assigned a set of nodes for the duration of her timeslot, and her job will be invoked on those nodes. During this time, she will be able to login to her nodes, which she will want to do if she's running an interactive job. If there are any errors with her job, she will be notified by e-mail. Once her job has completed or her time is up, whichever comes first, the datafiles she created are copied back to her home directory on the front end node.

Nonstandard use of Chiba City can entail endless variations of this scenario. A user might arrange to have dedicated access to the cluster for a long period of time—this requires administrator and, in some cases, management approval. Or a user might have a custom image to be tested and then arranged for installation on that user's nodes. Some people use the storage nodes as part of I/O experiments. Others use the visualization nodes, sometimes in conjunction with the jobs on the computing nodes, and other times as a completely separate activity.

Currently, we have about one hundred active users on Chiba City. We expect to add several hundred more in the next few months as a result of changes in the allocation policies on some of our other supercomputers.

Since its installation, Chiba has been used for many different types of activities. Notable among these are the following:

- Monte Carlo simulations in nuclear physics
- Computational optimization
- Parallel and numerical library development
- Distributed supercomputing development
- Communication library development
- File system development
- Astrophysical simulation
- Scalable system software development
- Visualization
- Genomics
- Automated reasoning
- Climate modeling of both Earth and Mars
- Molecular dynamics simulations
- Scalability testing of open source tools

A detailed description of these projects is beyond the scope of this chapter; this list is merely meant to give a feel for the different types of use that the cluster enables.

20.1.5 Final Thoughts on Chiba City

In this case study, we have described in detail the kinds of issues that we encounter when designing, building, and running a multipurpose large cluster. We hope that the topics discussed here will be useful to others who may find themselves in a similar situation.

Lessons Learned

This entire case study is about lessons that we've learned while running Chiba City. We still have a few that are worth mentioning.

- It is surprisingly difficult to run a job on the entire cluster. Most users don't care about this, but management would always like to confirm that a job has used every possible resource on the system. It seems like there is always at least one node that is down for hardware maintenance, or one network interface this is flaky, or a node that just isn't in the mood to play. We have actually run jobs on all of the nodes using both types of network, but these jobs take focused effort and are relatively rare.

- In a cluster, the hardware gets stressed beyond what any vendor expects because it is always being used, sometimes in ways that the designer never anticipated. We've had bad AGP and PCI slots, large-scale memory problems, fan lossage, bad cables, and everything else. Furthermore, when buying commodity hardware, one gets commodity quality. This hardware doesn't take abuse the way high-end supercomputing equipment does. It's a very good idea to invest in a three-year hardware maintenance option.

- When running a cluster like Chiba City, it is essential to have at least one person who lives in the Linux world. Two or three people is even better. Those people should follow the important Linux mailing lists, track bugs, and follow discussions on Web sites. The success of the cluster often rides on figuring out exactly which version of the kernel works best with which set of applications, or knowing that a particular feature will be available (or removed) in a few weeks.

Future Directions for Chiba

Chiba City has largely been a success. We would like for some portions of the system, notably the scheduler and the I/O system, to be more reliable and functional, but despite these failings, good science has been accomplished on the computer, both in the realm of computer science and in scientific simulation. The model that we use to manage and operate the cluster has worked well and shows every sign of scaling to a much larger cluster. We have a number of plans for software modifications to improve the system and to support new capabilities.

In the near future, the scalability work that has been started on Chiba City must continue to expand to larger and larger testbed systems. Many open scientific questions require systems that can deliver sustained petaflops of computation. It is not yet clear what the path to building a petaflop system is, but it is very likely that such a computer will be built from many tens or hundreds of thousands of individual computing components. As a community, in order to build such a system, we must have systems software that can operate a machine of that scale, and we must have algorithms and applications that can make reasonable use of it. Thus, while the computing industry forges ahead with building better and faster processors, we must have a strategy for connecting them together and making them run well. Scalability testbeds such as Chiba City are an important part of this plan, and we hope that research and activities in this space will continue to be expanded.

For more information on Chiba City and the software used to drive it, see `www.mcs.anl.gov/chiba`.

20.2 Jazz—A New Production Cluster

In 2002, Argonne determined that the Laboratory had a need for a production computing facility that would support the computing needs of scientists and engineers around the Lab. The Lab's Computational Science Advisory Committee discussed and studied the situation in detail and determined that a Linux cluster would be the appropriate way to satisfy the majority of the Lab's scientific computing requirements. Unlike Chiba City, which was limited to computer scientists and collaborators, this new cluster would be available to anyone at the Lab.

Thus, in October, we installed "Jazz," a 350-node Linux cluster purchased from Linux NetworX. Jazz achieved just over a teraflop on sustained Linpack benchmarks, putting it in the top 50 of the world's fastest supercomputers (or at least those that had been registered on the list). Although our goal had only been to install a cost-effective and efficient mid-range computer, it was interesting to see what it took to land towards the top of the top 500 list. A far more interesting fact was that we had a lot of company. The entire list, including the upper echelon, was loaded with clusters running Linux. Since we had installed Chiba City a mere three years earlier, the world of high-end computing had bought into (or been consumed by) Linux clusters in a serious way.

20.2.1 Different Worlds

While our plans for Jazz were built on our experience with Chiba City, we found that designing, installing, and running Jazz was quite different for a number of reasons.

First, the entire field of cluster computing on Linux had matured substantially. It was now possible to go to many different vendors and request some flavor of Linux cluster without first explaining what Linux was, why we wanted it, and how clusters worked. Vendors had experience with installing clusters. They had custom software suites, often built on open-source tools, for managing clusters.

That said, we found that buying a Linux cluster was still more complicated than buying an IBM SP or an SGI Origin 2000 simply because of the range of choices in hardware, interconnect, storage and software. One might say that buying an established supercomputer is a lot like buying a condo—you don't have any choice about where the walls go, but you choose your own furniture. In contrast, buying a Linux cluster today is like buying a house that hasn't been built yet. You sit down with the blueprints and the architect and discuss where to put toilets and whether or not to have a fourth bedroom.

A second reason that the experience was different was simply because the hardware had changed substantially in three years. Rather than looking at 500 MHz Pentium IIIs in a 2U case, we were looking at 2.4 GH Pentium IVs in a sub-1U case. This, of course, is something we've all grown to expect, but it's still entertaining. While the impact of Moore's Law is one of the main economic forces behind the technology industry, one could still make an argument that it's always better to delay your purchase by six months, when everything will be faster and cheaper.

Finally, and perhaps most importantly, Jazz was different then Chiba City because it was built for a different purpose.

20.2.2 Mission and Design

Jazz was designed from the outset to support serious production computing for a wide-range of users, namely the Argonne scientific computing community. Argonne is somewhat like a university campus in that it is divided into departments (or divisions, in Argonne's case) that operate relatively independently. For example, there's a chemistry division, a physics division, and a lot of engineering divisions.

Overall there are over thirty different divisions at Argonne, and Jazz was meant to be a technical computing resource for all of them.

Therefore, unlike Chiba City, Jazz was meant to be a "production" resource. It needed to perform well on a mix of code. It needed to be stable. We needed to make sure we had a happy user community, so we had to be helpful, answer questions, solve problems, and not crash the machine by trying out the latest Linux kernel to check out cool new features.

The need to be a production facility impacted the design in a number of ways:

- As part of the initial planning, we carried out a lot of benchmarks and testing on available systems using code that we expected to use on the system. We verified what we already knew—in most cases, application performance was directly related to the performance of the memory system. Anything that could be done to avoid memory bottlenecks and speed up memory was likely to be worth it. As a result, we decided to use nodes with just one CPU—the last thing we needed were multiple CPUs fighting over the memory bus, even if the price/performance ratio looked better on multiple CPU systems. We also decided to go with the best memory technology that we could afford. Benchmarks with Rambus were much better than the same tests with slower memory.

- We also knew from a survey of the application community that many of the applications were bound by the size of physical memory on a node. Thus we needed to try to maximize the amount of memory within budget constraints.

- Although we didn't expect every user to be running code that relied heavily on communications performance, we knew that many would, so we planned again on having a high-performance interconnect for the cluster.

- As described earlier, we knew from our experience with Chiba City that a global file system was essential. We knew that we had to have some way of having exactly the same file namespace on all nodes, even if the I/O performance on those files were bad.

- We also knew that the highest-performing code required fast I/O but could live with variable reliability for the sake of speed. Thus we expected that we would likely to have to have at least two different file systems installed (like our older SPs had had): a slow, global, reliable home file system, and a fast parallel file system.

- We'd had no end of troubles with OpenPBS on Chiba City, so we decided to use a more current resource manager. After surveying the options, we ended up buying PBS Pro.

- We knew that the system would require more human effort to support applications and operate in production mode for a large community than a cluster for a small number of users or purposes. Thus we planned on hiring four or five system administrators and application engineers.

- With a lot of users, and when allocating time on the machine to projects, the account and project system becomes a critical part of the infrastructure. We therefore anticipated that the time for "early user mode" would take longer than on previous systems, as we would be getting the allocation system working during that time.

- Being production means being fairly consistent. Because we expected to keep the software installation on the computing nodes relatively constant (as compared to Chiba City, where we load new images continually), we didn't feel that we needed as substantial a management infrastructure. Also, we had carried out a lot of testing of the management functionality of Chiba City, as reported in our team's paper at Cluster 2002 [36]. So, while Jazz still has mayors, it has many fewer than Chiba City did. The irony here is that in order to have a production facility, we felt that we could have fewer management systems, but this has turned out to be true.

- Finally, we needed the hardware on Jazz to be supported by a vendor. As part of the purchase, we specified that everything needed to have support for at least three years.

As a result, by knowing that we had to run a production facility and understanding the characteristics of the applications fairly well, we had a pretty solid definition of our requirements. In short, we had to have:

- single-CPU nodes with a lot of fast RAM

- a fast interconnect

- a rock-solid, but not necessarily fast, global file system

- a fast parallel file system

- reliable systems software

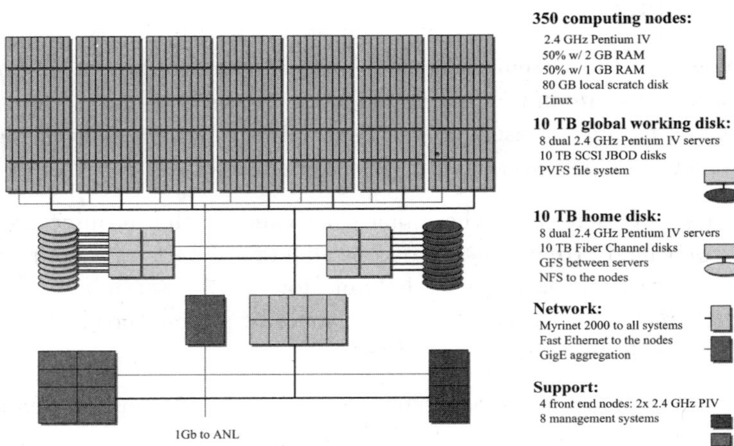
Jazz - the ANL LCRC Computing Cluster
350 computing nodes:
2.4 GHz Pentium IV
50% w/ 2 GB RAM
50% w/ 1 GB RAM
80 GB local scratch disk
Linux
10 TB global working disk:
8 dual 2.4 GHz Pentium IV servers
10 TB SCSI JBOD disks
PVFS file system
10 TB home disk:
8 dual 2.4 GHz Pentium IV servers
10 TB Fiber Channel disks
GFS between servers
NFS to the nodes
Network:
Myrinet 2000 to all systems
Fast Ethernet to the nodes
GigE aggregation
Support:
4 front end nodes: 2x 2.4 GHz PIV
8 management systems
1Gb to ANL

Figure 20.9: Argonne's Jazz Cluster

- good vendor support

This was the list that we took to the cluster vendors. From there, the question was how best to maximize the cluster parameters within our budget.

20.2.3 Architecture

The system that we ended up purchasing is illustrated in Figure 20.9. We purchased this cluster, Jazz, in its entirety from Linux NetworX.

The cluster consists of:

- 350 computing nodes. Each node has one 2.4 GHz Pentium IV. Half of the nodes have 2 GB of RAM, half have 1 GB. We ended up using DDR RAM for budget reasons after confirming that the performance was sufficient.

- 4 login nodes. These nodes are identical to the computing nodes, except that each has two CPUs and 2 GB of RAM.

- 8 home directory servers and 10 TB of FibreChannel disk. For home directory service, we went with a recommendation made by Linux NetworX and used a combination of GFS and NFS. GFS is a file system product from Sistina.

Each of these eight servers has joint access to a large GFS file system shared between them. Each then provides access to that file system to one eigth of the cluster using NFS. In this way, we avoid the scaling problems of NFS while maintaining consistency across all of the NFS servers.

- 8 PVFS servers and 10 TB of JBOD disk. For parallel I/O, we use eight servers running the Parallel Virtual File System exported to the entire cluster. Most users of this file system access it via MPI-IO interfaces.
- 8 management nodes. These nodes share a variety of duties including scheduler and job management, configuration management, monitoring, web services, and so on. As noted above, the management requirements for Jazz are substially lower than those of Chiba City because we rarely change the configuration of the entire system.
- Myrinet 2000. We selected Myrinet for the fast interconnect for the system because it was proven to scale to clusters this size (and larger), performs well, and wasn't overwhelmingly expensive. We seriously considered Gigabit Ethernet as an alternative, but the cost of well-performing GigE switches is still prohibitive, and the reliability of some GigE NICs under Linux is a problem.
- Fast Ethernet. Even with Myrinet, we felt that we need a rock-solid network for management and applications to fall back onto.

For management purposes such as remote power control and console management, Linux NetworX provided a proprietary solution—the ICEbox, which fulfilled the functionality of a collection of similar hardware that we'd found incredibly handy on Chiba City.

20.2.4 Installation

It's interesting to understand precisely what you're getting when you buy a cluster. The vendors are striving to be able to provide a turn-key system, but the definition of "turn-key" changes rather dramatically between a cluster that runs one application and a cluster than runs hundreds. We didn't expect to have a system that worked with no modification, nor did we expect to be handed 350 computers with no operating system, but we weren't sure where in the middle things would land.

On the hardware side, having installed a 256-node cluster ourselves, we had no particular desire to build a 350-node cluster. Fortunately, this was one of the many things that the vendors had taken on, and learned to do quite well, since we'd had the Chiba City barnraising. Linux NetworX installed Jazz without substantial help from us, although we needed to be involved from time-to-time to handle power attachments, floor space issues, cable routing decisions, and so on.

On the software side, it turns out that it would have been possible for us to stay similarly uninvolved. We would have ended up with Linux installed on every node, an environment for parallel computing that had MPI and PVM installed, the global file systems built, and Linux NetworX's "ClusterWorX" management software that could be used to build and configure nodes. This was substantially more than we could have imagined when installing Chiba City three years earlier, and was quite excellent in and of itself.

However, to run a production computing environment, we had to do quite a lot more work, such as installing extra software, building the user environment, building the allocation mechanisms, installing bug and request tracking systems, and adding our favorite set of management tools. Fortunately, the Linux NetworX folks understood that we were in a rush, so while they were working on software installs, we had joint access to the machine. We ended up working together on a lot of the detailed configuration.

As it turns out, it was very important for us to be involved during the software installation, because we needed to become very familiar with the configuration of the machine as a part of taking ownership of it. Also, there were several situations where we were able to ask the vendor to do things differently then they normally would have in order to accomodate our specific needs.

20.2.5 Software Environment

While it's not feasible to list the entire set of software packages that are installed on the cluster in this space, it is useful to describe the more essential tools available to users of the system.

This list of software refers to the software installed on the login nodes, which is where the users do the bulk of their work. The compute nodes have fully-populated Linux installations and all of the tools that might be necessary to have on compute nodes (such as libraries) but don't necessarily have every tool installed on them.

The Base Installation

- RedHat 7.2

- All the tools and languages you'd expect in a reasonable UNIX-based environment including X11, Perl, Python, the GNU tools, CVS, Bitkeeper, and so on.

The Development Environment

ABSoft Compilers	MPICH - multiple versions
NAG Compilers and Libraries	ROMIO
Intel Compilers and Libraries	MPICH-2
Portland Group Compilers	Globus
Totalview	Columbus
IDL	NetCDF
Matlab	NCAR
Gaussian	PETSc
StarCD	ScaLAPACK
Gnu compilers	

20.2.6 Going Production

When you buy a large machine from a vendor, one of the first major transition points in the lifecycle of that system is when the machine is turned over to you from the vendor. In our case, this happened after Linux NetworX had finished building the machine, installing the base software with a number extensions, configuring the file systems, teaching us about the tools that they delivered, and passing a number of tests confirming that the machine was operating correctly. While it was great to finally get to this point, our work was really just starting.

If this machine were going to run only a few applications or support only a few users, we could have started doing so immediately. Enough of the software was installed and enough of the system configured that we could have started using it for parallel jobs at this point. However, in order to turn it into a multi-user, multi-project resource, we had quite a few more things to complete.

For the next two months, we kept the system in "Configuration and Testing mode". During this time, we installed the majority of the programs listed in the previous section. We installed the Maui scheduler to work in conjunction with PBS Pro, and spent a lot of time configuring those. We began to create web pages with information for the user community. We put in an initial user account creation system, and began to slowly add users to the system. These were users who we knew would be comfortable on large and potentially unstable machines, users who could put the machine through its paces and give us lots of feedback on how it was working, what was missing, and so on. By the time we were done with this phase of testing, we probably had about ten user accounts on the system.

Once the system was relatively stable, we entered "Early User mode". At this point, we added accounts for anyone who asked, with the caveat that we were still specifically asking for feedback and that the machine might be taken down at any point to fix problems or reconfigure things. The bulk of our own effort at this point, beyond responding to user issues, was to focus on the account creation system and the allocation tracking system. (That said—responding to user issues took a huge amount of time.) In our division, we already have a comprehensive user account management system. We extended it to include the Jazz system, and then created web pages so that anyone at the Laboratory could easily request an account specific to Jazz and use those web pages to manage their account.

Like most multi-user production facilities, we planned for Jazz to be formally allocated. We had an allocations committee that would be making decisions about which projects at the Laboratory would be able to use the system and what percentage of the machine would be available to each project. The committee met several times to discuss allocation and scheduling policies, and our job was to make sure that those allocation policies could be implemented on the system. We used the "QBank" software [92], created by Pacific Northwest National Laboratory, to manage allocations.

After three months of Early User Mode, the cluster was stable, the majority of requested software was configured and installed, we had a fairly good start at the web-based documentation, and the account and allocation system was working. We were ready to shift formally into production mode.

We held a ribbon-cutting ceremony to mark the occasion, at which the Laboratory Director, Dr. Hermann Grunder, spoke and helped cut a ceremonial ribbon cable.

From this point onwards, we opened up the cluster to access by the entire Laboratory community and began to track allocations. Based on the policies set the allocations committee, any user at Argonne who got an account would be given 1000 CPU hours of initial startup time. To compute for longer than that, a user would need to submit a project request that explained the project in fairly substantial detail. The committee would then determine how much time on the machine to allocate—times of 20,000 hours and more are currently typical. Although we have the option of stopping any project that has run beyond its allocation, we're currently taking the more friendly approach of warning those projects that they're exceeding their allocated time and discussing the usage of the system with the allocations board. As the user community and usage on Jazz expands, this will no doubt become a more complex issue.

20.2.7 Jazz Status and Futures

Jazz is now really at the beginning of its life cycle. At the time of this writing, it has been in production mode for only a few months. Use of the cluster is expanding regularly, and we will begin outreach efforts across the Laboratory shortly.

Response from the user community has been exceptionally positive. The individual nodes are fast and responsive—the Pentium IVs and the memory system compare well to all other systems currently out there, although this will of course change as new technology is rolled out. The entire cluster is solid and reliable.

Although we are still early in the project, we can identify a number of essential bits of information that we have learned or confirmed:

- Both GFS and PVFS are working well. Having a global file system is proving to be just as critical as we had thought it would be.

- We're generally happy with the way that the vendors have embraced Linux clusters. Designing and purchasing this system was far simpler then what we went through with Chiba City, and the vendor handled installation and followup support quite well. Obviously, the experience of others in this case will depend on who their specific vendor is, but the point here is that there are now a number of professionals in the business who are doing a good job of this.

- That said, these clusters are still not simple. We've had some very serious headaches with the networks, the file systems, the schedulers, and in configuring the environment. We've overcome all of these (for the moment), but the situation is not yet optimal, and is nowhere near turn-key.

- Adequate and experienced staffing is essential. We have had the equivalent of three system administrators working full-time (and then some) on this project since its inception. Among the staff are people with experience on large-scale parallel computers, strong Linux backgrounds, and networking skills. As the user community grows, we are adding people who can focus on supporting applications with porting, parallelizing, and tuning code, as well as running seminars and tutorials. This is essential to the success of a production facility for a large user community.

We hope that Jazz, in its current configuration, will meet the needs of the Argonne computing community for the next three years. Our development and expansion focus during that time will be on application support and capabilities. If Jazz is operating correctly as a production facility, it will simply continue to work smoothly through the efforts of the systems administration team. Based on our experiences thus far with Jazz and with Linux clusters in general, we're confident that this goal is within reach.

21 Conclusions

William Gropp and Ewing Lusk

In this book we have tried to collect the information needed to build, use, and operate a Beowulf computer. The chapter authors have described the key issues and technologies associated with their individual topics, and then gone on to provide details associated with the current state of the art. We hope that this combination will not only guide you in making near-term decisions but also enable you to make informed choices in the future regarding hardware and software use with clusters.

21.1 Keeping Up To Date

In preparing this second edition of *Beowulf Cluster Computing with Linux*, nearly all authors were reminded how quickly software evolves by the number of changes in the details of installing and using the software packages described here. Fortunately, it is primarily the *details* that change; the concepts either remain the same or evolve much more slowly.

A number of approaches exist for keeping up to date. Nearly all of the software packages and some of the hardware items described in this book have web sites. We have tried to include as many as possible explicitly; if we haven't included the site you need, Google (`www.google.com`) is your friend.

The Beowulf mailing list (`beowulf@beowulf.org`) is an active, ongoing discussion of all Beowulf-related topics, for clusters both large and small. A number of specific technology areas also have newsgroups, such as `comp.parallel`, `comp.parallel.mpi`, and `comp.parallel.pvm`. Specific software often has its own mailing list and/or web site.

21.2 Future Directions for Clusters

It seems likely that Beowulf-style cluster computing will continue to grow, due to considerations of both supply (costs will continue to decrease, driven by commodity markets) and demand (more applications will come into existence and evolve to exploit parallelism to meet their computing resource requirements). As the use of clusters grows, we will see even more "integration vendors" that bundle pre-assembled hardware with increasingly professional software to provide turnkey solutions. At the same time, those seeking the most economical solutions will still be able to create their own quite capable parallel computers from components available at the nearest mall and software they can download for free. A wonderful thing about Beowulf computing is that the same technology underlies both approaches.

21.2.1 Clusters Get Faster

The amazing increases in CPU clock rates will continue, at least for the next few years, following the "doubling every 18 month" prediction of Moore's law. However, Moore's law, which is really an observation about the rate at which the size of features such as a transistor shrink on silicon wafer, cannot hold true indefinitely. If nothing else, feature sizes are rapidly approaching the dimensions of a single atom, where no further reduction will be possible (even if a gate can be built with a single atom). One possibility is to increase the CPU power by using parallelism; a number of research groups are already looking at such approaches. In some ways, these CPUs become little clusters. Other approaches look at different architectures, concentrating on a memory-centric, rather than processor-centric, computing model. Whatever the approach taken, we can expect that CPU's will continue to rapidly increase in performance.

The development that would have the greatest impact on the range of applications that can exploit cluster computing would occur if interconnection networks began behaving according to Moore's Law. So far, this has not been historically true, but recent developments are encouraging. The early parallel computer networks started at relatively low speed. (The Intel iPSC 1 used the original Ethernet to connect its nodes based on the Intel 80286 CPU.) There was a rapid increase through the time of the Intel Paragon and the ASCI Red machine, which had more than 100 MByte/second bandwidth between nodes. It is unfortunate that these early networks were never commoditized into high performance system area networks (the one exception being Myrinet, which grew out of Chuck Seitz's pioneering work with the Cosmic Cube, a machine that can be viewed as the ancestor of all cluster computers because it used commodity CPUs as the building block).

One solution to the problem of commodity, multi-vendor high-performance networking may be Infiniband. The original goals for Infiniband included doubling bandwidth at the same rate as Moore's law—every 18 months. Unlike latency, which is constrained by the speed of light to no less than about 1 ns/foot (3 ns/meter), increasing bandwidth is an engineering problem. Infiniband vendors are just beginning to sell large-scale switches this year. Time will tell whether Infiniband achieves its promise and provides a suitable cost-effective cluster network. Software will also be required; fortunately, support for MPI, both as part of the MPICH project and MVAPIBCH (`nowlab.cis.ohio-state.edu/projects/mpi-iba`), is already available.

21.2.2 Clusters Get Larger

This year (2003), multiple Linux clusters are being installed with more than a thousand nodes each. Even larger, "Beowulf-like" systems are coming soon, such as the 10,000-CPU Red Storm machine from Cray and the 64,000-CPU BG/L from IBM. These will be among the very most powerful computers in the world when they are installed. While you can't buy all of their components at the corner electronics store, many of the topics covered in this book are relevant to their design, system software, programming, use, and management. And in the future, the technology used in these machines may become more generally available.

One interesting open-source effort is the Scalable Systems Software project (`www.scidac.org/ScalableSystems`). In it a number of groups are collaborating on the development of a component architecture, with well-defined interfaces expressed in XML, for the systems software (schedulers, process managers, monitors, accounting systems, etc.) for large systems. The component structure makes it possible for alternate component implementations to evolve individually and interact with other, separately developed, components.

21.2.3 Clusters Get Smaller

Nodes developed for the game market have become capable enough to run Linux and thus serve as cluster building blocks. A number of sites have assembled clusters from Sony Playstation 2's. Continuing downward in size, as we noted above, increasing densities for transistors on a chip are leading in the direction of clusters that fit on a single chip. You can already buy small clusters that are in a single PC tower; desktop clusters will become common-place in the next few years. And someday soon, you may have a cluster in your PDA or cell phone.

21.3 Learning More

Although we hope we have done a lot more than "scratch the surface" of Beowulf-style computing in this book there is of course much more to learn in every area, and keeping current in any area of computing remains a challenge. We recommend the reading list in Appendix B, which includes some other books in this series from MIT Press. Suggestions for further study are also given in individual chapters.

To keep abreast of the latest research in cluster computing, you might consider attending any of the several annual conferences and workshops devoted to related topics. Examples include the IEEE Cluster Conference (all aspects of clusters), Supercomputing (both research papers and vendor exhibits, especially high-end machines), EuroPVM/MPI (both applications and implementation research on MPI and PVM), and the multiple conferences devoted to Linux and to parallel computing in general.

Now that you have finished this book, it is time to put your new knowledge into practice. Go forth and compute!

A Glossary of Terms

Beowulf-class system: commodity cluster employing personal computers or low-cost SMP servers to achieve excellent price-performance initially developed by the Beowulf project at the NASA Goddard Space Flight Center

bit: the fundamental unit of information representing a two-state value; a digital circuit capable of storing a two-state value

BLAS: basic linear algebra subroutines

bps: bits per second, a unit measure of data transfer rate

byte: a commonly addressed quantity of digital information storage of eight bits reflecting one of 256 distinct values

cluster: in the general sense, any interconnected ensemble of computers capable of independent operation but employed to service a common workload

commodity cluster: a cluster of commercial computing nodes integrated with a commercial system area network

constellation: a cluster of large DSM, SMP, or MPP computing nodes incorporating more microprocessors per node than there are nodes in the system

COW: cluster of workstations; an early project at the University of Wisconsin

DSM: distributed shared memory multiprocessor, tightly coupled cache coherent multiprocessor with non-uniform memory access

EPIC: Explicitly Parallel Instruction Computing

Ethernet: the first widely used and truly ubiquitous local area network operating at 10 Mbps

Fast Ethernet: a cost effective local area network based on the original Ethernet protocol that has become very popular with low end Beowulf-class systems; providing 100 Mbps

Gigabit Ethernet: a LAN that is the successor of Fast Ethernet providing peak bandwidth of 1 Gbps.

GNU: a project resulting in a number of open source and free software tools including the GNU C compiler and Emacs

GPL: GNU Public License; a legal framework protecting open source software

HDF: Hierarchical data format, both a file format and high level interface for I/O access in both sequential and parallel applications

HPL: High Performance Linpack

Infiniband: a system-area network designed to provide high performance and to provide a path for rapid improvement in network bandwidth.

ISA: Instruction Set Architecture

LAN: Local Area Network; a network employed within a single administrative domain such as a laboratory or office complex, connecting PCs and workstations together to file servers, printers and other peripherals, and to the Internet. Low cost LAN technology has been adopted to provide Beowulf-class systems with inexpensive moderate bandwidth interconnect

LED: Light Emitting Diode

Linux: the dominant Unix-like cross-platform operating system developed by a broad international community enabled by an open source code framework

Mbps: 1 million bits per second data transfer rate or bandwidth

Mega: prefix meaning 1 million or in the case of storage 2^{20}

message passing: An approach to parallelism based on communicating data between processes running (usually) on separate computers.

metadata: Used in the context of file systems, this is the information describing the file, including owner, permissions, and location of data

MPI: message passing interface, a community derived logical standard for the transfer of program messages between separate concurrent processes

MPP: Massively Parallel Processors

MTBF: Mean Time Between Failure

Myricom: vendor, distributor, and developer of the Myrinet network for commodity clusters

network: the combination of communication channels, switches, and interface controllers that transfer digital messages between Beowulf cluster nodes

NIC: network interface controller; usually the combination of hardware and software that matches the network transport layer to the computer node of a cluster

NOW: network or workstations, and early influential commodity cluster project at UC Berkeley

PC: see Personal Computer

PCI: the dominant external interface standard for PCs and workstations to support I/O controllers including NICs

Personal Computer or PC: mass market microprocessor based computer employed by both commercial and consumer users for everything from games to spreadsheets and internet browsers; emphasizing performance/cost for maximum market share, these nodes are the basis for low cost Beowulf-class clusters

PVFS: Parallel virtual file system

PVM: Parallel Virtual Machine, a library of functions supporting an advanced message-passing semantics

QSW: high bandwidth network employed in very large clusters, specifically the SC series developed by Compaq

Quadrics: commercial vendor of networking hardware and software. See QSW

RISC: Reduced Instruction Set Computer

ROMIO: Portable implementation of MPI-IO interface (not an acronym)

RWCP: major Japanese initiative to develop robust and sophisticated cluster software environment

SAN: System Area Network; a network optimized for use as a dedicated communication medium within a commodity cluster

Scheduler: a software tool which is part of the node operating system or system middleware that manages the assignment of tasks to cluster nodes and determines the timing of their execution

SMP: Symmetric MultiProcessor, tightly coupled cache coherent multiprocessor with uniform memory access

SSE: Streaming SIMD Extensions

WAN: Wide Area Networks used to connect distant sites, even on a continental scale

B Annotated Reading List

This appendix contains an annotated reading list of books and papers of interest to builders and users of Beowulf clusters.

Jack Dongarra, Ian Foster, Geoffrey Fox, William Gropp, Ken Kennedy, Linda Torczon, and Andy White, editors. *Sourcebook of Parallel Computing.* Morgan Kaufmann, 2003. A collection of chapters written by many of the leaders in the field of parallel computing, including overviews of parallel computer architecture, programming models, algorithms. Also included are descriptions of applications that have successfully used parallel computing.

Ian Foster. *Designing and Building Parallel Programs.* Addison-Wesley, 1995. Also at: `http://www.mcs.anl.gov/dbpp/`. A general introduction to the process of creating parallel applications. It includes short sections on MPI and HPF.

William Gropp, Steven Huss-Lederman, Andrew Lumsdaine, Ewing Lusk, Bill Nitzberg, William Saphir, and Marc Snir. *MPI—The Complete Reference: Volume 2, The MPI-2 Extensions.* MIT Press, Cambridge, MA, 1998. An annotated version of the MPI Standard; this contains additional examples and discussion about MPI-2.

William Gropp, Ewing Lusk, and Anthony Skjellum. *Using MPI: Portable Parallel Programming with the Message Passing Interface,* 2nd edition. MIT Press, 1999. A tutorial introduction to the MPI Standard, with examples in C and Fortran.

William Gropp, Ewing Lusk, and Rajeev Thakur. *Using MPI-2: Advanced Features of the Message-Passing Interface.* MIT Press, Cambridge, MA, 1999. A tutorial introduction to the MPI-2 Standard, with examples in C and Fortran. This is the best place to find information on using MPI I/O in applications.

Brian W. Kernighan and Dennis M. Ritchie. *The C Programming Language.* PTR Prentice Hall, 2nd edition, 1988. The original book describing the C programming language.

John M. May. *Parallel I/O for High Performance Computing.* Morgan Kaufmann, 2001. A thorough introduction to parallel I/O including MPI I/O and higher-level libraries such as HDF.

Evi Nemeth, Garth Snyder, Scott Seebass, and Trent R. Hein. *Unix System Administration Handbook.* Prentice Hall PTR, 3rd edition, 2001. A comprehensive and practical book on Unix system administration, it covers all major varieties of Unix, not just Linux.

Peter S. Pacheco. *Parallel Programming with MPI.* Morgan Kaufman, 1997. A good introductory text on parallel programming using MPI.

Gregory F. Pfister. *In Search of Clusters: The Ongoing Battle in Lowly Parallel Computing, 2nd ed.* Prentice Hall, Englewood Cliffs, NJ, 1995 edition, 1998. A delightful book advocating clusters for many problems, including for commercial computing. It has nice sections on parallel programming and (as part of his argument for clusters) a good discussion of shared-memory systems and the issues of correctness and performance that are often brushed under the rug. See Pfister's annotated bibliography for more books and articles on clusters.

Marc Snir, Steve W. Otto, Steven Huss-Lederman, David W. Walker, and Jack Dongarra. *MPI—The Complete Reference: Volume 1, The MPI Core,* 2nd edition. MIT Press, Cambridge, MA, 1998. An annotated version of the MPI-1 Standard, it contains more examples than the official copy and is a good reference on MPI.

Thomas L. Sterling, John Salmon, Donald J. Becker, and Daniel F. Savarese. *How to Build a Beowulf.* MIT Press, 1999. The original and best-selling Beowulf book. Includes a discussion of building and testing Beowulf node hardware.

W. Richard Stevens. *Advanced Programming in the UNIX Environment.* Addison-Wesley, Reading, MA, USA, 1992. A thorough and highly readable reference on programming under Unix.

W. Richard Stevens. *UNIX Network Programming: Interprocess Communications*, volume 2. Prentice-Hall, Upper Saddle River, NJ 07458, USA, second edition, 1998. A companion to Stevens' excellent book on sockets and XTI, this book covers POSIX and System V interprocess communication mechanisms including shared memory, remote procedure calls, and semaphores.

W. Richard Stevens. *UNIX Network Programming: Networking APIs: Sockets and XTI*, volume 1. Prentice-Hall PTR, Upper Saddle River, NJ 07458,

USA, second edition, 1998. An excellent reference for network programming under Unix; it provides a highly readable and detailed description of all aspects of Unix socket programming.

David Wright, editor. *Beowulf.* Penguin Classics, 1957. A highly regarded translation (into prose) of the Beowulf Epic.

C Annotated URLs

Below is a sampling of URLs that are helpful for those building or using a Beowulf. This is not an exhaustive list, and we encourage the reader to browse the Web for other sites. A good place to start is the general Beowulf Web sites.

C.1 General Beowulf Information

`www.beowulf.org`: The original Beowulf Web site. See also the Beowulf mailing list at `www.beowulf.org/mailman/listinfo/beowulf`.

`beowulf-underground.org`: The Beowulf Underground provides "unsanctioned and unfettered information on building and using Beowulf systems." It is a site that allows the Beowulf community to post brief articles about software, documentation, and announcements related to Beowulf computing. Each article includes links to Web sites and downloads for the various items. A separate commercial and vendor area keeps free software well delineated. Moderators work to keep the material brief and on topic and to prevent abuses. This is the one stop for all things Beowulf.

`dsg.port.ac.uk/sigwulf`: The special interest group (SIG) on Beowulfs. Provides material material for teaching courses on cluster computing.

C.2 Node and Network Hardware

`www.cs.virginia.edu/stream`: The STREAM Benchmark provides a simple measure of the performance of the memory system on a node. This site also includes results for a wide variety of platforms, from PC nodes suitable for a Beowulf, to workstations, to supercomputers.

`www.tomshardware.com`: Aimed at hobbyists building their own computers, this is a good site for general background on node hardware and includes up-to-date instructions on building your own node.

C.3 Network Security

`www.securityfocus.org`: An up-to-date, searchable security exploit information service that supplies descriptions, discussions, solutions, and exploit codes on a per vulnerability basis.

`www.cert.org`: Very complete, includes vendor responses to vulnerabilities, but holds back vulnerability information until vendors have had time to respond.

C.4 Performance Tools

`www.netlib.org/benchmark/hpl`: Home of the High Performance Linpack Benchmark

`www.mcs.anl.gov/mpi/mpptest`: Performance tests for MPI, including a guide for how *not* to measure communication performance.

C.5 Parallel Programming and Software

`www.mpi-forum.org`: The official MPI Forum Web site, contains Postscript and HTML versions of the MPI-1 and MPI-2 Standards.

`www.mcs.anl.gov/mpi`: A starting point for information about MPI, including libraries and tools that use MPI and papers about the implementation or use of MPI.

`www.mcs.anl.gov/mpich`: Home of the MPICH and MPICH2 implementations of MPI. Download source, documentation, and Unix and Windows versions of MPI from here. Also check the bug list page for patches and announcements of releases.

`www.netlib.org`: A valuable collection of mathematical software and related information.

`www.csm.ornl.gov/pvm`: PVM home page.

`www.mcs.anl.gov/romio`: Home of the ROMIO implementation of the I/O chapter from MPI-2. ROMIO is included in MPICH and LAM but can also be downloaded separately. Information on tuning ROMIO for performance can be found here.

`hdf.ncsa.uiuc.edu`: Home of HDF. Included here are I/O libraries; tools for analyzing, visualizing, and converting scientific data; and software downloads, documentation, and support information.

`www.parl.clemson.edu/pvfs`: Home of PVFS, a parallel file system designed for Beowulf. This site includes online documentation, FAQ, source code downloads, mailing lists, developer's area, and research papers about PVFS.

www.cs.dartmouth.edu/pario: Home of the Parallel I/O Archive. This includes a list of projects in parallel I/O, people working in parallel I/O, and conferences on parallel I/O. Its biggest claim to fame is an extensive annotated bibliography of parallel I/O resources.

C.6 Scheduling and Management

www.openpbs.org: The OpenPBS site is the official Web site for the open source version of PBS. Maintained by Altair, it offers downloads of software, patches, and documentation, and it hosts FAQs, discussion lists, searchable archives, and general PBS community announcements.

www.pbspro.com: Focused on the Professional Version of PBS, the PBS Pro Web site includes software downloads, documentation, evaluation versions, beta releases of new software, news, and information for the PBS administrator.

www.supercluster.org: The Supercluster Web site contains documentation for the Maui scheduler and Silver metascheduler. It also includes cluster-relevant research in areas of simulation, metascheduling, data staging, allocation management, and resource optimization.

www.scyld.com: The Scyld Web site provides information on the profession version of the Scyld Beowulf product. Scyld was recently acquired by Penguin Computing (www.penguincomputing.com).

www.cs.wisc.edu/condor: The Condor Project Homepage provides access to software, documentation and reports.

gridengine.sunsource.net: The Grid Engine Web site provides access to software, documentation, mailing lists, and other resources.

References

[1] Paul Albitz and Cricket Liu. *DNS and BIND.* O'Reilly & Associates, Inc., Sebastopol, CA 95472, 4th edition, 2001.

[2] Stephen F. Altschul, Thomas L. Madden, Alejandro A. Schaffer, Jinghui Shang, Zheng Zhang, Webb Miller, and David J. Lipman. Gapped BLAST and PSI-BLAST: a new generation of protein database search programs. *Nucleic Acids Res.*, 25:3389–3402, 1997.

[3] Sridhar Anandakrishnan. Penguins everywhere: GNU/Linux in Antarctica. *IEEE Software*, 16(6):90–96, Nov/Dec 1999.

[4] E. Anderson, Z. Bai, C. Bischof, J. Demmel, J. Dongarra, J. Du Croz, A. Greenbaum, S. Hammarling, A. McKenney, S. Ostrouchov, and D. Sorensen. *LAPACK Users' Guide.* SIAM, Philadelphia, 1992.

[5] Thomas E. Anderson, Michael D. Dahlin, Jeanna M. Neefe, David A. Patterson, Drew S. Roselli, and Randolph Y. Wang. Serverless network file systems. *ACM Transactions on Computer Systems*, 14(1):41–79, February 1996.

[6] Aztec home page. `http://www.cs.sandia.gov/CRF/aztec1.html`.

[7] Zhaojun Bai, James Demmel, Jack Dongarra, Axel Ruhe, and Henk van der Vorst. *Templates for the Solution of Algebraic Eigenvalue Problems, A Practical Guide.* SIAM, 2000.

[8] Satish Balay, Kris Buschelman, William D. Gropp, Dinesh Kaushik, Matt Knepley, Lois Curfman McInnes, Barry F. Smith, and Hong Zhang. PETSc web page. `http://www.mcs.anl.gov/petsc`, 2001.

[9] Satish Balay, Kris Buschelman, William D. Gropp, Dinesh Kaushik, Matt Knepley, Lois Curfman McInnes, Barry F. Smith, and Hong Zhang. PETSc

users manual. Technical Report ANL-95/11 - Revision 2.1.5, Argonne National Laboratory, 2002.

[10] Satish Balay, William D. Gropp, Lois Curfman McInnes, and Barry F. Smith. Efficient management of parallelism in object oriented numerical software libraries. In E. Arge, A. M. Bruaset, and H. P. Langtangen, editors, *Modern Software Tools in Scientific Computing*, pages 163–202. Birkhauser Press, 1997.

[11] Daniel J. Barrett and Richard Silverman. *SSH, The Secure Shell: The Definitive Guide.* O'Reilly & Associates, Inc., Sebastopol, CA 95472, 1st edition, 2001.

[12] Richard Barrett, Michael Berry, Tony F. Chan, James Demmel, June Donato, Jack Dongarra, Victor Eijkhout, Roldan Pozo, Charles Romine, and Henk van der Vorst. *Templates for the Solution of Linear Systems: Building Blocks for Iterative Methods.* SIAM, Philadelphia PA, 1994. `http://www.netlib.org/templates/`.

[13] Luiz André Barroso, Jeffrey Dean, and Urs Hölzle. Web search for a planet: The Google cluster architecture. *IEEE Micro*, 2003.

[14] David M. Beazley. *Python Essential Reference.* New Riders Publishing, second edition, 2001.

[15] L.S. Blackford, J. Choi, A. Cleary, E. D'Azevedo, J. Demmel, I. Dhillon, J. Dongarra, S. Hammerling, G. Henry, A. Petitet, K. Stanley, D. Walker, and R.C. Whaley. *ScaLAPACK Users' Guide.* SIAM, 1997.

[16] BLAS web page. `http://www.netlib.org/blas`.

[17] Peter J. Braam. The Lustre storage architecture. Technical report, Cluster File Systems, Inc., 2003.

[18] Tim Bray. Bonnie file system benchmark. `http://www.textuality.com/bonnie/`.

[19] Ron Brightwell, Tramm Hudson, Arthur B. Maccabe, and Rolf Riesen. The Portals 3.0 message passing interface. Technical Report SAND99-2959, Sandia Technical Report, November 1999.

[20] Surendra Byna, William Gropp, Xian-He Sun, and Rajeev Thakur. Improving the performance of MPI derived datatypes by optimizing memory-access cost. Technical Report ANL/MCS-P1045-0403, Mathematics and Computer Science Division, Argonne National Laboratory, 2003.

[21] B. Callaghan, B. Pawlowski, and P. Staubach. NFS version 3 protocol specification. Technical Report RFC 1813, Sun Microsystems, Inc., June 1995.

[22] Philip H. Carns, Walter B. Ligon III, Robert B. Ross, and Rajeev Thakur. PVFS: A parallel file system for Linux clusters. In *Proceedings of the 4th Annual Linux Showcase and Conference*, pages 317–327, Atlanta, GA, October 2000. USENIX Association.

[23] CERT web site. `http://www.cert.org`.

[24] Chaco web page. `http://www.cs.sandia.gov/~bahendr/chaco.html`.

[25] Albert Cheng and Michael Folk. HDF5: High performance science data solution for the new millennium. In ACM, editor, *SC2000: High Performance Networking and Computing. Dallas Convention Center, Dallas, TX, USA, November 4–10, 2000*, pages 149–149, New York, NY 10036, USA and 1109 Spring Street, Suite 300, Silver Spring, MD 20910, USA, 2000. ACM Press and IEEE Computer Society Press.

[26] Averg Ching, Alok Choudhary, Kenin Coloma, Wei keng Liao, Robert Ross, and William Gropp. Noncontiguous I/O accesses through MPI-IO. In *Proceedings of the Third IEEE/ACM International Symposium on Cluster Computing and the Grid (CCGrid2003)*, May 2003.

[27] Avery Ching, Alok Choudhary, Wei keng Liao, Robert Ross, and William Gropp. Noncontiguous I/O through PVFS. In *Proceedings of the 2002 IEEE International Conference on Cluster Computing*, September 2002.

[28] Douglas Comer. *Internetworking with TCP/IP, Volume 1: Principles, Protocols, and Architecture.* Prentice Hall, Inc., Englewood Cliffs, NJ 07632, 4th edition, 2000.

[29] Peter F. Corbett and Dror G. Feitelson. The Vesta parallel file system. In Hai Jin, Toni Cortes, and Rajkumar Buyya, editors, *High Performance Mass Storage and Parallel I/O: Technologies and Applications*, chapter 20, pages 285–308. IEEE Computer Society Press and Wiley, New York, NY, 2001.

[30] Cray Research. *Application Programmer's Library Reference Manual*, 2nd edition, November 1995. Publication SR-2165.

[31] David E. Culler, Richard M. Karp, David A. Patterson, Abhijit Sahay, Klaus E. Schauser, Eunice Santos, Ramesh Subramonian, and Thorsten von Eicken. LogP: towards a realistic model of parallel computation. *ACM SIGPLAN Notices*, 28(7):1–12, July 1993.

[32] I. S. Dhillon. *A new $O(n^2)$ Algorithm for the Symmetric Tridiagonal Eigenvalue/Eigenvector Problem.* PhD thesis, Computer Science Division, University of California, Berkeley, California, 1997.

[33] Chris DiBona, Sam Ockman, and Mark Stone. *Open Sources: Voices from the Open Source Revolution.* O'Reilly & Associates, Inc., 1999.

[34] Jack Dongarra. Performance of various computers using standard linear equations software. Technical Report Number CS-89–85, University of Tennessee, Knoxville TN, 37996, 2001. `http://www.netlib.org/benchmark/performance.ps`.

[35] Jack J. Dongarra, Iain S. Duff, Danny C. Sorensen, and Henk A. van der Vorst. *Solving Linear Systems on Vector and Shared Memory Computers.* SIAM, Philadelphia, 1991.

[36] R. Evard, N. Desai, J. Navarro, and D. Nurmi. Clusters as large-scale development facilities. In *Proceedings of the 2002 IEEE International Conference on Cluster Computing*, September 2002.

[37] FFTW web page. `http://www.fftw.org`.

[38] Fluent web page. `http://www.fluent.com`.

[39] G. C. Fox, S. W. Otto, and A. J. G. Hey. Matrix algorithms on a hypercube I: Matrix multiplication. *Parallel Computing*, 4:17–31, 1987.

[40] Matteo Frigo and Steven G. Johnson. FFTW: An adaptive software architecture for the FFT. In *Proc. 1998 IEEE Intl. Conf. Acoustics Speech and Signal Processing*, volume 3, pages 1381–1384. IEEE, 1998.

[41] The galley parallel file system. `http://www.cs.dartmouth.edu/~dfk/nils//galley.html`.

[42] Gaussian web page. `http://www.gaussian.com`.

[43] Al Geist, Adam Beguelin, Jack Dongarra, Weicheng Jiang, Bob Manchek, and Vaidy Sunderam. *PVM: Parallel Virtual Machine—A User's Guide and Tutorial for Network Parallel Computing.* MIT Press, Cambridge, Mass., 1994.

[44] W. Gropp and E. Lusk. Scalable Unix tools on parallel processors. In *Proceedings of the Scalable High-Performance Computing Conference, May 23–25, 1994, Knoxville, Tennessee*, pages 56–62, 1109 Spring Street, Suite 300, Silver Spring, MD 20910, USA, 1994. IEEE Computer Society Press.

[45] W. D. Gropp, D. K. Kaushik, D. E. Keyes, and B. F. Smith. Towards realistic performance bounds for implicit CFD codes. In *Proceedings of Parallel CFD'99*, pages 241–248, 1999.

[46] William Gropp, Steven Huss-Lederman, Andrew Lumsdaine, Ewing Lusk, Bill Nitzberg, William Saphir, and Marc Snir. *MPI—The Complete Reference: Volume 2, The MPI-2 Extensions.* MIT Press, Cambridge, MA, 1998.

[47] William Gropp, Ewing Lusk, Nathan Doss, and Anthony Skjellum. A high-performance, portable implementation of the MPI Message-Passing Interface standard. *Parallel Computing*, 22(6):789–828, 1996.

[48] William Gropp, Ewing Lusk, and Anthony Skjellum. *Using MPI: Portable Parallel Programming with the Message Passing Interface,* 2nd edition. MIT Press, Cambridge, MA, 1999.

[49] William Gropp, Ewing Lusk, and Debbie Swider. Improving the performance of MPI derived datatypes. In Anthony Skjellum, Purushotham V. Bangalore, and Yoginder S. Dandass, editors, *Proceedings of the Third MPI Developer's and User's Conference*, pages 25–30. MPI Software Technology Press, 1999.

[50] William Gropp, Ewing Lusk, and Rajeev Thakur. *Using MPI-2: Advanced Features of the Message-Passing Interface.* MIT Press, Cambridge, MA, 1999.

[51] William D. Gropp and Ewing Lusk. Reproducible measurements of MPI performance characteristics. In Jack Dongarra, Emilio Luque, and Tomàs Margalef, editors, *Recent Advances in Parallel Virtual Machine and Message Passing Interface*, volume 1697 of *Lecture Notes in Computer Science*, pages 11–18. Springer Verlag, 1999. 6th European PVM/MPI Users' Group Meeting, Barcelona, Spain, September 1999.

[52] Michael Hasenstein. The logical volume manager (LVM). Technical Report Whitepaper, SuSE Inc., 2001.

[53] Don Heller. Rabbit: A performance counters library for Intel/AMD processors and Linux. `www.scl.ameslab.gov/Projects/Rabbit/`.

[54] J. M. D. Hill, B. McColl, D. C. Stefanescu, M. W. Goudreau, K. Lang, S. B. Rao, T. Suel, T. Tsantilas, and R. H. Bisseling. BSPlib: The BSP programming library. *Parallel Computing*, 24(14):1947–1980, December 1998.

[55] James V. Huber, Jr., Christopher L. Elford, Daniel A. Reed, Andrew A. Chien, and David S. Blumenthal. PPFS: A high performance portable parallel file system. In Hai Jin, Toni Cortes, and Rajkumar Buyya, editors, *High Performance Mass Storage and Parallel I/O: Technologies and Applications*, chapter 22, pages 330–343. IEEE Computer Society Press and Wiley, New York, NY, 2001.

[56] Craig Hunt. *TCP/IP Network Administration.* O'Reilly & Associates, Inc., Sebastopol, CA 95472, 3rd edition, 2002.

[57] S. A. Hutchinson, J. N. Shadid, and R. S. Tuminaro. Aztec user's guide: Version 1.1. Technical Report SAND95-1559, Sandia National Laboratories, 1995.

[58] IEEE/ANSI Std. 1003.1. Portable operating system interface (POSIX)–part 1: System application program interface (API) [C language], 1996 edition.

[59] Iperf home page. `http://dast.nlanr.net/projects/iperf`.

[60] Alan H. Karp. Bit reversal on uniprocessors. *SIAM Review*, 38(1):1–26, March 1996.

[61] Jeffrey Kephart and David Chess. The vision of autonomic computing. *IEEE Computer*, pages 41–50, January 2003.

[62] David Kotz. Disk-directed I/O for MIMD multiprocessors. In Hai Jin, Toni Cortes, and Rajkumar Buyya, editors, *High Performance Mass Storage and Parallel I/O: Technologies and Applications*, chapter 35, pages 513–535. IEEE Computer Society Press and John Wiley & Sons, 2001.

[63] LAPACK software. `http://www.netlib.org/lapack`.

[64] C. Lawson, R. Hanson, D. Kincaid, and F. Krogh. Basic linear algebra subprograms for FORTRAN usage. *Transactions on Mathematical Software*, 5:308–323, 1979.

[65] Edward K. Lee and Chandramohan A. Thekkath. Petal: Distributed virtual disks. In *Proceedings of the Seventh International Conference on Architectural Support for Programming Languages and Operating Systems*, pages 84–92, Cambridge, MA, October 1996.

[66] J. Li, W.-K. Liao, A. Choudhary, R. Ross, R. Thakur, W. Gropp, and R. Latham. Parallel netCDF: A scientific high-performance I/O interface. Technical Report ANL/MCS-P1048-0503, Mathematics and Computer Science Division, Argonne National Laboratory, May 2003.

[67] Xiaoye S. Li. *Sparse Gaussian Eliminiation on High Performance Computers.* PhD thesis, University of California at Berkeley, 1996.

[68] Josip Loncaric. Linux 2.2.12 TCP performance fix for short messages. `www.icase.edu/coral/LinuxTCP2.html`. This web site is no longer available.

[69] LS-Dyna web page. `http://www.lstc.com`.

[70] Alex Martelli and David Ascher, editors. *Python Cookbook.* O'Reilly and Associates, 2002.

[71] John D. McCalpin. STREAM: Sustainable memory bandwidth in high performance computers. `http://www.cs.virginia.edu/stream/`.

[72] Message Passing Interface Forum. MPI: A Message-Passing Interface standard. *International Journal of Supercomputer Applications*, 8(3/4):165–414, 1994.

[73] Message Passing Interface Forum. MPI2: A message passing interface standard. *International Journal of High Performance Computing Applications*, 12(1–2):1–299, 1998.

[74] Jeffrey Mogul and Steve Deering. Path MTU discovery. Technical Report IETF RFC 1191, Digital Equipment Corporation WRL and Stanford University, November 1990. `http://www.ietf.org/rfc/rfc1191.txt`.

[75] P. Mucci, S. Brown, C. Deane, and G. Ho. Papi: A portable interface to hardware performance counters. `icl.cs.utk.edu/projects/papi/`.

[76] NAMD web page. http://www.ks.uiuc.edu/Research/namd/.

[77] Nastran web page. http://www.mscsoftware.com/products/products_detail.cfm?S=74&PI=7&M=0.

[78] Nils Nieuwejaar and David Kotz. The Galley parallel file system. *Parallel Computing*, 23(4):447–476, June 1997.

[79] Nils Nieuwejaar, David Kotz, Apratim Purakayastha, Carla Schlatter Ellis, and Michael Best. File-access characteristics of parallel scientific workloads. *IEEE Transactions on Parallel and Distributed Systems*, 7(10):1075–1089, October 1996.

[80] Bill Nowicki. NFS: Network file system protocol specification. Technical Report RFC 1094, Sun Microsystems, Inc., March 1989.

[81] NWChem web page. http://www.emsl.pnl.gov:2080/docs/nwchem/nwchem.html.

[82] Emil Ong, Ewing Lusk, and William Gropp. Scalable Unix commands for parallel processors: A high-performance implementation. In Jack Dongarra and Yiannis Cotronis, editors, *Proceedings of Euro PVM/MPI*. Springer Verlag, 2001.

[83] OpenMP Web page. www.openmp.org.

[84] ParMetis web page. http://www-users.cs.umn.edu/~karypis/metis/parmetis/index.html.

[85] Chrisila Pettey, Ralph Butler, Brad Rudnik, and Thomas Naughton. A rapid recovery Beowulf platform. In Henry Selvaraj and Venkatesan Muthukumar, editors, *Proceedings of Fifteenth International Conference on Systems Engineering*, pages 278–283, 2002.

[86] PLAPACK web page. http://www.cs.utexas.edu/users/plapack/.

[87] Jon Postel, editor. Transmission control protocol. Technical Report IETF RFC 793, Information Sciences Institute, University of Southern California, September 1981. http://www.ietf.org/rfc/rfc0793.txt.

[88] Kenneth W. Preslan, Andrew Barry, Jonathan E. Brassow, Russell Cattlelan, Adam Manthei, Erling Nygaard, Seth Van Oort, David C. Teigland, Mike Tilstra, Matthew O'Keefe, Grant Erickson, and Manish Agarwal. A 64-bit,

shared disk file system for Linux. In *Proceedings of the Eighth NASA Goddard Conference on Mass Storage Systems and Technologies*, March 2000.

[89] Kenneth W. Preslan, Andrew P. Barry, Jonathan E. Brassow, Grant M. Erickson, Erling Nygaard, Christopher J. Sabol, Steven R. Soltis, David C. Teigland, and Matthew T. O'Keefe. A 64-bit, shared disk file system for Linux. In *Proceedings of the Seventh NASA Goddard Conference on Mass Storage Systems*, pages 22–41, San Diego, CA, March 1999. IEEE Computer Society Press.

[90] The parallel virtual file system. `http://www.pvfs.org`.

[91] Using the parallel virtual file system. `http://www.parl.clemson.edu/pvfs/user-guide.html`.

[92] QBank: A CPU allocations bank. `http://www.emsl.pnl.gov:2080/docs/mscf/qbank-2.10/`.

[93] Red Hat Linux 9: Red Hat Linux Customization Guide. Red Hat web site. `http://www.redhat.com/docs/manuals/linux/RHL-9-Manual/pdf/rhl-cg-en-9.p%df`.

[94] R. Reussner, P. Sanders, L. Prechelt, and M Müller. SKaMPI: A detailed, accurate MPI benchmark. In Vassuk Alexandrov and Jack Dongarra, editors, *Recent advances in Parallel Virtual Machine and Message Passing Interface*, volume 1497 of *Lecture Notes in Computer Science*, pages 52–59. Springer Verlag, 1998. 5th European PVM/MPI Users' Group Meeting.

[95] R. K. Rew and G. P. Davis. The unidata netCDF: Software for scientific data access. *Sixth Int'l. Conf. on Interactive Inf. and Processing Sys. for Meteorology, Oceanography, and Hydrology*, February 1990.

[96] R. Ross, D. Nurmi, A. Cheng, and M. Zingale. A case study in application I/O on linux clusters. In *Proceedings of SC2001*, November 2001.

[97] Robert B. Ross. *Reactive Scheduling for Parallel I/O Systems.* PhD thesis, Dept. of Electrical and Computer Engineering, Clemson University, Clemson, SC, December 2000.

[98] Youcef Saad. *Iterative Methods for Sparse Linear Systems.* SIAM, Philadelphia, PA, 2003. Originally published by PWS Publishing Company, Boston, 1996; this edition is available for download from `http://www.cs.umn.edu/~saad`.

[99] K. Schloegel, G. Karypis, and V. Kumar. Parallel multilevel algorithms for multi-constraint graph partitioning. In *Proceedings of EuroPar-2000*, 2000.

[100] Frank Schmuck and Roger Haskin. GPFS: A shared-disk file system for large computing clusters. In *First USENIX Conference on File and Storage Technologies (FAST'02)*, Monterey, CA, January 28-30 2002.

[101] SecurityFocus web site. `http://www.securityfocus.org`.

[102] S. Shepler, B. Callaghan, D. Robinson, R. Thurlow, C. Beame, M. Eisler, and D. Noveck. NFS version 4 protocol. Technical Report RFC 3010, Sun Microsystems, Inc., Hummingbird Ltd., Zambeel, Inc., and Network Appliance, Inc., December 2000.

[103] Joseph D. Sloan. *Network Troubleshooting Tools.* O'Reilly & Associates, 2001.

[104] Quinn O. Snell, Armin R. Mikler, and John L. Gustafson. NetPIPE: A network protocol independent performace evaluator. In *IASTED International Conference on Intelligent Information Management and Systems*, June 1996. `http://www.scl.ameslab.gov/netpipe/paper/netpipe.ps`.

[105] Marc Snir, Steve W. Otto, Steven Huss-Lederman, David W. Walker, and Jack Dongarra. *MPI—The Complete Reference: Volume 1, The MPI Core,* 2nd edition. MIT Press, Cambridge, MA, 1998.

[106] D. C. Sorensen. Implicit application of polynomial filters in a k-step Arnoldi method. *SIAM J. Matrix Anal.*, 13:357–385, 1992.

[107] T. Sterling, D. Savarese, D. J. Becker, J. E. Dorband, U. A. Ranawake, and C. V. Packer. BEOWULF : A parallel workstation for scientific computation. In *International Conference on Parallel Processing, Vol.1: Architecture*, pages 11–14, Boca Raton, USA, August 1995. CRC Press.

[108] Thomas L. Sterling, John Salmon, Donald J. Becker, and Daniel F. Savarese. *How to Build a Beowulf.* MIT Press, 1999.

[109] Hal Stern, Mike Eisler, and Ricardo Labiaga. *Managing NFS and NIS.* O'Reilly & Associates, Inc., Sebastopol, CA 95472, 2nd edition, 2001.

[110] W. Richard Stevens. *TCP/IP Illustrated, Volume 1: The Protocols.* Addison-Wesley Publishing Company, Reading, MA 01867, 1994.

[111] W. Richard Stevens. *UNIX network programming: Networking APIs: Sockets and XTI*, volume 1. Prentice-Hall PTR, Upper Saddle River, NJ 07458, USA, second edition, 1998.

[112] SuperLU web page. `http://www.nersc.gov/~xiaoye/SuperLU/`.

[113] Rajeev Thakur and Alok Choudhary. An Extended Two-Phase Method for Accessing Sections of Out-of-Core Arrays. *Scientific Programming*, 5(4):301–317, Winter 1996.

[114] Rajeev Thakur, Alok Choudhary, Rajesh Bordawekar, Sachin More, and Sivaramakrishna Kuditipudi. Passion: Optimized I/O for parallel applications. *IEEE Computer*, 29(6):70–78, June 1996.

[115] Rajeev Thakur, William Gropp, and Ewing Lusk. On implementing MPI-IO portably and with high performance. In *Proceedings of the 6th Workshop on I/O in Parallel and Distributed Systems*, pages 23–32. ACM Press, May 1999.

[116] Rajeev Thakur, Ewing Lusk, and William Gropp. A case for using MPI's derived datatypes to improve I/O performance. In *Proceedings of SC98: High Performance Networking and Computing*, November 1998.

[117] Rajeev Thakur, Robert Ross, Ewing Lusk, and William Gropp. Users guide for ROMIO: A high-performance, portable MPI-IO implementation. Technical Report ANL/MCS Technical Memorandum No. 234, Mathematics and Computer Science Division, Argonne National Laboratory, May 2002.

[118] C. Thekkath, T. Mann, and E. Lee. Frangipani: A scalable distributed file system. In *Proceedings of the Sixteenth ACM Symposium on Operating System Principles (SOSP)*, October 1997.

[119] TotalView Multiprocess Debugger/Analyzer, 2000. `www.etnus.com/Products/TotalView`.

[120] J. L. Traeff, R. Hempel, H. Ritzdoff, and F. Zimmermann. Flattening on the fly: Efficient handling of MPI derived datatypes. In J. J. Dongarra, E. Luque, and Tomas Margalef, editors, *Recent Advances in Parallel Virtual Machine and Message Passing Interface: 6th European PVM/MPI Users' Group Meeting*, volume 1697 of *Lecture Notes in Computer Science*, pages 109–116. Springer Verlag, 1999.

[121] The treadmarks distributed shared memory (DSM) system. `www.cs.rice.edu/~willy/TreadMarks/overview.html`.

[122] Trilinos web page. `http://software.sandia.gov/trilinos/index.html`.

[123] M. Vilayannur, A. Sivasubramaniam, M. Kandemir, R. Thakur, and R. Ross. Discretionary caching for I/O on clusters. In *Proceedings of the Third IEEE/ACM International Symposium on Cluster Computing and the Grid (CCGrid2003)*, May 2003.

[124] Larry Wall, Tom Christiansen, and Jon Orwant. *Programming Perl*. O'Reilly and Associates, third edition, 2000.

[125] R. Clint Whaley, Antoine Petitet, and Jack J. Dongarra. Automated empirical optimizations of software and the ATLAS project. *Parallel Computing*, 27(1–2):3–35, January 2001.

[126] Omer Zaki, Ewing Lusk, William Gropp, and Deborah Swider. Toward scalable performance visualization with Jumpshot. *High Performance Computing Applications*, 13(2):277–288, Fall 1999.

[127] Robert L. Ziegler. *Linux Firewalls*. New Riders Publishing, 2nd edition, 2001.

[128] Zoltan web page. `http://www.cs.sandia.gov/Zoltan/`.

Index

I

J

K

L

M